PRACTICAL
BUSINESS ENGLISH

PRACTICAL
BUSINESS ENGLISH

Colleen Vawdrey
Utah Valley Community College

Ted D. Stoddard
Brigham Young University

R. DerMont Bell
Brigham Young University

IRWIN
Homewood, IL 60430
Boston, MA 02116

Sponsoring editor:	Craig S. Beytien
Editorial coordinator:	Jeanne Warble
Marketing manager:	Kurt Messersmith
Cover design:	Nancy Serensky
Cover image:	Photomicrography by Herb Comess
Project editor:	Karen Smith
Production manager:	Bob Lange
Art coordinator:	Mark Malloy
Compositor:	Impressions, Inc.
Typeface:	11/13 Times Roman
Printer:	Von Hoffmann Press

Library of Congress Cataloging-in-Publication Data

Vawdrey, Colleen.
    Practical business English / Colleen Vawdrey, Ted D. Stoddard, R.
DerMont Bell. — Instructor's ed.
       p.   cm.
    Includes index.
    ISBN 0-256-11562-1 (instructor's ed.). — ISBN 0-256-10274-0
    1. English language—Business English. 2. English language—
Grammar—1950– 3. English language—Rhetoric. 4. Business
writing. I. Stoddard, Ted D. II. Bell, R. DerMont. III. Title.
PE1479.B87V39   1993
808′.06665—dc20   92–17684

Printed in the United States of America
1 2 3 4 5 6 7 8 9 0 VH 9 8 7 6 5 4 3 2

Colleen Vawdrey has a bachelor's degree and a master's degree from Brigham Young University and has recently received her doctorate from Utah State University with an emphasis in Business Communication. She is currently an assistant professor in the Office Technology and Administration Department at Utah Valley Community College in Orem, Utah.

Dr. Vawdrey began one of the first high school business English/communication courses in Utah and taught at that level for many years. She has also taught business communication and business English as separate courses at the community college level and as a combined course at the university level.

Her dissertation research in the area of communication found that students' ability to edit and write correctly is related to their knowledge of grammar and punctuation principles. The exercises of *Practical Business English* reflect this philosophy of progressing from knowing the rules to applying them in editing and writing.

Ted D. Stoddard is professor of management communication in the Marriott School of Management at Brigham Young University in Provo, Utah. He received his doctorate from Arizona State University in 1967. During every year of his three-decade academic career, he has taught courses in undergraduate business communication.

Dr. Stoddard is currently the coordinator of undergraduate business writing at Brigham Young University. Several years ago, he developed the model for BYU's undergraduate course in business writing—a unique course that is competency-based and that offers advanced-writing general-education credit to any student at BYU.

A distinctive component of BYU's competency-based course is the English grammar module that Dr. Stoddard helped develop. The learnings in this module are centered around Irwin's grammar-review textbook coauthored by Dr. Stoddard, *Effective Writing: A Practical Grammar Review*. Numerous dimensions of *Practical Business English* are spinoffs of Dr. Stoddard's work with the grammar module in BYU's competency-based business-writing program.

R. DerMont Bell is presently professor of management communication at Brigham Young University. He has a bachelor's degree and a master's degree from BYU and a doctorate from the University of Southern California.

He currently teaches advanced writing to undergraduate university students. The course he teaches includes a strong emphasis on English grammar and satisfies the university's general-education requirements in advanced writing. His teaching assignments have emphasized—in addition to business writing—research methods and principles of testing and evaluation.

Dr. Bell has served as department chair and as department coordinator of undergraduate business communication at BYU. He is a coauthor of *Effective Writing: A Practical Grammar Review*, Irwin's widely used, hands-on approach to the study of effective grammar usage.

He is a member of various professional organizations in business and education and has served in the past as the national president of Delta Pi Epsilon, a national graduate honorary society in business education.

We wrote *Practical Business English* with you, the student, uppermost in our minds. We also naturally kept your teacher in mind as we planned, wrote, and revised our materials.

Practical Business English came to life because of the felt needs expressed by several publics. In our academic careers, we have taught business English to thousands of students who repeatedly cried out to us for improved learning materials. Our personal visits with scores of teachers gave us insights into their expressed needs for improved business English instructional materials. And countless visits to teachers by representatives of our publisher, Richard D. Irwin, Inc., verified the interest in and need for a practical textbook to deliver business English learnings.

We of course would have no reason to write a business English textbook unless we felt we could improve on the textbooks already in use. The message that improvements were possible and were needed came to us time and again from our own students, from other teachers' students, and from teachers such as yours. If your teacher has adopted *Practical Business English* to help teach you business English, we feel gratified for the chance to help you master the critically important material you'll find in our textbook.

You might naturally wonder how *business English* differs from *English*. In reality, the two are identical. However, in a business environment, we can make the rules and principles of English come alive because their relationships with real life are clearly understood. Business English gives you the fundamentals to help you communicate clearly and correctly. In the "real world" associated with making a day-to-day living, you will find nothing more important to your success than the ability to communicate effectively. In fact, once you leave the classroom and enter the world of work, you probably will find your course in business English has been one of the most valuable, if not **the most valuable**, course in your entire academic curriculum.

We assure you that the rules and principles of business English are not difficult to master. At the same time, we admit they are sometimes frustrating—probably because of the terminology associated with business English. We encourage you to pay special attention to the terms and to master them routinely as a first step in each lesson. The terms are logically named and will usually make sense to you if you will answer the question, *Why is this term given this name?*

As you undoubtedly realize, English as a language contains many exceptions and inconsistencies to the rules. In *Practical Business English*, we typically take a stance in favor of consistency. We do explain the "shades of gray," but we advocate one way of doing things to help make the learning process easy. We think you'll appreciate this approach.

We use the imperative mood (which you'll learn about in Lesson 13) in stating the rules of business English. As such, the rules have the flavor of directives for you to follow—much like commands. We understand that "life will not come to a standstill" if you deviate from some of these directives on occasion. However, throughout the textbook, we expect you to follow the directives precisely in all the exercises.

When you can apply the directives correctly in your own writing, you'll feel the **power** of knowing business English. You'll **know** what is right and what is wrong, and you'll probably have a certain smug feeling because of that knowledge. The ability to apply the rules correctly is known as *transfer of learning*, and your foremost goal throughout your study of business English should be to achieve the ability to apply the directives correctly in your own writing.

Organization of This Textbook

The following units are in *Practical Business English*:

1. Reviewing the Basics

2. Using Verbs

3. Punctuating Your Writing

4. Using Connectives

5. Selecting Nouns and Pronouns

6. Ensuring Agreement and Reference

7. Using Modifiers

8. Dealing with Language Usage

9. Developing Effective Writing Techniques

10. Generating Business Correspondence

Your teacher may decide to skip some of the lessons in some of the units or to teach the units in a sequence other than the one shown above. Such decisions are normal—reflecting the legitimate academic freedom that teachers enjoy. As you read further, you'll understand more about our rationale for the organization of *Practical Business English*; and you'll understand why your teacher might choose to cover the lessons in a sequence different from the one in the textbook.

Special Features

The following items are special features of *Practical Business English*. These features are designed intentionally for you, the student, or for your teacher.

Personal-writing style—We help make you feel you are part of the learning process by using first- and second-person personal pronouns in discussions, rules, and learning hints. The rules are stated in the imperative mood to give the feeling and force of commands rather than ''nice-to-do statements.''

Pretest-posttest—For each lesson, we provide a pretest for you to use in a self-check environment before you study the lesson. We then provide a posttest so you can check your understanding after studying a lesson.

Terminology—We do not provide an isolated glossary for the entire text. Instead, we provide a terminology section in every lesson so you can study the terms with the corresponding lesson.

Learning hints—Where appropriate, we use a learning hint to help you understand the rule, the rule's applications, or the ''shades-of-gray'' implications of the rule.

Frequently used and abused rules—In determining which business English rules to include, we selected those rules that are both frequently used in the business world and frequently abused by students or business workers. Through this process, we eliminated dozens of rules that have little or no real relevance to the communication process.

Levels of exercises—We prepared exercises according to their levels of difficulty. Level A exercises contain dichotomous questions (such as true-false questions); Level B, multiple-choice and matching questions; and Level C, editing, intensive-editing, composition, and cumulative-editing questions. The levels permit you or your teacher to select appropriate questions for your learning abilities.

Quantity of exercises—We provide almost 300 pages of exercises. You'll get lots of practice applying the rules of each lesson.

Editing in Level C exercises—For transfer-of-learning purposes, our Level C exercises require extensive editing (which goes beyond mere proofreading). These editing exercises will truly help you transfer a lesson's learnings to a real-world environment.

Cumulative editing/cycling—We cycle a lesson's learnings through Level C cumulative-editing exercises in succeeding lessons in the unit in which the lesson appears and in the two units following the unit of introduction. Such repetition will help reinforce prior learnings.

Independent lessons and units—If desired, you or your teacher can rearrange the sequence of the textbook's units and lessons. Level C cumulative-editing activities tend to thwart using a different sequence than the one in the text, but you or your teacher can easily avoid this problem by eliminating the Level C cumulative-editing activities.

Transfer-of-learning philosophy—True-false and multiple-choice questions do little to foster transfer of learnings from the time you study a lesson to the time you apply the lesson's content in real-world situations. To help achieves transfer of learnings, we use extensive editing activities. If you can edit sentences containing business English errors, you will be significantly better prepared to recognize such errors in your own writing.

Comprehensive test bank with explanations—We provide your teacher with a test bank of 1,000 objective questions. In the hard-copy version, we provide not only answers but also explanations for correct answers and for incorrect answers. We also give a rule number or a page number from which the question is derived. We provide the test bank in both a hard-copy version in the *Instructor's Resource Manual* and in an electronic-file version.

Intentional omissions of appendices—You will not find any appendices in *Practical Business English*. Instead, the materials that are usually located in business English textbooks' appendices are included in Unit 1. Material in an appendix often leaves the user with the feeling the material is relatively unimportant and need not be mastered. However, the typical appendix material found in Unit 1 is indeed important; and we feel that including this material in regular lesson format gives a clear signal about the value of the material. Your teacher will make appropriate decisions about which lessons in Unit 1 you are to study. On your own, you can profitably study any of them that are not assigned by your teacher.

Functional instructor's edition—Your instructor has a special spiral-bound instructor's edition of *Practical Business English*. This instructor's edition contains answers to all the exercises.

Transparencies—We provide about a hundred acetate transparencies for your teacher to use in teaching the content of *Practical Business English*. We think you will be pleased with the ways these transparencies will enhance the course.

Spelling and frequently misspelled words—We include a separate lesson on spelling rules. The lesson also includes a 150-word list of words that occur frequently in the business vocabulary and that are frequently misspelled by students and business people. You're in good company if you make spelling blunders. We advocate your use of an electronic speller in your writing, but we also maintain you should be accountable for mastering the spelling of the most frequently occurring misspelled words in the business vocabulary.

Number usage—We include a separate lesson on number usage from the business-world perspective. We have selected a limited number of rules reflecting those that are frequently used in business correspondence. If you'll master the rules we've selected, you'll make very few errors in using numbers in your writing.

Introduction to writing—If your teacher wants you to do writing assignments in your business English course, we provide Units 9 and 10 for that purpose. In Lesson 34, we introduce you to writing requirements for the sentence and the paragraph. In Lesson 35, we cover accessing techniques—a very distinctive lesson. In Lesson 36, we teach the prewrite, write, and rewrite strategies. And in Unit 10, we introduce you to the writing of business and personal correspondence. You'll enjoy these writing lessons.

Language usage—We feel language usage is part of business English, although we admit that language usage is not grammar. We provide four lessons associated with language usage: Lesson 5—''Confusing Words''; Lesson 31—''Wordy Expressions''; Lesson 32—''Confusable Words''; and Lesson 33—''Nonsexist Writing.'' Your use of the English language will naturally improve as a result of these lessons.

Comprehensive index—The index for *Practical Business English* has been prepared with you distinctively in mind. You'll find it very useful in helping you find material in the text.

Software tutorial—As of the first printing of *Practical Business English*, we are planning a software tutorial to help you study business English. Your teacher will know whether this tutorial is available and will decide whether to use it in your business English course.

Information inside covers—On the pages inside the front and back covers of the textbook, you will find four useful resource sources: (1) the 150 frequently misspelled words we emphasize, (2) the irregular verbs you should know, (3) a mini-glossary containing the lesson numbers of the most significant terms in the text, and (4) a listing of typical editing symbols used by many teachers of business English.

Supplementary Materials

We have prepared the following supplementary materials to help your teacher in the teaching of business English:

> *Instructor's Edition of Practical Business English*
> *Instructor's Resource Manual for Practical Business English*
> Transparencies
> CompuTest 3 Software

Outcomes

As you begin your study of business English, you may have similar feelings to those of many of our students. That is, you may be fearful of the material because of negative experiences in the past. Or you may think you're going to be bored because you cannot see the value of English skills in your life.

After business English students have finished school and are working in the ''real world,'' they inevitably give an excellent report about their business English classes. In fact, they typically say that business English was the most valuable course of all courses taken. You may indeed give similar feedback to your business English teacher.

A comprehensive list of outcomes of your study of business English is not possible. However, we invite you to examine the following outcomes in anticipation of the positive things to come from your business English course. In studying *Practical Business English*, you'll learn to do at least the following to one degree or another:

Identify and use parts of speech.
Know the differences between phrases and clauses.
Spell correctly, especially frequently misspelled words.
Use confusing words correctly.
Use numbers correctly according to business-world standards.
Capitalize correctly.
Use abbreviations correctly.
Use the dictionary.
Distinguish among verb tenses.
Distinguish among verb moods.
Distinguish between active and passive voice.
Punctuate correctly.
Understand the nature of coordination and subordination.
Use prepositions correctly as connectives.
Choose correctly between subjective and objective case.
Use relative pronouns correctly.
Use possessive case correctly.
Write sentences in which the subject and the verb agree.
Achieve agreement between pronouns and their antecedents.
Use adjective and adverb modifiers correctly.
Use and punctuate compound and consecutive modifiers correctly.
Avoid misplaced and dangling modifiers.
Reduce the number of wordy expressions used.
Choose correctly between selected confusable words.
Use nonsexist wording.
Write grammatically correct sentences.
Write paragraphs with acceptable unity and length.
Employ effective access techniques.
Use prewrite, write, and rewrite techniques.
Format letters and memorandums correctly.
Write good-news messages.
Write bad-news messages.
Write persuasive messages.

As you can see, you're going to master hundreds of new learnings and skills as a result of your business English course.

Acknowledgments

We acknowledge the assistance given by those teachers who reviewed *Practical Business English* during one phase or another. Specifically, we thank the following individuals for their support:

Jean Embree, *Sawyer College of Business*
Joan Ryan, *Lane Community College*
Carolyn Quantrille, *Spokane Falls Community College*
Mary Ellen Metwalli, *Chaffey College*
Ella Butler, *Los Angeles Southwest College*
Yolanda Grisolia, *California State–Long Beach*
Kathy Grimes, *Trend Colleges*
Jean Rohrer, *Hagerstown Business College*
Richard Swanson, *Sanford Brown College*
Martha S. Johnson, *Hamilton Business College*
Jane Irvin, *Gateway Community College*
Aneida Brownstein, *Drake Business College*
Jennifer Getz, *Heald Business College–Walnut Creek*
Barbara Weeks, *Heald Business College–Sacramento*
Marge Harris, *Itasca Community College*

We also acknowledge the special assistance and encouragement given us by two individuals at Richard D. Irwin, Inc.—Craig S. Beytien, sponsoring editor, and Karen Smith, project editor. Without their help, we would not have completed this textbook.

And we thank the personnel of the Fifth Floor Word Processing Center in the Marriott School of Management at Brigham Young University. We give a special thanks to Nina Whitehead, the supervisor who so effectively coordinated much of the word processing of our manuscript.

Colleen Vawdrey
Ted D. Stoddard
R. DerMont Bell

CONTENTS

UNIT 1   REVIEWING THE BASICS   2

   1. Parts of Speech   5
   2. Sentence Components and Types   17
   3. Spelling   31
   4. Confusing Words   47
   5. Number Usage   61
   6. Capitalization   75
   7. Abbreviations   89
   8. Dictionary Usage   105

UNIT 2   USING VERBS   120

   9. Orientation to Verbs   123
   10. The Simple Tenses   143
   11. The Perfect Tenses and Progressive Forms   157
   12. Verbals   171
   13. Mood   187
   14. Voice   201

UNIT 3   PUNCTUATING YOUR WRITING   218

   15. The Comma for Joining Independent Clauses   221
   16. The Semicolon for Joining Independent Clauses   233
   17. Introductory Clauses, Phrases, and Words   247
   18. Series, Interrupters, Appositives, and Appendages   261
   19. Other Punctuation   279

UNIT 4   USING CONNECTIVES   298

   20. Connecting, Coordinating, and Subordinating   301
   21. Prepositions   317

UNIT 5   SELECTING NOUNS AND PRONOUNS   334

   22. Subjective- and Objective-Case Pronouns   337
   23. Relative Pronouns   353
   24. Plural Nouns   365
   25. Possessive Nouns and Pronouns   377

UNIT 6   ENSURING AGREEMENT AND REFERENCE   392

   26. Subject-Verb Agreement   395
   27. Pronoun-Antecedent Agreement and Reference   407

UNIT 7   USING MODIFIERS   422

28. Adjectives and Adverbs   425
29. Compound, Coordinate, and Consecutive Modifiers   443
30. Misplaced and Dangling Modifiers   459

UNIT 8   DEALING WITH LANGUAGE USAGE   476

31. Wordy Expressions   479
32. Confusable Words   499
33. Nonsexist Writing   513

UNIT 9   DEVELOPING EFFECTIVE WRITING TECHNIQUES   528

34. Writing Sentences and Paragraphs   531
35. Accessing Business Documents   547
36. Using Prewrite, Write, and Rewrite Strategies   565

UNIT 10   GENERATING BUSINESS CORRESPONDENCE   578

37. Correspondence Formats   581
38. Good-News Messages   591
39. Bad-News Messages   601
40. Persuasive Messages   611

Index   619

PRACTICAL
BUSINESS ENGLISH

LESSONS IN THIS UNIT

1. PARTS OF SPEECH
2. SENTENCE COMPONENTS AND TYPES
3. SPELLING
4. CONFUSING WORDS
5. NUMBER USAGE
6. CAPITALIZATION
7. ABBREVIATIONS
8. DICTIONARY USAGE

As you think about the title of Unit 1, ''Reviewing the Basics,'' you might be tempted to ask yourself, ''Why is the material in this unit any more 'basic' than everything else in this text?'' Such a question is logical. Some students and some instructors might consider nearly everything in the textbook to be ''basic'' in nature.

However, for several reasons, you can be assured that your curriculum needs a business English course and that the course requires an appropriate textbook. Yes, much of the material in any business English textbook is ''basic''—meaning that the material reflects the fundamental building blocks of good business writing. The realistic need for students to master these basics at a higher level than they already have justifies this text's ''basic'' contents.

Often in business English textbooks, much of the material you will find in this textbook's Unit 1 appears in an appendix at the end of the book. To us, that suggests the material is unimportant

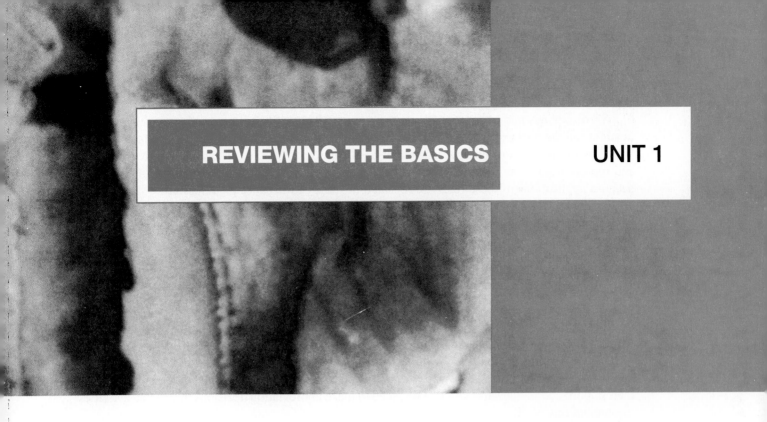

REVIEWING THE BASICS   UNIT 1

or is less important than the rest of the material in the book. We simply don't subscribe to that thinking. We feel Unit 1's contents are important, so we have chosen to present the material in Unit 1 as part of the textbook rather than in an appendix.

You and your instructor will decide the extent to which you need to review or study the lessons in Unit 1. To help you decide the approach you will follow, we draw your attention to our thinking and approach to Unit 1.

We have found that many students have a poor understanding of how business English works and are weak in the use of the "jargon" of business English. Those deficiencies begin with the parts of speech and sentence components and types. Throughout this book, we must assume you do have *some* knowledge, so if you lack such understandings, you will profit from a thorough review of the "basics" covered in Lessons 1 and 2.

We also know many students have rather serious spelling problems, so we approach "spelling basics" in a unique way. We realize how helpful electronic spellers are to writers, but we also realize you may not always have access to such spellers. Therefore, in Lesson 3, we give you some practical rules of spelling and introduce you to 150 of the most frequently used and most frequently misspelled words of the business vocabulary. We ask you to master the spelling of at least these frequently misspelled words, especially because we repeat them in selected exercises in some of the subsequent lessons. You'll be amazed at your growth in spelling power if you *do* master these frequently used—and frequently misspelled—words.

We follow a similar philosophy concerning the "confusing words" in Lesson 4. Most of your problems with the words in this lesson are not spelling dilemmas. Instead, they are word-choice decisions that you repeatedly face. The "confusing words" we have selected are based on the frequency with which they occur in the business vocabulary. We expect you to master these words because you will use them in some of the subsequent lessons.

All disciplines and occupations have their unique ways of handling numbers in written documents, and the business world is especially careful to request preferred usage. Therefore, Lesson 5 deals with the rules of number usage that are commonly reflected in business correspondence and reports. Again, we ask you to master the number-usage rules at the beginning of the book, because applications of these rules are repeated in some of the subsequent lessons.

Capitalization rules are generally uniform among disciplines, but we find that students usually need either a review or an initial exposure to capitalization rules. Lesson 6 reviews the rules of capitalization that are common in the business world. Once again, we expect you to master these rules because of their importance and because they appear in selected activities in some of the subsequent lessons.

We all use abbreviations in our day-to-day writing-related activities. However, the business world, much like other disciplines, has unique requirements for using or not using abbreviations in business writing. In Lesson 7, you will find rules about abbreviations that can generally be applied to any discipline. Thus, you will want to master the rules for abbreviations because of their importance and because you will be asked to make abbreviation decisions in selected activities throughout this book.

Lesson 8 of this unit deals with the dictionary. Everyone uses the dictionary at one time or another. However, we feel your use of this important tool will be significantly enhanced if you know and practice effective dictionary usage. We do not use dictionary learnings throughout this textbook, but we do encourage you to master dictionary usage as an important dimension of your study of business English.

Of the eight lessons in Unit 1, all are important to your study of business English; but five of them are very crucial because you will be repeatedly exposed to their contents, rules, or principles. At the beginning of the course, resolve to master everything in Unit 1; and be certain you are ready to make repeated judgments and decisions about the following five components of Unit 1:

The frequently misspelled words in Lesson 3

The confusing words in Lesson 4

The rules for numbers in Lesson 5

The rules for capitalizations in Lesson 6

The rules for abbreviations in Lesson 7

The contents of Lessons 3 through 7 will influence and guide you throughout much of this textbook. This impact is a reflection of the psychological learning principle of repetition—you will be exposed over and over to the frequently misspelled words, confusing words, number rules, capitalization rules, and abbreviations rules. As you determine your plan for mastering Unit 1, and especially Lessons 3 through 7, your individuality will help you know how much of Unit 1 you have already mastered and how intensively you must study and how much you must memorize to gain an appropriate mastery of this unit.

A study of English grammar fundamentals begins with the parts of speech. All words fit into one of eight parts of speech. The purpose of this lesson is to acquaint (or maybe reacquaint) you with these parts of speech. Your ability to identify these categories and to understand their functions in grammar is important in mastering business English.

All eight parts of speech are presented as an overview in this lesson. They will then be studied in depth in succeeding units in the text.

Pretest

Identify each part of speech in the following sentences.

1. Yes! You should send quickly for some information and prizes.
2. Alas, they will find the project very interesting yet without purpose.

Key: (1) Yes—interjection; you—pronoun; should send—verb; quickly—adverb; for—preposition; some—adjective; information—noun; and—conjunction; prizes—noun; (2) Alas—interjection; they—pronoun; will find—verb; the—adjective; project—noun; very—adverb; interesting—adjective; yet—conjunction; without—preposition; purpose—noun.

Terminology

Adjective—A modifier of a noun or a pronoun. Adjectives answer such questions as *what kind? which one?* or *how many?*

Kathleen wore **that cute pink** blouse.

Adverb—A modifier of a verb, adjective, or other adverb. Adverbs answer such questions as *how? when? where?* or *to what extent?*

Eric ran **away very fast**.

Antecedent—The noun for which a pronoun substitutes.

Chiaki found the **book** lying on **its** side in **her** room.

Article—A category of adjectives that includes the words *a, an,* and *the.*

The student needed **a** sweater and **an** umbrella.

Common noun—A noun that names a general category of persons, places, things, or ideas.

The **members** of the **committee** discussed **loyalty** within the **company**.

Conjunction—A connector of words, phrases, or clauses to show relationships.

Shreedhar **or** Keisha will be available, **but** Mark **and** Alan have other commitments.

Helping verb—A verb added to the main verb to form a verb phrase.

Kent **has been** helping Craig with the project.

Interjection—A word or phrase used to express emotion or surprise. Interjections are not used often in business writing.

Oh, I understand now.

Linking verb—A verb that shows the state of being in a sentence. Forms of the verb *to be* are the most common linking verbs. Sense verbs such as *taste* and *smell* are also considered linking verbs.

Noun—The word or phrase that names a person, place, thing, or quality.

David showed his **honesty** by returning the **money**.

Preposition—A word used in a sentence to show relationships. Prepositions most often occur in phrases with nouns or pronouns.

In the fall, everyone **except** Judy will be promoted.

Pronoun—A word used to substitute for a noun.

She and Michael took **her** sister with **them**.

Proper noun—A noun that names a specific person, place, thing, or quality and that is usually capitalized.

Connie rode **Amtrak** to **New York**.

Verb—The word or group of words that describes the action or state of being in the sentence.

Emma **has been** loyal and **should receive** a raise.

Nouns

*Use
T1-1
here*

Nouns name persons, places, things, or qualities.

The **doctor** has been providing the necessary care. (person)

The **university** decided to assume that function. (place)

Each **plan** has a different strong point. (thing)

Honesty is still perceived to be the best policy. (quality)

Nouns generally tell what you are writing about and often serve as subjects of sentences. Most nouns name things that can be seen (with the exception of qualities such as loyalty). They provide the visual images of the sentence.

Nouns can be either singular (referring to one item) or plural (referring to two or more items). This distinction will become important since you must make the verbs and pronouns agree with the nouns. You will study this topic in detail in Unit 5.

Nouns can also be classified as common or proper. **Common nouns** name general categories such as a student or a course. **Proper nouns** name specific items such as *Edward* or *Business English 101*. You should remember to capitalize most proper nouns.

Pronouns

Pronouns are used to substitute for nouns. Pronouns avoid the need to repeat nouns or to create awkward messages. Compare the following sentences:

When Mary's class was over, Mary went to Mary's car.

When Mary's class was over, she went to her car.

Because pronouns are noun substitutes, they may also serve as subjects of sentences. Like nouns, pronouns name something that can usually be visualized. However, readers may easily become confused if pronouns are not used carefully.

Effective writers are careful to be sure the reader knows to what idea the pronoun refers. This reference word is known as the **antecedent**.

Ricardo told Marianna he was ready for the meeting.

The reader knows the pronoun *he* refers to Ricardo. But what about the following sentence?

The manager told Bruce he needed an updated agenda.

Who needed the agenda—Bruce or the manager?

Pronouns are classified according to their use—called case. The details of pronoun use will be presented in depth in Unit 5.

Verbs

Verbs are usually the action words in the sentence. Because verbs are the words that make the sentence "move," they are usually considered the most important part of the sentence. Every sentence **must** contain a verb to be complete. Many times a sentence may contain a verb phrase. When this situation occurs, all verbs except the last one in the phrase are known as *helping verbs*. Some sentences have more than one verb; in these cases, the verbs are known as compound verbs.

We **should have known** she **was telling** us the truth.

The helping verbs are **should have** and **was**. The main verbs in this compound example are **known** and **telling**.

Sometimes verbs will show a state of being or condition rather than action. Such verbs are called *linking verbs*. Forms of the verb *to be* are the most common linking verbs. Other common state-of-being verbs include verbs related to the senses (see, feel, touch, etc.).

Geri **is** the new district manager.

Michel **has been** ready for over an hour.

Verbs are the most complex part of the sentence and include many properties that are important to your study of business English. Because your understanding of these properties is vital to your mastery of business communication, we have chosen to present them at the beginning of your study—in Unit 2.

Adjectives

Modifiers are words that make the sentence interesting. Although your writing may be considered complete with limited use of modifiers, the reader will not "picture" what you are saying as easily without the use of these modifiers.

Adjectives are one type of modifier. They clarify your writing because they describe nouns and pronouns. Adjectives answer such questions as *what kind? which one?* or *how many?*

That policy offers the **best** benefits of **three** plans.

Which one?—*that*
What kind?—*best*
How many?—*three*

The words *a*, *an*, and *the* are known as **articles**. These common words also function as adjectives in a sentence.

A book and **an** apple are on **the** table.

Adverbs

Use
T1-2
here

Adverbs are another kind of modifier; and they describe verbs, adjectives, and other adverbs. Adverbs answer such questions as *how? when? where?* or *to what extent?* The most common adverb ending is *ly*.

Yesterday Jose completed the job **here exceedingly well**.

How?—*well*
When?—*yesterday*
Where?—*here*
To what extent?—*exceedingly*

Although business writing does not tend to use modifiers to the same degree that creative writing does, you will find them important to your study of business English. They will be discussed in depth in Unit 7.

Prepositions

Prepositions are a type of connective. They show relationships within a sentence by connecting the object (a noun or pronoun) with another part of the sentence. By learning to recognize prepositional phrases, you will also discover that finding the subject of a sentence will be easier because prepositional phrases cannot act as simple subjects. Sentence subjects will be discussed in Lesson 2.

The winners **of the contest** were chosen last week.

You should select the preposition that indicates the relationship you want to establish—position, direction, time, or something else.

Position		Direction	
above	*above* the room	**at**	*at* the back
beneath	*beneath* the book	**down**	*down* the stairs
by	*by* the car	**from**	*from* the box
in	*in* the class	**to**	*to* the meeting
near	*near* the house	**up**	*up* the hill
outside	*outside* the door		

Time		Miscellaneous	
after	*after* the game	**about**	*about* the merger
before	*before* next week	**except**	*except* the president
during	*during* intermission	**for**	*for* her benefit
since	*since* yesterday	**of**	*of* importance
until	*until* tomorrow	**without**	*without* hope

Conjunctions

Conjunctions are another type of connector and are used to join words, phrases, or clauses in a sentence. Both conjunctions and prepositions are often overlooked parts of sentences. However, their importance in relating one item to another within the message will become evident to you as you study their characteristics.

Classifications of conjunctions include coordinating, subordinating, correlative, and conjunctive adverbs.

Sherry **and** Jose are working on that project. (coordinating)

You may go **when** your replacement arrives. (subordinating)

Neither Eric **nor** David has finished school. (correlative)

We are trying; **however**, we have not succeeded. (conjunctive adverb)

Unit 4 discusses all types of connectives as they relate to business writing.

Interjections

Interjections are words that are used to show emotion or strong feelings. They are often punctuated with an exclamation mark, although a comma may be used also.

No, you should not worry about that situation.

Wow! I am very impressed with your accomplishment.

*Use
T1-3
here*

Since interjections do not commonly cause problems in business writing, they will not be emphasized in this textbook.

Posttest

Mark the words in the sentences according to the following key:

Adj = adjective	N = noun
Adv = adverb	Prep = preposition
Con = conjunction	Pro = pronoun
Int = interjection	V = verb

1. You should know and use grammar principles correctly.

2. Approval of your teacher is required before the test.

Key: (1) You—pro, should know—v, and—con, use—v, grammar—adj, principles—n, correctly—adv; (2) Approval—n, of—prep, your—pro (used as adj), teacher—n, is required—v, before—prep, the—adj, test—n.

LEVEL A

Name _____

Exercise 1–1   On the lines below, write **T** if the statement is true and **F** if the statement is false.

_T_ 1. Pronouns are words used in a sentence to replace nouns.

_F_ 2. A sentence cannot function without both a noun and a verb.

_T_ 3. Adjectives and adverbs are both modifiers, but they are used to modify different words.

_T_ 4. Both prepositions and conjunctions are types of connectors.

_F_ 5. The verb in a sentence always shows action.

_F_ 6. Although common nouns are usually capitalized, proper nouns are always capitalized.

_T_ 7. Interjections may or may not include exclamation marks.

_T_ 8. Prepositions usually occur in phrases and show relationships within sentences.

_T_ 9. Conjunctions may join one entire clause with another.

_T_ 10. Adverbs most commonly end in *ly*.

Exercise 1–2   Write **N** for bold words that are nouns and **V** for bold words that are verbs.

_V, N_ 1. Please **check** your **mail** daily.

_N, V_ 2. You should sign your **check** before you **mail** it.

_N_ 3. The **blind** does a good job of blocking the sun.

_V_ 4. The sun will **blind** the football team at this angle.

_N, V_ 5. The **ground** will be white as long as the weather keeps **snowing.**

_V, N_ 6. Your car is **grounded** as long as the **snow** keeps falling.

_V_ 7. If you **rock** the canoe, we may all fall in.

_N_ 8. Jeremy gathered some beautiful **rocks** on the shore.

_N_ 9. That gold **watch** is very elegant.

_V_ 10. Please **watch** your step as you walk.

_V_ 11. Because my car is broken, I must **walk** to work this week.

_N_ 12. The **walk** around the gardens is well kept by the gardener.

_N_ 13. After the candidate **search** ended, we went to dinner to celebrate.

_V_ 14. Will you help me **search** for the missing report?

Exercise 1–3 Write **Adj** for bold words that are adjectives and **Adv** for bold words that are adverbs.

Adj 1. All **new** automobiles will be delivered in time for your sale next week.

Adj 2. The items on your **afternoon** schedule for tomorrow must be postponed.

Adv 3. The Jazz did a good job of **consistently** outscoring opponents because of the home-court advantage.

Adj 4. Joni did a **better** job of completing the report than any other member of the department did.

Adv 5. Joni completed the report **better** than anyone else in the department.

Adv 6. How **well** did Shirlee do in her interview yesterday?

Adj 7. Colette has found the **proper** way to sell her ideas to the president.

Adv 8. Did Pierce find a way to handle the problem with the customer **properly**?

Adj 9. Vickie found **beautiful** flowers on her desk when she arrived this morning.

Adj 10. We had an order placed for **ten** copies of our new software program.

Exercise 1–4 Write **C** if the statement is correct and **I** if the statement is incorrect.

C 1. The sentence *My brother has taken a new job with a consulting company* contains a pronoun.

I 2. The sentence *You did not voice opposition; we implemented the plan* contains a conjunction.

I 3. The sentence *Three plans were considered before we made the final decision* contains both an adjective and an adverb modifier.

I 4. In the sentence *Nobody wanted to see Ms. Lindsay leave the company for another position*, the word *for* is a conjunction.

I 5. In the sentence *Mick continues to give good advice, even though he is no longer our consultant*, the word *consultant* is an adjective.

C 6. The sentence *Do not let anyone convince you we are losing sales to the competition* contains three pronoun examples.

C 7. The sentence *I will call Lindy in the morning to arrange an appointment with Dr. Hayward* contains two prepositional phrases.

C 8. The sentence *The whole reason for our meeting is to increase efficiency in the department* contains a linking verb.

LEVEL B

Name _____

Exercise 1–5   Underline each verb or verb phrase and indicate whether the main verb in each sentence is an action verb (**A**) or a linking verb (**L**).

L ___ 1. One of the major goals is managing our resources.

A ___ 2. Four important skills will help with the task.

A ___ 3. Involve the employees in the task as much as possible.

A ___ 4. Some people may ignore the most basic solutions.

L ___ 5. After some time, your answer will be easy to recognize.

L ___ 6. Failure is usually a chance for eventual success.

A ___ 7. Effective managers share information with other people.

A ___ 8. After my evaluation, I highly recommend this expansion.

Exercise 1–6   Indicate the part of speech for each of the bold words in the following sentences.

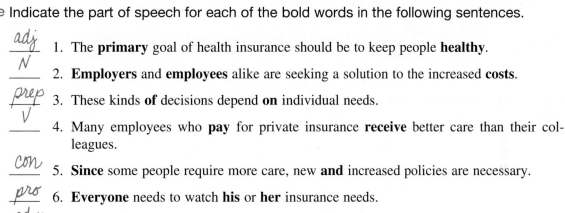

adj ___ 1. The **primary** goal of health insurance should be to keep people **healthy**.

N ___ 2. **Employers** and **employees** alike are seeking a solution to the increased **costs**.

prep ___ 3. These kinds **of** decisions depend **on** individual needs.

V ___ 4. Many employees who **pay** for private insurance **receive** better care than their colleagues.

con ___ 5. **Since** some people require more care, new **and** increased policies are necessary.

pro ___ 6. **Everyone** needs to watch **his** or **her** insurance needs.

adv ___ 7. Competition **very** often affects medical needs **adversely**.

adj ___ 8. **Cost-saving** ideas might include **some** group insurance policies.

prep ___ 9. **Under** the present system, tough decisions must be made **about** alternatives.

V ___ 10. Determining what services **can be provided** is important, and the decision **will be made** soon.

adv ___ 11. These decisions are **often** difficult and cannot be made **quickly**.

con ___ 12. **Before** the change, employees could not choose their health care plan **but** were forced to conform.

N ___ 13. **Availability** of the latest **technology** gives patients the best **care** possible.

pro ___ 14. **No one** is denied care as long as **his** or **her** needs can be met.

Exercise 1–7   Indicate the correct answer for each question.

willing, able
the

1. On the line at the left, list all the adjectives in the following sentence: *Marty is willing and able to edit our proposal before we send it to the printer.*

our, we
it

2. On the line at the left, list all the pronouns in the above sentence.

has requested,
continue, started

3. List all the verbs in the following sentence: *Mr. Williams has requested that I continue the project you started in August.*

Mr. Williams,
project, August

4. List all the nouns in the above sentence.

quickly,
definitely

5. List all the adverbs in the following sentence: *By completing their project quickly, we will definitely guarantee correct implementation by the incoming committee.*

correct,
incoming, the

6. List all the adjectives in the above sentence.

and, although

7. List all the conjunctions in the following sentence: *During the meeting, we discovered Mr. Romero and Ms. Tucker are not qualified for their jobs, although they are receiving top pay.*

during, for

8. List all the prepositions in the above sentence.

Exercise 1–8   Label all parts of speech in the following sentences.

    Pro   N   Prep   Adj   Adj   N   Adv   V   Adj   Adj   N
1. Our choice of a new plan now is the best option.

    Adv   N   V   Adj   N   Prep   Pro   N
2. Actually, Todd knows the details about our decision.

    N   Prep   N   V   V   V   Con   V
3. Restrictions of policies will be noted and followed.

    Prep   Adj   N   Adj   N   V   V   Adv
4. With recent advances, the economy has benefited greatly.

    Adv   N   V   Pro   N   Prep   Adj   N
5. Today, technology aids our competition in world markets.

LEVEL C

Name _____

Exercise
1-9

Underline the nouns in the following sentences. Then replace each noun with another noun. No. 0 is provided as an example.

    Ken   type   customer   article

0. Tom discusses a new breed of people in his textbook.

1. The activities of executives include both people and things.

2. Top employees understand the importance of helping others.

3. Success in business means one must go beyond the ordinary.

4. Professionals are concerned with the management of the company.

5. Most firms can improve service by analyzing procedures.

6. All facts must be considered when the selection is made.

7. Two main issues evolve from the dispute.

Exercise
1-10

Indicate whether the bold word is an adjective (adj) or an adverb (adv). Then replace each bold modifier with another modifier. No. 0 is provided as an example.

                                practical

  adj   0. Parents should teach children **sound** money management.

  adj 1. A **flexible** budget is critical to achieving goals.

  adv 2. Children will budget **enthusiastically** with some help.

  adj 3. A savings program is **effective** in planning for the future.

  adj 4. **Three** principles can be applied to money management.

  adv 5. Set goals that will **accurately** reflect needs and wants.

  adj 6. Too many people do not have a **workable** budget.

adv   7. Conservative spending is **only** difficult at first.

adv   8. **Too** many uses for money may be the source of conflict.

adj   9. You should learn to live by **these** basic principles.

adj   10. Use savings for planned, **short-term** purchases.

Exercise 1–11

1. Compose a sentence containing at least five adjectives. Mark them.

_____

_____

2. Compose a sentence containing both an action verb and a linking verb. Mark each.

_____

_____

3. Compose a sentence containing both a common and a proper noun. Label each.

_____

_____

4. Compose a sentence containing three prepositional phrases. Mark them.

_____

_____

5. Compose a sentence containing two pronouns. Mark the pronoun and draw an arrow to the antecedent for each.

_____

_____

6. Compose a sentence containing three adverbs. Mark them.

_____

_____

SENTENCE COMPONENTS AND TYPES

LESSON 2

Being able to communicate clearly requires that both the reader and the writer get the same meaning from the message. You must adhere to certain ''rules of the trade'' to ensure that the words you put on paper will be clear to your intended reader. In written communication, the sentence is the basic unit you must understand.

Sentences are classified in several ways. In this lesson, we will look at sentences to become more familiar with the components that make sentences both correct and clear.

Sentence Components

Every sentence must contain both a subject and a predicate. However, sometimes the subject is understood, as in the imperative sentences discussed later in this lesson. Sentences may also contain complements to complete their meaning. You must be able to distinguish among the elements of subjects, predicates, and complements to understand sentence structure.

Subjects. The simple subject is the noun or pronoun that is the topic of the sentence. That is, the subject tells *who* or *what* the sentence is about. As you learned in Lesson 1, subjects are almost always nouns or pronouns. Some sentences have two or more subjects that are called compound subjects. The complete subject includes the simple or compound subject and any subject modifiers needed to complete the meaning.

The greatest assets in a business are the employees.

Assets is the simple subject; *the greatest assets in a business* is the complete subject.

Both managers and employees in a business are great assets.

The compound subject is *managers* and *employees*; *both managers and employees in a business* is the complete subject.

Understanding sentence subjects is important. As you will find throughout your study of business English, finding the true subject of a sentence (the simple subject) is essential in making predicates and other sentence components agree.

Predicates. The simple predicate is the verb of the sentence. Some sentences may have two or more verbs called compound verbs. The complete predicate includes the simple or compound verb and any modifiers and complements needed to complete the thought.

Managers have promoted individual initiative in employees.

Have promoted is the simple predicate or verb; *have promoted individual initiative in employees* is the complete predicate.

People are motivated by self-interest and want success.

The compound predicate is *are motivated* and *want*; *are motivated by self-interest and want success* is the complete predicate.

Complements. Complements are used to complete the thought of the sentence. Three complements are direct objects, indirect objects, and subject complements.

Direct objects are nouns or pronouns that complete the sense of an action verb. They usually answer the questions *whom?* or *what?* In the following example, *responsibility* is the direct object and answers the question *what?*

Good managers give employees **responsibility.**

Indirect objects are nouns or pronouns that complete the sense of an action verb and that precede direct objects. These indirect objects usually answer the questions *to whom?* or *to what?* or *for whom?* or *for what?* In the following sentence, *employees* is an example of an indirect object and answers the question *to whom?*

Good managers give **employees** responsibility.

Both the direct and indirect objects follow the action verb *give*.

Subject complements are nouns, pronouns, or adjectives that complete the sense of a linking verb. They describe the subject.

A good manager is **understanding**.

Understanding is an adjective and is the subject complement following the linking verb *is*.

The leader of the discussion group was **Glenn**.

The best candidate for the position will be **she**.

Glenn is the noun complement of the linking verb *was*. *She* is the pronoun complement of the linking verb *will be*. As a novice student of business English, you may challenge the use of *she* instead of *her*. When you study pronouns in Unit 5, you will learn about pronoun usage. For now, simply know that a pronoun may be used to complete the thought of a linking verb.

Pretest

Mark the items below using the following classifications:

F	Fragment	**SM**	Simple sentence
RO	Run-on sentence	**CM**	Compound sentence
CS	Comma splice	**CX**	Complex sentence

1. Examples of unethical behavior appear daily in the media action must be taken immediately to counter this trend.

2. Although a myriad of factors influence ethics, two stand out.

3. In order to determine who can best teach ethical principles.

4. Few people question the fact that education affects ethical beliefs, but many persons question the impact of this effect.

5. Values formed long ago cannot be completely changed in a short time.

6. Strong arguments for teaching ethics exist, many managers are introducing ethics programs in their companies.

Key: (1) RO—two independent clauses should be separated with a semicolon or joined with a comma plus *and*; (2) CX—dependent clause followed by independent clause; (3) F—incomplete idea; (4) CM—two independent clauses with correct punctuation; (5) SM—one independent clause; (6) CS—two independent clauses incorrectly punctuated with comma only).

Terminology

Clause—A group of words with a subject and a verb.

Comma splice—A sentence containing two independent clauses that are joined with a comma only.

Complement—A word, phrase, or clause in the predicate used to complete the meaning of the sentence.

Complex sentence—A sentence containing one independent clause and at least one dependent clause.

Compound-complex sentence—A sentence containing at least two independent clauses and at least one dependent clause.

Compound sentence—A sentence containing two or more independent clauses and no dependent clauses.

Declarative sentence—A sentence stating fact and ending with a period.

Dependent clause—A group of words containing a subject and a verb but not expressing a complete thought.

Direct object—A sentence complement of an action verb. Direct objects usually answer the questions *whom?* or *what?* about the subject and its verb.

Exclamatory sentence—A sentence that expresses strong feeling, fact, or opinion and that ends with an exclamation mark.

Fragment—A group of words that is incorrectly expressed as a sentence.

Imperative sentence—A sentence that issues a command. Imperative sentences have an understood *you* subject.

Independent clause—A group of words that has a subject and a verb and that can stand alone.

Indirect object—A sentence complement of an action verb. Indirect objects usually answer the questions *for whom?* or *for what?* or *to whom?* or *to what?* and precede direct objects.

Interrogative sentence—A sentence that asks a direct question and ends with a question mark.

Inverted order—A sentence not stated in the usual sequence of subject, verb, and complement. Questions are often expressed in inverted order.

Normal order—A sentence stated in the usual sequence of subject and verb followed by any complements.

Phrase—A group of words without a subject and a verb.

Polite request—A sentence containing a request for action rather than an answer. Although similar to an interrogative sentence, a polite request ends with a period.

Predicate—The sentence component containing the verb and other words to complete the thought. The simple predicate is the verb.

Run-on sentence—A sentence containing two independent clauses without punctuation or a conjunctive joiner to join the clauses.

Subject—A word or group of words explaining the topic of the sentence. Subjects are either nouns or pronouns.

Subject complement—The sentence component that completes a linking (state-of-being) verb. The subject complement describes the subject and can be a noun, a pronoun, or an adjective.

Sentence Patterns

Sentences most commonly begin with the subject. Although many patterns are possible, the most frequent ones are discussed here. You should become skilled at recognizing the patterns.

Use T2-1 here

Subject/Verb. Sometimes a sentence will contain only a subject and verb with no completers necessary.

Jose is working.

Maria cried.

Subject/Action Verb/Direct Object.   Action verbs often require an answer to the questions *what?* or *whom?* to complete the thought.

> Yuki enjoys school.
>
> Chris likes Toni.

School answers *what* Yuki enjoys, and *Toni* answers *whom* Chris likes. You can readily see that the sentences would not make sense without these direct-object completers.

Subject/Action Verb/Indirect Object/Direct Object.   When answering the questions *to whom?* or *to what?* or *for whom?* or *for what?*, use an indirect object along with the direct object to complete the thought. The indirect object will precede the direct object.

> Melba gave her the book.
>
> Mother bought Michael the car.

The pronoun *her* answers *to whom* the book was given; likewise, the noun *Michael* answers *for whom* the car was bought.

Use T2-2 here

Subject/Linking Verb/Subject Complement.   The component after a linking verb is a noun, a pronoun, or an adjective that describes the subject.

> Larry has been busy.
>
> Verna is an accountant.

Inverted Order.   Although sentences most commonly begin with the topic first (the subject) and then tell about the topic (verb), you probably already know that this order is not always followed. Sometimes the elements in a sentence will not appear in normal order beginning with the subject. Questions are good examples of inverted-order sentences. Many times you may want to return these sentences to normal order in your mind to help you ''sort out'' the elements into correct parts.

Inverted	**Normal**
Will you go with me?	You will go with me.
Under the bed are the slippers.	The slippers are under the bed.

Sentence Types

To understand the different types of sentences, you must know the differences among phrases, dependent clauses, and independent clauses. Phrases are groups of words that do not contain a subject and a verb. They can function as adjectives, adverbs, nouns, or verbs within the sentence. Although dependent and independent clauses both contain subjects and verbs, the dependent clause cannot function alone as a sentence. It must ''depend'' on another part of the sentence.

Use T2-3 here

Phrase	in the room
Dependent clause	if he was in the room
Independent clause	he was in the room

As you can see, the independent clause could be a sentence; but the phrase and the dependent clause need more information for the thought to be complete. Understanding the differences among phrases, dependent clauses, and independent clauses is extremely important to your study of business English. When you study punctuation in Unit 3, you will realize the importance of being able to distinguish among these elements.

Sentences can be classified by structure—the number and kinds of clauses included in the sentence.

Use T2-4 here

Simple Sentences.   A simple sentence contains only one independent clause and no dependent clauses.

> Nick paid the check.

Compound Sentences.   A compound sentence contains at least two independent clauses and no dependent clauses.

> Nick paid the check, and Terry left the tip.

Use T2-5 here

Complex Sentences.   A complex sentence contains one independent clause and at least one dependent clause.

> Although Nick paid the check, Terry left the tip.

Compound-Complex Sentences.   A compound-complex sentence is a combination that includes at least one dependent clause and at least two independent clauses.

> Although the rest of us were not aware, Nick paid the check; and Terry left the tip.

A skilled writer will combine sentence types when writing to add variety and to avoid the monotony that can occur when only one sentence type is used.

Sentence Problems

Use T2-6 here

Beginning writers frequently experience some common problems with sentences. Avoiding these problems will give you a definite advantage as you strive to improve your written communication skills. We will stress three common sentence problems. Because they are so important in writing, you will find them again in the punctuation and connectives sections of the text.

Sentence Fragments.   A fragment is a group of words that is punctuated as a sentence. The fragment may be a phrase or a dependent clause. Remember, however, that neither of these can function as a sentence.

> To determine how the task should be done.

> Since individuals are forced to make value judgments daily.

Run-on Sentences.   A run-on sentence contains two independent clauses without punctuation or a conjunctive joiner to join the clauses. Careful writers ensure that correct punctuation is used to join the clauses.

> A business community is a good place for ethical examples individuals are forced to make value judgments daily.

Use T2-7 here

Comma Splices.   A comma splice contains two independent clauses that are joined with a comma only. As the punctuation and connectives lessons will clearly point out, you have several choices to correct these sentences. However, you need to realize now that a comma cannot perform the joining function by itself.

> A business community is a good place for ethical examples, individuals are forced to make value judgments daily.

Sentence Categories

Another way to classify sentences is by their intent. We will recognize five categories of sentences.

Declarative Sentences.   A declarative sentence states a fact or presents information. These sentences are the most common and end with a period.

> People develop ethical behavior by modeling others.

Interrogative Sentences.   An interrogative sentence asks a direct question and ends with a question mark.

> Do people develop ethical behavior by modeling others?

Imperative Sentences.   An imperative sentence issues a command and has an understood *you* subject.

> Develop ethical behavior by modeling others.
>
> [*You*] develop ethical behavior by modeling others.

Exclamatory Sentences.   An exclamatory sentence expresses strong feeling, fact, or opinion and ends with an exclamation mark.

> You must develop ethical behavior!

Polite Requests.   A polite request differs from a question by requesting action rather than an answer. Although similar to an interrogative sentence, the polite request ends with a period.

> Will you please develop ethical behavior.

Posttest

For each sentence below, mark the simple or compound subject **S**; underline the complete subject once; mark the simple or compound predicate **P**; underline the complete predicate twice; mark direct objects **DO**; and mark indirect objects **IO**.

1. Students' character and personality are determined early.

2. Many educators are teaching ethics.

3. Personal experience will give them credibility.

Classify each sentence below as simple **SM**, compound **CM**, complex **CX**, or compound-complex **CC**. Then, classify each sentence as declarative **D**, interrogative **IN**, imperative **IM**, exclamatory **E**, or polite request **PR**.

4. Do managers and educators realize ethics is shaped by family and church long before an individual joins a company?

5. Although adherence to ethics is not always a written rule, it is expected.

6. Adopt the code of ethics for your business, and expect your employees to follow it.

Key: (1) Students' character and personality are determined early. (2) Many educators are teaching ethics. (3) Personal experience would give them credibility. (4) CX, IN; (5) CX, D; (6) CM, IM.

LEVEL A

Name _____

Exercise 2–1   On the lines below, write **T** if the statement is true and **F** if the statement is false.

_T_ 1. A sentence may have more than one subject.

_F_ 2. The simple predicate is the main verb only and does not include the helper verbs.

_F_ 3. A subject complement may be a noun or adjective and follows an action verb.

_T_ 4. A sentence may be complete with a subject and verb and may not require any complement.

_T_ 5. An indirect object may be a noun or pronoun and may answer the question *for whom* or *for what*.

_F_ 6. The statement *In the parking terrace are the automobiles* illustrates a normal order sentence.

_T_ 7. An independent clause may also be classified as a simple sentence.

_F_ 8. Joining two independent clauses with only a comma is an acceptable procedure.

_T_ 9. A dependent clause may also be classified as a sentence fragment.

_T_ 10. An imperative sentence will be written without a subject since the subject is understood.

Exercise 2–2   Write **S** if the group of words is a complete sentence and **NS** if the group of words cannot stand alone as a sentence. The end-of-sentence punctuation has been omitted.

_NS_ 1. Have been involved in business for 20 years

_NS_ 2. If less than a tenth of the energy stored as heat were converted each year

_S_ 3. The source of thermal energy is simply warm seawater

_S_ 4. Less than 5 percent of the incoming warm water is turned into steam

_NS_ 5. In a typical open-cycle system where the working fluid is warm seawater

_S_ 6. To complete the cycle, cold seawater condenses the steam

_NS_ 7. As long as you have plans to attend the seminar the last part of June

_S_ 8. All employees will be tested

_S_ 9. Call for your free brochure today

_NS_ 10. In September, when the students have left their summer jobs and have returned to school

_NS_ 11. If tickets are not available for the concert on your first choice of dates

_S_ 12. Having completed the planning stage, we began the project

_NS_ 13. The purpose of the project that has been outlined in detail

Exercise 2–3   For each item below, write **S** on the line if the statement is a simple sentence and **CM** if the statement is a compound sentence.

    _S_   1. Our office building is in need of repair on the outside and remodeling on the inside.

    _CM_   2. We have called an interior decorator, but he is out of town until next week.

    _CM_   3. Find out the measurements of the conference room, and report them to me as soon as possible.

    _S_   4. The ceiling in Mr. Jackson's office is stained from the last rainstorm.

    _CM_   5. Corporate headquarters have not agreed to pay for the renovations, nor do they intend to approve new furniture.

For each item below, write **CX** on the line if the statement is a complex sentence and **CM** if the statement is a compound sentence.

    _CX_   6. When the carpenters repair the roof, they plan to install a new chimney.

    _CX_   7. Because we want to take advantage of the furniture sales, we must choose the color schemes now.

    _CM_   8. We have agreed to install partitions in the word-processing center, yet the administrative assistants are not pleased.

    _CX_   9. We plan to replace the blue shades in the offices with a peach shade that is currently a more popular color.

    _CM_   10. The project will be finished in time for our seminar; thus, we can have an open house at that time.

Exercise 2–4   On the lines below, write **C** if the statement is correct and **I** if the statement is incorrect.

    _I_   1. In the sentence *Among the new courses offered is Principles of Marketing*, *courses* is the simple subject.

    _C_   2. The sentence *The newly hired professors and the incoming freshman students are eager to begin a new semester* contains a compound subject.

    _I_   3. The sentence *Dan plans to take courses in the morning and work in the afternoon* is a compound sentence with two subjects.

    _I_   4. The sentence *Networking with other students is important for any college student* contains a compound verb.

    _C_   5. In the sentence *The bookstore, which is located on the second floor of the student center, will not open until 10 a.m.*, *bookstore* is the simple subject.

    _I_   6. Because the sentence above is a simple one, *is* and *will open* are the compound verb.

    _I_   7. In the sentence *After completing registration, do you plan to buy your textbooks?*, *you* and *registration* are the compound subjects.

    _C_   8. In the sentence above, *do plan* is the simple verb.

LEVEL B

Name _____

Exercise
2–5

Match each sentence below with one of the following letters to indicate the problem. If the item is a correct sentence, use **S**.

F   Fragment   **CS**   Comma splice
RO   Run-on sentence   **S**   Correct sentence

_S_   1. Artificial intelligence imitates human reasoning.

_F_   2. To further develop this type of software.

_CS_   3. The most successful application is the expert system, this system acts as a consultant.

_S_   4. These systems will not only improve your firm's capabilities but also cut costs in the long run.

_CS_   5. You are right, the machine sounds too good to be true.

_RO_   6. Artificial intelligence is hard to define it is not defined the same way by everyone.

_F_   7. The job of the knowledge engineer, who is the link between the software developer and the end user.

_RO_   8. Expert systems are important they involve creating equipment with human-like ability.

Exercise
2–6

Match each sentence below with one of the following letters to indicate the sentence type.

SM   Simple   **CX**   Complex
CM   Compound   **CC**   Compound-complex

_CM_   1. Industrial robots have been around for about 25 years, and they now perform a wide variety of tasks.

_SM_   2. Significant improvements have been made in robotics technology in recent years.

_CM_   3. When programming a robot arm, an operator selects from the choices; a worker can then teach it to see new parts.

_CX_   4. As prices fall, robots will become more attractive to potential users.

_SM_   5. Advances in technology and in image processing have led to the development of new software.

_CM_   6. Robots have become more effective in industry; however, they are being used more often in medical research.

_CX_   7. Because some applications require computers to sort through databases, an effort to increase speed has begun.

_SM_   8. In the environment, the greatest demand will be for programmers and systems analysts with experience.

Exercise
2–7

Match each sentence below with one of the following letters to indicate the sentence category. Then insert the correct end-of-sentence punctuation.

D   Declarative   **E**   Exclamatory
IN Interrogative   **PR**   Polite Request
IM Imperative

_IN_   1. In this decade of hostile takeovers, are management accountants in demand or in peril ?

_D_   2. Many accountants ask whether they should be concerned about the consequences .

_PR_   3. Will you please outline the advantages of each situation .

_D_   4. How fast you can progress will depend on your communication and technical skills .

_IM_   5. Don't be afraid to gain experience while aspiring to your goals .

_IN_   6. Do you mind getting involved with untried specialties ?

_IM_   7. Since advanced preparation is necessary, begin now to plan for the future .

_E_   8. As Harry Truman knew, those who can't take heat should stay out of the kitchen !

Exercise
2–8

Indicate the correct answer for each question.

1. On the line below, write the simple subject of the following sentence: *Along with the shoes, Julianne also bought a matching purse.*

   Julianne

2. Write the simple verb of the following sentence: *Sheila and her husband have been waiting at least four hours for you to arrive.*

   have been waiting

3. Write the compound subject of the following sentence: *Neither Mrs. Gill nor the student-body officers has a valid suggestion for the next assembly.*

   Mrs. Gill, student body officers

4. Write the simple subject of the following sentence: *The new red convertible with all the electronic equipment is on sale today only.*

   Convertible

5. Write the compound verb of the following sentence: *Randy, along with his office colleagues, has agreed with the plan and will implement it immediately.*

   has agreed, will implement

6. Write the complete predicate of the following sentence: *Dimitri's involvement with the project has involved too much of his spare time lately.*

   has involved too much of his spare time lately

LEVEL C

Name _____

Exercise
2–9

In the following sentences, underline the simple or compound subject once and the simple or compound verb twice. Then replace each subject. No. 0 is provided as an example.

characteristics
0. The <u>qualities</u> of ineffective and effective managers <u>are described</u> in the article.

1. Their primary <u>roles</u> as effective managers <u>are</u> mentor and developer.

2. <u>Developing</u> good traits and <u>improving</u> on those already acquired <u>are</u> important challenges.

3. <u>Reasons</u>, rather than excuses, <u>are</u> highly <u>recommended</u> as learning tools.

4. The <u>descriptions</u> of each quality in a manager <u>instruct</u> and <u>inspire</u> potential executives.

5. Major <u>reform</u> of the foreign trade system <u>began</u> last year.

6. After six months of planning, the <u>leaders</u> can <u>determine</u> the best plan to use.

7. The first three <u>conditions</u> <u>require</u> updated technology.

8. Trade <u>officials</u> <u>propose</u> a plan to establish a better balance of trade.

Exercise
2–10

Compose sentences using the designated patterns and then identify each element.

1. Subject/verb/direct object

_____

_____

2. Subject/verb/indirect object/direct object

_____

_____

3. Subject/linking verb/subject complement

_____

_____

4. Inverted order and the same sentence in normal order

_____

_____

5. Compose a simple sentence. Mark the subject and verb.

_____

_____

6. Compose a compound sentence. Mark the subject(s) and verb(s).

_____

_____

7. Compose a complex sentence. Mark the subject(s) and verb(s).

_____

_____

8. Compose a compound-complex sentence. Mark the subject(s) and verb(s).

_____

_____

Accurate spelling is a vital component of any written document. A writer must ensure that all words are spelled correctly; otherwise, the reader may make the assumption that the writer is not totally literate and, therefore, may not be inclined to take the action desired by the writer.

A writer's inability to spell correctly need not be a reflection on his or her intelligence or ability to succeed in life. However, readers often evaluate writers in a negative sense if the writers do not use correct spelling in their written presentations.

Today, electronic spellers do wonders for writers who are not good spellers. However, two electronic-speller downfalls are obvious: (1) writers do not use them often enough, and (2) writers rely too much on them and, therefore, do not proofread to pick up incorrect word choices that are missed by the spellers.

Accurate spelling is primarily rooted in rote memorization. However, if you have spelling deficiencies, you can significantly improve your spelling ability if you master a few rules that will help you learn to spell frequently occurring, frequently misspelled words.

The approach of this lesson is twofold: (1) to introduce you to a few fundamental rules of spelling and (2) to introduce you to 150 of the most frequently occurring, most frequently mis-spelled words in the business vocabulary. Then, in selected lessons, you will be exposed repeatedly to those 150 words; and you will be expected to master them. Your mastery of them will involve your ability to remember the rules of spelling and, if necessary, to memorize the correct spellings.

Pretest

Circle all misspelled words in the following sentences. Write the correct spellings for each of the misspelled words at the end of each sentence.

31

1. I recomend that you accomodate all the calender items Ms. Markham thinks are necessary for the forthcoming curiculum meeting.

2. The concensus of the group is that we should pursuade you to develope the questionaire after you design the brochure.

3. When you receive the pamplet, do not be surprized or embarassed at some of the arguements in it.

4. If nesessary, employes can deduct their mileage and miscellanious expenses incurred while attending the morgage hearings.

5. I truely hope we ask Mr. Yost to be a permanant advisor to the Extention Division because of his excellent writting skills.

6. To the surprize our our bookeeper, I found some surplus flurescent lights in the temporary storage area.

7. Each of your dependants will have an oppertunity to decide his or her own curriculum at our school.

8. We are hopefull we can develope more practical pronounciation guides than the ones we have been using.

9. You are elegible to recieve a scholarship, even though you transferred in the middle of the year.

10. Was Mr. Brooks greatful when he passed his driver's lisence test on the first attempt?

Key: (1) recommend, accommodate, calendar, curriculum; (2) consensus, persuade, develop, questionnaire; (3) pamphlet, surprised, embarrassed, arguments; (4) necessary, employees, miscellaneous, mortgage; (5) truly, permanent, extension, writing; (6) surprise, bookkeeper, fluorescent; (7) dependents, opportunity; (8) hopeful, develop, pronunciation; (9) eligible, receive; (10) grateful, license.

Terminology

Abstract noun—A noun that cannot be clearly visualized, such as *independence, faith,* and *courage.*

Concrete noun—A noun that can be clearly visualized, such as *tree, horse,* and *table.*

Consonant—The alphabet letters *b, c, d, f, g, h, j, k, l, m, n, p, q, r, s, t, v, w, x, y,* and *z,* all of which are letters other than vowels.

Derivative—A word formed from another, chiefly by the addition of such word elements as prefixes and suffixes to roots, stems, and words. *Rename, named,* and *naming* are derivatives of *name.*

Mnemonic—A memory device, such as a formula or a rhyme, used as an aid in remembering (pronounced with short vowels—*ni mon' ik*).

Prefix—A letter, syllable, or word added to the beginning of a word to change its meaning, such as *a*drift, *pre*determine, and *over*growth.

Suffix—A letter, syllable, or word added to the end of a word to change its meaning, such as breez*y,* friend*ly,* walk*ing,* and friend*ship.*

Syllable—A unit of spoken or written language consisting of a single letter or a group of letters that forms one sound.

Vowel—The alphabet letters *a, e, i, o,* and *u.* The letters *w* and *y* sometimes serve as vowels (as in *awl* and *rhyme*).

Rules

1. **In a one-syllable word ending in consonant-vowel-consonant, double the final consonant before adding a suffix that begins with a vowel.**

Word	Suffix	New Word
bag	-ed	bagged
bet	-or	bettor
big	-est	biggest
run	-er	runner
sin	-ing	sinning
tan	-ing	tanning
ton	-age	tonnage

   Do not apply Rule 1 if the final consonant is not pronounced. For example, in *show*, the final consonant is silent and therefore is not doubled in *showing*.

   For words such as *quiz*, notice the *u* has the sound of a consonant. Therefore, you can apply Rule 1 in such spellings as *quizzes* and *quizzing*.

2. **In a two-syllable word that ends in consonant-vowel-consonant and that is accented on the second syllable, double the final consonant before adding a suffix that begins with a vowel.**

Word	Suffix	New Word
acquit	-al	acquittal
admit	-ance	admittance
begin	-er	beginner
occur	-ence	occurrence
prefer	-ed	preferred

When the suffix is added to some words, such as *confer* (*CON fer ence*), the accent changes to the first syllable. In most of these words, you will not double the final consonant of the root word.

In words such as (*CAN celed*), the preferred business-world usage is *canceled* instead of *cancelled*, although both are listed as correct in most dictionaries.

When you do not pronounce the final consonant in words such as *bestow*, the ''double'' rule does not apply. In these instances, spellings such as *bestowed* and *bestowing* result.

3. **Drop the final *e* before adding a suffix that begins with a vowel.**

Word	Suffix	New Word
desire	-able	desirable
desire	-ous	desirous
excuse	-able	excusable
include	-ing	including
please	-ant	pleasant
rare	-ity	rarity

In some words, such as *usable*, the dictionary permits both *usable* and *useable*. However, the preferred business-world usage is the first dictionary option, *usable*, which reflects Rule 3 correctly.

You should conclude that the final *e* is retained if a suffix beginning with a consonant is added. Because each suffix in such words as the following begins with a consonant, the final *e* in the root word is retained:

Word	Suffix	New Word
improve	-ment	improvement
tire	-less	tireless
large	-ly	largely
remote	-ness	remoteness

Dictionary usage contrasts with business-world preferences again and produces some exceptions you should consider, such as *acknowledgment* and *judgment*.

Other exceptions to Rule 3 involve words that end with the soft sound of *ge* or *ce*. The *e* is typically retained when *able* or *ous* is added, as in *changeable, manageable, noticeable,* and *outrageous*.

4. **Following a soft *c*, write the *e* before the *i* when these two letters are sequential. Write the *e* before the *i* when the two are pronounced with the sound of *long a*.**

You probably learned this rule through the mnemonic statement "Use *i* before *e* except after *c* or when sounded like *a* as in *neighbor* and *weigh*."

Some examples of soft *c* are *conceive, deceive, deceit, receipt,* and *receive*. Some examples of long *a* are *neighbor, reign, sleigh,* and *vein*.

In most other words, the *i* is written first. Some examples of *i* before *e* are *belief, relief, shriek,* and *yield*.

Some common words are exceptions to Rule 4's statements, and you will need to give special attention to such words as *counterfeit, forfeit, height, seize,* and *weird*.

5. **Distinguish between the two parts of a word that is made up of a prefix and a root.**

Several misspelled words are comprised of a prefix and a familiar word (such as *un* + *noticed* to form *unnoticed*). If you are aware of a few common prefixes, you can help yourself avoid the misspelling of such words as the following:

dis + appear	disappear
il + legible	illegible
il + logical	illogical
inter + racial	interracial
mis + spell	misspell
over + ripe	overripe
re + commend	recommend
under + rate	underrate
un + natural	unnatural

Learning Hint 1. Create a mnemonic device (a memory helper) for any word you have difficulty mastering.

Many times, you have undoubtedly used mnemonic devices to help you remember things. We suggest you intentionally create a mnemonic device to help you remember the spelling of troublesome words.

For example, note the slight difference between *defendant* and *dependent*. Assume you have a pet ant who lives in your ant farm. Assume further you have to go to court to defend your ant who is accused of embezzlement. You'll remember easily that *defendant* is spelled with an *a* because you will *defend* your *ant*; and you'll then remember that *dependent* is different from *defendant* and is not spelled with an *a*.

Here are a few other mnemonic devices:

all right (not alright)—Always two words in business communications. Although some dictionaries recognize the existence of *alright,* the business world does not accept this spelling. Associate *all right* with *all correct* or *all wrong.*

argument (not arguement)—Say to yourself, "I lost an *e* in that argument."

believe (not beleive)—Remember that you can't be*lie*ve a *lie.*

calendar (not calender)—The D.A.R. (Daughters of the American Revolution) will check the calen*dar* before setting their next convention date.

cemetery (not cemetary)—The c*e*m*e*t*e*ry is a place we can get to with ease (*e's*).

definite (not definate)—De*finite* comes from the word *finite.*

embarrass (not embarass)—Double *r* plus double *s* = double trouble.

grammar (not grammer)—Don't *mar* your writing with poor gram*mar.*

occurrence (not occurence)—An occurrence may be a *curr*ent event.

parallel (not paralell)—*All* the lines are par*all*el (the word *all* appears in the word *parallel*).

privilege (not priviledge)—You won't spell privilege with a *d* if you'll remember this sentence: It is my privi*leg*e to stand on one *leg.* The word *leg* appears in *privilege.*

pronunciation (not pronounciation)—The *nun* knows how to use correct pro*nun*ciation.

pursue (not persue)—I *pur*sued the pickpocket who took my *pur*se.

recommend (not reccomend or recomend)—*Recommend* is simply *re* plus *commend.*

separate (not seperate)—To se*par*ate means to tear a*part.*

superintendent (not superintendant)—The superintend*ent* collects the *rent.*

supersede (not supercede)—Both the first and third syllables begin with *s*.

surprise (not surprize or suprize)—You *sur*ely won't get a prize with that sur*prise*!

We suggest you use your own ingenuity to create mnemonic devices to help you spell troublesome words.

Learning Hint 2. Master the spelling of frequently occurring, frequently misspelled words in the business vocabulary.

The words in the following list not only are frequently misspelled but also occur frequently in day-to-day business activities. Obviously, we could add many other words to the list, depending on where we draw the line in terms of frequency of occurrence.

The following words will be used repeatedly in several subsequent exercises. We suggest you begin now (1) to recognize the words in the list and (2) to master the spellings of the words. In all instances, we give the American-usage spelling. We do not include words that may not be spelling problems so much as word-choice problems (such as *principal* versus *principle*). We cover these kinds of words in Lesson 4, which deals with confusing words.

Where applicable, such as in *judgment*, we have starred the words that have more than one spelling in some dictionaries. The starred version represents the preferred (if not obligatory) spellings in the business world. We also typically list only one of a frequently misspelled word's derivatives (for example, we list only *occurrence*, but *occurring* and *occurred* are other *occur* derivatives that could be on the list).

Table 3–1
Frequently Misspelled Words

absence	calendar	definite	fluorescent
accessible	canceled*	dependent	foreign
accidentally	careful	describe	forfeit
accommodate	catalog	description	fulfill
acknowledgment	category	desirable	gauge
acquaintance	cemetery	develop	grammar
acquisition	changeable	disappear	grateful
adolescence	commitment	disappoint	grievous
alignment	committee	eligible	harass
all right	comparative	embarrass	height
a lot	competent	employee*	helpful
analyze	competitive	enclosure*	hindrance
apparent	concede	entrepreneur	hopeful
argument	conceivable	equipped	implement
attendance	congratulate	equivalent	incidentally
beginning	consensus	exaggerate	interference
believe	consistent	excellent	irrelevant
beneficial	convenience	existence	judgment*
benefited*	criticism	explanation	label
bookkeeper	curriculum	extension	liable
brief	deductible	familiar	liaison
brochure	defendant	feasible	library

Table 3–1			
(concluded)			
license	perceive	recommend	surprise
likable*	permanent	reference	synonymous
maintenance	permissible	referring	temporary
mileage	persuade	remuneration	thorough
miscellaneous	possession	restaurant	transferred
misspell	practical	rhythm	traveler*
mortgage	preferred	satellite	truly
necessary	prejudice	separate	usable
noticeable	presence	serviceable	vacuum
obsolescent	privilege	similar	visible
occasionally	procedure	sincerely	volume
occurrence	prominent	sizable*	withhold
omission	pronunciation	sophomore	writing
opportunity	pursue	summarize	yield
pamphlet	questionnaire	superintendent	
parallel	receive	supersede	

*Preferred business-world spelling.

(handwritten in margin: Use T3-1 here)

Posttest

Circle all misspelled words in the following sentences. Write the correct spellings for each of the misspelled words at the end of each sentence.

1. We benefited by your attendence at the resturant hearings, and we definately appreciate the visable role you assumed.

2. Mr. Mendoza has two sophmore dependants who are eligible to recieve the libary-research scholarship money.

3. Are you familiar with the fluoresent lights that are discribed on page 19 of the Ex-Cel Lighting's temperary catalogue?

4. Incidentaly, I am hopeful we can impliment alot of your suggestions for safeguarding the rights of defendents.

5. I am surprized that you feel alright about the agreement for a sizable aquisition of additional land for the cemetary expansion.

6. Joanie accidently mispelled several words when she took the essay examination covering her grammer class.

7. What explaination can we give for our dissappointing performance during the second quarter?

8. The pamplet on mortgage lending practices discribes fully our committment to serve the citizens.

9. I am not exaggerating when I say that our physical faciliites are equiped to provide all accomodations for 500 seminar participants.

10. Can you reccommend a member of the libary staff who is qualified to help us develop our questionaire?

Key: (1) attendance, restaurant, definitely, visible; (2) sophomore, dependents, receive, library; (3) fluorescent, described temporary, catalog; (4) incidentally, implement, a lot, defendants; (5) surprised, all right, acquisition, cemetery; (6) accidentally, misspelled, grammar; (7) explanation, disappointing; (8) pamphlet, describes, commitment; (9) exaggerating, equipped, accommodations; (10) recommend, library, questionnaire.

LEVEL A

Name _____

Exercise 3–1 On the lines below, write **T** if the statement is true and **F** if the statement is false.

_T_ 1. The business world prefers *canceled* to *cancelled*, although both are correct in some dictionaries.

_T_ 2. *Win* is a one-syllable word ending in consonant-vowel-consonant; therefore, the final consonant is doubled before the *-ing* suffix is added.

_F_ 3. *Desireable* is an exception to the rule that the final *e* is dropped before a suffix is added that begins with a vowel.

_T_ 4. To add the *-ence* suffix to the two-syllable word *concur*, you double the final consonant because the suffix begins with a vowel.

_F_ 5. *Arguement* and *judgement* are examples of preferred dictionary spellings.

_F_ 6. *Changable* and *noticable* are examples of Rule 3—drop the final *e* before adding a suffix that begins with a vowel.

_T_ 7. "Use *i* before *e* except after *c* or when sounded like *a* as in *neighbor* and *weigh*" is an example of a mnemonic statement.

_T_ 8. A good way to avoid misspelling *misspell* and *recommend* is to recognize that such words are made up of a prefix and a root.

_T_ 9. The first *m* in the word *mnemonic* is not pronounced.

_F_ 10. In spite of what else might be said, you need not worry if you have spelling deficiencies because the electronic speller will solve your spelling dilemmas.

Exercise 3–2 If the first word in the parentheses is spelled correctly, mark **A**. If the second word is correct, mark **B**.

_A_ 1. In my (absence/abcense), please answer the telephone.

_A_ 2. Yes, those expenses are (deductible/deductable).

_B_ 3. He feels like he is operating in a (vaccum/vacuum).

_B_ 4. The (superintendant/superintendent) will be gone next week.

_B_ 5. Those two words are (synonomous/synonymous) words.

_A_ 6. The matter is a very (grevious/grevous) one.

_A_ 7. I (exaggerated/exagerrated) when I gave my report.

_A_ 8. (Congratulations/Congradulations) on receiving the award!

_A_ 9. Hank will be the (liaison/liason) with your office.

_B_ 10. You'll get excellent (milage/mileage) with your new car.

Exercise **Write C** if all frequently misspelled words are spelled correctly; **write I** if any is mis-
3–3 spelled.

C 1. Please give your acknowledgment to the curriculum committee.

I 2. Don't be disapointed if the library is closed.

I 3. "Less likely" is an excellent example of comparitive degree.

I 4. I perceive that she is a hinderance to the committee.

I 5. Yes, the sattelite dish is definitely serviceable.

C 6. His views on the mortgage are truly irrelevant.

I 7. The rhythm of the song is alright!

I 8. Your interferance in the matter is embarrassing.

C 9. He is an entrepreneur—not merely a bookkeeper!

I 10. I concede; you indeed have alot of time on your hands.

Exercise **Write A** if the first word is the preferred business-world spelling; **write B** if the second
3–4 word is preferred.

B 1. My cousin is a worldwide (traveller/traveler).

A 2. Several of us (benefited/benefitted) from the work of Ms. Conklin.

A 3. Much to my dismay, we (canceled/cancelled) our reservations to fly to Hawaii.

B 4. My uncle is disappointed with the (judgement/judgment) rendered in the *State v. McKendricks* case.

A 5. One of the (employees/employes) wants to take two weeks of vacation time during the Christmas holidays.

A 6. Abdul is certainly a very (likable/likeable) person when you get to know him.

B 7. Did you include the proper (inclosure/enclosure) with the Dallas project letter?

B 8. What (explaination/explanation) can we give for March's increase in our water bill?

B 9. In April, we will begin the new rate for (milage/mileage) reimbursement.

A 10. Personal interest is no longer a (deductible/deductable) item.

B 11. We were (dissappointed/disappointed) with the second-quarter income.

A 12. The (consensus/concensus) of the council is that a new garage must be built.

B 13. Dr. Barney is not the (prominant/prominent) judge mentioned in Ms. Willow's testimony.

B 14. The (critcizm/criticism) of Dr. Barney's actions severely damaged his credibility as a judge.

LEVEL B

Name _____

Exercise
3–5

Write the letter that identifies the sentence containing no misspelled words.

_a_ 1. *a.* We gave a competitive bid for the fluorescent lights.
     b. Your explaination is a very feasable one.
     c. Are you writting the revised questionnaire?

_c_ 2. *a.* I am greatful for the more-than-adequate remuneration.
     b. We sincerely appreciate your help on the calender.
     c. Barbra accidentally benefited from the transaction.

_c_ 3. *a.* The priviledge is mine to fulfill the assignment.
     b. He is witholding information about the restaurant.
     c. In his presence, I briefly described our dilemma.

_c_ 4. *a.* She is a very practicle and honest employee.
     b. Ben occasionaly harasses the other workers.
     c. The information in the pamphlet is obsolescent.

_b_ 5. *a.* We are hopeful that the defendent will cooperate.
     b. For your convenience, we will grant the extension.
     c. We can see no concievable reason for his attendance.

_a_ 6. *a.* Your presence at the meeting will be helpful.
     b. Yes, the cemetary is equipped with sprinklers.
     c. We cannot accomodate your request for 50 catalogs.

_c_ 7. *a.* The guage on the dashboard is very visible.
     b. We hope to pursuade you to use the new labels.
     c. He needs to develop better pronunciation habits.

_c_ 8. *a.* Yes, we received the grammer text in today's mail.
     b. The necessery information is now in Melba's possession.
     c. Brent transferred during his sophomore year.

_b_ 9. *a.* Volume 2 is very similiar to Volume 1.
     b. Are you familiar with the temporary restraining order?
     c. Beginning next month, we will have seperate offices.

_c_ 10. *a.* The traveler is definitely a likeable person.
     b. The new brochure supercedes all previous publications.
     c. The dependents are not eligible for the tax breaks.

_b_ 11. *a.* The foriegn assignment will be beneficial for her.
     b. We will implement the miscellaneous suggestions next week.
     c. We have reached a concensus on the property acquisition.

_a_ 12. *a.* We have a definite reason for being disappointed with the results.
     b. In your absence, the maintainance crew will be working until almost midnight.
     c. The best explaination I can give is that I was not eligible to participate.

_b_ 13. _a._ The sophomores were surprized with the voting results.
       _b._ You were very helpful in doing a thorough analysis of our budget needs.
       _c._ We are writting to ask your opinion about our obsolesent computers.

_c_ 14. _a._ Beginning March 1, the proceedures for travel reimbursement will change.
       _b._ Did we get the new lables to mail the fall catalogs?
       _c._ I'm delighted you will be our liaison with the cemetery personnel.

_a_ 15. _a._ Each of the entrepreneurs provided helpful information to us.
       _b._ When will you be able to develope the new cirriculum guidelines?
       _c._ I'm pleased to congradulate you for your consistent attendance record.

_c_ 16. _a._ We definately want to implement your suggestions next quarter.
       _b._ My work at the library is merely an extention of the work you did.
       _c._ Jed has a competitive advantage because of his height.

Exercise 3–6 Look up the rule number and the related discussion that reflects the correct spelling of the word, and write the rule number on the first line. Then spell the word correctly on the second line. If no rule directly applies, write **O** on the first line.

_1_ 1. bigest _biggest_   _3_ 7. desireable _desirable_

_2_ 2. admitance _admittance_   _3_ 8. improvment _improvement_

_5_ 3. ilogical _illogical_   _2_ 9. cancelled _canceled_

_4_ 4. hieght _height_   _4_ 10. yeild _yield_

_5_ 5. ommission _omission_   _5_ 11. dissappoint _disappoint_

_3_ 6. judgement _judgment_   _O_ 12. surprize _surprise_

Exercise 3–7 Write the letter that corresponds to the correct spelling of the word.

_b_ 1. (_a_) liabel; (_b_) liable; (_c_) lieble; (_d_) liebel

_c_ 2. (_a_) lisence; (_b_) lisense; (_c_) license; (_d_) licence

_a_ 3. (_a_) maintenance; (_b_) maintainance; (_c_) maintainence; (_d_) maintenence

_d_ 4. (_a_) adolesence; (_b_) adolecense; (_c_) adolesense; (_d_) adolescence

_c_ 5. (_a_) similiar; (_b_) simillar; (_c_) similar; (_d_) similair

_c_ 6. (_a_) existance; (_b_) existanse; (_c_) existence; (_d_) existense

_d_ 7. (_a_) equivelent; (_b_) equivalant; (_c_) equivallent; (_d_) equivalent

_a_ 8. (_a_) prejudice; (_b_) predjudice; (_c_) prejudise; (_d_) prejidice

_b_ 9. (_a_) incidently; (_b_) incidentally; (_c_) incidentely; (_d_) incidentelly

_d_ 10. (_a_) referance; (_b_) referrence; (_c_) referrance; (_d_) reference

LEVEL C

Name _____

Exercise 3–8   Create a mnemonic device to help you remember each of the following frequently misspelled words.

1. Existence _____

2. Exaggerate _____

3. Maintenance _____

4. Permissible _____

5. Consensus _____

6. Similar _____

7. Liaison _____

8. Synonymous _____

9. Serviceable _____

10. Pamphlet _____

Exercise 3–9   Edit the following sentences by underlining all the frequently misspelled words; then spell correctly the words that are misspelled.

1. If the *opportunity* oppertunity arises, we will undertake a thorough review of our mileage-reimbursement *procedures* proceedures.

2. I am hopeful that Wilson Chemicals will *pursue* persue its commitment to make its research findings *accessible* accessable to us.

3. As you will see in the *enclosures* inclosures, we have truly attempted to write a readable *description* discription of our library acquisitions procedures.

4. My only *criticism* criticizm of the document is that the writer has not been careful in employing *parallel* paralell construction in his *writing* writting.

5. One former *acquaintance* aquaintance, Ms. Marshall, is extremely *competent* competant—as you will see from her credentials when she worked as a prominent attorney.

6. When I <u>summarized</u> the data, I discovered that a <u>sizeable</u> increase in sales revenue was appar-
   sizable   *appar-*
   ent
   <u>ant</u> in each of last quarter's sales.

7. I <u>concede</u> that <u>Catagory</u> I represents a <u>permanent</u> increase in operating costs for the <u>alinement</u>
   Category   *alignment*
   equipment.

8. When I <u>analyzed</u> the data, I found them to be <u>useable</u> and to support the <u>consistant</u> increase
   usable   *consistent*
   in quarterly sales over the past year.

9. <u>Incidently,</u> Calvin Carmichael simply <u>disappeared</u> and <u>forfieted</u> his bail after the fourth occur-
   Incidentally   *forfeited*
   <u>rence</u> of his arrest for drug abuse.

10. In <u>referring</u> to the situation, Yul said he <u>prefered</u> not to divulge the names of the <u>eligable</u>
    preferred   *eligible*
    <u>employees.</u>

11. Our bid <u>definately</u> will be <u>competetive,</u> and we are <u>hopeful</u> that our product is <u>equivalent</u> to
    definitely   *competitive*
    the one specified.

12. The <u>maintainance</u> workers' questions were <u>grievious</u> ones, but they seemed <u>irrelevant</u> to us.
    maintenance   *grievous*

13. Are you <u>familiar</u> with the <u>grammer</u> and <u>pronounciation</u> rules that deal with <u>Category</u> II vio-
    grammar   *pronunciation*
    lations?

14. In the document, the following words were <u>mispelled</u>: traveler, <u>enterpreneur,</u> and <u>restuarant.</u>
    misspelled   *entrepreneur*   *restaurant*

15. We <u>cancelled</u> our Bahamas trip when we <u>recieved</u> word about our <u>acquisition</u> of the Denver
    canceled   *received*
    <u>mortgages.</u>

16. If that decision is <u>alright</u> with you, we will offer the <u>renumeration</u> to all of the <u>temporary</u>
    all right   *remuneration*
    <u>employees.</u>

Exercise 3–10

Composition

Use at least two frequently misspelled words in writing the following sentence components and types that are discussed in Lesson 2. Remember to spell the words correctly!

1. Complex sentence _____

   _____

2. Compound sentence _____

   _____

3. Fragment _____

   _____

4. Dependent clause _____

   _____

5. Inverted-order sentence _____

   _____

6. Imperative sentence _____

   _____

7. Run-on sentence _____

   _____

8. Polite request _____

   _____

9. Interrogative sentence _____

   _____

10. Exclamatory sentence _____

   _____

11. Comma splice _____

_____

12. Declarative sentence _____

_____

Exercise 3–11 Write a sentence in which one of the frequently misspelled words serves the following functions:

Compo-
sition

1. Direct object _____

_____

2. Subjective complement _____

_____

3. Subject _____

_____

4. Indirect object _____

_____

5. Verb _____

_____

6. Adjective _____

_____

CONFUSING WORDS — LESSON 4

A strong vocabulary is an important tool to the effective writer. Using the right word in the right way at the right time is the mark of the successful communicator. Writing ability is definitely strengthened by vocabulary power. Being able to use words with precision and judgment is an asset to any writer.

Some words that writers may want to use are troublesome because they are easily confused with other words. These words are referred to here as **confusing words**. The improper choice of such words distracts and—sometimes—irritates the reader. The words in this category are perfectly good words, however, and may be used to good effect by the skillful writer who makes the correct choice.

Confusing words typically have similar sounds, similar spellings, or similar meanings. Sometimes they have all of these characteristics. The careful writer is aware of these similarities and is able to make the proper choices essential to correct and effective writing.

This lesson introduces you to 41 sets of confusing words. Some of these words are used more often than others in typical business writing, but all of them are words a business writer will find useful. Each word is defined and subsequently used in context to illustrate its correct use. You will also encounter these words again at selected places in the text. You are expected to become familiar with them and to be able to use them correctly in your writing.

A writer's misuse of any of the confusing words in this lesson might cause the reader to misunderstand the message or to react negatively to the writer. In the business world, for example, readers expect, if not demand, writers to correctly use such confusing words as *affect/effect, capital/capitol, it's/its,* and *principle/principal*; and any misuse of such words might raise a red flag of illiteracy in the minds of readers.

Obviously, we could have included many more pairs of confusing words in this lesson than we have included. Watch for additional confusing words in your writing, and be sure you choose the correct word in every instance. In Lesson 32, you'll find many other words that are similar to those in Lesson 4.

| Pretest |

Underline all incorrectly used (confusing) words in the following sentences. At the end of each sentence, write the correct words to be substituted for the words you underlined. No. 0 is provided as an example.

0. A change in the counsel's policy is thought to be eminent; therefore, employee moral is likely to improve. (council's, imminent, morale)

1. As one important communication media, television has already surpassed all the high-performance criterion set by many of its most-imminent critics.

2. Weather it's too early to proceed with a new design for office stationary is not yet known.

3. If you allow yourself to be lead further in the wrong direction, you are likely to encounter problems.

4. To illicit the desired response, prepare an implicit written agreement to indicate that we are all ready to observe the ethical and morale demands of the community.

5. Do you expect the principle architect to effect the committee's selection of a building cite?

6. The council may waver and loose momentum if it continues to move further away from its proper role in the community.

7. The advise given by the pastor of St. Michael's Parish proved to be altogether fitting for the personnel with the exception of the school principle from Rolling Hills Academy.

8. Anyone of there recommendations for the proposed advertising campaign should be evaluated on the basis of merit rather than from the point of view of personnel biases.

9. Every one on the strategic planning task force expects most of the criterion to be ultimately changed for selecting building cites on the East Coast and in the Hawaiian Islands.

10. According to Mr. Sodderry, the stationary supply store—and the barber shop, to—in the state capital building will need repairs bad if further neglect is allowed to occur.

Key: (1) medium, criteria, eminent; (2) Whether, stationery; (3) led, farther, (4) elicit, explicit, moral; (5) principal, affect, site; (6) lose, farther; (7) advice, principal; (8) any one, their, personal; (9) Everyone, criteria, eventually, sites; (10) stationery, too, capitol, badly.

| Frequently Confused Words |

advise—to recommend or to counsel (v.)

advice—opinion about what to do; recommendation (n.)

affect—to influence; to modify; to pretend to have or feel (v.)

effect—result or impression (n.); to accomplish or bring about (v.)

altogether—entirely (adv.)

all together*—everyone gathered, or unified

already—previously (adv.)

all ready*—completely prepared

anyone—written as one word when the emphasis is on *any* (person)

any one—written as two words when (1) *one* is stressed; (2) followed by an *of* prepositional phrase; or (3) one of a number of things is stressed

bad—an adjective (She felt *bad* about the decision.)

badly—an adverb (She behaved *badly* at the party.)

capital—a city or town; wealth or resources (n.)

capitol—a statehouse; a building occupied by Congress or other lawmakers (n.)

compliment—to say something good about someone; to praise (v.); a polite greeting (n.)

complement—something that completes or makes perfect (n.); to add to or to serve as a complement to (v.)

criterion—a standard of judging; a principle by which a correct judgment may be formed (n.)

criteria—plural of criterion

council—a group of people called together to give advice, talk things over, or settle questions (n.)

counsel—act of talking things over (v.); advice; person who gives legal advice (n.)

device—mechanical invention; machine; apparatus, plan, scheme, trick (n.)

devise—to think out; to plan, to contrive, to invent (v.)

disburse—to pay out; to expend; to spread out (v.)

disperse—to scatter; to diffuse; to separate or move apart (v.)

elicit—to bring or draw out; to evoke (v.)

illicit—unlawful; prohibited; not permitted (adj.)

eminent—high in office, rank, or public esteem; lofty (adj.)

imminent—impending; near at hand; threatening to occur (adj.)

eventually—at some time in the future; coming later (adv.)

ultimately—last; farthest; most extreme (adv.)

everyone—written as one word when the emphasis is on *every* (person)

every one—written as two words when (1) *one* is stressed; (2) when followed by an *of* prepositional phrase; or (3) one of a number of things is stressed.

except—to leave out; to exclude (v.); with the exclusion of (prep.)

---

* Some writers regard *all together* and *all ready* as redundant expressions. They reason that the words *together* and *ready* are accurately descriptive of the conditions or circumstances to which they apply and that *all* is therefore superfluous when used with these terms.

accept—to take something offered; to receive with favor (v.)

explicit—expressed precisely, distinctly (adj.)

implicit—implied; understood though not expressed (adj.)

farther—refers to distances (adv.)

further—indicates degree or quantity (adv.)

illusion—a misconception or false impression (n.)

allusion—an indirect or implied reference (n.)

imply—to suggest or state indirectly (v.)

infer—to draw a conclusion; to deduce (v.)

it's—contraction for *it is* or *it has*

its—possessive case of pronoun *it*

later—more late; late in a greater degree; subsequently; afterward

latter—second of two; more recent; nearer the end

lead—to guide; to go in advance (v.); acting or serving as a leader (adj.); a heavy, soft, metallic element (n.)

led—past tense and past participle of lead (v.) (Paula *led* the discussion.)

likely—probably (adv.); credible (adj.)

liable—obligated; responsible (adj.)

loose—not fastened; not strict; free (adj.); to release (v.)

lose—not have any longer; be unable to find; fail to keep, preserve, or maintain (v.)

medium—a means of communication or conveyance; the middle or midst (n.)

media—the plural of *medium* (n.)

moral—concerned with principles of right and wrong in conduct or character (adj.)

morale—mental attitude; courage; hope, confidence (n.)

passed—past tense of *pass*; moved onward; proceeded (v.)

past—ended; over; belonging to a previous time (adj.)

personal—individual; private; done in person; directly by oneself—not through others

personnel—persons employed in any work or service

precede—to go before

proceed—to go on after having stopped; to move forward; to take place

principle—fundamental belief; rule of action or conduct (n.)

principal—most important, main (adj.); capital sum; head of school; leader (n.)

sight—thing seen; power of seeing, vision; device to assist in taking aim or observing

site—position or place of anything, such as *the landing site*

cite—to quote something or someone; refer to; mention as an example; summon to appear, as before a law court

stationary—fixed in place; not movable

stationery—writing materials

than—expresses comparison or diversity; rather, better, otherwise (adv.)

then—refers to time or place; immediately or soon afterward; next in order of time or place (conj.)

there—in or at that place (adv.); used to introduce a sentence or clause

their—of or belonging to them (possessive pronoun)

to—denotes direction or introduces an infinitive

too—in addition; more than enough; to such a degree

waiver—an intentional relinquishment of a known right or advantage; an express statement of relinquishment (n.)

waver—to sway; to vacillate; to be unsettled in opinion (v.)

weather—atmospheric state with respect to conditions of temperature, pressure, or humidity (v.); to bear up against and come through (v.)

whether—a term used to introduce alternatives: *Ask whether he prefers meat or fish.* (conj.)

who's—contraction for *who is* or *who has*

whose—possessive case of pronoun *who*

your—possessive form of *you*

you're—contraction of *you are*

Use
T4-1
here

Posttest

Underline all incorrectly used words in the following sentences. At the end of each sentence, write the correct words that should be substituted for the words you underlined.

1. You're file in the personal office will be reviewed at a latter date.

2. Management deserves to be complemented on the addition of improved retirement benefits as a complement to the other principle employee benefits offered by your firm.

3. Who's council will be followed in the selection of a suitable sight for the conference?

4. Will the Board of Directors approve the one principal criteria illicited from the bank for raising needed capital?

5. Alice Liu lead yesterday's discussion on the effectiveness of stationery devises in the construction of the badly needed storage facility.

6. The evidence indicates your definitely wrong if you believe Rufus Berger is liable to support a waver of graduation requirements.

7. The teacher refused to except the later of the two wavers proposed at the angry student's request by the director of the personnel department.

8. Whether your liable to be selected as the firm's chief representative to the conference in Washington, D.C., the nation's capitol, is less then certain at this time.

9. May I ask whose likely to eventually device an alternative plan to the one sited by the firm's morale officer as the most promising solution to the problem?

10. The deadline has past for the finance officer to disperse the travel funds requested by the members of the advisory counsel who have all ready made plans to attend the Charleston meetings.

Key: (1) Your, personnel, later; (2) complimented, principal; (3) Whose, counsel, site; (4) criterion, elicted; (5) led, stationary, devices; (6) you're, likely (or you are, likely), waiver; (7) accept, latter, waivers; (8) you're, likely, capital, than; (9) who's, devise, cited; (10) passed, disburse, council, already.

LEVEL A

Name _____

Exercise 4-1

On the lines below, write **T** if the statement is true; write **F** if the statement is false.

__T__ 1. The term *counsel* may be used as either a noun or a verb; *council* is used only as a noun.

__F__ 2. The word *lead* is used properly in the sentence, *The company was lead through a difficult period by a competent manager.*

__F__ 3. *All together* should be used to indicate *entirely* or *completely.*

__T__ 4. As an adverb, *badly* is properly used to describe an action word such as *wrote* or *performed.* (The student wrote badly; the team performed badly tonight)

__F__ 5. The words *waver*, *liable*, and *degrade* are all included in the group of confusing words presented in this chapter.

__T__ 6. In the sentence, *Please effect a change in the company's performance*, the word *effect* serves as a verb.

__T__ 7. To conclude that vocabulary power is an important criterion in good writing is to *infer* something.

__F__ 8. To indicate distance rather than degree or quantity, a writer should use the word *further.*

__F__ 9. *Than* and *then* are interchangeable in business writing because they have essentially the same meaning.

__T__ 10. *Principal* rather than *principle* should be used to refer to the chief administrator of a high school.

Exercise 4-2

Within the parentheses in each of the following sentences, underline the word that is the correct choice for the intended meaning.

1. What (<u>advice,</u> advise) do you have for the beginning writer?

2. If the meeting is held in the restaurant, what time can you be (their, <u>there</u>)?

3. The salesman (<u>already,</u> all ready) has met his quota for the second quarter.

4. Who do you believe (eventually, <u>ultimately</u>) will be the winner?

5. Honesty, as a (<u>moral,</u> morale) principle, is important to the success of our company.

6. A good attitude is (<u>likely,</u> liable) to (<u>affect,</u> effect) your evaluation.

7. Both reports are well written, but the (later, <u>latter</u>) one is more complete than the first one.

8. The speaker did not mean to (<u>imply,</u> infer) that she held a contrary view.

9. (Anyone, <u>Any one</u>) of the reporters is qualified to (precede, <u>proceed</u>) with the investigation.

10. I, (to, <u>too</u>), believe that overly (lose, <u>loose</u>) regulations may result in safety violations.

11. I am not qualified to (<u>advise,</u> advice) you on that question.

12. He was (their, there), but she was here.

13. Jana wants to go (to, too), but the (principle, principal) has refused to give permission.

14. As the parade (past, passed) by, Donnie exclaimed, "What a (cite, sight)!"

15. As you (precede, proceed), you should know that your inspection will (precede, proceed) a similar review by Valerie Bates.

16. If you (affect, effect) an air of indifference, you will have a definite (affect, effect) on the outcome.

17. The criticism is offensive because the foreman expressed it (bad, badly).

18. Any attempt to (elicit, illicit) (elicit, illicit) behavior may be subject to prosecution.

19. Only six (council, counsel) members were present when the discussion of future (council, counsel) business was held.

20. I expect to see Tomika Yurasaka (later, latter) in the day if the (later, latter) of the two proposals I gave you is approved.

Exercise 4–3 Write **C** if the bold word is correctly used for the meaning intended. Write **I** if the bold word is incorrectly used.

_C_ 1. Thank you for your kind words; I appreciate the **compliment**.

_C_ 2. Can you tell me **who's** likely to receive the promotion?

_C_ 3. The firm has now interviewed **everyone** who applied for the job.

_I_ 4. A schedule of proposed writing assignments **ultimately** will be announced by the teacher.

_I_ 5. The customary midterm examination for this course is **eminent**.

_C_ 6. The announcement made no reference to any of the **criteria** discussed earlier.

_I_ 7. You should have no **allusion** about the difficulty of the task you have been assigned.

_C_ 8. The best efforts of all concerned are **implicit** in the discussion.

_C_ 9. No matter what **their** views may be, the auditors must rewrite the report.

_I_ 10. As soon as you **site** the delivery truck, tell the guard to open the gate.

_I_ 11. Place an order for 700 paper dobbers from Rutex, Inc.; **than** notify Miss Writely in Shipping.

_C_ 12. **Disperse** the 24 vans in our motor pool among our six branches west of the Mississippi.

_C_ 13. We have been told not to overlook radio as an effective advertising **medium** in our fall campaign.

_I_ 14. The new course to be offered to college seniors is entitled Principles of Ethical and **Morale** Behavior in Business.

LEVEL B

Name _____

Exercise
4–4

Write the letter that identifies the sentence that does not misuse a confusing word.

_a_ 1. a. How can you infer from the evidence presented that profits will increase in the coming year?
   b. Advise may be cheap, but it also may be useful.
   c. As a compliment to your office decor, the Persian rug is a striking addition.

_c_ 2. a. I understand the appointment of a new principal is eminent.
   b. No matter whose in charge, the rules should be applied consistently.
   c. The new policy is a good example of a badly conceived idea.

_a_ 3. a. The committee's work must precede the actual announcement.
   b. Without proper guidelines, most workers may loose sight of company objectives.
   c. As an effective communications media, the newspaper offers advertisers many advantages.

_b_ 4. a. The jury is already to announce its verdict.
   b. Extensive repairs will be required to the exterior of the capitol.
   c. Weather the construction funds are approved or not, the remodeling can begin immediately.

_b_ 5. a. Riot police were called in to disburse the unruly crowed.
   b. A further explanation of the Board's intentions is expected shortly.
   c. Neither of the two interviews was altogether satisfactory, but the later one was better than the first.

_a_ 6. a. Because the present system is not working adequately, Miss Wardle has been asked to devise a new approach.
   b. On the advice of legal council, the firm has withdrawn its offer.
   c. Every one we talked to preferred Plan B.

_c_ 7. a. No further attempts will be made to illicit a revised proposal.
   b. We are not surprised by the affect of Regulation 4011.
   c. The idea that you can get something for nothing is an illusion.

_b_ 8. a. Although the matter was discussed, an implicit understanding was never drafted.
   b. The quality of stationery used for office correspondence definitely should be upgraded.
   c. Under no circumstances can there bid be accepted.

_a_ 9. a. In times past, expectations were much different.
   b. A quick response is liable to produce the desired outcome.
   c. Your absolutely right to demand a full review of you're credit record.

_b_ 10. a. Leadership is the single most-important criteria in selecting a new president.
   b. The debate team is expected ultimately to overcome its competition at the meet.
   c. We can't be sure weather their attorney will waiver in her demands, but we hope so.

b 11. *a.* Your new in town, aren't you?
    b. Speaking of the weather, is snow expected today?
    c. The commander reports that moral is high among the troops.

a 12. *a.* Do not waver in your convictions.
    b. Your request for a waver of the calculus requirement has been approved.
    c. Are you willing to wave your right to an appeal?

b 13. *a.* I am going to the movie, to—no matter what you say!
    b. Zola can cite chapter and verse to support our position.
    c. The firm's personal office is located on the first floor.

c 14. *a.* Mr. Cloyder recently past away.
    b. Dorita works in the stationary shop on the corner.
    c. When you get there, call me.

c 15. *a.* Who's keys are these?
    b. Bonita will proceed you in line.
    c. Your task is to disburse the funds as they are needed.

c 16. *a.* I hope you will except my excuse for this late assignment.
    b. Can anyone here throw the javelin further than Billy Bob can?
    c. In her report, did the supervisor make any allusion to my absences?

b 17. *a.* Although nothing was stipulated verbally or in writing, the agreement between us is explicit.
    b. Her work is not altogether satisfactory.
    c. Danger is definitely eminent!

b 18. *a.* Lilah wants to enroll very bad.
    b. Your compliment is sincerely appreciated.
    c. All the essential criterion have been satisfied.

a 19. *a.* The streets of the capital are in need of repair.
    b. Gino's performance is liable to surprise you.
    c. The latch on the screen door must be lose.

c 20. *a.* I don't know weather you are right, but I hope so.
    b. The later suggestion is better than the first one.
    c. Our attorney gave us good counsel.

a 21. *a.* It's too late to change your mind now.
    b. Car No. 10 was the eventual winner.
    c. That practice is both elicit and unethical.

b 22. *a.* You will be hired if you can device a solution to our problem.
    b. The distance from Denver to Phoenix is farther than the distance from Phoenix to Tucson.
    c. May I introduce Dr. Boris Pasternak, the imminent author and lecturer.

LEVEL C

Name _____

Exercise 4–5   Write **C** if no misuse of a confusing word occurs. Write **I** if one or more confusing words are used incorrectly. Then underline the confusing words in **every** sentence and edit all incorrect sentences. No. 0 is provided as an example.

_____**I**_____ 0.   Can you site the specific rule that effects the selection of new counsel members?
cite ... *affects* ... *council*

_____**C**_____ 1.   The Engineering Department set four criteria for an improved mechanical device to control the production-line conveyor.

_____**I**_____ 2.   Mr. Brandon asked me to complement you on your excellent presentation to the council.
compliment

_____**I**_____ 3.   David says he can go no further in completing the principle part of the project until the weather improves.
farther ... *principal*

_____**I**_____ 4.   Who's car is parked in site of the entrance to the plant?
Whose ... *sight*

_____**I**_____ 5.   Do you believe Mrs. Chen meant to infer that Roger will be assigned to our team in March?
imply

_____**I**_____ 6.   The sample is a bad one; it's quality is not typical of those that preceded it.
its

_____**I**_____ 7.   To few counsel members will be in town next week to consider the appointment of Sandra King as director of the personnel office.
Too ... *council*

_____**I**_____ 8.   According to Agatha's report, the principal believes that the level of moral throughout the school is high.
morale

_____**I**_____ 9.   The probable effect of the imminent revision is any one's guess.
anyone's

_____**I**_____ 10.   All together, their achievements have been sited more than a dozen times in the media.
Altogether ... *cited*

_____**C**_____ 11.   Stationary missile launchers in that zone exceed the number agreed to previously and must be dispersed over a greater geographical area.

_I_ 12. During the planning meeting, allusion was made to the explicit terms of the agreement
to purchase a building cite _(site)_ on the outskirts of the nation's capital.

_I_ 13. The economy performed badly last year, as an analysis of anyone _(any one)_ of the four fiscal
periods will show.

_I_ 14. We have been asked weather _(whether)_ Mr. Dukakis is qualified to advice _(advise)_ the city counsel _(council)_ on
how to effect an altogether higher performance level in its work.

_I_ 15. Joseph has all ready _(already)_ elicited suggestions from everyone _(every one)_ of the officers except Mr.
Roskelly.

_I_ 16. Both criteria the agency approved are likely to farther _(further)_ weaken its ability to precede _(proceed)_
with its plans to improve employee morale.

_I_ 17. The driver may lose his license after being sighted _(cited)_ for recklessness when he past _(passed)_ a
school bus on a hill.

_C_ 18. All the speakers except Ms. Bianchi signed a waiver of the requirement that papers
prepared for publication be passed along to the editorial committee for review.

_I_ 19. The principal believes that everyone _(every one)_ of the currently enrolled students will eventually _(or ultimately)_
graduate.

_I_ 20. Citing company policy, the personal _(personnel)_ officer announced that any one _(anyone)_ who's interested
may proceed with plans to register for night school.

_I_ 21. Does any one _(anyone)_ feel badly _(bad)_ about the affect _(effect)_ of Miss Kellopp's advise _(advice)_ on the eventual
outcome?

_I_ 22. Its _(It's)_ true that further changes in the guidelines were made as a result of the council _(counsel)_
received at the meeting in the capital _(capitol)_ building.

Exercise 4–6   Review the subject matter studied in this and previous lessons by composing sentences as instructed in the following exercises:

Cumulative Review

1. Illustrate the subject/predicate/indirect object/direct object pattern in which the word **principal** serves as the indirect object.

_____

_____

2. Use **compliment** in a simple sentence that contains a pronoun and the pronoun's logical antecedent. Underline the antecedent.

_____

_____

3. Use **effect** as a verb and also as a noun in a complex sentence. Underline **effect** as a verb.

_____

_____

4. Use the three articles **a**, **an**, and **the** in a compound sentence that also contains the word **farther**.

_____

_____

5. Write an interrogative sentence that contains a phrase and that uses the word **liable**. Underline the phrase.

_____

_____

6. Write a compound-complex sentence that uses the words **media, personal,** and **advice.** Use both an indirect object and a direct object. Underline the indirect object once; underline the direct object twice.

_____

_____

7. Use *eventually* and *ultimately* in a declarative sentence that contains at least one conjunction and one interjection. Underline the conjunction once; underline the interjection twice.

_____

_____

Exercise
4–7

Cumula-
tive

Review

Mark the following sentences to indicate whether they are simple (**SM**), compound (**CM**), complex (**CX**), or compound-complex (**CM-CX**). Then edit the sentences to correct errors in spelling or in the confusing words you have studied previously. Item 0 is provided as an example.

_SM_ 0. Mr. Dayton is the ~~defendent~~ *defendant* ~~who's passed~~ *whose past* behavior is suspect.

_SM_ 1. Your ~~judgement~~ *judgment* on the purchase of the building site is important to us.

_CM_ 2. The most important ~~criteria~~ *criterion* is salary, but good working conditions are also ~~desireable.~~ *desirable*

_CM_ 3. To ~~yeild~~ *yield* the desired results, an improved ~~devise~~ *device* has been installed; and improved assembly procedures definitely will be used.

_CX_ 4. Is the distribution of questionnaires to all club members ~~permissable,~~ *permissible* even though the members are ~~all ready~~ *already* participating in the project?

_SM_ 5. The proposed ~~renumeration~~ *remuneration* to be given to Mr. Doyle and to Mrs. Kolling ~~supercedes~~ *supersedes* the sizable payment promised earlier for ~~there~~ *their* highly ~~visable~~ *visible* efforts as members of the regional ~~counsel~~ *council* advisory team.

_CM_ 6. Miss Venetto may ~~surprize~~ *surprise* you; she, ~~to,~~ *too,* is ~~liable~~ *likely* to recommend Warren's termination.

_CM_ 7. Where is the ~~prefered~~ *preferred* building site, and what is ~~it's~~ *its* expected cost?

_CM-CX_ 8. The ~~proceedure~~ *procedure* is known to ~~every one,~~ *everyone* even though ~~its~~ *it's* new; and the ~~maintenence~~ *maintenance* costs are ~~similiar~~ *similar* to those in the ~~passed.~~ *past*

_CX_ 9. A ~~florescent~~ *fluorescent* gauge is the ~~principle~~ *principal* device in the ~~vaccum~~ *vacuum* mechanism, according to Professor Durtschi, the ~~imminent~~ *eminent* designer.

_CX_ 10. Yes, even if the new stationery logo is ~~dissapointing,~~ *disappointing* it still meets the one important ~~criteria~~ *criterion* already approved by the ~~Superintendant~~ *Superintendent* of ~~Personel.~~ *Personnel*

NUMBER USAGE   LESSON 5

Perhaps no area of written expression encounters a greater diversity of views concerning correct application than number usage. Writers and reference manuals alike have conspicuously different notions about the proper use of numbers in business writing. Although some relatively uniform guidelines are generally adhered to by most authorities, practices vary considerably even among the experts.

Reasonableness and consistency are important characteristics of effective number usage. Reasonableness occurs when numbers are used in a sensible and logical way. Consistency is present when uniformity in usage is emphasized while allowances are made for legitimate and helpful exceptions. The number-usage standards in this lesson are based on these two important characteristics.

The rules for number expression presented in this lesson represent widely recognized number-expression conventions in the business world. They emphasize the most frequently occurring situations.

Rule No. 1—the rule of ten—may be considered the base or umbrella rule governing number usage in general. Rules 2 through 12 stipulate sensible and useful exceptions to the general guidelines provided in Rule No. 1.

Study carefully the following guidelines for number usage. Your mastery of these rules will give you confidence when you use numbers in your writing—something you will do often as a writer.

Pretest

Underline all misused numbers in the following sentences. Then, at the end of each sentence, write the preferred usage for the errors you underlined. No. 0 is provided as an example.

0. 1st-quarter sales showed an increase of <u>twenty</u> percent in each of our two western divisions. (First, 20)

1. Exactly eleven copies of the announcement were mailed on March 1st to our office on Fourth Street.

2. An increase of 15% in overhead costs is expected by the 3-member task force assigned to evaluate our twelve regional offices.

3. A meeting has been scheduled at 7 o'clock for the finance group to consider the $3,000,000 loss experienced by the company during the past two and one-half years.

4. 15 auditors worked on the project for 3 months and eleven days at a cost of hundreds of thousands of dollars.

5. The fee of $162.00 is less than 2/3 the amount charged by the two mechanics who performed similar work for us last year.

6. The first one-half mile of the ten-kilometer route was completed in $1^{7}/_{8}$ minutes with a temperature reading of seventy degrees.

Key: (1) 11, March 1; (2) 15 percent, three-member, 12; (3) seven o'clock, $3 million or 3 million dollars, $2^{1}/_{2}$; (4) Fifteen, 11 days; (5) $162, two-thirds; (6) 10-kilometer, 70 degrees.

Terminology

Cipher—A zero (the number 100 contains two ciphers).

Definite number—An exact number, one that can be precisely expressed (a check for *$1,000*; a class of *30* students).

Indefinite number—A number that is not clearly defined or determined; without fixed or specific limit (a crowd of *thousands*; a woman in her *thirties*).

Mixed number—A number containing a fraction ($8^{1}/_{2}$; *$20.10*).

Ordinal—A number denoting order or degree (*first, second, tenth*); figures expressed with the ordinal endings *nd* (second), *rd* (third), *st* (twenty-first), or *th* (sixth).

Rule of ten—The number usage standard requiring numbers that do not exceed ten to be written out (*one; six; nine*). Numbers above ten are expressed as figures (*11; 50; 236*).

Whole number—An integer; a number without a fraction (*$5; 105* degrees; *47* pounds).

Rules

1. **Write out numbers from one to ten inclusive. Use figures to express numbers over ten.**

    Sarah requested *nine* copies of the production report.
    A group of *six* students attended the conference for *three* days.

    The project was completed in just *15* working days.
    The office products show recorded *840* visits to its *21* exhibits.

    Learning Hint 1.   Express whole numbers in millions or higher in combined word and figure form.

    With more than *1 billion* people, China has the world's largest population. At present, the U.S. has
      less than *300 million* people.

2. **Spell out numbers that begin sentences.**

    Seven new accounts were approved by the manager in just one day.
    Twenty-five of our finest sales representatives will be honored at the Seattle meeting.

    Learning Hint 2.   If a number at the beginning of a sentence is more than two words, recast the sentence to place the number elsewhere and avoid an awkward construction.

    NO   215 boys are registered for summer camp.
          8,500 or more students are expected to enroll spring term in Lincoln Community College.

    YES   About 215 boys are registered for summer camp.
          Lincoln Community College expects at least 8,500 students to enroll spring term.

3. **Express numbers in a related group in the same manner. If the largest number is more than ten, express all numbers in the group as figures.**

    The purchase order specified *three* chairs, *five* lamps, and *one* desk.
    The research study included *53* executives, *210* employees, and *1,330* customers.
    Crown City's summer baseball league is comprised of *2* divisions, *10* teams, and approximately *200*
      players.

    Learning Hint 3.   If unrelated numbers appear in the same sentence, the *rule of ten* (Rule No. 1) governs their expression.

    In less than *four* weeks, the firm expects to hire *12* drivers, *3* mechanics, and *1* dispatcher.
    A total of *21* athletes from Valley High earned *seven* gold medals, *nine* silver medals, and *five* bronze
      medals in the meet's *12* events.

4. **If two numbers occur consecutively, spell out the smaller number to avoid confusion. If the larger number is the first word of a sentence, however, express the smaller number as a figure.**

    Our study group will need *14 three*-ring binders.
    The plans call for only *two 4*-bedroom units to be built.
    Five 3-act plays will be performed during the month of May.

5. **Write percentages in figures followed by the word** *percent* **(except in statistical material).**

> The interest rate will be *8 percent.*
> An increase of *100 percent* in sales volume is expected this year.
> What *percent* of your employees have college degrees?

6. **Except in legal documents, write amounts of money in figures. Express even sums of money without the decimal and ciphers. Use figures without the decimal, and spell out** *cents* **when stating amounts less than $1. Express round sums of money in millions or higher in combined word and figure form.**

> The cost of the book is *$5.*
> I paid *$120.30* for my new power saw.
> Admission fees are *$10* for adults and *$6.25* for children.
>
> The pens you requested are *79 cents* each.
> The cost of electricity to use your stereo is just *3 cents* per hour.
>
> The building is projected to cost about *$13 million* (or *13 million dollars*).
> Construction costs of more than *$600 million* (or *600 million dollars*) were recorded in the county in August.

7. **Use figures to express whole numbers and fractions. Spell out and hyphenate fractions that stand alone.**

> We estimate that *2¼* more days will be required.
> The job will be completed in less than *one-half* the time expected.

8. **Express decimal fractions in figures. If a decimal fraction is not preceded by a whole number, use a cipher before it (unless the decimal fraction itself begins with a cipher).**

> The average score on the exam was *75.2.*
> The runner clocked a time of *10.86* seconds.
>
> The correct weight is *0.55* gram.
> The second measurement differed from the first by just *.02* gram.

9. **Use figures to express time when** *a.m.* **and** *p.m.* **are used. Do not use the colon and ciphers with even hours. When minutes and hours are shown together, use a colon to separate the figure for the hour from the figure for the minutes. Spell the hour in full when** *o'clock* **is used.**

> The class meets on Mondays at *9 a.m.*
> The meeting adjourned at *4:30 p.m.*
>
> Both the *two o'clock* flight and the *six o'clock* flight were canceled.
> The seminar will begin promptly at *2 p.m.*, a rest break is scheduled for *3:30*, and final discussions will conclude at *five o'clock.*

10. **When the word** *number* **precedes a number, express the word** *number* **as a capitalized abbreviation (singular—No.; plural—Nos.) and use a figure to express the number itself.**

> The player with *No. 22* on her shirt is the team captain.
> Your report is Item *No. 7* on the agenda.

Learning Hint 4.   Show plurals of figures by the addition of *'s*.

How many *100's* were earned on the test?
An ice skater's mastery of figure *8's* is not easily achieved.

11. **Use figures to express distances (except fractions of a mile or of a kilometer), measures, dimensions, weights, and temperatures.**

8 meters, one-fourth kilometer, 2 grams, 3 meters by 5 meters, 70 degrees, 10 tons
The basketball player is *7 feet 6 inches* tall and weighs *240 pounds*.
A *2-meters-by-4-meters* sign has been placed *three-fourths of a kilometer* south of Intersection No. 6.
The weight was incorrectly recorded as *10 pounds* instead of *10 grams*.
The runner covered the final *nine-tenths of a mile* in *105-degree* heat in a time of *3³/₄ minutes* to set a school record for the *4-mile* run.

12. **Spell out ordinal numbers that require no more than two words. However, use figures with ordinals for street names above *Tenth*. In dates, use figures with ordinals when the day precedes the month or appears alone; use figures *without* ordinals when the day follows the month.**

The *twenty-fifth* candidate was selected for the *sixth*—and final—place on the team.
On her *107th* attempt of the season, Bonnie Klue—for the *first* time in her career—set a league record in the high jump.
The sports arena on *15th* Street is the site of the *Eighth* Annual Winter Games.
The youth competition will conclude on the *23rd of June*. If the adult events cannot get under way as early as *June 25*, they will be delayed until the *30th*.

Use
T5-1
here

Posttest

Underline all misused numbers in the following sentences. Then, at the end of each sentence, write the preferred usage for the errors you underlined.

1. One hundred twenty pages of the manuscript containing four bar graphs, eight tables, and twenty-one footnote references were misplaced for over two weeks.

2. On September 10th, Carrie Disha will celebrate her 1st anniversary as supervisor of the branch office on Sixteenth Avenue.

3. In just three days with the help of two aides, Mr. Martini traveled twelve hundred miles, gave ten speeches, attended fourteen meetings, and held six interviews.

4. Less than 50% of the group attended the 7 o'clock dinner, even though tickets costing $30.00 each were purchased in advance by over three-fourths of the group members.

5. Phyllis Larsen, ranked No. 1 in the five-thousand-meter event, collapsed in 99-degree heat on August 2nd just two and one half minutes into the race.

6. At $27.00 a carton, the pencils cost over 18 cents each—an increase of ten percent over our last order on the fifteenth of May.

Key: (1) 4, 8, 21; (2) 10, first, 16th; (3) 1,200, 10, 14, 6; (4) 50 percent, seven o'clock, $30; (5) 5,000, August 2, 2½; (6) $27, 10 percent, 15th.

LEVEL A

Name _____

Exercise
5–1

On the lines below, write **T** if the statement is true; write **F** if the statement is false.

__T__ 1. The rule of ten says that, in general, numbers above ten are written as figures.

__T__ 2. Numbers that begin sentences should always be spelled out.

__F__ 3. The number *one hundred* should not be used to begin a sentence.

__F__ 4. All numbers in the same sentence must be either written out or expressed as figures—they cannot be expressed both ways.

__T__ 5. In the sentence, *A group of 15 18-year-old students arrived early, 15* should be spelled out.

__F__ 6. In normal business writing, percentages should be expressed by figures followed either by the word *percent* or by the percent symbol (%).

__F__ 7. The word *cents* should not be used to express sums of money.

__F__ 8. Figures are always used to express miles and kilometers.

__T__ 9. Some ordinal numbers are expressed as figures; others are written out.

__T__ 10. The word *number* should be expressed as an abbreviation when it precedes a figure.

__F__ 11. A figure may be expressed in plural form by the addition of *es*.

__T__ 12. Fractions that are not accompanied by whole numbers should be written out and hyphenated.

Exercise
5–2

Within the parentheses in each of the following sentences, underline the number that illustrates correct usage.

1. Madge paid the entire bill of (<u>$145</u>, $145.00).

2. Of the questions asked on the questionnaire, only (<u>2 of 10</u>, two of ten) were answered correctly.

3. (25, <u>Twenty-five</u>) days were required to complete the journey.

4. The carton contained (7 ten-pound, <u>seven 10-pound</u>) bags of sugar.

5. Losses are expected to total over ($35,000,000; <u>35 million dollars</u>).

6. The two styles of binders shown in the brochure sell for ($.75 and $1.00, <u>75 cents and $1</u>), respectively.

7. The survey revealed that approximately (two-fifths, <u>2/5</u>) of our Las Vegas employees have been with us less than (5, <u>five</u>) years.

8. The order specified (<u>16</u>, sixteen) jackets—all size (<u>42s</u>, 42's).

9. The elapsed time between the two flashes of light was exactly (.9, <u>0.9</u>) seconds.

10. The afternoon performance begins at (2:00 p.m., 2 p.m.); the evening performance begins at (7, seven) o'clock.

11. The (first-, 1st-) place prize in the writing contest is ($1,000, one thousand dollars).

12. Tax returns are due on the (15, 15th) day of April—not on May (1, 1st), as reported in the *Daily Bugle*.

Exercise 5–3 Write **C** if the bold number is correctly used. Write **I** if the bold number is incorrectly used.

I 1. The width of the driveway was determined to be just over **seven** meters.

C 2. The patient's body temperature was recorded as near normal with a thermometer reading of **98.5** degrees.

I 3. A **#1** ranking was achieved at the end of the season by the team from Collins, NV.

I 4. All evening classes must end no later than **9:45 o'clock**.

I 5. **Forty-seven and two-thirds** cubic feet of asphalt was needed to repair the road.

C 6. The evening's activities concluded with a **five-**course dinner at a cost of $15 for each course.

C 7. **Twelve** letters, 15 memos, and 25 other documents were located in the secretary's files.

I 8. The letter requested payment within **10** days of an overdue balance of $285.

I 9. The university announced that **two hundred fifty** scholarships will be awarded for the coming year.

C 10. Expect to pay a service charge of **2 percent** for a loan with the terms you desire.

C 11. About $3\frac{1}{2}$ pages of court testimony were transcribed in less than **one-half** hour.

C 12. Since the mail goes out at **five o'clock**, deliver your outgoing mail to the post office by 4:45 p.m., if possible.

I 13. The research lab is located on the **4th** floor of Building No. 5.

C 14. The **Eighth** Street exit leads directly to the conference center on Twenty-Second Avenue.

C 15. A **30-feet by 40-feet** reception area is planned for the Memphis branch office.

I 16. The **First** of the year will bring dozens of changes in company policies.

C 17. In **two** weeks, 10 computers and 15 monitors will be exchanged for the five new laser printers we requested for the communications center.

C 18. At a price of $85.50 each, the four chairs delivered today will cost **$342**.

I 19. The annual **.99-cent** sale will be held this year on Saturday, September 12.

I 20. In the past one-half hour, the outside temperature reading has changed only **.6** degree.

LEVEL B

Name _____

Exercise
5–4

Write the letter that precedes the sentence in which there are no errors in number usage.

_b_ 1. *a.* On August 19th, we expect a visit from the vice president of the West Coast Region.
    b. Sometime before the first of the month, all travel costs must be analyzed.
    c. No expense summaries can be submitted after the 31 of March.

_a_ 2. *a.* The latest test shows the average mileage for this vehicle to be 37 miles per gallon.
    b. An all-time low temperature reading of minus twenty-two degrees was recorded yesterday in Mountain Falls.
    c. Rita's recipe for shepherd's stew calls for exactly two cups of chopped onions.

_b_ 3. *a.* Sonata #5 is the final number on the program.
    b. The two entries are sponsored by Dytron, Inc. and are identified as Nos. 3 and 4, respectively.
    c. Candidate number six was disqualified for cheating.

_a_ 4. *a.* A seven o'clock meeting has been called for tomorrow morning.
    b. The train left the station at nine p.m. sharp.
    c. Your appointment with the dentist has been changed to 3:00 p.m. today.

_b_ 5. *a.* $3^1/_2$ hours will be needed to complete the task.
    b. Just over three-fourths of the employees voted to return to work.
    c. Approximately $^1/_3$ of the group replied to the questionnaire during the final $2^1/_2$ weeks.

_c_ 6. *a.* The total distance was a surprising .90 meters.
    b. Even a change in temperature of less than 0.05 degree can be accurately recorded.
    c. The average number of children per household in the state is 1.8.

_a_ 7. *a.* Diggins Auto advertised 15 nine-passenger vans in Sunday's newspaper.
    b. A maximum of 6 29-cent hot dogs will be sold to any one customer.
    c. A total of thirty 3-day ski passes will be given to contest winners.

_a_ 8. *a.* Perfect scores of 100 percent were earned by six people.
    b. Five percent of the boys and 15% of the girls were honored as student scholars.
    c. The current 5% sales tax will increase to $5^1/_2$% in January.

_c_ 9. *a.* The attorney's fee of $250 per hour was considered excessive by all 3 clients.
    b. A one-way flight is $85.00; the round-trip fare is $160.00.
    c. The total amount collected of $98,000 represents an average contribution of less than 5 cents for each citizen of the state.

_a_ 10. *a.* The group consisted of 25 students, 6 teachers, and 2 counselors.
    b. During the 3-day conference, Mrs. Ponza attended 12 meetings, 4 seminars, and 2 news briefings.
    c. A tour group of 40 adults, 15 teenagers, and six children under 12 years of age arrived in Honolulu on the 10th of December.

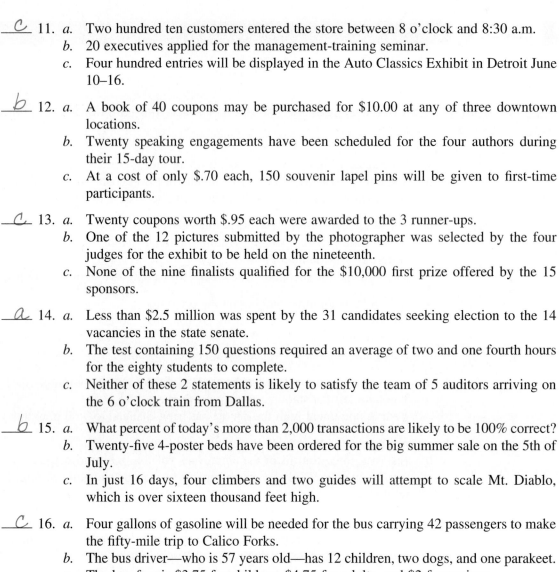

_c_ 11. _a._ Two hundred ten customers entered the store between 8 o'clock and 8:30 a.m.
     _b._ 20 executives applied for the management-training seminar.
     _c._ Four hundred entries will be displayed in the Auto Classics Exhibit in Detroit June 10–16.

_b_ 12. _a._ A book of 40 coupons may be purchased for $10.00 at any of three downtown locations.
     _b._ Twenty speaking engagements have been scheduled for the four authors during their 15-day tour.
     _c._ At a cost of only $.70 each, 150 souvenir lapel pins will be given to first-time participants.

_c_ 13. _a._ Twenty coupons worth $.95 each were awarded to the 3 runner-ups.
     _b._ One of the 12 pictures submitted by the photographer was selected by the four judges for the exhibit to be held on the nineteenth.
     _c._ None of the nine finalists qualified for the $10,000 first prize offered by the 15 sponsors.

_a_ 14. _a._ Less than $2.5 million was spent by the 31 candidates seeking election to the 14 vacancies in the state senate.
     _b._ The test containing 150 questions required an average of two and one fourth hours for the eighty students to complete.
     _c._ Neither of these 2 statements is likely to satisfy the team of 5 auditors arriving on the 6 o'clock train from Dallas.

_b_ 15. _a._ What percent of today's more than 2,000 transactions are likely to be 100% correct?
     _b._ Twenty-five 4-poster beds have been ordered for the big summer sale on the 5th of July.
     _c._ In just 16 days, four climbers and two guides will attempt to scale Mt. Diablo, which is over sixteen thousand feet high.

_c_ 16. _a._ Four gallons of gasoline will be needed for the bus carrying 42 passengers to make the fifty-mile trip to Calico Forks.
     _b._ The bus driver—who is 57 years old—has 12 children, two dogs, and one parakeet.
     _c._ The bus fare is $3.75 for children, $4.75 for adults, and $2 for seniors.

_a_ 17. _a._ On March 5, notebooks will sell in the bookstore for $1 each—or 85 cents each if a customer buys three or more.
     _b._ Meet me at the corner of 16th and Stratford by 3 o'clock if you want to save one dollar on the third matinee of _The Smoking Gun_ now showing at the Palace.
     _c._ Sammy ranked 107th in his class of 640 students at the end of his 3rd year in law school.

_b_ 18. _a._ The next 6 performances of _Arsenic and Old Lace_ are scheduled for December 4th–9th in the theater on the 1st floor of the Drama Center on 12th Avenue.
     _b._ Dennis paid $13,000 for a 3/4-ton pickup that gets 20 miles per gallon in temperatures that exceed 100 degrees.
     _c._ In their first meet of the season, the 8 members of the Kansas University gymnastics team recorded scores that included several 9.5's but very few 10's.

LEVEL C

Name _____

Exercise 5–5

Mark **C** if no number-usage errors occur; mark **I** if one or more number-usage errors occur. Then underline the number-usage errors in sentences where they occur and edit the sentences to remove the errors. No. 0 is an example.

___I___ 0. Of the <u>10</u> *(ten)* sales representatives who attended the <u>fifteen</u> *(15)*-day seminar, only two received certificates.

___I___ 1. Ninety passengers demanded refunds averaging <u>$255.00</u>. *($255.)*

___I___ 2. The federal budget, for the <u>4th</u> *(fourth)* consecutive year, is expected to exceed <u>one</u> *($1)* trillion <u>dollars.</u>

___I___ 3. The recorded time of <u>four</u> *(4)* hours, 12 minutes, and 31 seconds fell short of the old record by <u>one and a half</u> *(1½)* minutes.

___I___ 4. Six trucks and <u>fifteen</u> *(15)* cars were impounded by <u>7</u> *(seven)* Dawson City police officers in a period of 21 days.

___I___ 5. The 12 jurors agree that the award of <u>$1,500,000</u> *($1.5 million)* is <u>50%</u> *(50 percent)* higher than expected.

___C___ 6. George Tidwell's two-hour presentation to 50 twenty-year veterans was the third and final event of the day.

___I___ 7. Less than <u>10%</u> *(10 percent)* of the samples satisfied the <u>6-point</u> *(six-point)* standard required by the three scientists.

___C___ 8. A $5 registration fee is customary; a discount of 75 cents is given to those who sign up the first day.

___I___ 9. Zodiac stock rose to 18³/₄ points during the month—a gain in value of $6, or <u>47%</u>. *(47 percent)*

___I___ 10. Final exams for classes meeting at <u>9:00</u> *(9)* a.m. will be <u>2</u> *(two)* hours in length and will be held at 3:30 <u>o'clock</u> *(p.m.)* Monday, April <u>17th</u>. *(17)*

_I_ 11. Player No. 11 picked up her 5th [*fifth*] foul with 2 [*two*] minutes remaining in the game.

_I_ 12. A technical foul was assessed against the Dragons by the 3 [*three*] officials when 2 [*two*] number 6s [*No. 6's*]

appeared on the floor at the same time.

_I_ 13. The July 4th [*4*] holiday will be celebrated this year by over 4,000,000 [*4 million*] people in the state's

six largest cities.

_I_ 14. At 8 p.m., the 12th Avenue bus carrying 33 passengers was reported to be stalled near

the 1st [*First*] Street bridge.

_I_ 15. In less than 18 months, Lennis grew approximately four [*4*] inches to reach a height of six [*6½*]

and one half feet.

_C_ 16. Sixty thousand ceiling tiles measuring 9 inches by 12 inches were required to complete

the $500,000 project.

_I_ 17. Twelve 4-poster beds were to be sold at $210 each—a 30% [*30 percent*] discount—on November

2nd. [*2.*]

_I_ 18. Janowicz, Inc. ranks No. 178 on the Fortune 500 list and, in its 20th [*twentieth*] year of operations,

announced a $.95 [*95-cent*] stock dividend—good news for its 1.3 million stockholders.

_I_ 19. The fifth storm of the season brought a drop of twenty [*20*] degrees in overnight tempera-

tures; the city's Emergency Assistance Center received over 350 calls for help in its 6 [*six*]

branch offices.

_I_ 20. The witnesses testified that four 9's were among the seven numbers on the license plate

of the 18-wheel truck seen leaving the scene of the 3-car [*three*] accident.

_I_ 21. 16 [*Sixteen*] girls and 21 boys enrolled in the 10-and-over-swimmers' [*ten*] class scheduled to begin

Monday morning, August first [*1*], at 9 [*nine*] o'clock.

Exercise
5–6

Use the suggested abbreviations to identify the sentence category in which each of the following sentences belongs. Also, insert the correct end-of-sentence punctuation and correct any misspelled words. Item 0 is an example.

Cumula-
tive
Review

D   Declarative   **EX**   Exclamatory
IN Interrogative   **PR**   Polite Request
IM Imperative

                    license   maintenance
__IM__   0. Renew your lisence as a maintenence technician by June 30.

                                              grateful   pamphlet
__PR__   1. Will you please tell your secretary that I am greatful for the phamplet she sent me .

            satellite   dependent   writing   their
__IN__   2. Which sattelite companies are dependant on competent writting specialists for there

existence ?

                        employes definitely
__EX__   3. In the future, all employes definately must submit their mileage logs without fail to the

bookkeeper
bookeeper !

            attendance committee   accommodate
__IM__   4. Alert the attendence comittee that the catalog cannot accomodate further additions to

curriculum
the curiculum .

            superintendent congratulated   competent
__D__   5. The superintendant congradulated his competant staff on the excellent appearance of

the cemetary grounds .

            sophomore embarrassed   grammar   prominent
__IN__   6. The surprised sophmore was embarassed by the grammer used in the prominant entre-

preneur's speech, was she not ?

                            vacuum
__PR__   7. Miss Holte, will you ask the vaccuum sales representative to step into my office after

            bookkeeper
he talks to the bookeeper .

                                                            briefly
__EX__   8. Once and for all, never take a company car from the motor pool—even breifly—unless

            license
you have your driver's lisence with you /

                                        yield   satellite   recom-
__IM__   9. Inquire immediately whether Radex, Inc. will yeild the necessary satellite time recco-

mended
mended for the overseas broadcast of the Albany conference

Exercise 5–7 Mark each item with the appropriate abbreviation to indicate the item's proper classification, and correct any misused numbers or improperly used (confusing) words.

Cumulative Review

F	Fragment	**SM** Simple Sentence
RO	Run-on Sentence	**CM** Compound Sentence
CS	Comma Splice	

_F_ 0. Although *every one* [everyone] was informed of the *surprizing* [surprising] change in the time of the meeting to be attended by all ten visitors from Taiwan.

_SM_ 1. The curriculum meeting scheduled for Friday at ~~9~~ *nine* o'clock has been changed to Monday at 1 p.m.

_CS_ 2. Ask the ~~restuarant~~ *restaurant* manager to attend the conference on July ~~12th~~ *12* he should attend all three ~~principle~~ *principal* meetings.

_CM_ 3. The printer was delivered to the ~~capital~~ *Capitol* building today, but ~~it's~~ *its* price of ~~$1,000.00~~ *$1,000* is one fourth more than expected.

_RO_ 4. The ~~temperary~~ *temporary* headquarters on ~~Twentieth~~ *20th* Street is ~~4~~ *four* blocks from the ~~Foriegn~~ *Foreign* Affairs Office I can walk there in ~~10~~ *ten* minutes.

_F_ 5. Due to the ~~truely practicle~~ *truly practical* approach used by the ~~3~~*three*-member committee appointed to consider suggestions from the student ~~counsel~~ *council* to improve school attendance.

_SM_ 6. You may take no more than one month to complete the ~~three thousand~~ *3,000*-mile inspection tour of ~~everyone~~ *every one* of our 14 satellite assembly plants.

_CM_ 7. Over ~~30%~~ *30 percent* of our ~~employes~~ *employees* have ~~past there~~ *passed their* 60th birthday, but fewer than ~~10~~ *ten* are expected to ~~loose~~ *lose* income this year because of ~~miscelaneous~~ *miscellaneous* health problems.

_CM_ 8. The firm's business ~~lisence~~ *license* will be ~~forfieted~~ *forfeited* on the ~~31~~ *31st* of December; however, a ~~temperary~~ *temporary* permit may be obtained by ~~any one who's~~ *anyone whose* application is approved by the licensing committee.

CAPITALIZATION LESSON 6

Through capitalization, we use uppercase letters to give emphasis or to show importance to the word capitalized. From a reverse perspective, of course, we do not give emphasis or show importance if we do not capitalize a word.

To employ business English properly, we should know when to capitalize and when not to capitalize. That sounds easy enough. However, as with so many components of the English language, differences of opinion exist about what should and should not be capitalized. In addition, the rules of capitalization reflect numerous exceptions and inconsistencies that must be internalized by the truly effective writer. In fact, no set of capitalization rules can be universally applicable.

In some instances, a reliable dictionary may be an authoritative source to answer some of the questions that arise about capitalization. However, even the dictionary will not answer all questions.

The rules that follow are appropriate for general usage. They may not apply totally to a specialized situation, such as a government office or an advertising agency. And rules of capitalization may vary from one company to another.

Many additional rules could be presented in this lesson, such as the obvious rule that the first word in a sentence is capitalized. However, the rules that follow reflect frequently occurring capitalization questions more than the frequency of occurrence of all capitalization. The rules are presented according to general topics associated with capitalization.

Pretest

With a **C** or an **I**, indicate whether the capitalization is correct or incorrect in the following sentences. Then correct all capitalization that is wrong.

1. Melba Goldstein, my Algebra teacher, plans to circle the entire Earth next summer—probably beginning in Mid-June.

2. The Professor spent the entire Summer in the South doing research for his book, *The Flora and Fauna within the State of Florida.*

3. Please tell state representative LeRay English what you think the major concerns of the State of Nevada should be during the Twenty-First Century.

4. You are right; Professor Victor Westin teaches Business Writing I every fall and winter semester in the Management Communication Department.

5. Did your Mom pay the ticket at the local Police Department before or after she talked with our Mayor?

KEY: (1) algebra, earth, mid-June; (2) professor, summer, Within; (3) State Representative, state, twenty-first century; (4) C; (5) mom, police department, mayor.

Rules of Capitalization

1. *Academics*—**Capitalize academic subjects only when reference is made to a specific course title. Capitalize all names of languages. Capitalize academic degrees when used with the name of an individual, but do not capitalize degrees when used with the word *degree*. Do not capitalize *freshman, sophomore, junior, senior,* or *graduate*.**

   During my sophomore year, I will take word processing, American history, and Spanish.

   Susie's favorite courses are Algebra I, Early American Novels, and Business English.

   Our college offers both a bachelor of science in business and a master's degree in business administration.

   Jose Ortega, Doctor of Philosophy, will talk to us about the merits of the bachelor's degree.

2. *Astronomical bodies*—**Capitalize names of specific planets, stars, and other astronomical bodies. Do not capitalize *sun, moon,* or *earth* unless they are used in connection with the capitalized names of other astronomical bodies.**

   The four planets that are nearest our sun are Mercury, Venus, Earth, and Mars.

   You are correct; Earth is minuscule in size compared to the Milky Way.

   She traveled around the earth twice during those ten years.

3. *Businesses and organizations*—**Capitalize the names of companies, associations, schools, political parties, foundations, clubs, hospitals, religious groups, etc., according to the preference of the business or organization. Unless special emphasis or distinction is required, do not capitalize the short form of an organization when the short form is used**

in place of the full name (e.g., *the company*) unless the short form is intended to invoke the full authority of the organization. Capitalize organizational terms when they designate proper-noun, actual names of units in the business or organization (e.g., *Advertising Department* but not *an advertising department*).

The Faith of Our Fathers is authored by James Cardinal Gibbons of the Catholic Church, and the book presents the principal tenets of the Church.

The Book of Mormon: Another Testament of Jesus Christ is published by The Church of Jesus Christ of Latter-day Saints (the Mormons). (This capitalization is preferred by the Church.)

A Man for All Seasons will be reviewed by majors in the Drama Department of the College of Eastern Utah.

When you come to the company headquarters, I'll give you a copy of Marketing's procedures manual.

4. *Calendar items*—**Capitalize days of the week, months of the year, holidays, religious days, and specific calendar-oriented events. Capitalize historic events and imaginative names given to historical periods. Do not capitalize seasons unless they are personified or refer to a specific time period or event. Do not capitalize the names of decades and centuries.**

Monday, December 5	the Christian Era
New Year's Eve	fall, winter, spring, summer
Civil War years	Come, gentle Spring.
Martin Luther King Day	Fall Semester 1992 (but, fall semester)
Good Friday	during the eighties
the Great Depression	in the twenty-first century

5. *Compass terms*—**Do not capitalize points of the compass unless they refer to a particular region or are used as part of a proper name. Capitalize *northern, southern, eastern,* and *western* when they refer to the people in a region and to their cultural, social, or political activities. Do not capitalize these words if they refer to the general location, geography, or climate of a region.**

west of the Pecos
south of the border
the Deep South
the North Pole
He is originally from the Middle West but now lives in the South.
Go north on Interstate 15 and then east on Interstate 80.
I am going out West after my three years on the East Coast.
Southern hospitality
Northern Ireland
westerly winds

6. *Derivatives of proper nouns or adjectives*—**Do not capitalize derivatives of proper nouns or adjectives that have acquired a common meaning.**

bone china
roman numerals
plaster of paris
manila envelope
diesel
watt
french dressing

7. *Family titles*—Capitalize family titles only when they stand alone or when they are followed by a personal name.

> Jack said, ''Will you take me to the movies, Uncle?''
> I haven't heard from my Aunt Josie for a month.
> I called my mother and father last night.
> I called Mom and Dad last night.
> Is your grandfather still living?
> I expect Grandmother Moses to live another ten years.

8. *Government bodies, officials, and titles*—Capitalize the names of countries, international organizations, and city, county, state, and national bodies. Capitalize such terms as *Police Department* if the term refers to the organization in an official capacity. Capitalize *federal* and *state* only when they are part of an official name or proper noun. Capitalize titles of high-ranking officials at the state, national, and international levels when the titles precede, follow, or take the place of a name.

> Federal Trade Commission
> the House of Representatives (or the House)
> Federal Bureau of Investigation (or the Bureau)
> the British Commonwealth
> Scott Matheson, Governor of Utah
> George Bush, President
> We attended meetings of our local board of education.
> The Alpine District Board of Education meets next Monday.
> Why are you not subject to federal and state laws?
> I wrote the Federal Deposit Insurance Corporation.

9. *Hyphenated words*—Capitalize hyphenated words as you would if you used them separately or in conjunction with another rule of capitalization. Capitalize a hyphenated prefix only when it is the first word of a sentence. When the prefix precedes a proper noun, capitalize only the proper noun.

> Spanish-American
> English-speaking countries
> President-elect Wengreen
> mid-December blues (but mid-winter blues)
> non-Methodist friends
> ex-President Reagan

10. *Names/nicknames*—Capitalize names/nicknames when they are used to designate particular people, places, or things.

> the First Lady
> the Windy City
> Old Ironsides
> the Beehive State
> the Coast (West Coast)

11. *Nationalities, races, languages, and religions*—Capitalize all nationalities, races, languages, and religions. Do not capitalize *black* and *white*.

Mexican-American   French
Afro-American   Negro
Chinese   Methodist
Caucasian   Judaism

12. *Nouns preceding numbers or letters*—**Capitalize a noun that precedes a letter or a number indicating sequence. However, do not capitalize** *line, note, page, paragraph, size,* **and** *verse.*

Table 15
Appendix A
Lesson 15
Exercise 22
Column 2
Invoice 43-386
Purchase Order 12-344
Chapter IX
Policy No. 3-45-623 (*No.* is not necessary to precede the number or letter in these kinds of terms.)
page 29
size 16

13. *Personal titles*—**Capitalize personal titles when they precede the person's name. Do not capitalize a title when it follows the person's name unless the person is a high-ranking government official or unless you want to give special recognition to the position. Do not capitalize a personal title that precedes a person's name if a comma occurs between the title and the name (that is, the name is in apposition to the title). Do not capitalize occupational designations or classes of positions.**

Professor Emory Sonderegger
Dr. William Sawaya
Martin Harris, associate professor
Joseph Smith, mayor of Springville
Ben Donaho, coordinator of purchasing, will submit the request.
Paula Goodson plans to apply for the job as accountant for the company.

14. *Product and trade names*—**Capitalize trademarks, brand names, proprietary names, and names of commercial products. Do not capitalize the common noun following the name of a product.**

Westinghouse refrigerator
Ivory soap
Grade A beef
IBM personal computers

15. *Publications, literary and artistic works, and headings*—**Capitalize all words in titles of literary works, artistic works, and headings except the articles, conjunctions, and prepositions mentioned in Learning Hint 1.**

How to Succeed in Business Without Really Trying (book)
The Enemy Within (book)
''An Analysis of the Use of Punctuation in Business Correspondence'' (article)
Two newspapers I read every day are *The Daily Herald* and the *Christian Science Monitor.*
The title of his article is ''What to Listen For.''

Learning Hint 1.   Be consistent in capitalizing the words in titles, subtitles, headings, subheadings, names of businesses, and names of organizations. In general, capitalize all words with four or more letters. In addition, capitalize all nouns, pronouns, adjectives, verbs, adverbs, and subordinate conjunctions, regardless of length. Capitalize articles (*a, an, the*) and coordinate conjunctions (*and, but, or, nor, for, so, yet*) only when they are the first or last words. Capitalize prepositions only when they are four or more letters in length or when they are the first or last words. Finally, do not capitalize the *to* in infinitives.

Learning Hint 2.   As you look at the above examples, you will see that some are italicized. For many years, underscoring of typewritten material has been a way to show italics. With the advent of word-processing software, a writer can easily use true italics rather than use the underscore. However, the underscore still signifies italics.

In conjunction with Rule 15, the titles of books, pamphlets, poems, magazines, newspapers, movies, plays, musicals, operas, radio and television shows, musical compositions, paintings, and pieces of sculpture are capitalized and italicized.

In business correspondence, the titles of literary and artistic works are sometimes keyed in solid capitals to signify italics. Presumably, this practice originated so the typist would not have to backspace on the typewriter to use the underscore for italics. In business correspondence and reports, you may choose among the underscore, solid caps, or true italics to show italics. In this textbook, we will always use true italics when italicizing material.

Use T6-1 here

Posttest

With a **C** or an **I**, indicate whether the capitalization is correct or incorrect in the following sentences. Then correct all capitalization that is wrong.

1. All of the concerned caucasians and Black Afro-Americans met with the Sociology Professor in room 210 of the college of business building.

2. Sally purchased the China dolls during her trip to the far east last Spring.

3. We will appoint a Grievance Committee sometime during the Third Quarter as directed in Item 12 of the Division Head's memo.

4. Yes, Paul used my IBM personal computer last fall to write his senior thesis, ''The Case against Government Intervention in El Salvador.''

5. Did you notice grandfather's change of opinion after he visited with the Governor in Mid-May?

Key: (1) Caucasians, black, sociology professor, Room, College of Business Building; (2) china, Far East, spring; (3) grievance committee, third quarter, division head's; (4) Against; (5) Grandfather's, governor, mid-May.

LEVEL A

Name _____

Exercise 6–1 On the lines below, write **T** if the statement is true and **F** if the statement is false.

_F_ 1. *Business English* is capitalized in every instance.

_T_ 2. *Sun, earth,* and *moon* are capitalized only when used in connection with the names of other astronomical bodies.

_T_ 3. The short form of an organization's name is capitalized only when the short form invokes the full authority of the organization.

_F_ 4. *Fall, winter, spring,* and *summer* are always capitalized in business correspondence.

_T_ 5. Points of the compass are not capitalized unless they designate definite regions or are part of a proper name.

_F_ 6. *Use small Roman numerals* reflects correct capitalization.

_F_ 7. We always capitalize such terms as *Police Department* and *Board of Education*.

_F_ 8. *Federal* and *State* are almost always capitalized in business correspondence.

_F_ 9. Whenever a hyphenated prefix is used with a proper noun, the prefix is capitalized.

_T_ 10. We should not capitalize *page, paragraph,* or *size* when they precede a letter or a number indicating sequence.

_T_ 11. The names of all languages are capitalized.

_F_ 12. The capitalization in this sentence is correct: *I hope to receive my Master's Degree in April.*

_F_ 13. *Freshman, sophomore, junior,* and *senior* are capitalized in educational correspondence.

_F_ 14. The capitalization in this sentence is correct: *I work full time in an Advertising Department.*

_F_ 15. The names of historic events are capitalized, but imaginative names given to historical periods are not capitalized.

_F_ 16. *Northern, southern, eastern,* and *western* are always capitalized.

_T_ 17. The capitalization in this sentence is correct: *I bought four bottles of french dressing.*

_T_ 18. Family titles, such as *uncle* and *grandfather,* are capitalized when they stand alone.

_F_ 19. *Federal* should always be capitalized in governmental correspondence.

_T_ 20. Hyphenated words are capitalized as you would if you used them separately or in conjunction with another rule of capitalization.

Exercise 6–2 Assume that each of the following phrases comes at the end of a sentence. Mark **C** if the capitalization is correct and **I** if the capitalization is incorrect.

_I_ 1. taking business management 100.

_C_ 2. refer to Exhibit II.

_I_ 3. on flight 1776 from Boston.

_I_ 4. working for this Company.

_C_ 5. the annual parking-lot sale.

_I_ 6. during the Spring.

_I_ 7. the club's Constitution.

_I_ 8. license No. 200251.

_I_ 9. in a large Accounting Department.

_I_ 10. living out west.

_I_ 11. traveling West on Interstate 80.

_I_ 12. study lesson 6 tonight.

_I_ 13. enjoy Indian summer.

_C_ 14. studied business law last fall.

_C_ 15. Old Man Winter.

_I_ 16. elected to the U.S. senate.

_C_ 17. talks like a Southerner.

_C_ 18. the Communications Department.

_I_ 19. plan to be a Sophomore.

_I_ 20. in room 574.

_C_ 21. drawn with india ink.

_I_ 22. seen _Gone With The Wind_.

_I_ 23. performed a Herculean task.

_I_ 24. South of Pioneer Park.

_I_ 25. the democratic party candidate.

_I_ 26. on labor day.

_I_ 27. to Timpanogos cave.

_I_ 28. near lake ontario.

_I_ 29. at the Hotel.

_I_ 30. listen to a Rock Band.

Exercise 6–3 Mark **C** if the capitalization is correct; mark **I** if the capitalization is incorrect.

_I_ 1. I'm from the midwest.

_C_ 2. He plans to attend college.

_I_ 3. I lived in the west last year.

_C_ 4. I very much enjoy English.

_I_ 5. His Grandfather is still alive.

_I_ 6. Ben is a Sophomore this year.

_I_ 7. Xu is the new Class President.

_C_ 8. My uncle is a Catholic priest.

_C_ 9. Take the test in the Tanner Building.

_I_ 10. What on Earth are you doing?

_C_ 11. Fire Prevention Week begins Monday.

_I_ 12. The Westerly winds will blow.

_I_ 13. Please buy some French dressing.

_C_ 14. The governor of Idaho will speak.

_I_ 15. Have you seen the President-Elect?

_I_ 16. We're going to the sunshine state.

_I_ 17. The data are found in table 23.

_I_ 18. Have you converted to islam?

_I_ 19. I've done my Spring cleaning.

_I_ 20. We sold the old Mimeograph machine.

_I_ 21. We hiked along Squaw Peak trail.

_I_ 22. We watched the Cuban Rumba.

_I_ 23. Rod stayed at the embassy suites hotel.

_I_ 24. Please sing us an irish ballad.

| LEVEL B |

Name _____

Exercise   Write the letter that identifies the sentence with correct capitalization.
6–4

_c_ 1. *a.* My father was an active Democrat during Post-World War II.
    b. Please go to room 215 to take the Graduate Management Aptitude Test.
    c. He is an Afro-American student from the Big Apple.

_b_ 2. *a.* The church believes in the rites of the Sacrament and of Baptism.
    b. Yes, Northern Idaho is my favorite part of the West.
    c. We have established Campus Cleanup Week during the third week of fall semester 1992.

_c_ 3. *a.* We bought some Turkish Towels while we were in eastern Europe.
    b. I get to introduce the Governor of Utah at the opening game of the Pioneer Baseball League.
    c. State Senator-elect Parker wants to help us get a police department in Escalante.

_a_ 4. *a.* Ms. Bronson was interviewed on KSL Television about her experiences with the Hotpoint dishwasher.
    b. I hope to get the job of Foreman in the northern assembly division.
    c. Juanita Munoz, Chairperson of the Department, will speak on Government Ethics at the symposium.

_c_ 5. *a.* According to Mr. Clements, the birds are a mixture of the Rio Grande and eastern wild turkeys.
    b. Clements, who is a Past President of the National Federation of Wild Turkeys, will speak on Tuesday.
    c. The mayors have talked about the issue openly, and the Chamber of Commerce has represented both cities in the past.

_b_ 6. *a.* The Jazz Basketball star, Karl ''the mailman'' Malone, will be on the nominating committee.
    b. I hope to take courses in business for my bachelor's degree and then go to law school.
    c. The parade route will take us through Downtown Provo and will terminate at the East Bay Industrial Park.

_b_ 7. *a.* Vernal City Attorney Bud Gregerson is familiar with the environmental response, compensation and liability act.
    b. Individuals who speak any Southeast Asian language are needed to tutor refugees in learning English.
    c. ''The Crisis Line is open 24 hours a day,'' said director Monte Willes.

_a_ 8. *a.* The dispute resulted in an investigation by school board officials and the Department of Social Services.
    b. The Cold Fusion Institute will receive funding of $5 million next Fall.
    c. ''A Day In The Life Of Charley Jones'' is the title of the drama department's play.

_b_ 9. _a._ During the Great Depression of the Thirties, my Grandfather was lucky to have work most of the time.

  _b._ The House will ask for a roll-call vote on provisions of the new Vocational Education Act.

  _c._ When we reached the canal zone, we went through the canal in record time.

_a_ 10. _a._ As you will see in Column 1, the air-pollution levels in the city of Payson are far too high.

  _b._ About Mid-August, the Art Gallery in Lehi will exhibit my Mother's paintings.

  _c._ The mower was ruined by a Nylon stocking, according to Art Monson, the Campus Grounds Coordinator.

Exercise 6–5 On the first line below, indicate any capitalization rule numbers reflected in the sentence's bold words (more than one rule number may be reflected in each sentence). On the second line, mark **C** if all of the bold words' capitalization is correct and **I** if any capitalization is incorrect.

_13_ _C_ 1. Newspapers are a critical part of the **mass media**, according to Eugene Gholdston, **associate publisher** of _The Daily Universe_.

_3_ _I_ 2. Recycling containers will be placed on the ASU **Campus** by the **physical facilities division**.

_8_ _I_ 3. The **Savings and Loan** scandal touched five **Senators** and the **president's** son.

_5_ _I_ 4. Young **Democracies** in **eastern** Europe are being threatened.

_8_ _I_ 5. Margaret Thatcher is the first woman **Prime Minister** in English **History**.

_13_ _I_ 6. Dr. Gallagher, **Professor** of **Spanish**, will be on leave for one **Quarter**.

_15_ _I_ 7. The heading in question is ''Where **The** Heat Comes **From**.''

_2_ _C_ 8. Which is nearer the **Sun**—the planet **Venus** or the planet **Earth**?

_7,4,5_ _I_ 9. My **grandfather** was born in the **Twentieth Century** and lived in **upstate** New York.

_12,11_ _I_ 10. You do not have to indicate on **form** 1040 whether you are **White** or **Black**.

_1,2_ _I_ 11. In **Physics**, we studied the magnetic fields of the **sun** and the **moon**.

_3,1_ _C_ 12. Our **company** will sponsor your registration in **Computer Science** 404.

_6,5_ _I_ 13. Use **Roman** numerals in your outline for your essay about the **West**.

_7,5_ _C_ 14. My **grandmother** told me today she is moving to the **west** side of town.

_9,5_ _I_ 15. We are suffering a **Mid-July** heat wave so common in the **Deep South**.

_10,9_ _I_ 16. The **city of angels** is where the **Spanish-Speaking** Americans live.

_11,12_ _C_ 17. You'll find the information about the **Arabs** in **Chapter** 26.

_13,11_ _C_ 18. Carl Pope, **professor of English**, talked to us about **creative writing**.

_14,5_ _I_ 19. We bought a **Hotpoint** stove top for our home on the **West** side of town.

_13,14,11_ _I_ 20. **Associate Professor** Newell Dudley wrote _Writing without Bias._

LEVEL C

Name _____

Exercise 6–6 Mark **C** if the capitalization is correct. Mark **I** if any capitalization is incorrect. Then edit all incorrect capitalization.

_C_ 1. In 1853, Minister Gadsden sought a larger natural boundary with Mexico, including all of Lower California.

_I_ 2. In 1919, a peace conference was held at Versailles, with President Wilson speaking for The United States.

_I_ 3. The first Atomic-Powered Submarine, the *Nautilus*, was launched at Groton, Connecticut.

_I_ 4. Oppenheimer, known as "the Father of the Atomic Bomb," was accused of Communist sympathies.

_I_ 5. At that time, the President's proposed budget called for expenditures of over $62 billion for the next Fiscal Year.

_I_ 6. Robert Weaver, Secretary of the Department of Housing and Urban Development, was the first Negro to become a Cabinet officer.

_I_ 7. The use of a Poll Tax was ruled unconstitutional by the supreme court in *Harper v. Virginia Board of Elections*.

_I_ 8. Nader's book, *Unsafe At Any Speed*, criticized the automakers for their lack of safety concerns.

_C_ 9. No, the First Lady is not from the Gopher State.

_I_ 10. The River in question is the Colorado River, which claimed the Professor's life last Summer.

_I_ 11. Steven Benedict, Jr. plans to run for the office of attorney general next Fall.

_C_ 12. Vice President Linton recommended me to be general manager of our divisional office in San Antonio.

_I_ 13. The President of the company saw the need to hire the new Cost Accountants.

_C_ 14. I want you to tell me, Doctor, whether the Salk vaccine will be available.

_C_ 15. Mayor-elect Payne plans to put his uncle, Charles Huggins, on the city's payroll.

_I_ 16. Incidentally, Grandfather is pleased that you are the new President of the American Society for Training and Development.

_C_ 17. Talk to Mr. Ky in Corporate Communications first, and then visit with Ms. Speck in Marketing.

_I_ 18. I was directed by Chairman Weaver to be sure the guidelines meet all Federal and State laws.

_C_ 19. When you get to the zoo, be sure to spend some time in the Gorilla House.

_I_ 20. Which would you rather visit—the north pole, the west coast, or the deep south?

_I_ 21. We went North to Blackfoot and then West to Arco.

_I_ 22. The movie is about Prohibition during the Roaring Twenties.

Exercise 6–7

Composition

1. Compose a sentence containing a family title, a high-ranking government title, and a compass term.

_____

_____

2. Compose a sentence containing a season of the year, a local government body, and the name of a local business.

_____

_____

Exercise 6–8

Cumulative Editing

Edit the following sentences to reflect what you have learned from Lessons 3 through 6.

1. The ~~S~~upreme ~~C~~ourt _pursued_ ~~persued~~ the ~~C~~onstitutionality of the Federal Wages and Hours Act; the ~~c~~ourt also _proceeded_ ~~proceded~~ to review disputes between ~~L~~abor ~~U~~nions in relation to the Sherman Antitrust Act.

2. _Incidentally,_ ~~Incidently,~~ Thomas Bradley was not _surprised_ ~~surprized~~ when he won the runoff election ~~too~~ _to_ become the first ~~B~~lack ~~M~~ayor of Los Angeles.

3. The ~~S~~ecretary of agriculture _apparently_ ~~aparently~~ has a _personal_ ~~personnel~~ hobby of listening to ~~alot~~ _a lot_ of Beethoven and reading ~~N~~ineteenth-~~C~~entury ~~E~~nglish poetry.

4. _Three_ ~~3~~ times in a row, ~~p~~rofessor Rodriguez _congratulated_ ~~congradulated~~ and _complimented_ ~~complemented~~ the ~~twenty~~ _20_ American ~~L~~iterature ~~C~~ourse _sophomore_ ~~sophmore~~ students who had read _Moby Dick_.

5. Although Harry has an _excellent_ ~~exeellant~~ knowledge of ~~P~~hilosophy, he did not get the ~~oppertunity~~ _opportunity_ to test out of ~~you're~~ _your_ ~~p~~hilosophy 201 course.

6. According to the ~~S~~enator from Illinois, _every one_ ~~everyone~~ of the ~~d~~emocrats doubted that ~~there~~ _their_ presidential candidate would ~~recieve~~ _receive_ ~~consistant~~ _consistent_ support in the ~~W~~est and in the ~~S~~outh.

7. We ~~conceeded~~ *conceded* that ~~1/4~~ *one-fourth* of our ~~middle ages~~ *Middle Ages* ~~Libary~~ *Library* holdings are inadequate; however, Miss Palmer, our ~~Head Libarian~~ *Head Librarian*, promised that she will not ~~loose site~~ *lose sight* of our goal to make ~~sizeable~~ *sizable* improvements by ~~Spring~~ *spring* of next year.

8. My ~~2nd~~ *second* term paper is about the ~~affects~~ *effects* that the most ~~prominant~~ *prominent* ~~french~~ *French* and ~~english~~ *English* ~~Kings~~ *kings* and ~~Queens~~ *queens* had on the ~~renaissance~~ *Renaissance* ~~period~~ *Period* (at least during the ~~Fifteenth~~ *fifteenth* ~~Century~~ *century*).

9. In my March ~~3rd~~ *3* paper, I ~~discribe~~ *describe* ~~Antiquity~~ *antiquity* as the "Golden Age" because ~~Reason~~ *reason* prevailed and ~~Civilization~~ *civilization* permitted a natural ~~persuit~~ *pursuit* of ~~Truth~~ *truth*.

10. As part of ~~it's curiculum~~ *its curriculum*, the ~~College~~ *college* will offer ~~4~~ *four* sections of ~~principals of entre-perneurism~~ *Principles of Entre-preneurism*.

11. The ~~counsel~~ *Council* of ~~general~~ *General* ~~education~~ *Education* is located on the ~~4th~~ *fourth* floor of the Widtsoe ~~building~~ *Building*, which is ~~fifty~~ *50* yards ~~South~~ *south* of the Brimhall ~~tower~~ *Tower*.

12. After the ~~3 defendents~~ *three defendants* attended ~~Church~~ *church*, they ~~aparently travelled five~~ *apparently traveled 5* miles to the ~~sight~~ *site* of the new ~~Cemetary~~ *cemetery*, which is on ~~south~~ *South* ~~university~~ *University* ~~avenue~~ *Avenue*.

13. The ~~Superintendant~~ *superintendent* directed ~~1/5~~ *one-fifth* of her students to use the ~~Computers~~ *computers* in ~~room~~ *Room* ~~twelve~~ *12* to help ~~sumarize~~ *summarize* the ~~principle~~ *principal* ~~Statistical~~ *statistical* implications reflected in ~~table six~~ *Table 6*.

14. The new ~~Pastor~~ *pastor* of ~~you're~~ *your* ~~Church~~ *church* is from Australia; he's ~~carefull~~ *careful* to ~~advice~~ *advise* his congregation that he speaks "~~australian~~ *Australian*."

15. When we reached the southern Utah part of the ~~west~~ *West*, we were ~~dissappointed~~ *disappointed* that ~~every one~~ *everyone* did not speak with a "Southern Utah ~~Twang~~ *twang*."

16. The ~~1st~~ *first* verse of the poem, *Come ~~gentle spring~~ Gentle Spring*, ~~truely~~ *truly* inspired me to start my poem with the verse "Stay away miserable ~~Winter~~ *winter*."

Obviously, an abbreviation is a shortened form of a word or a phrase. We have come to accept the use of abbreviations to save time and space.

In business correspondence or in instances where a formal or semiformal style of writing is employed, we tend to use abbreviations sparingly. In general, the following advice may be good advice for many business-writing situations: *When in doubt, spell it out.*

However, we do commonly use some abbreviations in all kinds of writing, such as the following situations:

Preceding or following personal names (*Mr., Ms., Mrs., Jr., Sr., Ph.D.*)

As part of an organization's legal name (*Co., Inc., Ltd.*)

Expressions related to time (*a.m., p.m., EDT, B.C., A.D.*)

Names of companies or organizations (*IBM, GE, YMCA, NAACP, UCLA, BYU*)

In some business-writing situations, such as on business forms or in tables or lists, we might abbreviate items we would not normally abbreviate—such as days of the week, names of the months, or units of measure.

As with so many style questions, the various disciplines typically have unique idiosyncrasies associated with the use or nonuse of abbreviations. Business writing is a case in point. Any business writer should be familiar with the frequently occurring instances when abbreviations are or are not used. Related to the use or nonuse of abbreviations are style issues of punctuation, spacing, and capitalization.

The rules of abbreviation that follow reflect the typical, most frequently occurring instances when abbreviation decisions face the business writer. Many additional rules could be included. You will perhaps have to consult a formal style manual to answer some of your future questions about abbreviations. As you master the rules of abbreviation that follow and as you write business documents, you should keep the following general directives in mind:

1. As much as possible, keep abbreviations out of running text, except in technical matter.

2. Typically restrict general abbreviations, such as *etc.* (and so forth), *e.g.* (for example), and *i.e.* (that is), to parenthetical references.

3. Restrict your use of "scholarly" abbreviations, such as *et al.* and *cf.*, to documentation notes in scholarly publications.

4. Spell out the full term and put the abbreviation in parentheses immediately following for any abbreviation that may not be familiar to your reader.

5. Be consistent in employing an abbreviation in the same way throughout a document.

6. Employ appropriate and consistent punctuation, spacing, and capitalization with abbreviations.

You might also distinguish among pure abbreviations, shortened words and nicknames, acronymns, and contractions—all of which have a similar "flavor." For example:

Abbreviations: *Mr., p., vol., e.g., no., Geo., IBM, YMCA*

Shortened words and nicknames: *memo, exam, condo, Tom, Dick, the Fed*

Acronymns: *EPCOT, BASIC, ZIP, NOW, laser, radar*

Contractions: *won't, isn't, gov't, '92*

Finally, most of the rules have exceptions. Although some of the common exceptions are noted, space will not permit a complete explanation of all of them.

Pretest

With a **C** or an **I**, indicate for each sentence whether all abbreviations are correct or incorrect. Then correct all abbreviations that are wrong.

1. Most university profs. today must have a Dr. of philosophy degree or its equivalent to receive tenure.

2. While I was in NYC, I stayed at the Y.M.C.A. located on 64th St.

3. During my 1st year in Ariz., I was delighted that the state used mountain standard time rather than MDT.

4. According to Professor Stauffer, the speed limit in downtown St. George is 25 miles per hour.

5. I wrote to my bro., Bill, in Tempe, AZ, to get information on Ariz. State's Ed. D. program.

Key: (1) professors, doctor of philosophy or Ph.D.; (2) New York City, YMCA, Street; (3) first, Arizona, MST or mountain daylight time (for consistency); (4) C; (5) brother, Arizona, Arizona, Ed.D or doctor of education.

Terminology

Acronym—A shortened form derived from the initial letters of the words that make up the complete form and pronounced like a word. For example, *OPEC* is the *Organization of Petroleum Exporting Countries.*

Contraction—A shortened word or words in which an apostrophe indicates omitted letters or words. For example, *don't* is the contraction for *do not.*

Rules

1. *Capitalization*—**In general, use the capitalization that coincides with the capitalization of the word being abbreviated: capitalize proper-noun abbreviations and do not capitalize common-noun abbreviations.**

   International Business Machines = *IBM*
   District of Columbia = *D.C.*
   Genesis = *Gen.*
   ante meridiem = *a.m.*
   Some exceptions: postscript = *P.S.*; mountain standard time = *MST*; anno Domini = *A.D.*

2. *Punctuation and spacing*—**In general, use a period at the end of an abbreviation; use no periods or spaces in all-capital abbreviations; use periods but no spaces in all-lowercase abbreviations; and use periods and spaces in two-word abbreviations.**

   Single words: *Ms., Jr., Wed., Oct.*

   All capitals: *AICPA, IRS, MIT.* Exceptions: Use periods in academic degrees (*B.S., M.S., Ph.D.*); geographic names (*U.S.S.R., U.S.A*); and some miscellaneous instances (*B.C., A.D.*).

   All lowercase: *i.e., f.o.b., a.m.* Exceptions: *rpm, mph, in, ft*—when they occur frequently on forms or in tables.

   Two-word: *op. cit., gr. wt., Lt. Col., N. Mex.*

3. *Personal names with abbreviations*—**Always use *Mrs., Mme., Ms., Mr.,* and *Dr.* when they are used with personal names. Spell out long military, religious, and honorable titles in formal situations; but abbreviate such titles in informal situations if the surname is accompanied by a first name or initials. Do not abbreviate *Reverend* or *Honorable* if the word *the* precedes their use. Always abbreviate *Jr., Sr.,* and *Esq.* when they follow personal names.**

   Dr. Martin will speak to *Mr.* and *Mrs.* Jex on Tuesday.

   Miss Lopez left early today, but *Ms.* Owens stayed for the entire class period.

   I will talk to *Professor* Popham and *Reverend* Miller about the seminary program.

   The *Honorable* Jake Garn, *Sr.* will speak at the graduation exercises.

4. *Compass directions*—**Write out and capitalize compass directions that are used as nouns. Write out and do not capitalize compass directions that are used as adjectives. Write out cardinal compass directions that precede street names in addresses; abbreviate other compass directions that precede or that follow street names. Follow postal regulations for compass directions in envelope addresses.**

Noun: Jason lived in the *South* for several years.
Adjective: We live in the *southern* part of town.

Cardinal compass directions in addresses: 422 *North* Palisade Drive
Other compass directions in addresses: 2258 Matthew, *NW*; 1142 *SW* 1200 Street
Compass directions in envelope addresses: 4015 *N* 480 *E*; 422 *N* PALISADE DR

5. *States, districts, territories, and provinces*—**If space must be conserved, use the standard abbreviation for states, districts, territories, and provinces; otherwise, spell out these items. In addresses, use the two-letter abbreviations for states, districts, territories, and provinces.**

Alabama	Ala.	AL
Alaska	Alaska	AK
Arizona	Ariz.	AZ
Arkansas	Ark.	AR
California	Calif.	CA
Colorado	Colo.	CO
Connecticut	Conn.	CT
Delaware	Del.	DE
District of Columbia	D.C.	DC
Florida	Fla.	FL
Georgia	Ga.	GA
Guam	Guam	GU
Hawaii	Hawaii	HI
Idaho	Idaho	ID
Illinois	Ill.	IL
Indiana	Ind.	IN
Iowa	Iowa	IA
Kansas	Kans.	KS
Kentucky	Ky.	KY
Louisiana	La.	LA
Maine	Maine	ME
Maryland	Md.	MD
Massachusetts	Mass.	MA
Michigan	Mich.	MI
Minnesota	Minn.	MN
Mississippi	Miss.	MS
Missouri	Mo.	MO
Montana	Mont.	MT
Nebraska	Nebr.	NE
Nevada	Nev.	NV
New Hampshire	N.H.	NH
New Jersey	N.J.	NJ
New Mexico	N. Mex.	NM
New York	N.Y.	NY

North Carolina	N.C.	NC
North Dakota	N. Dak.	ND
Ohio	Ohio	OH
Oklahoma	Okla.	OK
Oregon	Oreg.	OR
Pennsylvania	Pa.	PA
Puerto Rico	P.R.	PR
Rhode Island	R.I.	RI
South Carolina	S.C.	SC
South Dakota	S. Dak.	SD
Tennessee	Tenn.	TN
Texas	Tex.	TX
Utah	Utah	UT
Vermont	Vt.	VT
Virgin Islands	V.I.	VI
Virginia	Va.	VA
Washington	Wash.	WA
West Virginia	W. Va.	WV
Wisconsin	Wis.	WI
Wyoming	Wyo.	WY
Alberta	Alta.	AB
British Columbia	B.C.	BC
Manitoba	Man.	MB
New Brunswick	N.B.	NB
Newfoundland	Newf./Nfld.	NF
Northwest Territories	N.W.T.	NT
Nova Scotia	N.S.	NS
Ontario	Ont.	ON
Prince Edward Island	P.E.I.	PE
Quebec	Que.	PQ
Saskatchewan	Sask.	SK
Yukon Territory	Y.T.	YT

Note those instances in which no official abbreviation has been designated: Alaska, Guam, Hawaii, Idaho, Iowa, Maine, Ohio, and Utah.

6. *Government agencies, business organizations, labor unions, societies, associations, broadcasting stations*—**Use all-capital letters with no periods or spaces for government agencies, business organizations, labor unions, societies, associations, and broadcasting stations.**

EEOC = Equal Employment Opportunity Commission
FBI = Federal Bureau of Investigation
NYSE = New York Stock Exchange
AFL-CIO = American Federation of Labor and Congress of Industrial Organizations
ASCAP = American Society of Composers, Authors, and Publishers
ABC = Association for Business Communication
NBC = National Broadcasting Corporation

Learning Hint 1.   Write the name of an organization or group according to its preference. The letterhead is a good guide to such preferences. The following terms are often abbreviated in the names of business organizations:

Bro. = Brother   Inc. = Incorporated
Bros. = Brothers   Ltd. = Limited
Co. = Company   Mfg. = Manufacturing
Corp. = Corporation   Mfrs. = Manufacturers

Learning Hint 2.   *United States* is typically abbreviated if it is used as part of the name of a government agency. When *United States* is used as an adjective, it is often abbreviated. When it is used as a noun, it is spelled out.

U.S. Department of Agriculture or USDA
U.S. Air Force or USAF
the United States government
across the United States

7. *Time of day and time zones*—Use *a.m.* and *p.m.* (lowercase and without spaces) in expressions of time. Where desirable, use abbreviations for standard time zones or daylight saving time.

7 a.m.; 10 p.m.
EST = eastern standard time
CST = central standard time
MST = mountain standard time
PST = pacific standard time
EDT = eastern daylight time
CDT = central daylight time
MDT = mountain daylight time
PDT = pacific daylight time

8. *Measurements*—Spell out units of measure in nontechnical writing. Abbreviate them in technical and scientific work, on business forms such as invoices, and in tables.

Learning Hint 3.   Units of measure are often abbreviated without periods, although either form is correct. The singular abbreviation is used for both singular and plural forms.

in or in. = inch or inches
ft or ft. = foot or feet
yd or yd. = yard or yards
oz or oz. = ounce or ounces
lb or lb. = pound or pounds
qt or qt. = quart or quarts
gal or gal. = gallon or gallons
mpg or m.p.g. = miles per gallon

Learning Hint 4.   Metric units of measure generally follow the same guidelines as other units of measure. However, a period is not used following metric units of measure. Also, some metric expressions are abbreviated in nontechnical writing.

m = meter
g = gram
L = liter (Note the capitalization.)
d = deci (as in decimeter—dm)
c = centi (as in centimeter—cm)

m = milli (as in milliliter—ml)
da = deka (as in dekameter—dam)
h = hecto (as in hectogram—hg)
k = kilo (as in kilometer—km)

The box is 30 *cm* long.
Our camera requires 35*mm* film.
The bale weighs 100 *kg*.
Our trip was almost exactly 100 *km* long.
We traveled no faster than 100 *km/h*. (Note the diagonal mark to express *per*.)

9. *Foreign expressions*—**In foreign expressions, distinguish between short words and abbreviations; use periods with abbreviations only.**

ad hoc = for a particular purpose
cf. = compare
e.g. = for example
et al. = and other people
etc. = and other things, and so forth
ibid. = in the same place
i.e. = that is
non seq. = it does not follow
re = in the matter of
supra = above
viz. = namely

10. *Symbols*—**Except on business forms and in tables and statistical writing, do not use symbol abbreviations. Always use the ampersand (&) in a company name if the company prefers the ampersand's use.**

@ = at
& = and
% = percent
$ = dollars
¢ = cents
° = degrees
= = equals
= number (before a figure) or pounds (after a figure)
' = feet
'' = inches
× = by, multiplied by
Kelly & Company

Use T7-1 here

Posttest

With a **C** or an **I**, indicate for each sentence whether all abbreviations are correct or incorrect. Then correct all abbreviations that are wrong.

1. The Rev. McQueen received his Dr. of Divinity degree about five years after he was Lt. Gov. of the state.

2. I'm certain that Ms. Pulaski completed her Ph.D. thesis before she began her work with UNESCO.

3. Doctor Helen Garcia was born in East L.A. but has lived most of her life in Albuquerque, NM.

4. During the 2nd year of Mister Cochran's work with the Co., he participated actively in the I.O.O.F.

5. On Wed., we shipped the parts to Edward Christensen, Junior, FOB Excel Corporation's dock in San Antonio, TX.

Key: (1) Reverend, doctor of divinity or D.D., lieutnant governor; (2) C; (3) Dr., East Los Angeles, New Mexico; (4) second, Mr., company, IOOF; (5) Wednesday, Jr., f.o.b., Texas.

LEVEL A

Name _____

Exercise 7–1 On the lines below, write **T** if the statement is true and **F** if the statement is false.

_T_ 1. In business correspondence, we normally do not abbreviate days of the week and names of the months.

_T_ 2. Abbreviations such as *i.e.* and *e.g.* are usually restricted to parenthetical references.

_F_ 3. *UFO* is an example of an acronymn.

_F_ 4. The proper abbreviation for *International Business Machines* is *I.B.M.*

_F_ 5. You have your choice of using or not using periods in academic-degree abbreviations (such as *PhD* or *Ph.D.*).

_F_ 6. Compass directions that are used as nouns are abbreviated and capitalized.

_F_ 7. The correct abbreviation for *Utah* is *Ut.*

_F_ 8. *Federal Bureau of Investigation* may be abbreviated either as *F. B. I.* or *F.B.I.*

_T_ 9. When *United States* is used as an adjective, it is often abbreviated.

_F_ 10. Abbreviations for units of measure must always be followed by periods (such as *in.* or *oz.*).

_F_ 11. The correct abbreviation for *New Mexico* is *N.M.*

_F_ 12. An acronym is a contraction.

_T_ 13. Periods but no spaces are used in all-lowercase abbreviations.

_F_ 14. *Reverend* and *Honorable* are always abbreviated when they are titles.

_T_ 15. Broadcasting stations are abbreviated in all-capital letters without periods.

_T_ 16. A period is not used following metric units of measure.

_F_ 17. *Non. seq.* and *supra.* are correct foreign-expression abbreviations.

_T_ 18. In general, common-noun abbreviations are not capitalized.

Exercise 7–2 Mark **C** if correct abbreviation rules are followed; mark **I** if they are not.

_I_ 1. Prof. Adams teaches statistics.

_C_ 2. I met Dr. Baramki when I taught at NYU.

_I_ 3. Were you born in Nebr. or Iowa?

_I_ 4. The lost-and-found sale will be held next Sat.

_I_ 5. While I was at the P.O., I bought the stamps.

_I_ 6. I hope to tour through G. Britain next summer.

_I_   7. Mark Bowman, my M.D., now sees patients on weekends.

_I_   8. By 3 PM, she will complete her part of the project.

_I_   9. Are you going to your phys. education class today?

_C_ 10. Reverend Hilton will speak at the funeral.

_I_ 11. You'll find the table on pg. 24 of the report.

_I_ 12. I won't have to take Eng. or Hist. my senior year.

_I_ 13. Please stop by my office the next time you're in L.A.

_I_ 14. The search committee will select a new pres. by May 10.

_I_ 15. Marcie spent the entire summer in Mont.

_I_ 16. Do you like Eastern daylight time?

_C_ 17. *Gal* and *gal.* are both correct abbreviations of *gallon.*

_I_ 18. We averaged 35 miles/gal. on the trip.

_I_ 19. Use *et. al.* if four or more persons are the authors.

_I_ 20. My brother, Geo. Parker, Jr., will be with me.

Exercise 7–3   Mark **C** if correct abbreviation rules and the related spacing guidelines are followed; mark **I** if they are not.

_I_   1. The keynote address was delivered by David Chichester, Ph. D.

_I_   2. The terms are $462.50, f. o. b. Nauvoo, Illinois.

_I_   3. Our representative, Mr. L.M. Adams, will visit you on March 3.

_C_   4. Martin worked for two years as secretary to Ms. K. M. Kowalski.

_I_   5. The building is on the corner of Bryant and Victory Sts.

_C_   6. Please deliver the package directly to C. M. Yeltsin, Esq.

_I_   7. We have hired Ms. Matilda Gregory, R. N., to help us take care of Grandmother Parkinson.

_I_   8. Be sure to use the correct Z.I.P. codes when you compile the new mailing list.

_C_   9. The people lived in the area from 90 B.C. to 120 A.D.

_I_ 10. According to the rumors, General Schwarzkopf's I.Q. is 170.

_I_ 11. Beginning January 1, we will not accept any more c. o. d. orders.

_I_ 12. As you know, Lieutenant Robert F. Matthews is a close friend of mine.

_I_ 13. Have you ever visited Disneyworld and the E.P.C.O.T. Center?

_I_ 14. Her correct street address is 13284 Montrose, Southwest.

_I_ 15. Several good word-processing packages are available, e. g., WordPerfect® and Wordstar®.

LEVEL B

Name _____

Exercise
7–4

Write the letter that identifies the correct sentence.

_b_ 1. *a.* University profs. at USC typically must have a Ph.D. or its equivalent.
   b. Doctor Bronson decided to add a P.S. to his complaint letter.
   c. For the 1st time in a decade, we got snow in Phoenix, AZ.

_b_ 2. *a.* My brother, Ed., plans to work for G.E. when he gets his M.S. degree.
   b. Joseph Hanson, Jr. is now a lieutenant colonel in the U.S. Air Force.
   c. J. C. Penney Company is located in the S.E. corner of the new Univ. Mall.

_c_ 3. *a.* On Wed., April 3, we will fly to Washington, DC.
   b. Mister Jones was present for the dedication of the new ROTC facility.
   c. The street address on the envelope was correctly typed as 6690 NW YORK ST.

_b_ 4. *a.* Geo. will be in S. Calif. to attend the Rose Bowl Parade.
   b. In your M.S. thesis, use *ibid.* to footnote something that is in the same place as the prior footnote.
   c. I hope to spend the entire summer in Cardston, Alta., Can.

_c_ 5. *a.* You'll find the information on pp. 96–98 of Dr. Paul's book.
   b. Dr. Martha Ragan, M.D., will speak in Saint Louis on January 12.
   c. In February, Reverend McCabe will tour the MGM Studios with us.

_c_ 6. *a.* At 10 a.m., Wm. Ryan has an appointment with me at the Better Bus. Bureau.
   b. Jeffery Cottle, Atty. at Law, has now moved his offices to 2256 N. University Ave.
   c. Senator Garn has a special interest in activities of the WHO.

_b_ 7. *a.* I lived in the N.E. for the 3rd time when I got out of the Air Force.
   b. Which does Dr. Bates prefer—ASCII or EBCDIC?
   c. Do you want to work for the F.H.A. or the I.C.C.?

_b_ 8. *a.* Garn spent Sept. 2 rewriting the creation story from the book of Gen.
   b. At Garrison Pulleys, Inc., we do not use postscripts for afterthoughts.
   c. You can see the special on NBC next Thurs. at 8:30 a.m. EST.

_c_ 9. *a.* Stater Bros. will lease new facilities at our Center Street office complex.
   b. We're pleased to be moving to the southern US sometime next Dec.
   c. The correct abbreviations are *New Mex.* and *No. Dak.*

_c_ 10. *a.* What should Kent say if he doesn't want to serve on the AAUP ad. hoc. committee?
   b. Liz. has three reasons for declining (viz, her busy schedule, her health, and her lack of interest).
   c. Dr. Dale Zabriski, Sr. will accompany Lt. Col. Sue Gaston to the meetings at MIT.

_c_ 11. *a.* Yes, my youngest brother, Nidal, plans to get his Ph. D. in electrical engineering in June.
   b. The quotation from Ventura Electronics was f. o. b. our loading dock.
   c. I must master the spelling of several words (e.g., *receive, recommend,* and *pursue*).

_a_ 12. _a._ Our meeting with Vice President McNicholls is scheduled for next Tuesday at 10 a.m.
      _b._ Jessica is looking forward to substituting gymnastics for her phys. ed. class.
      _c._ The full name of the disciplined employee is Bentley Echols Stafford, Junior.

_c_ 13. _a._ Did you get your PhD degree from the University of New Mexico?
      _b._ Did you take your philosophy class from Prof. Tidwell or Prof. Wixom?
      _c._ I belong to the Association for Business Communication (ABC).

_a_ 14. _a._ The program will begin at 8 a.m., MDT.
      _b._ We plan to begin promptly at 7 P.M., mountain daylight time.
      _c._ Is your 5 p.m. starting time M.S.T. or P.S.T.?

_c_ 15. _a._ I got 30 m.p.g. on my trip to North Dakota.
      _b._ The honey comes in 10 lbs. buckets or 5 gal. cans.
      _c._ Willy won the 50-yard dash but not the 4-mile run.

_b_ 16. _a._ Hughie misspelled three words (I.E., _receive, seize,_ and _brief_).
      _b._ I am not a member of the ad hoc committee for rank and advancement.
      _c._ Harper Redford et. al. are the authors of _Cry No More._

_a_ 17. _a._ In January, the Honorable Joseph Van Dyke will speak on our campus.
      _b._ Do you have the latest A.I.C.P.A. announcement?
      _c._ The order was shipped via TransWest Trucking F.O.B. our dock in Nephi.

_c_ 18. _a._ Doctor Rulon Parker, Jr. will meet you for lunch in the Wilkinson Center.
      _b._ When you receive you PH.D. degree, will you return to Snowflake, Az.?
      _c._ Reverend Wilcox is from the northern part of Alberta, Canada.

Exercise 7–5 Write the letter that identifies the correct match. If necessary, consult a dictionary for assistance.

A acronymn   D common-noun abbreviation
B shortened word   E foreign expression
C proper-noun abbreviation   F incorrect; no match possible

_D_ 1. a.m.   _C_ 11. Ltd.

_A_ 2. FORTRAN   _B_ 12. exam

_B_ 3. condo   _E_ 13. ibid.

_C_ 4. Exod.   _F_ 14. MPG

_F_ 5. G.M.A.T.   _F_ 15. M.B.A.

_A_ 6. FICA   _D_ 16. APB

_A_ 7. P.S.   _D_ 17. d.b.a.

_F_ 8. Ida.   _D_ 18. FWD

_C_ 9. Sask.   _B_ 19. re

_C_ 10. Dr. Zhivago   _A_ 20. NATO

LEVEL C

Name _____

Exercise 7–6 Mark **C** if all abbreviations are correct. Mark **I** if any is incorrect. Then edit all incorrect sentences.

_**I**_ 1. Send the form to ~~N.A.S.C.A.R.~~ *NASCAR*, ~~Attn.~~ *Attention* of Volunteer Coordinator, 401 White ~~St.~~ *Street*, Alexandria, ~~Va.~~ *VA* 22314.

_**I**_ 2. Request Catalog ~~#9~~ *No. 9* to see our complete selection of material and accessories by ~~lb.~~ *pound* ~~&~~ *and* ~~yd.~~ *yard*.

_**I**_ 3. ~~Mister Thos.~~ *Mr. Thomas* Weiss has resided at 1818 ~~N. Wash. St.~~ *North Washington Street* since ~~Feb.~~ *February* of 1988.

_**I**_ 4. Mark exercises every ~~Mon.~~ *Monday* and ~~Wed.~~ *Wednesday* ~~A.M.~~ *a.m.* and refuses to send for the ~~Dr.~~ *doctor* for something as trivial as a cold.

_**I**_ 5. The Boy Scouts of America (~~B.S. of A.~~ *BSA*) went through the ~~So. bldgs.~~ *south buildings* and accomplished a very successful used-clothing drive.

_**C**_ 6. Dr. Greene used the 1/4 hp motor that ran at 1,500 rpm with 90 percent efficiency.

_**I**_ 7. Augustus reigned from 27 ~~b.c.~~ *B.C.* to 14 ~~a.d.~~ *A.D.*

_**I**_ 8. ~~Prof.~~ *Professor* Alice Smith met Professor Paz at the ~~Assoc.~~ *Association* for ~~Bus. Comm.~~ *Business Communication* convention in San Antonio, ~~Tx.~~ *Texas*.

_**C**_ 9. According to the vice president, Smith & Company, Inc. will establish its corporate headquarters in Ft. Worth, Texas.

_**I**_ 10. I have to take my ~~math.~~ *mathematics*, ~~Eng.~~ *English*, and ~~hist.~~ *history* exams next ~~Mon.~~ *Monday* and ~~Tues.~~ *Tuesday*.

_**I**_ 11. ~~Jere.~~ *Jeremiah* 42–44 tells about the flight of the Jews to Egypt when Jerusalem fell in 586 B.C.

_**I**_ 12. As ~~Rev.~~ *Reverend* Timothy lay dying, he sought comfort in reciting the 23rd Psalm.

_C_ 13. You will find Dr. Doolittle's discussion about St. Louis on pages 36–38.

_I_ 14. James Jefferson, ~~Senior~~ is the ~~J.P.~~ in Oasis, ~~Ut.~~
Sr.   justice of the peace Utah

_I_ 15. Sun Valley, ~~Ida.~~ is the birthplace of ~~Sen. Benj.~~ Stokes.
Idaho   Senator Benjamin

_I_ 16. The ~~Xmas~~ pageant will be presented this year at Hillcrest ~~Jr.~~ High School.
Christmas   Junior

_I_ 17. I am not familiar with the documentation system that ~~Doctor~~ Mendenhall recommends
Dr.
(~~ibid,~~ ~~op cit,~~ and ~~loc cit~~).
ibid. op. cit.   loc. cit.

_C_ 18. Representative Nguyen will speak about IQ tests during the 11 p.m. TV broadcast on

ABC.

_I_ 19. ~~Rev.~~ Marshall was a ~~govt.~~ worker for six years and a ~~univ.~~ faculty member for four
Reverend   government   university

years.

_I_ 20. In the ~~p.s.~~ to his letter, Clark Madsen, R.N. asked me to ~~rsvp~~ if I am able to attend his
P.S.   r.s.v.p.

wedding ceremony.

_I_ 21. Garth Holman, ~~atty.~~ at law, will speak at our monthly C.P.A. meeting in ~~Aug.~~
attorney   or CPA   August

_I_ 22. ~~Gov.~~ Lee is supportive of the high-rise apartments being built in the ~~N.W.~~ part of our
Governor   northwest

subdivision.

Exercise 1. Compose a sentence containing an acronym, a shortened word, and an academic-degree
7–7   abbreviation.

Composi- _____
tion
          _____

          2. Compose a sentence containing the standard abbreviations and the ZIP abbreviations for
             three states near the one in which you live.

          _____

          _____

Exercise 7–8

Edit the following sentences to reflect what you have learned from Lessons 3 through 7.

Cumulative Editing

1. After ~~10~~ [ten] months, the FBI gave the ~~explaination~~ [explanation] that John Madden got ~~lose~~ [loose] from them in Meridian, ~~Miss.~~ [Mississippi], but was found hiding in the home of ~~Doctor~~ [Dr.] Roscoe Bush.

2. ~~Supt.~~ [Superintendent] Tex Rasmussen has ~~4~~ [four] ~~S~~[s]isters (ranging in age from ~~twelve~~ [12] to 26 years) and a ~~surprizingly~~ [surprisingly] young ~~M~~[m]other.

3. At the ~~preceeding conf.~~ [preceding conference], Dr. Gordon Christensen, D.D.S. gave us the results of his ~~comparitive~~ [Comparative] research involving ~~four hundred eighty-two~~ [482] children.

4. ~~Incidently, Chas.~~ [Incidentally, Charles] Dickens' *The Christmas Carol*, the most-celebrated ~~Xmas~~ [Christmas] story of the past ~~2~~ [two] centuries, will be read on ~~Dec. 23rd.~~ [December 23.]

5. At least ~~4~~ [four] leaders from the ~~N.I.H.~~ [NIH] ~~comittee~~ [committee] were ~~dissapointed~~ [disappointed] when they conferred with ~~U.N.~~ [or UN] ~~Rep. Geo.~~ [Representative George] Jenkins at his home on ~~Fifty-Third St.~~ [53rd Street] in ~~N.Y.~~ [New York].

6. The performance at the ~~8th St.~~ [Eighth Street] theater started ~~1 hr.~~ [one hour] ~~latter~~ [later] than ~~alot~~ [a lot] of us anticipated.

7. Ned Freeman, ~~Junior's~~ [Jr.'s] ~~U~~[u]niversity recently added ~~2~~ [two] new ~~Libary~~ [library] Science ~~personell~~ [personnel] — Helen Twyman, ~~MS~~ [M.S.], and Wanda Scott, ~~Doctor of Philosophy.~~ [Ph.D.]

8. Between ~~sixty-five~~ [65] and ~~70%~~ [70 percent] of the ~~U. of C.~~ [University of California] students approved the antismoking ordinance after the ~~dr's.~~ [doctor's] speech; ~~every one~~ [everyone] else refused to pass ~~judgement~~ [judgment] on it.

9. ~~You're principle~~ [Your principal] sculpture of ~~Saint~~ [St.] Peter weighs almost 1,500 ~~lbs.~~ [pounds] and is much more ~~practicle~~ [practical] than the one you did of St. Paul.

10. ~~Begining~~ [Beginning] on ~~p. eight~~ [page 8], you'll find the principal telephone numbers of the U.S. ~~S~~[s]enators; on ~~p. ten~~ [page 10], you'll find their ~~D.C.~~ [District of Columbia] home addresses.

11. As I ~~adviced~~ [advised] you, the books, which once cost as little as a ~~Q~~[q]uarter, now ~~occasionaly~~ [occasionally] sell for as much as ~~five dollars and ninety-five cents~~ [$5.95].

12. The ~~Vice Pres~~. of our Student ~~Counsel~~ ~~definately~~ gets to preside at ~~1 mtg~~. every ~~4~~ weeks.
    vice president — *s* — *council* — *definitely* — *one meeting* — *four*

13. The ~~proceedures~~ call for the local Movie Theater to show a Humphrey Bogart Film on the ~~1st. Mon~~. of every ~~mo~~.
    procedures — *m* — *t* — *f* — *first Monday* — *month*

14. I finally ~~conceeded~~ that all fish measuring less than ~~ten ins~~. had to be thrown back into Mirror ~~Lk~~.
    conceded — *10 inches* — *Lake*

15. Mr. ~~&~~ Mrs. Troy Yeltsin hope ~~there~~ ~~3-yr~~.-old filly is ~~elegible~~ to be entered in the ~~Saint~~ Patrick's ~~day~~ race.
    and — *their three-year* — *eligible* — *St.* — *D*

Exercise 7–9

Cumulative Editing

Mark **C** if all numbers, capitalizations, and abbreviations are used correctly; mark **I** if any number, capitalization, or abbreviation is used incorrectly. Then edit all incorrect items.

I 1. When we bought the house, the interest on the ~~f.h.a.~~ ~~mortgate~~ was 5½%.
FHA mortgage — *percent*

I 2. You'll find the poem on ~~Page~~ 4 in *Best Poems ~~Of~~ ~~The~~ Old West*.
p — *o* — *t*

I 3. Since receiving my ~~Ed. D~~. degree, I have taught for ~~6~~ years at the ~~Univ~~. of New Mexico.
Ed.D. — *six* — *University*

I 4. The lot on Ft. Ticonderoga Drive in the Apple Ridge ~~subdivision~~ is ~~one~~ of 12 we are considering.
S — *1*

I 5. The correct billing notation is "~~e. o. m~~.," which means "~~End of Month~~."
e.o.m. — *e* — *m*

I 6. The special photocopy rate for the entire month of ~~Febr~~. is $.05 per page.
February — *5 cents*

C 7. W. W. Clyde & Son, Inc. is one of four construction companies being considered for the 600 South Street project.

I 8. The price of the fabric, as advertised on ~~T.V~~., is ~~$5.00~~ per ~~sq. yd~~.
TV or television — *$5* — *square yard.*

I 9. We plan to take ~~Jr~~., our ~~3~~-year-old stallion, to Dr. Martin Lowell, ~~D. V. M~~.
Junior — *three* — *D.V.M.*

I 10. I will be in Mt. Vernon on ~~Fri~~., ~~Oct~~. 6, and will plan to stop by your ~~Company~~ at ~~one~~ p.m. for a short meeting.
Friday October — *c* — *1*

DICTIONARY USAGE LESSON 8

In theory, unabridged dictionaries contain every word accepted for use in the English language. In actuality, an unabridged dictionary cannot contain every word because new words are created daily. As you can see, an unabridged dictionary contains hundreds of thousands of words—reflecting the richness of the English language.

An abridged dictionary, on the other hand, may contain from a few thousand to almost 200,000 words. The dictionaries we use on a day-to-day basis for home, school, and business purposes are nearly always abridged dictionaries. They vary not only in length but also in the types of information they contain. We tend to think of the dictionary as a source of definitions and pronunciations, but a good abridged dictionary provides a gold mine of additional information if we know how to use it.

Many writers consider the dictionary to be the most useful general reference book available. We feel the dictionary should not be considered the supreme authority we consult to settle all arguments about words and their meanings; but instead, we suggest the dictionary be viewed as a record of the ways language is actually used as of the publication date of the dictionary—with the clear understanding that usage frequently changes.

The business world frequently consults the dictionary to resolve issues of usage and pronunciation. For example, although some dictionaries offer a variety of acceptable spellings and pronunciations for some words, the business world advocates using a dictionary that gives the ''preferred'' spelling and pronunciation first. For spelling purposes, for example, we prefer *judgment* to *judgement*. For pronunciation purposes, we prefer to pronounce coupon as *koopon* rather than as *kyoopon*.

Most of us learn what words mean and how to use them by reading and by listening to others speak. However, we can learn that information—and considerably more—by using a good dictionary. We are suggesting that we take time on occasion literally to ''read the dictionary.'' That suggestion, of course, is much broader in scope than the suggestion to ''consult the dictionary.''

The dictionary can be an excellent supplementary textbook for your business English course. We include this material about the dictionary in Unit 1 so you will be aware of the value of a dictionary to your study of business English. Your instructor, of course, will determine the emphasis given to the dictionary as a supplemental tool.

Pretest

With a **T** or an **F**, indicate whether each statement is true or false.

1. The typical dictionary we use in a business office is an unabridged dictionary.

2. *Archaic* is the dictionary usage label used to identify a word that is part of the nonstandard vocabulary of a given culture.

3. *Best* is the adjectival comparative of *good* and the adverbial comparative of *well*.

4. A syllable consists of a vowel alone, a vowel with one or more consonants, or two or more vowels with one or more consonants.

5. An antonym is a word having a meaning that is the same or nearly the same as that of another word.

6. The only pronunciation guide found in most dictionaries is located in the ''front matter.''

7. *Go* is an example of a verb with inflections shown in the dictionary.

Key: (1) F—abridged; (2) F—this is slang and *archaic* refers to terms once common but now rare; (3) F—superlative; (4) T; (5) F–synonym; (6) F—front matter and bottom of the page; (7) T.

Terminology

Abridged dictionary—A shortened version of an unabridged dictionary. Nearly every dictionary used in business offices is an abridged dictionary.

Antonym—A word having a meaning opposite to that of another word. *Light* is the opposite of *dark*.

Archaic—The dictionary usage label used to identify a word that was once common but that now is used rarely.

Colloquial—The dictionary usage label used to identify a word that is used in informal or conversational speaking.

Comparative—The second degree of comparison of an adjective or an adverb. *Better* is the adjectival comparative of *good* and the adverbial comparative of *well*.

Dialect—The dictionary usage label used to identify a word that is commonly used in one geographic area but is little used in other areas. The entry sometimes is labeled *regional* and also includes the geographic area of usage.

Etymology—The derivation of a word or an account or explanation of the origin and history of a word. An etymology traces the history of a word from one language to another as far back in time as can be determined with reasonable certainty.

Homonym—A word that has the same sound and often the same spelling as another word but that differs in meaning, such as *roll* and *role*.

Idiom—A phrase or an expression whose meaning cannot be understood from the ordinary meanings of the words in it. *Give in* is an English idiom meaning *yield*.

Inflection—A change in the form of a word to show case, number, gender, person, tense, mood, voice, or comparison. For example, the suffixes *-est* and *-ed* are common inflections in English.

Intransitive—Refers to a verb (such as *sit* or *go*) that does not have an object to complete its meaning. Usually labeled *intr.* in the dictionary.

Obsolete—The dictionary usage label used to identify a word that is no longer in active use except in quotations or in an intentional archaic expression.

Slang—The dictionary usage label used to identify a word that is part of the nonstandard vocabulary of a given culture or subculture.

Superlative—The highest degree of comparison of an adjective or an adverb. *Best* is the adjectival superlative of *good* and the adverbial superlative of *well*.

Syllabication—The process of dividing a word into syllables. A syllable is a word or part of a word pronounced as a unit that usually consists of a vowel alone or a vowel with one or more consonants.

Synonym—A word having a meaning that is the same or nearly the same as that of another word. *Speak* is a synonym for *talk*.

Transitive—Refers to a verb that requires an object to complete its meaning. Usually labeled *tr.* in the dictionary.

Unabridged dictionary—A complete dictionary that is not shortened or condensed. Theoretically, an unabridged English dictionary contains every word used in the English language.

Discussion

Whether consulting or reading the dictionary, we will get much more from our efforts if we learn to recognize and to use the various features of our dictionaries. Among the typical components and ways in which dictionaries can be used are the following:

Front matter.   The preliminary pages of a dictionary usually contain information about dictionaries and the English language and show you how to use your dictionary. Each dictionary is typically distinctive, so you will want to study the front matter carefully to make the best use of your dictionary.

Back matter.   The pages following the words beginning with the letter *z* often contain useful information in the form of charts, lists, and special supplements. For example, you might find biographical entries, geographic entries, abbreviations, and information about colleges and universities.

Spelling.   The entries will confirm correct or preferred spellings. The business world typically uses the first spelling of a word as the preferred spelling.

Syllabication.   The entries will confirm the correct places to divide words at their syllables. Most dictionaries show the between-syllable breaks with a centered dot. If a compound word has a centered dot, the word is written as one word. If the compound has a hyphen, the result is a compound expression that is always hyphenated. If two words have neither a centered dot nor a hyphen, they are written as two words. If you cannot find an entry for a compound word or phrase, you can usually assume the words are written separately without a hyphen.

The syllabication guides are useful to help you divide words at the ends of lines. When you are using adequate word-processing software, however, you can turn on the hyphenation command and let the software do the dividing of words at the ends of lines.

Pronunciation.   Dictionaries use pronunciation symbols and accent marks (stress marks) to help you pronounce words correctly. You will find a detailed pronunciation guide in the front matter of your dictionary, and you will find a summary of the pronunciation guide at the bottom of each set of pages. If more than one pronunciation of a word is shown, the preferred pronunciation is usually given first—and that is the one used in the business world.

Definitions.   The definitions in a dictionary help assure you that you have selected the correct word for the occasion. If a word has more than one meaning or definition, the most common or accepted is usually given first.

Parts of speech.   The entries contain an italicized or boldfaced label that indicates what part of speech the entry represents. The labels are abbreviated but are easy to identify. The spelling, pronunciation, and meaning for a word may differ, of course, when the word functions as different parts of speech; so you must be careful to use the entry's information that coincides with the part of speech with which you are concerned.

Inflections.   Nouns, verbs, adverbs, and adjectives often change form grammatically. These changes, such as *child* to *children*, are called *inflections*. Regular noun plurals, regular verb tenses, and comparatives are not shown in dictionaries. However, irregular nouns or unusual plurals, verbs with irregular tenses or difficult spellings, and adverbs or adjectives with irregular comparatives or superlatives are usually shown. This information is often invaluable in helping you choose the correct inflected form.

Etymology.   A brief history or origin of a word, known as the *etymology* of the word, is given in most dictionaries and sometimes includes the year the word was first used. The preliminary pages of the dictionary contain a key to the etymological abbreviations. The etymology of a word is not only interesting but also useful in helping you remember the definition of the word.

Usage notes.   Associated with selected entries, your dictionary may contain usage notes to help you determine the acceptability of words in writing and in speaking and to confirm correct usage of words that are commonly misused or confused. For example, check your dictionary to see if it contains a usage note for *affect* versus *effect*.

Usage labels.   Usage labels are provided to indicate how or where a word is used. In that respect, some words are unacceptable in business writing. The following labels are commonly used to signal usage information to the reader:

Archaic—Word surviving from a previous period.

Obsolete—Word that is no longer in use or a word's definition that is no longer in use.

Colloquial or *informal*—Word used in casual writing or conversation.

Slang—An informal word that may be used occasionally for effect.

Nonstandard or *substandard*—The word does not conform to accepted usage among educated speakers and writers.

Dialect, South, Brit., etc.—Word used in certain regions of the country or the world.

Synonyms and antonyms.   Although the best place to find synonyms and antonyms is in a thesaurus, the dictionary often provides limited information about synonyms and antonyms. Synonyms, or words that have similar meanings, are shown after some word definitions; antonyms, or words that have opposite meanings, appear less frequently and are found following synonyms.

Guide words.   Guide words are given at the top of each page or pair of pages to show you at a glance the first word and the last word defined on the page or pages. Guide words are extremely useful to speed up the process of finding words in the dictionary.

Idioms.   For some words, the dictionary may label idiomatic usage of the words. This process helps us understand the meaning of special or unique phrases that are called idioms—expressions that are peculiar to themselves grammatically or that cannot be understood from the individual meanings of their elements. For example, *keep company* is an idiom associated with the definition of *company*.

Figure 8–1, part of a sample page from *Webster's Ninth New Collegiate Dictionary*, illustrates several of the above elements of dictionary entries.

Posttest

With a **T** or an **F**, indicate whether each statement is true or false.

1. You will find an unabridged dictionary in most business offices.

2. An inflection is an expression whose meaning cannot be understood from the ordinary meanings of the words in it.

3. If you know the etymology of a word, you will automatically know how to pronounce the word.

4. *More fully* is the superlative of *full*.

5. In most dictionaries, if a compound word is written with a hyphen, the result is a compound expression that is always hyphenated.

6. If a word is nonstandard, it will be a word used distinctively in certain geographic areas of the country.

7. Guide words are used to show the various inflections of a word.

Key: (1) F—abridged; (2) F—idiom; (3) F—derivation, origin, or history of the word will be known; (4) F—the comparative of *full*; (5) T; (6) F—dialect; (7) F—to show the first and last words defined on the page or pages.

Figure 8–1

Sample Dictionary Entries

Guide words ——————————————————

Entry and word division ——————— **co·he·sive** \kō-'hē-siv, -ziv\ *adj* (ca. 1721) : exhibiting or producing cohesion or coherence ⟨a ~ social unit⟩ ⟨~ soils⟩ — **co·he·sive·ly** *adv*

Inflections ————————————————— **co·he·sive·ness** *n*

co·ho \'kō-(,)hō\ *n, pl* **cohos** *or* **coho** [origin unknown] (1869) : a rather

Scientific name ———————— small salmon (*Oncorhynchus kisutch*) with light-colored flesh that is native to both coasts of the No. Pacific and is stocked in the Great Lakes

co·hort \'kō-,ho(ə)rt\ *n* [MF & L; MF *cohorte*, fr. L *cohort-, cohors* —

Etymology ———————————— more at COURT] (15c) **1 a** : one of 10 divisions of an ancient Roman legion **b** : a group of warriors or soldiers **c** : BAND, GROUP **d** : a group of individuals having a statistical factor (as age or class membership) in common in a demographic study ⟨a ~ of premedical students⟩

Definition with examples showing ——— **2** : COMPANION, COLLEAGUE ⟨a silk hat materialized in the air beside

use of word in context   me . . . and my special, only technically unassigned ~ grinned up at me —J. D. Salinger⟩

co·hosh \'kō-,hash\ *n* [of Algonquian origin; akin to Natick *kōshki* it is rough] (1796) : any of several American medicinal or poisonous plants: **a** : BLACK COHOSH **b** : BLUE COHOSH **c** : BANEBERRY

co·iden·ti·ty \,kō-ī-'den(t)-ət-ē, ,kō-ə-'den(t)-\ *n* (1927) : identity between two or more things

Variant pronunciations —————— **¹coif** \'kȯif, *in sense 2 usu* 'kwäf\ *n* [ME *coife*, fr. MF, fr. LL *cofea*] (14c) **1** : a close-fitting cap: as **a** : a hoodlike cap worn under a veil by nuns **b** : a protective usu. metal skullcap formerly worn under a hood of mail **c** : a white cap formerly worn by English lawyers and esp. by serjeants-at-law; *also* : the order or rank of a serjeant-at-law **2** : COIFFURE

Variant spellings ——————— **²coif** \'kȯif, 'kwäf\ *vt* **coiffed** *or* **coifed**; **coif·fing** *or* **coif·ing** (15c) **1** : to cover or dress with or as if with a coif **2** : to arrange (hair) by brushing, combing, or curling

coif·feur \kwä-'fər\ *n* [F, fr. *coiffer*] (1847) : a male hairdresser

coif·feuse \kwä-'fə(r)z, -'f(y)üz\ *n* [F, fem. of *coiffeur*] (1870) : a female hairdresser

Pronunciation ——————— **coif·fure** \kwä-'fyü(ə)r\ *n* [F, fr. *coiffer* to cover with a coif, arrange (hair), fr. coif (1631) : a style or manner of arranging the hair

coif·fure . . . **1** : being . . . eautifully ~ . . . **2** : having . . . es of connect . . . ows, layer . . . ings **4** . . . postage stamps; *also* : a stamp from such a roll

¹coin \'kȯin\ *n* [ME, fr. MF, wedge, corner, fr. L *cuneus* wedge] (14c) **1**

Stylistic usage ——————— *archaic* **a** : CORNER, CORNERSTONE, QUOIN **b** : WEDGE **2** : a usu. flat piece of metal issued by governmental authority as money **b** : metal money **c** : something resembling a coin esp. in shape **3** : a standard or valid mode of expression ⟨perhaps wisecracks . . . are respectable literary ~ in the U.S. —*Times Lit. Supp.*⟩ **4** : something having two different and usu. opposing sides — usu. used in the phrase *the other side of the coin* ⟨I'm in it for the ~ —Sinclair Lewis⟩ **5** : MONEY

Part-of-speech label ——————— **²coin** *vt* (14c) **1 a** : to make (a coin) esp. by stamping : MINT **b** : to convert (metal) into coins **c** : to shape (a piece of metal) in a mold or die **2** : CREATE, INVENT ⟨~ a phrase⟩ — **coin·er** *n* — **coin money** : to get rich quickly

³coin *adj* (1559) **1** : of or relating to coins ⟨a ~ show⟩ **2** : operated by coins ⟨a ~ laundry⟩

coin·age \'kȯi-nij\ *n* (14c) **1** : the act or process of coining **2 a** : COINS **b** : something (as a word) made up or invented

co·in·cide \,kō-ən-'sīd, 'kō-ən-,\ *vi* **-cid·ed; -cid·ing** [ML *coincidere*, fr. L

Date ——————————————— co- + *incidere* to fall on, fr. *in-* + *cadere* to fall — more at CHANCE] (1719) **1 a** : to occupy the same place in space or time **b** : to occupy exactly corresponding or equivalent positions on a scale or in a series **2** : to correspond in nature, character, or function **3** : to be in accord or agreement : CONCUR

Synonym ——————————— *syn* see AGREE

~in·ci·dence \kō-'. . . səd-ən(t)s, . . . (t)s\ *n* (160 . . .) . . . the act or eve . . . . . .en at . . . . . .e by acc . . . ~ . . . seem . . . . . . connection; *also* : any of these occurrences

co·in·ci·dent \-səd-ənt, -sə-,dent\ *adj* [F *coincident*, fr. ML *coincident-, coincidens*, prp. of *coincidere*] (1563) **1** : of similar nature : HARMONIOUS ⟨a theory ~ with the facts⟩ **2** : occupying the same space or time ⟨~ events⟩ *syn* see CONTEMPORARY — **co·in·ci·dent·ly** *adv*

Stress marks ——————— **co·in·ci·den·tal** \(,)kō-,in(t)-sə-'dent-ᵊl\ *adj* (1800) **1** : resulting from a coincidence **2** : occurring or existing at the same time — **co·in·ci·den·tal·ly** \-'dent-lē, -ᵊl-ē\ *adv*

coin lock *n* (1926) : a lock released by the insertion of a coin

coin machine *n* (1920) : SLOT MACHINE

coin–op \'kȯi-,näp\ *n* (1961) : a self-service laundry where the machines are operated by coins

Regional label ——————— **co·in·sur·ance** \,kō-ən-'shùr-ən(t)s, *chiefly Southern* (')kō-'in-,\ *n* (1889) **1** : joint ass . . . mption of risk (as b . . . two underwriters) with another **2** . . . insur . . . . . . rope] . . . h the ins . . . . . . arse . . . ated . . . the outer husk of a co . . . nut

Pronunciation key ———————
\ə\ **abut** \ᵊ\ **kitten**, F **table** \ər\ **further** \a\ **ash** \ā\ **ace** \ä\ **cot, cart**
\aù\ **out** \ch\ **chin** \e\ **bet** \ē\ **easy** \g\ **go** \i\ **hit** \ī\ **ice** \j\ **job**
\ŋ\ **sing** \ō\ **go** \ȯ\ **law** \ȯi\ **boy** \th\ **thin** \th\ **the** \ü\ **loot** \ù\ **foot**
\y\ **yet** \zh\ **vision** \à, ḵ, ⁿ, œ, œ̄, ᵫ, ᵫ̄, ʸ\ *see* Guide to Pronunciation

LEVEL A

Name _____

Exercise 8–1   If the italicized word is used correctly, mark **C** on the lines below; if the word is incorrect, mark **I**. Consult the dictionary to verify your choices.

I   1. Will we be able to use the data to *illicit* the facts we need?

I   2. Martha's story about the demonstration was very *credulous*.

C   3. By the time Bryant returned home, we had *hardly* any pizza left.

C   4. Do you agree that retaking the exam is a *plausible* thing to do?

I   5. From my *prospective*, I tend to agree with the executive committee.

C   6. The fund, which has not been *dispersed* at the death of the retiree, becomes part of the deceased's estate.

I   7. The one *criteria* that we advocate most is that of honesty.

I   8. Benjamin desires to *proceed* Amy in the graduation line.

C   9. You will have to fill out the *waiver* form to get permission to exclude the health class from your required courses.

I   10. One of the *principle* reasons I am going is to hear you give the keynote address.

Exercise 8–2   Mark **A** if the first word is correct; mark **B** if the second word is correct. Consult the dictionary to verify your choices.

A   1. I noticed a warm friendship (among/between) the three students.

B   2. Edison made many attempts to (discover/invent) the electric light.

A   3. John developed the (habit/custom) of going to sleep immediately following the ten o'clock news.

A   4. The movie had (scarcely/hardly) begun when the power went off.

B   5. You impugned my (character/reputation) with your false accusations.

B   6. The monastery is 3 miles (further/farther) than we expected.

B   7. The new desks for the classroom will be (stationery/stationary) because they will be bolted to the floor.

B   8. You have my permission to try to (illicit/elicit) any response you can from Tamara Lynn.

B   9. The (sight/site) of the new civic center will be about 2500 North Main Street.

A   10. (Eventually/Ultimately), we will equip the offices with refrigerated air conditioning.

Exercise 8–3 Mark **A** if the first word is the better choice; mark **B** if the second word is the better choice. Consult the dictionary to verify your answers.

_A_ 1. Can you (visualize/see) the way the building will look when it is built?

_B_ 2. I noticed the geese tended to (crowd/flock) together.

_A_ 3. The collapse of the roof was caused by (faulty/injurious) construction techniques.

_B_ 4. My visit to the hot climate of Vera Cruz had a(n) (iniquitous/deleterious) effect on my health.

_A_ 5. You are impolite when you (stare/look) at beggars on the street!

_A_ 6. The figures in the 1849 letter are now (illegible/ineligible).

_B_ 7. The Delta Airport will get a new (hanger/hangar) under provisions of the bill.

_B_ 8. Ms. Moss certainly has some unique (incites/insights) about the proposed itinerary.

_B_ 9. Marti reached an (amiable/amicable) agreement with the other members of her group.

_B_ 10. The reference manual is an (authoritarian/authoritative) source of information.

_A_ 11. Please send us the (balance/remainder) of the money that is due.

_A_ 12. Virgil has a problem with (continuous/continual) hiccuping.

_A_ 13. Veronica (deprecated/depreciated) Joshua for his weak performance.

_A_ 14. Faith will not talk about the incident because she is (discreet/discrete).

_B_ 15. A person who is conceited and boastful is an (egoist/egotist).

_B_ 16. My grandparents (immigrated/emigrated) from England last year.

_A_ 17. Our inventory showed we have (fewer/less) lawn mowers than we thought.

_A_ 18. Courtney told me he finally feels (well/good) following his illness.

_B_ 19. Edison was indeed an (ingenuous/ingenious) inventor.

_B_ 20. The left-over war (material/materiel) will be stored at Hill Air Force Base.

Exercise 8–4 Mark **A** if the first word is the better choice; mark **B** if the second word is the better choice. Consult the dictionary to verify your answers.

_B_ 1. A(n) (numismatist/ornithologist) is a student of birds.

_A_ 2. (Entomology/Etymology) is the study of insects.

_B_ 3. (Floriculture/Graphology) is the study of handwriting.

_B_ 4. A(n) (referee/umpire) is a football official who rules on plays.

_B_ 5. (Lacrosse/Jai alai) is a game in which the ball is carried with a racket.

LEVEL B

Name _____

Exercise 8–5   Using the dictionary, show the pronunciation and accent marks for these foreign words and expressions and give a brief definition of each.

1. ad hoc _Concerned with a particular end or purpose_
2. carte blanche _Full discretionary power_
3. esprit de corps _Common spirit among group members_
4. faux pas _A blunder_
5. hors d'oeuvres _Appetizer foods_
6. laissez faire _Deliberate abstention from interference_
7. per diem _By the day_
8. rendezvous _A place appointed for assembling or meeting_
9. status quo _Existing state of affairs_
10. vice versa _With the order changed_

Exercise 8–6   Write one homonym, one synonym, and one antonym for each of the following words. Consult the dictionary for help if necessary.

Words	Homonyms	Synonyms	Antonyms
capital	Capitol	Chief	subordinate
coarse	course	rough	delicate, fine
here	hear	in this place?	there?
peace	piece	tranquility	discord
principal	principle	main	secondary
break	brake	smash	mend
buy	by	purchase	sell
fore	for, four	in front	aft

Exercise 8–7   Write the correct pronunciation and accent, part of speech, and a brief definition for each of the following pairs of misused words.

decease _Verb — die_
disease _noun — illness_

incite ___*verb — stimulate to action*___

insight ___*noun — wisdom and understanding*___

persecute ___*verb — oppress because of principles or beliefs*___

prosecute ___*verb — bring before a court of law*___

prophecy ___*noun — thing told about the future*___

prophesy ___*verb — tells what will happen*___

emigrant ___*noun — person who leaves own country to settle in another*___

immigrant ___*noun — person who comes into a foreign country to live there*___

Exercise 8–8 Using the dictionary, write two words or phrases on each blank to illustrate each term.

1. archaic ___*outdated; antiquated*___

2. colloquial ___*conversational; not used in formal speech*___

3. dialect ___*pattern of speech of a particular people; idioms*___

4. idiom ___*language expression of a particular people; dialect*___

5. slang ___*language peculiar to a particular group; informal language*___

Exercise 8–9 Using the dictionary, show the pronunciation and accent marks of each word.

1. encyclopedia _____ 11. juice _____

2. harmonious _____ 12. peripheral _____

3. brought _____ 13. picture _____

4. martyr _____ 14. guarantee _____

5. linguistic _____ 15. transcend _____

6. genuine _____ 16. pneumonia _____

7. khaki _____ 17. naive _____

8. comparable _____ 18. sacrilegious _____

9. reservoir _____ 19. condolence _____

10. aluminum _____ 20. irrelevant _____

LEVEL C

Exercise
8–10

Name _____

Look up each of the following words in the dictionary, and then compose a sentence containing the word.

1. ingenuous _____

_____

2. diffident _____

_____

3. liaison _____

_____

4. assiduous _____

_____

5. salacious _____

_____

Exercise
8–11

What information do you find in your dictionary on the spelling of these pairs of words? Are the spellings interchangeable? If so, which form would you use and why?

1. aesthetic/esthetic _Interchangeable spellings; aesthetic preferred_

2. carat/karat _Variant spellings. Carat used for precious stones; karat used for gold_

3. favor/favour _Variant spellings. Favour used in Britain; favor used in the U.S._

4. gaol/jail _Variant spellings. Jail is used in U.S.; gaol is used in Britain._

5. sac/sack *Sac is associated with fluid-containing structures in plants and animals; a sack is a bag.*

Exercise 8–12

Write the dictionary pronunciations for the following words. Then compose a sentence in which you use the word. Circle the pronunciation that reflects the word as used in your sentence.

1. creek _____

_____

2. greasy _____

_____

3. herb _____

_____

4. leisure _____

_____

5. poinsettia _____

_____

Exercise 8–13

Using the dictionary, answer the following questions by composing a complete sentence.

1. In what kind of writing could you appropriately use the word *gimmick*?

_____

_____

2. If a woman *rests on her laurels*, what is she doing?

_____

_____

3. What is the past tense of *bear* in the sense of *carry*?

_____

_____

4. What is the plural of *ghetto*?

_____

_____

5. In what kind of writing could you appropriately use the word *whence*?

_____

_____

6. What is the origin of *assassin*?

_____

_____

7. To what extent has *fiasco* retained its original meaning?

_____

_____

8. Where are the Carpathian Mountains?

_____

_____

9. Is Mexico City larger or smaller than Tokyo in population?

_____

_____

10. How long is a furlong?

_____

_____

**Exercise
8–14**

Compose a sentence that satisfies the statement or question. Consult the dictionary for help when necessary.

1. What is the preferred pronunciation of *divulge*?

_____

_____

2. Divide *fraternize* into syllables by placing a small dot between syllables.

_____

_____

3. What does the Latin word *male* mean?

_____

_____

4. Compose a sentence in which you use an *oxymoron*.

_____

_____

5. Which syllable receives the primary stress in the preferred pronunciation of *convex*?

_____

_____

6. What is the difference between *prophecy* and *prophesy*?

_____

_____

7. Can an *immoral* person also be an *amoral* person?

_____

_____

8. What is the difference between an *alumnus* and an *alumna*?

_____

_____

LESSONS IN THIS UNIT

9. ORIENTATION TO VERBS

10. THE SIMPLE TENSES

11. THE PERFECT TENSES AND PROGRESSIVE FORMS

12. VERBALS

13. MOOD

14. VOICE

The verb is the strongest part of speech. If we are to become familiar with verbs so we can make them do our bidding, we must understand their peculiar characteristics—or their properties. We must also understand how verbs change form (how they are inflected) to indicate these characteristics.

A major hurdle to overcome in understanding verbs is to master the terminology associated with them. That terminology is not difficult to understand when you realize each term is logically selected according to its function. We have tried to define and illustrate the terms carefully to help you understand them.

The verb has five properties—number, person, tense, mood, and voice. In this unit, we will study three of those properties—tense, mood, and voice. In the unit on agreement, we will study number and person.

As the strongest part of speech, the verb is the heart of a sentence. Because verbs describe what the subject is doing or what is being done to the subject, they bring the sentence to life. And

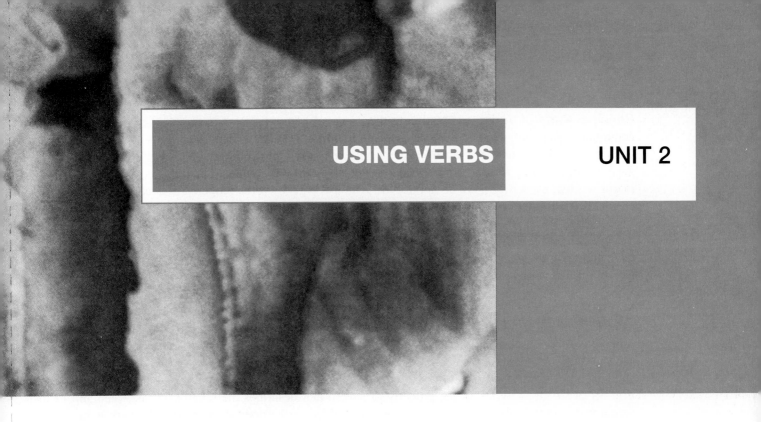

because the verb describes the subject's action, condition, or state of being, the verb is often thought of as the "motor" of the sentence—the "thing" that makes the sentence "go." We cannot form a sentence without a verb.

Action verbs may express physical actions (e.g., *run, jump, sing*) or mental actions (e.g., *think, believe, recommend*). Linking verbs do not express action but join or link one part of the sentence to another part (e.g., *is, are, am, was, were, seem, look, feel, taste, smell*).

Classes of Verbs.   Verbs have two main classes—transitive and intransitive.

A *transitive* verb is a verb that requires an object to complete its meaning. An *intransitive* verb is a verb that does not have an object to complete its meaning. Sometimes, the same verb may be transitive in one instance and intransitive in another. Linking verbs are always intransitive.

Perhaps the main reason for us to distinguish between transitive and intransitive verbs is to help us choose the correct verb form of troublesome verbs—especially *lie/lay, sit/set,* and *rise/raise.* You will recall from Lesson 8 that you can determine whether a verb is transitive or intransitive by consulting the dictionary.

Tenses of Verbs.   *Tense* is the property of the verb that reflects the time of an action or a state of being. That is, tense equals time.

From a writing perspective, we must learn to write about things as they were, as they are, or as they will be. To deal with time adequately in our writing, we must understand the three simple tenses (present, past, and future), the three perfect tenses (present perfect, past perfect, and future perfect), and the progressive companion forms of these six tenses. Mastery of tense involves coping with inflections of verbs (conjugations of verbs) and understanding the roles of helping (auxiliary) verbs.

Principal Parts of Verbs.   Identifying the principal parts of a verb is part of the process of conjugating that verb. (To *conjugate* a verb is to identify the inflections or alterations of that verb among the various tenses of the verb.) The term *conjugation* by itself may be enough to scare us away from mastering the parts of verbs. However, if we do not conjugate English verbs properly in our writing, especially if we do not use the principal parts of verbs properly, our readers might consider us semiliterate.

We can easily form the principal parts of regular verbs (e.g., *walk, walked, walked*), but we almost have to memorize the principal parts of irregular verbs (e.g., *do, did, done*). Verb conjugation will be closely allied with our study of tense.

Moods of Verbs.   *Mood* is the property of the verb that expresses the way a writer regards an assertion—as a declarative statement or a question (indicative mood); as a command or request (imperative mood); or as a hypothesis, a wish, a doubtful or impossible condition, or a contrary-to-fact condition (subjunctive mood).

Voices of Verbs.   *Voice* is the property of a verb that describes the relationship between an action verb and the subject of the verb. When the subject is the doer of the action, the verb is in the active voice. When the subject is the receiver or the result of the action, the verb is in the passive voice. Linking verbs, of course, are neither active nor passive.

Verbals.   A *verbal* is a word that reflects the nature of a verb but functions as a noun, an adjective, or an adverb. The three verbals are gerunds, participles, and infinitives.

Though the terms *gerund, participle,* and *infinitive* sound ominous, they are relatively simple to understand. A significant outcome of understanding verbals is our ability to avoid one major red flag of illiteracy—the dangling modifier. Another important outcome is the ability to use the appropriate verbal in connection with the tense of the main verb.

Subject/Verb Agreement.   Another red flag of illiteracy we want to avoid is the clause in which the subject and the verb do not agree. Subject/verb agreement is naturally related to our study of verbs. However, we will deal with subject/verb agreement in Unit 6.

Resolve now to put in whatever time and effort are necessary for you to learn as much as you can about verbs. Your efforts will pay large dividends throughout your study of business English and your career in the business world.

ORIENTATION TO VERBS

Of the eight parts of speech, the verb seems to cause the greatest number of learning problems. Perhaps that is because verbs have a larger number of inflectional forms (alterations to the basic forms) than any other part of speech. The inflection of verbs is called *conjugation*; verbs are conjugated according to person, number, tense, mood, and voice.

The two required components of every sentence are the subject and the verb. The verb tells what the subject does (active verb), what something else does to the subject (passive verb), or what the subject is (linking verb). In addition, the verb is used to make a statement, to ask a question, or to give a command. For example:

To make a statement:

We *use* the X-L floppy disks almost exclusively.
We *purchased* a new computer for the receptionist.

To ask a question:

Do we *use* the X-L floppy disks exclusively?
Have we *purchased* a new computer for the receptionist?

To give a command:

Use the X-L floppy disks exclusively.
Purchase a new computer for the receptionist.

Because the verb is so closely allied to the subject, we can increase the readability, interest, and power of our writing by judiciously selecting the correct or most appropriate verbs. For example, notice how our feelings toward Mr. Gonzalez change according to the verb selected:

Mr. Gonzalez *complimented* his students.
Mr. Gonzalez *praised* his students.

Mr. Gonzalez *applauded* his students.
Mr. Gonzalez *eulogized* his students.
Mr. Gonzalez *glorified* his students.

If we are to choose the best verb or the appropriate form of the verb, we must understand the properties of the verb—person, number, tense, mood, and voice. (Tense, mood, and voice are covered in this unit; person and number are covered in Unit 6.) To indicate these properties, we either change the form of the verb or add helping verbs to the main verb.

Pretest

With a **C** or an **I**, indicate whether the italicized verb is correct or incorrect. Then correct all verbs that are wrong.

1. Has Victoria *became* engaged during the holidays?

2. The lake *was froze* so solid that we walked across.

3. Matthew *has did* an especially fine job of cleaning the room.

4. We definitely *foreseen* the accident before it occurred.

5. Be sure you *lay* down for an hour's nap this afternoon.

6. We *have* already *set* through four of the playoff games.

7. Please inform Harold when the bread *has raised*.

Key: (1) I, become; (2) I, was frozen; (3) I, has done; (4) I, foresaw (5) I, lie; (6) I, have sat; (7) I, has risen.

Terminology

Auxiliary verb—See *helping verb*.

Complement—Follows a linking verb and is a noun, an adjective, or a pronoun in the complete predicate. Unlike an object, a complement is related to the subject rather than to the verb. A noun used as a complement is a *predicate noun*; an adjective used as a complement is a *predicate adjective*; and a pronoun used as a complement is a *predicate pronoun*. All of these are often called the *subject complement*. For example:

Predicate noun: The dog is a *terrier*.
Predicate adjective: She is *independent*.
Predicate pronoun: The person responsible is *he*.

Conjugation—The result of the inflected forms of a verb that indicate person, number, tense, mood, and voice.

Finite verb—The principal verb of a clause. A term used to distinguish a main verb (*sing*) or a verb phrase (*will sing*) from a verbal (*sung, singing, to sing*). A verbal is a nonfinite verb in the form of a gerund, participle, or infinitive. A verbal cannot by itself function as a predicate.

Helping verb—A verb such as *have, can,* or *will* that is used with a main verb to form a verb phrase; also called an auxiliary verb.

Infinitive—The present-tense form of a verb (with or without *to*)—for example, *walk* or *to walk.*

Inflection—An alteration that occurs in the form of a word to show a specific meaning or grammatical relationship to some other word or group of words. For example:

Nouns: man, men; man's, men's
Verbs: see, saw, seen, seeing
Pronouns: *I, my* car, a car for *me*
Adjectives: a *good* person, a *better* person, the *best* person
Adverbs: frequently, *more* frequently, *most* frequently

Intransitive verb—A verb that does not have an object to complete its meaning. (For example: Bread *rises.* The ball *was hit* by the boy.) Among the many intransitive verbs are linking verbs, which are always intransitive.

Irregular verb—A verb that does not form its past tense and past participle by the addition of -*d* or -*ed* to the stem of the infinitive—for example, *begin, began, begun.*

Linking verb—A verb that links its subject to the subject complement in the form of a predicate noun, a predicate adjective, or a predicate pronoun. Common linking verbs are *become, seem, appear, feel, look, taste, smell, sound,* and forms of the verb *be* (*is, am, are, was, were, be, been,* and *being,* which are also called *state-of-being verbs*).

Main verb—A sentence's one verb that expresses an action or a state of being; the last verb in a verb phrase.

Mood—The property of the verb through which we show the manner of the action. Through the *indicative mood,* we state a fact or ask a question. Through the *imperative mood,* we express a command or make a request. Through the *subjunctive mood,* we make a supposition, state a hypothesis, make a recommendation, or make a statement that is contrary to fact. For example:

Imperative mood: Get out of the room!
Indicative mood: The time has come for you to leave the room.
Subjunctive mood: You should leave the room now.

Nonfinite verb—A verbal (gerund, participle, or infinitive) functioning as a noun, an adjective, or an adverb. A nonfinite verb cannot stand as the only verb in a sentence—for example, *running* as both a gerund and a present participle, *jumped* as a past participle, and *to sing* as an infinitive.

Number—The inflectional (altered) form of a verb that indicates whether the verb is singular or plural.

Object—In connection with verbs, the person or thing that receives the action of the verb. An object may be a word, a phrase, or a clause. For example:

Word: The boy hit the *ball.*
Phrase: He prefers *to ski.*
Clause: I did not know *that you are ill.*

Participle—A verb form usually ending in *-ing* or *-ed*. A participle may be combined with helping verbs to form verb phrases with different tenses. When a participle is a word standing alone, it is a verbal and functions as a modifier.

Person—Changes in the form of pronouns and verbs to indicate whether a person is speaking (*I am*—first person), is spoken to (*you are*—second person), or is spoken about (*it is*—third person). Only personal pronouns and verbs change their forms to show person; nouns are always third person.

Predicate—The verb and whatever words are related to it in a sentence; the part of a sentence that tells what the subject does or what is done to the subject or what state of being the subject is in. A *simple predicate* is (1) the main verb when it does not have helpers or (2) the verb phrase when the main verb has helpers. A *complete predicate* consists of a verb and its complement along with any modifiers.

Predicate adjective—See *complement*.

Predicate noun—See *complement*.

Predicate pronoun—See *complement*.

Principal parts—The forms of a verb from which the various tenses are derived: the present tense or present infinitive (*see, walk*), the past tense (*saw, walked*), and the past participle (*seen, walked*).

Regular verb—A verb that forms its past tense and past participle when *-d* or *-ed* is added to the basic form of the verb. For example: *hope* becomes *hoped*; *walk* becomes *walked*.

State of being—The outcome of a verb that denotes existence. Forms of *be* are used to show state of being: *am, is, are, was, were, be, been, being*.

Tense—The verb property that indicates the time of a verb action—whether it happened in the past, is happening in the present, or will happen in the future. English verbs have five categories of tense: *present, past, future, progressive,* and *perfect*.

Transitive verb—A verb that requires an object to complete its meaning. (For example: The boy *hit* the ball.) Some verbs may be either transitive or intransitive. (For example: Maria *sang* a song. Maria *sang* at the funeral.)

Verb—A word that indicates action, condition, or process. For example: *talk, is, become*.

Verbal—Verb forms used as nouns, adjectives, or adverbs. The three verbals are gerunds, participles, and infinitives. (See *nonfinite verb*.)

Verb phrase—A verb consisting of the main verb and its helpers. A verb phrase serves as the simple predicate of a clause.

Voice—The verb property through which we show whether the subject acts (*active voice*) or is acted upon (*passive voice*).

Discussion

Your mastery of the material in the following discussion will help you understand and use verbs correctly.

Main Verbs and Helping Verbs.   A sentence may have only one verb that expresses an action or a state of being. We call such a verb a *main verb*. For example:

> Carl *drove* to the store.
> Harriet *is* our best candidate.

Or a sentence may have a combined unit of two or more verbs. We call the result a *verb phrase*. For example:

> I *will be transferred* in March.
> Suzie *has completed* the examination.

The main verb is always the last verb in a verb phrase. The other verbs in the phrase are called helping (or auxiliary) verbs; and the principal helping verbs are *is, am, are, was, were, be, been, being, have, has, had, may, must, ought, can, might, could, would, should, shall, will, do, does,* and *did*. No verb phrase can be longer than four words—three helping verbs and the main verb. Ten of the helping verbs, *can, could, may, might, must, ought, shall, should, will,* and *would,* are **always** used as helping verbs and are **never** used as main verbs.

The helping verb is often separated from the main verb by a modifier or, in a question, by the subject. For example:

> The personal computer *has* certainly *changed* the office.
> How *have* computers *changed* your inventory system?

Closely related to the verb phrase is the *predicate*, which tells what the subject does, what is done to the subject, or what state of being the subject is in. The simple predicate is either the verb or the verb phrase. The complete predicate is the verb and its complement along with any modifiers. For example:

> Dr. Ralph *testified*. (simple predicate)
> Energetic workers *accomplish a great deal of work*. (complete predicate)

Linking Verbs.   Linking verbs do not express action. Instead, they express a condition or a state of being. Because linking verbs are always intransitive, they never take objects.

The most common linking verbs are forms of *to be—am, is, are, was, were—*and verb phrases ending in *be, been,* or *being*. Other verbs commonly used as linking verbs are *seem, appear, become, sound, taste, smell, feel, remain, stay,* and *look*. One way to recognize linking verbs is to substitute the word *is* in place of the verb. Usually, if that substitution can be made, the verb is a linking verb. For example:

> She *looks* beautiful. = She *is* beautiful.
> The bread *tastes* moldy. = The bread *is* moldy.

Linking verbs link a complement (a predicate noun, a predicate adjective, or a predicate pronoun) to the subject. The result is that the subject and the complement apply to the same person or thing. Because of this characteristic, the linking verb is equivalent to the equal sign in an algebraic equation. For example:

> If A = B, then B = A.
> If the man is he, then he is the man.

Principal Parts of Verbs.   The verb has three principal parts: present tense (present infinitive), past tense, and past participle (the past participle always has a helper). A good way to recall these parts is to substitute those of any regular verb or irregular verb for the following:

Regular Verbs: I *play* today.
I *played* yesterday.
I *have played* every day this week.

Irregular Verbs: I *swim* today.
I *swam* yesterday.
I *have swum* every day this week.

Be sure you do not misuse the past tense and the past participle. We form the past tense and past participle of regular verbs by adding *-d* or *-ed* to the present infinitive: *bake, baked, baked; ask, asked, asked.*

Verbs that form the past tense and the past participle by a vowel change as well as by the occasional addition of an ending are called irregular verbs: *do, did, done; ride, rode, ridden.*

For example, the writer of the following sentences has confused the tenses:

The dog *has bit* me several times. (has bitten)
Harold *drunk* the entire quart of milk. (drank)
Snow *has fell* for an entire day. (has fallen)
We *done* all the work in less than a day. (did)
Yesterday I *ask* for permission to take the test. (asked)
We are *suppose* to take the exam today. (supposed)

The dictionary is an excellent source to verify the correct forms of the past tense and the past participle. If no additional forms follow the main entry, you will know the verb is regular (formed with the endings *-d* or *-ed*). If additional forms (inflections) are listed, you will know the verb is irregular. The English language has thousands of regular verbs but fewer than 200 irregular verbs.

Use
T9-1
here

For your reference and mastery, Table 9–1 contains the principal parts of most of the troublesome irregular verbs. Study them thoroughly; memorize and practice those that cause you difficulty; and substitute them in the sentences discussed above.

Table 9–1					
Frequently Occurring Irregular Verbs					
Present Tense (Infinitive)	**Past Tense**	**Past Participle**	**Present Tense (Infinitive)**	**Past Tense**	**Past Participle**
arise	arose	arisen	build	built	built
be (am/is/are)	was/were	been	buy	bought	bought
bear	bore	borne	cast	cast	cast
begin	began	begun	catch	caught	caught
bend	bent	bent	choose	chose	chosen
bite	bit	bitten	come	came	come
bid	bid	bid	cost	cost	cost
blow	blew	blown	deal	dealt	dealt
break	broke	broken	dig	dug	dug
bring	brought	brought	do	did	done

Table 9–1
(concluded)

Present Tense (Infinitive)	Past Tense	Past Participle	Present Tense (Infinitive)	Past Tense	Past Participle
draw	drew	drawn	say	said	said
drink	drank	drunk	see	saw	seen
drive	drove	driven	seek	sought	sought
eat	ate	eaten	sell	sold	sold
fall	fell	fallen	send	sent	sent
feed	fed	fed	set	set	set
feel	felt	felt	sew	sewed	sewn
find	found	found	shake	shook	shaken
fling	flung	flung	shine	shone	shone
fly	flew	tlown	show	showed	shown (or showed)
freeze	froze	frozen			
get	got	gotten (or got)	shrink	shrank	shrunk
give	gave	given	shut	shut	shut
go	went	gone	sing	sang	sung
grow	grew	grown	sink	sank	sunk
hang (to suspend)	hung	hung	sit	sat	sat
have	had	had	sleep	slept	slept
hear	heard	heard	slide	slid	slid
hide	hid	hidden (or hid)	speak	spoke	spoken
hit	hit	hit	spend	spent	spent
hold	held	held	split	split	split
keep	kept	kept	spread	spread	spread
know	knew	known	spring	sprang	sprung
lay (to place)	laid	laid	stand	stood	stood
lead	led	led	steal	stole	stolen
leave	left	left	stick	stuck	stuck
lend	lent	lent	strike	struck	struck
let	let	let	swear	swore	sworn
lie (to recline)	lay	lain	sweep	swept	swept
lose	lost	lost	swim	swam	swum
make	made	made	swing	swung	swung
mean	meant	meant	take	took	taken
meet	met	met	teach	taught	taught
pay	paid	paid	tear	tore	torn
prove	proved	proved (or proven)	tell	told	told
put	put	put	think	thought	thought
quit	quit	quit	throw	threw	thrown
read	read	read	wear	wore	worn
ride	rode	ridden	weep	wept	wept
ring	rang	rung	win	won	won
rise	rose	risen	wind	wound	wound
run	ran	run	write	wrote	written

Use T9-2 here

A related dimension of regular and irregular verbs is the compound verb—a verb to which another verb, a preposition, an adverb, a noun, or a syllable is attached as a prefix. Compound regular verbs form their past tenses and past participles just like regular verbs do. Compound irregular verbs form their past tenses and past participles according to their verb halves. For example, the three principal parts of *write* are *write, wrote,* and *written,* so the three principal parts of *typewrite* are *typewrite, typewrote,* and *typewritten.*

Follow the same procedures for the compound irregular verbs in Table 9–2 that were suggested for the other irregular verbs. That is, study the compound irregular verbs thoroughly; memorize and practice those that cause you difficulty; and substitute them in the sentences discussed above.

Table 9–2					
Sample Compound Irregular Verbs					
Present Tense (Infinitive)	Past Tense	Past Participle	Present Tense (Infinitive)	Past Tense	Past Participle
become	became	become	oversee	oversaw	overseen
behold	beheld	beheld	repay	repaid	repaid
broadcast	broadcast	broadcast	typewrite	typewrote	typewritten
foresee	foresaw	foreseen	understand	understood	understood
forget	forgot	forgotten	undertake	undertook	undertaken
forgive	forgave	forgiven	underwrite	underwrote	underwritten
handwrite	handwrote	handwritten	withdraw	withdrew	withdrawn
mistake	mistook	mistaken	withstand	withstood	withstood
overdo	overdid	overdone			

Transitive and Intransitive Verbs.   As you know, a sentence typically contains a noun or a pronoun as its subject and a verb (or a verb phrase) as its simple predicate. However, the mere presence of both a noun and a simple predicate does not necessarily make a meaningful sentence. For example:

> The manager wrote.

That word group is not a meaningful thought. It lacks the information about what the manager wrote and therefore needs an object of the transitive verb *wrote*—a word that tells us what the manager wrote. For example:

> The manager wrote the letter.

Letter is the direct object of the verb *wrote* because *letter* tells us what the manager wrote.

To determine the object of a verb, ask yourself *Whom?* or *What?* after the verb. For example: The manager wrote . . . what? The letter. *Letter* is the object of the verb *wrote*. Henry likes . . . whom? Nancy. *Nancy* is the object of Henry's liking.

Many verbs, of course, do not require objects. For example:

> Jesus *wept.*
> The manager *travels.*

The verbs *wept* and *travels* do not have objects. *A verb that requires an object for meaning is called a transitive verb* because the action *transfers* to the object. *A verb that does not require an object for meaning is called an intransitive verb* because the action is complete in itself. (The action in the verb does not transfer from the subject through the verb and to the object of the action.) For example:

Transitive: Jack *sent* the *report* today.
Marion *drives* his *car* twice a week.
Mark *attended class* yesterday.

Intransitive: Jack *sleeps* on a waterbed.
Marion *drives* on the left side of the road.
Mark *attends* on Tuesdays only.

We present this discussion about transitive and intransitive verbs so you can learn to use correctly the principal parts of six troublesome verbs: *lie, lay, sit, set, rise,* and *raise.* The key to understanding and using these verbs properly is in knowing the difference between transitive and intransitive verbs.

The principal parts of *lie* and *lay,* which you must memorize, are as follows:

Use
T9-3
here

Present	Past	Past Participle
lie	lay	lain
lay	laid	laid

Lie and *lay* have different meanings. *To lie* means *to recline* and is intransitive, and *to lay* means *to place* and is transitive. For example:

I *lie* on the couch. (present tense)
I *lay* on the couch yesterday. (past tense)
I *had lain* on the couch two days until you arrived. (past-perfect tense)

I *lay* the book on the desk each morning. (present tense)
I *laid* the book on the desk yesterday. (past tense)
I *had laid* the book on the desk, as you directed. (past-perfect tense)

Because *lie* is intransitive, it **never** requires an object to complete its meaning. Because *lay* is transitive, it **always** requires an object to complete its meaning.

The principal parts of *sit/set,* which you must memorize, are the following:

Present	Past	Past Participle
sit	sat	sat
set	set	set

Sit and *set* have different meanings. *To sit* means *to be seated* and is intransitive, and *to set* means *to place* and is transitive. *Sit* **never** requires an object because it is intransitive. *Set* **always** requires an object because it is transitive—it requires a word that tells us what was set. For example:

The boys normally *sit* on the north end. (present tense)
The boys *sat* on the south end yesterday. (past tense)
The boys *had sat* on either the north end or the south end until they got 50-yard seats. (past-perfect tense)

He *sets* the manual on my credenza. (present tense)
He *set* the manual on my credenza yesterday. (past tense)
He *had* always *set* the manual on my credenza until you told him not to do so. (past-perfect tense)

The principal parts of *rise* and *raise*, which you must memorize, are as follows:

Present	Past	Past Participle
rise	rose	risen
raise	raised	raised

To rise means *to get up* and is intransitive, and *to raise* means *to lift* and is transitive. *Rise,* as an intransitive verb, **never** requires an object to complete its meaning. *Raise,* a transitive verb, **always** requires an object to complete its meaning—to tell the reader what was raised. For example:

I *rise* by 7 a.m. most mornings. (present tense)
I *rose* at 6 a.m. yesterday. (past tense)
I *had risen* before 7 a.m. every morning until my alarm clock broke. (past-perfect tense)

I *raise* the windows myself. (present tense)
Sue *raised* the windows today. (past tense)
We *had raised* the windows every morning until we were told to keep them closed. (past-perfect tense)

Note the *i's* in the verbs *lie, sit,* and *rise*; and note that *intransitive* begins with *i. Lie, sit,* and *rise* are intransitive and do not require objects. On the other hand, *lay, set,* and *raise* are transitive and therefore require objects to complete their meanings.

Note also that if you ask the question *what?* after one of these verbs and get no answer, you know the verb is intransitive and must be *lie, sit,* or *rise.* If you get an answer to *what?*, you know the verb is transitive and must be *lay, set,* or *raise.*

Posttest

With a **C** or an **I**, indicate whether the italicized verb is correct or incorrect. Then correct all verbs that are wrong.

1. We *payed* the invoice last Thursday.

2. When you *blowed* up the balloon, did you get dizzy?

3. We *had* individually *spoke* to everyone before you arrived.

4. Mark *had handwrote* the speech before he typed it.

5. I *lay* on the bed for about an hour this morning.

6. *Do* you and Quentin *set* together at the assemblies?

7. The sun *had raised* to the twelve o'clock position before I awoke.

Key: (1) I, paid; (2) I, blew; (3) I, had spoken; (4) I, had handwritten; (5) C; (6) I, do sit; (7) I, had risen.

LEVEL A

Name _____

Exercise 9–1 On the lines below, write **T** if the statement is true and **F** if the statement is false.

_T_ 1. Helping verbs are also known as auxiliary verbs.

_F_ 2. The term *verb phrase* is synonymous with the term *complete predicate*.

_F_ 3. The three principal parts of verbs are present tense, past tense, and present participle.

_T_ 4. When the past participle of a regular verb is formed, *-d* or *-ed* is added to the present tense.

_T_ 5. The principal parts of *lead* are *lead, led, led*.

_T_ 6. The principal parts of *undertake* are *undertake, undertook, undertaken*.

_F_ 7. A transitive verb is a verb that does not require an object.

_F_ 8. *To lay* means *to recline* and therefore is intransitive.

_T_ 9. *To sit* means *to be seated* and therefore is intransitive.

_T_ 10. *Rise* is an intransitive verb that never requires an object to complete its meaning.

Exercise 9–2 Mark **C** if the correct principal parts of the verb are shown. Mark **I** if the correct principal parts are not shown.

_I_ 1. bring, brang, brung

_I_ 2. dig, dug, digged

_C_ 3. freeze, froze, frozen

_I_ 4. lie, lay, laid

_I_ 5. write, wrote, wrote

_I_ 6. swing, swang, swung

_C_ 7. speak, spoke, spoken

_I_ 8. weep, wept, weeped

_I_ 9. sit, set, set

_I_ 10. sew, sewed, sewed

_I_ 11. tell, told, telling

_I_ 12. sink, sunk, sunk

_I_ 13. shine, shone, shined

_C_ 14. shut, shut, shut

_C_ 15. sweep, swept, swept

_I_   16. tear, teared, teared

_C_   17. quit, quit, quit

_I_   18. steal, steal, stolen

_C_   19. handwrite, handwrote, handwritten

_I_   20. withdraw, withdraw, withdrawed

Exercise 9–3   Write **A** if the first verb is correct; write **B** if the second verb is correct.

_A_   1. The dough will (rise/raise) by 10 a.m.

_B_   2. The sun had (raised/risen) before the alarm went off.

_B_   3. The store is (rising/raising) its prices today.

_A_   4. The papers have (lain/layed) on my desk for two days.

_B_   5. The group is (lying/laying) the blame on Mr. Yates.

_A_   6. We have (laid/lain) more carpeting today than you have.

_A_   7. We did nothing but (lie/lay) in the shade today.

_B_   8. We (set/sat) in the outer office for almost an hour.

_A_   9. We desire to (sit/set) in the front row today.

_B_   10. Be sure you (set/sit) close to the window exit.

Exercise 9–4   Write **C** if the verb or verb phrase is correct. Write **I** if the verb or verb phrase is incorrect.

_I_   1. These plants have growed rapidly during my vacation.

_I_   2. How many of the dishes were broke during the move?

_I_   3. Have you went to Brigham City yet?

_I_   4. Some of the tomato plants were froze last night.

_C_   5. We had spoken to Marcia before the meeting.

_C_   6. The sweater has shrunk because you washed it.

_I_   7. Ms. Western done all she could to help us.

_I_   8. Have you began to collect your data yet?

_I_   9. The cab driver winded in and out of the city traffic.

_I_   10. We have chose Mr. Southern to coach our team.

LEVEL B

Name _____

Exercise 9–5   Write the letter that identifies the sentence with correct verb usage.

_c_   1.   *a.*   Have you seen my glasses? I last seen them this morning.
     b.   I drove the pickup all the way to California. Have you ever drove one that far?
     c.   Mark gave me two books yesterday. I have given one of them to Betty.

_b_   2.   *a.*   Bryant hasn't ate much meat this month.
     b.   The evidence proved to me that a deer had lain in the scrub oak.
     c.   Yolanda run 22 miles for the heart campaign.

_b_   3.   *a.*   Mary and Gary done all the work in about an hour.
     b.   Oran has drunk at least six soft drinks this morning.
     c.   Yesterday, I ask Luiz to attend the executive committee meeting.

_c_   4.   *a.*   When have you became eligible to run for vice president?
     b.   The turret lathe was bidded by Ironton Machine Tools at the lowest price of all bidders.
     c.   When you return from England, you can say you have driven on the left side of the road.

_a_   5.   *a.*   We lent Ms. Richards the Equitable Mortgage file yesterday.
     b.   We payed our Equitable Mortgage payment by the 15th of the month.
     c.   After you have ate lunch at the Gizmo, we want you to visit our downtown offices.

_c_   6.   *a.*   In April, Bill run in the Boston Marathon; he has run in it twice before.
     b.   Jeannie wore her new swimsuit today, and that is the first time she has wore it.
     c.   The Crowthers have come to our cabin only once this year; they normally come four times a year.

_a_   7.   *a.*   Jennifer swam in the first race today; she has swum in four events during the competition.
     b.   The first-period bell was rang while you were in the gymnasium.
     c.   Lt. Majors shrunk once from doing his duty, but he never shrunk a second time.

_c_   8.   *a.*   Mr. Carson begun the meeting about an hour late.
     b.   Apparently, Ms. Yeates has forgot to tell everyone about the meeting.
     c.   Mr. Marx, who is our best sales representative, has met his quota already.

Exercise 9–6   Underline each subject once and each verb or verb phrase twice. Above each verb or verb phrase, write **R** if the main verb is a regular verb and **I** if the main verb is an irregular verb.

1.   Effective <u>writing</u> <u>depends</u> upon a knowledge of both principles and rules.
                       R

2.   <u>Tense</u> <u>means</u> time. As a good writer, therefore, <u>you</u> <u>will keep</u> the time order of events straight.

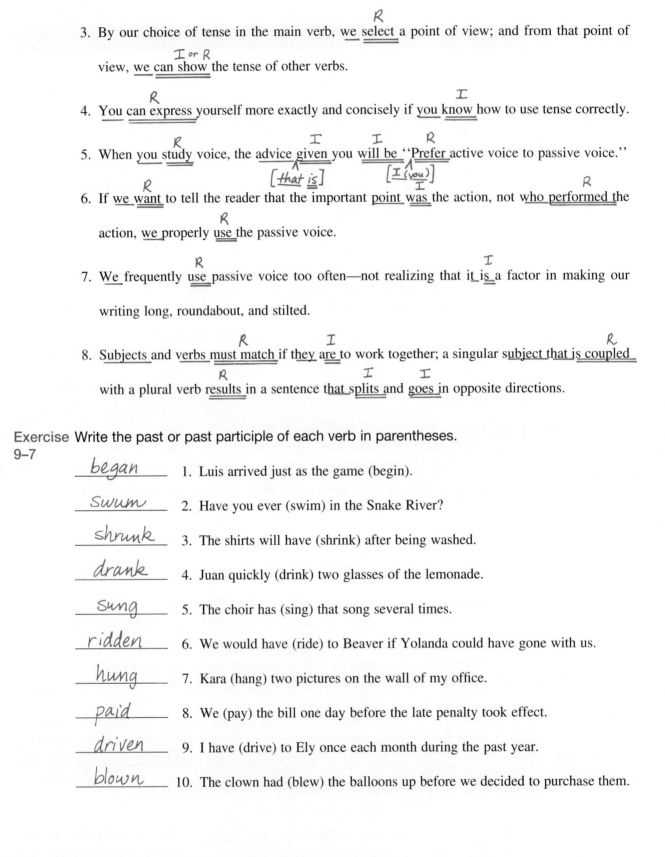

3. By our choice of tense in the main verb, we select a point of view; and from that point of view, we can show the tense of other verbs.

4. You can express yourself more exactly and concisely if you know how to use tense correctly.

5. When you study voice, the advice given you will be "Prefer active voice to passive voice."

6. If we want to tell the reader that the important point was the action, not who performed the action, we properly use the passive voice.

7. We frequently use passive voice too often—not realizing that it is a factor in making our writing long, roundabout, and stilted.

8. Subjects and verbs must match if they are to work together; a singular subject that is coupled with a plural verb results in a sentence that splits and goes in opposite directions.

Exercise 9–7 Write the past or past participle of each verb in parentheses.

____began____ 1. Luis arrived just as the game (begin).

____swum____ 2. Have you ever (swim) in the Snake River?

____shrunk____ 3. The shirts will have (shrink) after being washed.

____drank____ 4. Juan quickly (drink) two glasses of the lemonade.

____sung____ 5. The choir has (sing) that song several times.

____ridden____ 6. We would have (ride) to Beaver if Yolanda could have gone with us.

____hung____ 7. Kara (hang) two pictures on the wall of my office.

____paid____ 8. We (pay) the bill one day before the late penalty took effect.

____driven____ 9. I have (drive) to Ely once each month during the past year.

____blown____ 10. The clown had (blew) the balloons up before we decided to purchase them.

LEVEL C

Name _____

Exercise
9–8

In each sentence, underline each verb or verb phrase. Mark **C** on the line if the verbs and verb phrases are correctly used. Mark **I** if any verb or verb phrase is incorrectly used. Then edit all incorrect verbs.

_**I**_ 1. I was <u>setting</u> [*sitting*] quietly when someone suddenly <u>set</u> a newspaper in front of me.

_**I**_ 2. The lake <u>kept</u> <u>raising</u> [*rising*] until it finally <u>had raised</u> [*risen*] above the high-water mark.

_**I**_ 3. While the employees <u>were laying</u> the carpet, the supervisor <u>was laying</u> [*lying*] down in the back room sound asleep.

_**C**_ 4. The pamphlets that <u>were lying</u> on the desk <u>had lain</u> there for at least a week.

_**I**_ 5. Several times in Hawaii I <u>set</u> [*sat*] on the beach while I <u>watched</u> the sun <u>set</u> in the west.

_**I**_ 6. When the sun <u>raised</u> [*rose*] this morning, I <u>realized</u> that my head <u>had not risen</u> from my pillow for eight hours.

_**I**_ 7. We <u>had forgot</u> [*forgotten*] to take our umbrellas to San Antonio, so we <u>bought</u> new ones from a street vendor.

_**I**_ 8. I was truly <u>shook</u> [*shaken*] up by the news that the volcano <u>had blew</u> [*blown*] its top this morning.

_**I**_ 9. The bat <u>has bit</u> [*bitten*] Laurie on the hand, so we <u>have went</u> [*gone*] to the doctor's office.

_**I**_ 10. As soon as I <u>got</u> to the river, I <u>casted</u> [*cast*] the bait into the pool and promptly <u>caught</u> a 2-pound fish.

_**I**_ 11. Que <u>has broken</u> with tradition and <u>has chose</u> [*chosen*] to bring his camper rather than his tent.

_**C**_ 12. Although Zola <u>forgot</u> to bring the bacon, she <u>has been forgiven</u> for her oversight.

_**I**_ 13. Edward <u>swore</u> to all of us that he <u>had slidden</u> [*slid*] down the slope only once.

_I_ 14. When you have ~~rode~~ _ridden_ the range with Tex, you <u>will have been swept</u> up in the immensity of the land.

_I_ 15. Yes, we ~~seen~~ _saw_ the culprits who ~~done~~ _did_ the dirty deed.

_I_ 16. After he ~~winded~~ _wound_ the clock, Kent ~~sat~~ _set_ the key on the mantle.

_I_ 17. Jolene has ~~bore~~ _borne_ her grief well and has ~~began~~ _begun_ to recuperate from her husband's death.

_C_ 18. I <u>have eaten</u> poi only once, and that one experience <u>has kept</u> me from eating poi again.

_I_ 19. Jack would have ~~wore~~ _worn_ his cowboy hat but <u>had</u> already <u>let</u> Jake <u>borrow</u> it.

_I_ 20. Olga has ~~went~~ _gone_ to more meetings than I <u>have,</u> and I'<u>m</u> sure she has ~~payed~~ _paid_ more attention to the details than I <u>have.</u>

Exercise 9–9 Compose sentences that contain the past participles of both verbs that are indicated.

Composition

1. begin, hide

   _____

2. know, drive

   _____

3. bring, freeze

   _____

4. pay, go

   _____

5. spend, shake

   _____

Exercise
9–10

Compose sentences that reflect the directives indicated.

Compo-
sition

1. An intransitive verb other than *lie*, *sit*, or *rise*

_____

2. Two linking verbs

_____

3. Two past-tense verbs

_____

4. Three helping verbs in one verb phrase

_____

5. Two transitive verbs

_____

Exercise
9–11

Edit the following sentences to reflect what you have learned in Lesson 9 and to correct any frequently misspelled words or misused confusing words.

Cumula-
tive
Editing

1. ~~Apparantly,~~ *Apparently* ~~writting~~ *writing* is not a single operation but is best ~~broke~~ *broken* down ~~too~~ *to* a process consisting of preplanning, ~~writting~~ *writing*, and revising.

2. I ~~payed~~ *paid* attention to ~~you're~~ *your* excellent comparison of ~~writting~~ *writing* and an iceberg—the ~~visable~~ *visible* one-ninth reflects what you see and the ~~invisable~~ *invisible* eight-ninths reflects prewriting and revising.

3. No matter what kind of ~~writting~~ *writing* you have ~~chose~~ *chosen* to do, you must ~~percieve~~ *perceive* the ~~affect~~ *effect* of good preplanning.

4. To my surprise, I have ~~occasionaly drew~~ *occasionally drawn* the conclusion that prewriting is not merely a means of discovering something to write about; it involves willingness and desire to ~~set~~ *sit* down to think my own ~~personnel~~ *personal* thoughts.

5. Incidently, I have began to realize that the most interesting and affective subjects for writting are those about which we either have some knowledge or about which we want to develope some knowledge.

6. I seen alot of my writting as something that has came from the principle ideas and impressions that I have obtained from various sources and have made a familliar part of myself.

7. I conceed that my prewriting and writing have became complimentary processes, and I have began to write only after I have persued what I plan to say and how I plan to say it.

8. I beleive I payed a grievious price before I learned that time spent in preplanning saves time in writting and also helps make the finished product free from the affects of errors.

9. I have knew for the passed year that not even a skilled employe is equiped to preplan, write, and proofread all at the same time.

10. I finally have came to the realization that skilled writers knew from long experience that there first drafts are only the begining of the writting process.

Exercise 9–12

Cumulative Editing

Edit the following sentences to reflect what you have learned in Lesson 9 and to correct any frequently misspelled words, misused confusing words, and number-expression violations.

1. One researcher has wrote implicitly that a sixteen-cent tax increase could feasably discourage nearly 32,000,000 teenagers from smoking.

2. Dr. Mobley lead me too beleive that smoking-related deaths raised to 300 thousand in 1984 and that the increase represented a loss of 3.6 million years in terms of shortened life spans.

3. I seen you're Exhibit #2 on page #4, and I seen that the 131 words yeilded seven sentences, with an average length of 14 words.

4. I am carefull in advicing that the 5-year survival rate for malignant melanoma has went to 100% if the lesion is excised while it is less than .75 millimeters thick. However, the rate has went to about 50% when the lesion is 3.00 millimeters deep.

5. Latter, the doctor had gave Barbara helpfull instructions to minimize exposure to ultraviolet radiation if she would stay out of the sun from 10:00 AM to 2:00 PM each day.

6. To my surprize, the lifetime incidence of malignant melanoma has all ready went from one in fifteen hundred people to one in every 150.

7. Yes, everyone of the doctors have wrote that the babies of teenage mothers definately have high rates of illness, including low birth weight (under 5.5 pounds).

8. 15% of pregnant teens have became pregnant again within one year as a result of elicit relations; 30% have became so within 2 years.

9. Incidently, if you have chose the OK 92 printer, remember that it's tractor-feed paper can be anywhere from 3'' to 9.5'' wide.

10. According to the imminent bookeeper's explaination, a byte is a basic unit of information consisting of 8 bits; and a byte can represent any number between zero and 256.

Exercise 9–13

Cumulative Editing

Edit the following sentences to reflect what you have learned in Lesson 9. Also, spell all frequently misspelled words correctly, use all confusing words correctly, and apply capitalization and abbreviation rules correctly.

1. The Principle had all ready began the Curiculum Meeting in room number 444 of the Brimhall science building.

2. The Broshure shows on p. 4 that Utah, also knowed as the beehive state, has several National Parks disbursed throughout the Southern part of the state.

3. To get to you're S.L.C.C. class on Diesel maintainance, go N. on interstate 15 until you reach the 45th south exit. Then go W. until you reach Redwood road. Then, after one block North, you are their.

4. The likeable Doctor Mark Ekins, President of the Jefferson institute, has spoke twice to my American history class during the later half of the last two Wed. classes.

5. In his term paper, Vincent accidently done the wrong thing by saying that saturn, not pluto, is the ninth-largest planet and is further away from the sun than any other planet.

6. The Vice Pres. of academics at Southern Univ. telled every one in attendance at the Faculty Meeting yesterday that he reccomends an Economics Department be initiated at the School.

7. Next Spring, during the 4th week of spring quarter 1992, we are liabel to undertake an in-depth analysis of the great depression in Am. Hist. 101.

8. Can you beleive that my Mother and my Father turned me lose to go to Church in Saint Petersburg by myself when I were eight years old?

9. The Alpine School Dist. board of education will set in executive counsel meeting next Tues. evening to discuss Supt. Baird's criticizm about the overpass that we need so bad on Freedom Blvd.

10. I had forgot that the data in column 2 of table 4 aparently infer that more than one School District in the City may have a higher no. of Caucasians than Blacks.

As you know, the different forms a verb may take are referred to as *tenses*. Changes in tense in English verbs are shown by inflection or by the use of helping verbs.

As their main function, verbs describe an action or a state of being on the part of the subject. However, verbs also tell *when* an action took place or *when* the state of being existed—and this property of the verb is the *tense* of a verb.

Use T10-1 here

Tense relates to time from the point of view of the writer or speaker. For example, consider the act of *working*.

> If you say, "I *am working* today," you are looking, from the standpoint of the *present* time, at an action that is taking place *now*.

> If you say, "I *worked* 40 hours last week," you are looking, again from the standpoint of the present time, at an action that happened in the *past* (last week).

> If you say, "If I *work* next week, I *will have worked* 80 hours this month," you are placing yourself in the *future* (next week) and speaking from that point of view.

> If you say, "I told Rex yesterday that I *had worked* 40 hours last week," you are speaking, from the point of view of some time in the past (yesterday), of an action that was completed even before that "past time."

Verb tense gives us the ability to delineate such events in relation to time. In English, we use three simple tenses (*present, past,* and *future*) to express an action that is simply occurring. And we use three compound tenses—called *perfect*—to express an action that we consider to be completed. To be *perfected* means to be *completed*. (The perfect tenses are discussed in detail in Lesson 11.)

Each of the six tenses has a companion form called the *progressive* form, which tells us that the action named by the verb is a continued or a progressive action. The progressive consists of the present participle (the *-ing* form of the verb) plus the proper form of the verb *to be*. (The progressive forms are discussed in detail in Lesson 11.)

143

Use
T10-2
here

Table 10–1			
The Most Frequently Used Verb Tenses			
Tense	**I**	**he, she, it**	**we, you, they**
Present (now; immediate present)	ask	asks	ask
Present-progressive (continuing present)	am asking	is asking	are asking
Present-perfect (past time extending to the present; past participle plus *have* or *has*)	have asked	has asked	have asked
Past (started and completed in past)	asked	asked	asked
Past-progressive (continuing period in past)	was asking	was asking	were asking
Past-perfect (a time in the past before another past time; past participle plus *had*)	had asked	had asked	had asked
Future (will happen in the future)	will ask	will ask	will ask
Future-progressive (future time extending from the present)	will be asking	will be asking	will be asking
Future-perfect (will be completed in the future; past participle plus *have* plus *will*)	will have asked	will have asked	will have asked

The simple, perfect, and progressive tenses are shown in Table 10–1. In this lesson, we will study only the simple tenses—present, past, and future.

Pretest

Mark the sentence **C** if all elements of tense are correct; mark the sentence **I** if any element of tense is incorrect.

1. Yes, the manager done well when he suggested the policy change.

2. My birthday was last week, so my roommate buys me a stuffed animal.

3. The report will probably lay on Mr. Smith's desk all day.

4. You are correct—the scoutmaster at the jamboree was my next-door neighbor.

5. Ms. Everett said, "Smoking is now prohibited in all offices."

6. We are nearly froze by the time we finished our ice-fishing adventure.

7. My secretary had the cleanest desk because he cleans it before he leaves work each day.

Key: (1) I—use past tense *did*; (2) I—use past tense for both verbs *was* and *bought*; (3) I—use intransitive *lie*; (4) I—use present tense *is* to signal a permanent truth; (5) C; (6) I—to avoid a shift in tense, use past tense *were frozen* to agree with past tense *finished* or use *are frozen* and *finish* to signify present tense for both actions; (7) I—change one or more of the verbs to eliminate the shift in tense from past to present.

Terminology

Future tense—The form of the verb that, in relation to time, shows an action, state of being, or condition that is associated with the future and that will occur in the future. Future tense = still to come.

Historical present—The use of the present tense to make more vivid the description of some past action through a restatement or summarization of the facts from a book, report, letter, etc. For example: "Mr. Jones *states* in his letter . . ." or "Jesus *says*, 'Ask, and it shall be given you. . . .'"

Past tense—The form of the verb that, in relation to time, shows an action, state of being, or condition is associated with the past and came to an end in the past. Past tense = over and done with.

Perfect tenses—The forms of the verb that, in relation to time, show an action is perfected or completed. Past-perfect tense = started and completed in the past before some other past action. Present-perfect tense = started in the past and continuing in the present. Future-perfect tense = will be completed in the future in relation to another event.

Present tense—The base form of the verb that, in relation to time, points to something happening now, something done regularly or habitually, or something about to happen in the immediate future; also used for expressing universal truths and the historical present. Present tense = now or usually.

Progressive tenses—The forms of the verb that, in relation to time, show an action or event in progress. Progressive-tense verb forms are phrases consisting of a form of *be* plus a present participle (the present tense—plus -*ing*).

Shift in tense—An illogical or unnecessary change from one verb tense to another, resulting in confusion about the sequence of events as reflected in the verbs.

Simple tenses—Present, past, and future tenses. The simple tenses do not include the perfect tenses or the progressive forms.

Tense—The verb property through which is shown the time of a verb action—whether it happened in the past, is happening in the present, or will happen in the future. English verbs have five categories of tense: *present, past, future, progressive,* and *perfect.*

| Rules |

1. **Use the present tense to (*a*) indicate present action or state of being; (*b*) state universal or relatively permanent truths, facts, or opinions; (*c*) indicate action that is habitual or customary; (*d*) reflect the historical present; or (*e*) indicate the future.**

Present action or state of being. The primary use of present tense is to describe an action that is happening in the present (now) or to describe a state of being that exists at the present time. For example:

> You *bring* happiness to my life.
> My father *drinks* only soft drinks.
> Julia *is* the new president.
> Mario *is running* for the office of treasurer.

Universal or relatively permanent truths. The funeral speaker who said, ''The man we are eulogizing *was* my uncle,'' did not use the present tense properly. Even though the man is dead, he is still the speaker's uncle. This situation reflects the use of present tense to state universal or relatively permanent truths, facts, or opinions. For example:

> Lincoln *is* the capital of Nebraska.
> My teacher clearly taught that water *seeks* its own level.
> I learned early that two plus two *are* four.

Habitual or customary actions. Regardless of the tense of other verbs in a sentence, the present tense is used to indicate habitual or customary actions. For example:

> When I'm not traveling, I *jog* every day.
> Lolita always *eats* in the company cafeteria.
> Since becoming president, Mr. Bushman *leaves* the office at 4:30 every day.

Historical present. The historical present (sometimes called the *present viewpoint*) is used when we write about happenings in a work of literature or when we quote or paraphrase someone who wrote a letter, an article, a book, etc. Novice writers have a tendency to write about such events in the past tense. The novice writer reasons that if the happening has already been written about, it must have happened in the past.

Such incidents are best written about in the present tense. In literature, the rationale for the present tense is that the happenings of literature are unchangeable and therefore are permanently true. The next time we read the play, Hamlet will kill Claudius just like the last time we read the play. Or in an article in *Business Week*, the article and the author's thinking still exist in their present form and are unaffected by time. For example:

> Lucifer and the legions of evil *are* always exerting forces upon the unsuspecting Faustus.
> In his memorandum, Mr. Brown *states* that we *are* the employees who will move to Boston next spring.

Future time. The present tense is often used to express future time in relation to the present. For example:

We *need* your report by Friday.
Tomorrow I *go* (or *will go*) to Bryce Canyon National Park.
As soon as Ms. Hall *arrives*, we will begin the meeting.

2. **Use the past tense to express past time.**

Obviously, the past tense describes an action or state of being that occurred some time in the past. We normally use the past tense with relative ease.

We do, however, need to be careful in using the past-tense form, rather than the past participle, for the past tense. That is, we use the past participle, not the past tense, with helping verbs to form other tenses. Regular verbs cause us no difficulty because the past tense and past participle are the same. However, the irregular verbs cause difficulties such as the following:

NO   I *have went* to my last executive committee meeting.
       We *done* a good job selecting the candidate.

YES   I *have gone* to my last executive committee meeting.
       We *did* a good job selecting the candidate.

We also must watch that we do not confuse past tense with present-perfect tense. Remember that the present-perfect tense describes an action that may have started some time in the past but that continues up to, and perhaps through, the present. For example:

I *worked* at Thiokol for ten years. (past tense)
I *have worked* at Thiokol for ten years. (present-perfect tense)

Use of past tense in the first sentence implies that I no longer work at Thiokol. The present-perfect tense in the second sentence signals that I still work at Thiokol.

I *lost* my glasses. (The past tense signals that I lost the glasses some time in the past and that I may or may not have found them.)

I *have lost* my glasses. (The present-perfect tense extends the action into the present, so the reader can safely assume the glasses are still missing.)

3. **Use the future tense to indicate that an action will take place some time in the future or that a state or condition will exist some time in the future.**

We form future tense by placing *will* or *shall* before the present-tense form of the verb. For example:

I *will be* attending the meeting on Friday. (a simple statement of condition for the future)

Employees *shall* not *take* food into the conference room. (a statement of action that carries the weight of a command for the future)

A few years ago, conventions of usage prescribed specific instances when *will* and *shall* were to be used. Today, the distinction between the two has largely disappeared.

However, some writers continue to use *will* to express ordinary future tense and *shall* to emphasize something to indicate a determination (much like a command) that something must be done or must not be done. That is, to some writers, *will* is used to express the simple future;

Some writers also advocate that we should use *shall* with the first person and *will* with the second and third persons. However, to express anger or other strong emotions, we should use *will* with first person and *shall* with second and third persons.

In the exercises, we recommend either that you use *will* in all situations or that you distinguish between *will* and *shall* according to the above conventions.

4. **Within a sentence, avoid illogical shifts from one tense to another.**

A "shift in tense" occurs when a writer changes from one tense to another within the sentence. An **illogical** shift in tense results if the relationship of the tenses is not logical. For example:

> I *observed* him as he *keyboards* the material. (The shift is an illogical one from past tense to present tense.)

> Rico *intercepts* the pass and *shoots*, but he *missed*. (The shift is an illogical one from present tense to past tense—the most common illogical shift.)

Obviously, the way to correct an illogical shift is to change one of the verb forms so the same tense is used to talk about the same time.

Some shifts are logical. For example:

> Columbus *discovered* that the earth *is* round. (The logical shift from past tense to present tense reflects the permanent truth of the earth's roundness.)

> Dr. Ralph *said*, "I *will participate* in the debate." (This is a logical shift from past tense to future tense.)

Posttest

Mark the sentence **C** if all elements of tense are correct; mark the sentence **I** if any element of tense is incorrect.

1. I heard on the evening news that interest rates raised unexpectedly today.

2. Ned brought in the order on Monday, so Mr. Kirkham took us to dinner Tuesday evening.

3. The reason I returned the fan is that the on-off switch was broken.

4. Frankly, Bart dealt me the worst poker hands I've ever seen.

5. The accident occurred in front of my house yesterday, and the ambulance gets there in less than 15 minutes.

6. We were delighted with the results when we saw the finished project you supervised.

7. The new painter we hired paints the entire living room by the time Maria returned.

Key: (1) I—use intransitive past tense *rose*; (2) C; (3) I—use present tense *is* to signal a permanent truth; (4) I—use past tense *dealt*; (5) I—change *gets* to *got* to eliminate the shift in tense from past to present; (6) C; (7) I—correct the shift in

LEVEL A

Name _____

Exercise 10–1   On the lines below, write **T** if the statement is true and **F** if the statement is false.

_F_   1. "The dead person *was* my brother" is a correct application of past tense.

_F_   2. The primary use of present tense is to state habitual or customary actions.

_T_   3. Present tense can be used to express future time.

_T_   4. "I have went to great lengths to solve the problem" reflects incorrect use of the past participle.

_F_   5. Past-perfect tense is used to describe an action that was started and completed in the past.

_T_   6. Future tense is formed by using *will* or *shall* before the present tense form of the verb.

_F_   7. To express anger or other strong emotions, we use *shall* with first person and *will* with second and third persons.

_T_   8. "Kris *learned* that Kaminaljuyu *is* in Guatemala City" reflects a logical shift in tense.

_F_   9. "Roman *watched* Teresa as she *conducts* the meeting" reflects a logical shift in tense.

_F_   10. The verb property that tells when an action took place is known as *voice*.

Exercise 10–2   Write the **past tense** of each verb in parentheses.

Sold   1. Harmon's Pontiac (sell) the demonstrator cars.

rang   2. Mr. Marshall (ring) the bell to start the event.

took   3. Sally (take) the deposit to First Security Bank.

paid   4. After Jose received his wages, he (pay) all his bills.

saw   5. While I was there, I (see) the portfolio on June's desk.

Chose   6. Eleanor (choose) to attend the College of Eastern Utah.

wore   7. Nedra (wear) her new formal to the dance on Friday.

met   8. Coach Edwards (meet) with the new football recruits this morning.

swam   9. Paul (swim) a mile the first time he began his exercise program.

climbed   10. Richard (climb) the tree to pick the last apples.

Exercise
10–3

Mark **C** if no illogical shift in tense is evident; mark **I** if the sentence contains an illogical shift in tense.

_I_ 1. I worried because I hear nothing for two weeks.

_I_ 2. When Mr. Acuna entered, the audience rises.

_I_ 3. The Records Office evaluates my application and decided to admit me.

_C_ 4. For four years in a row, I attended summer camp; and I enjoyed every minute of the experiences.

_I_ 5. After I was at Lake Powell for two weeks, I receive word that Mr. Western offers me a job.

_C_ 6. Franz commented that his father, whom we met recently, is from Berlin.

_I_ 7. We learned that Ms. Valgardson was the person who uses the copy machine after hours.

_I_ 8. He walks to his office today and noticed the flowering shrubs for the first time.

_C_ 9. What is the name of the book representative who just left your office?

_I_ 10. When Val was a young man, he enrolls for evening courses at Henagar Business College.

Exercise
10–4

Write **C** if the correct past-tense, present-tense, or future-tense verbs are used. Write **I** if incorrect verbs are used.

_I_ 1. Mayor Jenkins issued a news release at the next City Council meeting.

_I_ 2. Yes, Ms. Sonderegger has mailed the Brighton contract yesterday.

_I_ 3. Ms. Gruwell demonstrates the WordPerfect® software to us tomorrow morning.

_I_ 4. Prior to last Monday, we always will submit our travel requests to Ms. Marshall.

_C_ 5. In six months, I shall attend my son's graduation ceremony.

_I_ 6. Whenever you will treat a customer with courtesy, you create goodwill.

_C_ 7. Yes, members of my staff investigated the Carmichael incident last month.

_I_ 8. On Monday, I process all the resumes we received last week.

_I_ 9. Presently, our accountant periodically will require us to submit our books to him for review.

_C_ 10. As you suspected, each of the Idaho Falls sales reps received a large year-end bonus.

LEVEL B

Name _____

Exercise 10–6   Underline the verb or verb phrase in each sentence. Then write **Past, Present, or Future** to identify any simple tense you have underlined. Nothing will be written on some of the blanks.

_____ 1. The installer <u>will have completed</u> the installation of your air-conditioning system by noon tomorrow.

Present 2. We <u>are</u> pleased to have the opportunity to share experiences with you.

Future 3. Who <u>will be</u> in charge of the meetings during Ms. Kroeger's absence?

Present 4. <u>Does</u> the city <u>give</u> you the option of having either one or two of the new trash containers?

Past 5. Neither Ms. Francis nor Ms. Turnbull <u>was</u> present at Tuesday's meeting.

Past 6. Whom <u>did</u> Mr. Aidukaitis <u>advise</u> you to contact for assistance with your tax return?

Future 7. We <u>will consider</u> carefully every suggestion from Mr. Blanchard and Ms. Bishop.

_____ 8. Mr. Albawab <u>will have cashed</u> the check before Monday.

_____ 9. The bridge over the creek <u>had collapsed</u> once before.

_____ 10. You <u>will be given</u> more responsibility in the future.

Exercise 10–7   Write the letter that identifies the sentence containing a simple-tense verb.

c 1. *a.* I wish you had notified Mr. Allred yesterday.
   b. Margie has left good instructions for completing the project.
   c. We were denied admission to the county fair.

a 2. *a.* Margie always seeks my recommendations for fun-and-games ideas.
   b. Our employees will have been paid their bonuses before the Christmas vacation.
   c. Brighton High and Skyline High have competed with each other in football for 25 years.

b 3. *a.* Ms. Allsup has applied for the job two times in the past year.
   b. The investments will pay you handsome dividends.
   c. Both Ms. Barnes and Ms. Beeson have been successful in using the new learning laboratory.

a 4. *a.* Julie is given every opportunity to decide the dates for her yearly vacations.
   b. David would have been given more responsibility if you had recommended that possibility.
   c. We have ordered new posture chairs for all of the new employees.

_a_ 5. _a._ I am annoyed by the actions of the employees in the shipping room.
   _b._ We will have shipped your order by the first of the month.
   _c._ We have already shipped a partial order via Acme Fast Freight.

Exercise Write the letter that identifies the sentence with the correct tense(s).
10–8

_a_ 1. _a._ The police ringed the building while the detectives searched it.
   _b._ Eric is the person who brang the cheese crisps for everyone.
   _c._ As you can well imagine, Lisa has spended more money than she should have spent.

_c_ 2. _a._ When the race was over, the runners layed down on the grass and rested.
   _b._ Seeing that Stewart had swam the river, we decided to swim across ourselves.
   _c._ Andrea correctly noted that Sacramento is the capital of California.

_b_ 3. _a._ In his memo, Mr. Cahoon states that we were the employees who raised the issue.
   _b._ On April 22, we will leave to spend a week in New England.
   _c._ As of last month, I will have worked at the hardware store for ten years.

_b_ 4. _a._ You should have seen what I seen when I went to the circus.
   _b._ When the party began to get wild, we knew that the fun had just begun.
   _c._ My friend drunk continuously all evening but assured me that he would not get drunk.

_a_ 5. _a._ Since her promotion, Ms. Chao expects us to take no more than a half-hour lunch break.
   _b._ When I'm not on company business, I swam each night in the hotel pool.
   _c._ Although the bell rung, the students refused to come in after recess.

Exercise For each verb on the left, write the correct simple tenses on the lines that follow the
10–9   verb.

	Past	**Present**	**Future**
1. order	I _ordered_	you _order_	we _will order_
2. keeps	we _Kept_	she _Keeps_	they _will Keep_
3. stole	you _stole_	we _steal_	it _will steal_
4. won	he _won_	I _win_	you _will win_
5. tears	they _tore_	it _tears_	I _will tear_
6. seen	it _saw_	they _see_	he _will see_
7. went	she _went_	you _go_	they _will go_
8. sang	I _Sang_	he _sings_	she _will sing_
9. bring	you _brought_	I _bring_	we _will bring_
10. drives	he _drove_	you _drive_	they _will drive_

LEVEL C

Name _____

Exercise 10–10   Write **C** if the sentence contains only simple-tense verbs; write **I** if the sentence contains verbs other than simple-tense verbs. Then edit all **I** sentences so the verbs are simple-tense verbs.

_I_   1. Dictionaries ~~have differed~~ *differ* not only in the information they include but also in the way they ~~have presented~~ *present* the information.

_C_   2. The best dictionary in the world will be of little value unless you know how to read and how to interpret the information it provides.

_I_   3. The front matter of a dictionary ~~will have explained~~ *explains* the organization of entries.

_I_   4. You will ~~have looked~~ *look* carefully at a dictionary page of entries to see how words and phrases are handled.

_C_   5. A little time spent in learning to use your dictionary can make it very useful to you.

_I_   6. Your dictionary will ~~have given~~ *give* two spellings for a word when usage ~~has been~~ *is* divided.

_I_   7. Dictionaries ~~have divided~~ *divide* words into units by means of small dots or spaces.

_I_   8. Word-division techniques ~~had enabled~~ *enable* you to see each part of the word clearly.

_I_   9. In writing, we ~~will have divided~~ *divide* a word at the end of a line only where the dictionary ~~will have shown~~ *shows* a division.

_I_   10. Because English ~~has shown~~ *shows* itself to be phonetically inconsistent, dictionaries ~~have used~~ *use* a system of special symbols to show how words ~~have been~~ *are* pronounced.

_C_   11. The pronunciation key at the bottom of the page will illustrate, with familiar words, the sounds represented by the symbols.

_I_ 12. Dictionaries often ~~have listed~~ _list_ two or more pronunciations for a word when usage will ~~have been~~ _is_ divided.

_I_ 13. Although the first pronunciation ~~has~~ usually ~~been~~ _is_ the more common one, it will not necessarily be preferred by all writers.

_I_ 14. Dictionaries ~~will~~ _are_ often ~~be~~ considered important for what they ~~have told~~ _tell_ us about the meanings of words.

_I_ 15. To a reader, a dictionary will ~~have been~~ _be_ used for finding the meanings not only of unfamiliar words but also of familiar words that will ~~have been~~ _be_ used in new senses.

_C_ 16. In looking for the meaning of a word in context, you must ordinarily isolate the right group of definitions before you can find the meaning for which you are looking.

_I_ 17. Some dictionaries ~~had given~~ _give_ the oldest meaning first, and other dictionaries ~~had given~~ _give_ the most common one.

_I_ 18. At the end of the entry, you ~~shall have found~~ _will find_ one or more idioms listed.

_I_ 19. My dictionary ~~has required~~ _requires_ or ~~has forbidden~~ _forbids_ a particular meaning or use of a word.

_C_ 20. You must exercise judgment in deciding whether a particular word will be appropriate in a particular context.

_I_ 21. A dictionary definition ~~has been~~ _is_, for the most part, a record of the specific meaning of a word.

_I_ 22. Most dictionaries ~~will have included~~ _include_ frequently used words and expressions from foreign languages.

Exercise 10–11   Compose sentences that contain the requested verbs.

Compo-
sition

1. The past-tense forms of *ride* and *shake*

   _____

   _____

2. The future-tense forms of *meet* and *sell*

   _____

   _____

3. The present-tense forms of *shake* and *shine*

   _____

   _____

4. The past-tense forms of *throw* and *spend*

   _____

   _____

5. The future-tense forms of *sing* and *sleep*

   _____

   _____

Exercise 10–12   Edit the following sentences to make all the verbs in each sentence coincide with the simple tense shown in parentheses. Also, edit the sentences to reflect material from Lessons 1 through 10.

Cumula-
tive
Editing

1. ~~Accept~~ *Except* in questions, I ~~percieved~~ *perceive* that verbs usually ~~will have followed~~ *follow* the subject. (present)

2. In meaning, ~~you're~~ *your* verbs ~~have indicated~~ *indicate* Action, Condition, or Process. (present)

3. ~~Incidently~~ *Incidentally*, each ~~Principle Verb~~ *principal verb* ~~will have been~~ *had* one word or a phrase and ~~may add~~ *added* letters or ~~change~~ *changed* internally to indicate Person, ~~No.~~ *number*, Tense, and Voice. (past)

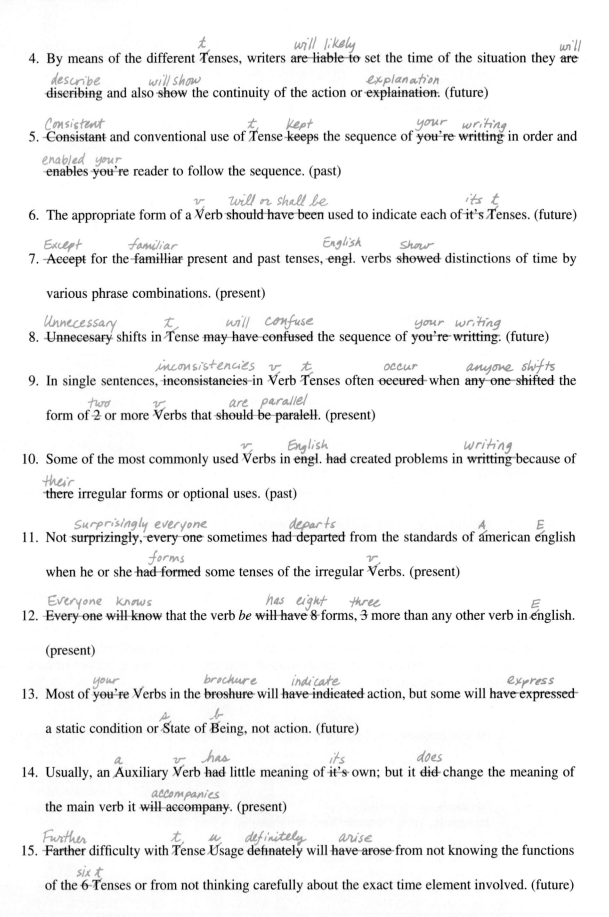

4. By means of the different ~~t~~ Tenses, writers ~~are liable to~~ *will likely* set the time of the situation they ~~are~~ *will*
~~discribing~~ *describe* and also ~~show~~ *will show* the continuity of the action or ~~explaination.~~ *explanation.* (future)

5. ~~Consistant~~ *Consistent* and conventional use of ~~t~~ Tense ~~keeps~~ *kept* the sequence of ~~you're writting~~ *your writing* in order and
~~enables you're~~ *enabled your* reader to follow the sequence. (past)

6. The appropriate form of a ~~v~~ Verb ~~should have been~~ *will or shall be* used to indicate each of ~~it's~~ *its* ~~t~~ Tenses. (future)

7. ~~Accept~~ *Except* for the ~~familliar~~ *familiar* present and past tenses, ~~engl.~~ *English* verbs ~~showed~~ *show* distinctions of time by
various phrase combinations. (present)

8. ~~Unnecesary~~ *Unnecessary* shifts in ~~t~~ Tense ~~may have confused~~ *will confuse* the sequence of ~~you're writting.~~ *your writing.* (future)

9. In single sentences, ~~inconsistancies~~ *inconsistencies* in ~~v~~ Verb ~~t~~ Tenses often ~~occured~~ *occur* when ~~any one shifted~~ *anyone shifts* the
form of ~~2~~ *two* or more ~~v~~ Verbs that ~~should be paralell.~~ *are parallel.* (present)

10. Some of the most commonly used ~~v~~ Verbs in ~~engl.~~ *English* ~~had created~~ problems in ~~writting~~ *writing* because of
~~there~~ *their* irregular forms or optional uses. (past)

11. Not ~~surprizingly, every one~~ *Surprisingly everyone* sometimes ~~had departed~~ *departs* from the standards of ~~american~~ *A*merican ~~english~~ *E*nglish
when he or she ~~had formed~~ *forms* some tenses of the irregular ~~v~~ Verbs. (present)

12. ~~Every one will know~~ *Everyone knows* that the verb *be* ~~will have 8~~ *has eight* forms, ~~3~~ *three* more than any other verb in ~~english.~~ *E*nglish.

(present)

13. Most of ~~you're~~ *your* Verbs in the ~~broshure~~ *brochure* will ~~have indicated~~ *indicate* action, but some will ~~have expressed~~ *express*
a static condition or ~~S~~tate of ~~B~~eing, not action. (future)

14. Usually, an ~~A~~uxiliary ~~v~~ Verb ~~had~~ *has* little meaning of ~~it's~~ *its* own; but it ~~did~~ *does* change the meaning of
the main verb it ~~will accompany.~~ *accompanies.* (present)

15. ~~Farther~~ *Further* difficulty with ~~t~~ Tense ~~u~~ Usage ~~definately~~ *definitely* will ~~have arose~~ *arise* from not knowing the functions
of the ~~6~~ *six* ~~t~~ Tenses or from not thinking carefully about the exact time element involved. (future)

THE PERFECT TENSES AND PROGRESSIVE FORMS

The Perfect Tenses.   As you know, *tense* refers to the form of the verb that indicates time. You also know that the concept of *perfect* applied to tense means the action is *perfected* or *completed*. On a time continuum, actions in a perfect tense are perfected or completed before actions in a corresponding simple tense. You form all the perfect tenses by using one or more helping verbs with the past participle of the verb.

Table 11–1 shows the time framework and the formation procedures for the perfect tenses. Memorize this table if you want to master the perfect tenses.

The Progressive Forms of the Six Tenses.   Each of the six tenses has a companion form called the *progressive form.* As its name implies, the progressive signals that the action named by the verb is a continued or a progressive action at the time of the verb tense. Although not truly a tense, the progressive shows how an ongoing action occurred at the time of any tense.

We might view the present participle as the fourth principal verb part. For any tense, the progressive form uses the proper form of *be* plus the *present participle* of a verb as the main verb. For example, the progressive forms of the verb *to walk* are as follows:

Use T11-1 here

Table 11–1		
The Time Framework and the Formation of Perfect Tenses		
	Past-Perfect	**Present-Perfect**	**Future-Perfect**
Time	Action was started and completed in the past before some other past action.	Action was started in the past and continues in the present.	Action will be completed in the future in relation to another event.
Form	Use **had** + past participle.	Use **have** or **has** + past participle.	Use **will** or **shall** + **have** + past participle.

Present tense: I am walking; he is walking

Present-perfect tense: I have been walking; he has been walking

Past tense: I was walking; he was walking

Past-perfect tense: I had been walking; he had been walking

Future tense: I shall be walking; he will be walking

Future-perfect tense: I shall have been walking; he will have been walking

As you can see, the present participle is always the main verb; and the form of *be* always appears before it as a helper.

Because tense is time, the progressive is merely an alternative form showing *how* as well as *when* an action occurs. For example, notice the progression of time in the following tenses of *walk*:

Past-Perfect	Past	Present-Perfect	Present	Future	Future-Perfect
John *had walked*	John *walked*	John *has walked*	John *walks*	John *will walk*	John *will have walked*
John *had been walking*	John *was walking*	John *has been walking*	John *is walking*	John *will be walking*	John *will have been walking*

Thus, if we substitute the progressive form for a simple or a perfect tense, we show that the action is continuing during the time of the tense:

Use T11-2 here (handwritten note in margin)

Mary *talks* on the phone.
Mary *is talking* on the phone.

Mary *has taken* her examination.
Mary *has been taking* her examination.

By June, Mary *will have worked* for six months.
By June, Mary *will have been working* for six months.

Pretest

Mark the sentence **C** if all elements of tense are correct; mark the sentence **I** if any element of tense is incorrect.

1. Zeke has completed his research last Friday and will have been sending you the results next Thursday.

2. When Wendell had returned, Martha had finished preparing the notes for his presentation.

3. We will have examined the manuscript carefully by the time you arrive next Monday.

4. Abraham was researching the report as thoroughly as he can.

5. Peter is researching the report when he noticed the errors you made.

6. Leila will be checking with you periodically to see if you need additional resources.

7. Roscoe will be translating the document into Spanish last week when I spoke to him, and he will have already translated it into French before he started the Spanish translation.

Key: (1) I—use past tense *completed* and future tense *will send*; (2) I—use the past tense *returned* so the past perfect *had finished* can occur in proper sequence; (3) C; (4) I—use the present progressive *is researching*; (5) I—use the past progressive *was researching*; (6) C; (7) I—use past-perfect tenses *had translated* and *had* already *translated* to avoid a shift in tense and to show these actions were completed before other actions in the sentence. (Other alternatives are possible for some of the sentences.)

Terminology

Past participle—A verb form that typically ends in *-d* or *-ed* in the case of regular verbs (as in *filed* and *watched*) or that is irregularly formed in the case of irregular verbs (as in *seen* and *sung*).

Perfect participle—A verb form consisting of *having* plus the past participle (as in *having filed* and *having watched*).

Perfect tenses—The time of a verb's action denoting that the action is completed or perfected.

Present participle—A verb form that ends in *-ing* (as in *using* and *making*). The present participle is formed when *-ing* is added to the present-tense verb.

Progressive form—A verb phrase that consists of a present participle used with a form of *be* and that denotes continuous action.

Rules

1.   Use the past participle to form the perfect tenses.

The **present-perfect tense** is formed with *have* or *has* plus the past participle. The present perfect signals two actions:

First, action just completed at the present time:

> Mr. Bush *has* just *arrived* at the hotel.
>
> We *have worked* on the report this morning.

Second, action that began in the past and that continues into the present:

> I *have been* a Thiokol employee for ten years. (and still am)
>
> Zeke *has held* the job for six years. (and still does)

Be wary of such present-perfect tense illogical thinking as the following:

> NO   The druggist *has filled* the prescription last week.
>   We *have completed* the project yesterday.

YES The druggist *has filled* the prescription.
The druggist *filled* the prescription last week.
We *have completed* the project.
We *completed* the project yesterday.

The **past-perfect tense** is formed with *had* plus the past participle. The past perfect signals action that was completed *before another past action*. **We use the past perfect when we need to show that two actions happened at different times in the past.**

I *had finished* (past-perfect tense) reading the report before you *reached* (past tense) the office.

I already *had mailed* the letter when you *called*.

If we are merely showing that one action happened in the past, we use past tense rather than past-perfect tense. When we use past-perfect tense rather than past tense for such instances, we find ourselves feeling the need to add something to the sentence to complete its meaning. For example:

NO I *had finished reading* the report. (before you reached the office?)
I already *had mailed* the letter. (when you called?)

YES I *finished reading* the report.
I already *mailed* the letter.

Distinguish carefully between past tense and past-perfect tense. To do so, remember that the past tense describes an event that happened at any time in the past. Remember further that the past-perfect tense must describe an event that happened *before* another event in the past. For example:

When I *returned*, Wilma *finished* the report. (The two past-tense verbs signal that both actions happened at about the same time in the past.)

When I *returned*, Wilma *had finished* the report. (Although both actions occurred in the past, the past perfect *had finished* signals that this action was completed before the past-tense action.)

The **future-perfect tense** is formed with *shall have* or *will have* plus the past participle. The future perfect names an action or condition that will be completed by (or before) some specified time in the future. For example:

I *will have been* a Thiokol employee for ten years next Monday.

We *will have filled* all the orders by 10 a.m.

In summary, the perfect tenses are formed as follows:

past-perfect: *had* + past participle

present-perfect: *have* or *has* + past participle

future-perfect: *will* or *shall* + *have* + past participle

2.   **Use the present participle to form the progressive tenses.**

The **present-progressive tense** indicates action still in progress and consists of the verbs *am, is,* or *are* plus the present participle. For example:

Wesley *is writing* the report as rapidly as he can.

The **past-progressive tense** indicates action in progress sometime in the past and consists of the verb *was* or *were* plus the present participle. For example:

Ms. Padre *was trying* to find a job when she contacted me.

The **future-progressive tense** indicates action that will be in progress in the future and consists of the verb *will be* or *shall be* plus the present participle. For example:

We *will be working* with you for about two weeks.

The **present-perfect-progressive**, the **past-perfect-progressive**, and the **future-perfect-progressive** tenses coincide with the simple-perfect tenses. They express an action that was or will be completed at the time of another action and express a continuing action. These tenses consist of the present participle plus the verbs *has been, have been, had been, will have been,* and *shall have been.* For example:

We *have been shipping* the new model since January 1. (present-perfect-progressive)

We *had been shipping* the new model until we received your letter. (past-perfect-progressive)

By July 1, we *will have been shipping* the new model for six months. (future-perfect-progressive)

3.   **Within a sentence, avoid illogical shifts from one tense to another.**

As you learned in Lesson 10, a shift in tense occurs when you change from one tense to another within a sentence. An **illogical** shift in tense results if the relationship of the tenses is not logical. Problems with illogical shifts are compounded when you must make decisions among simple, perfect, and progressive forms. For example:

I *will be observing* him as he *has keyboarded* the material. (The shift is an illogical one from future-progressive to present-perfect.)

Rico *had intercepted* the pass and shot, but he *will miss.* (The shift is an illogical one from past-perfect to future.)

As you learned in Lesson 10, the way to correct an illogical shift in tense is to change one or more of the verb forms so the time periods reflected in the verbs are logical.

Posttest

Mark the sentence **C** if all elements of tense are correct; mark the sentence **I** if any element of tense is incorrect. Then correct the tenses in all sentences that are incorrect.

1. The budget committee will have reviewed the snow-removal appropriations by the time the City Council meets next Tuesday.

2. Cinderella was running to her coach as rapidly as she can.

3. J. D. will be speaking in Dallas last week when I called him, and he will have already spoken in San Antonio before he spoke in Dallas.

4. Sue Ellen had jogged twice in the park last week and will be jogging one more time next Thursday.

5. Bentley will be working part time while he goes to summer school.

6. While Arturo had been cleaning the fish, Antonio finishes the preparations for cooking the meal.

7. Marsha is comparing the group means when she realized the procedure error we made.

Key: (1) C; (2) I—use present tense *runs* and present tense *can run* to report the tenses in a literary event; (3) I—use past-perfect *had spoken* and past-perfect *had* already *spoken* to avoid shifts in tense and to show that the events in the past-perfect tenses occurred before the events in the past tenses; (4) I—use past tense *jogged* and future tense *will jog*; (5) C—could also be *will work*; (6) I—use past progressive *was cleaning* and past tense *finished*, or use past tense *cleaned* and past tense *finished*, or use present tense *cleans* and future tense *will finish*, or use present tense *cleans* and present tense *finishes* if you are writing about a literary event; (7) I—use past-progressive *was comparing* with past tense *realized*. (Other alternatives are possible for some of the sentences.)

LEVEL A

Name _____

Exercise 11-1 On the lines below, write **T** if the statement is true and **F** if the statement is false.

_F_ 1. On a time continuum, actions in a perfect tense are completed after actions in a corresponding simple tense.

_F_ 2. Past-perfect tense is formed with *have* or *has* plus the past participle.

_T_ 3. Each of the six tenses has a companion form called the progressive form.

_T_ 4. The progressive form uses the proper form of *be* plus the present participle of a verb as the main verb.

_F_ 5. "John will have been walking" is an example of past perfect progressive.

_T_ 6. The present-perfect tense is used to show action just completed at the present time.

_T_ 7. The present-perfect tense is used to show action that began in the past and that continues into the present.

_F_ 8. We use the past-perfect tense to show that two actions happened at the same time in the past.

_F_ 9. The past participle is used to form the progressive tenses.

_T_ 10. The present-progressive tense consists of the verbs *am, is,* or *are* plus the present participle.

Exercise 11-2 Mark **A** or **B** to show the correct choice that answers the question.

_B_ 1. Which sentence indicates that Ms. Grimley is no longer office manager?
A. When the celebration begins, Ms. Grimley will have been office manager for five years.
B. When the celebration begins, Ms. Grimley would have been office manager for five years.

_B_ 2. Which sentence shows that Cherie continues to obey her father?
A. Because she wishes to please her father, Cherie had obeyed him faithfully.
B. Because she wishes to please her father, Cherie has obeyed him faithfully.

_A_ 3. Which sentence shows that Erik improved his attendance record?
A. Because Erik had been constantly late for work, he had been a problem to Mr. Roberts.
B. Because Erik had been constantly late for work, he was a problem to Mr. Roberts.

_B_ 4. Which sentence indicates that Que decided not to attend before the meeting began?
A. Because the City Council meeting would already be in session, Que has decided not to attend.
B. Because the City Council meeting would already have been in session, Que had decided not to attend.

_A_ 5. Which sentence implies that the conversation is still going on?
   A. Does Oprah know how long she has been talking with Sam?
   B. Does Oprah know how long she had been talking with Sam?

Exercise 11–3 Mark **C** if all verb tenses are correct; mark **I** if any tense is incorrect.

_I_ 1. After I have answered the request for a quotation, I sent the information to Mr. Wesley.

_C_ 2. Jeannie will have received notification of her acceptance before she receives her diploma.

_I_ 3. Mrs. Cox will be telephoning Mr. Cox before he had arrived at the office.

_I_ 4. The error in the invoice had been discovered after the mail was picked up for the day.

_C_ 5. We discovered the error in the invoice while UPS was picking up the package.

_I_ 6. I will be mastering the software when I had received adequate guidance in using it.

_I_ 7. Before the inventory is taken, I had made several suggestions for expediting the procedures.

_I_ 8. Dr. Crandall will have been teaching for 30 years before he is retiring.

_C_ 9. After Johnny had been late three days in a row, Ms. Hardy finally reprimanded him.

_I_ 10. Mr. Dixon will be remembering that he will have been teaching the square dance to us.

Exercise 11–4 Mark **A** if the first verb is correct; mark **B** if the second verb is correct.

_B_ 1. The flag was (risen, raised) when the celebration began.

_A_ 2. I will be (laying, lying) the finished report on your desk tomorrow morning.

_B_ 3. Be sure to bring the stapler that is (setting, sitting) on the outer office desk.

_B_ 4. I barely had (layed, laid) my briefcase down when Mr. Hansen called me to the podium.

_B_ 5. After I had (laid, lain) down for about ten minutes, my headache went away.

_A_ 6. The moon will be (rising, raising) over the mountain while you tell your campfire stories.

_A_ 7. Before Clyde reaches the finish line, Henry (will have passed, passed) him.

_B_ 8. We (will have done, will be doing) everything we can for our uncle before his death.

_A_ 9. We (had written, are writing) letters to our sister before her birthday last May 10.

_A_ 10. My dad certainly (will spend, had spent) a lot of time in front of his television set before the football season ends.

LEVEL B

Name _____

Exercise 11–5 Using the list below, write the letter that identifies the tense of the verb form shown.

A   Simple-past
B   Simple-present
C   Simple-future
D   Past-perfect

E   Present-perfect
F   Future-perfect
G   Past-progressive
H   Present-progressive

I   Future-progressive
J   Past-perfect-progressive
K   Present-perfect-progressive
L   Future-perfect-progressive

_A_ 1. froze
_B_ 2. hide
_F_ 3. will have sunk
_K_ 4. has been stealing
_L_ 5. will have been riding
_A_ 6. drank
_E_ 7. has identified
_G_ 8. was dealing
_J_ 9. had been thinking
_H_ 10. am progressing
_C_ 11. will be sold
_L_ 12. shall have been seeking
_H_ 13. is seeking
_F_ 14. will have overflowed
_C_ 15. will be underwritten

_A_ 16. overdid
_B_ 17. speaks
_J_ 18. had been teaching
_E_ 19. has transpired
_D_ 20. had wept
_I_ 21. shall be seeking
_H_ 22. is taking
_E_ 23. have preferred
_A_ 24. thought
_B_ 25. throw
_E_ 26. has taken
_A_ 27. flung
_A,B_ 28. set
_D_ 29. had given
_J_ 30. had been holding

Exercise 11–6 Each bold verb is in the present-perfect tense. On the lines below, change each verb to the past-perfect tense and then to the future-perfect tense.

	Past-Perfect	**Future-Perfect**
1. Some runners **have finished** already.	had finished	will have finished
2. The secretary **has identified** the error.	had identified	will have identified
3. She **has screened** the incoming calls.	had screened	will have screened
4. We **have kept** very accurate records.	had kept	will have kept

	Past-Perfect	**Future-Perfect**
5. Jack **has promised** no such thing!	had promised	will have promised
6. The customers **have visited** our store.	had visited	will have visited
7. The wait **has seemed** like an eternity.	had seemed	will have seemed
8. Virginia **has given** her approval.	had given	will have given

Exercise 11–7 On the lines below, write the tense that is requested for each verb.

	Past-Perfect	**Past-Perfect-Progressive**	**Future-Perfect-Progressive**
1. dig	had dug	had been digging	will have been digging
2. slide	had slid	had been sliding	will have been sliding
3. catch	had caught	had been catching	will have been catching
4. kneel	had knelt	had been kneeling	will have been kneeling
5. split	had split	had been splitting	will have been splitting
6. bid	had bid	had been bidding	will have been bidding
7. eat	had eaten	had been eating	will have been eating
8. lay	had laid	had been laying	will have been laying

Exercise 11–8 Write the letter that identifies the sentence containing correct verb tense(s).

_a_ 1. _a._ I have enjoyed learning about the effects of radiation.
    _b._ Until I researched the effects of tanning, I will have been an avid sunbather.
    _c._ I will have been looking forward to your critique of my work next week.

_b_ 2. _a._ His report exposes the effects of tanning and will offer suggestions to counteract those effects.
    _b._ Mr. Shorts said that tanning is becoming a serious issue.
    _c._ Millions of people will have taken beach vacations next summer.

_c_ 3. _a._ The radiation absorbed by the body will have been returned in the future as a form of skin cancer.
    _b._ Many parts of my body had been affected when I expose it to the sun.
    _c._ About half a million new cases of skin cancer occur each year.

_b_ 4. _a._ People should be covering their bodies when they have gone to the beach.
    _b._ You should avoid exposing your skin to the sun between 10 a.m. and 2 p.m.
    _c._ Early detection of skin cancer was a skill that Dr. Stanton possesses.

LEVEL C

Name _____

Exercise 11–9   Mark **C** if all tenses are correct in the sentence. Mark **I** if any tense is incorrect. Then edit all incorrect tenses. (Some answers may vary depending on your perceived time perspective.)

_I_   1. Recent research ~~will have been revealing~~ *reveals* that tanning ~~was~~ *is* not a healthy habit.

_I_   2. Some doctors have ~~went~~ *gone* so far as to say, ''Americans are addicted to tanning—and the result ~~was~~ *is* an epidemic of skin cancer.''

_I_   3. Although many detrimental effects are caused by overexposure to the sun, skin cancer ~~will have been~~ *is* the most serious.

_I_   4. When ultraviolet B rays penetrate the skin, cells ~~are producing~~ *produce* melanin, a pigment that rises to the surface and ~~will have been~~ *is* visible as a tan.

_C_   5. Getting too much sun too quickly denies your skin the chance to produce enough melanin.

_I_   6. Although no health benefits ~~had been~~ *are* derived from tanning, many health threats exist.

_I_   7. Children who get a bad sunburn ~~had doubled~~ *double* their chances of developing malignant melanoma later in life.

_I_   8. Many sunbathers ~~will have been~~ *are* unwilling to give up tanning.

_I_   9. The edges of basal cell carcinoma often ~~will be exhibiting~~ *exhibit* spidery red lines, and the tumor may appear translucent or pearly.

_I_   10. As the tumor ~~will have been increasing~~ *increases* in size, its surface usually ~~has become~~ *becomes* more irregular.

Exercise 11–10   Compose sentences that contain the verb tenses shown.

Composition

1. Present perfect progressive of fly

_____

_____

2. Future perfect of seek

_____

_____

3. Past perfect of loosen

_____

_____

4. Future perfect progressive of steal

_____

_____

5. Present perfect of sing

_____

_____

6. Past perfect progressive of ride

_____

_____

Exercise 11–11   Edit the following sentences to reflect what you have learned from Lessons 3 through 4 and 9 through 11.

Cumulative Editing

1. By the time ~~alot~~ *a lot* of ~~you're~~ *your* typical employees ~~will have retired~~ *retire*, they will ~~earn~~ *have earned $1 million* over ~~$1,000,000~~.

2. I *have* held the position of ~~bookeeper~~ *bookkeeper* for over two years now, and I ~~will be~~ *am* enjoying the job and ~~it's~~ *its* duties immensely.

3. The sales clerk told me she ~~all ready~~ [already] sold the last computer that ~~will be advertized~~ [was advertised] in the ~~catalogue~~ [catalog].

4. We ~~percieved~~ [perceived] immediately that Ms. Underhill, our former vice ~~principle~~ [principal], ~~was~~ [is] easier to get along with than Mr. Ross.

5. The students in Apartment 3 have ~~payed there maintainance~~ [paid their maintenance] fees and ~~began~~ [have begun] to pack for ~~there~~ [their] return to California.

6. Arthur ~~sweared~~ [swore] that he had never ~~swam~~ [swum] the Colorado River as ~~your beleiving~~ [you believe] he did.

7. Several years will ~~have past~~ [pass] before I ~~seen~~ [see] the dusty ~~traveller~~ [traveler] again.

8. Before I realized what ~~will be~~ [was] happening, the conductor entered the car, ~~will be taking~~ [took] tickets from passengers, and then ~~ultimately disapeared~~ [eventually disappeared] into the next car.

9. Once we ~~agreed~~ [agree] on our study ~~proceedures~~ [procedures], Nellie will ~~be dispersing~~ [distribute] study assignments to ~~every one~~ [everyone] who ~~will be~~ [is] willing ~~too~~ [to] participate.

10. Once Shelby graduates, he will ~~have been recieving~~ [receive] several job offers at different tourist ~~sights~~ [sites] in Los Angeles.

Exercise 11–12   Edit the following sentences to reflect what you have learned from Lessons 5 through 7 and 9 through 11.

Cumulative Editing

1. The lifetime incidence of malignant melanoma skin cancer ~~will have been going~~ [has gone] from one in every ~~fifteen hundred~~ [1,500] people to ~~one~~ [1] in every ~~one hundred fifty~~ [150]—a ~~10-fold~~ [ten-fold] increase. [Tense desired: began in the past; continues into the present]

2. The ~~5~~ [five]-year survival rate for malignant melanoma ~~had approached~~ [approaches] 100% [percent] if the lesion ~~will have been~~ [is] excised while it is less than ~~.75~~ [0.75] millimeters thick. The rate ~~had dropped~~ [drops] to about 50% [percent] when the lesion ~~was three~~ [is 3] millimeters deep at the time of excision. [Tenses desired: present, recurring, constant events]

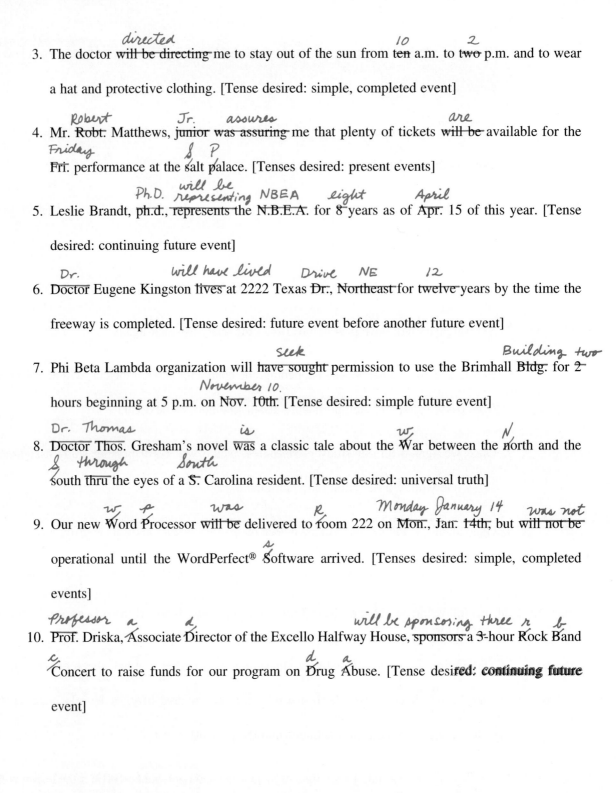

3. The doctor ~~will be directing~~ *directed* me to stay out of the sun from ~~ten~~ *10* a.m. to ~~two~~ *2* p.m. and to wear

   a hat and protective clothing. [Tense desired: simple, completed event]

4. Mr. ~~Robt.~~ *Robert* Matthews, ~~junior~~ *Jr.* ~~was assuring~~ *assures* me that plenty of tickets ~~will be~~ *are* available for the

   ~~Fri.~~ *Friday* performance at the *S* ~~salt~~ *P* ~~palace~~. [Tenses desired: present events]

5. Leslie Brandt, ~~ph.d.~~ *Ph.D.*, ~~represents~~ *will be representing* the ~~N.B.E.A.~~ *NBEA* for ~~8~~ *eight* years as of ~~Apr.~~ *April* 15 of this year. [Tense

   desired: continuing future event]

6. ~~Doctor~~ *Dr.* Eugene Kingston ~~lives~~ *will have lived* at 2222 Texas ~~Dr.~~ *Drive*, ~~Northeast~~ *NE* for ~~twelve~~ *12* years by the time the

   freeway is completed. [Tense desired: future event before another future event]

7. Phi Beta Lambda organization will ~~have sought~~ *seek* permission to use the Brimhall ~~Bldg.~~ *Building* for ~~2~~ *two*

   hours beginning at 5 p.m. on ~~Nov. 10th.~~ *November 10.* [Tense desired: simple future event]

8. ~~Doctor Thos.~~ *Dr. Thomas* Gresham's novel ~~was~~ *is* a classic tale about the *W*~~W~~ar between the *N* ~~north~~ and the

   S ~~south~~ ~~thru~~ *through* the eyes of a ~~S.~~ *South* Carolina resident. [Tense desired: universal truth]

9. Our new *W*~~W~~ord *P*~~P~~rocessor ~~will be~~ *was* delivered to *R*~~r~~oom 222 on ~~Mon., Jan. 14th,~~ *Monday January 14* but ~~will not be~~ *was not*

   operational until the WordPerfect® *S*oftware arrived. [Tenses desired: simple, completed

   events]

10. ~~Prof.~~ *Professor* Driska, *A*~~A~~ssociate *D*~~D~~irector of the Excello Halfway House, ~~sponsors~~ *will be sponsoring* a ~~3~~ *three*-hour *R*~~R~~ock *B*~~B~~and

    C~~C~~oncert to raise funds for our program on *D*~~D~~rug *A*~~A~~buse. [Tense desi~~red: continuing future~~

    event]

A *finite verb* is the principal verb of a sentence or a clause. A finite verb can serve as the only verb of a sentence. On the other hand, a *nonfinite verb* functions as a noun, an adjective, or an adverb. Participles, infinitives, and gerunds are nonfinite verbs known as *verbals*. A nonfinite verb cannot stand as the only verb in a sentence.

Verbals have some of the characteristics of verbs—including tense. Participles have three tenses; gerunds and infinitives both have two tenses. Because verbals reflect time, or tense, we must understand them to deal adequately with some of the rules of tense.

Use T12-1 here

Participles. A participle is a verb form that may function as a part of a verb phrase (was *singing*, had *completed*); as an adjective (the *smoking* car, the *completed* project); or as a nonfinite verb (The chairperson, *smiling* broadly, left the room.).

The participle has three tense forms: present, past, and perfect. Notice how these tenses are formed:

> Present participle: talking, writing
>
> Past participle: talked, written
>
> Perfect participle: having talked, having written

As you now know, the past participle is usually used as part of a verb phrase; we need not spend additional time on the past participle.

The present participle refers to action happening at the *same time* as the action of the main verb. For example:

> Answering the phone, Ben confirms his appointment. (The main verb is in the present tense; therefore, the present participle *answering* carries the idea of present time.)

Answering the phone, Ben confirmed his appointment. (With the change in the tense of the main verb to the past, the time of the participle is also changed to the past.)

The perfect participle refers to action occurring *before* the action of the main verb. For example:

Having finished the report, Ben is planning to leave. (The time reflected in the perfect participle *having finished* took place before the present-tense main verb.)

Having finished the report, Ben was preparing to leave. (The time reflected in the perfect participle *having finished* took place in the past, prior to the past-tense main verb.)

Use T12-2 here

Infinitives. Technically, an infinitive is a present-tense verb; and an infinitive phrase is a present-tense verb preceded by the word *to*. Throughout this textbook, we will mean *infinitive phrase* when we use the word *infinitive*.

Infinitives are used mainly as nouns and less frequently as adjectives or adverbs. Infinitives may have subjects, objects, complements, or modifiers.

We're concerned with two tense forms of the infinitive: the present and the perfect.

Present: to talk, to write

Perfect: to have talked, to have written

The present infinitive names an action occurring at the *same time* as the action of the main verb. For example:

I am trying to finish the assignment today. (Both actions are taking place at the same time in the present.)

I was trying to finish the assignment by May 1. (Both actions took place at the same time in the past.)

I will try to finish the assignment by noon. (Both actions will happen at the same time in the future.)

The present infinitive also expresses future time with the help of a time modifier. For example:

I hope to graduate in April. (I hope now to graduate in the future.)

John wanted to sell the computer next month. (John wanted in the past to sell the computer at some future time.)

The perfect infinitive expresses action occurring *before* that of the main verb. For example:

I am happy to have served on the committee. (I am happy now to have served in the past.)

The choice between the present infinitive and the perfect infinitive is simple if you will remember the following guidelines: (1) the present infinitive is used to express action simultaneously with, or later than, that of the main verb; (2) the perfect infinitive is used to express action prior to that of the main verb; (3) the present infinitive is used whenever the main verb reflects any form of past tense; and (4) the present infinitive is used if the main verb is preceded by *has*, *have*, or *had*.

In isolated instances, we might argue that the action in a perfect infinitive precedes the action in a past-tense main verb. In this textbook, however, we will always stress the use of the present infinitive in connection with the use of any form of past tense in the main verb.

Use T12-3 here

Gerunds.   The gerund is a verb ending in -*ing* that functions as a noun. In other words, a gerund is a present participle used as a noun.

When a present participle is used as a subject, a complement, an object, or an appositive, it functions as a noun and is called a *gerund* rather than a participle. And when a participial phrase functions as a noun, it is called a *gerund phrase* rather than a participial phrase. Throughout this textbook, the term *gerund* will be used to refer either to a gerund or to a gerund phrase.

Technically, gerunds have two tense forms: present and perfect. The present tense of the gerund refers to an action happening at the present time:

> *Talking* out loud will get your teacher's attention.

The perfect tense of the gerund refers to an action that was completed *before* the time of the main verb:

> I attribute my success to *having married* the right person.

In dealing with gerunds in this textbook, we will be concerned almost exclusively with the present tense. We will not stress the tense of gerunds in relation to rules of usage, although you will readily see that tense rules for gerunds coincide with tense rules for present and perfect participles.

Learning Hint 1.   Most verbs are action words (*run, jump, sing, swim,* etc.). Verbals are almost always derived from action verbs and, as such, retain the actions of the verbs from which they are derived.

Because of the action inherent in verbals, novice writers sometimes mistakenly think they have written a sentence when they really have written a sentence fragment. Such sentences frequently contain a verbal, but not a verb. For example:

> Thelma, *straining* her back while tying her shoes in the morning.

> The photographs, *having been delivered* to the family only one day after the wedding.

> The cowboy, to get the attention of his friends and *to impress* Ms. Morley.

You must, of course, be wary that you do not write sentence fragments thinking they are sentences. As you work with verbals, be especially careful to avoid fragments.

Pretest

Mark the sentence **C** if all elements of verbal usage are correct; mark the sentence **I** if any element of tense is incorrect.

1. I hoped to have gone to the movies on my birthday next month.

2. I would like to have lived in the days of King Arthur.

3. I would have liked to live in the days of King Arthur.

4. Walking the two miles to the museum, Boyd found himself tired from the exertion.

5. Talking to his former classmates, Ben relished the fond memories of his teenage years.

6. Ed says that his skiing prowess is the result of his having skied at Sundance at least once each week for the last three winters.

7. Having consulted his future son-in-law, Mr. Tang was evaluating the pros and cons of investing in an apartment complex.

8. Ms. Perotti would have liked to have gone to the Canadian Rockies for her vacation, but her work schedule prevented her from doing so.

9. Mr. Wahinehookae, having been detained for four hours at the Salt Lake International Airport because of foggy weather.

10. When Ms. Schaefermeyer returned from her vacation to Key West, she committed herself to completely finish the graphics section of the Warren report within a week's time.

Key: (1) I—use the present infinitive *to go* following the past-tense verb *hoped* to show that you are still hoping *to go*, not *to have gone*; (2) C—the perfect infinitive *to have lived* expresses time prior to that of the main verb *would like*; (3) C—The present infinitive *to live* is used for time contemporaneous with that of the main verb *would have liked*; (4) I—the walking occurred before the finding, so the perfect participle *having walked* should be used; (5) C—the talking occurred contemporaneous with the relishing; (6) C—the action in the perfect gerund preceded Ed's current skiing prowess; (7) C—the perfect participle *having consulted* correctly precedes the action of *was evaluating*, the main verb; (8) I—a present infinitive, *to go* in this instance, should be used following a past-tense main verb or following a main verb that is preceded by *have*; (9) I—containing a verbal but not a verb, this item is a fragment; (10) I—*to completely finish* is an unnecessary split infinitive.

Terminology

Finite verb—Full verbs in sentences and clauses. Derived from the Latin *finis*, meaning *end* or *limit*. Finite verbs can be limited in person by a pronoun or subject (I walk, he walks); in time by a tense form (he walks, he walked); or in number through singular or plural forms (she sings, they sing). (*See nonfinite verb.*)

Fragment—A group of words that is an incomplete statement but that is punctuated as a complete sentence.

Gerund—The verb form (verbal) used as a noun and always ending in *-ing*.

Infinitive—The verb form (verbal) used chiefly as a noun and less frequently as an adjective or an adverb; almost always made up of *to* plus a verb form. (A principal part of a verb is the present tense—also called an infinitive. For our purposes, *infinitive* will be used in connection with *to* plus a verb form.)

Nonfinite verb—Verbals (participles, gerunds, and infinitives) that cannot serve as predicates to make full sentences. Nonfinite verbs are sometimes called *unfinished verbs*. (*See finite verb*.)

Participle—The verb form (verbal) used as an adjective. A participle's ending varies according to inflection and spelling (e.g., *-ing, -ed, -t, -en*).

Perfect infinitive—The words *to have* plus the past participle form of the verb (*to have run, to have jumped, to have sung*).

Present infinitive—The word *to* plus a present-tense verb (*to run, to jump, to sing*).

Perfect participle—The past participle form of a verb plus a *having* helper (*having run, having jumped, having sung*).

Present participle—A present-tense verb with *-ing* added to it (*running, jumping, singing*).

Verbal—Verb forms (gerunds, participles, and infinitives) used as nouns, adjectives, or adverbs. Verbals may take objects, complements, and modifiers. Infinitives may have subjects.

Rules

1. **Use a present participle to refer to action happening at the same time as the action of the main verb.**

   By itself, a present participle cannot indicate the **exact** time of an action. By definition, when a participial construction is used, the tense sequence of the present participle coincides with the tense of the main verb in the independent clause. For example:

   > *Taking* the chair lift, Leila *shows* her intention to ski down the north slope. (Because the main verb is in the present tense, the present participle *taking* carries the idea of present time.)

   > *Taking* the chair lift, Leila *showed* her intention to ski down the north slope. (With the main verb's change to past tense, the present participle *taking* now carries the idea of past time.)

2. **Use a perfect participle to refer to action occurring before the action of the main verb.**

   By itself, a perfect participle cannot indicate the **exact** time of an action. By definition, when a participial construction is used, the perfect participle must be used if the writer needs to show that the time sequence of the participle occurred before the tense shown in the main verb. For example:

   > *Having dictated* the letter, Mr. Quest *is contemplating* his next move. (The perfect participle shows that Mr. Quest finished dictating the letter before he contemplates his next move.)

   > *Having dictated* the letter, Mr. Quest *was contemplating* his next move. (Again, the perfect participle signals that Mr. Quest finished dictating the letter and then contemplated his next move.)

3. **Use a present infinitive to name an action occurring at the same time as the action of the main verb or to express future time.**

By itself, a present infinitive cannot indicate the **exact** time of an action. By definition, when an infinitive construction is used, the present infinitive shows that the action of the infinitive (*a*) coincides with the main verb's tense or (*b*) expresses future time. For example, the following infinitives coincide with the main verb's tense:

I *am trying* my best *to complete* the project today.

I *was trying* my best *to complete* the project before the due date.

I *will try* my best *to complete* the project by 4 p.m.

I *tried* my best *to complete* the project yesterday.

The following infinitives express future time:

I hope *to complete* the project by next Tuesday.

I planned *to ask* your permission.

We had hoped *to win* the tournament.

Learning Hint 2.   Do not confuse the infinitive phrase with the prepositional phrase introduced by the preposition *to*. When the present tense of a verb follows the word *to*, you will know for certain that the construction is an infinitive phrase. However, for *to* to be a preposition, it must introduce an object, which will usually be a noun or a pronoun. For example:

Infinitive phrases: I want *to visit* my father.
                      Melba tried *to stay* awake.

Prepositional phrases: I went *to* a video party.
                         Melba came *to* the cafeteria.

Learning Hint 3.   Traditional grammar authorities have long maintained that the infinitive should not be split (the *to* should not be separated from the verb by another word). In line with this thinking, the phrasing in the following sentences is not appropriate:

Maxine told me *to never ask* her for help again.

I was unable *to completely finish* the report on time.

Today, grammar authorities generally agree that a split infinitive is not necessarily wrong unless it is awkward and can be avoided easily. We recommend that you understand fully the nature of a split infinitive, that you use the split infinitive sparingly, and that you split the infinitive only when you can obviously or more comfortably or specifically do so than not. In that respect, consider the following split and unsplit infinitives:

Clear: Really, we want you *to applaud.*

Unclear: We want you really *to applaud.*

Unclear: We want you *to applaud* really.

Clear: We really want you *to applaud.*

Clear: We want you *to really applaud.* (split infinitive)

Clear: We plan *to urgently request* your applause. (split infinitive)

4. **Use a perfect infinitive to express action occurring before that of the main verb.**

In using the infinitive construction, sometimes you must signal to the reader that the action in the infinitive occurred before the action of the main verb. In such situations, the perfect infinitive is used. For example:

> Mr. Martin appears *to have been* drunk last evening.

> I am happy *to have known* him for the past three years.

5. **Use a present infinitive following past-tense main verbs or following main verbs that are preceded by *has, have,* or *had*.**

Following past-tense main verbs or following any main verb that is preceded by *has, have,* or *had*, be especially careful because the present infinitive, not the perfect infinitive, is normally used to show that the infinitive action coincides with the action of the main verb. For example:

> NO   We *wanted to have honored* you at the banquet.
> We *had hoped to have shipped* the parts today.
> We *should have liked to have represented* you at the meetings.

> YES   We *wanted to honor* you at the banquet.
> We *had hoped to ship* the parts today.
> We *should have liked to represent* you at the meetings.

Occasionally, you may find an instance in which the action in the infinitive indeed preceded the past-tense action of the main verb. In that situation, Rule 4 will apply; and you can use a perfect infinitive following the past-tense main verb. In this textbook, however, we avoid such situations; so you will know you can consistently apply Rule 5.

Posttest

Mark the sentence **C** if all elements of verbal usage are correct; mark the sentence **I** if any element of tense is incorrect.

1. By buying the diamond-studded bracelet in Idaho, I had hoped to have avoided paying sales tax.

2. Having visited his grandparents in Michigan, Monte tells them once more about his life-long ambitions.

3. Marcia desperately wanted to have seen *Gone with the Wind* when she was a child.

4. Having swum in the olympic-sized pool, Greg admitted that the hotel pool is not large enough.

5. Participating in the spring stock-car races proved to be the diversion that Helen had been seeking.

6. I would like to have seen Lionel's face when his mother told him the story.

7. When he had finished with the Brownsville project, Mr. Labarbera, contemplating the satisfaction of taking a well-earned vacation.

8. As soon as Ms. Mittleman agreed to work for our advertising agency, she committed herself to thoroughly review her priorities for both work and recreation.

9. When I visited with Ms. Vonspeierman, she indicated that she would have liked to have participated in our seminar but could not do so because of other commitments.

10. Having accepted the offer to attend law school at Columbia, Fawn found herself in a turmoil as she tried to deal with her need for off-campus housing.

Key: (1) I—the present infinitive *to avoid* is used following the past perfect *had hoped*; (2) I—the present participle *visiting* must be used to show that the action of visiting coincides with the action of telling; or use *told* to show that the action of visiting occurred before the action of the main verb; (3) I—the present infinitive *to see* is required following the past tense verb *wanted*; (4) C—the perfect participle *having swum* correctly shows that the action of swimming occurred before the action of admitting; (5) C—correct gerund usage; (6) C—the perfect infinitive *to have seen* expresses time prior to that of the main verb *would like*; (7) I—containing a verbal but not a verb, this item is a fragment; (8) I—*to thoroughly review* is an unnecessary split infinitive; (9) I—a present infinitive, *to participate* in this instance, should be used following a past-tense main verb or following a main verb that is preceded by *have*; (10) C—the perfect participle *having accepted* correctly precedes the action of *found*, the main verb.

LEVEL A

Name _____

Exercise 12–1   On the lines below, mark **T** if the statement is true and **F** if the statement is false.

_F_ 1. A nonfinite verb can serve as the only verb of a sentence.

_T_ 2. The present participle is used to show action happening at the same time as the action of the main verb.

_F_ 3. The perfect participle is used to show action happening at the same time as the action of the main verb.

_F_ 4. Examples of infinitives are *running, jumping*, and *singing*.

_F_ 5. The present infinitive is used to express action occurring before that of the main verb.

_F_ 6. The perfect infinitive is used if the main verb is preceded by *has, have,* or *had*.

_T_ 7. Gerunds function as nouns.

_F_ 8. *Having dictated the letter* is an example of a present participle.

_T_ 9. The tense sequence of a present participle coincides with the tense of the main verb in the independent clause.

_T_ 10. The present perfect infinitive is used to express action occurring before the action of the main verb.

_T_ 11. A participle's ending varies according to inflection and spelling.

_T_ 12. By itself, a perfect participle cannot indicate the exact time of an action.

_F_ 13. *Deciding to dictate the letter* is an example of a perfect infinitive.

_F_ 14. *To completely finish* is an example of a perfect infinitive.

_T_ 15. A present infinitive is used following a main verb preceded by *has, have,* or *had*.

_F_ 16. Verbals are almost always derived from state-of-being verbs.

_T_ 17. Participles have three tenses; gerunds and infinitives have two tenses each.

Exercise 12–2   Mark **C** if the tense of the infinitive is correct; mark **I** if the tense is incorrect.

_I_ 1. The majority of the employees preferred to have been enrolled in Plan B of the medical insurance.

_I_ 2. The employees are pleased to be instructed so carefully in fire-control procedures. [Intent: the instructions took place last week]

_C_ 3. I am attempting to finish the Benson Institute project today. [Intent: both actions are happening in the present]

_C_ 4. I was attempting to finish the Benson Institute project before you asked for it. [Intent: both actions happened at the same time in the past]

C 5. I shall try to finish the Benson Institute project before you ask for it. [Intent: both actions are happening at the same time in the future]

I 6. Mr. Gregerson appeared to have been drunk during tonight's office party.

I 7. I would have liked to have spent the entire week of May 3 in San Diego.

I 8. Mr. Rogers had expected to have verified the accuracy of his data before the meeting begins tomorrow.

I 9. My present objective is to have played football for the Arizona State Sun Devils.

I 10. Interjections were sometimes used to have shown disgust or disappointment.

C 11. The Budget Committee had promised to prepare the revised salary schedule by May 1.

I 12. As a result of the incident, Winn resolved to never ask for Paul's assistance again.

Exercise 12–3 For sentences 1 through 4, mark **A** if the tense of the first participle is correct; mark **B** if the tense of the second participle is correct. For sentences 5 through 12, mark **C** on the blank if the tense of the participle is logical; mark **I** if the tense is illogical.

B 1. (Having spoken/Speaking) to the student, the teacher paced back and forth in front of the room. [Intent: the speaking and the pacing occurred simultaneously]

A 2. (Having evaluated/Evaluating) the test results, the teacher decided to prepare a new test. [Intent: the evaluating preceded the deciding]

B 3. (Having listened/Listening) to the group's comments, Dr. Warner changed her opinion of the situation. [Intent: the listening and the change occurred simultaneously]

A 4. (Having learned/Learning) that the seminar had been taught yesterday, Margaret began expressing her irritation to me. [Intent: the learning preceded the expressing]

C 5. Running down the hall, Fred tripped and spilled the jelly beans.

I 6. Saying what he wanted to say, Fred quietly closed the door behind him as he left the room.

C 7. Feeling discouraged and depressed, Duane did not keep his appointment with Dr. Jeffries.

I 8. Hugh, straining his back from the lifting, later found himself facing back surgery.

I 9. Writing for three hours, Euna finally completed the term paper at midnight.

C 10. Members of the class, understanding that Ms. Jacoby had counseled them correctly, looked at each other in amazement.

I 11. The dead dog, snarling wickedly and foaming at the mouth, was diagnosed with a case of rabies.

I 12. Having irrigated until morning, the farmer paused frequently to gaze at the stars.

LEVEL B

Name _____

Exercise
12–4

Each of the following sentences contains two verbals. Underline each one of them. Then identify each verbal in the order it appears and classify it as follows: **G**—gerund; **P**—participle; **I**—infinitive.

P *I* 1. <u>Dressed</u> in his rented tuxedo, Clyde appeared <u>to be</u> very handsome.

P *I* 2. <u>Realizing</u> that the meeting might start late, Marjorie went to the copy center <u>to run</u> additional agendas.

I *G* 3. Am I <u>to understand</u> that <u>driving</u> to Albuquerque will require the use of two rental cars?

P *I* 4. <u>Running</u> the fourth leg of the relay race, Sue was determined not <u>to fall</u> behind.

G *I* 5. <u>Training</u> your kitten <u>to use</u> the litter box might require a certain amount of patience.

I *G* 6. Yes, Carma earned money <u>to pay</u> her way through the MBA program by <u>teaching</u> an economics course.

P *I* 7. <u>Having assessed</u> the damages to the car, the adjuster decided <u>to declare</u> it unsalvageable.

I *I* 8. <u>To appear</u> as calm as he could, Troy decided <u>to take</u> a tranquilizer before his speech.

P *G* 9. <u>Rested</u> thoroughly at the base camp, the climbers found the <u>going</u> easier the fourth day.

P *I* 10. His mind <u>dazed</u> because of the blow to the head, Gerald tried <u>to collect</u> his wits before the next move.

Exercise
12–5

Write the letter that identifies the item with the correct tense or verbal usage.

c 1. *a.* The model cars made from our company's plastic and sold throughout North America.
   b. Inventing the new plastic, we had hoped to have used it in our line of antique model cars.
   c. Having realized the value of the new plastic, Dr. Knott recommended that we patent the process immediately.

b 2. *a.* Dr. Kissling, the head surgeon, is anxiously waiting to have told us about the ambulance's arrival.
   b. The Red Cross nurses have tried to convince us that the ambulance will arrive shortly.
   c. The medical personnel, anxiously awaiting the arrival of the ambulance to take the wounded to the field hospital.

_b_ 3. _a._ I feel that spring is the time really to appreciate the Rockies.

   _b._ To appreciate a 1957 Chevy fully, I think you have to actually drive one.

   _c._ You must try the Purple Turtle's milk shakes to appreciate them truly.

_a_ 4. _a._ Lying still and pretending to be dead, the child escaped injury during the exchange of gunfire.

   _b._ The child pretended to have been dead so she could escape injury during the gunfire.

   _c._ The small child, lying still and pretending to be dead during the exchange of gunfire.

_a_ 5. _a._ Having arranged a meeting to introduce her son-in-law, Mrs. Kaze is now preparing the refreshments.

   _b._ Having prepared the refreshments, Mrs. Kaze had arranged a meeting to introduce her son-in-law.

   _c._ Mrs. Kaze, arranging a meeting to introduce her son-in-law, is now preparing the refreshments.

_c_ 6. _a._ We are endeavoring to have raised our children in a drug-free environment.

   _b._ To have raised our children in a drug-free environment, we try to have helped them select the right friends.

   _c._ To be sure our children do not use drugs, we are helping our children select their friends.

_c_ 7. _a._ The personnel manager wanted to have seen the resume before she interviewed Mr. Trumbo.

   _b._ Interviewing Mr. Trumbo, the personnel manager had wanted to have reviewed his resume before she conducted the interview.

   _c._ Having looked at the resume, the personnel manager wished she had reviewed it before she interviewed Mr. Trumbo.

_a_ 8. _a._ Had we realized the consequences, we would have attempted to verify the boy's whereabouts on Halloween night.

   _b._ All four of us, worrying about Halloween night's impact on the boy.

   _c._ We should have asked to have verified the boy's whereabouts on Halloween night.

_b_ 9. _a._ Knowing the results, we are trying to have changed our travel reservations today.

   _b._ After reviewing the situation, we earnestly desire to schedule our travels as we requested in our March 10 letter.

   _c._ In reading your letter, we now want to have traveled to Spain as part of our itinerary.

_c_ 10. _a._ He appears to be a highly qualified administrator. [Intent: he no longer is a highly qualified administrator]

   _b._ She appears to have been a gifted artist. [Intent: she continues to be a gifted artist]

   _c._ He is honored to have paid for the meal out of his own pocket. [Intent: he presently has feelings about an action from the past]

_b_ 11. _a._ We raised some questions about his doing the job adequately. [Intent: to express time before the main verb]

   _b._ The group raised several questions about his having completed the work on schedule. [Intent: to express time before the main verb]

   _c._ During the meeting, Beth and I would have liked to have questioned him about his failure to have completed the work. [Intent: to express correct times following the main verb]

LEVEL C

Name _____

Exercise
12–6

Write **C** if the sentence reflects logical tense sequences; write **I** if the sentence violates logical tense sequences. Then edit all sentences marked **I**.

_I_ 1. George Washington is viewed by Americans ~~to have been~~ *as* the father of their country.

_C_ 2. These beautiful Canada geese, migrating in huge flocks at this time of the year, are landing at suitable resting places along the way.

_C_ 3. Skiing at Snowbird this spring turned out to be the diversion Ronnie had been seeking.

_I_ 4. All members of the office staff ~~are~~ *were* delighted to be included in last week's fund-raising activities. *(or: are delighted to have been included)*

_I_ 5. We shall try to ~~have collected~~ *collect* the survey data by the time you return from Guadalajara.

Exercise
12–7

Compo-
sition

Using the suggested topic, compose a sentence that fulfills the directives given.

1. The next presidential election—use a present infinitive to express future time.

_____

_____

2. Abraham Lincoln—use a perfect participle to refer to action occurring before the action of the main verb.

_____

_____

3. Your best friend—use a perfect infinitive to express action occurring before that of the main verb.

_____

_____

4. The last dinner you ate—use a present infinitive following a past-tense main verb.

_____

_____

5. Your favorite TV show—use a present participle to refer to action happening at the same time as the main verb's action.

_____

_____

Exercise 12–8

Explain why each sentence has an error in tense.

1. We are attempting to have completed the report by tomorrow.

   A present infinitive is needed to reflect the same tense as the main verb.

2. Ms. Kim appears to be ill at yesterday's luncheon.

   A perfect infinitive will show that the time of the infinitive occurred before the time of the main verb.

3. We had hoped to have stopped payment on the check in time.

   A present infinitive is used following a past-perfect main verb.

Exercise 12–9

Edit the following sentences to correct any errors in verbals.

1. ~~Having taken~~ *Taking* the examination before the deadline, Claudine signaled her intention to do well in the course. (Intent: the action of the verbal took place at the same time as the action of the main verb)

2. ~~Anticipating~~ *Having anticipated* a positive response from her teacher, Claudine decided to take the examination before the deadline. (Intent: the action of the verbal took place before the action of the main verb)

3. Claudine hopes to ~~have completed~~ *Complete* the writing examination by next Tuesday.

complete

4. Claudine will try her best to ~~have completed~~ the writing examination several days before the deadline. (Intent: The action of the verbal occurred at the same time as the action of the main verb)

5. As you suspected, Claudine decided to thoroughly prepare for the examination and to ~~com-~~
completely
~~pletely~~ finish her lab work one week before the term's end.

have been
6. Claudine appears to ~~be~~ interested in completing her course requirements ahead of schedule.

(Intent: the action in the verbal occurred before that of the main verb) *(or to be interested in having completed)*
finish
7. According to Mr. Burrill, Claudine wanted to ~~have finished~~ her course assignments one week before the term's end.

complete
8. Claudine has decided to ~~have completed~~ her lab work before any of the other students complete theirs.

reward
9. Mr. Burrill decided to ~~have rewarded~~ any student who completes his or her lab work ahead of schedule.

successfully
10. To ~~successfully~~ complete the course ahead of schedule, Claudine was determined to ~~have~~
finish
~~finished~~ all lab assignments one week early.

Exercise 12–10   Edit the following sentences to reflect what you have learned from Lessons 3 through 4 and 9 through 12.

Cumulative Editing

requires   *complete*   *your advertising pamphlet*
1. Our present objective ~~had required~~ us to ~~have completed~~ Phase I of ~~you're advertizing pamplet~~ by 5 p.m. today.

has commitment
2. Having initiated the plan for early-morning workouts, Ms. King ~~had~~ a ~~committment~~ to have
invite everyone
~~invited every one~~ to participate.

You're   W   select   personal
3. ~~Your~~ right. we would have liked to ~~have selected~~ our own ~~personel~~ candidate to ~~have~~ run for
superintendent
state school ~~superintendant~~.

4. After ~~having recieved~~ [receiving] your ~~advise~~ [advice], George was determined to ~~have repeated~~ [repeat] the experiment one more time.

5. ~~Incidently~~ [Incidentally], living in a Desert Shadows condominium ~~has appeared too have been~~ [appears to be] a good decision for us to ~~make~~ [have made].

6. I was very honored to ~~have recieved~~ [receive] your letter asking me to ~~have participated~~ [participate] in Business Awareness Week ~~latter~~ [later] this month.

7. In ~~having reacted~~ [reacting] to your suggestions, I am ~~writting~~ [writing] to ~~have informed~~ [inform] you that I will ~~except~~ [accept] your invitation.

8. According to the ~~broshure~~ [brochure], home ownership today ~~had appeared to have been~~ [appears to be] related to living in a house rather than in an apartment.

9. A ~~similiar~~ [similar] federal law that ~~had been deviced to have prevented~~ [is devised to prevent] hospitals from turning away indigent patients faces a court test today.

10. After having recorded ~~it's~~ [its] biggest-ever monthly gain in March, the Michigan survey's confidence index ~~liably~~ [likely] will ~~have declined~~ [decline] sharply in April.

11. In the six countries for which detailed age information is available, moving rates were con-~~sistantly~~ [sistently] high for preschool children and for ~~there~~ [their] parents.

12. The lower prime rate directly ~~effects~~ [affects] many small businesses~~, but~~ [. However,] the continued reluctance of businesses to ~~have borrowed~~ [borrow] could ~~have limited~~ [limit] the impact of the reduction.

13. The ~~surprize talk of a~~ [surprise] merger of Citizens Trust and Peoples First National ~~latter~~ [later] this year was supposed to ~~have been~~ [be] a model for bank mergers everywhere.

14. Although the economy remains weak in much of the nation, a new survey ~~had~~ [has] turned up a few ~~hopefull~~ [hopeful] signs that the economy may be about to ~~have bottomed~~ [bottom] out.

You have learned that tense is a property of the verb. A second property of the verb is known as *mood*, which refers to the mode, manner, or way in which a statement is intended to be understood. That is, *mood* is the term used to describe a writer's attitude toward the subject as it is expressed by the form of the verb.

Through our choice of mood, we can direct our readers to regard a statement (a dependent or an independent clause) as a simple statement of fact, a question, a command, a statement with a degree of improbability or impossibility, or a statement contrary to fact. As writers, we select one of three moods to signal the manner in which our ideas are to be understood:

1. The *indicative mood* is used to make a statement of fact or to ask a question.

2. The *imperative mood* is used to make a request, to make a suggestion, or to give a command.

3. The *subjunctive mood* is used to express a wish, a statement of doubt, or an impossible fact.

Indicative Mood.   We use the indicative mood very naturally. Sentences other than questions in the indicative mood literally *indicate* something, a point that will help you remember the term *indicative mood*. By definition, a question is also an indicative-mood sentence. For example:

> The time has come for us to leave the room.
>
> Why don't we leave the room right now?

Imperative Mood.   Though we may not realize it, we are using the imperative mood when we give orders, give direct instructions, or make certain kinds of requests. The subject of a verb in the imperative mood is always *you* and is usually omitted or understood from the context. For example:

> Get out of this room!

Use T13-1 here

Use T13-2 here

Use
T13-3
here

Subjunctive Mood.   In modern English, the subjunctive mood has steadily decreased in usage. However, we usually use the subjunctive mood when we express contrary-to-fact, impossible, or improbable conditions. We also usually use the subjunctive mood to make certain requests, to give indirect commands, to express wishes, or to make recommendations. For example:

> We should leave the room immediately.
>
> If I were you, I would leave the room.

Pretest

Mark the sentence **C** if the intended mood is used; mark the sentence **I** if an incorrect mood is used.

1. The company needs to give every blue-collar worker a 5 percent pay raise. (Recommendation desired)

2. A move to revive individual retirement accounts is gaining momentum in Congress. (Statement of fact desired)

3. I wish my uncle was a member of the Supreme Court. (Contrary-to-fact statement desired)

4. Just how far will the fans go in boycotting the team won't be known until ticket sales can be tabulated? (Conclusion desired)

5. If I were you, I would make plans now to supplement your Social Security when you retire. (Contrary-to-fact statement desired)

6. Those retired people who believe music making shouldn't stop with retirement should join the National Senior Symphony. (Conclusion desired)

7. Join the National Senior Symphony to support those people who believe music making need not stop with retirement. (Recommendation desired)

Key: (1) I—worded as a statement of fact or a conclusion rather than as a recommendation; (2) C; (3) I—*were* rather than *was* must be used to show that the uncle is not a member; (4) I—the terminal punctuation for a conclusion is a period rather than a question mark; (5) C; (6) I—a subjunctive-mood recommendation is made rather than an indicative-mood conclusion; (7) C—an imperative-mood statement or a subjunctive-should statement can be used to make recommendations.

Terminology

Conclusion—In business writing, a decision that is reached after facts or findings have been deliberated. Conclusions are stated in indicative mood.

Imperative mood—A statement (clause) that gives a command, makes a request, or gives directions. In business writing, policy and procedure directives are commonly stated in imperative mood. Recommendations are also often stated in imperative mood—especially when the recommender wants his or her recommendations to be absolute in tone and without any feeling of doubt.

Indicative mood—A statement (clause) that states a fact or asks a question. The majority of sentences we write are written in the indicative mood. In business writing, findings are usually stated in indicative mood.

Mood—The form of the verb that is used to indicate the manner or mode in which an action or state is viewed. English has indicative, imperative, and subjunctive moods.

Recommendation—A statement made about the counsel or advice that something be done. In business writing, recommendations are most often stated in the *subjunctive should*. The subjunctive should is appropriate for recommendations because the recommender has no assurance the reader will follow the advice given in the recommendations. That is, the subjunctive-should recommendation reflects the *doubt* that is inherent in such a recommendation. If the writer desires to recommend something without any doubt about the necessity of its being implemented, the imperative mood rather than the subjunctive should is appropriate.

Subjunctive mood—A statement (clause) that reflects a wish, a condition contrary to fact, an improbable situation, or an impossible situation.

Subjunctive should—The use of *should* as a subjunctive-mood statement. The subjunctive should is commonly used to express recommendations because doubt commonly exists that recommendations absolutely will be implemented.

Rules

1. **Use the indicative mood to make a statement of fact or to ask a question.**

We use the indicative mood in almost all our writing and speaking. Most of the writing in this textbook is in the indicative mood. We use indicative naturally in writing declarative or interrogative sentences. For example:

> Mr. Santos was ill when the budget committee met last Tuesday.

> Why didn't Mr. Santos notify me he was ill?

In business writing, we use the indicative mood to report most things as they are, as they were, or as they will be. In examining that statement, you will notice that our choice of tense might require more conscious attention than our choice of mood. We naturally use indicative mood to report facts or findings and to draw conclusions.

In an *if/then statement*, the writer may use indicative mood if the *if* statement is considered to be true or probable. In indicative-mood *if/then* statements, the verbs *was* and *is* are used with *will, can,* and *shall* (as opposed to the subjunctive-mood verb *were* that is used with *would, should,* and *could*). For example:

> If your assessment *is* true, we *will* need a third grinding machine. (True situation—we need the third machine)

> If your assessment *were* true, we *would* need a third grinding machine. (Contrary-to-fact situation—we do not need the third machine)

2. **Use the imperative mood to express a command, make a request, or give directions.**

The imperative mood is the command form of the verb. The subject of an imperative-mood sentence is seldom expressed but is always the pronoun *you*. For example:

Read the instructions carefully before attempting to assemble this unit.

Insert the cotter pin through the hole in the shaft and bend the pin as shown.

Please send the usual thank-you letter to Mr. Wilde.

We use the imperative mood rather naturally. Perhaps our greatest mistake is in not using it enough. The imperative mood is especially useful in business writing for giving commands, detailing directions or instructions, making requests, and stating strong recommendations. Business writers widely use the imperative mood (''command language'') for writing procedures or instructional material. Notice that all this unit's rules (which are intended to be ''commands'' or directives) are stated in the imperative mood.

Often, you will want to soften the impact of an imperative mood statement by improving its tone. One way to improve tone is to include the word *please* along with the verb. You can also make a request when *please* is not needed to improve the tone. For example, contrast the imperative-mood tone in the following sentences:

Return the questionnaire by January 15.

Please return the questionnaire by January 15.

Let us help you return the questionnaire by enclosing a stamped, addressed envelope for your use.

3. **Use the subjunctive mood to make statements you think are not true, possible, or probable.**

Contrary-to-fact, or untrue, statements refer to situations that do not exist or that are not real and therefore require the use of subjunctive mood. Impossible or improbable statements also require the subjunctive mood.

The subjunctive mood typically uses the verb *were*:

I wish I *were* able to help you.

If only he *were* capable of returning the money he stole!

He looks as though he *were* very successful.

In all such statements, you can **feel** they are contrary to fact.

If/then statements are often expressed in subjunctive mood because the writer believes the statements to be untrue, impossible, or improbable. In subjunctive if/then statements, the subjunctive verb *were* is usually used with *would, could,* and *should*:

If this report *were* true, we *would* have to buy new machinery.

If the newly hired writer *were* properly trained, he *would* know how to write the proposal.

If I *were* elected to Congress, I *would* try to cut taxes.

As if and *as though* are always subjunctive because they mean "not really, but pretending or supposing that . . . ."

She spoke *as if* she were in favor of adopting the proposal.

The report was presented *as though* it were the final decision.

Past-tense verbs used to express present or future events also create the subjunctive mood:

The report was presented as though it *represented* the final decision.

If I *won* the election, I would cut taxes.

If I *told* you about the new project, I would be fired immediately.

Wishes are always expressed in the subjunctive because wishes are ideas that are not true (at least not at the present, or no one would have to wish):

I wish the report *were* finished.

I wish we *could refund* your money.

Indirect commands are also part of the "make-believe" world of the subjunctive mood:

Don asked that the report *be prepared* for the meeting.

We suggest that a task force *be assigned* to consider the idea.

All *would, could,* and *should* statements are subjunctive-mood statements. In that respect, the subjunctive should is an excellent way to make a recommendation:

We *should* sell the old machines and purchase new ones.

Students *should* preregister if they desire to avoid a late-registration fee.

The subjunctive should is a natural way to make a recommendation because the recommender has no assurance that the recommendation will be followed. As such, especially in the business world, the subjunctive-should recommendation is used to express a contingent or hypothetical action.

In appropriate examples above, notice that *would, could,* and *should* are helping verbs. Other helping verbs that set up the subjunctive mood are *may, might,* and *ought.*

A relic of the past is the subjunctive-mood noun clause. We do not use the subjunctive very often in such instances, but its use is correct. Perhaps the primary thing to remember is the possibility of using the subjunctive for noun clauses. For example:

If night school *be* your desire, go for it.

Mr. Martin has requested our department *make* the changes.

4. Avoid illogical shifts in mood within a sentence.

From the tense lessons, you already understand the nature of a *shift*. A writer's consistency in his or her point of view is also important in relation to mood.

Most illogical mood shifts are indicative to imperative shifts, although other shifts also occur quite frequently. A shift in mood is confusing to the reader because the shift suggests the writer has changed his or her way (manner) of looking at conditions:

NO Assign a locker to each freshman student, and then you can permit the students to check out gym clothes. (Shift from imperative to indicative mood)

YES Assign a locker to each freshman student, and then permit the students to check out gym clothes. (Both imperative-mood statements)

NO A summary of your findings should be prepared, and then make plans to present your report at the next board meeting. (Shift from subjunctive to imperative mood)

YES You should prepare a summary of your findings, and then you should make plans to present your report at the next board meeting. (Both subjunctive-mood statements)

Be aware that not all mood shifts are illogical. In that respect, remember that every clause is either indicative, imperative, or subjunctive. Within a sentence, watch for the "illogical feel" that occurs if the shift in mood from one clause to another is an illogical shift.

Posttest

Mark the sentence **C** if the intended mood is used; mark the sentence **I** if an incorrect mood is used.

1. Next fall, many business schools will begin teaching environmental management as part of their curricula. (Statement of fact desired)

2. Do you understand why the federal government will probably cut research payments to several universities? (Conclusion desired)

3. The Boston office should pare management and professional ranks by encouraging career switches. (Recommendation desired)

4. If I was going to fail the course, I would drop it before the drop period ends. (Contrary-to-fact statement desired)

5. The North Word Processing Center should invest in spreadsheet software. (Conclusion desired)

6. Do you know that universities have routinely been overbilling the government for years? (Indicative mood desired)

7. If I were going to college this fall, I would be able to play the violin in the school orchestra. (Contrary-to-fact statement desired)

Key: (1) C; (2) I—an indicative-mood question is asked rather than an indicative-mood conclusion; (3) C; (4) I—the *if* clause is in indicative mood, and the independent clause is in subjunctive mood; but both must be in the subjunctive mood; (5) I—worded as a recommendation, not a statement of fact; (6) C; (7) C.

LEVEL A

Name _____

Exercise 13–1 On the lines below, mark **T** if the statement is true; mark **F** if the statement is false.

_F_   1. The indicative mood is used to make a request.

_T_   2. *The police should attempt to locate the lost boy* is a subjunctive-mood statement.

_T_   3. The subject of a verb in the imperative mood is always *you.*

_F_   4. Conclusions are best stated in the subjunctive mood.

_T_   5. Business-report recommendations may be stated in either the imperative mood or the subjunctive should.

_T_   6. *If your thinking is correct, you will pass the test* is an indicative-mood statement.

_F_   7. Wishes are best expressed as statements of fact in the indicative mood.

_F_   8. *If/then* statements are always expressed in the subjunctive mood.

_F_   9. *State your request, and then please get on with your work* represents an illogical shift in mood.

_F_ 10. The subjunctive mood often uses the past-tense verb *was.*

_T_ 11. *If your thinking were correct, we will need a new computer* contains a shift in mood.

_F_ 12. Perhaps our greatest mistake with the imperative mood is in using it too much.

_F_ 13. An imperative-mood statement is a command; we cannot improve its tone.

_T_ 14. A clause that begins with *as though* must always be a subjunctive-mood statement.

_T_ 15. As helping verbs, *may, might, could, should,* and *ought* set up the subjunctive mood.

Exercise 13–2 Write **C** if the mood in the sentence is correct; write **I** if the mood is incorrectly stated.

_I_   1. The law requires that you are 16 years old before you ride a motorcycle.

_I_   2. Grandpa continues to treat me as if I was still a baby.

_C_   3. If I were rich, I would buy a new car.

_I_   4. I wish that I was you so I could take a trip to Hawaii!

_C_   5. I move that the meeting be adjourned.

_I_   6. If what you say is true, we would have no need to fear for our lives.

_C_   7. Were it not for health hazards, smoking would be less of a threat to lung problems.

_I_   8. If the hamburger was spoiled, we could smell it.

_I_   9. Mr. Wight is certainly acting as though he is wealthy.

_C_ 10. If Glenn was at the party, I certainly didn't run into him.

Exercise 13–3 Write **C** if the statement fulfills the requested condition. If otherwise, write **I**.

_C_ 1. Even for a person who plans for medical care, the unpredictability of medical needs may result in bills beyond the person's financial means. (Statement with an expression of doubt)

_C_ 2. To find out if you qualify for medical financial assistance, contact our business office. (Strong recommendation)

_I_ 3. Because we care about our community, the charity services we offer go beyond assisting with medical bills. (Recommendation desired)

_I_ 4. Please take a moment to acquaint yourself with the women who faithfully serve on the board. (Statement of fact desired)

_C_ 5. Members of the governing board have made valuable contributions to the hospital facilities. (Conclusion desired)

_I_ 6. A different hospital department is featured each quarter. (A mild command desired)

_I_ 7. Many charities have memorial programs, probably because the memorials are ideal for helping worthy causes. (Contrary-to-fact statement desired)

_I_ 8. We should focus our attention on special events and on estate-planning seminars. (Statement of fact desired)

_I_ 9. The know-your-hospital program could give residents a close look at health-care progress and trends. (Statement of fact desired)

_C_ 10. Tax exemption helps not-for-profit hospitals help the community. (Statement of fact desired)

Exercise 13–4 Mark **A** on the blank if the first verb is correct; mark **B** if the second verb is correct.

_B_ 1. They request that Ms. Parker (speaks/speak) with them immediately.

_A_ 2. I wish that Dale (were/was) coordinating the project.

_B_ 3. If I (was/were) you, I would move to New York.

_B_ 4. Ms. Williams insists that her refund (is/be) mailed today.

_A_ 5. The Security Office requires that each employee (present/presents) proper identification each morning.

_B_ 6. If Mr. Janda (was/were) in town, I am certain he would attend the meeting.

_A_ 7. I wish that I (were/was) going with you to Helena.

_A_ 8. The committee has asked that our office (supervise/supervises) the investigation.

_A_ 9. If the meat (is/were) left out, it will spoil.

_B_ 10. If the cheese (was/were) spoiled, we could tell by the taste.

LEVEL B

Name _____

Exercise 13–5 Write the letter that matches each sentence with the intended mood for the statement being made: **A**—Indicative mood; **B**—Imperative mood; **C**—Subjunctive mood.

_C_ 1. I wish you were the king of England.

_B_ 2. Please pass the salt and pepper.

_C_ 3. I demand that the damage be reported immediately.

_A_ 4. If Doran was on television as he claimed, he probably appeared in a commercial.

_A_ 5. Ms. Evans has completely reorganized the company's accounting department.

_A_ 6. Did Ms. Evans consult you during the reorganization?

_B_ 7. Please return the enclosed questionnaire by July 12.

_C_ 8. Mr. Williams should be at the Thursday meeting.

_B_ 9. Let us help you make out your own tax return.

_C_ 10. We would appreciate your forwarding this information promptly.

Exercise 13–6 Write the letter that identifies the sentence in which mood is correctly used.

_C_ 1. *a.* Use the data stamp when the letter arrives, and then you should show the letter to me.
   b. He looks as though he was very successful at the race track.
   c. This report looks as though it were prepared by a novice writer.

_b_ 2. *a.* If only we had known, we can have spoken to Dr. McKell.
   b. We should not repeat in public what was discussed at the executive board meeting.
   c. I will replace the burned-out light globes if I were taller.

_a_ 3. *a.* If his testimony at the trial is true, Ms. Carrasco is indeed guilty of perjury.
   b. If the Simpson case was assigned to me, I would do my best to defend Mr. Simpson.
   c. Had the first payment been made in April, the second is due in October.

_a_ 4. *a.* Mr. Ruckelshaus is worried he may have to give up his dream of being an architect. (The writer desires to express doubt)
   b. The court ruled that police may detain an individual without a warrant for 48 hours without a court finding that the arrest was improper. (The writer wants to make a recommendation)
   c. In your new executive role, plan to spend about 40 percent of your time on professional tasks. (The writer wants to make a statement of fact)

_C_ 5. *a.* I wish Jacoby was our sales representative.
   b. Art knows that Brandy were not in Portland on Monday.
   c. If Jack had been at the meeting, he would have dominated the conversation.

_c_ 6. *a.* Plan the commercial around the Ford model, and then you should contact Ms. Jex for assistance.

    b. The fraternity members want to have a crash course in business law, so you should tailor your seminar to their interests.

    c. Give your presentation at the Embassy Suites in Salt Lake City, and then make arrangements to hold the next seminar at the Granada Royale in Scottsdale.

_b_ 7. *a.* You should recognize the many reasons for losing weight; be sure you select the best weight-management program for your needs.

    b. The hospitals simply would not be as caring and compassionate as they are without the service our volunteers provide.

    c. You do have several options, and we should be happy to help you get the care you need.

_c_ 8. *a.* Jill were definitely wrong in expressing her opinion of Mr. Ingle.

    b. I am the one who suggested that Sorrel is granted a leave of absence.

    c. If Sydney was in Rexburg, he undoubtedly visited our showroom there.

_a_ 9. *a.* If your statement were true, we would not be selling the book on hospital services.

    b. Although my home decorator were here yesterday, she did little to solve the dispute.

    c. Carlton suggested that the office is closed for one week during the holidays.

_c_ 10. *a.* Our resource needs would be more easily solved if our sales force were larger and if Junius was still in charge.

    b. All of us know that if Mr. Jenks were systems manager, he will initiate changes in the accounting system.

    c. If I were qualified for the job, I would apply for the position you advertised.

_a_ 11. *a.* While we were in California, Edwin spent money as though it grew on trees.

    b. I will not be in the office on Monday; however, you should be able to reach me at home.

    c. Use your home-equity loan to buy that new automobile, or you may simply apply for one of our low-interest auto loans.

_b_ 12. *a.* Reporting your findings at the meeting should be limited to ten minutes; then be sure you state your recommendations succinctly.

    b. Eliminate any gender bias during your interviews, and practice active listening when the interviewees are talking.

    c. Help us deliver the conference packets on Saturday; then will you please help mail the registration forms on Monday?

_c_ 13. *a.* We want to hold a family reunion; you should find out who will attend.

    b. Schedule a boat for the reunion, and then you should notify everyone.

    c. If I were in charge, I would hold the reunion at Flaming Gorge on July 5.

_a_ 14. *a.* Had I not agreed to be in Salem on Monday, I would be able to help you.

    b. I will not be here on Monday; call me, however, on your mobile phone.

    c. I wish I was going to be here Monday to help with the Crosby account.

| **LEVEL C** |

Name _____

Exercise
13–7

Write **C** if the mood indicated in parentheses is reflected in the sentence. Write **I** if the sentence reflects a different mood. Then edit all **I** sentences so they reflect the moods indicated.

_I_   1. ~~Our~~ head accountant ~~must approve~~ all out-of-state travel requests. (imperative mood)
Get approval from our   *for*

_C_   2. Ms. Tolbert usually represents the vice president at the grievance committee meetings. (indicative mood)

_I_   3. All employees ~~have been~~ informed that Mr. Jacobs is retiring on December 31. (subjunctive mood)
should be

_I_   4. ~~Will you~~ please show Mr. Reagen his new office while I am in San Francisco. (imperative mood)
P

_C_   5. Mr. Reagen requested that Mr. Winstone meet him at the airport. (subjunctive mood)

_I_   6. Ms. Tomlinson ~~is~~ pleased with the progress we have made in remodeling her office. (subjunctive mood)
should be

_I_   7. ~~Ask~~ Mr. Reagen to call Ms. Tomlinson as soon as he arrives at the airport. (indicative mood)
is supposed

_I_   8. ~~Fax~~ this order to Warner Brothers the first thing tomorrow morning. (subjunctive mood)
T   *should be faxed*

_I_   9. ~~The~~ findings ~~will be summarized,~~ and the final reports ~~will be delivered~~ by Tuesday afternoon. (imperative mood)
Summarize the   *deliver*

_I_   10. If Mr. Maxwell ~~had known~~ the facts, he ~~would not have assigned~~ Mr. Kidwell to teach the course. (indicative mood)
knows   *will not assign*

Exercise 13–8

Using the subjects indicated, compose sentences that reflect the mood indicated.

Composition

1. Your basketball experience (subjunctive mood).

   _____

   _____

2. Your desire to visit Las Vegas (indicative mood).

   _____

   _____

3. Your primary directive to your friend who has borrowed your new car (imperative mood).

   _____

   _____

Exercise 13–9

Edit the following sentences to correct any errors in mood or to satisfy the stipulations in parentheses.

Editing

1. I wish I ~~was~~ *were* the person responsible for the parking-lot recommendations.

2. We ~~need to~~ *should* build a multiple-level parking lot south of the Clark Building. (Recommendation desired)

3. If the initiative were approved by the voters, it ~~will~~ *would* dismantle the state's Department of Alcoholic Beverage Control. (The probability of these actions occurring is doubtful)

4. The black smoke billowing from the plant's smokestack ~~would~~ *will* continue for a full week. (Statement of fact desired)

5. Preregistration for summer term should begin in about two weeks, so ∧*you should* pay attention to the new procedures for telephone registration.

6. The Division of Wildlife Resources ~~should~~ *must* restrict the hunting season to the first two weeks in October. (Conclusion desired)

7. I don't think that more money for another hunting stamp ~~would~~ *will* improve anything (Statement of fact desired)

8. If Parley's analyses ~~were~~ *are* correct, we ~~would~~ *will* need to back up our files every night. (Statement of fact desired)

The company must sell its
9. ~~We should sell our~~ fleet of company cars and purchase new ones. (Conclusion desired)

10. Our analyses show we need to purchase new company cars; therefore, we ~~should~~ *can* place the order by the end of the month.

11. Invite Governor Snelling to speak at commencement, and then ~~you can~~ tell his daughter we have honored her request.

Please
12. ~~I want you to~~ request Parker Scowcroft to attend the art exhibit as a representative of the company. (A statement in the form of a polite directive is desired)

13. Call today to order your $5 double-pepperoni pizza, and ~~we will appreciate your telling~~ *tell* your neighbors about the offer.

Exercise
13–10   Edit the following sentences so they no longer contain shifts in either tense or mood.

Cumula-
tive
Editing
1. ~~Word process~~ *Had you word processed* your report ~~so it looks~~ *to make it look* professional, ~~and~~ you ~~should~~ *would* have received a good grade on it.

2. Add a bibliography at the end of your report, and then ~~you may~~ consider the report completed.

You should mail
3. ~~Mail~~ your application by June 1, ~~and you should be receiving~~ *if you want to receive* a response within two weeks.

4. Our meetings will ~~have~~ run for two full days; your schedule ~~should~~ *will have to* accommodate our needs.

attend
5. We considered the invitation to ~~have attended~~ the ceremony a compliment; you also reflect a positive attitude about your being invited.

Exercise 13–11

Edit the following sentences that reflect number-usage, tense, or mood errors.

Cumula-
tive
Editing

1. The building will ~~have contained~~ *contain* 41,350 square feet and will have ~~sixteen~~ *16* office suites.

2. Give the free blood-pressure checks from ~~eight~~ *8* a.m. to ~~ten~~ *10* a.m., and then ~~you should~~ begin making the cancer-screening appointments at 10:30 a.m.

3. Last year, IHC ~~will have~~ provided over ~~twelve million dollars~~ *$12 million* in charity care; ~~please change~~ next year's goal ~~to~~ *will* reflect that level of charity cases.

4. In 1990, the federal government paid hospitals only ~~$.63~~ *63 cents* for each dollar of care that ~~will be~~ *was* provided under government health programs.

5. Health-care costs were nearly ~~six~~ *6* percent higher this year than last year, and costs ~~should be~~ *probably will be* nearly ~~eight~~ *8* percent higher next year than this year.

Exercise 13–12

Edit the following sentences to correct all confusing-word, tense, or mood errors.

Cumula-
tive
Editing

1. If I could possibly help Mr. Todd round up the horses that are ~~lose~~ *loose*, I ~~will~~ *would* do it.

2. Continuing education for lawyers ~~had been all ready becoming~~ *already has become* a casualty of the current recession.

3. In the future, law firms ~~viewed~~ *will view* continuing legal education as an easy budget cut; program administrators ~~should except~~ *will be expected to accept* that view.

4. The cutbacks have ~~took~~ *taken* a toll on ~~everyone~~ *every one* of the educational institutions; last year, for example, the Institute for Continuing Legal Education ~~will have~~ filed for bankruptcy court protection.

5. ~~Do~~ *You should* not have any ~~allusions~~ *illusions* about our status; we ~~liably~~ *likely* should be able to avoid filing for bankruptcy.

6. ~~The~~ *Please understand the* date for filing our quarterly tax return is ~~eminent~~ *imminent*, so be sure you get the paperwork in order as soon as possible.

You have learned that tense and mood are two properties of the verb. Voice is a third property of the verb.

In understanding voice, we must understand the distinction between active voice and passive voice. And we must not make the mistake of thinking that every verb is either active or passive. Some verbs are neither active nor passive but are known as linking verbs or as state-of-being verbs.

We also will help our understanding of voice if we understand the distinction between transitive and intransitive verbs.

Some of us have the mistaken notion that passive voice is taboo and therefore incorrect. Actually, either active voice or passive voice is grammatically correct. The choice between active or passive is the writer's option. Good advice, however, is that given to business writers:

Prefer the active voice to the passive voice.

However, we obviously cannot follow that imperative-mood directive unless we understand active voice and passive voice and can verbalize the differences between the two. At that point, we can more easily follow two other common directives related to voice:

1. Use the active voice to emphasize the performer of the action.

2. Use the passive voice to deemphasize the performer of the action (and therefore to emphasize the object of the action).

Although we state "rules" associated with this lesson on voice, these rules are really directives for you to follow if you want to write as effectively as you can. In the final analysis, you, the writer, must decide whether to use active voice, passive voice, or a linking-verb construction.

Pretest

Mark the sentence **C** if everything associated with voice is correct. Mark the sentence **I** if it violates anything associated with voice.

1. Mr. McGee made an excellent presentation at this morning's board meeting. (Passive voice is used)

2. An excellent presentation was made by Mr. McGee at this morning's board meeting. (Active voice is used)

3. Mr. McGee seemed ill during most of this morning's board meeting. (Active voice is used)

4. Mr. McGee has been an excellent employee for several years. (Passive voice is used)

5. The meeting agenda will be printed in Friday's newsletter, and the secretaries will distribute newsletters to everyone on the fourth floor.

6. The salespeople discussed the procedures for fourth-quarter reporting, and everyone contributed pertinent suggestions to improve the process.

7. The tardy slips will be collected by Ms. Midgley next week. (The writer desires to de-emphasize the performer of the action)

8. Ms. Midgley will collect the tardy slips next week. (The writer desires to emphasize the performer of the action)

Key: (1) I—the sentence is in the active voice; (2) I—the sentence is in the passive voice; (3) I—the verb *seemed* is a linking verb and is neither active nor passive; (4) I—the verb *has been* is a linking verb and is neither active nor passive; (5) I—the sentence contains a shift from passive voice to active voice; (6) C–both clauses are in the active voice; (7) C—the passive voice deemphasizes the performer of the action, Ms. Midgley; (8) C—the active voice emphasizes the performer of the action, Ms. Midgley.

Terminology

Active voice—Results when the subject is the doer of the action indicated by the verb.

Intransitive verb—A verb that does not require an object to complete its meaning.

Linking verb—A verb that connects the subject with the subject complement (predicate noun, pronoun, or adjective). The various forms of *to be* are the most commonly used linking verbs and are also frequently called *state-of-being verbs*. Other commonly used linking verbs are *seem, appear, feel, look, taste, smell,* and *sound*; such linking verbs are not usually called state-of-being verbs.

Passive voice—Results when the subject is being acted upon. Formed with the past participle of a verb plus a *be* verb helper (*is, are, am, was, were, be, been, being*).

Past participle—The verb part that typically ends in *-ed* for regular verbs or that is formed irregularly for irregular verbs and that cannot function as a predicate without a helper. In this lesson, the helper used with the past participle is a form of the verb *be*. The past participle plus a *be* verb helper form the passive voice.

State-of-being verb—Forms of the verb *be* (*is, are, am, was, were, be, been, being*). State-of-being verbs are also called *linking verbs*.

Subject complement—A noun, pronoun, or adjective that follows an intransitive linking verb and that completes the sense of the verb. Also called a *predicate complement* or a *predicate nominative*. Depending on the part of speech it is, a subject complement may be called a *predicate noun*, a *predicate pronoun*, or a *predicate adjective*.

Transitive verb—A verb that requires an object to complete its meaning.

Voice—The form of a transitive verb that indicates whether the subject performs the action or whether the subject is being acted upon. A verb with a direct object is in the *active voice*. When the direct object of an active-voice sentence becomes the subject, the verb is in the *passive voice*.

| Rules |

Use T14-1 here

1. **Use active voice to show that the subject performs the action in the sentence.**

   When a verb is in the active voice, the subject of the clause is the performer of the action:

   > The boy hit the ball.

   > Monte manages the company.

   Most sentences we write should be in the active voice. In general, we should use the active voice whenever possible because it is more direct and economical than the passive voice. Therefore, especially in business writing, the following directive is appropriate:

   > Prefer the active voice to the passive voice.

   Whenever we use the active voice, we select an action verb and then use a subject that is responsible for the action in the action verb.

Use T14-2 here

2. **Use passive voice to show that the subject receives the action of the verb.**

   When a verb is in the passive voice, the subject is acted upon by the verb:

   > The ball was hit by the boy.

   > The company is managed by Monte.

   Therefore, a verb is passive if its action is performed upon the subject.

   Obviously, the secret to preferring the active voice to the passive voice lies in understanding both active voice and passive voice. Of the two, passive voice is clearly the more difficult to understand by the novice writer.

   The passive voice consists of some form of the verb *be* as a helper plus a past participle. In that respect, remember that *have* plus a past participle creates the perfect tenses and that *be* plus a past participle creates the passive voice. Remember also that forms of *be* are the following: *is, are, am, was, were, be, been, being*. And note that only action verbs can be in the passive voice because only action verbs can have direct objects. (The direct objects of active-voice sentences become the subjects of their passive-voice counterparts.)

Note how we can form the active voice and the passive voice in the simple and the perfect tenses, and note how a form of *be* plus the *past participle* is required for passive voice:

Present	Mr. McAllister *takes* vitamins every day. (active)
	Vitamins *are taken* every day by Mr. McAllister. (passive)
Past	Robert *took* the test on Monday. (active)
	The test *was taken* by Robert on Monday. (passive)
Future	Kristen *will take* the test on Tuesday. (active)
	The test *will be taken* by Kristen on Tuesday. (passive)
Present Perfect	Martin *has taken* a long time to write the book. (active)
	A long time *has been taken* by Martin to write the book. (passive)
Past Perfect	Gail *had completed* the sculpture. (active)
	The sculpture *had been completed* by Gail. (passive)
Future Perfect	We *will have completed* our review by March 12. (active)
	Our review *will have been completed* by March 12. (passive)

Although we prefer the active voice to the passive voice, the passive voice has its place in business writing. Specifically, you should use the passive voice when you want to de-emphasize the doer of the action. For example, passive voice will typically be preferred in such an instance as the following:

Active: **You** failed to enclose the questionnaire.

Passive: The questionnaire was not enclosed.

Also, you will typically use passive voice when you do not know who the doer of the action was:

The company car was stolen.

My wallet was mailed to me.

In the active voice, a transitive verb will always have an object. You can locate the object by asking *What?* or *Whom?* after the verb.

You can always consult the dictionary to determine whether a verb is transitive or intransitive or both. Remember that many verbs can be either transitive or intransitive according to usage.

Unless you know whether a verb requires an object to complete its meaning, you may not use it correctly in your writing. For example, *rise, lie,* and *sit* are intransitive verbs; therefore, no other words are needed to complete their meanings. But notice also that they are active-voice verbs:

NO	The bread *raises.*
	The men *set* at the table.
	I *laid* on the bed yesterday.
YES	The bread *rises.*
	The men *sit* at the table.
	I *lay* on the bed yesterday.

3.   Use a linking verb to express a condition that requires neither active nor passive voice.

Linking verbs are neither active nor passive voice. They are always intransitive and therefore never take objects. The most-common linking verbs are forms of the verb *to be* (*am, is, are, was, were, be, been, being*). These *be* verbs are also commonly called *state-of-being verbs*. Additional linking verbs are such verbs as *appear, become, feel, look, remain, seem, smell, sound, stay,* and *taste*. Technically, these linking verbs are not state-of-being verbs, although some textbooks refer to them as such. To determine whether a verb other than a state-of-being verb is a linking verb, try to substitute a state-of-being verb in its place. If the sentence still has meaning, the verb is a linking verb. For example:

You *look* beautiful! also has meaning as: You *are* beautiful!

A linking verb is followed by a subject complement in the form of a noun, a pronoun, or an adjective (often called *predicate noun, predicate pronoun,* or *predicate adjective*). As a noun or a pronoun, a subject complement names the same person or thing referred to by the subject. As an adjective, a subject complement describes the subject in some way. For example:

The dog is a *collie*. (The subject complement is a noun.)

The person responsible is *he*. (The subject complement is a pronoun.)

My brother is *intelligent*. (The subject complement is an adjective.)

The subject complement as a pronoun oftentimes causes problems for writers. We will cover the predicate pronoun in depth in the unit on pronoun case.

4.   Within a sentence, avoid illogical shifts in voice.

Illogical shifts can occur not only in tense and mood but also in voice. An illogical shift in voice can be distracting or confusing to a reader.

Shifts in voice usually occur in complex or in compound sentences. Although a shift might occur within a paragraph or a document, we prefer to restrict ourselves to the sentence itself in trying to recognize and to change illogical shifts in voice.

Illogical shifts in voice can occur from active to passive or from passive to active. Within a sentence, we also can feel the awkwardness of a shift involving a linking-verb construction and an active-voice or passive-voice construction. Usually, these shifts reflect a shift in subject between clauses. Therefore, we advocate that you usually avoid mixing active, passive, or linking-verb constructions within a sentence. Obviously, we will run into situations in which we disagree about what is an illogical shift among active, passive, or linking-verb constructions.

Here are some examples of illogical shifts in voice:

Daniel enjoyed hunting deer in the fall, but fishing was also enjoyed throughout the year by him. (Reflects a shift from active voice to passive voice)

Cora's Saturdays are devoted to library study, and she takes a full load of courses every semester. (Reflects a shift from passive voice to active voice)

Active voice is easy to use, and our managers use active voice routinely in their writing. (Reflects a shift from a linking-verb construction to active voice)

Posttest

Mark the sentence **C** if all elements associated with voice in this lesson are correct. Mark the sentence **I** if it violates any element of this lesson's voice discussion or rules.

1. Ms. Mellor did an excellent job of handling the flowers for Mr. McKinnon's funeral. (Active voice is used)

2. The revised report will be reviewed by Mr. Miles early Tuesday morning. (The writer desires to emphasize the performer of the action)

3. The representatives discussed the old procedures carefully, and the revised procedures were distributed today to all members of the office staff.

4. Ms. Mellor sent the flowers to the Huntsman Funeral Home. (Active voice is used)

5. The results of the election will be known late Tuesday by Mr. Minor, and the results will be given to us early Wednesday morning.

6. The flowers were sent to the Huntsman Funeral Home by Ms. Mellor. (Passive voice is used)

7. Early Tuesday morning, Mr. Miles will review the revised report. (The writer desires to deemphasize the performer of the action)

8. Ms. Mellor looked totally depressed throughout the funeral this morning. (Passive voice is used)

Key: (1) C; (2) I—the performer, Mr. Miles, is deemphasized through the passive voice; (3) I—the sentence contains a shift from active voice to passive voice; (4) C; (5) C—both clauses are in the passive voice; (6) C; (7) I—through active voice, the performer, Mr. Miles, is emphasized; (8) I—the verb *looked* is a linking verb and is neither active nor passive.

LEVEL A

Name _____

Exercise
14–1

On the lines below, mark **T** if the statement is true; mark **F** if the statement is false.

_F_ 1. Passive voice is used to emphasize the performer of the action.

_F_ 2. English is concerned with three voices: active, passive, and state of being.

_T_ 3. An intransitive verb is a verb that does not require an object to complete its meaning.

_F_ 4. State-of-being verbs are such verbs as *be verbs* and *taste, smell,* and *feel.*

_T_ 5. Voice indicates whether the subject performs the action or whether the subject is being acted upon.

_F_ 6. The passive voice consists of some form of a *be verb* or *have* plus a past participle.

_T_ 7. The passive voice does have its place in the business world.

_T_ 8. You can locate the object of a transitive verb in the active voice by asking *what?* or *whom?* after the verb.

_F_ 9. Any verb used in the passive voice is an intransitive verb.

_T_ 10. *Rise, lie,* and *sit* are intransitive verbs.

_T_ 11. In general, we should use the active voice whenever possible because it is more direct and economical than the passive voice.

_F_ 12. Forms of *be* are the following: *is, are, am, has, have, had, was, were, be, been,* and *being.*

_F_ 13. *The check was not enclosed* is in the active voice.

_F_ 14. All linking verbs are active-voice verbs.

Exercise
14–2

Mark **A** if the verb is in active voice; mark **B** if the verb is in passive voice.

_B_ 1. The Zion's Bank check was endorsed by Pedro.

_A_ 2. Mayor Jenkins will lay the cornerstone of the City Center next week.

_B_ 3. Your check should have been deposited by Toni yesterday.

_A_ 4. Your office staff refused to give me your home telephone number.

_A_ 5. We have called all members of the committee three times.

_B_ 6. A copy of the minutes was sent to me in the hospital.

_B_ 7. Your request for transfer may be reviewed by Ms. Brigham tomorrow morning.

_A_ 8. Everyone wants a significant raise.

_B_ 9. The goodwill of our customers is valued highly by company management.

_A_ 10. At the time, Mr. and Mrs. Ueberroth were hurrying to the graduation ceremonies.

Exercise 14–3 — Write **T** if the verb is transitive; **I** for intransitive; **A** for active voice; **P** for passive voice; and **N** for neither active nor passive voice. Each sentence will have two answers.

_IA_ 1. During the play, we should sit close to the exit.

_TA_ 2. Yes, the salvage crew has raised the sunken ship.

_IP_ 3. A copy of our Invoice No. 2335 was faxed to you today.

_IN_ 4. The food at the new French restaurant was excellent.

_IN_ 5. The current recession, for all its problems, is not entirely bad.

_TA_ 6. Within the next month, hundreds of baseball players will file claims for their share of the collusion award.

_IP_ 7. The revised figures on population growth were analyzed by our team of statisticians.

_IA_ 8. Mr. Fernaldo's secretary refused to give me an appointment for next Monday.

_IA_ 9. With the right amount of yeast, the dough will rise properly.

_IA_ 10. I sat in the doctor's office for over an hour.

Exercise 14–4 — Mark the sentence **C** if all elements associated with voice in this lesson are correct. Mark the sentence **I** if it violates any element of this lesson's voice discussion or rules.

_C_ 1. JoAnn excused herself from the meeting because of illness. (Active voice is used)

_I_ 2. The quarterly tax return will be completed in the near future. (The writer desires to emphasize the performer of the action)

_I_ 3. The budget committee discussed the new salary procedures, and copies of the new procedures were given to the entire office staff.

_C_ 4. Whales are believed by some scientists to be as intelligent as humans. (The writer desires to deemphasize the performer of the action)

_C_ 5. The racquetballs were delivered to the Foothill Sports Center by Victor Quigley. (Passive voice is used)

_C_ 6. The results of the fish kill will be known next spring, and the results will be published in all newspapers in the state.

_I_ 7. Students enjoy our campus very much, and our university is being attended in greater numbers than ever before.

_I_ 8. By next Wednesday morning, Ms. Kilman will have located the missing statistical report. (The writer desires to deemphasize the performer of the action)

_I_ 9. Mr. Martinez looked unhappy throughout his daughter's wedding. (Passive voice is used)

_I_ 10. Vice President Germann is very smart. (The subject complement is a noun)

LEVEL B

Name _____

Exercise
14–5

Using the list below, write the letters that identify the tense, mood, and voice of the verb.

A	Past tense	G	Indicative mood
B	Present tense	H	Imperative mood
C	Future tense	I	Subjunctive mood
D	Past-perfect tense	J	Active voice
E	Present-perfect tense	K	Passive voice
F	Future-perfect tense	L	Linking-verb construction

BGL   1. Copyright law for copying software is clear.

EGK   2. Software users have been allowed to make one copy of the software for use as a backup.

DGK   3. For an upgrade, the user had been sold just one license by the software maker.

BGL   4. Any contract involving more than $500 is subject to my approval.

BHJ   5. Don't put any embarrassing information on your electronic mail system.

FGL   6. Users of our electronic mail system will have been careful about their messages.

AGK   7. The privacy issues were settled in the California courts.

CGJ   8. Will you get caught for copying software?

EGJ   9. Software companies have not accepted the copying practices.

BGL   10. Using electronic mail is writing in at least one respect.

Exercise
14–6

Write the letter identifying the sentence that reflects the correct application of all elements of voice as discussed in this lesson.

b   1. *a.* The droning of the housefly reminded me of childhood days at my grandfather's farm. (Linking verb is used)
      b. Doll dresses were sewn by my cousin and me. (Passive voice is used)
      c. The kitchen smells at Grandmother's were wonderful. (Passive voice is used)

a   2. *a.* Last summer, we returned to the Hobble Creek cabin of our honeymoon days. (Intransitive verb used)
      b. Immediately behind the cabin, Hobble Creek flows noisily down the canyon. (Transitive verb used)
      c. No television or radio is found in the Hobble Creek cabin. (Linking-verb construction used)

_c_   3. _a._   At the picnic, the aroma of grilled hot dogs and caramel corn mixed with the smell of gunpowder from firecrackers. (Passive voice used)

     _b._   Gibbonsville is considered one of the premier campgrounds in the wilderness area. (Linking-verb construction used)

     _c._   Children on three-wheeled bikes wait in the parking lot for their races to begin. (Intransitive verb used)

_a_   4. _a._   The fireworks display is an extraordinary display to climax the celebration. (Intransitive verb used)

     _b._   Throughout the day, the clowns have mingled freely with the children. (Passive voice used)

     _c._   The root beer tastes wonderful after an afternoon of baseball. (Active voice used)

_c_   5. _a._   The boys have eaten the watermelons without concern for the adults. (Passive voice used)

     _b._   The youngsters prepare for the treasure hunt, getting ready to hunt the coins in the pile of yellow straw. (Transitive verb used)

     _c._   Gibbonsville is the perfect place for reunion, reflection, and renewal. (Linking-verb construction used)

Exercise 14–7   Write the letter that identifies the sentence without a shift in tense, mood, or voice.

_c_   1. _a._   Apex Equipment has designed a new forklift truck, and the truck is engineered for simplicity of use.

     _b._   We should purchase one of the trucks, but our year-end surplus was fully expended last week.

     _c._   On the truck's controls, a concave shape signifies the up-down lever; and a convex shape identifies the tilt control.

_b_   2. _a._   Widespread use of the discount program could reduce travelers' fares, so don't be overly anxious to purchase tickets too far in advance.

     _b._   The fees are being imposed by foreign airlines, although similar fees are being considered by domestic carriers.

     _c._   Business travelers normally pay the highest fares, and the lowest fares are usually paid by vacation tour groups.

_c_   3. _a._   During their conversation, Mack grumbled about the work load while Marion discusses the change of supervisors.

     _b._   According to Matilda, if she were rich and if her father was still alive, her life would be different.

     _c._   Recently, Grandfather Herman had to enter a nursing home; but he did not like it.

_a_   4. _a._   At one point during the hike, Lon literally ran to catch up; but he soon found himself unable to keep up the pace.

     _b._   Ms. Kontas told me, ''Take a deep breath, and then you should just speak normally.''

     _c._   On Fridays, Riley mowed and trimmed the lawn; but the other days of the week were devoted to fishing.

_b_   5. _a._   With much concern, the girls rebooted the computer; but some of the components were ruined by the lightning strike.

     _b._   The printer was broken yesterday, but it was fixed by noon today.

     _c._   The decision to sell half the holdings was arrived at by the board of directors, and I completed the sale the following Monday.

LEVEL C

Name _____

Exercise   Write **C** if the sentence reflects the voice indicated in parentheses. Write **I** if the sen-
14–8   tence reflects a different voice. Then edit all I sentences so they reflect the voice indi-
           cated.

_I_   1. You should make ~~your request~~ for a transfer in writing. (Passive voice used)
            Should be made

_I_   3. ~~A decision was reached today by the committee.~~ (Active voice used)
            The committee reached a decision today.

_I_   4. Lanny's nomination to the committee ~~was seconded by Julio.~~ (Active voice used)
            Julio seconded

_C_   5. By Friday, the junior prom queen will have been selected. (Passive voice used)

_I_   6. Donn ~~is eager~~ to pursue the High Uintahs hunting trip. (Active voice used)
            wants

_C_   7. The damaged 747 finally landed safely at Salt Lake International. (Active voice used)

_I_   8. ~~Troy's new novel is being praised by most members of our book club.~~ (Linking-verb
            Most members of our book club are complimentary of Troy's new book.

          construction used)

_I_   9. ~~The company was founded initially by my grandmother.~~ (Active voice used)
            My grandmother founded the company initially.

_C_   10. Lieutenant Hyatt has examined the crime scene with his usual attention to detail. (Active

           voice used)

Exercise   In each sentence, change passive voice to active voice or active voice to passive voice.
14–9

Editing   1. ~~The wrecked automobile was~~ quickly sold ~~by the insurance company.~~
              The insurance company   *the wrecked automobile.*

          2. Cynthia, my best friend, ~~was chosen~~ as homecoming queen.
               We chose

          3. ~~Mr. Konakis was~~ urged ~~by the students~~ to rewrite the last act of the play.
               The students   *Mr. Konakis*

          4. ~~The state troopers stopped~~ all traffic going north on Interstate 15 *was stopped by the
             state troopers.*

          5. ~~The volcanic eruption in Hawaii destroyed~~ several homes within a few hours *by the
             volcanic eruption.* *were destroyed*

6. Yesterday, ~~someone stole~~ Mr. Juliano's new Mercedes, *was stolen by someone.*

The metric system is used by most
7. ~~Most~~ of the world today. ~~uses the metric system.~~

We bruised many ~~~~ *we*
8. ~~Many~~ of the peaches that ~~were picked~~ ~~by us~~ on Friday. ~~were bruised slightly.~~

~~~~ *I was*
9. ~~With great patience, my Uncle Loren~~ taught ~~me~~ how to play golf, *by my Uncle Loren, who used great patience.*

Mr. Keller ~~~~ *one tour member's name*
10. ~~One tour member's name was~~ accidentally left off the final list. ~~by Mr. Keller.~~

Exercise 14–10

Write a sentence that fulfills the directive.

Composition

1. A sentence containing two passive-voice verbs.

_____

_____

2. A sentence containing two active-voice verbs.

_____

_____

3. An active-voice sentence with a transitive verb.

_____

_____

4. A sentence with a shift from active to passive voice.

_____

_____

Exercise 14–11

Revise each sentence to eliminate any shift in tense, mood, or voice.

Cumulative Editing

Kurt mowed the lawn.
1. ~~The lawn was mowed by Kurt, and~~ I should have raked the grass cuttings.

does
2. The road map shows the cities and roads, but it ~~did~~ not show the counties.

3. Most employees are congratulated for their accomplishments, ~~which helped them stay motivated.~~ *and are motivated by the congratulations.*

4. Kathy ~~was~~ *is* required to stay on the dialysis machine, and her husband is ~~able~~ *permitted* to take her to the hospital each time.

5. The knobs and dials have been replaced by a touch screen, and the operators' ~~reduced their~~ training time and errors, *have been reduced.*

6. The new camera was judged one of the best consumer ~~products; decide~~ *products. You may decide* for yourself whether such a judgment is equitable.

7. ~~The~~ *Corrine passed the* final exams ~~were passed by Corinne~~, but she ~~is not excited~~ *expressed no excitement* about her grades.

8. If the seeds had been planted according to directions, the refund ~~can~~ *could* be sent as stipulated in the warranty.

9. ~~An internship is more vital than ever~~ *You should know the importance of an internship, and*; you should pursue a summer internship with Fuqua Electronics.

10. Harry Truman was considered a defeated candidate, ~~who is~~ *but he was* elected President of the United States.

Exercise 14–12   Edit the following sentences to correct all tense, mood, voice, frequently misspelled words, and confusing-word errors.

Cumulative Editing

1. Has Toni ~~did~~ *done* her share by ~~recomending~~ *recommending* an appropriate design for the new ~~stationary~~ *stationery*?

2. Please confirm ~~weather~~ *whether* the tomatoes ~~definately~~ *definitely* were ~~growed~~ *grown* in ~~you're~~ *your* sister's hothouse.

3. ~~Everyone~~ *We purchased every one* of the defective ~~fluoresent~~ *fluorescent* lights ~~was purchased~~ from Higbee Electric, so *we must* change our source of supply next time we order.

4. I wish I ~~had went~~ *had gone* with Cassie to the ~~personel~~ *personnel* office at the ~~begining~~ *beginning* of the month.

5. Please ~~pursuade every one~~ *persuade everyone* to be tested for drug use, and ~~you should~~ report your knowledge of any ~~elicit~~ *illicit* drugs.

6. ~~T~~*The* criteria for success, ~~was developed by Ms. Fowles,~~ *Ms. Fowles developed* but Ms. Coombs ~~surprized~~ *surprised* us all when she disagreed with Ms. Fowles' ~~arguements~~ *arguments*.

7. I should have ~~wrote~~ *written* to Opal, ~~whose~~ *who's* responsible for the ~~broshure; but the broshure was not~~ *brochure. However, I did not receive* ~~recieved by me~~ *the brochure* until this morning.

8. We ~~truely~~ *truly* appreciate your consulting role with the City ~~Counsel~~ *Council*, and ~~your name was suggested~~ *we have suggested you* as a replacement for the ~~imminent~~ *eminent* Mr. Frandsen.

9. ~~Incidently~~ *Incidentally*, the ~~defendent~~ *defendant* agreed ~~too have completed~~ *to complete* the civic service if ~~its recomended by~~ the judge, *recommends the service.*

10. ~~Ultimately~~ *Eventually*, Ms. Barlow will ~~have persued~~ *pursue* the job as vice ~~principle; so~~ *principal. Therefore,* Mr. Beeman should let his interest be known.

Exercise 14–13 Edit the following sentences to correct all tense, mood, voice, and number-usage violations.

Cumulative Editing

1. The office staff ~~will have~~ mourned the ~~forty~~ *40*-year-old senator who ~~had~~ died in a plane crash last May ~~30th~~ *30*.

2. Savings rates today remain 25% *percent* above the levels of ~~2~~ *two* years ago, so investors ~~are counseled~~ *we counsel* to use our money-market savings plan.

3. By January ~~1st~~ *1*, more than ~~three thousand~~ *3,000* individuals *will* have been trained on our high-tech equipment.

4. The least-expensive policy, ~~having expected~~ *which we expect* to cost anywhere from $20.00 *20* to $40.00 *40* in monthly premiums, will contain only certain core benefits.

5. Part A, which pays hospital bills for ~~34,000,000~~ *34 million* persons, is financed by a fixed-rate payroll tax of 2.9~~%~~ *percent* per worker.

6. We agreed to ~~have concluded~~ *conclude* from our research in ~~thirteen~~ *13* medical centers that therapy ~~could~~ ~~save four thousand~~ *saves 4,000* lives a year.

7. Mr. Anthony regularly visits ~~2~~ *two* hospitals, ~~thirty~~ *30* and ~~sixty~~ *60* miles away; and ∧ *his wife teaches* the Bible-study classes. ~~are taught by his wife.~~

8. If you are ~~fifty~~ *50* or over, you can easily join AARW~~,~~ *& by filling out and mailing* ~~just fill out and mail~~ the coupon along with your $5.~~00~~ check.

9. Annual dues include $3.60 for *Modern Living* and ~~$.95~~ *95 cents* for the *AARW Bulletin*, and ~~a one~~ *your* ~~thousand-dollar~~ *membership includes a $1,000* accidental-death policy ~~is included with your membership.~~

10. Gilmer, 62 at the time, was told her job was abolished; ~~the firm assigned~~ her duties ∧ *were assigned* to a newly hired ~~twenty~~ *20*-year-old worker.

Exercise 14–14

Cumulative Editing

Edit the following sentences to correct any misuse of tense, mood, voice, abbreviations, or capitals.

1. ~~Doctor~~ *Dr.* Gallup, a supporting member of ~~M.A.D.D.~~ *MADD*, recently agreed to serve as a ~~c~~ *C*apitol ~~h~~ *H*ill lobbyist; ∧ *we reached* our decision to work with him ~~was reached~~ after much deliberation.

2. ~~Cmdr.~~ *Commander* Williams will ~~have~~ *note* ~~noted~~ that the river has become a significant problem to the ~~c~~ *C*oast *G*~~g~~uard and the ~~US~~ *U.S.* taxpayer.

3. The American ~~s~~ *S*ociety for ~~t~~ *T*raining and ~~d~~ *D*evelopment estimates that 60 percent of ~~N.~~ *North* America's largest companies now offer leadership training, but ~~the percent was estimated to be higher~~ ~~than that by Geo. Steed.~~ *George* Steed *estimates the percent to be chigher.*

4. ~~Gen.~~ *General* Motors has developed a clear, protective coating to go on top of paint~~,~~ *;* the coating should protect the paint from acid rain.

5. Dr. Salina, ~~c~~ Chief of ~~s~~ Surgery at the ~~Ut~~. *Utah* Valley ~~Med~~. *Medical* Center, announced his findings at the ~~A.S.C.O.~~ *ASCO* Convention; ~~and his report was applauded by~~ everyone in attendance, *applauded his report.*

6. Lee Nay, the ~~v~~ Vice ~~p~~ President of the ~~N~~. *New* Jersey ~~p~~ Plant, has proposed a plan to ~~have told~~ *tell* potential buyers how much used cars ~~were~~ *are* actually worth.

7. ~~Prof. Wm.~~ *Professor William* Noyes, a ~~Prof~~. *professor* of ~~N~~atural ~~R~~esources at the ~~Univ~~. *University* of ~~N. Mex.~~, *New Mexico* wants **to build the** facility on ~~C~~ity-owned property.

8. "Original products like macaroni and cheese are showing growth," says **Lucinda Sabey,** ~~p~~ President of Midway Associations, ~~Incorporated~~, *Inc.* a ~~N.Y.~~ *New York* ~~M~~arket ~~R~~esearch firm.

9. The ~~s~~ supreme ~~c~~ court ruled that ~~f~~ Federal ~~l~~ Law does not require ~~S~~ hareholders to make what ~~will~~ ~~be~~ *is* believed a futile request to the directors to ~~have filed~~ *file* a lawsuit.

10. You are invited to tour several major ~~W~~ineries in ~~S~~. *South* Australia on camelback, so ~~c~~ call our ~~C~~amel ~~F~~arm for more information.

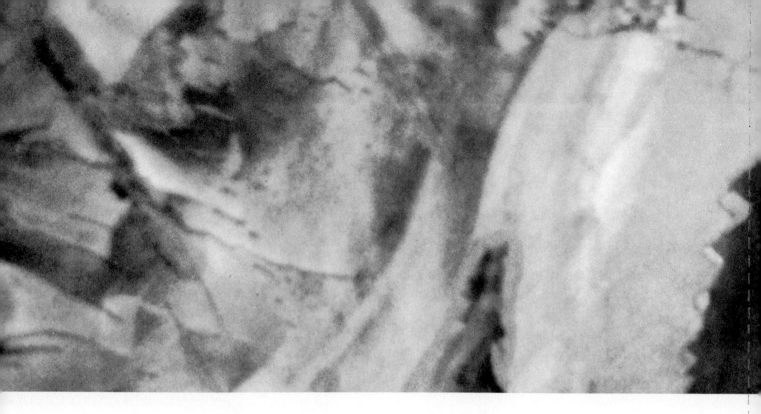

LESSONS IN THIS UNIT

15. THE COMMA FOR JOINING INDEPENDENT CLAUSES
16. THE SEMICOLON FOR JOINING INDEPENDENT CLAUSES
17. INTRODUCTORY CLAUSES, PHRASES, AND WORDS
18. SERIES, INTERRUPTERS, APPOSITIVES, AND APPENDAGES
19. OTHER PUNCTUATION

Properly applied punctuation helps your reader understand your message. Improper punctuation slows down the communication process and can cause confusion for your reader.

We have all experienced the frustration that comes because of the exceptions and inconsistencies in the English language. On occasion, perhaps you have criticized the ''authorities'' who make the usage rules and wished you could be responsible for making the rules more consistent. Undoubtedly, you have experienced these feelings as you learned and used the rules of punctuation. For example, note the punctuation differences (inconsistencies) in the following sentences:

John wrote the report and Jane mailed it today.
John wrote the report, and Jane mailed it today.
John wrote the report; and Jane mailed it today.

At the store I purchased apples, oranges and bananas.
At the store I purchased apples, oranges, and bananas.
At the store, I purchased apples, oranges, and bananas.

Which sentences in the above examples are punctuated correctly? If you have explored the

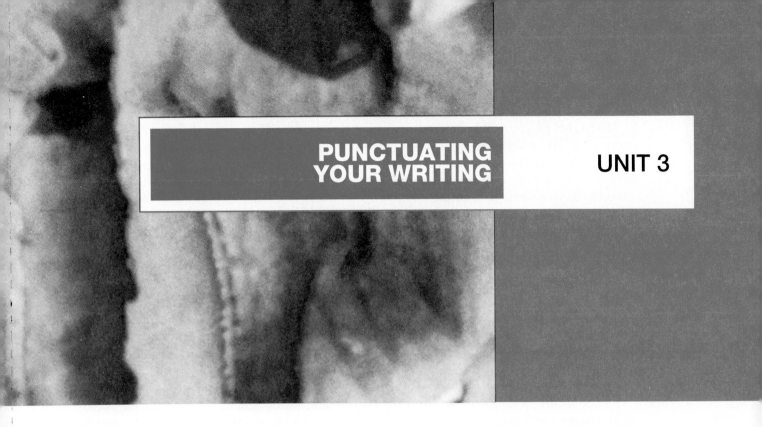

various style manuals in disciplines such as English, journalism, and business, you will know that all of the sentences might be punctuated correctly—depending on the style manual and the discipline.

In the business world, we try to be **consistent** in applying the rules of punctuation. We recognize the potential exceptions and inconsistencies; but we then decide on a consistent, rational, and preferred application of the various rules. From teaching and learning perspectives, that approach makes the process of mastering the various rules of punctuation much easier.

If this textbook were a comprehensive usage handbook, we might introduce you to almost 100 different rules of punctuation. However, in Lessons 15 through 18, we have restricted our scope of punctuation coverage to those rules that are most frequently used and also most frequently abused. The rules in these lessons are those that are generally crucial if you are to avoid any chance of miscommunication. Then, in Lesson 19, we introduce you to several other rules of punctuation that are nice to know but that do not necessarily cause miscommunication if they are misapplied.

When you have mastered the rules in this unit, you can *intentionally* influence your reader to help him or her understand your message. That is, through the correct application of the rules in the unit, you can reflect one or more of the following objectives of punctuation usage and choice:

1. To force pauses at appropriate points.

2. To increase or decrease the amount of emphasis.

3. To clarify the meaning of the thought you are communicating.

4. To give variety to your writing.

5. To signal changes in direction or thought.

6. To punctuate according to acceptable business standards.

Even though you will learn to use punctuation intentionally so you can accomplish one or more of the above objectives, you need to keep in mind that the best punctuation is nearly inconspicuous. That is, the punctuation is ''there''; but the reader is not necessarily conscious of its presence. In general, your reader will be conscious of the punctuation you use only when the meaning of your message is unclear.

When you master the punctuation rules in Unit 3, you will be ''home free'' most of the time as you punctuate your writing. That is, you will know you have punctuated your writing correctly; and you will be assured your punctuation will not be a stumbling block to your reader's comprehension of your message.

Therefore, we suggest you think of punctuation as an aid to good sentence structure. You will not necessarily make poorly written sentences clearer by merely adding punctuation here and there in sentences. You must first write a clear sentence and then be sure the punctuation is correct to increase the clarity of the sentence.

To be totally successful in mastering the rules of punctuation, you must *internalize* the vocabulary that goes with the punctuation rules. Therefore, as with all units in this textbook, give special attention to understanding the terms found at the beginning of each lesson; and be grateful the terminology also applies to most other lessons in the text.

Finally, remember that common sense will help you recognize when some kind of punctuation is necessary. From that point, realize that your mastery of the punctuation rules in Unit 3 will ensure your choosing the correct and best mark of punctuation!

You will first be introduced in Lessons 15 and 16 to the punctuation used to join independent clauses in compound sentences. In Lesson 17, you will explore the punctuation following introductory clauses, phrases, and words. Then, in Lesson 18, you will learn about punctuation used for items in the middle of a sentence and preceding appended items at the end of a sentence. Finally, in Lesson 19, you will be exposed to selected miscellaneous rules of punctuation that are infrequently used and that admittedly are not as important as the punctuation rules covered in Lessons 15 through 18.

Punctuation involving compound modifiers and consecutive, parallel adjectives will be covered later in the textbook. In many English usage textbooks, the hyphen used with compound modifiers and the comma used with consecutive, parallel adjectives are often presented along with other punctuation marks. Because compound modifiers and consecutive, parallel adjectives are modifiers in the true sense of the word, we present the rules for these modifiers in the modifiers unit, Unit 7.

One doctoral dissertation showed that, for business-writing purposes, 27 rules of punctuation accounted for 97 percent of all punctuation used. As we look at those 27 rules, we find that several, such as the colon following a salutation in a business letter, need not be given singular attention. Therefore, we will limit our punctuation exposure to a relatively few rules; and if you can master these few, you will be able to use the correct punctuation in nearly every instance.

THE COMMA FOR JOINING INDEPENDENT CLAUSES

Remember that a clause is a group of words with a subject and a verb. Remember also that an *independent* clause (also known as a *main* clause) can "stand alone." That is, it can be a simple sentence when the first word is capitalized and a terminal punctuation mark is placed at the end.

As you know from Lesson 2, when one independent clause is combined with another independent clause and no dependent clauses are involved, the independent clauses form a compound sentence. This combining process is referred to by some style manuals as a *joining* of the independent thoughts, whereas other style manuals refer to the process as a *separating* of the independent thoughts.

In this text, we view the process as a joining process. That is, when we join two independent clauses, we want to reflect the relationship between the clauses; and we use punctuation to help the joining process.

Generally, the choice of what punctuation to use when you join independent clauses is your option. As a writer, you know best how closely related (or widely separated) the thoughts in the independent clauses are. Your role is to choose the punctuation that comes closest to conveying the intended meaning to your reader.

How do you decide which punctuation to use when you join two independent clauses? The answer to that question is found when you answer the following questions:

1. How important is the idea expressed by each clause?

2. How closely related are the thoughts in the clauses?

3. How much and what kind of emphasis do I want to give to each clause?

4. Do I want to use a "conjunctive joiner" to help join the clauses?

5. What kind of conjunctive joiner do I want to use?

Obviously, you have several punctuation options from which to choose when you join independent clauses to form a compound sentence. When you understand the implications of the various options, you can then select the option you desire so you *can influence* your reader in the way you desire as a writer.

Pretest

With a **C** or an **I**, indicate whether the punctuation is correct or incorrect in the following sentences. Then punctuate the sentences marked **I**.

1. He sat at his computer this morning, and made a preliminary draft of his speech.

2. Lisa arrived at 8:30 but she left soon after.

3. Rachel went to medical school and became a physician; but Timothy opted to attend the seminary to become a minister.

4. The Cougars have the conference's leading quarterback, the Cowboys have outstanding running backs.

5. About a hundred people set out to climb Mt. Timpanogos only 25 succeeded during the July 4 event.

6. Randolph has no intention of completing the course nor is he willing to petition for an incomplete in the course.

Key: (1) I—no comma; (2) C or I but I in this text; comma before *but*; (3) C—comma in place of semicolon is also correct; (4) I—change comma to semicolon or add *but* following comma; (5) I—semicolon before *only* or add comma and *but* before *only*; (6) I—comma before *nor*.

Terminology

Clause—A "group" of words with a subject and a verb. A group might consist of only two words, as in *Christina laughed*. A group might also consist of one word with an understood subject, as in *Stop!*

Comma splice—A sentence containing two independent clauses that are joined with a comma only.

Compound sentence—A sentence containing two or more independent clauses and no dependent clauses. The writer has the task of joining the independent clauses by using correct connecting devices—punctuation and conjunctive joiners.

Conjunctive joiner—A word or phrase used to join two independent clauses. The only conjunctive joiner used in Lesson 15 is the coordinating conjunction.

Coordinating conjunction—Any one of seven conjunctions (*and, but, or, nor, for, so, yet*) used to join independent clauses.

Independent clause—A group of words that can stand alone. An independent clause is also called a *main clause*. By itself, it can be a simple sentence.

Run-on sentence—A sentence containing two independent clauses but containing no punctuation or conjunctive joiner to connect the two clauses.

Rules

Use
T15-1
here

1. **Use a comma preceding a coordinating conjunction that joins two independent clauses.**

We use seven coordinating conjunctions in English: *and, but, or, nor, for, so,* and *yet*. Each signals a particular meaning to the reader, and the choice of which to use is usually easy to make. Note that all the coordinating conjunctions are short. Each is a one-syllable word.

The comma tells your reader that the first independent clause has ended and that the second is about to begin.

NO   I like your writing style and I want you to teach it to Jose.

YES   I like your writing style, and I want you to teach it to Jose.

Learning Hint 1.   Some style manuals suggest the comma may be omitted when the two independent clauses are short (usually five or fewer words).

John did the research and Antonio wrote the report.

For all exercises in this text, we require you **always** to use the comma before the coordinating conjunction. The comma forces a pause between the independent thoughts and helps ensure that the reader will not misread the sentence.

Learning Hint 2.   If neither punctuation nor a conjunctive joiner is used to join the independent clauses of a compound sentence, the result is called a *run-on sentence*.

NO   Mr. Gamache cannot attend the meeting he will be in St. Louis on the 13th.

A run-on sentence is one of the most flagrant grammatical blunders. Its seriousness is reflected by the fact that some writing authorities refer to it as a red flag of illiteracy.

Use
T15-2
here

2. **Do not join two independent clauses with a comma only.**

If a comma by itself is used to join two independent clauses, the result is called a *comma splice*.

NO   Ms. Durtschi missed her flight on Monday, she finally arrived on Wednesday.

The word *splice* signifies the writer is trying to join the two independent thoughts with a comma only. The comma splice is another serious punctuation blunder some writing authorities label a red flag of illiteracy.

To correct a comma splice, you have the option of using any of the appropriate rules in either Lessons 15 or 16. In Lesson 15, your choice is a comma preceding a coordinating conjunction, as follows:

Ms. Durtschi missed her flight on Monday, but she finally arrived on Wednesday.

In Lesson 15, you will concentrate on the comma preceding a coordinating conjunction to join two independent clauses. Do not apply the semicolon when you are joining independent clauses until you do the exercises in Lesson 16.

Use T15-3 here

3. **Do not use a comma to separate compound elements that are not independent clauses but that are joined with a conjunction.**

For example:

NO   The stock market went down yesterday, but appears to be rebounding today.

YES   The stock market went down yesterday but appears to be rebounding today.

For some reason, novice writers often have a tendency to put a comma before a conjunction. Rule 1 tells us we put the comma before the conjunction only when we are joining two independent clauses in a compound sentence—not when we are separating two other compound elements such as the compound verbs *went* and *appears*.

Posttest

With a **C** or an **I**, indicate whether the punctuation is correct or incorrect in the following sentences. Then punctuate the sentences marked **I**.

1. We invited every graduate of the Class of 1985 to attend our Homecoming Gala we were delighted when about 75 percent of those invited attended and participated.

2. Bob taught the class but I graded the papers.

3. I prepared the handouts for the oral presentation at the San Antonio conference last month, Ms. Chan gave the presentation and answered the follow-up correspondence.

4. Ms. Redd completed the Athena Project yesterday, and gave the final report to me this morning.

5. Mr. Boyter does not want to take his own car to the Springville seminar for he desires to ride with us in the company car.

6. The Personnel Grievance Committee did indeed conduct a thorough review of your complaint; but at least two members of the committee had preconceived biases about your actions.

Key: (1) I—following *Gala*, use a comma and *and*; or use a semicolon; (2) C or I but I in this text because a comma is required before *but*; (3) I—change comma to semicolon or add *and* following the comma; (4) I—no comma; (5) I—comma before *for*; (6) C—comma in place of semicolon is also correct.

LEVEL A

Name _____

Exercise 15–1 On the lines below, write **T** if the statement is true and **F** if the statement is false.

_F_ 1. A phrase is a group of words with a subject and a verb.

_F_ 2. A clause that can stand alone and thus be a simple sentence is called a dependent clause.

_F_ 3. When two independent clauses are joined together in a sentence, the result is known as a complex sentence.

_T_ 4. Choosing among the correct options for joining independent clauses is the writer's option.

_T_ 5. Different conjunctive joiners impact (influence) a reader in different ways.

_F_ 6. The seven coordinating conjunctions are *and, but, or, for, so, yet,* and *thus.*

_T_ 7. Throughout the text, you will be required to always use punctuation preceding a coordinating conjunction in a compound sentence.

_F_ 8. A run-on sentence is the same thing as a comma splice.

_T_ 9. Both the run-on sentence and the comma splice are considered to be red flags of illiteracy.

_F_ 10. Good punctuation advice is, *Put a comma before a conjunction most of the time.*

Exercise 15–2 Mark **C** if the punctuation is correct; mark **I** if the punctuation is incorrect.

_I_ 1. We recently traveled to Idaho, and went down the Salmon River.

_I_ 2. Conder played the first half at the quarterback position, Eardley played quarterback during the second half.

_I_ 3. Two of the employees signed the agreement but three others refused to do so.

_C_ 4. I know why everyone likes ice cream, but I think 4 gallons is too much to buy.

_C_ 5. Scott has a solution, and I think he will share it with us tomorrow.

_I_ 6. Brooks reported that he has finished the project, and that he is ready to begin work on the exit report.

_I_ 7. His rates are inexpensive and his work is excellent.

_I_ 8. We lost our luggage on the Boston flight, we recovered everything two weeks later.

_I_ 9. We expect to be through by March 15, thus we hope to arrive in Delta on March 22.

_I_ 10. The tenants did extensive damage to the apartment the manager did not discover the damage until the tenants had moved.

Exercise 15–3 Write **C** if the two independent clauses are joined correctly; write **I** if they are joined incorrectly.

_I_ 1. Nikki refused to drink the water, she thought it was polluted.

_I_ 2. Vaughn overhauled his car last week, thus it is now ready to drive to Yonkers.

_I_ 3. Mr. Reimschissel is having trouble learning to ski just last week he crashed into a tree for the third time.

_C_ 4. Everyone in the group considered a college education to be a must, yet four group members refused to take the college-admission examination.

_I_ 5. We have not enrolled Gwen in the soccer camp nor have we seriously considered doing so.

_I_ 6. Don't delay write your senator today!

_C_ 7. The Festival of Independence will be enjoyable, for you will gain a new appreciation of the freedoms you have.

_I_ 8. Robyn admitted she had donated blood so Derek felt he should also donate a pint.

_I_ 9. Ms. Reynauld ordered the software, Ms. Reiger taught the staff how to use it.

_C_ 10. Mr. Orehoski wants to fly to Hawaii for the convention and also wants to take two of his children with him.

Exercise 15–4 Mark **Y** (for **yes**) if the clauses are joined correctly with punctuation and a coordinating conjunction; mark **N** (for **no**) if the clauses are not joined with a coordinating conjunction or if they are punctuated incorrectly.

_N_ 1. In Pineview, plantations nestle among oaks draped with Spanish moss and scarlet poinsettias line the narrow streets.

_Y_ 2. Everything may seem tranquil, but it's not.

_N_ 3. The focus of attention is the satellite dish that the Optsitnik Company wants to put on top of its building, but that the preservationists have blocked.

_N_ 4. Optsitnik has branches in many small towns, but has just one broker in each office.

_Y_ 5. Mr. Optsitnik says that satellite dishes provide an essential communications link and give investors everything from faster stock-order executions to economic updates from Optsitnik headquarters.

_N_ 6. The dishes are an important symbol of high-tech prowess, thus associated brokerage firms desire to have one.

_Y_ 7. The advice given by objectors is, ''Disseminate your information the historic way, and don't clutter our city's skyline.''

_N_ 8. Optsitnik has appealed in county court, and notes that the zoning board initially granted a variance.

LEVEL B

Name _____

Exercise
15–5

Write the letter that matches the reason associated with each sentence's punctuation and/or conjunctive joiner.

A   Comma splice
B   Run-on sentence

C   Sentence correct
D   None of the above

_B_ 1. We spent the entire night in the airport we didn't get home until the next evening.

_A_ 2. Alysann has the answers, she'll share them at the study session.

_A_ 3. Professor Huffstutler taught the course during the first four weeks, Professor Martynski took over for the duration of the semester.

_B_ 4. Gretchen anticipates she will have the report completed by February 2 thus the Standards Committee will be able to start its work on February 3.

_A_ 5. Joe knows all of you like liver and onions, his landlady won't let him cook such things in the apartment.

_D_ 6. We ended up in Denver after one day, and then took two days to get to Pueblo.

_D_ 7. I concluded that you have the experience, and that your resume is entirely adequate.

_D_ 8. McDougall's Restaurant is nearby and the food is exceptional.

_B_ 9. The students wanted to rent the apartment the owner decided not to rent to students.

_C_ 10. Three of the students decided to go with us to the Comdex convention, but two others could not afford to pay the lodging expenses.

Exercise
15–6

Write the letter that identifies the one best sentence.

_b_ 1. a. I usually have difficulty starting to write a research paper this paper is no exception.
       b. The medical costs of drug abuse are high, and the current annual costs of drug abuse are about $60 billion.
       c. Many pros and cons exist for drug legalization, the cons of legalization outweigh the benefits of legalization.

_a_ 2. a. Many problems exist in college athletics today, and many forces around the country contribute to these problems.
       b. The biggest problems involving college athletics are athletes' education, and people's obsession with money.
       c. Some athletes who come from disadvantaged backgrounds do not have the tools to compete academically, unfortunately these students' academic skills do not match their superior athletic skills.

_c_   3. *a.*   Crime is perhaps an unavoidable problem today and authorities are desperately trying to stop it.

         b.   White-collar criminals are a new breed of thieves, they are not the typical streetwise, undereducated criminals.

         c.   We have no definite answers, but we must take corrective measures.

_a_   4. *a.*   People are either for or against euthanasia, and heated arguments exist on both sides of the issue.

         b.   Opponents are repulsed by the thought of active euthanasia and they do not think that passive euthanasia should be allowed.

         c.   Nevertheless, society should allow passive euthanasia because it is justifiable, however active euthanasia should not be tolerated.

_c_   5. *a.*   If the buying company lays off employees, the community may lose a portion of its tax base, and experience increased unemployment and welfare payments.

         b.   The Federal Government is considering requiring increased disclosure in takeovers, and various changes in the tax laws to regulate the use of leveraged buyouts.

         c.   Mergers are financial transactions that involve the buying and selling of a business, and leveraged buyouts are mergers that finance large portions of the purchase price of the transaction with debt.

_c_   6. *a.*   The students incur the costs of an extra year in school yet the accounting firms have to pay higher starting salaries to the students.

         b.   The number of people qualified to sit for the CPA exam has gradually increased, student supply is a short-run concern.

         c.   Class demand doubled during the year before the 150-hour requirement became law, and two graduating classes merged into one to meet the law's timetable.

_b_   7. *a.*   Office automation includes personal computers, local area networks, software, and printers, such items have become much more prevalent and useful in the last decade.

         b.   Users have more time to think smart and to think creatively, so faster decisions can be made.

         c.   Regular backup of files should be made security measures should be taken to safeguard information

_c_   8. *a.*   The volume of park visitors has tripled and annual concession revenues now exceed $500 million.

         b.   Congressman Omer argues that concessionaire contracts last too long, and that rents and fees are far too low.

         c.   Forty contracts are due for renewal this year, and 60 more will be considered in three years.

_c_   9. *a.*   The homeless are not found solely within big cities, they may be found in almost all areas of the country.

         b.   Many homeless are ordinary citizens some of these citizens are homeless because of economic reasons.

         c.   Some homeless are unwilling to do what is needed to overcome their homelessness, so they must bear much of the blame for their troubles.

LEVEL C

Name _____

Exercise
15–7

Edit the sentences by eliminating incorrect punctuation and by adding appropriate punctuation and coordinating conjunctions.

1. The laser printer has caught on quickly; *for* laser printers use one of the best software packages on the market—desk-top publishing.

2. Laser and ink-jet printers can handle graphics as well as text, and are now affordable and durable substitutes for impact printers.

3. We did not have adequate software for our use, so we had to develop our own software for our specific applications.

4. New versions of each software package are available, *and* the new versions often include sophisticated capabilities and functions.

5. The future of office automation looks good, for business can expect to see better graphics and better user interface.

6. Many would-be users are scared off by the large costs involved, and are afraid that no immediate monetary benefits will be found.

7. Some businesses have spent much money implementing a system, *but* they have not seen an expected increase in sales or profits.

8. Other companies have purchased large systems, but do not use the systems because of ineffective training.

9. Most crimes are money theft, but some are file manipulation.

10. The computer operator will usually blame the computer if data are lost, but having backups of data will eliminate the disaster factor of such data loss.

Exercise 15–8

Cumulative Editing

Edit the following sentences that reflect misuse of verb rules, frequently misspelled words, confusing words, and the rules in Lesson 15. Be especially watchful for shifts in tense, mood, or voice.

1. Many ~~prominant~~ *prominent* coaches and trainers provide steroids for ~~there~~ *their* athletes, ~~steroids are reccomended and prescribed by some physicians.~~ *and some physicians recommend and prescribe steroids.*

2. At least one short-term positive ~~affect~~ *effect* results for the athlete who ~~used~~ *uses* steroids *for* they ~~definately~~ *definitely* promote muscle development.

3. ~~No~~ *We have not verified any* conclusive evidence ~~has been verified~~ relative ~~too~~ *to* the extent of steroid use by athletes *,* but many athletes ~~truely~~ *truly* confirm that ~~the drugs are used.~~ *they use the drugs.*

4. ~~The~~ *An athlete should be advised that the* health risks of using steroids are great, *and* ~~an athlete should be~~ ~~adviced~~ *counseled* to look at the dangers of using steroids before being ~~pursuaded~~ *persuaded* about whether to take the drugs.

5. Steroids used by American athletes are produced ~~principly~~ *principally* in the United States, *but athletes sometimes are sent* ~~go~~ to Mexico or England for secondary sources of supply.

6. Steroids are ~~accessable~~ *accessible* from over-the-counter sources in Mexico *,* so some athletes go ~~their~~ *there* to obtain the drugs.

7. Most high-school steroid users have been ~~counciled~~ *Counseled* about steroids by their high-school coaches *,* but the *users* ~~coaches~~ often ~~gave the steroids to the users.~~ *are given steroids by the coaches.*

8. Major steroid dealers in the past regularly ~~send~~ *sent* out direct-mail ~~advertizing,~~ *advertising* *and* catalogs to athletic ~~personel.~~ *personnel.*

9. A pertinent issue related to steroid use is that an athlete experiences positive ~~affects~~ *effects* when taking steroids, *and* ~~an athlete is encouraged by~~ such ~~affects~~ *effects encourage the athlete* to continue using the drugs.

10. Some steroid users think that the body normally tells the user when to "cut ~~lose~~ *loose*," ~~but this message often is overridden by~~ the testosterone imperative to train hard *,* *but* *often overrides this message.*

11. A euphoric state with diminished fatigue ~~had been~~ *is* produced by steroids, so ~~consistant~~ *consistent* training

is enhanced.

**Exercise
15–9** Edit all number-usage, verb, and Lesson 15 punctuation errors in the following sentences. Use Lesson 15 punctuation rules for joining independent clauses.

Cumulative
Editing

1. Retired people do a lot of volunteer work, and say they ~~had desired~~ *desire* to help out even more.

2. Two out of five people ~~sixty~~ *60* or older ~~will have performed~~ *performed* some sort of volunteer activity

during the preceding year, or about ~~one and a half~~ *1.5* million people in that age group ~~were~~ *are*

volunteers as of the current month.

3. About ~~1/4~~ *one-fourth* of the nonvolunteers would donate time and effort if they ~~have been~~ *were* asked, *and* another

~~2~~ *two* out of ~~5~~ *five* say they might.

4. My grandmother wishes she ~~was~~ *were* a volunteer, but she ~~did~~ *does* not have transportation to travel the

~~five~~ *5* miles to the Senior Citizens Center.

5. Almost ~~3~~ *three* out of ~~5~~ *five* ~~will have been giving~~ *gave* time to religious organizations last year, and about

~~1/3~~ *one-third* ~~will be working~~ *worked* with social service agencies last year.

6. Today, civic and cultural organizations, and schools or other education groups ~~had been~~ *are* favorites for volunteer work.

7. Volunteers ~~provided~~ *provide* companionship, and render service through visits or phone calls.

8. A majority of volunteers from last year liked to ~~have given~~ *give* service to educational groups, *but* fewer

than 10% ~~percent~~ of last year's volunteers ~~had given~~ *gave* time to political parties or campaigns.

9. My grandfather opted to ~~have volunteered~~ *volunteer*, for service in the kindergarten program at Rose

Park Elementary School.

10. ~~Researching~~ *Having researched* the data thoroughly, I ~~will have~~ concluded that women volunteers outnumber

men.

Exercise Using Lesson 15 punctuation rules, make each sentence a correctly punctuated com-
15–10   pound sentence. Edit all capitalization and abbreviation errors.

Cumula-   1. H.U.D. issues a survey of construction lending each month, but the Survey sometimes raises
tive
Editing   questions about its reliability.

2. I think that Economists still believe the credit crunch exists, and don't believe H.U.D.'s

   numbers.

3. Prof. Oporto from Colo. State Univ. surveys 300 banks a month, and extrapolates Industry

   lending numbers from those responses.

4. Doctor Oflynn says her Agency will have to re-examine the numbers, but does not have the

   time to do so now.

5. Is Salt Lake City, Ut., the most affordable city in the Nation or does that honor belong to

   Milwaukee, Wisc.?

6. Geo. Poppen's measure of Housing Costs combines Rental and Homeowning Costs, but other

   surveys look only at the price of Ownership.

7. An Economist for the Home Builders group questions mixing rents and housing prices, but

   adds that Colo. State's conclusions on the affordablity of various cities are generally correct.

8. Many Apartment dwellers trade up into homes, so rents are important to consider in predicting

   Home Prices.

9. The Firm's study predicts that Housing Prices will jump in Dallas and Denver, but they will drop

   in Boston and Miami.

10. The urban land institute held its last convention in Dallas, and the group will hold its next con-

    vention in London.

THE SEMICOLON FOR JOINING INDEPENDENT CLAUSES

If a comma forces the reader to pause, a semicolon forces the reader to pause even more abruptly. In punctuating compound sentences and joining the independent clauses, the writer decides how abrupt the pause should be between the clauses and then selects the appropriate punctuation and conjunctive joiner. Clearly, novice writers underuse the semicolon as an emphasis device to force their readers to pause abruptly between independent clauses.

The semicolon is used to show a degree of separation that is intermediate between the comma and the period. As such, the semicolon is perhaps misnamed. The prefix *semi-* means *partial* or *having some of the characteristics of*. As such, the semicolon is not a partial colon; nor does the semicolon have many of the characteristics of the colon. Instead, the semicolon is more closely related to the comma and the period.

In fact, we might call the semicolon a *supercomma* or a *semiperiod*. That is, the semicolon does the same thing a comma does—forces a pause—except more dramatically. Or the semicolon performs the same function a period does—forces a pause—except less dramatically.

As a writer, you will do well to be judiciously selective in choosing among the comma, the semicolon, and the period. By choosing correctly, you can automatically signal to the reader the degree of relationship and the emphasis you want to show between two independent thoughts. Obviously, the closest relationship is shown with the comma; the next closest with the semicolon; and the least close with the period.

For example, observe and "feel" the closeness as well as the separation contrasts between clauses in the following sentences:

> Several of the supervisors feel they can solve the personnel problems, but none of them will volunteer to write the solution proposal.

> Several of the supervisors feel they can solve the personnel problems; however, none of them will volunteer to write the solution proposal.

Several of the supervisors feel they can solve the personnel problems; none of them will volunteer to write the solution proposal.

Several of the supervisors feel they can solve the personnel problems. But none of them will volunteer to write the solution proposal.

Several of the supervisors feel they can solve the personnel problems. None of them will volunteer to write the solution proposal.

Think about the following statement: *The semicolon should be used only between items of equal rank.*

When you internalize these thoughts, you will avoid using a semicolon to separate a subordinate clause or a phrase from the rest of the sentence—practices that might be considered additional red flags of illiteracy.

Pretest

With a **C** or an **I**, indicate whether the punctuation is correct or incorrect in the following sentences. Then punctuate the sentences marked **I**.

1. We will, of course, attempt to complete the East Bay Project by the deadline; but, as you know, we have had several serious delays.

2. The farmers are thinking about using an improved fertilizer; thus their crop yields will probably increase.

3. Professor Berrio has not paid his ABC dues, therefore, he is not eligible to vote this year.

4. Alice attended UVCC for her first two years then she transferred to USU to complete her baccalaureate degree.

5. After we had reviewed the grievance report thoroughly; however, we decided to put one more worker on the assembly line.

6. Salvatore read the help-wanted ads at the Employment Office; and went to the Computer Services Department where, as I expected, he obtained a part-time job.

Key: (1) C; (2) I—add a comma after *thus*; (3) I—replace the comma after *dues* with a semicolon; (4) I—add a semicolon after *years* to avoid a run-on sentence; (5) I—replace the semicolon with a comma because an independent clause does not precede the semicolon; (6) I—remove the semicolon because an independent clause does not precede it and because no punctuation is needed to separate the compound verb *read* and *went*.

Terminology

Conjunctive adverb—An adverb that is used to connect the independent clauses of a compound sentence. Typical examples are *however, therefore, nevertheless, thus, hence, moreover, otherwise,* and *consequently.*

Dependent clause—A group of words that contains a subject and a verb but that cannot stand alone—it is not a sentence. A dependent clause is also called a *subordinate clause*. As such, a dependent clause "depends" on the independent clause for meaning or is of lesser importance than the independent clause.

Phrase—A group of words without a subject and a verb. A phrase is used as a noun, an adjective, or an adverb.

Semiperiod—A word describing the role of a semicolon because the semicolon forces an abrupt pause—but not quite as abruptly as a period does.

Sentence interrupter—A word or phrase occurring in the middle of a sentence to achieve transition between thoughts. Such words and phrases are used to show addition, comparison, contrast, result, summary, or time. Typical examples are *moreover, in like manner, nevertheless, consequently, in other words*, and *in the meantime*.

Supercomma—A word describing the role of a semicolon because the semicolon forces a pause—much more abruptly than does a comma.

Transitional phrase—A phrase that is used to achieve transition between elements of a composition. In this lesson, transitional phrases are introduced to connect the independent clauses of a compound sentence. Typical examples are *in the same manner, on the other hand, on the contrary, in other words,* and *in the meantime*.

> ## Rules

Use T16-1 here

1. **Use a semicolon between closely related independent clauses not joined by a conjunctive joiner.**

   As stated previously, a compound sentence results when two independent clauses are joined in some way. The decision to join the two thoughts should not be arbitrary—the thoughts should be related to each other. When you use only a semicolon to join two independent thoughts, the thoughts should be **closely related**.

   As stipulated in Lesson 15, Rule 2, a comma splice results when two independent clauses are joined with a comma only. Most comma splices can be corrected if the comma is replaced with a semicolon. The semicolon is an extremely effective joiner because it forces a very abrupt pause between the independent thoughts. Most novice writers have not learned to use the semicolon to join independent thoughts and thereby to achieve the effectiveness of "spreading" the relationship between the thoughts.

   NO   We arrived at several solutions to the problem we submitted our report to Mr. Evans yesterday. (run-on sentence)

   We arrived at several solutions to the problem, we submitted our report to Mr. Evans yesterday. (comma splice)

   YES   We arrived at several solutions to the problem; we submitted our report to Mr. Evans yesterday.

   Learning Hint 1.   As explained in Lesson 15, Rule 1, a comma is normally used before a conjunction joining two independent clauses.

We arrived at several solutions to the problem, and we submitted our report to Mr. Evans yesterday.

Occasionally, you may want to change the comma in such sentences to a semicolon. Some authorities frown on this practice, but it is entirely correct if you desire to spread the relationship slightly between the two independent thoughts. That is, the semicolon is used to achieve a stronger break between the clauses than a comma allows.

Learning Hint 2.   The secret to applying Rule 1 is in being able to recognize the differences among independent clauses, dependent clauses, and phrases. When writers attempt to use Rule 1 without taking into account those differences, such sentences as the following result:

NO   We plan to end the rally in June; when the weather is still cool.

The committee intends to survey all eligible employees; at least those working in the downtown office.

Such uses of the semicolon are incorrect. In Learning Hint 4 of Lesson 18, you will learn one instance in which semicolons can be used to replace commas. Other than that one instance, we will consistently use the semicolon throughout this textbook to join the independent clauses in compound or compound-complex sentences. In fact, other than Learning Hint 4 of Lesson 18, you can safely apply the following approch to the semicolon:

An independent clause precedes and follows a semicolon.

When readers see a semicolon, they naturally expect to find an independent clause preceding it and an independent clause following it. Therefore, in any sentences you write or edit (other than the kind reflected in Learning Hint 4 of Lesson 18), a semicolon will be incorrect if it is not used in connection with independent clauses.

Learning Hint 3.   A colon may be used between independent clauses if the second clause summarizes or explains the first. You will rarely, if ever, use such punctuation; but it occasionally might achieve a desired relationship.

Faith precedes the miracle: the miracle cannot occur without faith.

Use T16-2 here

2. **Use a semicolon before and a comma following a conjunctive adverb or transitional phrase used to join two independent clauses.**

If a distinguishing characteristic of the coordinating conjunction is its shortness (*and, but, or, nor, for, so,* and *yet* are all one-syllable words), a conjunctive adverb is usually a multiple-syllable joiner (with the exception of *still, hence, then,* and *thus*). For example, typical conjunctive adverbs are *therefore, moreover, consequently, subsequently, however,* etc. Obviously, a conjunctive adverb is an adverb fulfilling the role of a conjunction—that is, the role of a conjunctive joiner.

The conjunctive adverb and the transitional phrase both serve similar purposes, and both have the same punctuation when joining the independent clauses in a compound sentence. Typical transitional phrases used as conjunctive joiners are *for example, in other words,* and *as a matter of fact.*

To punctuate a compound sentence with conjunctive adverbs and transitional phrases, use a semicolon preceding and a comma following the conjunctive joiner.

NO   Hideo does not know English, moreover, he is struggling with our customs.
Hideo does not understand English, at the same time, he is struggling with our customs.

YES   Hideo does not know English; moreover, he is struggling with our customs.
Hideo does not understand English; at the same time, he is struggling with our customs.

Learning Hint 4.   When a comma is used in a compound sentence in place of a semicolon and preceding a conjunctive adverb or a transitional phrase, a comma splice results—as explained in Lesson 15, Rule 2, which tells us not to join two independent clauses with a comma only.

NO   Senator Goodfellow expects to propose a 19.6 percent rate for assets held three years, however, sources say his final proposal will be closer to 15 percent.

YES   Senator Goodfellow expects to propose a 19.6 percent rate for assets held three years; however, sources say his final proposal will be closer to 15 percent.

Learning Hint 5.   Note that Rule 2 deals with the semicolon to help in joining two independent clauses in a compound sentence. Actually, both a joining function and a separating function occur when Rule 2 is employed. The punctuation and conjunctive joiner not only join the two thoughts but also denote the feeling of separation between the thoughts.

Some style manuals suggest that if a conjunctive adverb or a transitional phrase blends smoothly with the rest of the sentence and requires little or no pause in reading, the conjunctive joiner does not have to be set off with a comma. However, for consistency, we will always require the comma in all exercises in this text.

The distinctive punctuation in Rule 2 does not apply when such words as *however*, *moreover*, and *consequently* and such transitional phrases as *for example* and *in other words* are used as sentence interrupters. A sentence interrupter requires a comma preceding and following it, as defined in Rule 2 in Lesson 18.

NO   We decided; however, to go to the movies on Saturday.
Ms. Oligschlaeger's actions; in other words, seem to support my plan of action.

YES   We decided, however, to go to the movies on Saturday.
Ms. Oligschlaeger's actions, in other words, seem to support my plan of action.

*Use
T16-3
here*

3.   Use a semicolon between independent clauses joined by a coordinating conjunction if either of the clauses contains one or more internal commas.

Compound sentences frequently become long sentences containing many phrases, modifiers, etc. In the process, a sentence often contains several commas that can cause confusion and force the reader to read the sentence a second time.

Our order was prepared for envelopes, letterhead, and purchase orders, and invoices, letterhead, and shipping labels were sent instead.

In such situations, any confusion is avoided if the comma before the coordinating conjunction is changed to a semicolon.

Our order was prepared for envelopes, letterhead, and purchase orders; and invoices, letterhead, and shipping labels were sent instead.

Rule 3 is not presented as an absolute rule in some style manuals because readers are not always confused if a comma is used. On the other hand, replacing the comma with a semicolon is correct punctuation and will assure that no confusion results. For consistency, we will always require the semicolon in this textbook when one or both clauses in a compound sentence have internal commas.

Posttest

With a **C** or an **I**, indicate whether the punctuation is correct or incorrect in the following sentences. Then punctuate the sentences marked **I**.

1. Byron attended the first soccer camp in San Diego then he returned to Salt Lake City for our soccer camp.

2. Najib completed our driver's education course; and returned to Laramie where, as I predicted, he passed the driving examination on his first attempt.

3. Matilda hopes, obviously, that she will complete her bachelor's degree this year, but, as you anticipated, she will require one additional semester.

4. Ed Kamalu will not be able to go to San Antonio on November 15; hence he will not be able to participate on our panel.

5. When we arrived in Chicago to attend the meetings; therefore, we tried to contact you to have you clarify our roles on the committee.

6. We are attempting to improve our students' performances on the examination; consequently, we plan to offer several help sections this fall.

Key: (1) I—add a semicolon after *San Diego* to avoid a run-on sentence; add a comma after *then* to punctuate the conjunctive adverb correctly; (2) I—remove the semicolon because an independent clause does not precede it and because no punctuation is needed to separate the compound verb *completed* and *returned*; (3) I—internal punctuation on both sides of the coordinating conjunction requires the comma after *year* to be a semicolon; (4) I—the conjunctive adverb *hence* requires a semicolon preceding it and a comma following it; (5) I—*therefore* as used here is a sentence interrupter and does not join two independent clauses, so the semicolon should be replaced with a comma; (6) C.

LEVEL A

Name _____

Exercise 16–1   On the lines below, write **T** if the statement is true and **F** if the statement is false.

_F_   1. Novice writers tend to overuse the semicolon.

_T_   2. The semicolon might legitimately be called a ''supercomma'' or a ''semiperiod.''

_F_   3. When you join two independent clauses, you can show the closest relationship with the semicolon and the next closest with the comma.

_T_   4. The semicolon should be used only between items of equal rank.

_T_   5. In general, a semicolon signals that an independent clause precedes and follows the semicolon.

_F_   6. When a semicolon replaces a comma preceding the coordinating conjunction in a compound sentence, a closer relationship between the clauses results.

_T_   7. Conjunctive adverbs are frequently multiple-syllable adverbs used as conjunctive joiners.

_T_   8. A semicolon precedes and a comma follows conjunctive adverbs used as joiners in compound sentences.

_T_   9. A comma splice results when a comma is used before a conjunctive adverb or a transitional phrase in a compound sentence.

_F_   10. A colon is never used between two independent clauses in a compound sentence.

_F_   11. The semicolon is more closely related to the comma and the colon than to the period.

_F_   12. The closest relationship between clauses in a compound sentence is shown with the semicolon.

_T_   13. A semicolon that separates a subordinate clause from an independent clause might be considered a red flag of illiteracy.

_T_   14. *Thus, hence,* and *therefore* are examples of conjunctive adverbs.

_F_   15. A phrase is a group of words with a subject but without a verb.

_F_   16. A complex sentence results when two independent clauses are joined in some way.

_T_   17. All coordinating conjunctions are one-syllable words; most conjunctive adverbs are multiple-syllable words.

Exercise 16–2   Mark **C** if the punctuation is correct; mark **I** if the punctuation is incorrect.

_I_   1. I began this assignment by first reading Chapter 2, then I reread the chapter, making an outline as I went along.

_I_   2. Exhibit 1 is the 16th-grade informative abstract; marked with slashes to separate the independent clauses.

_C_ 3. Exhibit 5 contains the actual computations; and Exhibit 6 is the ''uncluttered'' version of the abstract.

_I_ 4. The index does very well in helping a writer to become more aware of the different levels of writing; thus, assisting the writer to manipulate the work as desired.

_I_ 5. Although the Gunning Fog Index has several weaknesses; it still is a very useful tool.

_I_ 6. At times, employees may be asked to write something for high-school dropouts; and, at other times, for a law firm.

_I_ 7. The opportunity to use the index in a professional career might not present itself very often, however, when the opportunity does arise, the index can be very useful.

_I_ 8. I am sure that in the future I will be grateful for the experience; when I am able to use my skills in my professional career.

_I_ 9. These are strange days for Blaine Posey; every consumer-products company's worst nightmare.

_I_ 10. One problem is long delays; as the FAA, according to the GAO, typically takes six weeks to process a single malfunction.

Exercise 16–3 If the punctuation and conjunctive joiner connect two independent clauses, write **Y** (for yes); if not, write **N** (for no).

_N_ 1. Our school has several problems; such as overcrowded classes and a lack of supplies.

_Y_ 2. My father buys a new automobile quite frequently; for example, this year he bought a Cadillac after buying a Corvette just 15 months ago.

_Y_ 3. When I tried to fix my lawnmower, I found that the engine, which I thought I could fix, was worn out; so I went to a small-engine dealer, Harvey's Gas Engines, and bought a new engine.

_N_ 4. Writing a term paper involves three processes; prewriting to develop an outline; writing to put meat on the outline; and rewriting to correct any errors.

_N_ 5. Mr. Hayes said that he cannot condone any kind of dishonesty; even if we show evidence that the ends justify the means.

_Y_ 6. Traffic in most big cities is becoming increasingly congested; but Houston is going in the opposite direction.

_N_ 7. Although Houston remains the seventh most-congested city; it has become steadily less so in the past five years.

_Y_ 8. JoAnn Lomax has several valid opinions about the traffic-survey study; hence, we will delay our final decision until we hear from her.

_Y_ 9. Houston attributes the easing of traffic problems to increased reliance on bus transit; in a similar fashion, Phoenix has cut congestion by designating lanes for high-occupancy vehicles.

LEVEL B

Name _____

Exercise   Write the letter that identifies the reason for the semicolon in each sentence.
16–4
   a   Between independent clauses joined by a conjunctive adverb.
   b   Between independent clauses not joined by a conjunction or a conjunctive adverb.
   c   Between clauses joined by a coordinating conjunction but having internal commas.
   d   No match possible.

   _b_   1. Feedback, which is returned information, assists the communication process; feedback
          helps communicators to understand each other.

   _d_   2. Intrapersonal communication helps to shape a communicator's feedback and nonverbal
          signs; which are both a part of face-to-face communication.

   _c_   3. Proper listening, a developed skill, helps to better communication; for it increases job
          performance, enhances learning, and helps build trust.

   _b_   4. Proper listening, a developed skill, helps communication; good listening increases job
          contentment, heightens learning, and helps build trust.

   _d_   5. Two poor listening habits are judging subjects as not worth your effort; and failing to
          observe nonverbal aids.

   _a_   6. Listening occurs for many reasons; consequently, distinct types of listening are required
          for distinct types of situations.

   _d_   7. The FAA's early-warning system for detecting trends in plane malfunctions is not work-
          ing; according to the findings of a congressional agency.

   _d_   8. Airlines report mechanical problems to the FAA, which puts them into a database; and
          mails summaries to airlines and manufacturers, as well as to FAA inspectors.

   _d_   9. The new tax, called the passenger facility charge, is supposed to raise $1.3 billion a
          year; with the money earmarked to fund airport expansion.

   _d_ 10. Airport groups disagree; saying the new tax will be a boon to travelers by financing
          improvements.

Exercise   Write the letter that identifies the one best sentence.
16–5
   _c_   1. *a.*   The articles available on the topic of managers are many, and, of course, I have not
                   had the time to locate all of them.
             b.   Some managers give themselves heart attacks and nervous breakdowns, still worse,
                   many are ''carriers'' of such illnesses; causing their employees to be ill.
             c.   Most managers exhibit some leadership skills; and most leaders, on occasion, find
                   themselves managing.

   _a_   2. *a.*   The two functions of leading and managing may overlap; yet leadership and man-
                   agement are not the same thing.
             b.   Managers are people who do things right, leaders are people who do the right thing.
             c.   Both roles are crucial but they differ profoundly.

_c_ 3. _a._ A manager is in the business of ''clarifying'' goals and tasks; and determining ''who is going to do what.''

     _b._ The surgeon arrives and starts giving commands prior to an operation; whereas the manager arrives only to perform the same action.

     _c._ Managers turn expectations of people into concrete agendas and action plans; in this sense, managers facilitate change.

_b_ 4. _a._ Many times when an organization tries to make the transition from a control style to a high-involvement management style; the manager is often seen as the villain who resists the change.

     _b._ Leaders provide high goals for the people in organizations; in addition, leaders see themselves as resources and helpers to the group.

     _c._ Managers know how to use questions to get the most information from others; as well as to win allies.

_c_ 5. _a._ Leaders are seldom seen as threats they recognize and reward all employees for effective performances.

     _b._ Leaders exist at every level of the organization, moreover, leaders usually prefer to influence than to command.

     _c._ Intimidation is not necessary when a person is a leader; moreover, trust is the underlying requirement in winning over employees.

_a_ 6. _a._ The effective leader is a ''bender'' rather than a ''breaker''; he or she is successful in making gradual changes in the strategy, structure, people, and processes.

     _b._ The leader relies on trusted subordinates to sketch in the details; and to keep the leader posted on progress.

     _c._ If managers suffer from managerial blind spots; such blind spots can stand in the way of advancement.

_c_ 7. _a._ Two blind spots that managers might reflect are inability to take criticism; and withdrawal from personal involvement with associates.

     _b._ Experts concur that unless you provide a vision of the reason why you show up every morning; you are not providing leadership.

     _c._ The managerial leader should be actively involved in meetings; moreover, he or she should make sure the meetings stay on track.

_b_ 8. _a._ The managerial leader must be willing to teach skills; to share insights and to give experience.

     _b._ Thanking people is an important part of taking care of them; thanking employees is taking care of their psychological health.

     _c._ A managerial leader should not simply solve problems; but should let subordinates solve most problems on their own.

_b_ 9. _a._ Some experts feel stress is caused by ''supervisory malfunction''; which means many supervisors do not know how to supervise.

     _b._ One in three citizens thinks about quitting work because of job stress; one in three expects to suffer job burnout in the near future.

     _c._ Much stress revolves around changes in the work environment, also, any perceived threats or demands might increase stress levels.

LEVEL C

Name _____

Exercise
16–6

On the lines below, write the lesson number (15 or 16); then, write the number of the rule or learning hint associated with the punctuation or conjunctive joiner in each sentence (i.e., 15-2). Then, edit all incorrect sentences. In some sentences, appropriate rules or learning hints to cover the punctuation needs have not yet been introduced; so do your best to punctuate these sentences correctly.

15-2; 16-2   1. Throughout history, philosophers have searched for the meaning of good and of

   evil; then, based on their findings, they have formed images of what they thought

   to be a utopian society.

LH2   2. The purpose of government is to defend and to secure appropriate blessings for the

   people of today, and for the people of tomorrow.

LH2   3. When the time came that humankind formed societies, each member of the society

   consented to obey the laws of the society.

16-2   4. Membership in a society is a privilege; thus, membership is not a God-given right.

16-3   5. People are free to choose to live in whichever society they desire; but, after choos-

   ing, they must accept and abide by the laws of that society.

(Rule not yet intro- duced)   6. Madison knew that people of the same interests, would unite and use the power of

   the group to obtain common goals.

LH 2   7. Because governments do not have the authority to restrict freedom without consent,

   domestic tranquility can exist only when freedom of speech is unrestricted.

15-3   8. Internal forces may seek to usurp power over the authorized government, and

   destroy the liberty of the people.

LH -2   9. Freedom of speech can be used to arouse people to the defense of their liberty, and

   to expose the evil desires of domestic forces wishing to gain power.

Exercise
16–7

Composition

1. Using the subject of skiing, compose a sentence containing a coordinating conjunction; and use internal punctuation in both of the independent clauses.

_____

_____

2. Using the subject of bicycle riding, compose a sentence containing a conjunctive adverb.

_____

_____

3. Using the subject of air pollution, compose a sentence containing a conjunctive transitional phrase.

_____

_____

4. Using the subject of graffiti, compose a compound sentence requiring a semicolon before a coordinating conjunction.

_____

_____

Exercise
16–8

Cumulative Editing

Edit the following sentences to reflect what you have learned from Lessons 2 through 16.

1. Erica Soto is the first student this year to ~~recieve~~ *receive* the ~~A~~*A*thlete-~~S~~*S*cholar award*a* ~~and~~*g* will probably ~~have been~~ *be* awarded the sportsmanship award next ~~S~~*S*emester.

2. Businesses need ~~L~~*l*and, ~~L~~*l*abor, ~~C~~*c*apital, and ~~M~~*m*anagement*,* to ~~have produced~~ *produce* the goods and services that consumers desire.

3. Athletes ~~were~~ *are* often ~~embarassed~~ *embarrassed* to discuss their use of ~~S~~*s*teroids;*they* fear ~~personel~~ *personal* disqualification or disapproval from peers.

4. Today's ~~a~~*A*merican laborer ~~will have been earning~~ *earns* one of the highest wage rates in the world*s* and ~~will pay~~ *pays* one of the lowest tax rates.

5. The proposed Rapid-Transit System will help to cut down on traffic congestion, but the system ~~was~~ *will be* much less convenient than automobiles.

6. Call me at home, or, ~~I should be happy to have you~~ make an appointment to talk to me in my office.

7. Athletes who are ~~being dependant~~ *dependent* on steroids ~~will~~ obtain them any way they can, but athletes usually do not need to ~~have worried~~ *worry* about finding a ~~principle~~ *principal* source of supply for the steroids.

8. Your idea ~~was~~ *is* good, but does not take into account the effects of double-digit inflation.

9. As a person consumes more of a product, the satisfaction ~~yeilded~~ *yielded* by the last unit of that product ~~had been decreasing~~ *decreases*.

10. We know that after our students complete the sixth grade, they have about a 75 percent chance of ~~having finished~~ *finishing* ~~High School~~ *high school*.

11. The independent clause is complete in meaning, whereas, the ~~dependant~~ *dependent* clause, for ~~it's~~ *its* meaning, ~~will have been depending~~ *depends* on the main clause.

12. Let me know ~~you're~~ *your* schedule, however, so I can ~~have called~~ *call* you when you are not studying.

13. Give me the answers to the sample test questions; I will copy the answers and give them to other members of our study group.

14. Joan intended to ~~have saved~~ *save* money from working this ~~Summer~~ *summer*, and then to go to ~~europe~~ *Europe* a year later than she originally ~~had~~ planned.

15. If ~~your~~ *you're* in a hurry, we will try to fill your order while you ~~have waited;~~ *wait* but we prefer to ship orders via ~~U.P.S.~~ *UPS*.

16. In 1970, about ~~1~~ *one* out of ~~6~~ *six* employed persons ~~will have~~ earned a living by doing clerical work; and over 80 percent of these people were women.

Exercise 16–9   Edit the following sentences that may contain Lessons 15 and 16 punctuation errors, number-usage errors, errors in frequently misspelled words, or confusing-word errors.

Cumulative Editing

1. Among ~~one hundred~~ *100* cities that applied for awards, 2/3 *two-thirds* have ~~implimented~~ *implemented* recycling programs; and almost ~~1/5~~ *one-fifth* of the programs are less than a year old.

2. Waste-disposal fees range from $5.00 a ton in Jackson, Tennessee, to $161.00 in Philadelphia.

3. Ann Arbor, Michigan, recycles toner cartridges from laser printers; Clifton, New Jersey, ~~accomodates~~ *accommodates* concrete and asphalt.

4. Minneapolis, an award winner, ~~persues~~ *pursues* the addition of a solid-waste fee to monthly utility bills, and households that recycle get a $7.00 discount.

5. Martin Marietta will ~~develope~~ *develop* a $3,000,000 *$3 million* robot, that will handle ~~alot~~ *a lot* of hazardous wastes at a ~~sight~~ *site* in Idaho Falls, Idaho.

6. Pomeroy Martin is a full-service firm with branches in Bellevue and Portland; ~~it's~~ *its* clients include Washington Life Insurance and the city of Seattle.

7. More efficient industrial motor systems ultimately offer high-~~volumn~~ *volume* electricity savings, but the systems are proving a hard sell.

8. ~~Alot~~ *A lot* of our best motors ~~all ready~~ *already* have efficiency ratings of almost 95%; *percent* ~~obsolesent~~ *obsolescent* motors are ~~liable~~ *likely* to have ratings below 90%. *percent.*

9. ~~Entreprenurs~~ *Entrepreneurs* often aren't willing to replace existing motors, even when a company president ~~conceeds~~ *concedes* that better motors pay for themselves in a few years through lower power bills.

10. Some utilities are ~~hopefull~~ *hopeful* they can change downtime associated with putting in new motors, however, in hopes of reducing ~~there~~ *their* need to invest in new power plants.

INTRODUCTORY CLAUSES, PHRASES, AND WORDS

As you can see by its title, this lesson deals with sentence elements that come at the beginning of a sentence or that precede an independent clause. In all situations, the rules introduced in this lesson are concerned with the comma.

Introductory implies that the dependent clause, phrase, or word precedes the independent clause. As such, these sentence elements are set off from the independent clause by commas. Here we see the ultimate function of the comma exemplified—to force the reader to pause following the introductory clause, phrase, or word. With adequate practice, you will naturally *feel* the need to pause after these introductory elements and to use the comma to express that feeling.

In line with our approach throughout this textbook, we will introduce and teach the rules in Lesson 17 from the principle of consistency. That is, in some instances, style manuals give us a choice of using or not using the comma following some introductory elements. We advocate that the comma **always** be used because it is correct and because the rules are easier to master when applied consistently.

Pretest

With a **C** or an **I**, indicate whether the punctuation is correct or incorrect in the following sentences. Then punctuate the sentences marked **I**.

1. Because we have not yet received your purchase order we cannot ship your replacement parts.

2. Martin has decided to apply for the supervisory position even though he is very happy in his current role.

3. Fifteen percent of our employees received bonuses this year, whereas only 10 percent did last year.

4. On Monday we hope to finalize the first-quarter progress report.

5. Checking for mistakes in the exit report, occupied about an hour of my time.

6. We provide excellent customer support; and, to help you learn how to use the software we want you to call our customer-assistance number any hour of the day or night.

7. Yes we will attend the graduation ceremony.

8. Indeed, I expect Marcie to graduate in the top 10 percent of her class.

Key: (1) I—use a comma following *order* to set off the introductory dependent clause; (2) I—use a comma following *position* to set off the nonrestrictive clause at the end of the sentence; (3) C; (4) I—use a comma following the short introductory prepositional phrase. In this textbook, all introductory prepositional phrases will be set off with commas; (5) I—the phrase is the subject of the independent clause and therefore should not be set off with a comma; (6) I—use a comma after *software* to set off the introductory verbal phrase; (7) I—set off the introductory word *yes* with a comma; (8) C.

Terminology

Adverbial clause—A dependent clause that functions as an adverb in relation to the independent clause. Adverbial clauses modify verbs, adjectives, or other adverbs and usually answer *When? Where? Why? How? To what degree?* or *Under what conditions?* An adverbial clause begins with a subordinating conjunction.

Complex sentence—A sentence containing one independent clause and at least one dependent clause.

Compound-complex sentence—A sentence containing at least two independent clauses and at least one dependent clause.

Essential—Synonymous with *restrictive*.

Nonessential—Synonymous with *nonrestrictive*.

Nonrestrictive—Applies to words, phrases, or clauses that are not needed to complete the meaning or structure of a sentence. Synonymous with *nonessential*. Nonessential sentence elements are typically set off with commas.

Restrictive—Applies to words, phrases, or clauses that are needed to complete the meaning or structure of a sentence. Synonymous with *essential*. Essential sentence elements are not set off with commas.

Subordinating conjunction—A word used to make an independent clause into a dependent (a subordinate) clause; a word used to join dependent clauses to independent clauses. Typical examples are *after, although, before, if, though,* and *when.*

Rules

Use T17-1 here

1. **Use a comma to set off a dependent clause that precedes an independent clause.**

   You have previously noted the differences between an independent clause and a dependent clause. In thinking about those differences, you'll recall that a dependent clause cannot stand alone—it is not a sentence. It is patterned like a sentence, with both a subject and a verb; but a dependent clause *begins* with a word that gives the reader the signal the clause cannot stand alone.

In one respect, you might conclude that a major difference between a dependent clause and an independent clause is the word used to introduce the dependent clause. Typical words used for that purpose are the following: *after, as, although, because, before, if, since, though, unless, until,* and *when*—which are called *subordinating conjunctions.*

For example, the following independent clauses are sentences:

You can predict.
John has finished the project.
Jane's work is satisfactory.

Notice how those independent clauses now change to dependent clauses when introduced with a subordinating conjunction:

If you can predict, . . .
Because John has finished the project, . . .
When Jane's work is satisfactory, . . .

The comma tells the reader that the introductory dependent clause has ended and that the main part of the sentence is about to begin.

NO   As soon as we heard the news we ran to congratulate him.
     If you succeed you have a chance of being elected.

YES   As soon as we heard the news, we ran to congratulate him.
      If you succeed, you have a chance of being elected.

We will **always** set off a dependent clause with a comma when the dependent clause precedes an independent clause. Most of the time, the dependent clause begins the sentence. Sometimes, however, the dependent clause is in the middle of a sentence but still precedes an independent clause. For example:

We received our order almost six months after we placed it; and when we complained about the delay, your shipping department refused to take any responsibility.

Use
T17-2
here

Learning Hint 1.   Rule 1 deals with dependent clauses that precede independent clauses. Are dependent clauses that *follow* independent clauses also set off by commas?

Most of the time, dependent clauses that follow independent clauses are *not* set off by commas. However, when the dependent clause is a nonrestrictive adverbial clause, it is set off by a comma. For example:

We failed to win the game, although we played our hardest.
We will not get the bid, as you have already discovered.
I will not vote for Dr. Howe, even though he is experienced.

If the adverbial clause that follows the independent clause is clearly restrictive, the adverbial clause is not set off with a comma. However, if a natural pause is evident, a comma is used.

Eun-Young will be pleased when she hears about her exam score.
We will announce the decision next Monday, when Ms. Cordova returns from Denver.

I hesitated to tell you because the results were not yet final.
I need the exit report by 4:30 tomorrow, because I must leave for the airport at 4:45.

Charlie predicted the score correctly before the game began.
Your order was shipped on May 20, before your fax arrived.

If you have difficulty determining whether a dependent clause following an independent clause is restrictive or nonrestrictive, simply use your good judgment to test whether a natural pause should precede the dependent clause. Adverbial clauses that are introduced with *although, though, even though,* and *as* are usually nonrestrictive; most other adverbial clauses are usually restrictive. (See Unit 5 for a discussion of punctuation associated with restrictive and nonrestrictive relative clauses.)

*Use
T17-3
here*

2. **Use a comma to set off an introductory phrase that precedes an independent clause.**

You will recall that a phrase is a group of words without a subject or a verb. Obviously, Rule 1 and Rule 2 are similar. Rule 1 deals with dependent clauses, and Rule 2 deals with phrases.

Learning Hint 2.   Some style manuals advocate that short prepositional phrases (five or fewer words) should not be set off by commas and that long prepositional phrases (more than five words) should be set off.

In the springtime we begin making plans to plant our crops.
In the spring of the year, we begin making plans to plant our crops.

In 1990 we began keeping adequate records of our profits and losses.
At the start of the summer of 1990, we began keeping adequate records of our profits and losses.

For consistency, we will **always** use a comma to set of a phrase that precedes an independent clause. We are **always correct** in following that practice; and doing so makes mastery of punctuation rational and consistent.

We could distinguish among various phrases that precede independent clauses. For example, we could discuss verbal phrases—participial, infinitive, and gerund; prepositional phrases; and introductory phrases that serve parenthetical or transitional functions. However, if you will develop a feel for **always** setting off a phrase that precedes the independent clause, you need not be concerned (for punctuation purposes) about the nature or function of the phrase.

In that respect, be sure you distinguish between phrases that precede independent clauses and those that are part of the independent clause.

NO   Taking advantage of the situation I lobbied for the necessary votes. (The phrase precedes the independent clause.)

Taking advantage of the situation, enabled me to lobby for the necessary votes. (The phrase is the subject of the verb.)

YES   Taking advantage of the situation, I lobbied for the necessary votes.
Taking advantage of the situation enabled me to lobby for the necessary votes.

Most of the time, introductory phrases begin the sentence. However, as with dependent clauses, the introductory phrase is sometimes located in the middle of a sentence but still precedes an independent clause.

We received our order almost six months after we placed it; after complaining about the delay, we obtained only a minor apology from your shipping department.

3.   Use a comma to set off an introductory, nonessential word that precedes an independent clause.

We have learned to be consistent in setting off introductory dependent clauses and phrases with commas. We will now extend the consistency principle to introductory, nonessential words that precede independent clauses.

Single, nonessential words that precede independent clauses are used to achieve transition, to give emphasis, or to show a particular attitude toward the meaning being conveyed.

Through these words, the writer can do such things as show addition (*also, besides, furthermore*); consequence (*accordingly, otherwise, therefore, thus*); concession (*anyway, however, nevertheless*); or sequence (*afterward, finally, first, next*). Or the writer can accomplish other objectives—such as reflect endorsement (*indeed*); show mild support (*apparently, presumably*); arouse emotion (*unfortunately, truthfully*); assume an honest position (*frankly, actually*); or reflect confirmation or disconfirmation (*yes, no*).

Typical examples of Rule 3's application are the following:

Lately, we have seen an increase in sales.
Furthermore, we desire you to absorb the Cleveland territory.
Incidentally, we had many good comments about your speech.
Alas, we must have discarded the April report.
Ideally, the sales conference should be held in Monterey.
Yes, you have my approval to take a week's vacation.
No, I do not agree with your evaluation of the situation.

Obviously, such introductory, nonessential words force the reader to pause. When they are used in an essential role, they do not force a pause and should not be followed by commas.

NO   However you may review the report to see if you concur.
         However, you review the report is up to you.

YES   However, you may review the report to see if you concur.
         However you review the report is up to you.

In some situations, the only way you can tell whether an expression is nonessential or essential is by the way you say it. Remember that the comma forces a pause following the introductory word. Therefore, in general, if your voice tends to *drop* as you say the word, the word is nonessential and should be set off with a comma.

| Posttest |

With a **C** or an **I**, indicate whether the punctuation is correct or incorrect in the following sentences. Then punctuate the sentences marked **I**.

1. As soon as you send us your purchase order we will ship your replacement parts within 24 hours.

2. Marco plans to resign shortly after Christmas, as he plans to return to Mexico right after the first of the year.

3. Linda is pleased with the raise we gave her though she still does not know the reasons for the raise.

4. In return, we expect you to work on alternate Sundays throughout the year.

5. To complete all your assignments on schedule requires appropriate discipline on your part.

6. You will be required to attend both sessions; and, in answering the questions of the workers you will have to be thoroughly familiar with the user's manual.

7. No, you will not be expected to conduct all of the exit interviews.

8. Unfortunately I will not be able to participate in next week's training sessions.

Key: (1) I—use a comma after *order* to set off the introductory dependent clause; (2) C; (3) I—use a comma following *her* to set off the nonrestrictive dependent clause at the end of the sentence; (4) C; (5) C; (6) I—use a comma after *workers* to set off the introductory phrase; (7) C; (8) I—use a comma to set off the introductory, nonessential word *unfortunately.*

LEVEL A

Name _____

Exercise
17–1

On the lines below, write **T** if the statement is true and **F** if the statement is false.

_F_   1. A subordinating conjunction is used to join two independent clauses to form a compound sentence.

_F_   2. A semicolon is used to set off a dependent clause that precedes an independent clause.

_T_   3. The word *nonrestrictive* means the sentence elements are nonessential and therefore are set off with commas.

_T_   4. You are always correct in using commas to set off short prepositional phrases that precede independent clauses.

_F_   5. *Taking advantage of the situation* is an example of a dependent clause.

_T_   6. Whenever you start a sentence with an introductory *yes*, you should use a comma following the *yes*.

_T_   7. In some situations, the only way you can tell whether an introductory expression is nonessential or essential is by the way you say it.

_F_   8. *When, if, as, because*, and *unless* are examples of coordinating conjunctions.

_F_   9. A complex sentence is a sentence containing at least two independent clauses.

_F_   10. Dependent clauses that follow independent clauses are almost always set off by commas.

_F_   11. An adverbial clause begins with a coordinating conjunction.

_T_   12. *After, although, before*, and *though* are examples of subordinating conjunctions.

_T_   13. A dependent clause begins with a word that gives the reader the signal the clause cannot stand alone.

_T_   14. A dependent clause that precedes an independent clause is always set off with a comma.

_T_   15. Adverbial clauses that are introduced with *although, though, even though*, and *as* are usually nonrestrictive clauses.

_F_   16. Prepositional phrases are always set off with commas.

_F_   17. Subordinating conjunctions are used to show addition, consequence, concession, or sequence.

_F_   18. Examples of introductory, nonessential words that show consequences are *also, besides, furthermore*, and *indeed*.

Exercise
17–2

Mark **C** if the punctuation is correct; mark **I** if the punctuation is incorrect.

_I_   1. As you know the problems that arise from television can be avoided, if proper supervision occurs.

I   2. In America television viewing by youth is an issue about which everyone should be concerned.

I   3. Children who spend a large part of their time watching television, do not do as well in school as those who watch less television.

I   4. Through television, children learn that conflicts can be settled, by using aggression.

C   5. As a result, children who watch too much TV may not develop the skills necessary for learning in school.

I   6. In tests children who did not watch TV scored higher than those who watched it.

C   7. Television is a good medium for education if TV is used correctly.

I   8. Children tend to watch the same types of TV programs as their parents. Thus, if the parents watch a lot of violence the kids watch violence too.

I   9. Yes the effects of TV violence have been researched repeatedly, although parents usually are not aware of the research results.

C   10. If practical, worthwhile activities are available for our children, we should turn the TV off.

Exercise 17–3   Write **C** if the punctuation in the sentence is correct; write **I** if the punctuation is incorrect.

I   1. Deborah likes to swim but Lance doesn't.

I   2. Adriana must pay back the loan, or have her wages garnisheed.

I   3. Whenever I leave my umbrella at home I inevitably experience rain.

I   4. I will not write to Wesley nor will I visit him again.

I   5. Yes I know what to do with the report.

C   6. After the one-week crash course, Bud was able to repair the brakes on most cars.

I   7. Everyone thinks that Alonzo is 50 years old although he is actually only 35.

I   8. By the way the Unita National Forest is among the top ten forests in terms of visitors it was the first national forest created in Utah.

I   9. Thanks to conservation efforts many areas that were destroyed before national forests were introduced have been restored to productive use; and certain species of wildlife have been introduced into places where they have not been seen for generations.

C   10. Last year, the Unita National Forest saw 3.37 million visitor days; and that's as if everyone in the state spent nearly two days in the forest.

I   11. Mr. Booth was born in Leadore in 1925, and received his early education in the Lemhi County schools; at age 20, he graduated from what is now Idaho State University.

C   12. Beginning September 1, all colleges in the state will be required to report their statistics for violent crime; therefore, we will be expected to centralize our crime-reporting procedures.

LEVEL B

Name _____

Exercise
17–4

Write **C** if the punctuation is correct; write **I** if the punctuation is incorrect. Then, write the letter that matches the reason for the **C** or the **I**. Some sentences reflect more than one answer.

A   introductory dependent clause
B   introductory prepositional phrase
C   introductory verbal phrase
D   introductory, nonessential word

E   nonrestrictive adverbial clause
F   restrictive adverbial clause
G   no match possible

___I, B___ 1. Through the efforts of Qi Wang we hope to finish the project on schedule.

___I, D, B___ 2. Yes if you insist I will accept the assignment.

___I, A, E___ 3. As Dr. Penrod entered the room he saw the two students although he did not know their names.

___I, C, F___ 4. Hurrying to the airport Jess broke the speed limit, because he got such a late start.

___I, D, C___ 5. Unfortunately, to get the necessary returns you will have to send out another follow-up letter.

___I, G___ 6. Passing the exam on my first try, enabled me to spend more time with my other classes.

___I, F___ 7. The store will not refund your money, unless you have your receipt.

___I, B___ 8. In return we expect you to work throughout the holiday season.

___I, G___ 9. However, you decide to allocate the expenses will be fine with me.

___C, E___ 10. We will cover your expenses, even though you do not have all the necessary documentation.

Exercise
17–5

Write the letter that identifies the one best sentence.

___b___ 1. a. Realizing her tenuous position Joan resigned from the committee.
         b. In effect, I do not have the necessary funds to make the trip.
         c. No, we cannot support your recommendation although James tried to change our thinking.

___a___ 2. a. By the time you have sold your stock in the corporation, you will be a rich woman!
         b. After hearing the good news she decided to sell her Prime News stock.
         c. Frankly, I don't want to sell my stock even though I would make a great deal of money, if I did so.

c   3. *a.* If appropriate steps are taken the adverse effects of TV on children can be minimized.
   b. The effects of TV watching by children can be harmful, if children watch the wrong programs.
   c. If parents are present, they can interact with their children, although children may not appreciate that interaction.

c   4. *a.* Many issues face employers, when they consider hiring prospective employees.
   b. Actually, in an effort to combat losses many employers have turned to employee testing.
   c. Detecting employees who are likely to steal is one primary purpose of screening potential employees.

a   5. *a.* As you know, employers have difficulties checking the backgrounds of workers thoroughly, as workers often are not long-term community residents.
   b. Merely accepting the test results, is easier than making the difficult choice of whether to hire or fire an individual.
   c. Feeling their privacy would be invaded; many people refuse to take a lie-detector test.

b   6. *a.* A lie detector works, by recording patterns of blood pressure, perspiration, and breathing, as responses to questions.
   b. Because lie-detector tests ease hiring decisions, employers are benefited by using the tests.
   c. The main issue is the production and safety rights of companies, against the privacy rights of employees.

a   7. *a.* In particular, I want to examine the legal and ethical questions when lie detectors are used in the workplace.
   b. Honesty is not found in all employees, in today's world.
   c. In many companies trust between employees and managers is imperative.

c   8. *a.* Hopefully, you will enjoy reading the report, when I submit it for your approval.
   b. One problem I encountered was trying to choose the best information, while researching the topic.
   c. Because so many students are writing papers, many of the resources I need are not always available.

b   9. *a.* The government has been criticized for spending millions of dollars, without having real evidence to support the spending.
   b. Nevertheless, the nation is making progress in its efforts to cut cholesterol.
   c. Despite the new questions a person is wise to cut back on high-fat foods.

c   10. *a.* In this report three different forms of discipline will be discussed.
   b. If your son is too young; he will not understand the punishment.
   c. Often, parents leave the disciplining of their children to others.

b   11. *a.* In addition recommendations on how to protect computers will be made.
   b. In 1977, Ryan wrote a book that became a classic for computer hackers.
   c. When Ryan's book first appeared it was regarded as science fiction.

LEVEL C

Name _____

Exercise 17-6   On the lines below, write the number of the Lesson (15, 16, or 17) and the number of the rule or learning hint associated with the punctuation or conjunctive joiner in each sentence. Then, edit all the incorrect sentences.

17-1
16-LH2   1. Although cholesterol is naturally produced, a person with a high amount has an elevated risk of heart disease.

17-3, 16-2   2. Today, most people know if their cholesterol levels are high; consequently, these people want to lower their cholesterol through the food they eat.

15-3, 17-3   3. Yes, the bill for cholesterol-related activities will amount to $20 billion a year, and will be paid mostly by individual patients.

17-1, 16-3   4. As you suspected, most studies deal with middle-aged men; but now the National Heart, Lung, and Blood Institute wants to study the effects of cholesterol on women.

16-3, 17-1   5. Cholesterol is dangerous by itself; but when a high cholesterol level is combined with other components, the factors become a deadly combination.

17-3
17-2
16-LH2   6. Nevertheless, after reading the article, I now know that high cholesterol is a much-greater problem than low cholesterol levels.

17-2
17-LH1
16-LH2   7. By introducing cholesterol-free food, the food market has helped efforts to combat high cholesterol, as you discovered in your survey.

17-1
16-1
16-LH2   8. As my research paper shows, scientists have developed many new drugs; these drugs have had a significant effect on lowering cholesterol counts.

16-1   9. The drugs' success is indisputable; they have lowered cholesterol in some patients by 50 percent.

17-2,
17-3, 16-2 10. Unfortunately, the long-term effects of some of the drugs have not yet been deter-

mined; in addition, some drugs that appear to be safe have unpleasant side effects.

17-2,
17-2, 16-3,
16-LH2 11. In one experiment, the cholesterol intake of a group of men was cut substantially;

but after seven years, the group's average cholesterol count was reduced by only

6.7 percent.

17-3, 15-3 12. Specifically, women, and people over age 65 seem to gain little from reducing cho-

lesterol and fat.

17-2
16-LH2 13. On the other hand, many scientists claim that their experiments have been successful,

and that even small improvements are a step in the right direction.

17-3, 17-1 14. Admittedly, if we want to reduce heart disease, the government must conduct cam-

paigns to make the public aware of the dangers of high cholesterol.

17-2, 16-1 15. As stated in the report, mounting evidence reveals that cholesterol reduction is more

complex than many people think; dieting and drugs do not necessarily ensure a longer

life.

17-2
16-LH2 16. Because of the danger of high cholesterol, people can benefit from knowing their

cholesterol levels.

17-2,
16-1, 17-1 17. For many fanatics, the cholesterol issue should not be taken so seriously; if temper-

ance is maintained, a person may as well enjoy a cholesterol-rich treat occasionally.

Exercise 17–7

Composition

1. Using the subject of automobiles, compose a compound-complex sentence containing an introductory dependent clause preceding the first independent clause, a conjunctive adverb joining the two independent clauses, and a prepositional phrase preceding the second independent clause.

_____

_____

2. Using the subject of automobiles, compose a complex sentence containing an introductory nonessential word and a nonrestrictive adverbial clause at the end of the sentence.

_____

_____

Exercise 17–8

Cumulative Editing

Edit the following sentences to reflect what you have learned from Lessons 2 through 17.

1. ~~Incidently~~ _Incidentally,_ many parents are ~~becoming~~ dissatisfied with ~~Public~~ and ~~Private~~ ~~Schools~~; some of these parents ~~will have been percieving~~ _perceive_ the advantages of educating ~~there~~ _their_ children at home.

2. Although many parents ~~had felt~~ _feel_ home schooling is best for their children, some parents ~~will have been having~~ _have_ difficulties ~~having educated~~ _educating_ their children at home because of uncooperative school ~~Principals~~ or ~~Superintendants~~. _Superintendents._

3. Many home schoolers ~~will be dissapointed~~ _are disappointed_ with ~~Public Education~~, because of ~~consistantly~~ _consistently_ bad ~~advise~~ _advice_ they have had.

4. By ~~having taught everyone~~ _teaching every one_ of their children in the home, parents are ~~liabel~~ _likely_ to monitor the exposure their children ~~will recieve~~ _receive_ from others.

5. Some students who ~~will be~~ _are_ intelligent ~~definately~~ _definitely_ cannot function in the traditional classroom, because each child ~~had personel~~ _has personal_ learning abilities.

6. Some parents ~~will be feeling~~ _feel_ ~~there~~ _their_ children are in ~~morale~~ _moral_ danger in ~~Public~~ ~~Schools~~; through home schooling, these parents are ~~hopefull~~ _hopeful_ they will control the environment to which ~~there~~ _their_ children are exposed.

7. According to ~~Prof.~~ *Professor* Marsh, home schooling ~~compliments~~ *Complements* children's needs, the school is not pushing children to advance for ~~calender~~ *calendar* reasons only.

8. Schools ~~recieve~~ *receive* no financial aid for home-schooled children in the §chool Đistrict, but are, sometimes asked to form a ~~liason~~ *liaison* with home schoolers to ~~have shared~~ *share* facilities, even though the shared-facility system often ~~are producing~~ *produces* unsatisfactory results.

9. According to ~~Doctor~~ *Dr.* Goldstein, to ~~have chosen~~ *choose* to educate home school children, ~~is apparently~~ *apparently* a public declaration in the belief and support of the family institution.

10. An example ~~was~~ *is* that in some §tates, to ~~have taught~~ *teach* the children at home, the parent must ~~have been~~ *be* a ~~Lisenced~~ *licensed* Ŧeacher, whereas, in other states, the parent needs only a Ħigh-§chool Điploma.

11. ~~You're~~ *Your* parents ~~will be seeing~~ *see* what the Public §chool has to offer, and ~~beleive~~ *believe* they can teach their children just as well at home.

12. ~~Your~~ *You're* correct; before home schoolers ~~will be educating~~ *can educate* their children without resistance, a change in thinking needs to be a ~~committment~~ *commitment* at all levels.

13. Regulation ~~will have been~~ *is* needed in home schooling to allow §tates to monitor the progress of the children; at the same time, a parent must ~~have been~~ *be* allowed to ~~have chosen~~ *choose* his or her children's ~~curiculum.~~ *curriculum.*

Believe us when we say the title of this lesson is a rational one. The title suggests we have a unique way of viewing the punctuation rules you'll learn next.

In this lesson, you'll deal mostly with punctuation rules that are internal to the sentence. You'll also acquaint yourself with the preferred punctuation to append a word or a phrase or certain kinds of dependent clauses to the end of an independent clause. Most of the punctuation in Lesson 18 concerns the comma; but you'll also learn about semicolons, parentheses, and dashes as they relate to the title of the lesson.

The word *series* is a plural noun. For a moment, try in vain to think of a singular form for *series*. In doing so, you'll realize that a series is a group of things of the same class coming one after the other in succession. Naturally, at this point, you might think about baseball and the *World Series*. In grammar, a series is a succession of coordinate elements in a sentence. To reflect a series, that succession must involve **three or more** items. If we have only two coordinate elements, we have a pair but not a series.

An *interrupter*, obviously, is something that interrupts. We could speak of interrupters in a sentence in terms of words, phrases, or clauses or as adjectives, parenthetical elements, nonrestrictive phrases or clauses, etc.; but we prefer to lump all such items into one concept we call an *interrupter*. You'll readily perceive that an interrupter "interrupts" the flow of a sentence so the writer can achieve some desired clarification, transition, or emphasis.

An *appositive* is a word or phrase that is "in apposition." That is, an appositive is a construction in which a noun or a noun phrase is placed with another word or phrase as an "explanatory equivalent." As such, an appositive merely adds information about a person or thing already identified. An appositive has much the same feel as an interrupter; but the two have slight distinctions with which you must be familiar.

"Something appended" is a simple way of describing an *appendage*. When we *append* something, we attach it to something else. At the end of a sentence, we sometimes need to append a word, phrase, or dependent clause to the main part of the sentence—such as this statement illustrates. The dash is a marvelous device to use with appendages so we can avoid sentence fragments, add clarification, or give emphasis. Right now, you probably are not very familiar with the dash for these purposes; but your writing will improve dramatically when you learn to append properly.

Pretest

With a **C** or an **I**, indicate whether the punctuation is correct or incorrect in the following sentences. Then punctuate the sentences marked **I**.

1. The house we plan to rent has four bedrooms, a dining room, a family room and a den in the basement.

2. We expect the principle of honesty, on the other hand to be exemplified by all employees.

3. Chapter 5, which tells about the California gold rush is very well written.

4. Jamie Jonas, our new vice president, will begin work on April 1.

5. The editor found several serious errors; run-on sentences, comma splices, and misplaced modifiers.

6. If you desire to go to the horse races; however, we will be delighted to accompany you.

7. One member of the class - Stacie Maag - agreed to give the Freedom Festival keynote address.

8. For our end-of-term social, Karley will order the pizza; Cammy will make a caesar's salad; and Dawna will provide home-made root beer.

9. Some common grammatical errors you should avoid are comma splices, run-on sentences, misuse of possessive case, dangling modifiers, and etc.

10. The business English class, that you recommend so highly, meets in the Marriott Building on Mondays and Wednesdays.

11. Jared's feelings about working on Saturdays, on the other hand, may influence Ms. Feddock to change his work schedule.

12. When we open our new store in West Valley City, we plan to offer a full line of sporting equipment; something we have not done at our Nephi store.

Key: (1) I—in this text, we will always use a comma preceding the conjunction in a series; in this sentence, the commas are additionally mandatory unless we want both the family room and the den to be in the basement; (2) I—use a comma following *hand* to set off *on the other hand* as an interrupter; (3) I—a comma must be used after *gold rush* to set off the nonrestrictive relative clause, *which tells about the California gold rush*; (4) C—*our new vice president*, an appositive, is correctly set off with commas; (5) I—use a dash to append the series to the independent clause; a colon could also be used; (6) I—*however*, as used here, is an interrupter—not a conjunctive joiner; (7) I—in the business world, we form a dash with two hyphens and with no space before or after the hyphens; and although commas are most often used to set off an appositive, parentheses or dashes may also be used; (8) C; (9) I—*etc.* means *and so forth*, so *and* should not be used preceding *etc.*; (10) I—*that clauses* are not set off with commas; (11) C; (12) I—a dash should be used rather than a semicolon to append a fragment to the independent clause.

Terminology

Appendage—A noun describing something that is appended to (added to) a principal object. For our purposes, an appendage is a sentence element (word, phrase, or clause); and the principal object is the independent clause of a sentence.

I can think of only one word to describe Mr. Boynton—*cautious.*
Swenson signed the letter with his usual closing—*with love and kisses.*
The statement was clearly stamped on every package—*Do not open until Christmas!*

Appositive—A noun or a noun phrase that identifies or explains its equivalent in the sentence. For example, *the house painter* is an appositive in the following sentence:

Mr. Jones, *the house painter*, is highly qualified.

We say the appositive, *the house painter*, is *in apposition* to its equivalent (*Mr. Jones*) because *Mr. Jones* and *the house painter* are placed side by side in the sentence. That the two are equivalent is proven because we could just as well word the sentence *The house painter, Mr. Jones, . . .* (and thereby make *Mr. Jones* the appositive).

Nonrestrictive—Synonymous with *nonessential* and used to designate a word, phrase, or clause that is descriptive of but not essential to the basic meaning of the sentence element with which it is associated.

Series—A plural noun that describes a group of coordinate elements (items of the same grammatical construction) coming one after the other in succession. A series requires three or more items that are preferably joined/separated by commas and that use a conjunction between the last two items. As we use the word *series* in relation to punctuation, notice we do so by using the term *a series*.

Rules

Use T18-1 here

1. **Use commas to separate words, phrases, or clauses in a series.**

By our definition, *a series* involves a succession of three or more coordinate elements in a sentence. We join (or separate) these coordinate elements with commas, and we usually place a conjunction between the last two elements. The elements are *coordinate* when they all reflect the same grammatical construction. If any one of the elements reflects a different grammatical construction than the others, then the series lacks *parallelism*. (In Unit 4, you will study the concept of *parallelism* in relation to coordinate items in a series.)

Items in a series can be words, phrases, or clauses. To be consistent and to avoid any chance of miscommunication, the business world prefers that we always use a comma before the conjunction.

NO   We will learn to write letters, memos and reports.
        You will present your exit report to Ms. Murphy, to Mr. Muhlback and to the executive board.

YES   We will learn to write letters, memos, and reports.
        You will present your exit report to Ms. Murphy, to Mr. Muhlback, and to the executive board.

Obviously, if phrases are used in a series, all the phrases must be the same kind of phrases. And we must not mix words, phrases, or clauses in any combination in a series.

NO   Master the rules for the comma, the semicolon, and be sure you understand the dash.
        Our feeling is that your presentation was accurate, it was well researched, and reflecting appropriate conclusions.

YES   Master the rules for the comma, the semicolon, and the dash.
        Our feeling is that your presentation was accurate, it was well researched, and it reflected appropriate conclusions.

Learning Hint 1.   Some disciplines (such as journalism) prefer to eliminate the comma preceding the conjunction in a series. Although this practice may not cause reader confusion in most instances, it can often force the reader to read the sentence a second time to get the intended meaning.

In this textbook, we ask you to be consistent by always using a comma preceding the conjunction in a series. By doing so, you will always reflect the items-in-a-series rule correctly; and you will help ensure that your reader understands the message of the sentence.

*Use
T18-2
here*

Learning Hint 2.   A series in a sentence requires a conjunction between the last two items in the series; moreover, the most frequently used conjunction in any series is *and*. By getting in the habit of putting a comma before the *and* in a series, novice writers often develop the habit of putting a comma before almost any *and* in the middle of a sentence.

The directors reviewed the salary schedule, and promised to do their best to raise wages.

In such constructions, notice that the conjunction joins only two coordinate elements and not three or more. That is, a series is not reflected in the sentence; and the comma is incorrectly used. In such instances, novice writers confuse Lesson 15, Rule 1 (use a comma before the conjunction that joins independent clauses in a compound sentence) and Lesson 18, Rule 1 (use commas to separate items in a series). Be certain you understand clearly these two rules and that you do not confuse the two.

Learning Hint 3.   *Etc.* is an abbreviation that stands for *et cetera*, which means *and so forth*. Inherent within the abbreviation is the conjunction that often occurs between the last two items in a series. When you use *etc.* with items in a series, do not use a second *and*:

NO   We bought pens, pencils, notebooks, paper, *and* etc. for the office.

YES   We bought pens, pencils, notebooks, paper, etc. for the office.

Learning Hint 4.   Rule 1 directs us to use commas to separate items in a series. As a writer, you also have the liberty of using semicolons to separate items in a series. Obviously, semicolons separate the items much more dramatically than commas do.

Writers seldom use semicolons in a series if each item in the series is short (such as single words or short phrases). However, if the items in a series are lengthy, semicolons might aid the readability of the series. Or if one or more of the items in the series contains internal commas, semicolons are usually considered mandatory to avoid comma confusion and aid readability.

> The President made the recommendation to protect American lives; to bring a sadistic, unprincipled criminal to justice; and to preserve the integrity of the treaty.

> Totally implantable hearts are being studied in Hershey, Pennsylvania; Cleveland, Ohio; and Salt Lake City, Utah.

2. **Use commas to set off internal sentence interrupters.**

You may not fully appreciate the benefits we derive from the ''lowly comma,'' but writers of some languages other than English are often envious of the English comma. Realizing that the comma forces the reader to pause and thereby to pay special attention to the reason for the pause, you will begin to appreciate the comma fully when you use it to set off internal sentence interrupters.

We're lumping several comma rules together in this rule—but all the rules reflect the concept of an interrupter. The interrupters that are impacted by Rule 2 are nonrestrictive modifiers, transitional elements, and parenthetical statements. A brief explanation of these interrupters follows. Notice that each is in the middle of the sentence and that each is set off with commas.

A **nonrestrictive modifier** is a nonessential subordinate clause or phrase that does not limit or define the term it modifies. That is, such a modifier does not *restrict* the term's meaning; and if the modifier were omitted, the meaning of the sentence would not change much.

> Many of the people in Guatemala, *who have lived in poverty for centuries*, desperately need our financial assistance.

Learning Hint 5:   In Unit 5, you will have an in-depth experience in working with nonrestrictive relative clauses. For now, simply remember the following: *which clauses* used as interrupters are set off with commas, but *that clauses* are not set off with commas. For example:

NO   The Finance Club *which* was organized last month will have its office in the Union Building.

The new automobile, *that* we purchased for tax purposes, cannot be used for personal reasons.

YES   The Finance Club, *which* was organized last month, will have its office in the Union Building.

The new automobile *that* we purchased for tax purposes cannot be used for personal reasons.

Transitional elements are used to achieve transition between thoughts. In Rules 2 and 3 from Lesson 17, we learned that such elements are set off with commas when the elements come at the first of a sentence. When such transitional elements as *furthermore, in addition, in the same manner, nevertheless, on the contrary, accordingly, in other words, furthermore,* and *however* appear in the middle of a sentence, they are set off on both sides with commas—unless they are performing as conjunctive joiners to join independent clauses.

We have many reasons, *however*, to support the new proposal.
The budget committee, *in other words*, does not support Mr. Munde's thinking.

Parenthetical statements distinctively reflect the idea of an interrupter. We call such sentence elements *parenthetical* because they are qualifying or explanatory statements that can be put inside parentheses.

Use T18-3 here

Learning Hint 6.   Often, interrupters can be set off with commas, dashes, or parentheses—especially in the case of parenthetical statements. As the writer, you have the option of deciding which to use. In general, dashes emphasize and parentheses deemphasize. For example:

I believe, even though the Dow Jones is up, that right now is a good time to sell your stock.
I believe—even though the Dow Jones is up—that right now is a good time to sell your stock.
I believe (even though the Dow Jones is up) that right now is a good time to sell your stock.

When you are choosing among commas, dashes, or parentheses, remember, in general, that commas and dashes emphasize the element being set off and that parentheses deemphasize the element.

3. **Use commas to set off appositives.**

An *appositive* is a noun or noun equivalent that is placed beside another noun to supplement or to complement the meaning of the first noun. An appositive has the same grammatical function as the noun to which it relates. In fact, a writer can usually reverse the order of the noun and its appositive without significantly changing the meaning. We say that the appositive is *in apposition* to the noun to which it relates. An appositive in the middle of a sentence is set off by commas; an appositive at the end of a sentence is preceded by a comma. For example:

My next-door neighbor, *Ms. Munk*, recently moved to Atlanta.
Ms. Munk, *my next-door neighbor*, recently moved to Atlanta.
The person who recently moved to Atlanta was my next-door neighbor, *Ms. Munk*.

4. **Use a dash to give emphasis, to show a sudden change in the structure of a sentence, or to append a fragment to an independent clause.**

As a mark of punctuation, the dash is a marvelous device to give emphasis to a sentence element or to append a word, phrase, or fragment to the independent clause. If any criticism can be directed toward novice writers in relation to the dash, it is that they tend to use it too infrequently.

As you know from Rule 2, the dash can be used to set off a sentence interrupter. As such, the dash gives more emphasis than either commas or parentheses.

One of the most useful things the dash can do is append a fragment to a sentence's independent clause. Consciously relate to that use if you have any tendency to write a ''sentence'' that is really just a fragment.

NO   Aimee's grammar errors were serious ones. Run-on sentences, comma splices, and dangling modifiers.

YES   Aimee's grammar errors were serious ones—run-on sentences, comma splices, and dangling modifiers.

See Rule 9 in Lesson 19 if you think a colon might be used in place of the dash.

Learning Hint 7.   In the business world, most keyboard dashes are formed with two hyphens with no space before or after the hyphens (--). For example:

NO   Only one person - Mr. Moudreaux - is eligible.
          Only one person -- Mr. Moudreaux -- is eligible.

YES   Only one person--Mr. Moudreaux--is eligible.

Admittedly, the practice of using two hyphens to form a dash is a carryover from the typewriter when a dash had to be longer than a hyphen and the keyboard did not accommodate a true dash. Today, printers often prefer an *em dash* to a two-hyphen dash. Adequate word-processing software will enable you to invoke an *em dash*, which is a solid-line equivalent to the length of two hyphens. For example, an *em dash* is made in WordPerfect® as follows: Control V, 4, 34. Except for illustrative instances, *em dashes* are used throughout this textbook.

Posttest

With a **C** or an **I**, indicate whether the punctuation is correct or incorrect in the following sentences. Then punctuate the sentences marked **I**.

1. Leonard Mackelprang, the driver of the car finally confessed to the hit-and-run accident.

2. When you arrive in Lake Tahoe, therefore, please feel free to stay at our summer cabin.

3. The central person in the investigation who turned out to be Alex Lynch, is Roland's brother-in-law.

4. The menu for breakfast during the deer hunt includes sourdough biscuits, bacon and eggs, and hot chocolate.

5. The housing report did not reach my office until Monday—probably an oversight on Gabriel's part.

6. Two of the Steamboat Springs hikers (Lance Nakagawa and Henry Nakai) were lost for about four hours.

7. From our perspective, as I'm sure you'll understand we hope to finish building the house in early October.

8. The type of grammatical errors Silas makes are the usual ones-dangling modifiers, mis-placed modifiers, comma blunders, etc.

9. Before Ila takes the algebra examination again, she plans to spend several hours in the learning resource center; something she has not done yet.

10. Nicollette's 1928 roadster, which she bought from her uncle who lives in Florida, will be in the July 4 parade.

11. Sun-Young's performance in the business English class, as I'm sure you know, represents an outstanding accomplishment—especially in light of her learning English just one year ago.

12. Holly will teach us about possessive case, Christopher has the assignment to cover past-perfect tense; and Brandt has volunteered to discuss misplaced modifiers.

Key: (1) I—the appositive, *the driver of the car*, must be set off on both sides with commas; (2) C; (3) I—the nonrestrictive relative clause interrupter, *who turned out to be Alex Lynch*, must be set off with commas; (4) C; (5) C; (6) C; (7) I—the dependent clause interrupter must be set off with commas; (8) I—a keyboard dash is made with two hyphens or with an em dash—but not with a single hyphen; (9) I—a dash, not a semicolon, is the most-appropriate way to append a sentence fragment to an independent clause; (10) C; (11) C; (12) I—either commas or semicolons should be used to set off the three independent clauses in a series—but not a mixture of the two.

LEVEL A

Name _____

Exercise 18–1   On the lines below, write **T** if the statement is true and **F** if the statement is false.

_F_   1. A *series* is a succession of two or more coordinate elements in a sentence.

_T_   2. A nonrestrictive sentence element is a nonessential element and is typically set off with commas.

_F_   3. The business world usually gives the writer the option of whether to use a comma preceding the *and* in a series.

_T_   4. In general, items in a series may be separated either with commas or with semicolons.

_F_   5. Typical sentence interrupters are misplaced modifiers, appositives, and parenthetical statements.

_F_   6. A *that* clause is an example of a nonrestrictive relative clause.

_T_   7. Interrupters can often be set off with commas, dashes, or parentheses.

_F_   8. In the business world, dashes may be made in one of two ways: (--) or (-).

_F_   9. The word *however* is an example of a sentence interrupter when used as a conjunctive adverb to join two independent clauses.

Exercise 18–2   Mark **C** if the punctuation is correct; mark **I** if the punctuation is incorrect.

_I_   1. A tax haven as you know, is a place of shelter or refuge from taxes.

_I_   2. The use of tax havens is legal, however, authorities are concerned with criminal use of havens.

_C_   3. Important features of tax havens are political stability; secrecy; accessibility and communication; low future taxation; and reasonable fees, duties, and miscellaneous taxes.

_I_   4. Some countries, although not considered tax havens allow special privileges that make them suitable as havens for limited purposes.

_I_   5. Legitimate tax-haven inquiries by other governments are often answered by little if any information.

_I_   6. Determining the full extent of these charges, is important, because they may completely offset the tax savings.

_C_   7. Communication facilities must be available—for example, telephone, telex, and television.

_C_   8. The activities of tax-haven countries include the placing of bank deposits; the creation of companies; and the formation of trusts.

_I_   9. The shipping industry particularly in Liberia, is encouraged to use havens; because a foreign corporation's shipping profits are exempt from U.S. tax under certain conditions.

Exercise 18–3 Mark **C** if the dash is used correctly; mark **I** if it is used incorrectly.

C 1. The local government officials want an improved road—but not at the expense of the canyon's aesthetics.

I 2. Stan the Man's Frozen Yogurt Shoppe—which is owned by Stanley Pons, will open three new mall stores in June.

I 3. The three administrators, Mr. Gray, Mr. Lundberg, and Ms. Lee—were asked to discuss year-round school.

I 4. Commissioner Denzil Maryboy-- a Navajo-- charged his fellow commissioners with dereliction of duty.

C 5. Mr. Hellinger said, ''My estimates reflect the costs of the care now being delivered—not what we should or shouldn't give.''

C 6. The economy may be crippled by the deaths of young adults—from bank managers to subsistence farmers.

I 7. Lifetime costs of caring for one patient - oft disputed and revised - now approach $85,000.

C 8. Many so-called angels—investors who back new companies—are turning away from high-tech investments.

I 9. Usually, venture capitalists prefer to invest—as early as possible in emerging technologies.

Exercise 18–4 Mark **C** if all commas in the sentence are correct; mark **I** if the sentence is incorrectly punctuated.

I 1. The ten questions, that Alix did not answer, were the most interesting ones.

C 2. Relatively few of your classes, however, are taught in the Tanner Building.

I 3. Three business recessions took place in the last decade, however, they were all short-lived.

I 4. Drunk drivers who are responsible for taking lives, obviously should have their licenses revoked.

C 5. Lincoln delivered his most-famous address at Gettysburg, site of one of the bloodiest Civil War battles.

I 6. The menu for the picnic included hamburgers, potato salad, root beer and watermelon.

I 7. I was happy to see the red, white, and blue flag, waving proudly in the breeze.

C 8. After the movie, Ellis and Jodi went home by taxicab because they preferred, as you can appreciate, to avoid the subway.

I 9. While his wife was in the hospital, Junior cleaned the house, and fixed meals, washed clothes, and helped his sons every evening with their homework.

LEVEL B

Name _____

Exercise 18–5   Write the letter that matches the reason associated with each sentence's punctuation. Some sentences may have more than one match.

A Series	E Appendage punctuation
B Nonrestrictive modifier	F Emphasis punctuation
C Parenthetical statement	G No match possible
D Appositive	

G,E,C   1. Because light can be focused through reducing lenses, this method produces details that are much smaller than those on the mask—allowing the mask, in turn, to remain large enough to be inspected and repaired.

B   2. Our computer will share the work, which the computer will complete at night, during a lunch break, or during any slack period lasting 15 minutes or more.

C   4. Workstations sold by Nu-Age Computers, for example, include an experimental program called Gotcha.

D,E   5. Richard Geyelin, Nu-Age's chief scientist, compares the process to recycling—noting that most computers are used only four hours a day.

D,B   6. Meg Shinker, head of general-interest books for Beacon Street Publishers, which published the book, says, ''I often quote dead people.''

B or C or F   7. The first two genetically engineered pesticides to reach the U.S. market—both of them developed by Morgan Corporation—may be approved for sale in July.

A   8. As you know, the director provides leadership in strategic planning; coordinates and manages administrative departments; and participates in the highest level of decision making.

G   9. According to the announcement sheet, the job requires a technical and business degree or equivalent, and strong cost-analysis skills.

D   10. The Business Education Fund, a $15 million loan fund for minorities, says its loans increased 90 percent last year.

Exercise 18–6   Write the letter that identifies the one best sentence.

C   1. *a.*   The cause of the traffic delay, apparently was a minor traffic accident.
   b.   Anthony Dolezal, an excellent photographer will accompany us on our trip.
   c.   The Salmon River, known as the River of No Return, is the only major North American river that flows north.

b   2. *a.*   The largest state in the nation - Alaska - is also my favorite state.
   b.   You should know, by the way, that other possible solutions may be discovered.
   c.   Dana Domenichello who owns three tire-repair shops will give the lecture on road safety.

_c_ 3. _a._ The quick-witted comedian, telling the jokes, is Norman Doerr, a cousin of mine.

 _b._ DKB Siding which manufactures the aluminum shingles will not be able to bid on the project.

 _c._ The 20-year service plaques will be given to Art Hobbs, Accounting Department; Andrea Dodds, Personnel Department; and Archie Dixon, Public Relations Department.

_a_ 4. _a._ The farmers were ready to plant their spring crops—and then the rains began.

 _b._ Three of the companies—you know their names, agreed to help in our cooperative-education project.

 _c._ The faulty software, the lack of a surge protector and the missing computer—all these problems will demand my attention tomorrow.

_a_ 5. _a._ Mr. Eagle decided to leave on Monday (as you suggested) and to stay in Palm Springs for a week.

 _b._ Notebooks, file folders, and computer ribbons—these are the three supply-room items, to which Ms. Dushku alluded in her memo.

 _c._ Three of the candidates—Mr. Dyke, Ms. Dymock and Ms. Elquist—have extensive political experience.

_b_ 6. _a._ When you are involved in zero-defect production—a goal we desire to reach this year.

 _b._ The problems we must overcome are the following: a shortage of raw materials; a lack of computer expertise; and inexperienced chemists.

 _c._ Marty Emmons, the new production analyst reported yesterday that the milling machine is broken; as a result, he will attend the machine-tool auction on Monday.

_c_ 7. _a._ The computer, that is in Room 28, will be given to Zeda when she begins work next week.

 _b._ As you may have heard ''The attorney, who represents himself or herself, has a fool for a client.''

 _c._ Pioneer Park, which was established in 1865, is noted for its massive shade trees.

_b_ 8. _a._ The new administrators who now lead the university, are dedicated, conscientious people.

 _b._ Our community-awareness group, as you may know, includes Patti Firl, parade coordinator; Russell Foushee, carnival supervisor; and Alice Fotu, Freedom Festival representative.

 _c._ We tend to think on the other hand, that you will receive partial compensation for the accident.

_a_ 9. _a._ The Eimco, Thiokol, and Hercules orders, which we have been expecting to receive any day, have been delayed—probably for two more weeks.

 _b._ Yesterday's market went up for most stocks in your portfolio—a few blue-chip stocks; however, declined in value.

 _c._ None of the employees naturally is willing to accept responsibility for the accident.

_c_ 10. _a._ The word-processing center will be responsible for the following nontyping tasks; answering the telephone; sorting the mail; and filing invoices.

 _b._ Ms. Gagon—a hard-working, competitive employee, was recently promoted to vice president.

 _c._ You will be wise to reflect three critical traits in your work—dependability, efficiency, and honesty.

LEVEL C

Name _____

Exercise 18–7   Write the number of the Lesson 18 rule or learning hint associated with the sentence's punctuation. Some sentences may reflect more than one rule or learning hint. Then, edit all incorrect sentences.

_LH5_   1. Bear River, which rises with the spring run-off, causes a great deal of damage in May.

_LH6_   2. Middle-aged people (most of whom do not get much exercise) often have back problems if they do heavy lifting.

_3, 4_   3. Maralise, one of our food-obsessed employees, told me that she could live on two foods: pizza and ice cream.

_LH6_   4. Members of the team—Will, Ben, Frank, Dave, and Jose—traveled to Challis in the same car.

_4, LH2_   5. Predict which horse will win the race, Saturday Runner, or Sure Bet.

_LH6, LH2_
_LH3, 1_   6. The four brothers—Erich, Bob, Blaine, and Boyd—look alike, and often go to games, movies, plays, and etc. together.

_LH 4_   7. Mr. Ridd thinks that our school should join the association; that Ms. Robinett, our English teacher, should represent us at meetings; and that all teachers should be required to attend meetings.

_4, LH3, 1_   8. Several complicated procedures are involved when we hire new employees, e.g., advertising the openings, interviewing the candidates, setting up training programs, and etc.

_3_   9. One of our systems analysts, Deanne Seals, will host the guests from Purdue University.

_____4_____ 10. A recent poll ranked homelessness as our No. 2 problem--directly behind the

deficit.

**Exercise
18–8**

Write the lesson number (15 through 18) and the number of the rule or learning hint associated with the sentence's punctuation. Some sentences may reflect more than one rule or learning hint. Then, edit all incorrect sentences.

_18-2, 16-1_   1. The topic of the paper, as you know, is software piracy; software piracy has become

a major problem in the software industry.

_18-LH2, 16LH2,
17-1, 18-2_   2. Although no one will argue that software piracy is legal and that it should be

condoned, experts, especially software manufacturers, differ in their solutions to

the problem.

_18-2,
16-LH2_   3. The problem we need to investigate is that of software piracy in the United States;

in comparison to international software piracy.

_18-1,
16-1, 17-2_   4. Corporations need to write, communicate, and enforce software policies; through

software policies, corporations can limit their software-piracy liabilities.

_17-2, 16-3_   5. From its foundations, the software industry has suffered problems with piracy; but

during the 1980s, the problem became more acute.

_17-2, 18-4,
16-LH2_   6. In spite of the risks involved, software copying is often condoned, especially

when PCs are installed in an office.

_18-2,
16-LH2,
18-LH5_   7. Most of the legal users of copy-protected software, as you know, find copy pro-

tection irritating because it does not allow the user to make a backup copy, that

is allowed under Section 117.

_17-2,
18-LH6_   8. According to Max Scofield, the sentiment among LAN managers—those who load

and maintain software packages, is that a less-irritating way of protecting software

ownership should be found.

17-2, 18-LH6,
16-3   9. In 1988, six leading software producers, (Aldus, Ashton-Tate, Autodesk, Lotus,

Microsoft, and WordPerfect) formed the SPA; and today the SPA represents 650

software publishers.

17-2
16-3, 18-2 10. To combat software piracy, the SPA conducts software audits; and, when necessary,

the SPA conducts raids on companies suspected of large-scale piracy.

Exercise 18–9

Compo-sition

Compose sentences that fulfill the directions given.

1. Using yourself as the subject, write a sentence containing an appositive.

   _____

   _____

2. Using yourself as the subject, write a sentence containing an end-of-sentence fragment connected to the independent clause with a dash.

   _____

   _____

3. Compose and punctuate correctly a sentence that contains four phrases in a series.

   _____

   _____

4. Compose a sentence using semicolons to punctuate three independent clauses in a series.

   _____

   _____

Exercise 18–10

Cumula-tive Editing

Edit the following sentences by correcting any frequently misspelled words, confusing words, or Lessons 15 through 18 errors.

1. The defendant, who's the cousin of a prominent judge, was surprised, that a change of venue was not recommended.

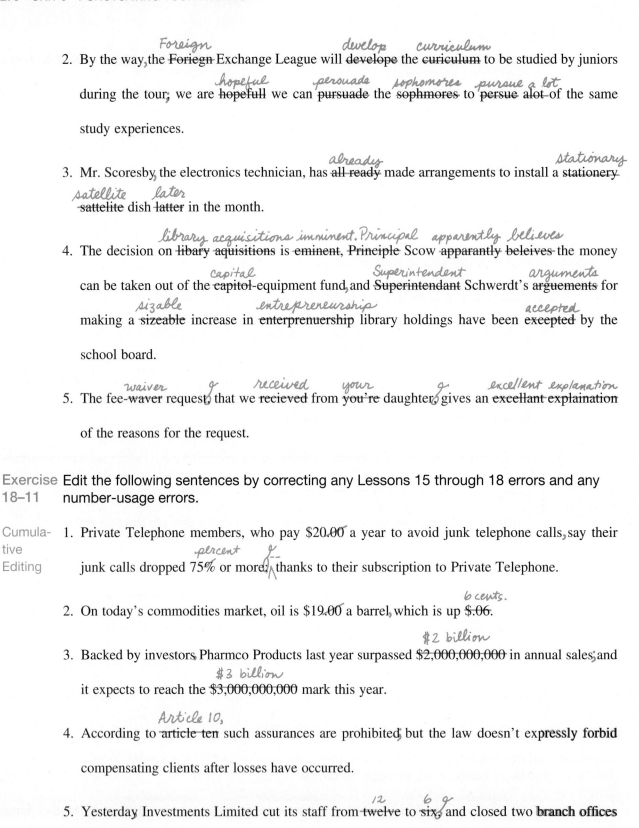

2. By the way, the ~~Foriegn~~ *Foreign* Exchange League will ~~develope~~ *develop* the ~~curiculum~~ *curriculum* to be studied by juniors during the tour; we are ~~hopefull~~ *hopeful* we can ~~pursuade~~ *persuade* the ~~sophmores~~ *sophomores* to ~~persue alot~~ *pursue a lot* of the same study experiences.

3. Mr. Scoresby, the electronics technician, has ~~all ready~~ *already* made arrangements to install a ~~stationery~~ *stationary* ~~sattelite~~ *satellite* dish ~~latter~~ *later* in the month.

4. The decision on ~~libary aquisitions~~ *library acquisitions* is ~~eminent,~~ *imminent.* ~~Principle~~ *Principal* Scow ~~apparantly beleives~~ *apparently believes* the money can be taken out of the ~~capitol~~ *capital* equipment fund, and ~~Superintendant~~ *Superintendent* Schwerdt's ~~arguements~~ *arguments* for making a ~~sizeable~~ *sizable* increase in ~~enterprenuership~~ *entrepreneurship* library holdings have been ~~excepted~~ *accepted* by the school board.

5. The fee ~~waiver~~ *waiver* request, that we ~~recieved~~ *received* from ~~you're~~ *your* daughter, gives an ~~excellant explaination~~ *excellent explanation* of the reasons for the request.

Exercise 18–11 Edit the following sentences by correcting any Lessons 15 through 18 errors and any number-usage errors.

Cumulative Editing

1. Private Telephone members, who pay $20.00 a year to avoid junk telephone calls, say their junk calls dropped 75% or more, *percent* thanks to their subscription to Private Telephone.

2. On today's commodities market, oil is $19.00 a barrel, which is up $.06. *6 cents.*

3. Backed by investors, Pharmco Products last year surpassed $2,000,000,000 *$2 billion* in annual sales, and it expects to reach the $3,000,000,000 *$3 billion* mark this year.

4. According to ~~article ten~~ *Article 10,* such assurances are prohibited, but the law doesn't ex**pressly forbid** compensating clients after losses have occurred.

5. Yesterday Investments Limited cut its staff from ~~twelve~~ *12* to ~~six,~~ *6,* and closed two **branch offices** in the process.

Exercise 18–12

Cumulative Editing

Edit the following sentences by correcting any Lessons 15 through 18 errors and any errors related to the verb unit.

1. ~~Go shopping~~ *When you shop* at Big Discount, the state's largest, brashest, and fastest-growing deep-discount chain, ~~and~~ you never know what price bargains you may find!

2. The stores keep prices down by buying in large volume, and ~~goods are bought by~~ the stores *buy goods* through special large-purchase discounts.

3. *Developers founded* Big Discount ~~has been founded~~ eight years ago in Dayton, Ohio; and the chain stores ~~are~~ *have* ~~making~~ *made* waves in retail-trade circles ever since.

4. ~~Having walked~~ *Walking* out of a Big Discount store in Pittsburgh and ~~having carried~~ *carrying* a bag full of X-tra film, Cheryl Smiley, a Carnegie Mellon graduate student, says, "If I had a choice I'd buy Nu-Film; but brand loyalty's not that important."

5. As of a month ago, Big Discount ~~will have~~ *had* developed a reputation for innovative merchandising, relentless marketing, and skillful negotiating with suppliers.

6. Competitors ~~had said~~ *say* Big Discount ~~had seemed~~ *seems* determined to ~~have taken~~ *take* over markets by cutthroat pricing and by forcing smaller operations out of business.

7. Big Discount officials will ~~have been denying~~ *deny* the company will have ~~had~~ a credit crunch, and *will* say the business is very profitable, although they won't ~~have given~~ *give* figures.

8. To ~~have accommodated~~ *accommodate* the supply, Big Discount needs to open new stores, and draw customers into existing stores, or else choke on its own inventory.

9. Big Discount does take care of its friends; company officials ~~will have paid~~ *pay* personal visits to manufacturers, ~~threw~~ *throw* parties for suppliers, and ~~promising~~ *promise* favorable display space in stores.

10. ~~Having entered~~ *Entering* a Big Discount store, shoppers ~~had been~~ *are* greeted by gleaming soft-drink machines; each can ~~will be selling~~ *is sold* for only 35 cents, a price many people haven't seen for ten years.

Exercise 18–13

Cumulative Editing

Edit the following sentences by correcting any capitalization, abbreviation, and Lessons 15 through 18 errors.

1. The two Universities schedule dozens of Freshman courses; in fact, this Fall, french, english, phil. 105, and math. 112 will be available. *[handwritten corrections: u over U (universities); f over F (freshman); F (Fall→fall); F (french→French); E (english→English); Philosophy over phil.; Mathematics over math.]*

2. I need two History courses, one Math. class and an Eng. class to complete my general-education requirements. *[handwritten corrections: h (History→history); mathematics over Math.; English over Eng.]*

3. The Vice President introduced Mr. Ungricht, the President of Goodenough Corporation, to my Mgmt. Professor, Dr. Turnbow. *[handwritten corrections: v, p (vice president); p (president); management over Mgmt.; p (professor)]*

4. At the Xmas party, my Grandfather and my Grandmother, told stories about growing up in southern Calif. *[handwritten corrections: Christmas over Xmas; g (grandfather); g (grandmother); S (southern→Southern); California over Calif.]*

5. I'll never forget my Father's last birthday; it was the last Fri. in Nov. we celebrated it on the banks of the Colo. River in Ariz. *[handwritten corrections: f (father); Friday over Fri.; November, and over Nov.; Colorado over Colo.; Arizona over Ariz.]*

6. According to my Uncle, if you enlist in the U.S. navy today, you'll be a Lt. in two years. *[handwritten corrections: u (uncle); N (navy→Navy); lieutenant over Lt.]*

7. You are correct in your observations; I enjoy the Thanksgiving Holidays more than I enjoy New Year's day. *[handwritten corrections: h (Holidays→holidays); D (day→Day)]*

8. After the Dinner on Pioneer Day, senator Udall introduced Ms. Unga to the Assoc. Dean of the College of Agric. *[handwritten corrections: d (Dinner→dinner); S (senator→Senator); associate over Assoc.; d (Dean→dean); Agriculture over Agric.]*

9. Cascade springs is a tourist attraction located somewhere in the west, Near Midway, Ut. I think, or near Flagstaff, Ariz. *[handwritten corrections: S (springs→Springs); W (west→West); n (Near→near); Utah, over Ut.; Arizona over Ariz.]*

10. My counselor, who has helped me tremendously, advised me to take spanish next year, and to avoid taking history or english. *[handwritten corrections: S (spanish→Spanish); E (english→English)]*

In Lessons 15 through 18, you have studied the most frequently used and most frequently abused rules of punctuation. By mastering the rules in Lessons 15 through 18, you will deal adequately with most of the punctuation needs in your writing.

In Lesson 19, you will study several other rules of punctuation; but these rules are rather infrequently used and therefore do not impact your writing as much as the rules in Lessons 15 through 18.

Obviously, we could study several other rules of punctuation beyond those in Lessons 15 through 19. However, we think you can deal adequately in most instances with other punctuation decisions, such as the following:

A period at the end of a declarative sentence: *My role as a supervisor will end in three months.*
A question mark at the end of a direct question: *Will you be able to speak at the Boston seminar?*
An exclamation point to express strong feeling: *Yes! We've decided to move our corporate head-quarters to Houston!*
A colon in expressions of time and proportions: *At 4:40 p.m. on Monday, we verified the ratio to be 2:1.*
A colon following salutations: *Dear Mr. Jones:*
A comma following a complimentary closing: *Sincerely yours,*
The diagonal (sometimes called a slash): *the secretary/treasurer; an either/or proposition*

Although we cannot give you absolutely valid figures, we think the rules we deal with in Lessons 15 through 18 cover about 80 percent of the punctuation decisions you must make in your writing. When we add the rules in Lesson 19 to those in Lessons 15 through 18, we think you will have explored about 95 percent of the punctuation decisions you must make in your writing. Therefore, if you **master** all the rules in Lessons 15 through 19, you'll **know** you're using punctuation correctly about 95 percent of the time!

Pretest

With a **C** or an **I**, indicate whether the punctuation is correct or incorrect in the following sentences. Then punctuate the sentences marked **I**.

1. Will you please get me a copy of Moby Dick from the public library?

2. The foremost question in my mind is whether we'll have to pay a late penalty.

3. I'm going to ask you Gail to be responsible for making our hotel reservations.

4. July 1, 1991 was the anticipated completion date for the road construction.

5. Eric Trafny, Jr. will receive an award for his outstanding leadership.

6. The name of the publishing company is S. A. Publishers, Inc.

7. Genoa, Nebraska is the small town where I spent the early days of my life.

8. Send the goods to me at 1402 52nd Avenue Meridian, MS 39301.

9. The traits I will emphasize in my talk are: dependability, reliability, and honesty.

10. According to Ben Franklin, 'a penny saved is a penny earned'.

11. Have you read Dr. Berhow's article, ''A Rationale for Lateness''?

12. As a club member, I got a significant discount when I ordered ''McCalls'' and ''Popular Science.''

13. Berntsen says, ''Such lawsuits force firms . . . to take the issues of software piracy seriously.''

14. According to Athey, ''No clear-cut solutions [exist] to solve the problem of software piracy.''

Key: (1) I—the sentence is a polite request and not a question, and *Moby Dick* must be italicized to show it is a book; (2) C—indirect questions do not require a question mark; (3) I—names used in direct address are set off with commas; (4) I—a comma is used to set off the year when the year follows the month and day; (5) C; (6) C—as far as we know, the company prefers to use a comma before *Inc.*; (7) I—a comma must follow *Nebraska*; (8) I—commas are used to set off the components of an address in a sentence; (9) I—the colon is extraneous and should not be used unless an expression such as *the following* is used; (10) I—double quotes must be used, and a period always goes inside the quote mark; (11) C; (12) I—magazine titles are italicized; (13) C; (14) C—brackets are used to make corrections or insertions in a direct quote.

Terminology

Ellipsis—A punctuation device used to show the omission of a word or several words in a direct quotation. In this textbook, an ellipsis consists of three periods. On a word processor, hard spaces are used between the periods; and soft spaces are used before and after the ellipsis.

Hard space—A word-processing command used to keep the letters or words together so that software does not divide the letters or the words at the ends of lines and does not insert additional spaces between the letters or words when right justification is used. The hard space, when combined with the items on the left and right of the hard space, is recognized by the software as being one word. Hard spaces are often used between the periods in an ellipsis (. . .) so the software will recognize the ellipsis as a ''word.''

Italics—A style of printing with the letters slanting to the right to give emphasis to whatever appears in italics. Italicized material is shown with underscores or with a true italics font. Some style manuals permit solid capitals for italicized material in business correspondence.

Soft space—The space between letters or words that results from one stroke of the keyboard space bar. A soft space is a signal to the word-processing software that one ''word'' has ended and another has begun. Some software will add additional space at the points of soft spaces if right justification is used.

Rules

1. **Use a period at the end of a polite request, a suggestion, or a command.**

   When you first read Rule 1, your reaction might have been, ''Everyone knows you put a period at the end of *a sentence*.'' A closer reading of the rule will verify the rule's distinctiveness.

   Polite requests, suggestions, and commands are often punctuated with a question mark. However, when you expect your reader to do something other than give an answer, the period is the correct punctuation:

   Will you please contact our office for further assistance.

   May we suggest you contact our office if you want personal assistance with your tax return.

   If you cannot attend the budget hearing, will you please send someone in your place.

2. **Use a period at the end of an indirect question.**

   The idea behind an indirect question is that we ''ask a question without really asking a question.''

   The only question Vince had was whether he would have to put in overtime to complete the project.

   Why Mr. Sears failed to file his income-tax return has never been explained fully.

3. **Use commas to set off names or titles used in direct address.**

   Names and titles used in direct address have the feel of sentence interrupters.

   We're hopeful, *Printha*, that you will give us your support.

   I want you to assume the leadership role, *Rick.*

4. **Use commas to set off the year when it follows the month and day.**

   Business communication requires rather specific procedures when you write about calendar events. Notice the correct formatting and punctuation for months, days, and years:

   I arrived on *April 15, 1992*, and began work on *April 16* in the assembly room. (preferred business style)

I arrived in *April 1992* and began work the day after I arrived. (notice the lack of commas when only the month and year are given)

I arrived on *15 April 1992* and began work on *16 April* in the assembly room. (preferred style for some disciplines other than business)

I arrived on the *15th of April, 1992,* and began work on the *16th of April.* (acceptable business style when the day precedes the month; notice the inclusion of ordinals in this example and the lack of ordinals in the above examples)

5. Use a comma to set off *Jr.* and *Sr.* following a person's name.

Most commonly, *Jr.* and *Sr.* are set off with commas when they follow a person's name—unless the person prefers otherwise. In this textbook, we will always require the comma to set off *Jr.* and *Sr.*

Harrison Scribner, *Jr.* has accepted the role of mediator.

Harrison Scribner, *Sr.*, the founder of the company, will continue to serve on the board of directors.

Note the lack of a comma in the following:

The award will be given to Richard Schwartzkopf *III.*

6. Use a comma to set off *Inc.* and *Ltd.* in a company name.

Unless a company prefers otherwise, as shown typically through the company letterhead, a comma is used to set off *Inc., Ltd.,* and similar expressions:

We gave the order to Seagull Book and Tape, *Inc.*

Did you buy stock in the Canadian firm of Baron's Oil, *Ltd.*?

7. Use commas to set off the name of a state, county, country, or the equivalent when it directly follows the name of a city.

For a vacation, we spent our time in *Blythe, California,* visiting with relatives.

My mother was born in *Bozeman, Gallatin, Montana,* on May 15, 1900.

We spent two days in *Mazatlan, Mexico,* before we traveled to *Tikal, Guatemala,* to meet my father.

8. Use commas to set off the components of an address used in a sentence.

My sister's address is Mrs. Luella Lekan, 6325 Ranchview Drive, Independence, Ohio 44131.

During our sabbatical, we lived at 3192 Foss Road, NE, No. 102, St. Anthony, MN 55421.

9. Use a colon between a clause and the material it introduces when the clause introduces the material with such expressions as *the following* and *as follows*.

NO   The four basic styles of leadership are: tells, sells, consults, and joins.

YES   The four basic styles of leadership are *as follows*: tells, sells, consults, and joins.

Note that a colon is not used immediately following a linking verb or a preposition.

10. Use quotation marks to enclose a direct quotation—the exact words of the person being quoted.

Merlin merely said, ''I won't go to the convention if it's held in November.''

According to Dr. Shepherd, ''Cellular telephone companies are fighting back against the fraud that's costing $200 million a year.''

In such sentences as the above, notice that a comma usually follows the introductory statement that precedes the quotation.

*Use
T19-1
here*

Learning Hint 1.   In business communications, commas and periods **always** go inside quotation marks.

In his speech, Leland used the statement ''win a few and lose a few.''

Leland used the statement ''win a few and lose a few,'' and Chiaki responded by saying, ''I've won a few and lost a lot.''

However, semicolons and colons go outside quotation marks:

Yesterday, Ms. Athey said, ''We will definitely finish by 5 p.m.''; however, we still worked until after 7 p.m.

Please bring me the following items from your ''tickler file'': the Veracruz project and the Guadalajara letters.

Question marks and exclamation points go inside the closing quotation mark when they apply only to the quoted material:

The question I did poorly on was, ''What do you expect for a salary?''

Question marks and exclamation points go outside the closing quotation mark when they apply to the entire sentence:

Are you tired of hearing Mr. Shin say ''Let's call it a day''?

Learning Hint 2.   The business world prefers that we always use double quotation marks for a quotation.

NO   The vendors claim they are fighting for their 'very existence.'

YES   The vendors claim they are fighting for their ''very existence.''

However, if we are using a quote within a quote, we use double quotation marks for the first quote and single quotation marks for the quote within the quote:

According to Mr. Allen, ''Such a policy, when *'policed and enforced,'* removes the copying activities from the scope of the employment.''

11. Use quotation marks to enclose the titles of magazine, journal, and newspaper articles; the titles of essays, poems, speeches, and sermons; the titles of chapters, sections, and lessons within a book; the titles of unpublished works such as term papers, reports, theses, and dissertations; and the titles of songs and short musical compositions.

The June 27, 1991, *Wall Street Journal* article is entitled ''Other Auto Makers May Run Ads Touting Their Nifty Turn Signals.''

Audrey Megerian's poem in the *Ensign*, ''Let Us Not Wait,'' is very much worth reading.

You'll find the discussion about semicolons in Lesson 16, ''The Semicolon for Joining Independent Clauses.''

The title of my term paper is ''Consumption of Fats and Oils in the Diet: Is the Taste Worth the Risk?''

Irving Berlin's composition, ''Deep Purple,'' is still my grandmother's favorite.

Learning Hint 3.   As explained in Learning Hint 1 of Lesson 6, you should be consistent in capitalizing the words in the titles of articles, essays, poems, book chapters, term papers, etc. In addition to enclosing such titles in quotation marks, we capitalize the words in titles as follows:

a. All words with four or more letters. (Some style manuals advocate capitalizing all words with five or more letters. We have chosen to capitalize all words with four or more letters in this textbook.)

b. All nouns, pronouns, adjectives, verbs, adverbs, and subordinate conjunctions, regardless of length.

c. Articles (*a, an, the*) and coordinate conjunctions (*and, but, or, nor, for, so, yet*) only when they are the first or last words in a title.

d. Prepositions only when they are four or more letters in length or when they are the first or last words in titles.

e. The *to* in infinitives only when it is the first word in a title.

''Getting Results With English Grammar''
''A Concise Explanation of English Grammar''
''How to Write Reports That Are Easy to Read''
''An Analysis to Determine the Frequency of Digits, Symbols, and Number Patterns Occurring in Business Communications''
''To Punctuate or Not to Punctuate—That Is the Question''

12. **Use italics to show cited or defined words; to designate foreign expressions that are not considered part of the English language; to designate the names of ships, trains, airplanes, and spacecraft; to show the titles of books, pamphlets, long poems, magazines, journals, and newspapers; and to show the titles of movies, plays, television and radio shows, musicals, operas, long musical compositions, paintings, and pieces of sculpture.**

Italics are shown either through underscores (this is an example of italics) or through ''true'' italics (*this is also an example of italics*). For years, the underscore was used on typewriters to signify italics. Today, true italics are possible with appropriate word-processing software—but you may still choose between underscores or true italics to show italics.

In order to is a wordy expression you should try to avoid.

The French expression, deja vu, refers to the illusion you have of already experiencing something actually being experienced for the first time.

My great-grandparents traveled up the Mississippi River to St. Louis on the *Chieftain*, a side-wheel paddle steamboat.

The Evening and the Morning Star was published in Kirtland, Ohio, from December 1833 through September 1834.

Harrison Ford starred in *Star Wars*, *The Empire Strikes Back*, and *Return of the Jedi*—three of the highest revenue-producing movies of all time.

Learning Hint 4.   For full titles of books, magazines, journals, newspapers, etc., an alternative to true italics or underscores is the use of solid capitals. Such titles may be keyed in solid capitals in the following situations: (1) in business correspondence—especially those situations in which titles occur frequently—and (2) in advertising and sales-promotion copy in which solid capitals are intended to give added access to the titles.

Have you received your copy of EFFECTIVE WRITING: A PRACTICAL GRAMMAR REVIEW?

BASIC BUSINESS COMMUNICATION
Fifth Edition
by Raymond V. Lesikar

Use T19-2 here

13. Use an ellipsis to show the omission of material in a direct quote.

An ellipsis is formatted with consecutive periods. The simplest procedure to follow when you use an ellipsis is to use a three-period ellipsis and to ignore end-of-sentence periods in relation to the ellipsis:

Animal rights has developed into a . . . controversial topic. Research laboratories have been broken into and severely damaged; . . . Bombs have been planted near cars of executives who are in charge of animal-research laboratories.

When you use word-processing software, the periods in the ellipsis are separated from each other by hard spaces and from the text by soft spaces. Punctuation on either side of the ellipsis may be retained or may be omitted.

If the ellipsis is used in the middle of a sentence, the sentence should read as if the ellipsis were not there. If the ellipsis is used between sentences, the result should read as two sentences; and the first word of the second sentence should be capitalized.

14. Use brackets to show the addition of words not included in the direct quote or to clarify the wording or content of the direct quote.

Brackets [as opposed to parentheses] are used to show any changes being made in a direct quote.

For example, if you desire to capitalize the first letter in the first word of a sentence following an ellipsis and if that letter is not capitalized in the original, brackets should be used around the letter to show that it is not capitalized in the original. Or bracketed insertions may be used in quoted material to clarify an ambiguity or to provide a missing word or letters. For example:

[S]cientists, at the beginning of the animal-rights movement, ignored the activist[s]. However, now that public support is becoming stronger for animal rights, scientists are beginning to defend [animal] research.

Posttest

With a **C** or an **I**, indicate whether the punctuation is correct or incorrect in the following sentences. Then punctuate the sentences marked **I**.

1. Guy is preparing an article on ''the office of the future''.

2. Nauvoo, Illinois, will be our second stop on our historical-sites tour.

3. Bernier makes his point by saying, ''Software copying is still extensive . . . and is often 'condoned' by corporate managers.''

4. The new vice president of operations is B. Kenneth Duffin Sr.

5. Will you please direct your sales representative to call on us regularly beginning January 1.

6. The extra features I want on the new company car are as follows; cruise control, air conditioning, and automatic transmission.

7. What we desire to know now is whether you plan to participate in our golf tournament?

8. Did you read the new article by Ms. Dunnaway, ''Welcome to Corporate America?''

9. On August 15, 1991, we completed the transition to the new computer system.

10. For many reasons that I won't mention, Jenae, we're extending your contract on the Seagull project.

11. On the other hand, Dunsmore says, ''(Many people) believe that animals should have the same rights that humans have.''

12. Mr. Dula's temporary mailing address is 1266 Kimberly Court, NE, Salem, Oregon 97303.

13. Yes, I have a job offer to work for Northern Forest Products Ltd.

14. Kent is fortunate; he has job offers at the *Deseret News* and *The Daily Herald.*

Key: (1) I—periods always go inside quote marks; (2) C; (3) C; (4) I—a comma must precede *Sr.*; (5) C; (6) I—a colon rather than a semicolon is required preceding the listing; (7) I—a period rather than a question mark follows an indirect question; (8) I–because the entire sentence is a question, the question mark should be outside the ending quotation mark; (9) C; (10) C; (11) I—brackets rather than parentheses are used to show that words have been added to the original quotation; (12) C; (13) I—a comma is required before *Ltd.*, unless the writer knows that the company prefers not to use a comma; (14) C— names of newspapers are italicized.

LEVEL A

Name _____

Exercise **On the lines below, write T if the statement is true and F if the statement is false.**
19–1

_F_ 1. An ellipsis is preferably formatted with three periods without spaces between the periods.

_T_ 2. You can legitimately show italics by underlining the material to be italicized.

_F_ 3. The following sentence is punctuated correctly: *Will you please have Ms. Wiggins fix my computer on Thursday?*

_T_ 4. A period rather than a question mark is used at the end of an indirect question.

_F_ 5. Titles used in direct address are preferably set off with dashes.

_T_ 6. The following sentence is punctuated correctly: *Will you please confirm whether January 15, 1994, is the centennial date for the birth of our company's founder, Wesley Jex Parkinson, Sr.*

_T_ 7. Commas and periods go inside quotation marks; semicolons and colons go outside quotation marks.

_F_ 8. In business correspondence, writers may use either single or double quotation marks as long as consistency is maintained.

_T_ 9. If an ellipsis is used between sentences, the result should read as two sentences; and the first word of the second sentence should be capitalized.

_F_ 10. Parentheses or brackets are used to show the addition of words not included in a direct quote or to clarify the wording or content of a direct quote.

Exercise **Mark C if the punctuation is correct; mark I if the punctuation is incorrect.**
19–2

_C_ 1. My father moved to Bergenfield, New Jersey, on June 1, 1992, and immediately began looking for work.

_I_ 2. The person responsible for the accident Mr. Shumate, is DeLoy K. Smiley, Sr.

_I_ 3. The question we want answered, Ms. Sinkinson, is whether the Bartlett Project will be finished this month?

_I_ 4. Will you please send the report to Sean Trauntvein, 998 Patterson Road, Santa Maria, CA 93454?

_I_ 5. Mr. Uibel said ''Tourism can impact culture through destruction or preservation''.

_C_ 6. According to Dr. Hagedorn, ''At some point, you have to let people 'have their say.' Oftentimes, you may give more credence to [protestors'] statements by suing the protestors than by ignoring their statements.''

_C_ 7. While visiting Cincinnati, Madge, I rode on the *Mississippi Queen*; and I spent a full day touring the offices of Markham and Harper, Inc.

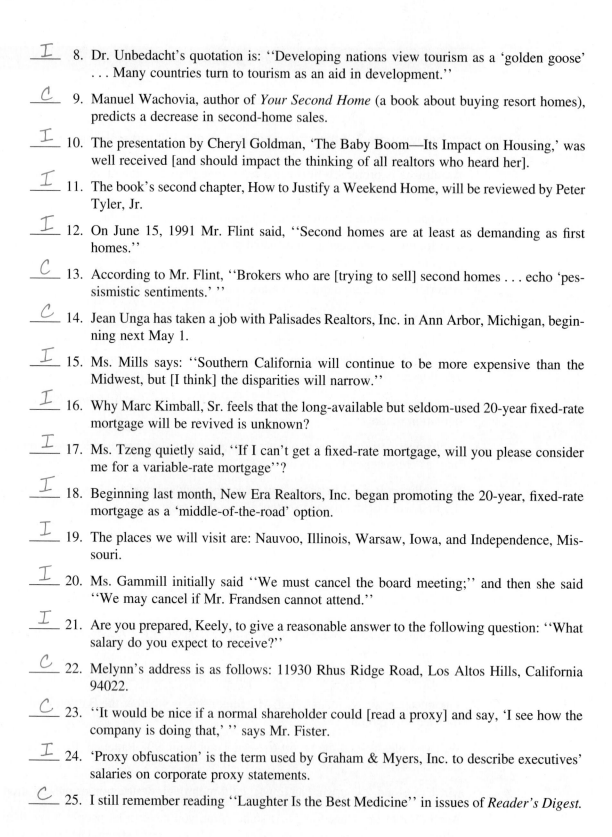

_I_   8. Dr. Unbedacht's quotation is: "Developing nations view tourism as a 'golden goose' . . . Many countries turn to tourism as an aid in development."

_C_   9. Manuel Wachovia, author of _Your Second Home_ (a book about buying resort homes), predicts a decrease in second-home sales.

_I_ 10. The presentation by Cheryl Goldman, 'The Baby Boom—Its Impact on Housing,' was well received [and should impact the thinking of all realtors who heard her].

_I_ 11. The book's second chapter, How to Justify a Weekend Home, will be reviewed by Peter Tyler, Jr.

_I_ 12. On June 15, 1991 Mr. Flint said, "Second homes are at least as demanding as first homes."

_C_ 13. According to Mr. Flint, "Brokers who are [trying to sell] second homes . . . echo 'pessismistic sentiments.' "

_C_ 14. Jean Unga has taken a job with Palisades Realtors, Inc. in Ann Arbor, Michigan, beginning next May 1.

_I_ 15. Ms. Mills says: "Southern California will continue to be more expensive than the Midwest, but [I think] the disparities will narrow."

_I_ 16. Why Marc Kimball, Sr. feels that the long-available but seldom-used 20-year fixed-rate mortgage will be revived is unknown?

_I_ 17. Ms. Tzeng quietly said, "If I can't get a fixed-rate mortgage, will you please consider me for a variable-rate mortgage"?

_I_ 18. Beginning last month, New Era Realtors, Inc. began promoting the 20-year, fixed-rate mortgage as a 'middle-of-the-road' option.

_I_ 19. The places we will visit are: Nauvoo, Illinois, Warsaw, Iowa, and Independence, Missouri.

_I_ 20. Ms. Gammill initially said "We must cancel the board meeting;" and then she said "We may cancel if Mr. Frandsen cannot attend."

_I_ 21. Are you prepared, Keely, to give a reasonable answer to the following question: "What salary do you expect to receive?"

_C_ 22. Melynn's address is as follows: 11930 Rhus Ridge Road, Los Altos Hills, California 94022.

_C_ 23. "It would be nice if a normal shareholder could [read a proxy] and say, 'I see how the company is doing that,' " says Mr. Fister.

_I_ 24. 'Proxy obfuscation' is the term used by Graham & Myers, Inc. to describe executives' salaries on corporate proxy statements.

_C_ 25. I still remember reading "Laughter Is the Best Medicine" in issues of _Reader's Digest_.

LEVEL B

Name _____

Exercise   Write the letter that identifies the one best sentence.
19–3

_b_   1. *a.* Will you please send me my stock certificate for Northwest Mining, Ltd.?
    b. My grandfather still lives in Ruston, Louisiana, in the home in which he was born.
    c. Charley's reasons for changing jobs are: better pay, realistic working hours, and longer vacations.

_c_   2. *a.* Will you please send the package to 13531 Grain Lane, San Diego, CA 92129?
    b. On December 19, 1985 Yolanda celebrated her 21st birthday in Villahermosa, Mexico.
    c. According to Vance's note, "Check No. 4336 was made out to LeRoy Forsythe, Sr."

_a_   3. *a.* I arrived in Cardston, Alberta, Canada, on March 12, 1986, and immediately began looking for a job.
    b. The question I have is why we don't offer a bonus in our company?
    c. Yes, Lennie Rafael Ganser, Jr. is a vice president at Middleton Machine Tools Inc.

_c_   4. *a.* "I'll speak at the conference," Ms. Foxborough said, "if I can use the multi-media room".
    b. The Kassar Pictures, Inc. situation is a classic instance of 'downsizing.'
    c. The title of Dr. Gabossi's dissertation is "An Experiment to Evaluate Various Access Techniques in Business Correspondence."

_b_   5. *a.* Ms. Foster's report concerns the increase in "reimbursement accounts;" however, she will not finish her report for two more weeks.
    b. Robert Feichko's new book, *The Male Chauvinist*, is a satire about today's "liberated male."
    c. If you are unable to finish your review by June 12, will you please give us a more-acceptable date?

_a_   6. *a.* For the audience's pleasure, Mr. Fasselin, will you please tell your stories about "office politics."
    b. Herb's new address is: 8081 Holland Circle, No. 7-J, Huntington Beach, CA 92647.
    c. For the first time in a month, Mr. Fugate didn't ask the question, "Will the recession never end"?

_a_   7. *a.* "Many small businesses," according to Mr. Lutz, ". . . are using newsletters [today] as a low-key marketing tool."
    b. Ms. Humphrey's new book, "The Art of Shopping at Garage Sales," has now sold 250,000 copies.
    c. I rode on Amtrak's "California Zephyr" from Ogden, Utah, to Los Angeles, California.

_c_   8. *a.* "We've offered (20-year) loans for some time, but we haven't promoted them," says Stephen Bennett.
    b. A recent issue of our bulletin contained articles entitled *Composite Fillings for Whiter Smiles* and *The Life Cycle of Plaque*.
    c. Mr. Craig asked very pointedly, "Have you seen Mountain View High School's production of *Death of a Salesman*?"

_b_ 9. _a._ Consultants must be ethical enough to say; ''You're okay now. You don't need my services anymore.''

  _b._ May we suggest that the tour should be in Cancun, Mexico, during the eclipse.

  _c._ Why Argus Bookstores, Inc. failed to carry Solomon Heiner's book, _For Men Only_, has never been explained fully?

_a_ 10. _a._ Did you see the Friday, July 12, 1991, eclipse while you were in Honolulu?

  _b._ Grant Henseler Jr.'s words were, ''Few cookbook specialties are as crowded . . . as low-calorie budget meals.''

  _c._ We want you to review the book by Grant Henseler, Jr., _Microwave Cooking Made Easy_, Marjorie and to recommend for or against its publication.

_c_ 11. _a._ According to Mr. Kraft, ''Any fast-food item that has ''light'' on it seems to do very well.''

  _b._ Mr. Kraft feels that the marketing meeting should be restricted strictly to a ''brain-storming session''.

  _c._ When a manufacturer develops a new line, ''We ask the firm to discontinue one of its products to save shelf space,'' says Douglas Kraft, Sr.

_c_ 12. _a._ The book by Thomas Howell, Jr., _Effective Business Writing_, contains a chapter entitled 'Choosing Between Active and Passive Voice.'

  _b._ I finished my article entitled ''Using Mood'' on August 12, 1990 but did not submit it to _The Business Writer's Journal_ until a year later.

  _c._ As you suspected, Dewey, I lived in Albuquerque, New Mexico, when I wrote ''Choose Your Style with Style.''

_b_ 13. _a._ ''We plan to expand our operations on June 1, 1993, said Ms. McDaniels, to Eugene, Oregon, in the Northwest.''

  _b._ You should know, Maria, that _persona non grata_ means ''one who is not acceptable.''

  _c._ Was it Red Henschke who said, ''We can't afford to be without computers today?''

_a_ 14. _a._ In your speech, be sure not to use the word _mad_ unless you mean ''insane.''

  _b._ While talking to the 911 operator, Mrs. Hoffman repeatedly yelled ''Help me; please help me''!

  _c._ Ms. Hoggatt said, ''Will you please be sure you do not confuse the words _affect_ and _effect_ in your theme?''

_b_ 15. _a._ The envelope marked 'Confidential—to be opened only by Ms. Helper' was delivered to us by mistake.

  _b._ I quoted Mr. Hislop as follows: ''Computers have become so routine that . . . [students] don't have to prove they can use them anymore.''

  _c._ At the conclusion of the meeting, Bud sang _A Poor Wayfaring Man of Grief_.

_c_ 16. _a._ Will you please read my term paper, _Understanding the Effects of Exercise on the Body_?

  _b._ We need to purchase three capital-equipment items: a fax machine, a laser printer, and a modem.

  _c._ My father told me, ''I saw _Gone With the Wind_ when I was 16 years old, and I want you to see it long before you are 16.''

LEVEL C

Name _____

Exercise 19–4   Edit the following sentences to reflect the punctuation guidelines in Lesson 19.

1. I still remember, Ms. Korenko, your exact words: "The word 'ain't' will not be tolerated in my classroom?".

2. The quotation I used is as follows: "[S]ome positive effects have been discovered concerning exercise [and osteoporosis] . . . [O]ne study determined that when a person exercises, the risk of fracture is decreased."

3. Were you at the meeting when he said, "Will you please tell me why we should decrease production"?

4. The chapter you asked about is "The Underscore as an Access Technique"; and the Business Communication Journal published the article in its August 1, 1992, newsletter.

5. My talk is entitled "Good Management Is the Best Medicine"; and the points I will emphasize (delete underline) are: teamwork, leadership, and coordination.

6. Mr. Stipp's company, Jethro, is called Occasional Greeting Cards, Inc.; and he runs it out of his home, 115 Hopi Court, Naperville, Illinois 60540.

7. Owners fear that once the pilot program ends, "[E]mployees will expect coverage and [owners] will have to carry the freight," Mr. Marsh says.

8. Will you please ask Toni to order Time and Newsweek for customers to read in our waiting room?

9. Our new office manager, William Karr, Jr., is vacationing in Aliquippa, Pennsylvania, until the 15th of March.

10. The question you did poorly on, Angelo, is "How can writers unintentionally offend their readers(?)"

Exercise 19–5

Edit the following sentences to reflect the punctuation guidelines in Unit 3.

Cumulative Editing

1. "Medical care is heavily influenced by teamwork," says Clark Kilgore, Sr., a professor at Northwestern University.

2. To help me with my report, will you please confirm whether death rates are lower in units with the best technology, and higher in units that treat a wide variety of illnesses?

3. Disappointed by the lack of accomplishments, such groups as Idaho Rivers Council, and Friends of the Northwest, see great promise in promoting state programs, and forging more regional pacts.

4. Just 12 percent of eligible firms took the offer; and three-quarters of those would have bought insurance anyway, according to Virginia Jowell, associate professor at Carnegie Melon.

5. Ms. Dunsmore says, "I particularly dislike one wordy expression, *each and every*, and ask that you avoid it entirely in your writing."

6. According to Dr. Billings, "One drug, naltrexone, may be the first medicine, that can help recovering alcoholics [avoid] relapse into heavy drinking(?)"

7. Mr. Kakatsidas, unfortunately, studied only 125 patients at the ICUs, but still found a twofold difference in death rates between the best and worst performers.

8. Ms. Neff, do you know which one of our employees said, "the love of money, not money, is the root of all evil?"?

9. Why Shannon O'Hearon, Jr.'s business, which employs his mother and a secretary, violates a rule against hiring people who live elsewhere to work in a resident's home has never been explained adequately.

10. The Matheson Health System, a Logan health-maintenance organization, established an "On-Call Nurse" program, to handle after-hours calls.

Exercise 19–6   Edit the following sentences to reflect guidelines from Units 2 and 3.

Cumulative Editing

1. JoAnn Collins is the student who ~~had thought~~ thinks that William Faulkner's short story, "Barn Burning," is as great a story as his novel, *Absalom, Absalom!*

2. ~~Having responded~~ Responding to the question, Zane said, "I'm Called Little Buttercup" is a song from Gilbert and Sullivan's operetta, *H.M.S. Pinafore.*"

3. For obvious reasons, Mr. O'Hearon, I wanted to ~~have~~ read the editorial, "A Legacy of Shame," in the July 14, 1991, issue of *The Daily Herald*.

4. When I ~~am~~ was in the ninth grade, I had to memorize Poe's *The Raven* and portions of Chaucer's *Canterbury Tales*.

5. In the Agatha Christie mystery, *Murder on the Orient Express*, Hercule Poirot rode the *Orient Express* and ~~solves~~ solved the murder of one of the passengers.

6. As our senior-class motto, Sherree will ~~have been proposing~~ propose "Forward Into Greatness" when we meet on Friday, October ~~14th~~ 14, to vote.

7. Ernest's answer on the exam ~~was~~ is indeed correct; "England's Turmoil," ~~that~~ which is Chapter 14 of Tuchman's *A Distant Mirror*, ~~did describe~~ describes the political situation in England during the fourteenth century.

8. Most of us ~~will~~ have heard "Water, water, everywhere, And all the boards did shrink; Water, water, everywhere, Nor any drop to drink," but few of us ~~will be remembering~~ remember that the lines are from *The Rime of the Ancient Mariner* by Samuel Taylor Coleridge.

9. I ~~will have~~ had been napping for about an hour when my father woke me and said, "Will you please do me a favor and mow the lawn today?"

10. I particularly ~~had liked~~ *like* the following quote from George Orwell's essay, "Politics and the English Language": "Most people ... would admit that the English language is in a bad way, but it is generally assumed that we cannot ... do anything about it."

Exercise 19–7

Edit the following sentences to reflect guidelines from Lessons 2 through 19.

Cumulative Editing

1. Mark Wessel, ~~whose~~ *who's* trying to sell his country home, says, "~~Its~~ *It's* not as if the market's depressed; ~~its~~ *it's* that the market has ceased to exist."

2. "Powerful forces are certain to promote reductions in regional disparities," says a report by Rafael Udy, a *P*rofessor of *R*eal *E*state at *T*he University of Idaho.

3. On a scale of ~~zero~~ *0* ("no influence") to ~~one hundred~~ *100* ("very influential"), the ratings averaged 20.

4. Martha Gibson, owner of a Springfield, ~~N.J.~~ *New Jersey,* newsletter, ~~will have said~~ *says* her professional subscriber list—lawyers, accountants, small-business people, and others who buy her newsletter— has grown ~~10-fold~~ *tenfold* in ~~10~~ *ten* years.

5. According to ~~Prof.~~ *Professor* Maughn's report, the gap in home prices between the *h*eartland and the *c*oasts is starting to narrow, and is expected to continue doing so throughout the next *d*ecade.

6. In 1973, the median resale price of a single-family home ~~had been~~ *was* $32,800 in the *n*ortheast, $31,000 in the *w*est, $29,000 in the *s*outh, and $25,300 in the *m*idwest.

7. Sheila Keele, a *s*enior *e*conomist at Morgan Stanley, says, "~~Its~~ *It's* like the pendulum is starting to ~~have swung~~ *swing* toward a more homogeneous national housing market; but it has a long way ~~too~~ *to* go."

8. In addition, Southwest Mortgage, based in Santa Fe, New Mexico, charges ~~two~~ *2* points to originate a ~~twenty~~ *20*-year loan, compared with ~~three~~ *3* points for a ~~thirty~~ *30*-year loan.

9. Only ~~six~~ [6] of the more than 2,000 lenders surveyed by S. W. Associates, a Pueblo, ~~Colo.~~ [Colorado] firm, have ~~similiar~~ [similar] products.

10. In March, the gap between the ~~east~~ [East] and ~~midwest~~ [Midwest] ~~shrinks~~ [shrank] to 85% [percent]; but the spread between the ~~west~~ [West] and ~~midwest~~ [Midwest] ~~had grown~~ [grew] to 88% [percent].

Exercise 19–8

Cumulative Editing

Edit the following sentences to reflect guidelines from Units 2 and 3. Correct frequently misspelled and confusing words.

1. ~~Every one~~ [Everyone] at the family reunion ~~gets~~ [got] into an ~~arguement~~ [argument] about whether Grandfather Bunker ~~was~~ [is] buried in the Bunkerville ~~Cemetary~~ [Cemetery] or in the Delta ~~Cem ary~~ [Cemetery].

2. ~~After~~ the discussion, we were going ~~altogether~~ [together] to the City ~~Counsel~~ [Council] meeting to ~~congradulate~~ [congratulate] the ~~m~~ mayor for ~~witholding~~ [withholding] his support from the ~~temporery restuarant~~ [temporary restaurant]-tax proposal.

3. If the suggestion ~~was alright~~ [is all right] with ~~you're~~ [your] parents, we'll ~~be making~~ [make] the camping equipment ~~accessable~~ [accessible] to all ~~you're sophmore~~ [your sophomore] friends.

4. If ~~your truely~~ [you're truly] a close ~~aquaintance~~ [acquaintance] of Eda Oakden, you'll ~~be feeling~~ [feel] bad if you don't ~~pursuade~~ [persuade] ~~every one~~ [everyone] to ~~have attended~~ [attend] her wedding reception.

5. We ~~conceed~~ [conceded] that our lighting system ~~was~~ [is] quite ~~obsolesent~~ [obsolescent], and then agreed to install ~~stationery~~ [stationary] ~~florescent~~ [fluorescent] lights throughout all offices at the State ~~Capital~~ [Capitol] Building.

6. Much to our ~~surprize~~ [surprise], we ~~had~~ reached a ~~concensus~~ [consensus] about the ~~curiculum~~ [curriculum] that ~~Principle~~ [Principal] Bayley's ~~comittee had reecomended too~~ [Committee recommended to] the school board.

7. ~~Superintendant~~ [Superintendent] Oberto ~~will have~~ said, "~~Its~~ [It's] not ~~feasable~~ [feasible] for us to ~~develope~~ [develop] the new courses this year, we're ~~hopefull~~ [hopeful] we can ~~have proceded~~ [proceed] with ~~there~~ [their] development next year."

8. ~~Travellers ocassionaly harrass~~ [Travelers occasionally harass] us about the ~~lose~~ [loose] gravel at the ~~sight~~ [site] of the ~~temperary~~ [temporary] road; a decision to ~~have persued~~ [pursue] the plan to oil the road is ~~considered to have been eminent.~~ [imminent].

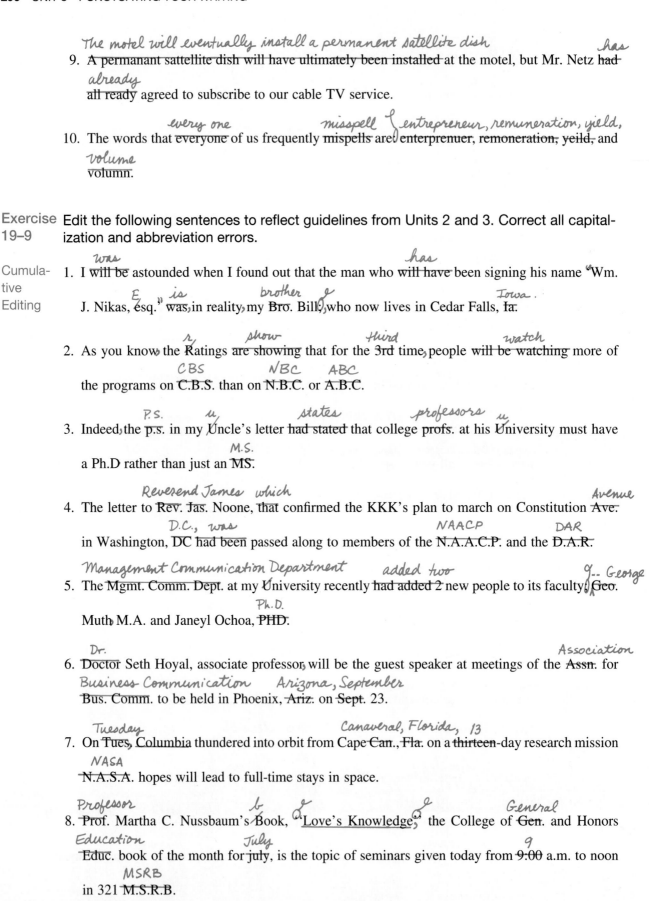

The motel will eventually install a permanent satellite dish

9. ~~A permanant sattellite dish will have ultimately been installed~~ at the motel, but Mr. Netz ~~had~~ *has*

already

~~all ready~~ agreed to subscribe to our cable TV service.

every one   *misspell*   {*entrepreneur, remuneration, yield,*

10. The words that ~~everyone~~ of us frequently ~~mispells are~~ ~~enterprenuer, remoneration, yeild,~~ and

volume

~~volumn.~~

Exercise 19–9   Edit the following sentences to reflect guidelines from Units 2 and 3. Correct all capitalization and abbreviation errors.

Cumulative Editing

was

1. I ~~will be~~ astounded when I found out that the man who ~~will have~~ *has* been signing his name "Wm.

E   *is*   *brother*   *&*

J. Nikas, ~~esq.~~" ~~was,~~ in reality, my ~~Bro.~~ Bill, who now lives in Cedar Falls, ~~Ia.~~ *Iowa.*

r,   *show*   *third*   *watch*

2. As you know, the ~~Ratings~~ ~~are showing~~ that for the 3rd time, people ~~will be watching~~ more of

CBS   *NBC*   *ABC*

the programs on ~~C.B.S.~~ than on ~~N.B.C.~~ or ~~A.B.C.~~

P.S.   *u,*   *states*   *professors u*

3. Indeed, the ~~p.s.~~ in my ~~U~~ncle's letter ~~had stated~~ that college ~~profs.~~ at his ~~U~~niversity must have

M.S.

a Ph.D rather than just an ~~MS.~~

Reverend James   *which*   *Avenue*

4. The letter to ~~Rev.~~ ~~Jas.~~ Noone, ~~that~~ confirmed the KKK's plan to march on Constitution ~~Ave.~~

D.C., was   *NAACP*   *DAR*

in Washington, DC ~~had been~~ passed along to members of the ~~N.A.A.C.P.~~ and the ~~D.A.R.~~

Management Communication Department   *added two*   *G-- George*

5. The ~~Mgmt. Comm. Dept.~~ at my ~~U~~niversity recently ~~had added 2~~ new people to its faculty, ~~Geo.~~

Ph.D.

Muth, M.A. and Janeyl Ochoa, ~~PHD.~~

Dr.   *Association*

6. ~~Doctor~~ Seth Hoyal, associate professor, will be the guest speaker at meetings of the ~~Assn.~~ for

Business Communication   *Arizona, September*

~~Bus. Comm.~~ to be held in Phoenix, ~~Ariz.~~ on ~~Sept.~~ 23.

Tuesday   *Canaveral, Florida, 13*

7. On ~~Tues,~~ Columbia thundered into orbit from Cape ~~Can., Fla.~~ on a ~~thirteen~~-day research mission

NASA

~~N.A.S.A.~~ hopes will lead to full-time stays in space.

Professor   *b*   *&*   *&*   *General*

8. ~~Prof.~~ Martha C. Nussbaum's ~~B~~ook, "Love's Knowledge," the College of ~~Gen.~~ and Honors

Education   *July*   *9*

~~Educ.~~ book of the month for ~~july,~~ is the topic of seminars given today from ~~9:00~~ a.m. to noon

MSRB

in 321 ~~M.S.R.B.~~

LESSONS IN THIS UNIT

20. CONNECTING, COORDINATING, AND SUBORDINATING
21. PREPOSITIONS

Connectives are words or punctuation marks that join sentence elements in a sensible way. Connectives are used to give clarity, consistency, and correct form to our writing. Just as road signs tell the automobile driver what to expect on the highway ahead, connectives signal the reader what is coming in a sentence. Connectives, then, are signals. As such, they tell the reader whether to expect a continuation of a particular thought, the addition of a similar thought, or the introduction of a different thought.

Connectives join sentence parts—words, phrases, and clauses. They also show relationships between ideas—a function referred to as *coordination* and *subordination*. And they contribute directly to *parallelism* (consistency) in the grammatical structure of a sentence—an important element in effective communication.

Frequently used connectives include coordinating conjunctions, correlative conjunctions, subordinating conjunctions, conjunctive adverbs, relative pronouns, prepositions, and certain punctuation marks. More will be said about these important sentence elements in Lessons 20 and 21.

All sentence classifications—simple, compound, complex, and compound-complex—use connectives. In fact, connectives are always present in compound, complex, and compound-complex sentences. And even simple sentences, which do not always require connectives, use these important joiners much of the time.

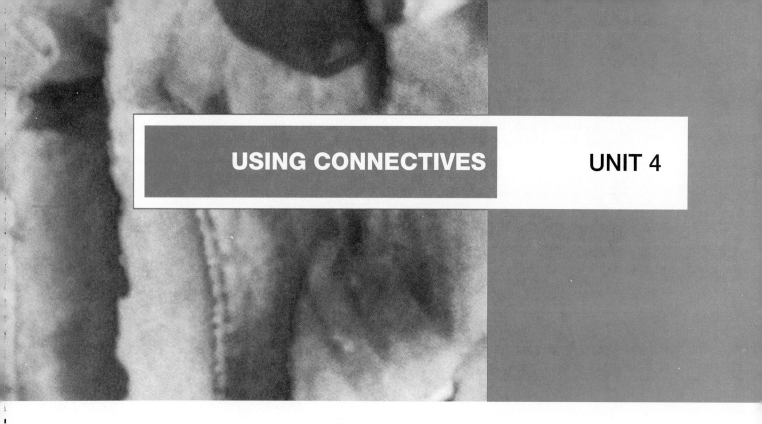

USING CONNECTIVES   UNIT 4

Note the following illustrations of sentence types with connectives in italics.

John left the office. (simple sentence with no connectives)

Jean *and* Louise traveled *to* Portland *and to* Seattle *by* train. (simple sentence with connectives)

Expense accounts were audited *on* March 1, *but* reimbursement checks will not be issued *before* March 15. (compound sentence)

After cashing his paycheck, Mr. Sanchez—*who* earns $500 weekly—bought a bicycle *for* his daughter. (complex sentence)

If you are late, you must wait *until* intermission *to* take your seat; *however,* the delay will be brief. (compound-complex sentence)

As a writer, you will want to use connectives properly to send clear and helpful signals that tell your reader where you are going in your thinking. Remember that the burden of clear communication rests primarily with the writer. Don't force the reader to guess what you mean. Using connectives properly will help you avoid ambiguity in your writing.

Connectives also help produce writing that feels comfortable to the reader. We could write without connectives if we wanted to, but such writing would seem strange indeed. Sentences would be short and choppy, and the language would feel rough and bumpy to the reader. Good writing has a sense of balance and order that comes in large measure from the skillful use of connectives to join sentence parts together in the right way.

Balance and good order in our writing are usually the products of parallel sentence structure. Language that is consistent and logical in grammatical form and meaning is said to be *parallel*. Such language is easier to understand than language that is not parallel, and parallel language is likely to feel ''right'' to the reader. The ability to write in a way that makes the reader comfortable with the language is one important mark of an effective writer.

As noted earlier, language conveys certain feelings to readers about the way the language itself is used. Writers often depend on the ''feel'' of the language to help them use connectives correctly. That's all right—to a point! Most of us get useful mileage from our ability to ''feel'' the language. Often, however, we will want to base our language usage on something more solid than feelings; we will want to understand the basics of correct language usage. When we can do that, our writing is likely to meet accepted standards of good expression.

An understanding of what connectives are and how they work is important to the competent writer and communicator. Use the guidelines and the exercises in the next two lessons to strengthen your writing power and to improve your communicative skills.

CONNECTING, COORDINATING, AND SUBORDINATING

LESSON 20

Sentences that are logically constructed contribute to easy reading and ready understanding. Logically constructed sentences are consistent—or *parallel*—in grammatical form. In fact, parallelism—or its absence—is often the difference between good writing and weak writing.

The proper use of connectives in all sentence classifications—simple, compound, complex, compound-complex—results in parallelism in our writing. Words, phrases, and clauses are correctly joined together to convey clearly and smoothly the writer's intended message.

Some connectives are used to join sentence parts that are equal—*coordinate*—in rank, such as two independent clauses. Other connectives join sentence parts that are unequal in rank, such as an independent clause and a dependent clause. When unequal sentence elements are joined, at least one of the elements is limited—or *subordinated*—by the connective that joins that element to the rest of the sentence.

Most connectives are words with which you are very familiar. Because they join sentence elements to each other, these words are sometimes referred to as *conjunctive joiners*. In addition, as you will see, certain punctuation marks function as connectives in our writing.

This lesson presents helpful guidelines in achieving parallelism in your writing—the proper connecting, coordinating, and subordinating of sentence parts. Study these guidelines carefully. When followed properly, they can help you strengthen the quality of your writing.

Pretest

Write **C** or **I** to indicate whether the use of connectives is correct or incorrect in the following sentences.

1. The seminar begins on Monday, January 10 but registration continues through Friday, January 7.

2. I plan to attend the seminar with Derek; however he is still recovering from surgery and may not be able to go.

3. The firm will pay 80 percent of the registration fee, therefore, each participant must pay $30 from personal funds.

4. While the seminar is relatively technical, most presentations are made with the beginner in mind.

5. Although most of this year's participants will be men; at least 40 women are expected to be present.

6. Last year's seminar was a huge success; this year's event is expected to be even better!

7. The student's answer not only was correct but also concise.

Key: (I) I—place a semicolon before the coordinating conjunction *but;* (2) I—place a comma after the conjunctive adverb *however;* (3) I—place a semicolon before the conjunctive adverb *therefore;* (4) I—Use a suitable subordinating conjunction such as *although* in place of the relative adverb *while (while* is used to indicate a duration of time); (5) I—use a comma instead of a semicolon after *men* to separate the dependent clause from the independent clause; (6) C; (7) I—Both correlatives should be followed by the same part of speech; for example, *The student's answer was not only correct but also concise.* (Both correlatives are followed by an adjective.)

Terminology

Connective—A word or punctuation mark that joins sentence parts to each other. Connectives frequently show relationships between the parts and provide desired emphasis in our writing. Conjunctions and prepositions are the most-important connectives.

Conjunctive adverb—A connective adverb such as *however* or *furthermore* that joins independent clauses to each other and that shows relationships between the clauses.

Coordinating conjunction—A connective word such as *and* or *but* that joins sentence elements of equal grammatical importance—words with words, phrases with phrases, and clauses with clauses.

Correlative conjunction—Conjunctions that are always used in pairs such as *either . . . or* and *not only . . . but also* to join words, phrases, and clauses that are grammatically equal in value or rank and to give desired emphasis to our writing. (The word *correlative* is properly pronounced **core-el-a-tiv**.)

Parallelism—The expression of two or more ideas of equal importance or rank in coordinate or consistent grammatical form (i.e., words joined to words, phrases joined to phrases, clauses joined to clauses).

Relative pronoun—A connective pronoun such as *that, who,* or *which* that functions as a conjunction in the dependent clause it introduces and connects to the rest of the sentence.

Relative adverb—A connective adverb that introduces a subordinate clause and connects it to the rest of the sentence. Relative adverbs in the English language are *where, when,* and *while.*

Subordinating conjunction—A conjunction such as *although* or *unless* that limits or subordinates the clause it introduces, resulting in an incomplete thought that depends on a main clause for complete meaning.

Rules

1. **Use a coordinating conjunction to join two independent clauses or to join other sentence elements (words or phrases) of equal grammatical rank or value. (See Lesson 15, Rule 1.)**

   The word *coordinate* means parallel—of equal importance or rank. A coordinating conjunction is used to join words, phrases, and clauses that are equal in importance or rank. The seven coordinating conjunctions in the English language are *and, but, or, nor, for, yet,* and *so.*

   Note the use of coordinating conjunctions in the following sentences to join sentence elements of equal importance. Remember that a clause contains both a subject and a verb; a phrase does not.

   You *and* I were selected as team leaders. (equal words joined by the coordinating conjunction *and*)

   Please send your reply to Mr. Bales *or* to Mrs. Purker. (equal phrases joined by the coordinating conjunction *or*)

   The vice president interviewed the candidates today, *but* his recommendation is not expected until tomorrow. (equal clauses joined by the coordinating conjunction *but*)

   Francesca did not meet the deadline agreed on, *nor* did she offer an explanation. (equal clauses joined by the coordinating conjunction *nor*)

   You received a promotion, *yet* you received no increase in salary. (equal clauses joined by the coordinating conjunction *yet*)

   Learning Hint 1.   Place a comma before a coordinating conjunction that joins two independent clauses.

   NO   Get the book from my office and return it to the library.

   YES   Get the book from my office, and return it to the library.

   Learning Hint 2.   Place a semicolon before a coordinating conjunction that joins two independent clauses if commas occur elsewhere in either of the independent clauses. (See Lesson 16, Rule 3.)

   NO   As you know, Mrs. Brooks will contact me, but I doubt she will call before the 15th.

   YES   As you know, Mrs. Brooks will contact me; but I doubt she will call before the 15th.

NO   I left my keys, my wallet, and my jacket at home, but, as you can see, I did remember to wear my glasses.

YES   I left my keys, my wallet, and my jacket at home; but, as you can see, I did remember to wear my glasses.

2. Use a conjunctive adverb to join two independent clauses and to show the relationship between the two clauses. (See Lesson 16, Rule 2.)

A careful choice of a conjunctive adverb used to join two independent clauses is important in giving your language the precise meaning intended. Some frequently used terms that function as conjunctive adverbs are the following:

accordingly	consequently	furthermore
hence	however	moreover
nevertheless	therefore	thus
similarly	still	

Joni has a high-school grade-point average of 3.85; *accordingly*, she will receive a scholarship to college.

The university will announce fall semester grades shortly; *thus*, we will know soon whether you qualify for admission to the program.

Farhan received only a *B–* this term in Business Writing; *however*, his grade was the highest in the class.

Learning Hint 3.   Transitional phrases such as *in fact, in the meantime, for example, in addition, in other words,* and *as a matter of fact* function as conjunctive adverbs in joining two independent clauses.

The textbook for the marketing course is new; *in fact*, the text is not yet available in the bookstore.

The work load in this course is heavy; *for example*, we are required to read two books and to write three papers in the first two weeks alone.

Learning Hint 4.   Place a semicolon immediately before and a comma immediately after a conjunctive adverb or transitional phrase.

NO   The school year is nearly over, thus vacation time is just around the corner.

The school year is nearly over; thus vacation time is just around the corner

YES   The school year is nearly over; thus, vacation time is just around the corner.

3. Use subordinating conjunctions to join unequal sentence elements (such as an independent clause and a dependent clause). (See Lesson 17, Rule 1.)

Some sentence elements are limited—or subordinated—by the conjunctions used to introduce them. These subordinated elements frequently are clauses that are not complete thoughts and cannot stand alone. They depend on a main clause in the same sentence for complete meaning. Some of the most frequently used subordinating conjunctions are the following:

after	if	though
although	how	unless
as	inasmuch as	until
as if	provided	when

as though	since	where
because	so that	whether
before	than	while

Before you report to the committee, double check your statistical analysis.

Provided your data are correct, a favorable decision on your proposal seems certain.

You should be able to begin the project in August *unless* unexpected obstacles develop.

Although $1 million has been collected, construction still has not begun.

Learning Hint 5.   As noted in Lesson 17, a comma is used to set off a dependent clause or an introductory phrase that precedes an independent clause. Most of the time, dependent clauses that follow independent clauses are not set off by commas. When the dependent clause is a nonrestrictive clause, however, it *is* set off by a comma. (See Lesson 17, Rule 2.)

NO   The construction crew will begin work on Tuesday, because Monday is a holiday. (The dependent clause that follows the independent clause is restrictive—essential to the meaning of the sentence—and should not be preceded by a comma.)

YES   The construction crew will begin work Tuesday, although the original plan called for work to start Monday. (The dependent clause that follows the independent clause is nonrestrictive—not essential to the meaning of the sentence—and should be preceded by a comma.)

Natural pauses precede nonrestrictive clauses and are helpful indicators that commas are needed where such pauses occur. On occasion, you will have to depend on your own good judgment to determine whether dependent clauses are nonrestrictive and, therefore, require commas to set them off.

4. **Use the relative pronouns *that, who, whom, which, whoever, whomever, whichever,* and *whatever* to show subordination of dependent clauses.**

The relative pronouns *that, who, whom, which, whoever, whomever, whichever,* and *whatever* are often used to introduce dependent clauses and to indicate the subordination of such clauses. Also, like conjunctions, these relative pronouns may be used to join the clauses they introduce to the rest of the sentence.

The evaluation form *that* is needed should be ready by 5 p.m. today.

The secretary *who* left the message on your answering machine is waiting for your call.

The customer with *whom* you spoke this morning is Mrs. Rada Voelker.

Whoever gets the promotion will receive an immediate increase in pay.

We hope you will provide *whatever* supplies are needed for the trip.

The principal indicated you should apply for *whichever* scholarships you prefer.

Remember to use *who* or *whom* to refer to people; use *which* or *that* to refer to things.

NO   The student *which* submitted the best paper is Suzy Bullen.

The student *that* submitted the best paper is Suzy Bullen.

YES   The student *who* submitted the best paper is Suzy Bullen.

Which never should be used to refer to people. On the other hand, *that* is sometimes used by some writers to refer to a particular class or type of people. For purposes of simplicity and consistency, however, this text uses only *who* or *whom*—never *that*—when referring to people.

Learning Hint 7.   Make the correct choice between *that* and *which* when one of these two relative pronouns is used to introduce a dependent clause. *That* is used to introduce a restrictive clause (one that is essential to the meaning of a sentence). *Which* is used to introduce a nonrestrictive clause (one that is **not** essential to the meaning of the sentence).

The use of *that* and *which* to introduce restrictive and nonrestrictive clauses will be discussed in depth in Lesson 23, "Relative Pronouns."

Use T20-2 here

5. Use the relative adverbs *where, when,* and *while* to show subordination and to introduce adjective clauses.

The relative adverbs *where, when,* and *while*—properly used—serve two purposes. They indicate subordination, and they connect the clauses they introduce to the rest of the sentence.

Remember that *where* relates to place or location, *when* indicates a fixed or stated period of time, and *while* indicates duration of time.

New York City is *where* the United Nations is located.

August is the month *when* applications for research funds must be submitted.

The demonstrators marched outside the building *while* the meeting was in progress.

Learning Hint 8.   Avoid using *when* and *where* in giving definitions.

NO   A comma splice is *when* two independent clauses are joined by a comma.

YES   A comma splice is the use of only a comma to join two independent clauses.

NO   A verb is *where* a word indicates action, condition, or process.

YES   A verb is a word that indicates action, condition, or process.

Also, avoid using *while* to show contrast or comparison. Instead, use words such as *although, though, but,* or *whereas.*

NO   *While* I committed two punctuation errors, I made no spelling mistakes.

YES   *Although* I committed two punctuation errors, I made no spelling mistakes.

NO   Profits are up and expenses are down in the Western Region, *while* just the opposite is true in the Southern Region.

YES   Profits are up and expenses are down in the Western Region, *whereas* just the opposite is true in the Southern Region.

Use T20-3 here

6. Use correlative conjunctions (connective pairs) to show parallelism in connecting coordinate—grammatically equal—words, phrases, and clauses.

Correlative conjunctions are always used in pairs. They promote parallelism, and they give appropriate emphasis to our writing. Some frequently used correlative pairs are

either . . . or   if . . . then
neither . . . nor   since . . . therefore
not only . . . but also   both . . . and
whether . . . or

Either the department secretary *or* the office supervisor will conduct the meeting.

Both the woman in the red dress *and* the girl in the blue sweater will receive cash awards.

If you will prepare the agenda, *then* I will schedule the facilities.

Learning Hint 9.   When correlative conjunctions are used, the writer can ensure that parallel grammatical form is fostered by making certain that each member of the pair is followed by the same part of speech or by the same grammatical construction.

NO   The plane was *not only* crowded *but also* it was late. (*Not only* is followed by an adjective; *but also* is followed by a pronoun.)

YES   The flight was *not only* crowded *but also* late. (Both *not only* and *but also* are followed by adjectives.)

NO   Your firm should *either* change its policy *or* it should explain why it won't. (*Either* is followed by a verb; *or* is followed by a pronoun.)

YES   Your firm should *either* change its policy *or* explain why it won't. (Both *either* and *or* are followed by a verb.)

NO   The panel will consider *whether* to continue the project *or* cancel it altogether. (*Whether* is followed by an infinitive phrase; *or* is followed by a verb.)

YES   The panel will consider *whether* to continue the project *or* to cancel it altogether. (Both *whether* and *or* are followed by an infinitive phrase.)

7. Use the semicolon to join independent clauses that are closely related but not connected by a coordinating conjunction or a conjunctive adverb.

Most connectives are words—''conjunctive joiners'' as they are referred to in this text. However, some punctuation marks—the semicolon, the comma, the dash, and the colon—also act as effective joiners of sentence parts.

The semicolon is particularly useful in joining independent clauses that are closely related to each other in meaning. When used alone, the semicolon substitutes for conjunctive joiners—words—that would otherwise be present.

The selection of the new vice president is expected today; most of us believe Dorothy Teague will be appointed.

Don't destroy the files until you hear from me; save them in case we need them again.

Learning Hint 10.   The semicolon—not the comma—is used without conjunctive joiners (words) to connect two closely related independent clauses. The common writing error of using only a comma for this purpose results in a comma splice.

NO   The office desk you requested costs $675, a less-expensive desk should be considered.

YES   The office desk you requested costs $675; a less-expensive desk should be considered.

Posttest

Write **C** or **I** to indicate whether the use of connectives is correct or incorrect in the following sentences.

1. The copy center has requested new equipment for the coming year; however, the present equipment is still in very good condition.

2. Ask for bids on a new Liston 775 copier, that particular model is a high-priority item.

3. The quality of new copying equipment is gradually improving, although the cost of such equipment is definitely rising.

4. The copy center secretary which was hired today will begin work on Monday.

5. Janae's sister was asked to not only attend the meeting but she also was invited to introduce the speaker.

6. Equipment obsolescence, Ms. Fleeter, is when existing equipment is no longer cost-effective.

7. Copy center personnel are unusually well trained, but they are among the most-efficient workers we have.

8. Since Miss Gozzi accepted our proposal, we can proceed at once; thus, a completion date of March 31 is realistic.

Key: (1) C; (2) use a semicolon instead of a comma to join these two closely related independent clauses; (3) use a conjunctive adverb such as *furthermore* or *in addition* instead of the illogical subordinating conjunction *although;* (4) use *who* instead of *which* as a relative pronoun that refers to a person; (5) use the correlative pair *not only . . . but also* properly to show parallel sentence structure (for example, *Janae's sister was invited not only to attend the meeting but also to introduce the speaker).* (6) do not use the relative adverb *when* to give a definition; (7) replace the coordinating conjunction *but* with *and* or *so* to clearly and logically convey the intended meaning; (8) C.

LEVEL A

Name _____

Exercise 20–1   On the lines below, write **T** if the statement is true; write **F** if the statement is false.

___F___ 1. The words *and, but, if,* and *for* are all examples of coordinating conjunctions.

___T___ 2. Conjunctive adverbs such as *furthermore* and *moreover* are used to connect sentence parts that are equal in rank or importance.

___F___ 3. The connective *nevertheless* is a transitional phrase.

___T___ 4. Some punctuation marks act as connectives; some do not.

___T___ 5. A subordinating conjunction such as *unless* is appropriately used to join sentence parts of unequal rank.

___T___ 6. The sentence *Judy lives in Tacoma; however, David lives in Seattle* reflects the proper use of connectives.

___T___ 7. A subordinated clause is less important to the meaning of a sentence than an independent clause.

___T___ 8. Closely related independent clauses may be joined either by a semicolon or by a coordinating conjunction that is preceded by a comma.

___F___ 9. The relative pronouns *which* and *that* are both suitable choices for introducing nonrestrictive clauses.

___T___ 10. The relative adverbs *where, when,* and *while* are used to show subordination in complex sentences.

___T___ 11. Correlative conjunctions are **always** used in pairs.

___F___ 12. *So* and *yet* are an example of a correlative pair.

Exercise 20–2   Write **C** if the bold connective is correctly used; write **I** if the bold connective is incorrectly used.

___C___ 1. This year's Thanksgiving Day parade has fewer entries than usual; **nevertheless**, it will take longer to pass the review stand than it did last year.

___I___ 2. You may apply for a credit card, if you wish; **and** your eligibility for credit privileges appears doubtful.

___C___ 3. **After** considering the matter carefully, the School Board agreed to the proposed name of Freedom High School.

___I___ 4. **Although** you were the first person to point out the problem, you deserve full credit for its elimination.

___C___ 5. If Zaki asks for a raise **and** if Mr. Toone approves, a salary adjustment will take place immediately.

___C___ 6. **While** the trial is in progress, the jury is to have no outside contacts.

_I_   7. The senator's letter **who** you received last week is a good example of tactful writing.

_I_   8. A new computer network, **that** will be welcomed by the staff, should be operational within ten days.

_I_   9. Don't expect additional funds for your research**,** the department's budget is overdrawn again.

_C_ 10. The new employee pay incentives will be announced **when** the sales conference ends on Saturday.

_I_ 11. **Neither** of us **or** any of you is on the Dean's List this semester.

_C_ 12. The announcement was a surprise **not only** to Mr. Shin **but also** to me.

Exercise 20–3   Write **C** if the use of connectives is correct; write **I** if the use of connectives is incorrect.

_C_   1. Wally and Tamara will travel to Atlanta to attend the Peach Festival and to visit Tamara's mother.

_I_   2. I can't find my car keys nor do I have an extra set.

_C_   3. Your letter did not arrive before noon because the mail was late today.

_C_   4. Several proposals will be made while the discussions are in progress.

_I_   5. No one will do a better job than Jim, though he is especially well qualified for the position.

_I_   6. The messenger that left the package works for the Riviera Delivery Service.

_C_   7. The announcement, which appeared in several newspapers, described an opening for a computer specialist who can speak both Russian and French.

_I_   8. The results of the tests are not yet known; consequently no decision on treatment can be made at this time.

_C_   9. The Payroll Department is where information on income-tax deductions can be obtained.

_C_ 10. A run-on sentence occurs if two main clauses are not joined by a connective, whereas the use of only a comma to connect two main clauses results in a comma splice.

_I_ 11. Please advise your client to hire the attorney that was recommended to her.

_I_ 12. The mayor of Lindon is both pleased with the contribution and he is willing to give the proposal his full support.

_I_ 13. All correspondence should be shredded, to avoid needless congestion in the files.

_C_ 14. We cannot, I am told, take further action until we hear from your committee.

_I_ 15. Mr. Frinze will announce his decision Wednesday; in the meantime you must try to be patient.

_I_ 16. Seven applicants were interviewed, seven applicants were rejected; the search for the right person goes on.

_C_ 17. Recreation facilities in this city are either poorly maintained or inconveniently located.

LEVEL B

Name _____

Exercise 20–4   For each of the following items, write the letter identifying the statement that reflects the preferred use of connectives.

c   1.   *a.*   Jay is available and he is unwilling to help.
      b.   Jay is available but he is unwilling to help.
      c.   Jay is available, yet he is unwilling to help.

c   2.   *a.*   The book on grammar, that you recommended, is the best I have seen.
      b.   The book on grammar which you recommended is the best I have seen.
      c.   The book on grammar, which you recommended, is the best I have seen.

a   3.   *a.*   Do not post the election results until the recount is complete.
      b.   Until the recount is complete do not post the election results.
      c.   As I said yesterday until the recount is complete, do not post the election results.

a   4.   *a.*   Please let me know where the audit will take place.
      b.   An audit is where the company's financial records are reviewed by professional accountants.
      c.   We expect to get reliable results where a professional audit is conducted.

b   5.   *a.*   If the store expands its inventory profits may improve.
      b.   Profits will increase if the store expands its inventory.
      c.   The store expanded its inventory and profits did, in fact, increase.

b   6.   *a.*   All employees have been given raises this year; moreover, the cost of living has increased.
      b.   The cost of living has increased; thus, we expect to receive raises this year.
      c.   Employees' raises are influenced by the cost of living; however, raises are given when the cost of living rises.

b   7.   *a.*   The oral presentation should last no longer than 30 minutes; accordingly you should keep one eye on the clock.
      b.   A short presentation will be appreciated; furthermore, a long message is unnecessary to achieve your objective.
      c.   Both long and short messages should be interesting, hence; you should prepare your presentations with that requirement in mind.

a   8.   *a.*   The truth of the matter is, as I think you know, both Rodney and Russell are unqualified for the job.
      b.   Rodney has attended only one training session, Russell has attended none at all.
      c.   Neither man is a good choice for the assignment; in fact Joseph Rooney now appears to be our best bet.

a   9.   *a.*   After completing all plans for the trip to Boston, please request the funds needed to cover our costs.
      b.   Provided your request is approved the finance officer, Sally Tribblet, will give you a check.
      c.   When you see Mr. Walling; tell him you will be out of the office during the weeks of September 10 and September 17.

_a_ 10. *a.* The manager of the St. Paul office, who is 39 years old, received this year's national performance award.

       b. An interesting point, that should not be overlooked, is the academic background of this year's winner.

       c. The award includes a cash prize of $5,000 which will be presented personally to the recipient by the president of the firm.

_c_ 11. *a.* We were told that either the supervisor in charge nor the employee will be held liable.

       b. Not only was the contract invalid, even the date and location of the performance were inaccurate.

       c. According to the record, Arthur Wiggley from Reno was both intoxicated and abusive when he was arrested.

_b_ 12. *a.* Do you know the woman that is in charge of the program?

       b. Your assignment is to introduce the speaker who was selected by the program director.

       c. Of all the participants listed in the printed program, the one which is best known is Bonita Chavez.

_c_ 13. *a.* The roads were unusually slick while the traffic was particularly heavy at the intersection where the accident occurred.

       b. While I can understand why the accident happened, I cannot accept the driver's explanation.

       c. While you talk to the driver and the witnesses, I will notify the police.

_c_ 14. *a.* The cause of the electrical problem was when an unexpected power outage occurred.

       b. A power outage is when the supply of electricity is interrupted.

       c. The time was exactly 1:35 a.m. when the equipment shut down in the plant.

_a_ 15. *a.* Invite both the president and the chairman of the board; tell both officers not to miss this important event.

       b. Send the invitations immediately; in addition find out by Friday who plans to attend.

       c. Be sure to overlook no one; and, expect a decidedly positive response.

_b_ 16. *a.* The revised publication date is November 1, the 60-day delay could not be avoided.

       b. Ms. Fisk has not prepared a new contract yet, nor does she have any intention of asking me to prepare one.

       c. A third author will be needed the work load is greater than expected.

_b_ 17. *a.* Neither the teacher or the principal plans to resign.

       b. The unit commander complimented the troops not only on their courage but also on their skill.

       c. Ronnee's explanation was either inaccurate or she failed to make herself clear.

_c_ 18. *a.* When I met Mrs. Urry, that also lives in East Mecklinburg, I was surprised by her youthful appearance.

       b. Your assignment will be to greet the customers while LaRane's duties will be explained to her later.

       c. The diagram on page 10, which is labeled Exhibit B, contains the information you want.

LEVEL C

Name _____

Exercise 20–5

Editing

Determine whether the bold connective words and punctuation are used correctly in the following sentences according to the guidelines given in Lesson 20. If not, edit them to make the necessary corrections. One of the sentences is correct in its present form.

1. Patients are to be admitted to the hospital as the need arises**; however,** emergency care always is to be given first priority.

2. Dr. Fulmer, Dr. Peranovski, and Dr. Chatwa are on 24-hour call, as announced previously; only Dr. Chatwa, ~~**therefore,**~~ *however* has an office in the hospital.

3. Hospital room rates will increase by approximately 10 percent at the end of the year, ~~**and**~~ *but* the quality of care is expected to remain unchanged.

4. Over 1,000 patients were admitted to the hospital last week**; yet,** the actual number of admissions is smaller than it was during the same period last year.

5. If you want to help where you are needed most, ~~**consequently**~~ you should assist the hospital administrator with the current fund-raising campaign.

6. Hospital facilities are not considered adequate at present; **on the contrary,** some doubt exists that the hospital meets the professional guidelines **that** govern its operations.

Exercise 20–6

Editing

Edit the following sentences according to the guidelines given in Lesson 20 for using connectives. Two of the items are correct in their present form.

1. If you get the draft written before noon, Barbara, call me at Ext. 2303.

2. I will not be able to write the evaluation, ~~and~~ *but* Rosalee Timme will be able to do it for me unless she is out of town.

3. The list of contributors is complete, although the number of people who contributed is smaller than expected.

4. Paul, Delilah, and Reva are among the finalists; but Neil and Sophia are not.

5. Only a few days remain to complete the survey, ~~while~~ *but (or whereas)* more than a month is available to analyze

 the data and to write the report.

6. Neither player heard that regulation uniforms not only are preferred but ~~they are also~~ *also are* required.

7. The recruiter who talked with you on Monday is the same one with ~~which~~ *whom* I spoke last week.

8. The typical waiting period for tax refunds takes approximately six weeks; nevertheless, some

 citizens receive refunds in less than half that time.

Exercise 20–7

Cumulative Editing

Edit the following sentences according to (1) the guidelines provided in Units 2 and 3 and (2) the guidelines presented in this lesson for the use of connectives. See if you can find the three sentences that use verbs, punctuation, and connectives correctly and, therefore, need no editing.

1. May I ~~lay~~ *lie* down for a short rest before we go to work?

2. Jamie has ~~chose~~ *chosen* to attend the university, I was told, following graduation from high school.

3. Will you and your sisters sit together at this evening's recital as we requested earlier?

4. The moon ~~raised~~ *rose* at nightfall to a cloudless sky; consequently, the evening air was cold and

 calm.

5. The players have ~~drank~~ *drunk* more liquid before the game than is good for them; ~~nevertheless,~~ *consequently* they

 will not play well.

6. Because the schedule has been changed, when are singers ~~suppose~~ *supposed* to practice for the concert?

7. When Lee finally ~~come~~ *came* to class, he discovered he had missed two quizzes and an exam.

8. I hope you haven't ~~forgot~~ *forgotten* either the assignment that is due tomorrow ~~nor~~ *or* the one that is due

 Friday.

9. The patient sat in a chair most of the morning but he became tired and is now ~~laying~~ *lying* on the

 bed.

10. The total cost of the furniture shipment will be ~~payed~~ *paid* by October 15 if all goes well.

11. The gardener ~~digged~~ *dug* around the base of each of the unhealthy trees and shrubs; ~~however,~~ *furthermore (or in addition)* he also added fertilizer to the soil.

12. The water level in the lake will have risen more than 8 feet by the end of the spring runoff if predictions are accurate.

13. Dr. Philatt, who lives in Dallas, reported that she did everything possible to make Mr. Rippee comfortable during his long stay in the hospital.

Exercise 20–8

Cumulative Editing

Edit the following sentences according to (1) the guidelines given in Unit 2 for the use of verbs and (2) the guidelines presented in this lesson for the use of connectives. Two of the sentences use both verbs and connectives correctly and need no editing; the other sentences contain errors and should be edited accordingly.

1. Bertram P. Haddaby, who arrived on the Mayflower, ~~was~~ *is* a direct ancestor on my father's side of the family.

2. May I compliment you on your work; you did a particularly good job of selecting the right personnel for the project.

3. When you have ~~went~~ *gone* to your last class of the semester, you will feel a great sense of real accomplishment and relief.

4. I *have* worked for Bastian Brothers for 30 years, but I hope to retire in the near future.

5. The driver called out the stops as the bus ~~travels~~ *traveled* along its route.

6. Although I recently had received a promotion, the boss informed me that my services ~~were~~ *are* no longer required.

7. The incident occurred without warning, but the supervisor ~~handles~~ *handled* the situation smoothly.

8. Dr. Zaid Rahman, the project leader, concluded that matter is eternal and indestructible; he ended his presentation with that comment.

9. As the conductor ~~approached~~ *approaches* the podium, the audience stands and applauds in appreciation.

10. For now, the auditor ~~will require~~ *requires* that we clear all payments with him, before we write the checks.

Exercise 20–9

Cumulative Editing

Edit the following items according to (1) the guidelines given in Unit 2 for the correct use of verbs and (2) the guidelines presented in this lesson for the use of connectives. Two of the items use both verbs and connectives correctly and need no editing; the others contain errors and should be edited accordingly.

1. Although she has not had voice lessons, Diedre would have liked to ~~have sung~~ *sing* the lead role in the spring musical.

2. The team captain had agreed to meet with the officials prior to the game despite Alain's statement to the contrary.

3. Our attorney, Lynne Souter, seemed to ~~have been~~ *be* confused during today's court hearing; perhaps her medication ~~is~~ *was* at fault.

4. After the injury, Robbie ~~had~~ promised never to ride a motorcycle again.

5. Jenny Benzer, ~~that~~ *who* won yesterday's race, said she would ~~like~~ *have liked* to run in last summer's marathon.

6. Speaking to his troops, the commander felt a surge of pride in their courage and accomplishments.

7. At his class reunion last month, Seann ~~listens~~ *listened* with fascination to his former classmates.

8. Playing in the Winter Games was even more exciting than Callie ~~expects,~~ *expected* as you correctly predicted.

9. If you ~~knew~~ *had known* the results in advance, would you *have wanted* ~~want~~ to be present when the announcement was made?

10. Are you certain that Warren Cole planned to ~~have completed~~ *Complete* the symphony before September's concert?

The importance of parallelism—consistency in sentence structure—was discussed briefly in the introduction to Unit 4 and in Lesson 20. You will recall from those discussions that parallelism is essential to effective writing and that connectives are useful aids in making our writing parallel in form and meaning.

Like the conjunctions and other joiners studied in Lesson 20, prepositions are used to connect sentence parts to each other. In fact, prepositions are among the most-important conjunctive joiners in the English language.

A preposition is a connecting word or group of words that joins the word, phrase, or clause that follows it with some other element in the sentence. When using prepositions, be careful to select the one that indicates the precise **position, direction, time,** or **miscellaneous relationship** you desire.

Some prepositions that are used often and that you are likely familiar with include the following:

Position		**Direction**	
in	*in* the letter	**to**	*to* the game
on	*on* the desk	**from**	*from* our stock
by	*by* the window	**toward**	*toward* the street
under	*under* the desk	**down**	*down* the street
above	*above* the desk	**up**	*up* the street
beside	*beside* the desk	**at**	*at* the intersection
across	*across* the room	**through**	*through* the window
against	*against* the wall		
inside	*inside* the building		
near	*near* the building		

	Time			**Miscellaneous**
before	*before* tomorrow		**of**	*of* the matter
after	*after* the meeting		**for**	*for* the reason
during	*during* the meeting		**about**	*about* time
until	*until* Tuesday		**with**	*with* us
within	*within* a week		**except**	*except* us
since	*since* yesterday			

Note that most prepositions consist of only one word; however, a few consist of two or more words.

Our choice of prepositions is often governed by usage or tradition rather than by the formal requirements of grammar. The difference in meaning between prepositions is often minor, yet that difference may be critical in conveying clearly the writer's intended meaning.

We depend on prepositions to help us make our writing feel right. Most of us do rather well in making prepositions work for us even if we haven't given much thought to how they function. Even so, the better we understand the role of prepositions in language usage, the more likely we are to make the correct choices when we use prepositions in our writing.

As writers, we want our writing to be clear, easy to understand, and comfortable to the reader. The ability to use prepositions correctly is a valuable tool in achieving that goal.

Pretest

Write **C** or **I** to indicate whether prepositions are used correctly or incorrectly in the following sentences.

1. Tell the finance officer to review carefully all future expense account statements for the purpose of eliminating inappropriate charges.

2. Instruct the finance officer to write up the results of his work at the end of each month.

3. Because of my illness, I will not be able for work until next week.

4. Professor Dallin has an understanding and an appetite for good literature.

5. The tutor has agreed to divide her time equally between you, Rachelle, and me.

6. I gave your notes to my secretary; I need to ask her if she knows where they are at.

7. The manager interviewed all of the candidates on Monday afternoon.

8. Jewel Larrabee is the only officer besides me who was in attendance at today's meeting.

9. We can achieve our goals by planning well, working hard, and by cooperating fully with each other.

10. The CEO will be with us only on Wednesday due to the fact that she will give the featured address at the NRTC conference in Atlantic City Thursday afternoon.

Key: (l) I—use the simple preposition *to eliminate* in place of the wordy preposition *for the purpose of eliminating;* (2) I—eliminate the superfluous preposition *up;* (3) I—use *to* rather than *for* as the correct idiomatic preposition; (4) I—use the preposition *of* to correctly complete the meaning of the noun *understanding;* (5) I—use *among* when referring to more than two people; (6) I—eliminate the superfluous terminal preposition *at;* (7) I—avoid using the preposition *of* after the words *all* or *both* unless *of* is essential to language clarity; (8) C; (9) I—observe good parallel form by using the preposition *by* to introduce *working hard;* (10) I—use the simple preposition *because* in place of the wordy phrasal preposition *due to the fact that.*

Terminology

Idiom—An expression that usage and tradition have established as ''correct'' whether or not it conforms to the conventions of formal grammar. (Examples: *Ms. Poppett is on the other line; this math problem is over my head.*)

Phrasal preposition—Two or more words that act together as one preposition. (*according to, for the purpose of, due to the fact that*)

Prepositional phrase—A group of words consisting of a preposition plus its object and any words that modify the object.

Simple preposition—A preposition consisting of a single, one-syllable word.

Split construction—A sentence structure that splits or divides closely related sentence elements and that requires different prepositions to complete two or more related words. (Example: *The candidate is trained **for** and familiar **with** the responsibilities of management.*)

Rules

1. **Use simple prepositions and other simple words rather than wordier phrasal constructions as connectives.**

   Good writing emphasizes conciseness. Wordiness, on the other hand, clutters our language and obscures its meaning. The use of simple prepositions and other simple words instead of multiple-word phrasal constructions strengthens our writing. However, because most of us have acquired the habit of using phrasal constructions, choosing a short, simple word often requires deliberate thought.

Choose	In place of
about, concerning	in regard to
after	subsequent to
because	due to the fact that
before	prior to
to	for the purpose of
if	in the event that
since, because	inasmuch as

   NO   May I talk with you *in regard to* your statement of expenses?

   YES   May I talk with you *about* your statement of expenses?

   NO   Please notify my secretary *in the event that* you cannot keep your appointment.

   YES   Please notify my secretary *if* you cannot keep your appointment.

2. Avoid using unnecessary prepositions.

Double prepositions and superfluous terminal prepositions are examples of using prepositions to excess. Wordiness and clumsy expression often occur if a writer uses prepositions where they serve no useful purpose.

NO   Will you write *up* the evaluation?

YES   Will you write the evaluation?

NO   Marni's office is near *to* the elevator.

YES   Marni's office is near the elevator.

NO   Only one name has been taken off *of* the list of candidates.

YES   Only one name has been taken off the list of candidates.

Learning Hint 1.   Avoid excessive use of prepositional phrases. Too many prepositional phrases in our writing makes our language awkward, cumbersome, and confusing. This writing weakness occurs often and should be avoided.

NO   The meeting should be scheduled *as soon as possible* and a complete discussion *of the problem* should be undertaken *in a constructive manner.*

YES   Schedule the meeting immediately and discuss the problem constructively.

NO   A set *of specifications* should be developed *by the architect for use by the contractors in the preparation of their bids.*

YES   The architect should develop the specifications the contractors need to prepare their bids.

Note that use of active voice helps eliminate unnecessary prepositional phrases.

Learning Hint 2.   May a preposition ever be placed at the end of a sentence? Yes—in certain circumstances. In times past, writers were admonished to avoid terminal prepositions. Even now, writers of formal English avoid end-of-sentence prepositions. In our day, however, most writers consider terminal prepositions acceptable if such prepositions contribute to the clarity and ''comfortableness'' of the sentence.

Consider these examples of end-of-sentence prepositions used in clear and natural expression:

Please find out where that report came *from.*

What political party does he belong *to*?

Here is the copy I wrote *on.*

How much inconvenience are you willing to put up *with*?

Some terminal prepositions, of course, result in awkward endings and should be avoided.

NO   Will you try the revised guidelines *out*?

YES   Will you try the revised guidelines?

NO   Deena knows where the file is *at.*

YES   Deena knows where the file is.

As a general rule, avoid ending a sentence with a preposition. However, make an exception to the rule when terminal prepositions contribute to clear and natural writing.

Learning Hint 3.   Avoid using the superfluous preposition *of* after *all* or *both* unless *of* is essential for language clarity.

NO   All *of* the printouts contain one or more errors.

YES   All printouts contain one or more errors.

NO   An examination of both *of* the purchase orders is required.

YES   An examination of both purchase orders is required.

YES   We hope that all *of* you will enroll in the training program. (*of* needed for clarity)

Use
T21-1
here

3. **Avoid the omission of prepositions needed to connect ideas of equal importance or to complete a split construction.**

Repeat those prepositions that introduce two or more thoughts of equal rank or value. Good parallel form often depends on this important but often disregarded practice.

NO   He asked *to* see our facilities and meet our staff.

YES   He asked *to* see our facilities and *to* meet our staff.

NO   The superintendent achieved his goals *by* working hard, listening to his employees, and devising fair and progressive policies.

YES   The superintendent achieved his goals *by* working hard, *by* listening to his employees, and *by* devising fair and progressive policies.

The term *split construction* refers to a sentence that requires different prepositions to complete two or more words. An awkward expression results if only one preposition is used when two or more prepositions are needed in such constructions. Be sure to use a **suitable** preposition for **each** word to be completed in the split.

NO   Melissa will apply and enroll *in* the University of Michigan in the fall.

YES   Melissa will apply *to* and enroll *in* the University of Michigan in the fall.

NO   Erik has an aptitude and a background *in* music composition.

YES   Erik has an aptitude *for* and a background *in* music composition.

4. **Use the preposition *between* to refer to two people, things, or collective groups; use *among* to refer to three or more people, things, or collective groups.**

For some reason, the between-among rule is frequently violated. It shouldn't be, however, because the usage guideline that governs these two prepositions isn't difficult to remember. Be alert to the circumstances that dictate which of these words is suitable for the purpose intended.

The campaign money was divided *between* the two candidates.

Just *between* you and me, I feel confident the offer will be accepted.

The championship game is *between* the Pirates and the Blue Sox.

Who *among* the five of us is qualified to be our leader?

Judge Waggoner divided the work *among* the three attorneys.

A disagreement *among* the members of the jury resulted in a voting deadlock.

Learning Hint 4.   Other prepositions that are frequently misused include the following:

beside/besides

in/into

like

Beside means *adjacent to*; *besides* means *in addition to.*

Please place the note pad *beside* the telephone. (*Beside* is used to indicate placement.)

What will I need *besides* a computer and a printer? (*Besides* is used to indicate something more.)

In refers to location or position; *into* indicates movement or a change of condition.

The fire extinguisher is *in* the foyer. (*In* is used to indicate location.)

Please take the patient *into* the examination room. (*Into* is used to indicate movement.)

The spring shower suddenly turned *into* a downpour. (*Into* is used to indicate change of condition.)

Like is often used to correctly introduce a noun or a pronoun; however, *like* should **not** be used as a conjunction to connect two clauses.

NO   I feel *like* the task never will be completed. (*Like* is used improperly as a conjunction.)

YES   I feel as though the task never will be completed.

Kent is *like* Doreen in his ability to think analytically. (*Like* is used correctly to introduce a noun.)

Use
T21-2
here

5. **Use idiomatic prepositions selectively to convey precise meaning and to avoid awkward expression.**

Idiomatic language is based primarily on usage or tradition rather than on the conventions of formal grammar. That's why Americans are likely to say *James is in the hospital* whereas the British say *James is in hospital.* Similarly, Americans say *Margaret is on vacation;* the British say *Margaret is on holiday.*

Idiomatic expression may or may not conform to established rules of grammar. The habit of expressing an idea in a particular way often overrides the customary demands of grammar conventions. What matters most in idiomatic language is clarity of expression, not grammatical purity. For that reason, we often hear—and write—such idiomatic expressions as

I think I'll turn in early tonight.

How did you catch that cold?

I'll have a go at it.

Did you agree to their proposal?

We will wind up this job today.

Her request is out of the question.

Don't give up on me yet.

I'm sorry you feel so blue.

In the English language, prepositions are probably used idiomatically more often than any other part of speech. Hundreds—perhaps thousands—of such usages exist. Consider the following examples:

Mr. Noring is going **on** vacation next week.
Mr. Noring is going **at** vacation next week.
Mr. Noring is going **in** vacation next week.
Mr. Noring is going **of** vacation next week.

The bid is **in** line with our estimate.
The bid is **at** line with our estimate.
The bid is **for** line with our estimate.
The bid is **about** line with our estimate.

All four examples in both groups of illustrations meet the demands of correct grammatical construction, yet only the first one in each group feels comfortable and conveys the precise meaning intended. The use of *on* rather than *at, in,* or *of* in the first group is idiomatically correct. The same is true of *in* rather than *at, for,* or *about* in the second group. A well-established usage tradition has made *on* and *in* the preferred idioms in these two expressions.

The point to be remembered is that idioms are an important part of our language, and they are used skillfully by effective writers. Even when idioms conflict with standards of conventional grammar, they contribute to language clarity because the reader is familiar with them and understands them readily.

Fortunately, most writers possess a generally good feel for idiomatic expressions. We usually encounter little or no difficulty in using such expressions properly. At times, however, the correct choice of idiom requires some thought if we are to avoid murky or clumsy writing. If uncertainty exists in the use of idioms, the writer has the responsibility of making certain that correct usage is observed. On these occasions, the dictionary or a good reference on idiomatic language can be a valuable resource.

Posttest

Write **C** or **I** to indicate whether the use of prepositions is correct or incorrect in the following sentences.

1. Both of you will be assigned to the Customer Service Center.

2. Josh is interested in, ready for, and excited about a new career opportunity in computer electronics.

3. Please take the storage cabinet down to the basement.

4. Notify all employees that in the event an emergency occurs, they must observe the new safety guidelines without fail.

5. Please find out where the old shipping records were taken to.

6. The contest among the seniors and the juniors for the most money collected was particularly close this year.

7. All supervisors are directed to be at attendance when the April staff meeting is held in Colorado Springs.

8. According to the minutes of the meeting, both employees were reprimanded for negligence and for insubordination.

9. The tour included visits to the Coliseum, the Hall of Deputies, and to the famous Fountain of the Gods.

10. The junior executive acted like he was surprised by the losses reported on this quarter's profit-and-loss statement.

Key: (l) C; (2) C; (3) I—the preposition *down* is unnecessary; (4) I—use the simple preposition *if* rather than *in the event*; (5) I—eliminate the superfluous terminal preposition *to*; (6) I—use *between* rather than *among* when referring to two collective groups; (7) I—use *in* rather than *at* as the correct idiomatic preposition; (8) C; (9) I—observe good parallel form by using the preposition *to* to introduce *the Hall of Deputies*; (10) I—avoid using *like* as a connective to join two clauses.

LEVEL A

Name _____

Exercise 21–1 On the lines below, write **T** if the statement is true; write **F** if the statement is false.

_T_ 1. Like a conjunction, a preposition is a connective term.

_T_ 2. *Among* is an example of a simple preposition.

_F_ 3. *Due to the fact that* is an example of a prepositional phrase.

_F_ 4. Phrasal prepositions and prepositional phrases are the same thing.

_F_ 5. Sentences should never end with a preposition.

_T_ 6. Double prepositions occur in the sentence *Narita's car is too near to the driveway.*

_T_ 7. Acceptable idiomatic language sometimes violates established grammar standards.

_T_ 8. *Among* is properly used when reference is made to more than two people or things.

_T_ 9. Double prepositions should always be avoided, but terminal prepositions are sometimes acceptable.

_F_ 10. *Wendy was surprised and delighted by her birthday present* illustrates the proper use of prepositions as connectives.

_T_ 11. The preceding item (No. 10) is an example of a split construction.

_T_ 12. The preposition *beside* refers to position or placement; *besides* means in addition to or something more.

_F_ 13. The preposition *like* is correctly used in the sentence *Katrina acts like nothing more remains to be done.*

_T_ 14. Excessive use of prepositional phrases weakens the following sentence: *The truck from the motor pool will be loaded by the workers and then it will be driven without delay to the receiving center of the Morton Tool Company.*

_T_ 15. The preposition *of* generally should not be used after *all* and *both*.

Exercise 21–2 Write **C** if the bold preposition is used correctly; write **I** if it is used incorrectly.

_I_ 1. Please be **to** your seats when the bell rings for class.

_I_ 2. Ms. Boyce has written the manufacturer a letter **in regard to** the defective product.

_I_ 3. Bob, please take your tool box **out to** the garage where it belongs.

_C_ 4. The contract stipulates that all **of** us are legally liable for any injuries that may occur.

_I_ 5. Mr. Weems has taken Lady and her puppies **out** for a walk.

_C_ 6. Fred Pavlak is the photographer whom I most want to work **with**.

_C_ 7. **To** whom should we forward this mail?

_I_   8. The foreman reported that all **of** the problems identified in your memo have now been corrected.

_C_   9. **Besides** a sleeping bag and a rain slicker, you should also bring a compass, a knife, and matches.

_I_ 10. Nothing succeeds **as** success.

_I_ 11. I doubt that Chief Dannic will agree **at** Officer Considine's suggestion.

_I_ 12. The choice of a winner in this year's essay contest apparently will be **between** Rhoda Tyler, Marta Kohn, and Enoc Fehr.

_C_ 13. The team is nervous **about** but well prepared **for** the championship game in Spokane.

_I_ 14. Please send Mr. Pritkin **in** the principal's office for his 3:30 appointment.

_C_ 15. The CEO has come to Sacramento **to** inspect our facilities, **to** interview our personnel, and **to** evaluate our performance.

Exercise 21–3   Write **C** if the use of prepositions is correct. Write **I** if the use of prepositions is incorrect.

_C_   1. Both men on the committee resigned because of poor health.

_C_   2. According to Francie, no one has yet been selected as class valedictorian.

_I_   3. The rest of the group will meet us up at the cabin on Lookout Mountain before nightfall.

_C_   4. Both of you must be present tomorrow morning when the winner is announced.

_I_   5. Inasmuch as the weather forecast calls for rain, the boss has postponed the company picnic.

_C_   6. Which university do you want your test scores sent to?

_I_   7. Mr. Danzig's name will not be taken off of his office door until the 15th.

_I_   8. The Civic Arena was built for concerts, athletic events, and for commercial exhibits.

_C_   9. The scuffle between the players began when one pushed the other out of bounds.

_I_ 10. Where did the building inspector go to after she left the meeting?

_I_ 11. Please total up your expenses and submit a request for an immediate reimbursement.

_I_ 12. We have been informed that the final decision is between Models B, D, and F.

_I_ 13. As a tennis pro, Lynda Compton claims she is in the top of her form.

_C_ 14. The security guard at the door refuses to let us in without a pass.

_C_ 15. Just among the four of us, Sandy Gilmour is likely to be our new department head.

_C_ 16. Which runway is Flight 302 landing on?

LEVEL B

Name _____

Exercise
21–4

Write the letter identifying the statement that reflects the preferred usage of prepositions.

_b_ 1. *a.* Prior to the meeting, Ms. Laramore prepared the agenda.
     b. A complete report is needed concerning Thursday afternoon's power failure.
     c. A board of inquiry has been appointed for the purpose of investigating the charges made against Thomas Housman.

_c_ 2. *a.* Please ask Karyl where she went to after leaving the office.
     b. Harvey went out to his car to get his briefcase.
     c. We are trying to determine what the opposing attorneys are up to.

_c_ 3. *a.* According to the manager, notifications should be sent to all of our customers.
     b. If you pay your entire bill within ten days, you may take the customary 3 percent discount off of the amount shown on the invoice.
     c. After reviewing your applications, the admissions committee decided that both of you will be admitted to the program.

_a_ 4. *a.* Mr. Margolis plans to visit the Hartford office and to interview each employee.
     b. As a team, we have committed ourselves to working hard, playing fair, and supporting each other.
     c. The survey revealed that our firm enjoys a reputation for honesty, for high-quality products, and good customer service.

_b_ 5. *a.* The conflict is between Ben, Kevin, and Wade.
     b. Among the members of the jury, only two have had previous courtroom experience.
     c. The race for the office of mayor this year is among the Progressive Party and the Liberal Party.

_c_ 6. *a.* I have been asked to sit besides Joan Princer and Kelli Wells during the presentation.
     b. Beside Mr. Wellington, Mr. Tooner and Mrs. Pozzini are expected to attend.
     c. Please place the file beside the telephone on the table.

_b_ 7. *a.* When will you take the computer printouts in the principal's office?
     b. Has the custodian moved the extra desk into the storage room yet?
     c. Miss Dana feels like her work is not appreciated.

_b_ 8. *a.* I'm willing to have a go to it.
     b. I'm willing to have a go at it.
     c. I'm willing to have a go for it.

_c_ 9. *a.* My secretary stayed home today because she is over the weather.
     b. We have decided we cannot agree for your proposal.
     c. Mr. Wembley isn't likely to give up on the Tucson project.

_a_ 10. *a.* The new copier will be placed in the word-processing center.
     b. We have finally discovered where the computer service center is at in your city.
     c. The purchasing department has ordered new printers for all offices inasmuch as our old printers are now obsolete.

_b_ 11. _a._ When you have read the proposal, please send it up to the vice president's office.

     _b._ Because you missed the planning meeting, your comments will not be considered.

     _c._ This month's production level is very near to the all-time record.

_b_ 12. _a._ The helicopter landing pad is in service up on the roof.

     _b._ May I see the scheduling plans you have been working on?

     _c._ All of the passengers must be cleared at the loading gate in the future.

_c_ 13. _a._ Plans have been made to test out our new winter clothing in cold weather.

     _b._ The choice is between Kansas City, Cincinnati, and St. Louis as next year's convention site.

     _c._ Justine will attend the workshop to get fresh ideas and to make new business contacts.

_a_ 14. _a._ Don is hoping for but skeptical about an opportunity to study abroad.

     _b._ Both accountants possess an interest and an aptitude for financial planning.

     _c._ All of the interviews will be held in the Board Room.

_c_ 15. _a._ The visitor is expected to arrive just prior to the lunch hour.

     _b._ Where do you recommend I go to for further graduate study?

     _c._ Whom is Quinn going to the dance with?

_b_ 16. _a._ Please tell Nancy to come in from out of the rain.

     _b._ Do you know where Ms. Bronson's flight is coming from?

     _c._ I will be absent from the ten o'clock meeting inasmuch as I have a prior appointment.

_a_ 17. _a._ Winston plans to enroll in school in the fall and to explore the possibility of majoring in industrial design.

     _b._ Despite your views to the contrary, I believe Mr. Pramer has been invited to New York to meet the CEO and be interviewed for a new job.

     _c._ Your test scores indicate that you are academically prepared, emotionally equipped, and deeply interested in a career in government service.

_b_ 18. _a._ You are entitled to one piece of carry-on luggage beside the two suitcases you plan to take with you on the plane.

     _b._ Among all the passengers, only one person was found with any medical training.

     _c._ If we expect to finish this project tomorrow, we should begin in the crack of dawn.

_a_ 19. _a._ Mr. Dart's performance is like Mr. Foster's in many respects.

     _b._ Miss Twaddle is behaving like she does not feel well today.

     _c._ Like it or not, we must present the revised health-insurance program like it has management's full support.

_a_ 20. _a._ Both candidates must be interviewed by both of you on Friday.

     _b._ All of us will be affected by both of the changes announced today.

     _c._ We have learned that all of you people in the Milling Division are eligible for all of the benefits described in the announcement.

_c_ 21. _a._ Please send Jerry out to get the briefcase in my car.

     _b._ The word-processing center is located up on the seventh floor.

     _c._ In his remarks, which entry did Mr. Torgeson appear to be most pleased with?

LEVEL C

Name _____

Exercise
21–5

Editing

Determine whether the bold prepositions are used correctly in the following sentences according to the guidelines given in this lesson. If they are not, edit them to make the necessary corrections. Two of the sentences are correct in their present form.

1. We are pleased to know that you are interested **in** and eager **for** new challenges.

2. When will you have your summary of the trustees' meeting written ~~**up**~~?

3. Call Dr. Krockett's office ~~**in the event**~~ *if* you experience any problems.

4. Have you taken any data off ~~**of**~~ Kyle's personnel records yet?

5. We have been advised that all ~~**of**~~ the employees in the Norman, Oklahoma, plant will be furloughed for three weeks in February.

6. Jill Claynor is the only manager ~~**beside**~~ *besides* you to be recognized for superior performance.

7. When you take each applicant ~~**in**~~ *into* your office, try to make the atmosphere as relaxed and as comfortable as possible.

8. Inform Mr. Reubens that we do not know where the key to the first aid cabinet is ~~**at.**~~

9. **Concerning** your recent request, a transfer to the St. Petersburg office at this time is not possible.

10. Travel funds amounting to $6,500 are to be divided equally ~~**between**~~ *among* the five employees in the public relations department.

11. Both ~~**of the**~~ speeches were excellent.

12. Louine is talking ~~**like**~~ *as though* her promotion is assured.

13. I am going to send the memo ~~**up**~~ to your office immediately, as you requested.

Exercise 21–6 Edit the following sentences according to the guidelines presented in this lesson on the use of prepositions. Three of the sentences are correct in their present form.

Editing

1. Try ~~out~~ the office furniture for two weeks; then tell us whether you want to buy it at a 10 percent discount.

2. Paula should know where these complaints came from.

3. We expect consumer prices to go ~~up~~ substantially higher in the coming year.

4. I plan to write the home office and ^to^ telephone the chief of personnel about the problem you reported earlier.

5. All of you with a master's degree will be given an opportunity to transfer to an overseas post.

6. Of all the entrants, Charla is the only one who is up to date with her homework, on time for all her classes, and in line with the school's academic requirements.

7. The coaches and the players on the team agreed to divide equally ~~between~~ ^among^ them the expenses related to their trip.

8. The manager seems ~~like she is~~ disappointed with our efforts thus far.

9. Professor Stauffer is planning to go ~~for~~ ^on^ leave next semester.

10. A follow-up report is expected ~~subsequent to~~ ^after^ the completion of the study.

11. Were you drawn ~~in to~~ ^into^ the discussion about changes in current working conditions?

12. The department head said he wants you to call him ~~up~~ before 4 p.m.

13. Thanks for your letter ~~in regard to~~ ^about^ housing costs in the Providence area.

14. Item 12 has been taken off ~~of~~ the list provided by the Purchasing Department yesterday.

15. Where should this package be delivered ~~to~~, Miss Torry?

Exercise 21–7

Cumulative Editing

Edit the following sentences according to (1) the guidelines given in Unit 3 for using punctuation and (2) the guidelines presented in this lesson for using prepositions. Can you find the two sentences that use both punctuation and prepositions correctly? The remaining sentences contain errors and should be edited accordingly.

1. We appreciate your interest in our company, and we look forward to talking with you personally ~~in regard to~~ *about (or concerning)* working for us.

2. Although we do not require employees to enroll in the company's health-insurance program, we recommend they do so.

3. Salary increases are given ~~for~~ *to* employees annually, provided the company is doing well.

4. Employee loyalty is important to us, the well-being of all ~~of~~ our workers, therefore, is a principal concern in our firm.

5. Daniel Porte has been with our company for 44 years; he has more seniority than any other worker.

6. Employee turnover in our company is extremely low; furthermore, we have a long list of applicants who are interested *in* and qualified for employment with our firm.

7. The moderate growth rate of the company, however, seems unlikely to create a strong demand for more workers.

8. The Employee Grievance Committee consists of Wayne Bidler, Sharon Smith, and Bella Abdul; and the committee holds meetings on the first and third Fridays of each month.

9. ~~In the event that~~ *If* important actions are taken by the committee, the employees affected are notified in writing.

10. Most employees appreciate the committee's efforts, although a few workers say the committee takes too long to mail ~~out~~ the letters that notify employees of action taken on complaints.

11. While you are ~~in~~ *on* leave next semester, the maintenance staff will refurbish the mail room, *the* cafeteria, and the storage area ~~down~~ in the basement.

Exercise
21–8

Cumulative
Editing

Edit the following sentences according to (1) the guidelines given in Unit 3 for using punctuation and (2) the guidelines presented in this lesson for using prepositions. You should determine whether any of the sentences use both punctuation and prepositions correctly and, therefore, require no editing.

1. At noon today, a special awards ceremony will be held in the atrium of the administration building ~~for the purpose of recognizing~~ *to recognize* this year's outstanding employees.

2. We met with our attorneys for over an hour; at that point, Reese suggested we try ~~out~~ a compromise plan that received immediate approval from all ~~of~~ those present.

3. You inquired in your letter whether we are prepared to meet the terms of your proposal; unfortunately, we cannot agree to your conditions.

4. The book, which I found ~~up~~ on the top shelf in my study, is the one you gave me more than a year ago.

5. Bring your financial ledgers, *your* computer printouts, and your most-recent profit-and-loss statement to the November 12 audit.

6. The buyers examined the latest designs, and placed an exclusive order ~~to~~ *with* Elegante Clothiers— a firm we like to do business with.

7. The new contract calls for immediate improvements in working conditions; opportunities to mediate future contract disputes; and better life insurance and retirement benefits for all workers.

8. When you walk ~~in~~ *into* the office, that will be yours from now on, I believe you will be delighted.

9. Both ~~of the~~ vice presidents, as a matter of fact, have advanced degrees from nationally recognized business schools.

10. As noted by the division manager, ''Our founder's prophetic statement that 'Maniac Apparel will be an international powerhouse one day' has proven to be entirely accurate.''

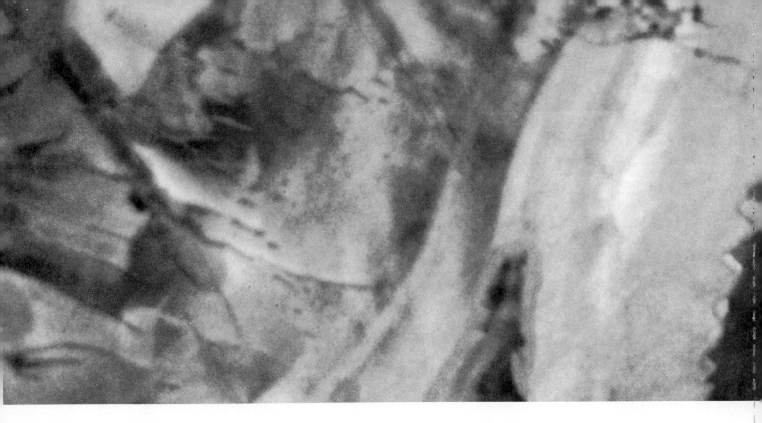

LESSONS IN THIS UNIT

22. SUBJECTIVE- AND OBJECTIVE-CASE PRONOUNS

23. RELATIVE PRONOUNS

24. PLURAL NOUNS

25. POSSESSIVE NOUNS AND PRONOUNS

As you are learning from your study of business English, each part of speech has different characteristics and unique potential problems for effective writers to master. Nouns change form regarding number. Making singular nouns plural may be a challenge, as many nouns are not considered "regular" in forming plurals. Another situation that often creates learning problems is the use of possessive nouns. Since an *s* is usually used for both plurals and possessives, many writers often have a problem determining the correct noun form in many situations. For instance, notice the similarity in sound in the following words:

companies   company's   companies'

Even though they are pronounced the same and we do not need to differentiate among them in oral communication, they are spelled differently and have different uses in written communication. As a careful writer, you will want to discern the differences between plurality and possession, master the different forms, and understand when each is appropriate.

The formation of noun plurals is covered in Lesson 24. The use of possessive nouns to show ownership is defined in Lesson 25. Besides understanding how to form possessives, you will learn when the use of these ownership words is appropriate in writing. Once you have mastered both plural and possessive nouns, you will discover how many misuses of these forms commonly exist and better appreciate the confusion created by people who don't use the forms correctly.

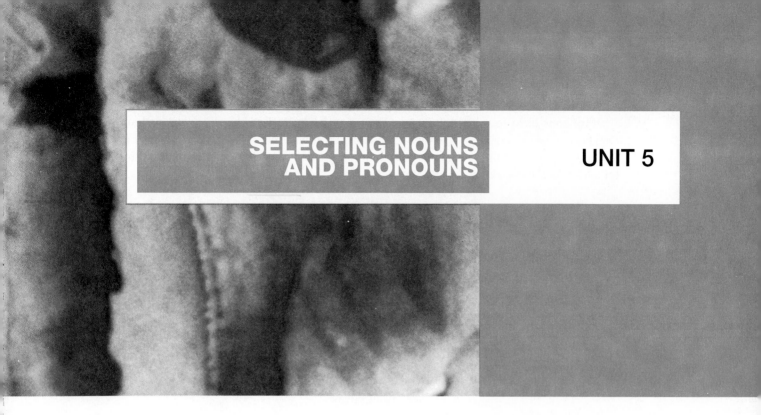

Pronouns are used to substitute for nouns. If we didn't have pronouns to substitute for nouns, the repetition of the nouns would often create awkward messages. Compare the following sentences:

When Sharon's class was over, Sharon met Todd; and Sharon and Todd went to Sharon's car.

When Sharon's class was over, *she* met Todd; and *they* went to *her* car.

As you can readily see, pronouns are very useful in effective writing. However, as a conscientious writer, you must take care to use the correct form of the pronoun.

Pronoun Properties.   Pronouns have four properties—number, person, gender, and case. Unlike nouns, which only change to indicate number, pronouns change forms to indicate all properties. These properties will be referred to often in the discussion of pronouns in both Unit 5 and Unit 6.

Number refers to total persons, things, or ideas being discussed. A **singular** pronoun refers to one, and a **plural** pronoun refers to two or more items.

He judged the book by *its* title. (singular)

Our team has always outscored *theirs*. (plural)

Person refers to the pronoun form indicating the speaker, the person spoken to, or the person spoken about. **First person** is used for the speaker or speakers, **second person** for the one or ones spoken to, and **third person** for the person(s) or thing(s) spoken about.

I will be sure to indicate *our* preference of seats. (first)

You may take *your* assistant to the meeting also. (second)

They weighed all views before making *their* choice. (third)

Pronouns have four **gender** forms. They may be masculine (*he, him, his*) or feminine (*she, her, hers*) when referring to specific individuals. Pronouns that refer to neither males nor females are neuter (*it, its*). Many pronouns are common gender since they can refer to both males and females (*they, them, their, theirs*).

> *He* took *his* report with *him* to the meeting. (masculine)
>
> *She* voiced *her* concerns about the decision. (feminine)
>
> The dog wagged *its* tail as *it* waited for the bone. (neuter)
>
> *They* brought *their* subordinates with *them*. (common)

Case refers to the function of the pronoun within the sentence. A pronoun functioning as the subject of a clause or as a subject complement will be in the **subjective** case, a pronoun functioning as the object of a verb or preposition will be in the **objective** case, and a pronoun showing possession or ownership will be in the **possessive** case.

> *We* showed the report to the client. (subjective)
>
> The client showed the report to *us*. (objective)
>
> The president showed *our* report to the client. (possessive)

Pronoun Categories. Pronouns are classified into several categories—for example, personal, relative, demonstrative, indefinite, interrogative, reflexive, and intensive. Some of these are more important to your study of business English than others.

Personal pronouns are the most-frequent category and include the words used to indicate the speaker, the one spoken to, or the person or thing spoken about. You will learn when to use subjective and objective cases of personal pronouns in Lesson 22 and possessive pronouns in Lesson 25.

Often classified as types of personal pronouns, **reflexive** and **intensive** pronouns always end with *self*. They are often misused and should normally be avoided. Lesson 22 will give more information on these categories.

Relative pronouns not only replace nouns but also show relationships between clauses in a sentence. Lesson 23 will explain the rules for using *who, whom, which*, and *that*.

The **demonstrative** pronouns refer to specific persons, places, things, or ideas. They often perform the function of adjectives in a sentence. The uses of *this, that, these*, and *those* will be included in Lesson 27.

Indefinite pronouns refer to a group or class of persons or things rather than to specific individuals. These pronouns may cause agreement problems with verbs and with antecedents and will be discussed in Lesson 26.

Interrogative pronouns are *who, whom, whose, which*, and *that*. They are used to ask questions. Although they are considered as a category, these pronouns used in this sense do not cause particular problems in writing; and we will not discuss them further in this text.

SUBJECTIVE- AND OBJECTIVE-CASE PRONOUNS

LESSON 22

As you learned in the unit introduction, pronouns may be divided into several categories. Of these groups, however, personal pronouns are the most common. You use these pronouns to refer to yourself and to other people.

You know from your study of Unit 1 that pronouns can substitute for nouns. Therefore, nouns and pronouns have the same functions—often as subjects of sentences. Also, like verbs, pronouns have other uses. Nouns do not change forms as they change functions, but pronouns do.

These personal pronouns take different forms, known as *cases*, as their function in the sentence changes. These cases are **subjective**, **objective**, and **possessive**. This lesson will deal with subjective case and objective case.

Many writers and speakers fail to distinguish between subjective-case and objective-case pronouns. The two cases are not interchangeable. How many children have you heard make such comments as ''Me and Ann are going to the party''? After being corrected and told the sentence should be ''Ann and I are going to the party,'' they become convinced *I* should always be used with a compound. This incorrect idea then becomes cemented into the adult's speaking and writing.

If you do not have a complete understanding of the differences between subjective and objective cases, you will find this lesson very helpful in increasing your understanding.

Sometimes, personal pronouns may include *self* and *selves* endings. With these endings, the pronouns become **reflexive** or **intensive**. Reflexive pronouns are used when the noun or pronoun has already been identified in the sentence. Intensive pronouns may be used to show emphasis in a sentence.

These *self* pronouns are often used incorrectly by writers who do not understand case. If writers cannot correctly distinguish between *I* and *me*, they believe that using *myself* will solve the prob-

Use
T22–1
here

Table 22–1			
Pronoun Cases			
	Subjective	*Objective*	*Possessive*	*Intensive Reflexive*
Singular				
First Person	I	me	my mine	myself
Second Person	you	you	your yours	yourself
Third Person	he	him	his	himself
	she	her	her hers	herself
	it	it	its	itself
Plural				
First Person	we	us	our ours	ourselves
Second Person	you	you	your yours	yourselves
Third Person	they	them	their theirs	themselves

lem. In reality, they have merely exchanged one grammatical problem for another. Reflexive and intensive pronouns are not interchangeable with either subjective- or objective-case pronouns.

Table 22–1 will be a helpful reference to you as you study personal pronouns in this lesson and in Lesson 25. We suggest that you memorize the information so you can readily recall the pronouns in each case.

Pretest

Mark the correct pronoun in each of the following examples:

1. The accountants, Daniel and (we, us), were impressed with the proposal.

2. The winner of the award was (he, him).

3. Mr. Joseph asked (she, her) to complete the report.

4. Sean and (she, her, herself) will be the honored guests.

5. The competition was between you and (I, me).

6. Jo asked if she could go with Mike and (she, her).

7. (We, Us) students will get higher grades if we study.

8. Juan is better at basketball than (I, me).

9. Franco had to convince (him, himself) before he could persuade anyone else.

10. Although Kanako understood English well, neither (she, her) nor (I, me) could translate the Japanese card.

11. All the registration forms should be sent to Madlyn and (we, us).

12. Dr. Haymond was able to fax the required information sooner than (I, me).

Key: (1) we—as an appositive, *we* renames the subject and is therefore in subjective case; (2) he—use subjective case after a linking verb; (3) her—use objective case for objects of verbs; (4) she—use subjective case as a subject; (5) me—use objective case as the object of a preposition; (6) her—use objective case as the compound object of a preposition; (7) we—*we* renames the subject and is therefore in subjective case; (8) I—complete the comparison *than I am*; (9) himself—refers to the subject already stated; the sentence could also be correct with *him* if the writer were referring to someone other than the subject; (10) she, I—use subjective-case pronouns as subjects of the independent clause; (11) us—use an objective-case pronoun as the object of a preposition; (12) I—complete the comparison *than I was*.

Terminology

Antecedent—The noun for which a pronoun substitutes. (*The president took the report with him. President* is the antecedent of the pronoun *him.*)

Appositive—A noun or pronoun word or phrase that follows and restates another noun or pronoun. The appositive functions the same way in the sentence as the noun or pronoun it complements. (*The editors, Allyson and he, finished the project.* The appositive *Allyson and he* restates *editors.*)

Intensive pronoun—A *self*-ending pronoun used to add emphasis to the sentence.

Objective pronoun—The form of a pronoun used as the object of a verb or preposition (*me, him, her, them*).

Reflexive pronoun—A *self*-ending pronoun used to refer to nouns or pronouns already identified in the sentence.

Subjective pronoun—The form of a pronoun used as a subject of a verb or a subject complement after a linking verb (*I, we, she, he*). Some texts call these pronouns *nominative* rather than *subjective*. Because *subjective* makes sense as the subject, we have chosen to use this term throughout the text.

Rules

You will have an easy time using pronouns correctly if you understand which pronouns are subjective and which are objective. Refer to Table 22–1 if you are unclear about any specific pronouns.

1. Use subjective pronouns as subjects of clauses.

> *They* worked hard at the job.
>
> Although *we* were early, the meeting started late.
>
> Both *she* and *I* wanted the promotion.

You may believe you can determine which pronoun to use strictly by the sound because you know *them worked hard* and *us were early* do not sound right and are incorrect pronoun uses. However, because pronouns are used incorrectly so often, some *wrong* pronouns may sound *right* to you. Therefore, you must understand the grammatical explanation of case to understand why certain pronouns are incorrect even though they may be commonly used.

You will recall from earlier lessons that every verb needs a subject. Find the verb in the clause and determine the subject of that verb. If you find the subject is the pronoun in question, you will know it must be in the subjective form. Also, if you find that the verb you have isolated is a linking verb, you can readily determine if the pronoun in question is a subject complement and therefore a subjective-case pronoun.

2. **Use subjective pronouns after state-of-being verbs.**

> NO   The new student is *her.*
> The project directors have been Dave and *me.*

> YES   The new student is *she.*
> The project directors have been Dave and *I.*

From your study of verbs, you understand state-of-being verbs. Because these verbs do not have objects (requiring objective pronouns), the pronoun forms are subject complements and are in the same form as the subject. Consider the linking verb as an equal sign. The information appearing on both sides must be the same. Therefore, the complement must be in the same form as the subject—subjective.

> *The new student = she*
>
> because you say *She* is the new student.

You cannot always rely on the "sound" of the pronoun to determine its correctness. Many speakers and writers incorrectly use an objective-case pronoun after a linking verb, and you may be one of those people who have heard and used the incorrect case so often that it sounds better to you than the correct case. Pay special attention to linking verbs used with pronouns until the correct forms become familiar to you.

3. **Use objective pronouns as the objects of verbs and prepositions.**

> John wanted *him* for the job.

John wanted (who?); the pronoun *him* is the direct object to complete the meaning of the verb. Therefore, the pronoun must be in the objective case.

> Did you address the letter to *him* or *her?*

The preposition *to* is part of the phrase to *him* and *her.* The objects of the preposition are the pronouns *him* and *her.* Therefore, they must both be in the objective case.

If you understand the application of subjective pronouns, using objective-case pronouns will be simplified. If the pronoun is not a subject or subject complement and is not possessive, it will be in the objective case.

4. Use objective pronouns as indirect objects in a sentence.

Ceara showed *him* the letter.

Using the same rationale described above, you can readily see an objective-case pronoun should be used. Because the pronoun is not the subject or a subject complement, it is in the objective case.

Although the preceding four rules dictate the use of personal pronouns in most situations you will encounter in business writing, the following hints will help you determine the correct pronoun in special cases.

Learning Hint 1.   When pronouns are part of a compound subject or compound object, separate them to determine the correct pronoun case.

Will Julie be able to go with (she, her) and (I, me)?

SEPARATE   Will Julie be able to go with *her*?
             Will Julie be able to go with *me*?

Therefore, the sentence should be

Will Julie be able to go with *her* and *me*?

Many people who think they understand pronouns and who never make an error when the pronouns are used separately have great difficulty when pronouns are in a compound. However, when you understand the grammatical property of case, you can see that *her* and *me* must be used since they are objects of the preposition and not subjects or subject complements.

Learning Hint 2.   When pronouns are used with the noun antecedent, omit the noun to determine the correct pronoun case.

Example A: (We, Us) teachers are also ready for a break.

OMIT NOUN—*We* are also ready for a break.

Therefore, the sentence should be

We teachers are also ready for a break.

Example B: You were correct to go along with (we, us) employees.

OMIT NOUN—You were correct to go along with *us*.

Therefore, the sentence should be

You were correct to go along with *us* employees.

Again, using your new knowledge of pronoun case, you can easily see that the pronoun *we* complements the noun *teachers*. Since *teachers* is the subject of the sentence, the pronoun *we* must be in the subjective case. Likewise, *employees* is the object of the preposition *with*. Therefore, the pronoun must be in the objective case—*us*.

Learning Hint 3. A pronoun in an appositive must be in the same case as the word it complements, called the **antecedent**. Mentally replace the noun antecedent with the pronoun from the appositive to determine which case is correct.

> Example A: The assistants, John and (she, her), were given the assignment.
>
> REPLACE NOUN—*She* [was] given the assignment. (In this case, of course, the verb must also be mentally changed to agree with the singular usage.)

Therefore, the sentence should be

> The assistants, John and *she*, were given the assignment.
>
> Example B: The assignment was given to the assistants, John and (she, her).
>
> REPLACE NOUN—The assignment was given to *her*.

Therefore, the sentence should be

> The assignment was given to the assistants, John and *her*.

Even though the sentences seem similar, the pronouns are different. By analyzing the sentences, you will find that the noun *assistants* is the subject of the first example and the object of the preposition in the second example. Therefore, the pronoun appositives must also be in the same case in each example.

Learning Hint 4. When pronouns are used in comparisons with *than* or *as*, complete the thought expressed to determine the correct pronoun case.

(handwritten margin note: Use T22-2 here)

> Example A: Mary was as confused by the idea as (she, her).
>
> COMPLETE—Mary was as confused by the idea as *she was*.

Therefore, the sentence should be

> Mary was as confused by the idea as *she*.
>
> Example B: Poor attitudes upset Mr. Kent as much as (I, me).
>
> COMPLETE—Poor attitudes upset Mr. Kent as much as *they upset me*.

Therefore, the sentence should be

> Poor attitudes upset Mr. Kent as much as *me*.

By analyzing the sentences using your knowledge of clauses, you can see that you actually have two clauses, one independent and one dependent. The problem arises because we shorten the dependent clause and omit the verb. If you mentally add the verb to the dependent clause, you will be able to tell whether the pronoun is the subject of the verb and is in the subjective case or is the object of the verb and is in the objective case.

5. **Use *self* or *selves* endings to show emphasis when the noun or pronoun has already been identified in the sentence.**

I will chair the project *myself.* (intensive)

We asked *ourselves* about chairing the project. (reflexive)

Intensive pronouns emphasize or ''intensify'' the pronoun already used in the sentence. **Reflexive** pronouns ''reflect'' or refer to a noun or pronoun already used in the sentence. These are the only two conditions that use *self* pronouns correctly.

Avoid using these *self*-ending words in situations in which subjective or objective pronouns should be used. Many people use *self* pronouns in other situations. If you are in doubt about whether to use a pronoun ending in *self* or *selves* in a specific situation, you will probably be more correct to avoid the *self* ending.

NO   Tiffany and *myself* will chair the project.

YES   Tiffany and *I* will chair the project.

NO   The project will be chaired by Tiffany and *myself.*

YES   The project will be chaired by Tiffany and *me.*

Some people make up their own *self* pronouns. Be sure you use only those forms that are considered correct; *ourself, themself, theirself,* and *theirselves* are not correct forms.

Posttest

Mark the correct pronoun in each of the following examples:

1. (We, Us) secretaries know that you wanted to increase the benefits.

2. The person responsible for the program was (she, her).

3. The two managers questioned (I, me) about the new employee.

4. I think the legislature's vote to give (they, them, themselves) a raise is a conflict of interest.

5. All the students except (he, him) finished the assignment.

6. Both (they, them) and (we, us) are potential buyers.

7. Dick wants the programmers, Haile and (we, us) to increase productivity.

8. No one was more excited to see him arrive than (I, me).

9. If we continue the project, we will surely put (us, ourselves) in jeopardy.

10. Scott made arrangements for both (he, him) and (I, me) to attend the premiere screening of the movie.

11. Evelyn asked for details about the position before she sent Jan and (I, me) the application.

12. Steve likes the idea of visiting Kiev more than (I, me).

Key: (1) we—*we* renames the subject and is therefore in subjective case; (2) she—use subjective case after a linking verb; (3) me—use objective case for objects of verbs; (4) themselves—refers to the subject already stated; the sentence could also be correct with *them* if the writer were referring to someone other than the subject; (5) him—use objective case as the object of a preposition; (6) they, we—use subjective case as subjects of verbs; (7) us—as an appositive, *us* renames the object and is therefore in objective case; (8) I—complete the comparison *than I was*; (9) ourselves—use *self* pronoun to emphasize the pronoun *we* already used; (10) him, me—use objective-case pronouns as objects of the preposition; (11) me—use objective-case pronoun as the object of the verb; (12)I—complete the comparison *than I do*.

LEVEL A

Name _____

Exercise 22–1

On the line, Write **T** if the statement is true and **F** if the statement is false.

_T_ 1. *Case* refers to the function of personal pronouns within a sentence.

_F_ 2. You can rely on whether the pronoun sounds "right" to determine the correct case.

_F_ 3. *They, he,* and *her* are all examples of objective pronouns.

_T_ 4. A subjective pronoun should always be used after a linking verb.

_F_ 5. Although objective pronouns should be used as objects of verbs and prepositions, subjective pronouns should be used as indirect objects.

_F_ 6. When pronouns are used in a compound phrase, the subjective form should always be used—for example, *Sylvia and I* rather than *Sylvia and me.*

_F_ 7. The pronoun *ourselves* is correct in any sentence if *we* or *us* has already been used in the sentence.

_T_ 8. The pronoun must always be in the same case as the appositive it complements.

_T_ 9. Completing the dependent clause of a comparison involving pronouns will help determine the correct pronoun case.

_F_ 10. The sentence *I would like you to accompany Toni and myself to the party* is correct because *myself* adds emphasis to the pronoun *I* already used in the sentence.

Exercise 22–2

Write **A** if the first pronoun is correct; write **B** if the second pronoun is correct.

_A_ 1. (We, Us) were the only ones available for the meeting.

_A_ 2. The only ones available for the meeting were (we, us).

_A_ 3. The new administrators chosen for the project were (she and I, her and me).

_B_ 4. Cliff asked for permission from both Sondra and (I, me).

_A_ 5. The only successful directors have been Clair and (he, him).

_A_ 6. The researchers, Taylor and (he, him), included data from your project in their report.

_B_ 7. The most-important data were found in the report completed by Willard and (I, me).

_B_ 8. The idea was more acceptable to the teachers than to (we, us).

_A_ 9. We were as successful with the program as (they, them).

_A_ 10. Marilyn and (I, myself) set goals for the entire department.

_A_ 11. Nobody can determine the solution except (them, themselves).

_B_ 12. Just between you and (I, me), let me assure you that Shelley was the cause of the problems.

_A_ 13. Everybody seemed more eager to experiment than (we, us).

_B_ 14. Anton accidentally hurt (him, himself) on the playground and needed stitches.

_A_ 15. Were (they, them) the ones who purchased this home?

_A_ 16. The person you should contact is (she, her).

_B_ 17. Please make reservations for my friend and (I, me) for dinner at 7 p.m.

_A_ 18. I am (he, him), the person who found the purse.

_B_ 19. Important guests like Mr. Minakas and (she, her) should receive special attention.

_A_ 20. You and (he, him) are in the final election.

_B_ 21. Special training is needed for (we, us) secretaries.

_A_ 22. The ones who requested the audit might have been (they, them).

_A_ 23. Are Susan and (she, her) training as medical assistants?

_B_ 24. This information should be kept confidential between you and (I, me).

Exercise 22–3 Indicate the correct pronoun case that should be used in each sentence by writing **S** for subjective case and **O** for objective case.

_S_ 1. Sherman and _____ will introduce you to the team.

_O_ 2. You will be introduced to the team by Sherman and _____ .

_O_ 3. Between you and _____ , we will find the best solution.

_O_ 4. We will find the best solution between you and _____ .

_S_ 5. Do you believe _____ will agree with our decision?

_S_ 6. The new director of the project will be _____ .

_S_ 7. After finishing the textbook, _____ was ready to write the term paper.

_O_ 8. The term paper was completed by _____ .

_S_ 9. The chairs of the department party will be Gary and _____ .

_S_ 10. Gary and _____ will be the chairs of the department party.

_S_ 11. The salespeople were more excited to begin the new project than _____ .

_S_ 12. _____ were more excited to begin the new project than the salespeople.

_S_ 13. The intruders may have been _____ .

_O_ 14. Special customers like Mr. Maroulakis and _____ must be given exceptional consideration.

_O_ 15. The results were presented to _____ employees.

LEVEL B

Name _____

Exercise 22–4 On the line, write the letter of the sentence that uses the correct application of pronoun case.

_b_ 1. *a.* Please congratulate the winner for the president and myself.
  b. The new insurance agents for the company are Mr. Josephs and he.
  c. Please congratulate the winner for the president and I.

_a_ 2. *a.* Please bring the lunch so we men will have something to eat.
  b. Did you mark the package ''Confidential'' specifically for Jake and I?
  c. Only one of the vice presidents—Shanna, Glenn, or her—will be selected for the board.

_c_ 3. *a.* Grades are the things that us students are most motivated by.
  b. The formal presentation given by my assistants, Anna and she, is scheduled for tomorrow.
  c. Grades are the things that most motivate us students.

_a_ 4. *a.* Do you believe he will help himself to the food before the party?
  b. If anyone is chosen as the new representative, it should be him.
  c. He indicates the information will be explained to Marilyn and he before a decision is made.

_b_ 5. *a.* Casandra left her money to her sons, Beau, Clifford, and he.
  b. After completing this assignment, you and I will be free to pursue other projects.
  c. I am more frustrated by this current problem than her.

_b_ 6. *a.* Despite protests from the public, the legislators voted themselfs a raise.
  b. After hearing the rumors, we convinced ourselves that the business was not stable.
  c. Obviously, Mr. Eckers and myself did not agree on the major points.

_b_ 7. *a.* The bonus will be given to he because he was selected as the outstanding employee.
  b. Please make sure the judges, you and she, give the bonus to the one selected as the outstanding employee.
  c. After the awards program, please send a copy of the news release to both the *Tribune* and myself.

_a_ 8. *a.* Gerald asked us, Jeanne and me, to interview the winner of the award.
  b. The new medical-insurance program will benefit new employees more than we.
  c. The new employees will benefit more from the medical-insurance program than us.

_a_ 9. *a.* Our supervisor asked Alice and me to interview the candidates.
  b. Us bank tellers must keep a close watch for counterfeit money.
  c. Could the person who was fired yesterday possibly be her?

_c_ 10. *a.* The open house for the new office was conducted by us, Fred and I.
  b. The late arrivals to the open house were them, Bill and Marshall.
  c. Every applicant except Adam and her was admitted to the program.

_b_ 11. _a._ Frankly, between you and I, let's hope the customers like the new products that were just delivered.
    _b._ The delivery people in that truck looked very much like Nick and him.
    _c._ As soon as the receipt is signed, the items will be delivered by Howard and she.

_c_ 12. _a._ Phyllis invited both Eden and I to the surprise party.
    _b._ The hosts of the party, Barry and her, were very gracious to the guests.
    _c._ At the end of the party, everyone thanked the Johnsons, Barry and her.

_c_ 13. _a._ The classes will be taught by Donna and myself.
    _b._ Our supervisor, Rusty Warner, asked Cord and I to finish the project.
    _c._ They did an excellent job of organizing the seminar themselves.

_c_ 14. _a._ We went to the hospital laboratory on the south side of the hospital ourself.
    _b._ When we arrived, only Ms. Harrison and her were available to do the blood tests.
    _c._ The results of the test were sent to Dr. Mineer by Dr. Giles herself.

Exercise 22–5 Underline each personal pronoun in the following sentences. Mark **C** if all pronouns in the sentence are used correctly and **I** if any pronoun is used incorrectly.

_I_ 1. Roberto was sure <u>he</u> could run the software better with the old computer than <u>her</u>.

_C_ 2. <u>We</u> better choose another restaurant because Eric does not like Mexican food as much as <u>I</u>.

_I_ 3. The computer specialists, Wallace and <u>me</u>, have taught <u>ourselves</u> the new software programs.

_C_ 4. The computer printout includes an expense summary for <u>them</u>, the salespeople in this territory.

_I_ 5. Mr. Gallatin has failed to pay the debt <u>you</u> owed to the creditors, Mr. Lloyd and <u>they</u>.

_I_ 6. The three supervisors—Merrill, Karin, and <u>myself</u>—signed the contract for the loan.

_C_ 7. At the end of the grace period, <u>they</u> and <u>I</u> hoped to have enough money to pay back the debt.

_C_ 8. The executives who voted in favor of the new policy are <u>they</u>.

_I_ 9. The loan was reviewed by <u>we</u> auditors and was found to be correct.

_C_ 10. Since only one administrator attended the conference and received the information, the presenter should be <u>she</u>.

_C_ 11. Could the advocates for the new procedures in <u>our</u> program have been <u>they</u>?

_I_ 12. The professors depended upon <u>we</u> students to finish the assignment this week.

_I_ 13. If <u>you</u> were <u>me</u>, what would <u>you</u> do to resolve the situation?

_I_ 14. Just between <u>you</u> and <u>I</u>, the decision will not be released until next week.

_C_ 15. If <u>I</u> were <u>she</u>, <u>I</u> would be careful about making the investment again.

| **LEVEL C** |

Name _____

Exercise   Write **C** if the pronouns in the sentence are correct and **I** if any pronouns are incorrect.
22–6   Then edit all incorrect pronouns in the sentences.

_I_   1. Neither Monica nor ~~myself~~ heard anything about the excursion. *(I)*

_I_   2. How much do they, Mr. Stewart and ~~him,~~ know about the historical significance? *(he)*

_I_   3. James would enjoy traveling with either Dr. Pine or ~~myself.~~ *(me.)*

_I_   4. Your outstanding achievements please your mother as much as ~~I.~~ *(me.)*

_I_   5. The kindergarten teachers, LuVera and ~~her,~~ were convinced the children understood the lesson. *(she)*

_I_   6. Felicia and I have taught ~~ourself~~ the new software for the computer system. *(ourselves)*

_C_   7. Everyone but you and me was asked to critique the report.

_I_   8. Obviously, you are as busily involved in the project as ~~me.~~ *(I.)*

_I_   9. The company must choose between you and ~~he~~ for the new position. *(him)*

_I_   10. Most major newspapers refuse to print anything negative about ~~theirselves.~~ *(themselves.)*

_C_   11. Where in the city were you and he going when the accident occurred?

_C_   12. Mario tried to give the information to us employees before we left the office.

_I_   13. I would rather give the assignment to Allyson since she is more careful than ~~them.~~ *(they.)*

_C_   14. Among the most-important visitors to the corporation are Linda, Brad, and he.

_I_   15. Two of our vice presidents, Scott and ~~her,~~ were responsible for the new regulations. *(she)*

_I_   16. If you do not understand, please ask Mr. Josephs or ~~I~~ for help. *(me)*

_C_ 17. The first arrivals at the school for the picnic were we teachers.

_I_ 18. Tom will find completing the assignment easier than ~~her~~. *she.*

_I_ 19. The boys who were selected to receive the scholarship are Brad and ~~him~~. *he*

_I_ 20. I understand the award money will be divided between you and ~~I~~. *me.*

Exercise Compose a sentence that fulfills each directive.
22–7

Compo- 1. A sentence correctly using a pronoun ending in *self* or *selves*.
sition

_____

_____

2. A sentence using both a subjective and an objective pronoun.

_____

_____

3. A sentence using a pronoun after a state-of-being verb.

_____

_____

4. A sentence using a pronoun in a comparison with *as* or *than*.

_____

_____

5. A sentence using a pronoun in an appositive.

_____

_____

6. A sentence using a pronoun as the object of the verb.

_____

_____

7. A sentence using a pronoun along with a noun antecedent.

   _____

   _____

8. A sentence using a compound pronoun as a subject.

   _____

   _____

9. A sentence using a compound pronoun as the object of the preposition.

   _____

   _____

10. A sentence using two pronouns as a compound subjective complement.

   _____

   _____

Exercise 22–8

Cumulative Editing

Make any necessary corrections to pronouns, spelling, and punctuation in the following paragraph.

I ~~beleive~~ _believe_ a clear understanding of the ~~begining bookeeper~~ _beginning bookkeeper_ position is important₍ _y_ for both you and ~~I~~ _me_. This understanding will enable us to place ~~ourself~~ _ourselves_ in an ~~accessable~~ _accessible_ situation;and the employers, Mr. Evelyn and ~~him~~ _he_, can better determine our ~~eligable~~ _eligible_ qualifications for ~~permenant~~ _permanent_ employment. Several ~~competancies~~ _competencies_ are ~~neccesary~~ _necessary_ for you and ~~I~~ _me_ to take advantage of this ~~opper-tunity~~ _opportunity_. Besides ~~posessing~~ _possessing_ accounting ability, you and I need ~~excelent~~ _excellent_ communication skills,a ~~helpfull~~ _helpful_ manner, and a ~~noticable comittment~~ _noticeable commitment_ to both ~~they~~ _them_ and us. Although we will be asked about ~~personnel~~ _personal_ qualities and skills,many other employers consider these traits more important than ~~them~~ _they_.

Exercise
22–9

Edit the following paragraphs to correct all connective, punctuation, and pronoun errors.

Cumulative Editing

Our new book, called *Making Your Garden Work,* is ready to be mailed ;and it could reach your home by next week. The information that was gathered both by expert researchers and we~ (*us*) horticulturalists will be informative and profitable for you. Amateur gardeners like yourself~ (*you*) can take advantage of this information (*; s*) simply follow the information in Chapter 2 for vegetable gardens and (*in*) Chapter 3 for flower gardens. Your neighbors may already have taken advantage of our offer. Would you and them~ (*they*) be interested in the investment and (*in the*) secrets of making gardening easier? We are sure you will be as interested as them~ (*they*). You can be the one that will have~ (*with*) the finest garden in the city.

The material has been documented between~ (*among*) florists, farmers, and I~ (*me*), as the editor. You will not only be pleased with the growth but also with the fruits of your labors (*; I*) if not , simply return the book within 30 days ;and we will be happy to return the money you paid or to credit your account.

We are eager to help you as we have helped other valued customers. Our subscribers have more success in gardening than them~ (*they*) who have not used our information. Do not delay , ; send for your copy of our book today. The victors will be both you and us~ (*we*).

Relative pronouns actually perform two functions within the sentence. Like personal pronouns, they substitute for a noun antecedent. In addition, they also show relationships by joining a dependent clause to a main clause in the sentence. These dependent clauses introduced by a relative pronoun are often called *relative clauses*. Table 23–1 shows the cases of the most-common relative pronouns.

As a careful writer, you will want to take care to ensure that the antecedent for the relative pronoun is clear to the reader. You will find as you study this lesson that the antecedent will often help determine which relative pronoun to use.

Use
T23-1
here

Table 23–1

Relative Pronoun Cases

Subjective	Objective	Possessive
who	whom	whose
whoever	whomever	
which	which	
that	that	

Pretest

Mark the sentence **C** if the relative clause is written and punctuated correctly; mark **I** if the sentence is incorrect.

1. The employees which are on vacation have not heard about the new dental insurance plan.

2. Our company procedures manual, that outlines the benefits, has been changed to reflect the new plan.

3. Mr. Lindsay who has the respect of all employees is the best choice for the new position.

4. Please tell us whom you think should receive the bonus.

5. Give the new policy to whomever you wish to take charge of the implementation.

6. The announcer of the program is the one whom we agreed should receive the award.

7. That book which is lying on the table is the one I used for the course.

8. Who do you think should be selected to chair the committee?

Key: (1) I—use *who* to refer to people; (2) I—use *which* to introduce nonrestrictive clauses; (3) I—put commas around the relative clause because it is nonrestrictive; (4) I—use *who* because the pronoun should be in the subjective case; (5) C; (6) I—use subjective-case pronoun *who*; (7) I—use commas around the *which* clause if the clause is nonrestrictive; if the reader will not know what book is being discussed, use *that* for the restrictive clause; (8) C.

Terminology

Nonrestrictive (Nonessential) clause—A clause that is not essential to the meaning of the sentence. Nonrestrictive clauses are set off in the sentence, usually with commas.

Restrictive (Essential) clause—A clause that is essential to the meaning of the sentence. Restrictive clauses are not set off with punctuation.

Rules

Use T23-2 here

1. Use *that* to introduce restrictive clauses and *which* to introduce nonrestrictive clauses.

The accounting book *that* Mr. Dillon uses is the only one with colored examples.

The Irwin accounting book, *which* is on the shelf, has the information you need.

Restrictive clauses are essential to the sentence. If the clause *that Mr. Dillon uses* were omitted from the first example, we would not know which accounting book was the one with colored examples. The second example contains a nonrestrictive clause, however. We can omit the clause *which is on the shelf* and still know which book has the information we need.

Sometimes, restrictive and nonrestrictive clauses can be very similar. Notice the following examples:

The dog *that* has floppy ears can perform tricks.

My dog, *which* has floppy ears, can perform tricks.

In the second sentence, we know which dog is meant without the dependent clause. Therefore, we can omit the *which* clause and the sentence will still make sense. However, the sentence *the dog can perform tricks* may leave some confusion. As the writer, you must take care to be sure your meaning is clear to the reader.

You will also remember from your study of punctuation that restrictive clauses require no punctuation and that nonrestrictive clauses are set off with punctuation, usually commas.

Notice that commas are almost always used with *which* clauses and almost never used with *that* clauses. By using the correct relative pronoun and the correct punctuation (or no punctuation), you give clues to your reader about the nature of the relative clause.

My car, *which has a flat tire*, is in the garage.

The reader will still know what car is in the garage without the clause *which has a flat tire*. However, changing the sentence to read

My car *that has a flat tire* is in the garage.

indicates that I have more than one car and need to explain which one is in the garage by using a restrictive clause.

Learning Hint 1.   Be consistent in using relative pronouns to connect two or more related elements.

NO   The announcement *that* was sent yesterday and *which* requested your response is on your desk.

YES   The announcement *that* was sent yesterday and *that* requested your response is on your desk.

2. Use *who* or *whom* to refer to a person. Use *which* or *that* to refer to a thing.

NO   The person *that* has just been hired is in charge of the project.
     The person, *which* we have just hired, is in charge of the project.

YES   Mrs. Holden, *who* has just been hired, is in charge of the project.
      Mrs. Holden, *whom* we have just hired, is in charge of the project.

You were introduced to the use of relative pronouns in Lesson 20. Although *which* can never be used with people, *that* is sometimes used to indicate a class or type of people. However, in this text, we will use *who* or *whom* exclusively when referring to people to simplify your writing decisions.

The distinction between *who* and *whom* is not related to their use in restrictive or nonrestrictive clauses.

My nephew who is in college speaks Spanish fluently. (restrictive clause)

My nephew, who is in college, speaks Spanish fluently. (nonrestrictive clause)

The first sentence is restrictive since it tells which nephew speaks Spanish. The second example indicates I have only one nephew; therefore, the fact that he is in college is not essential to the rest of the sentence. In both examples, *who* is the correct pronoun to introduce the relative clauses.

The use of *who* and *whom* is related to case rather than to restrictive or nonrestrictive principles. You will recall the uses of subjective and objective cases from Lesson 22. *Who* is a subjective-case pronoun; *whom* is an objective-case pronoun. You should use the same rules you used in your study of Lesson 22 to determine which of these pronouns to use.

Use T23-3 here

Learning Hint 2.   Because the difference between *who* and *whom* or *whoever* and *whomever* may be difficult to determine, you can use the following steps to determine the correct form:

a. Isolate the *who/whom* clause. Ignore the words before the *who/whom* pronoun.

b. Arrange the clause in normal order (subject/verb/complement).

c. Substitute *he* or *him* for the *who/whom* word in question. (Because *he, who,* and *whoever* are all subjective pronouns, they serve the same function. Likewise, *him, whom,* and *whomever* are objective pronouns and function the same way in a sentence.) You might use the mnemonic device that both *him* and *whom* end in *m* and both are objective pronouns.

d. If *he* fits, the correct word will be *who* or *whoever*; if *him* fits, the correct word will be *whom* or *whomever*.

Example A: Did you see (who, whom) conducted the meeting?

a. Isolate the clause. (who/whom conducted the meeting?)

b. The clause is in normal order (subject/verb/ complement).

c. Substitute *he/him.* (**he** conducted the meeting.)

d. Did you see *who* conducted the meeting?

Example B: (Who, Whom) did you ask about the report?

a. Isolate the clause after *who/whom.* (In this case, use the entire sentence.)

b. Arrange in normal order. (you did ask who/whom about the report.)

c. Substitute *he/him.* (You did ask **him** about the report.)

d. *Whom* did you ask about the report?

Example C: We will distribute free samples of the product to (whoever, whomever) comes to the meeting.

a. Isolate the clause. (whoever/whomever comes to the meeting).

b. The clause is in normal order (subject/verb/complement).

c. Substitute *he/him.* (*he* comes to the meeting).

d. We will distribute free samples of the product to whoever comes to the meeting.

You can also implement the process described previously by finding the verbs and determining the subjects of the verbs. If you find the pronoun in question must function as the subject or subject complement of the linking verb, you will know it must be a subjective form—*who* or *whoever*.

Example A: Did you see who/whom conducted the meeting?

The verb *did see* is completed by the subject *you.* The verb *conducted* must be completed by the *who/whom* pronoun. Therefore, the pronoun must be in the subjective case—*who.*

Example B: Who/Whom did you ask about the report?

The only verb *did ask* is completed by the pronoun *you*. Because the verb is action rather than linking, the *who/whom* is not a subject complement. Therefore, the pronoun must be in the objective case—*whom*.

Example C: We will distribute free samples of the product to whoever/whomever comes to the meeting.

The verb *will distribute* is completed by the pronoun *we*. The verb *comes* must be completed by the *whoever/whomever* pronoun. Therefore, the pronoun must be in the subjective case—*whoever*.

Learning Hint 3.   Writers can often omit the word *that* in many clauses without distorting the meaning of a sentence. In fact, to improve the conciseness of a sentence, some writing authorities recommend the word *that* be deleted in most situations in which *that* functions as a subordinating conjunction. Compare the following sentences with and without the word *that*:

WITH	Some writing authorities recommend *that* we delete wordy expressions.
	Ms. Watkins thinks *that* she will reach a decision by next Monday.
WITHOUT	Some writing authorities recommend we delete wordy expressions.
	Ms. Watkins thinks she will reach a decision by next Monday.

Deciding whether to delete *that* from a sentence is largely a writer's option. However, when writers physically delete *that*, it is still part of the sentence—much like the understood-you subject in sentences such as *Do not overload this elevator!* That is, in most instances, a dependent clause still exists—even if *that* is not physically in the sentence:

Some writing authorities recommend (independent clause) we delete wordy expressions (dependent clause introduced with an *understood that* used as a subordinating conjunction).

In general, writers can usually eliminate the wordy *that* in the following situations:

1. When *that* is used to introduce a subordinate clause functioning as the object of a verb.

WITH	Henry says that he is poor.
WITHOUT	Henry says he is poor.

2. When *that* is used to introduce a subordinate clause stating a fact, wish, reason, or cause.

WITH	Jack hopes that he will win the race.
	I wish that Jack had won the race.
	Jack is glad that Jill think so much of him.
WITHOUT	Jack hopes he will win the race.
	I wish Jack had won the race.
	Jack is glad Jill thinks so much of him.

3. When *that* is used to introduce a subordinate clause modifying an adverb or adverbial expression.

WITH	The homeless will sleep anywhere that they can.
WITHOUT	The homeless will sleep anywhere they can.

4. When *that* is used to introduce a subordinate clause that is joined to an adjective or noun subjective complement.

      WITH   Bonnie is positive that she is right.

      WITHOUT   Bonnie is positive she is right.

5. When the subject of a relative clause is different from the referent of the phrase preceding the clause.

      WITH   Carl has the novel that I was reading.

      WITHOUT   Carl has the novel I was reading.

6. When a sentence contains more than one *that*.

      WITH   I told Marshall that the guidelines that he prepared meet with my approval.

      IMPROVED I told Marshall that the guidelines he prepared meet with my approval.

      WITHOUT   I told Marshall the guidelines he prepared meet with my approval.

As your writing proficiency increases, you can make intelligent, writer-option decisions about including *that* in or deleting *that* from a sentence. Two reasonable tests to help you decide whether to include or to delete a *that* are (1) Is *that* used as a subordinating conjunction to introduce a dependent clause? and (2) Does the sentence sound right if *that* is deleted?

Posttest

Mark the sentence **C** if the relative clause is written and punctuated correctly; mark **I** if the sentence is incorrect.

1. Mr. Finelli is not the type of executive which our corporation needs.

2. Business communication is the subject which will be the most beneficial to a new business employee.

3. The person who has the respect of all employees is the best choice for the new position.

4. The woman, who you were talking with, is my economics professor.

5. Please introduce us to the man who you have chosen to be the new president of the corporation.

6. Whom did you appoint as the parliamentarian for the meeting?

7. Paul's garage that is on Seventh East is where I take my car for repairs.

8. We did not know whom the caller could have been.

Key: (1) I—use *whom* to refer to a person when objective case is required; (2) I—use *that* to introduce restrictive clauses; (3) C; (4) I—use *whom* since the pronoun should be in the objective case. The relative clause could be either restrictive or nonrestrictive depending on the number of women who were involved in the conversation; (5) I—use *whom* since the pronoun should be in the objective case; (6) C; (7) I—use a *which* clause with commas around the resulting nonrestrictive clause; however, if Paul has more than one garage, then the sentence is correct; (8) I—use subjective-case pronoun *who*.

LEVEL A

Name _____

Exercise
23–1

On the line, write **T** if the statement is true and **F** if the statement is false.

F 1. Restrictive clauses contain commas because they are essential to the meaning of the sentence.

T 2. Clauses introduced by relative pronouns are known as relative clauses.

F 3. *Who* should introduce clauses in the objective case.

F 4. Clauses involving people may be introduced by either *who/whom* or *which*.

T 5. Nonrestrictive clauses involving inanimate objects should always be introduced by *which*.

F 6. Since both *whom* and *him* are subjective-case pronouns, you may substitute *him* to determine if *whom* is the correct pronoun to use.

T 7. To determine whether to use *who* or *whom*, you need to isolate the relative clause.

T 8. Putting the clause in normal order involves starting with the subject first.

T 9. Nonrestrictive clauses should always be set off with punctuation.

T 10. Relative clauses involving things may be introduced by either *that* or *which*.

Exercise
23–2

Write **A** if the first pronoun is correct; write **B** if the second pronoun is correct.

A 1. (Who, Whom) will be chairing the meeting?

A 2. My mother is the one (who, whom) has given the best advice.

B 3. Charles is the only one to (who, whom) you can go for assistance.

A 4. Give the information to (whoever, whomever) answers the phone.

A 5. Do you know (who, whom) can solve the confusion?

A 6. They are the ones (who, whom) have been assigned to answer the questions.

B 7. The science teacher is the one (who, whom) we can trust.

A 8. We did not know (who, whom) the investigators were.

A 9. Do you know (who, whom) the speaker will be?

B 10. The consultant (who, whom) you sent has been very helpful.

A 11. Did you say they were the guests (who, whom) arrived late?

A 12. A complimentary copy will be sent to (whoever, whomever) requests one.

B 13. No matter (who, whom) you appoint to the program, you are ultimately responsible for its success.

A___ 14. The American Funding Company charges a late fee to (whoever, whomever) they find does not meet the deadline.

A___ 15. Do you know the ones (who, whom) we believe are responsible for the trouble?

A___ 16. Save the most important recognition for (whoever, whomever) has reached the highest achievement.

A___ 17. That man was he (who, whom) was responsible for the positive remarks.

B___ 18. The task will be completed by (whoever, whomever) the supervisor assigns.

B___ 19. Dr. Reed is the person (who, whom) we contacted yesterday.

B___ 20. Ms. Chandler is a consultant (who, whom) we have known for over ten years.

Exercise 23–3 Mark **R** if the bold clause is restrictive and **N** if the bold clause is nonrestrictive to the sentence. All internal punctuation has been omitted.

R___ 1. We have elected the person **who will be the junior class president**.

R___ 2. Economics is the subject **that I enjoy most**.

R___ 3. Ora Lyn is the kind of person **whom we need in the division**.

N___ 4. Cy's grandson **whom we visited yesterday** has just graduated.

R___ 5. The person **whom we visited yesterday** has just graduated.

R___ 6. The colleague **who is in my office** has signed the agreement.

N___ 7. The agreement was signed by Mr. Jonas **who is in my office**.

R___ 8. The equipment **that we ordered** has not yet arrived from the warehouse.

N___ 9. Ms. Lundgren **who edited the newsletter** has agreed to continue for another year.

N___ 10. Would you proofread the Newton contract **which must be ready by morning**.

R___ 11. The funds **that have been earmarked for the planning committee** were deposited in the department account.

N___ 12. The Pulsiphers **who used to own the home** have moved to Idaho.

R___ 13. The agent **who has been working with the conference** is very accommodating to our needs.

N___ 14. Friday's experience **which gave me much stress** turned out to be a good one after all.

R___ 15. Moniece is the one **who we agreed is most qualified to be the office manager.**

N___ 16. Getting ready for the wedding, the bride **who was already late** found she had a flat tire.

R___ 17. The contract **that was signed by Mr. Thatcher** is the one presently in effect.

N___ 18. Your contract **which was signed by Mr. Thatcher** is presently in effect.

LEVEL B

Name _____

Exercise 23–4   On the line within each sentence, write the correct word (*who, whom, which,* or *that*). Then, insert any necessary punctuation.

1. The banquet will honor the person *who* **has served as president of the organization**.
2. Business Communication is the subject *that* **will be the most valuable**.
3. Dr. Seaver is the accountant *whom* **we need in the department**.
4. Mr. Tschudy, *whom* **we referred to a specialist,** will need surgery.
5. The person *who* **was referred to a specialist** will need surgery.
6. The colleague *who* **has been promoted** has mailed the invitations.
7. The invitations have been mailed by Ms. Barber, *who* **has been promoted**.
8. The rule *that* **I consider the most important** is discussed on page 8.
9. The dean *who* **signed the letter** has been reprimanded by the university president.
10. Benjamin's contract, *which* **must be mailed tomorrow,** is still sitting on my desk.
11. Brenda's secretary, *who* **is also her cousin,** requested the audit.
12. Each of the men *who* **will be speaking** has been allotted 15 minutes.
13. The corporation needs a specialist *who* **understands how the computer system operates**.
14. Pat Oyler, *who* **is a systems analyst,** has been called in for a conference.
15. Ms. Perlinski, *who* **used to work for us,** has been hired by your corporation.
16. The dog *that* **frightened the little girl** is really harmless.
17. My chihuahua, Brandy, *which* **frightened your daughter,** is really harmless.
18. To determine *who* **embezzled the funds**, the local police conducted an investigation.
19. Shakespeare, *who* **has been quoted often,** is noted for his classic novels.
20. The law of economics, *which* **involves supply and demand,** is the basis of free enterprise.

Exercise 23–5   Write the letter of the sentence that best uses Lesson 23 guidelines.

_c_ 1. *a.* Marsella is the employee whom we believe represents the company policy best.
    b. The expert, who spoke at our last fraternity meeting, referred to *The Wall Street Journal* article.
    c. Juanita is the one who will deliver the insurance policies.

_c_ 2. *a.* Can you recommend a specialist in the field which can help me?
    b. The finance expert, that I talked with, gave me some good advice.
    c. We refused to pay the pizza driver, who was an hour late.

a 3. *a.* The secretary who has been with the company the longest will get the promotion.
    b. Who do you think we should hire as the project consultant?
    c. The warehouse foreman is the one which ordered the supplies.

c 4. *a.* The announcements, who had been handwritten, were mailed yesterday.
    b. Mr. Nasterny who has been with the company the longest will get the promotion.
    c. I am sure you will never guess whom we saw at the movie.

b 5. *a.* The scholarship should go to whomever has the highest test score.
    b. Mr. Martin is determined to be the one who does the best job.
    c. Mr. Behrman, who I told you about, is the one who helped me the most.

c 6. *a.* The teacher who I told you about is the one who helped me the most.
    b. The portfolio which you mailed to me is not the correct one.
    c. Dr. Kent is the one whom I have asked to accompany me.

a 7. *a.* Education should address all aspects of life that a person is striving to improve.
    b. Our physical needs which are always present often take precedence over our emotional ones.
    c. Learning is anything, that succeeds in changing behavior.

a 8. *a.* Intellectualism is built on the premise that humans are naturally curious.
    b. Animals, who have natural curiosity, must possess intelligence also.
    c. The people, who are gregarious, enjoy being part of a group.

a 9. *a.* The systems analyst who has been assigned the task will not be back to work until Thursday.
    b. My grandmother is the one which I believe I most resemble.
    c. Mr. Loo that has been helping with the conference is very congenial to work with.

c 10. *a.* To determine who we want for the position, we will interview all applicants.
    b. The patient who needs surgery, is sitting in your waiting room.
    c. Mr. Smith, who is in your waiting room, is the one needing surgery.

b 11. *a.* Mr. Rivera asked for our report which included the latest sales figures.
    b. Mark Bailey's latest book, which is on the best-sellers list, has made an impact on the market.
    c. The May issue of the magazine which includes the information is on the table.

a 12. *a.* The vice president who is in charge of production has not yet completed the inventory.
    b. Roger Thomas who is in charge of production has not yet completed the inventory.
    c. The inventory has not yet been completed by the department which is in charge of production.

a 13. *a.* Do you have the manual, which explains the procedures for installing the hard drive?
    b. The manual, that explains the procedures for installing the hard drive, is on Ms. Brunson's desk.
    c. Ms. Brunson has the manual which explains the procedures for installing the hard drive.

b 14. *a.* Mr. Bronson, which signed the letter for Ms. Brett, has recently received a promotion.
    b. The secretary who signed the letter for Ms. Brett has recently received a promotion.
    c. The letter was signed by Mr. Bronson who recently received a promotion.

LEVEL C

Name _____

Exercise 23–6   Mark **C** if the sentence is correct. Mark **I** if the sentence is incorrect. Using your knowledge of Lessons 22 and 23, edit all incorrect pronouns and punctuation of who, which, and that clauses.

_I_   1. Although both Ranee and ~~myself~~ *I* plan to attend the meeting, the directors, Georgina and ~~him~~ *he*, will be out of town at that time.

_I_   2. If you were ~~me~~ *I*, you would be as excited about the new assignment as ~~me~~ *I.*

_I_   3. While we neighbors gathered for the party, our children‚ who were making plans for another party‚ were already at the park.

_C_   4. Charles is the only salesperson whom the president has invited to attend the upcoming board meeting with us executives.

_I_   5. Margaret is the secretary ~~that~~ *who* can be trusted to follow through with the awards banquet for Kelli and ~~she~~ *her*.

_I_   6. Ben‚ who I thought was the most qualified for the position‚ told me he was not interested.

_I_   7. Whoever gets the position will have to choose an assistant between Ron and ~~I~~ *me.*

_I_   8. The software ~~which~~ *that* he listed as his favorite includes educational computer information ~~which~~ *that* may be helpful to ~~we~~ *us* programmers.

_I_   9. The branch office ~~which~~ *that* is in Illinois and that is producing better than the others is the one ~~that~~ Lowell and ~~me~~ *I* will visit next month.

_C_   10. Do you know who would be a better choice for the executive assistant position than Mr. Rossini or he?

_I_   11. Other employees ~~which~~ *whom* we hired at the new warehouse are eager to help Blake and ~~I~~ *me* repair the assembly line.

_I_ 12. I am well acquainted with the architect who designed the sample and ~~that~~ *who* is now

working on an improved model.

_I_ 13. We received their bid, which was the lowest, after the deadline; therefore, Joseph and I

could not consider it.

_C_ 14. That line of clothing does not sell well in sections of the country that have a lot of

sunshine.

_I_ 15. This line of clothing does not sell well in Southern California, which has a lot of sun-

shine.

Exercise 23–7

**Compo-
sition**

Compose sentences that reflect the directives indicated.

1. A sentence using *who* to introduce a relative clause.

   _____

   _____

2. A sentence using *whom* to introduce a relative clause.

   _____

   _____

3. A sentence using *that* to introduce a relative clause.

   _____

   _____

4. Make changes to your sentence 3 so it will now use *which* to introduce the relative clause.

   _____

   _____

As you have already learned from your study of business English, each part of speech has different characteristics and unique potential problems for effective writers to master. The challenge of nouns is that of number. If all nouns were regular and if we formed their plurals by merely adding an *s* to the singular form, this lesson would be unnecessary. Because so many nouns do not follow this normal procedure, you will want to master the rules of plural nouns. As you study this lesson, you will find that many of these rules are familiar to you. Others may not seem so routine.

As we indicated in the unit introduction, many people have difficulty distinguishing between plural and possessive nouns. Once you have answered your questions about plurals, you will then be ready to tackle Lesson 25 to master possessives.

Pretest

Write the plural form of each noun.

1. class　　　　　　　　_____

2. Welch (surname)　　_____

3. community　　　　　_____

4. tooth　　　　　　　_____

5. teaspoonful　　　　_____

6. Ph.D.　　　　　　　_____

7. safe　　　　　　　　_____

8. piano　　　　　　　_____

9. series   _____

10. crisis   _____

11. datum   _____

12. courtesy   _____

13. Dobbs (surname)   _____

14. geese   _____

Key: (1) classes; (2) Welches; (3) communities; (4) teeth; (5) teaspoonfuls (preferred); (6) Ph.D.s; (7) safes; (8) pianos; (9) series; (10) crises; (11) data; (12) courtesies; (13) Dobbses; (14) geese.

Terminology

Compound noun—A noun formed by two words joined into a hyphenated phrase or by separate words with one meaning (_attorney-at-law, vice president_).

Foreign noun—An English word that originated in another language.

Single compound noun—A noun formed by two words joined into a single word (_toothbrush, letterhead_).

Rules

1. **Form the plural of most nouns by adding _s_ to the singular noun.**

   course   course*s*
   corporation   corporation*s*

   Because this rule governs "normal" nouns, you will not find these plurals illustrated in most dictionaries. Many rules exist for forming plurals of the "abnormal" nouns; therefore, you will commonly find the plural forms listed in the dictionary entry for each singular noun.

2. **Form the plural of nouns ending in _ch, sh, s, x,_ and _z_ by adding _es_ to the singular form.**

   lunch   lunch*es*
   wish   wish*es*
   business   business*es*
   box   box*es*

   The preceding two rules are also used to form the plurals of surnames. Because we do not want to change the internal spelling of a person's name, we just add an _s_ or _es_. You have often seen plurals of surnames written with an apostrophe. This method is incorrect, however, when you are indicating plurality rather than possession.

Johnson	Johnson*s*
Henry	Henry*s*
Jones	Jones*es*
Sanchez	Sanchez*es*

3. **Form the plural of nouns ending in a consonant plus *y* by changing the *y* to *i* and adding *es*. For nouns ending in a vowel plus *y*, simply add an *s*.**

secretary	secretar*ies*
factory	factor*ies*
holiday	holiday*s*
valley	valley*s*

4. **Form the plural of some irregular nouns by changing forms or adding endings.**

mouse	mice
woman	women
child	children

Such nouns do not fit a particular grouping, and you must memorize their plurals. Luckily, most of these plurals are already familiar to you.

Use T24-1 here

5. **Form the plural of compound words on the main word of the group, and form the plural of single compound words at the end.**

mother-in-law	mother*s*-in-law
president-elect	president*s*-elect
general manager	general manager*s*
bookcase	bookcase*s*

When using compound words, whether they are written with or without hyphens, you must take special care to make the correct word plural. For example, *mother-in-laws* is not a grammatically correct plural. If the words in the compound seem equal in importance, the last one should contain the plural.

In recent years, the trend has become more flexible in forming plurals. For example, *attorney general* becomes *attorneys general* in the plural form. However, most dictionaries will now show *attorney generals* as a correct plural also. Likewise, *teaspoonful*, once *teaspoonfuls* in the plural form, can also be written as *teaspoonsful*. In this text, however, we will use the preferred plurals, which follow Rule 5.

Learning Hint 1.   Some compound words become verbs if the plural is added to the main word in the group. For example, *write-off* becomes *writes off*—a verb rather than a plural word. In these instances, the plural is formed at the end of the compound—as in *write-offs*.

6. **Form the plural of abbreviations written in capital letters by adding *s*; add *'s* to the abbreviations written in small letters. An *'s* may also be added to show the plural of a word used as a word.**

> I decided to tear up all the *IOUs* from my colleagues. (The abbreviation uses capital letters and will not be confused with the plural *s*.)
>
> The kindergarten class has been studying the *abc's*. (The lowercase abbreviation of *abcs* may be confusing.)
>
> The editor deleted most of the *and's* in the paragraph. (Without the apostrophe, *ands* may be confusing to the reader.)

Although all texts do not agree with this rule of forming plurals of abbreviations, we have chosen this approach to simplify your learning; and this strategy will be followed throughout this text. Occasionally, some capital letters may cause confusion if only an *s* is added (*A, I, M, U*). In these instances, you may prefer to add *'s* to the letter.

7. **Form the plural of words ending in a vowel plus *o* by adding *s*. Form the plural of most words ending in a consonant plus *o* by adding *es*.**

ratio	ratio*s*
studio	studio*s*
hero	hero*es*
potato	potato*es*

This rule has many exceptions, however. Many musical terms end in consonant *o* and just add *s*.

alto	alto*s*
cello	cello*s*
piano	piano*s*

8. **Form the plural of some *f* or *fe* words by changing the *f* or *fe* to *v* and adding *es*. For others, simply add *s*.**

wife	wi*ves*
belief	belief*s*
sheriff	sheriff*s*

These words sometimes create difficulty in determining which ones change forms and which do not. Any words ending in *ff* will simply add *s*. Other words are dependent upon pronunciation. Some words, such as *safe*, become different words when the forms are changed to *saves*.

9. **Memorize the plurals of nouns with foreign origins.**

alumnus	alumni
stimulus	stimuli
analysis	analyses
basis	bases
parenthesis	parentheses
hypothesis	hypotheses

synopsis	synopses
criterion	criteria
bacterium	bacteria
datum	data
addendum	addenda
curriculum	curricula
phenomenon	phenomena
vertebra	vertebrae

Through use, some of these words have an English *s* ending that is now preferred.

	English Plural	**Original Plural**
memorandum	memorandums	memoranda
index	indexes	indices
medium	mediums	media

Many writers now use *data* for both singular and plural constructions. This form has not yet become universal in acceptance, however; and we will consider *data* a plural term in this text. Even though *mediums* is the preferred plural, when the intent is a channel of communication such as television, *media* is still preferred.

10. Distinguish between words that are the same in singular and plural form and those that are only singular or plural.

Singular	**Plural**	**Both Singular and Plural**
news	scissors	deer
mathematics	thanks	moose
arthritis	headquarters	sheep
economics	proceeds	athletics

Your dictionary will be a good source of help when you encounter a word about which you are in doubt.

Posttest

Write the plural form of each noun.

1. brush   _____

2. Richins (surname)   _____

3. journey   _____

4. foot   _____

5. trade-in   _____

6. C.O.D.   _____

7. life   _____

8. veto   _____

9. corps   _____

10. addendum   _____

11. thesis   _____

12. tomato   _____

13. Butters (surname)   _____

14. deer   _____

Key: (1) brushes; (2) Richinses; (3) journeys; (4) feet; (5) trade-ins—*trades in* becomes a verb; (6) C.O.D.s; (7) lives; (8) vetoes; (9) corps; (10) addenda; (11) theses; (12) tomatoes; (13) Butterses; (14) deer.

LEVEL A

Name _____

Exercise 24–1   On the line, Write **T** if the statement is true and **F** if the statement is false.

_F_   1. Like pronouns, nouns change form for number, case, and gender.

_T_   2. The most common way we form plural nouns is by adding *s* to the singular noun.

_F_   3. To avoid changing the spelling of surnames, we form plurals by adding an apostrophe and *s*.

_F_   4. We always form the plural of a singular noun ending in *y* by changing the *y* to *i* and adding *es*.

_F_   5. We form the plurals of musical terms ending in *o* by adding *es*.

_F_   6. We form the plurals of hyphenated compound nouns by adding the plural to the last word in the group.

_T_   7. Some words are the same for both the singular and plural forms.

_F_   8. We form the plurals of most nouns with foreign origin by adding *s*.

_T_   9. Some nouns have more than one correct plural form.

_F_ 10. We always form the plurals of abbreviations by adding *s*.

Exercise 24–2   Mark **S** if the word is singular; mark **P** if the word is plural. Mark **SP** if the word is the same in both singular and plural form.

_P_   1. Ed.D.s

_P_   2. Wilcoxes

_P_   3. pros and cons

_SP_   4. series

_P_   5. errata

_S_   6. alumnus

_P_   7. the's

_S_   8. curriculum

_S_   9. criterion

_P_ 10. bills of sale

_S_ 11. parenthesis

_SP_ 12. sheep

_P_ 13. bacteria

_P_ 14. emphases

_SP_ 15. headquarters

_S_ 16. basis

Exercise 24–3   Mark **C** if the plurals in the sentence are written correctly; mark **I** if the plurals are incorrect.

_I_   1. How many knifes and forks did you find in the drawer?

_I_   2. Have you tried the lunchs in the cafeteria since the new chefs began working?

_C_   3. The data we received yesterday show an increase in sales.

_I_ 4. We must reorder since our stock of radioes is getting very low.

_I_ 5. The front-page story is about the two thiefs who robbed the bank.

_I_ 6. The Mitchell's have not yet picked up their new automobile.

_I_ 7. Space exploration has shown us that the moon has many vallies.

_C_ 8. Do not accept any more C.O.D.s.

_C_ 9. Our attorneys have opened new offices just three blocks from our main branch.

_C_ 10. The news about the current market trends is not positive.

_I_ 11. Both my brother-in-laws have recently changed occupations.

_C_ 12. Their analyses of the situation were determined to be valid for our purposes.

_I_ 13. Next week the James's will move into their new home since the old one has been sold.

_I_ 14. All proceed from our garage sale will be donated to the local charity.

_I_ 15. This shade tree is the first to shed its leafs in the autumn.

_I_ 16. Both the lawns and the bushs outside the building need cutting.

_I_ 17. The Safety Commission is conducting a study to determine how many lifes seat belts can save.

_C_ 18. The scissors in the drawer have a broken handle.

_I_ 19. Had you learned your abcs by the time you started kindergarten?

_I_ 20. In our history class, we have been studying the different territorys that were purchased by the United States.

_I_ 21. All the crisis were solved before Mother and Dad came home from the concert.

_I_ 22. The owners of the corner market are the Thomas'.

_C_ 23. The only criterion we recommended was not approved by the committee.

_C_ 24. The addenda were included in the appendix to the recipe book.

_I_ 25. I asked Bill to build some shelfs for the storage room in my basement.

_I_ 26. Your thanks is all I need to know that you appreciated what I did.

_I_ 27. How many hypothesis did you test in your experimental study?

_C_ 28. I received four memorandums today from Ms. Crenshaw.

_I_ 29. After you have read the article, please tell me which of the two enclosed synopsis is better.

_I_ 30. You often have your choice among commas, parenthesis, or dashes for sentence inter-rupters.

LEVEL B

Name _____

Exercise 24–4 Write the plural form of each singular word.

1. batch   *batches*
2. tomato   *tomatoes*
3. pastry   *pastries*
4. tooth   *teeth*
5. crisis   *crises*
6. genetics   *genetics*
7. go-between *go-betweens*
8. mouse   *mice*
9. mass   *masses*

Exercise 24–5 Write the correct plural form of each bold word in the sentences. Use one line for each word.

tariffs   1. Due to pressure received from special interest groups, high **tariff** were imposed on the imported Japanese **cargo**.

cargoes   2.

statistics   3. The **statistics** presented to the group did not favor the decision of the **authority**.

authorities 4.

sisters-in-law 5. George's three **sister-in-law** are now all active **notary public**.

notaries public 6.

criteria   7. What **criterion** was used in the selection of the new **secretary**?

secretaries 8.

solos   9. The audience applauded until Enrico sang two more **solo** accompanied by the **cello**.

cellos   10.

CPAs   11. Our department **CPA** were the first to notice the **erratum** in the accounts.

errata   12.

stock clerks 13. Kent has asked the **stock clerk** to inventory the **goods** in our Main Street warehouse.

goods   14.

Trumans 15. During homecoming, the **Truman** will attend the assembly for all **alumnus**.

alumni 16.

emphases 17. The Japanese and American Import and Export Offices have added **emphasis** to **balance of trade** and import quotas.

balances of trade 18.

phenomena 19. Samples of many rare **phenomenon** were sent to **laboratory** throughout the nation.

laboratories 20.

Exercise 24–6 Write the letter of the sentence or sentences with correct noun usage. In some cases, more than one sentence may be correct.

b 1. *a.* Our daughter-in-laws and their grandchildren spent their vacation at the beach.
     b. The Us look like the Vs in your state abbreviations and may be read as Vermont instead of Utah.
     c. Our local market deals with all types of goods from teethbrushes to office supplys.

a,b 2. *a.* How much have the prices of tomatoes and potatoes changed over the last five years?
     b. The bookkeepers recently computerized the accounts-payable records.
     c. The committee could not reach a decision because the members had too many different point of views.

a 3. *a.* The headquarters of our office have been moved across town.
     b. I always misspell Mississippi with too many *is*.
     c. The Johnson's have been on vacation for the past six weeks.

a,c 4. *a.* The athletes have swum laps in those swimming pools every day.
     b. The warehouse foremans have completed the requested inventory.
     c. Conflicting analyses of the problems were presented by the experts.

a 5. *a.* The freshmen and sophomores are sponsoring the upcoming proms.
     b. How many employees are entitled to leave of absences this year?
     c. Even though zeros and *O*'s look alike on the typewriter, they are not interchangeable on the computer.

c 6. *a.* Kathleen tore one of her contact lens and had to get it replaced.
     b. During the last three Februaries, I have missed more work than during any other months.
     c. When traveling abroad, you must become familiar with the foreign currencies.

a,b 7. *a.* With our new word-processing center, one secretary can handle the work of four bosses.
     b. Our hunting expedition netted four deer, two moose, and three geese.
     c. I have heard that the Gifford's are remodeling their basement.

a,b 8. *a.* I understand that the McDonald's franchises are extremely expensive.
     b. They require all customers to show their IDs to purchase alcohol.
     c. How many Debbie's do you have in your afternoon class?

LEVEL C

Name _____

Exercise 24–7 Mark **C** if the nouns in the sentence are written correctly; mark **I** if the sentence is incorrect. Then make any necessary corrections.

_I_ 1. When do you expect the ~~Roderick's~~ *Rodericks* to arrive from overseas?

_I_ 2. Our children are using too many ~~maybes~~ *maybe's* in their conversation.

_I_ 3. We will use these old computers as ~~trades-in~~ *trade-ins* when we buy new ones.

_I_ 4. The ~~Bushs~~ *Bushes* are planning to remodel the upstairs of their home next year.

_C_ 5. Why was the opening parenthesis omitted from this parenthetical remark?

_I_ 6. Do you know if either of the ~~propertys~~ *properties* is now up for sale?

_C_ 7. Copies of all correspondence and synopses of all reports are to be filed in my office.

_I_ 8. The ~~a.m.s~~ *a.m.'s* and ~~p.m.s~~ *p.m.'s* in this letter should be keyed in lowercase letters.

_C_ 9. The Foxes are planning to visit New Orleans next year for the Mardi Gras.

_I_ 10. Three ~~attorney-at-laws~~ *attorneys-at-law* have their offices in the Wrigley Building.

_I_ 11. What was the ~~bases~~ *basis* for selecting the new building site on Pioneer Avenue?

_I_ 12. Has the ~~criteria~~ *criterion* for making textbook selections been established?

_C_ 13. How many *the*'s were used in the last paragraph of this form letter?

_I_ 14. Did the dinner guests eat both ~~halfs~~ *halves* of the birthday cake?

_I_ 15. Many writers are unable to use their ~~thats~~ *that's* and ~~whiches~~ *which's* correctly.

_C_ 16. How many cupfuls of flour does that new recipe need?

_I_ 17. Do you think many ~~storeses~~ *stores* in this mall will be open tonight?

_I_ 18. Please have the ~~bookcase~~ *bookcases* moved to our new conference room.

_I_ 19. Three ~~diagnosis~~ *diagnoses* were included in the report sent to Ms. Bartok's doctor.

_I_ 20. The children had been spoiled so long they had learned to be real ~~shows-off.~~ *show-offs.*

_I_ 21. Both the 1980 and 1990 ~~census~~ *censuses* revealed increased growth throughout the state.

_I_ 22. The ~~itinerarys~~ *itineraries* for my Chicago and Portland trips arrived on the same day.

_C_ 23. The proxies on the vote were all received by last Friday.

_C_ 24. How many courts-martial were performed during the Civil War?

_C_ 25. The recipe called for two teaspoonfuls of salt, but I added only one.

_I_ 26. The six ~~thesis~~ *theses* that have been written this year were reviewed by the committee.

Exercise 24–8

Cumulative Editing

Edit the following paragraphs to correct all errors from your knowledge of Unit 3 punctuation, Unit 4 connectives, and Lessons 22 through 24 plurals and pronouns.

Your awareness ∧*of* and interest in our new ~~industrys~~ *industries* is satisfying to us. Many other people~~s~~ who live in Utah and Salt Lake ~~vallies~~ *valleys* ⨍ have added positive comments. Large ~~quantitys~~ *quantities* of mail have been received in our ~~branchs~~ *branches* all over the country. Other ~~companys~~ *companies* ~~which~~ *that* have followed our lead have received exciting results from their initial ~~analysises~~ *analyses* of their ~~surveyes.~~ *surveys.* Our promise to our ~~customer's~~ *customers* is that we will continue to be among the ~~trends-setter at~~ *trendsetters in* the field. Anyone~~s~~ ~~whom~~ *who* has worked with ~~we~~ *us* leaders ⨍ knows our commitment to you is strong.

Please contact our representatives in your area, the ~~Krebs's. While~~ *Krebses. Although* we can answer some questions, your personal sales representatives can provide details ~~in regard to~~ *about* places where specific help is ~~at.~~ *available.* The best ones to tell ~~your~~ *you* of our successes are ~~them.~~ *they.* They have brochures about upcoming ~~activitys~~ *activities* ~~which~~ *that* may be of interest to the ~~familys~~ *families* in your area.

You have learned about subjective- and objective-case pronouns. In this lesson, we will study the possessive case. Our study will include not only pronouns but also nouns. One of the challenges of English grammar is the fact that an *s* is used to make words both plural and possessive.

Possessive nouns and pronouns are used to show ownership. The alternative to the possessive form is the use of prepositional phrases. Although prepositional phrases may be a better choice in some instances, they are more wordy and cumbersome in most writing. For example, notice the difference in the following sentences:

> *The office of Dr. Murphy* seemed ominous as the *upcoming operation of the patient* was discussed with *the family of the patient.*

> *Dr. Murphy's office* seemed ominous as the *patient's upcoming operation* was discussed with *his family.*

As you can readily see, possessive nouns and pronouns are helpful in effective writing because the message is not only shorter but also easier to follow. However, the misuse of possessive case is a common red flag of illiteracy. Many people do not understand the difference between plurals and possessives and simply add apostrophes at random. Two actual signs seen recently illustrate the point:

Womens Health Care Clinic (new plural of *women*?)

Keep *Animal's* on Leash (what part of the animal?)

In both instances, readers can easily see that those involved in the preparation of these signs have much to learn about using the possessive case. As you study this lesson, keep in mind what you know about plurals and resolve to master the differences so your own writing will be free of these red flags.

Pretest

Mark the sentence **C** if the possessive nouns and pronouns are correct. Mark the sentence **I** if any possessive form is incorrect, and then correct the error.

1. We have to put down a two months' deposit for the apartment.

2. Both the mens' and the ladies' departments are located on the second floor of the store.

3. Do you believe Charles's new car was more damaged in the accident than Bettys?

4. Has your mother's-in-laws home been sold?

5. The professor and secretary's offices were both redecorated.

6. I was concerned about Cord resolving to change his attitude.

7. Our geography book was called *The World and It's People*.

8. The corporation's consultant's suggestions should be implemented.

Key: (1) C; (2) I—*men's*; (3) I—*Charles'* and *Betty's*; (4) I—*mother-in-law's*; (5) I—*professor's*; (6) I—*Cord's*; (7) I—*Its*; (8) I—*suggestions of the corporation's consultant*.

Terminology

Compound noun—A noun formed by two words joined into a single word, by two words joined into a hyphenated phrase, or by separate words with one meaning (*courtroom, attorney-at-law, vice president*).

Gerund—A verb form ending in *ing* used as a noun.

Joint ownership—Two or more owners possessing something together.

Possessive case—The form of a noun or pronoun used to show a person or thing owning or possessing something.

Separate ownership—Two or more owners possessing items separately.

Rules

Use T25-1 here

1. **Form the possessive of a noun not ending in *s* by adding an apostrophe and *s*; form the possessive of a noun ending in *s* by adding only an apostrophe.**

   The personnel director evaluated ten *applicants'* resumes for the *executive's* position.

   When you understand this one rule, you can form most possessive nouns correctly. Many people have the mistaken belief that possessives are formed by adding apostrophe *s* to singular words and an apostrophe to plural words. Although this rule is correct in many instances, it does not work in all situations. Compare the singular and plural possessives of these words:

Singular	Singular Possessive	Plural	Plural Possessive
student	student's	students	students'
boss	boss'	bosses	bosses'
business	business'	businesses	businesses'
alumnus	alumnus'	alumni	alumni's

As you can see, forming the possessive case is related to whether the word already ends in *s* (as stated in Rule 1) rather than whether the word is singular or plural.

Learning Hint 1.   Follow the same procedure outlined in Rule 1 to form the possessive of names. If the name already ends in *s*, add only an apostrophe. Some books indicate that you should add apostrophe and *s* to words and names ending in *s* if the possessive form is pronounced with an additional *s* sound. We have chosen to simplify your writing decisions, however, by consistently using Rule 1 in all instances.

Sandra	Sandra's
Charles	Charles'
Lois	Lois'
Ms. Simmons	Ms. Simmons'

Use T25-2 here

Learning Hint 2.   When you understand how to add the possessive case, your next challenge is to determine which word should contain the possessive form. Ownership may be shown in two ways: by using the possessive case and by using prepositional phrases. Therefore, you can mentally change the sentence to a form using a prepositional phrase to determine if a possessive noun or pronoun is appropriate. If you are unsure whether you have a possessive situation, use these steps to help you:

1. Create a prepositional phrase to find the ownership word. If the prepositional phrase makes sense, you know you have a possessive situation.

2. Look at the ownership word to determine whether it already ends in *s*. Then apply Rule 1.

Example: Give your boss thirty days notice before quitting.

(Should *thirty days notice* be possessive?)

1. Create a prepositional phrase—*notice of thirty days*.
Since the phrase makes sense, you know you have a possessive situation.

2. Look at the ownership word and apply Rule 1.
Since *days* ends in *s*, the possessive form should be *days'*.

Give your boss thirty *days'* notice before quitting.

Learning Hint 3.   Some texts distinguish which words can be made possessive. These books contain rules about which inanimate objects may show possession and which cannot. However, in this text, we stipulate that all nouns have the potential to become possessive if something is owned.

the *car's* motor

the *computer's* keyboard

Learning Hint 4.   Sometimes the thing owned may be omitted from the sentence. By mentally completing the thought, you can ascertain the ownership word.

Tom's desk was moved to the west side by *Cliff's*.

Even though the item owned by Cliff is not included, you can complete the thought.

Tom's desk was moved to the west side by *Cliff's* [*desk*].

Use
T25-3
here

2. **Write all possessive personal pronouns without an apostrophe.**

Your dog wagged *its* tail when the visitors arrived with *their* snacks.

Many writers confuse possessive personal pronouns with contractions. If the intent is to show ownership, no apostrophes should be used. Compare the following words that are often confused:

The program is known for *its* objectivity, and *it's* being continued for another season. (*its*—possessive pronoun; *it's*—contraction for *it is*)

You're to be commended for *your* effort in solving a potential problem. (*you're*—contraction for you are; *your*—possessive pronoun)

They're leaving *their* boots out *there* on the porch. (*they're*—contraction for *they are*; *their*—possessive pronoun; *there*—a place)

Whose luggage are you using for the trip; and *who's* accompanying you? (*whose*—possessive pronoun; *who's*—contraction for *who is*)

Learning Hint 5.   Some indefinite pronouns are written with apostrophes. (Does *anyone's* book show the correction on page 4?) Most often, indefinite pronouns include *else*; and the possessive is formed at the end. (Does *everyone else's* book also show the correction?)

3. **Form the possessive of a compound noun by adding** *'s* **to the end.**

My *sister-in-law's* office is downstairs.

Your *stepchild's* report card has improved.

Remember that the plural of a compound is formed by adding the *s* to the main word in the group. But the possessive form will always be added to the last word or the end of the single compound. For a plural possessive compound word, you may find the *s* sound to be repetitive.

My *sisters-in-law's* offices are downstairs.

Your *stepchildren's* report cards have improved.

4. **To show joint ownership, add the possessive to the last owner; to show separate ownership, add the possessive to each owner.**

Judy and Marla's apartment needs cleaning.

Judy's and Marla's apartments need cleaning.

Notice the difference in the two examples. Look at the thing owned (in this case *apartment*) to give you a clue about ownership. Because the first example shows only one apartment, the reader can quickly determine that Judy and Marla own it together. Because the second example shows two apartments, the reader assumes that each person is a separate owner.

Learning Hint 6.   When pronouns are used in joint or separate ownership, be sure the pronoun is in the possessive form.

NO   They wanted to see *Jerry and I's* masterpiece.

YES   They wanted to see *Jerry and my* masterpiece. (joint ownership)
They wanted to see *Jerry's and my* masterpieces. (separate ownership)

5.   Use a possessive-case noun or pronoun before a gerund.

NO   The president was unhappy with *them leaving* early.
I appreciate *Roberta taking* the time to help me.

YES   The president was unhappy with *their leaving* early. (possessive pronoun)
I appreciate *Roberta's taking* the time to help me. (possessive noun)

The rationale of this rule is that the emphasis in these examples is on the action rather than on the person. The president was unhappy about the act of leaving, not unhappy about the people. You specifically appreciate the time she took rather than appreciating Roberta.

6.   Use a prepositional phrase rather than a possessive form to avoid an awkwardly constructed sentence.

NO   The party will take place at *a friend of mine's house.*
The editor in chief's secretary's telephone is ringing.

YES   The party will take place at *the house of a friend of mine.*
The telephone of the editor in chief's secretary is ringing.

Some complex ideas may result in awkward-sounding sentences. To avoid this problem, we may decide that prepositional phrases are better choices than possessive constructions. Simplicity is, after all, the best approach to clear writing.

Posttest

Mark the sentence **C** if the possessive nouns and pronouns are correct. Mark the sentence **I** if any possessive form is incorrect, and then correct the error.

1. The express mail finally arrived after a weeks delay.

2. The husbands and wives club held monthly activities at the Country Club.

3. His responsibilities are no different from any other executive.

4. The notaries public's signatures were necessary on all forms.

5. Dr. Richards' and Mrs. Barker's offices are being moved upstairs.

6. The possibility of him arriving on time was discussed.

7. Mario was certain that your going to win the election.

8. The decision was based on my consultant's, Mr. Howsers, advice.

Key: (1) I—*week's*; (2) I—*husbands and wives'*; (3) I—*executive's*; (4) C, *notary publics'* is also correct; (5) C; (6) I—*his*; (7) I—*you're*; (8) I—*on the advice of my consultant, Mr. Howser.*

LEVEL A

Name _____

Exercise 25–1   On the line, write **T** if the statement is true and **F** if the statement is false.

_T_ 1. Possessive forms of nouns and pronouns are used to show ownership.

_T_ 2. Possession of nouns may be shown by the use of apostrophes or prepositional phrases.

_F_ 3. We form the possessive form of all singular nouns by adding *'s* to the nouns.

_F_ 4. Because all plural nouns already end in *s*, we make their possessive forms by adding just an apostrophe.

_F_ 5. Regardless of whether a name ends in *s*, we write the possessive form by adding *'s* to the name.

_T_ 6. If you are unsure whether a word should be in the possessive case, rearranging the sentence using a prepositional phrase will help.

_F_ 7. If the possessive form is to be used, the ownership word will always precede the thing owned.

_T_ 8. Possessive personal pronouns are always written without apostrophes.

_F_ 9. We show joint ownership by making both owners possessive.

_T_ 10. Sometimes we should prefer prepositional phrases over possessives to avoid awkward-sounding sentences.

_F_ 11. Possessive-case pronouns are not usually used with gerunds.

_F_ 12. We add *'s* to the main word to form the possessive of a compound noun.

Exercise 25–2   Mark **C** if the possessive nouns and pronouns in the sentence are written correctly; mark **I** if the sentence contains any incorrect possessive nouns or pronouns.

_I_ 1. Reading the report, the policeman asked if the stolen car was your's.

_C_ 2. I read in the newspaper that the Henries' home burned down last week.

_C_ 3. The artists' studios were desperately in need of new wallpaper.

_I_ 4. The repairman just arrived to fix Laurel and Chari's computers.

_C_ 5. At the recent concert, Hailey and Brian's duet won the top award.

_I_ 6. My brother's-in-laws farm is expanding to include animals as well as plants.

_I_ 7. Todays' inflationary prices are increasing faster than my salary.

_I_ 8. The Fox's vacation to Mexico had to be postponed since Kate's accident.

_I_ 9. My favorite place to shop is the womens' department at the mall.

_I_ 10. After reading your report, I can see that the project is well on it's way to success.

_I_ 11. The lease has been rewritten, and your next months' rent is due on the 10th.

_I_ 12. I know the fault is not our's, but do you really think it is theirs?

_C_ 13. Dr. Johnston and Dr. Bertleson's new book will be in the bookstores by the end of the month.

_I_ 14. That error is somebody elses, so don't blame me for the problem.

_C_ 15. All our children's clothing is now located on the second floor upstairs.

_I_ 16. Maxine's and Dan's home was recently sold for $2,000 more than they thought possible.

_I_ 17. The Appleton's automobile was totaled in the accident on I-15 during the snowstorm.

_I_ 18. The advancement of technology makes yesterdays' fiction often become tomorrow's facts.

_C_ 19. Have your daughters-in-law's businesses been merged into one corporation?

_I_ 20. I want to indicate to you that your well on your way to a promotion within the next six months.

Exercise 25–3 Mark **'s** or **s'** to show how the possessive form of the bold word should be made.

_s'_ 1. The four board **member** secretaries acted as tour guides during the grand opening.

_s'_ 2. The **accountant** plan is to computerize their records using the new software that was just installed.

_s'_ 3. My attorney is filing a suit because the company still owes me two **week** salary.

_s'_ 4. The **girl** shoe department now includes stockings and other accessories.

_'s_ 5. Our new building may not be ready on time because we have already had a **month** delay in beginning construction.

_'s_ 6. Both my **sisters-in-law** diamond rings have been lost in the last month.

_'s_ 7. **Yesterday** office procedures are quite different from those followed now.

_s'_ 8. Alex surpassed all our **racer** times in the marathon last week.

_s'_ 9. Three members of the **teacher** association agreed to support our proposal.

_'s_ 10. Everyone **else** luggage arrived on time; mine was the only one that was lost.

_s' or 's_ 11. Both the **computer** drives crashed within the last week, and my information is lost.

_'s_ 12. Were the results in the **textbook** index helpful to you in your research?

_'s_ 13. My living room furniture is more classic in design than **Nan**.

_s'_ 14. Wall Street in New York City is considered to be the heart of the **nation** financial district.

_s'_ 15. When I moved into my new apartment, I had to pay first and last **month** rent.

_'s_ 16. I don't believe his opinion on the project is better than **anyone else**.

_s'_ 17. Her photo album includes more pictures of the vacation in Israel than the **Holdaway**.

LEVEL B

Name _____

Exercise
25–4

Write the singular possessive form, the plural form, and the plural possessive form for each of the nouns.

Singular	Singular Possessive	Plural	Plural Possessive
1. wife	*wife's*	*wives*	*wives'*
2. salesperson	*salesperson's*	*salespeople* *salespersons*	*salespeople's* *salespersons'*
3. crisis	*crisis'*	*crises*	*crises'*
4. attorney-at-law	*attorney-at-law's*	*attorneys-at-law*	*attorneys-at-law's*
5. diagnosis	*diagnosis'*	*diagnoses*	*diagnoses'*
6. criterion	*criterion's*	*criteria*	*criteria's*
7. itinerary	*itinerary's*	*itineraries*	*itineraries'*
8. foot	*foot's*	*feet*	*feet's*
9. alley	*alley's*	*alleys*	*alleys'*
10. trustee	*trustee's*	*trustees*	*trustees'*
11. stimulus	*stimulus'*	*stimuli*	*stimuli's*
12. datum	*datum's*	*data*	*data's*
13. runner-up	*runner-up's*	*runner-ups*	*runner-ups'*
14. bookshelf	*bookshelf's*	*bookshelves*	*bookshelves'*
15. thesis	*thesis'*	*theses*	*theses'*

Exercise
25–5

Write the letter of the sentence or sentences with correct usage of possessive nouns and pronouns. In some cases, more than one sentence may be correct.

___b___ 1. *a.* The Rosses plane should arrive on time tomorrow from London.
     b. My father-in-law's business is located on the corner of Pennsylvania Street and Washington Avenue.
     c. Your organization dues include a years subscription to the monthly magazine.

___b,c___ 2. *a.* This companys financial position is questionable and should be checked further before any money is invested.
     b. Dawn and Karen's horse won first place in the county fair.
     c. Both my mother's and father's cars are in the repair shop.

___b,c___ 3. *a.* Please adjust the antenna since the televisions reception is very poor.
     b. My tooth's filling has fallen out; I must call the dentist.
     c. When I bought my new Honda, I did not notice that the new car's tires are very worn.

_a_   4. *a.* According to our latest figures, it's quite possible the contributions will exceed our goal.
  b. We want to keep all contributions confidential; I will appreciate receiving yours' personally at my home address.
  c. Did you realize that Sydnee's recent back surgery was more serious than our's?

_b,c_   5. *a.* The store manager has moved the ladies suits to the first floor.
  b. Martha and Don's computer must be upgraded before it can run the new software programs.
  c. Mr. Gosset helped support both his sons-in-law's wives while they finished their degrees.

_b,c_   6 *a.* Our supervisors' office is next to the elevator on the east side of the building.
  b. My new office is on the top floor next to the president's.
  c. If I were you, I would check the project's list of workers carefully.

_c_   7. *a.* The new editors' stories pleased his readers greatly.
  b. The two chiropractor's offices are located on the seventh floor.
  c. The dentist's assistant has been very helpful in filing my insurance papers.

_a_   8. *a.* The boys' sweaters were torn as the boys tried to crawl under the fence.
  b. The psychiatrists' office hours were clearly posted on her door.
  c. The chairman's status report included details on Raymond and I's proposed improvements to the department policy.

_c_   9. *a.* His brothers-in-law's reports are sent to a different vice president than yours'.
  b. The most valuable possession possible is a persons health.
  c. The employees' handbook was used for several months before the errors about benefits and vacation policies were noticed.

_a,c_ 10. *a.* Four former presidents' wives gathered at the White House for an afternoon tea.
  b. The sailors were told to be ready to ship out at a moments notice.
  c. Frank was not pleased with his wife's hair color and told her hairdresser.

_b_ 11. *a.* Mr. Morris's manager has been transferred to the San Diego office.
  b. The Revills' and Guymons' cabins are next to each other by the lake.
  c. Who's downtown store is having its sidewalk sale next week?

_c_ 12. *a.* Was your opportunity for advancement in this firm as good as it was in theirs'?
  b. Sydnee's and Morgan's duet was the hit of the recital that was held last week.
  c. Your brother and sister's business appears to be very successful.

_b,c_ 13. *a.* Aunt Ivies husband's friend recently visited us during our open house.
  b. Everyone else's positions seem more exciting and productive than ours.
  c. I understand your leaving the company has nothing to do with the new president.

_c_ 14. *a.* Have you had a chance to read Julie's and I's proposal for the conference?
  b. Ross's proposal seems to be the one that is most popular with management.
  c. I believe we will be successful if we accept her and Brooks' offer.

_a_ 15. *a.* Mr. Erickson and Ms. Rasmussen's course has received rave reviews from the participants.
  b. When your secretary's finish keying the report, will you please mail it to me?
  c. I cannot believe he expects us to change our plans with only five minutes notice.

LEVEL C

Name _____

Exercise   Mark **C** if the sentence is written correctly; mark **I** if any possessive nouns or pronouns
25–6   are incorrect. Then add the apostrophes and other necessary corrections.

_I_   1. Since Mrs. Jones' purse was stolen from her office, we are issuing keys for the desks.

_I_   2. Hans believes *you're* ~~your~~ the winner of the sales contest sponsored by the central office.

_I_   3. The children's requests for new playground equipment have been denied again this year.

_I_   4. A file of her current cases can be found in Ms. Thatcher's desk.

_C_   5. Our plan to initiate a new sales campaign this fall is more concrete than theirs.

_I_   6. Both the buyer's and the seller's *(or buyers' and the sellers')* signatures must be notarized on the contract.

_I_   7. The personnel managers' convention will be held in Dallas.

_C_   8. Please put the new typewriter ribbons in the desk's bottom drawer.

_C_   9. Our corporation is proud of its reputation for prompt service and dependability.

_I_   10. The testimony of all four witnesses supported the defendant's *(or defendants')* position.

_I_   11. Our community's resources have been combined to help us solve the drought problem.

_I_   12. Mr. Fillmore gave only a day's notice before he left the company for another job.

_C_   13. *The Herald Examiner*, Los Angeles' afternoon newspaper, includes a detailed story on James' accident.

_I_   14. Dr. McCarthy is not happy with Larry's coming late to her class each day when Larry seems to be on time for ~~your's~~. *yours.*

_I_   15. The experiences in today's business world are different from those in our ancestors' days.

_I_   16. The two editors in chief's remarks were published on the last page.

_I_   17. Mrs. Fletcher's appointment was at 9 a.m., but she arrived at 8:30 in time for ours.

_I_   18. The ten days' extension given on the contract has expired, and Becca's car will be repossessed at the same time as Paige's.

_I_   19. Some people believe *their* ~~there~~ only chance for success is at somebody else's expense.

_I_   20. Jessica became frustrated when she compared her achievements to Clark's and my ~~I's~~ records.

Exercise   Edit the following sentences by changing the bold prepositional phrases to possessive
25–7   forms.

1. The *teacher's textbooks* ~~textbooks of the teacher~~ were stacked on the floor beneath the bookcase.

2. Some of the *students' achievements* ~~achievements of the students~~ will be announced at the awards banquet.

class' appreciation

3. The **appreciation of the class** was expressed to all those guests present.

organization's members

4. Many **members of the organization** were pleased with the turnout for the event.

children's and adults' programs

5. The new format will be appealing for **programs of children and adults.**

faculty's and staff's offices

6. The **offices of the faculty and staff** must be cleaned before the new semester begins next

month.

agreement's language

7. The **language of our agreement** is too difficult for anyone without a law degree to understand.

New Year's resolutions

8. Are your **resolutions for New Year** going to last any longer than mine?

Exercise 25–8 Rewrite the following sentences to avoid awkwardly worded sentences.

1. The form has been filed in my attorney's, Mr. Rothgin's, office.

    The form has been filed in the office of my attorney, Mr. Rothgin.

2. Did you know Shelley's daughter's party is being held at my friend's, An Li's, house?

    Did you know the party of Shelley's daughter is being held at the house of my friend, An Li?

3. The Fourth of July's fireworks' display began at 9:30 and continued for at least 45 minutes.

    The fireworks' display on the Fourth of July began at 9:30 and continued for at least 45 minutes.

4. Mr. Olson's wife's piano has a beautiful walnut-wood finish.

    The piano of Mr. Olson's wife has a beautiful walnut-wood finish.

5. Do you agree with Allyson's company's motto for beating the competition?

    Do you agree with the motto of Allyson's company for beating the competition?

6. One of my friends' daughters was recently given a promotion to vice president of public relations.

_____

_____

Exercise 25–9   Edit the following document to correct any misuse of nouns or pronouns using principles you learned in Unit 5.

Cumulative Editing

Today's public relations professionals pursue an expanded and more ethical role than the

media and ~~them~~ *they* did a few decades ago. P. T. Barnum's philosophy was ''a sucker is born every

minute,'' and his practices exhibited ~~him~~ *his* taking advantage of the public's naivete. Public rela-

tions' disreputable beginning in its early eras has caused many people to distrust the profession-

als and misunderstand their role in modern business. Ivy Lee, ~~which~~ *who* is often called the ''Father

of Public Relations,'' instilled a more positive image for the Rockefeller family. Regardless of

Lee's success, others blamed public relations for coverups; and the negative reputation continued.

Some public relations' practitioners want to distinguish ~~theirselves~~ *themselves* from the fraud's by

licensing to define public relations as a profession. Those ~~who's~~ *whose* licensing requirements were

greatest are those ~~which~~ *who* intend to work as an individual's or organization's counselor. Although

licensing procedures will help define the practice, opposer's of the idea argue that society's pro-

tection does not hinge on ~~it~~ *its* being imposed on the public.

Exercise 25–10   Edit the following sentences to reflect the principles you learned in Units 3, 4, and 5 involving punctuation, connectives, and nouns and pronouns.

Cumulative Editing

1. Kellogg is introducing a new children's cereal, which is called Bigg Mixx, in an effort to increase

   ~~their~~ *its* market share; however, ~~it is too early to~~ *only time will* tell whether the product will have a positive

   impact.

2. If our company ~~concentrate their~~ *concentrates its* efforts on the current, successful products instead of *on* new

   ones, ~~they are~~ *it is* more likely to achieve ~~their~~ *its* goals.

3. In many urban schools, teachers do not have high regard ~~and~~ *for* expectations of their students,; this *attitude* results in low confidence in ~~them~~ *students* to succeed.

4. The students pick up on this lack of confidence, and end up performing to their teachers low expectations of them, and ~~they~~ develop no confidence (either in ~~theirselves~~ *the students themselves* or their peers.

5. Today, ~~not only are firms~~ *firms are not only* requiring clients to pay fees and expenses in advance but ~~they are~~ also tightening up their contracts' language.

6. ~~While~~ *Although* some governments have liberalized trade regulations by eliminating or reducing tariffs on most imported products, this *practice* has increased their gross domestic product, *has increased their* employment, and has decreased the public deficit.

7. The homeowner ~~which~~ *who* is already having difficulty must lower the price of the home to sell it and to get away from a house payment, that is probably too steep.

8. The banks' problems with property loans ~~are where~~ *occur when* defaults have increased; consequently, vacancy for office spaces ~~have~~ *has* increased in just a few years.

9. The keys to the solution ~~is~~ *are* public awareness, ~~providing~~ community workshops, and teamwork ~~between~~ *among* the three sectors of state and local governments, the federal government, and *the* private sector.

10. Alana was fired after she questioned all ~~of~~ managers' decisions ~~in regard to them~~ *about* reading electronic messages ~~between~~ *among* employees.

11. The lawsuit ~~which~~ *that* has been filed will probably be the first legal test of electronic privacy,; ~~which~~ *this situation* raises issues that will have widespread consequences ~~at~~ *in* the future.

12. In today's society of extremely competitive markets, ~~it is becoming evident that~~ the demand for lawyers' services is changing; and ~~they~~ *attorneys* are catering ~~toward~~ *to* their clients' wants.

LESSONS IN THIS UNIT

26. SUBJECT-VERB AGREEMENT
27. PRONOUN-ANTECEDENT AGREEMENT AND REFERENCE

Throughout our study of business English, we have separately considered nouns, pronouns, and verbs along with their unique characteristics. We are assuming you have mastered these grammar principles and will now be able to combine these parts of speech so they will "agree." In grammar, the term *agreement* means that elements of the sentence are in harmony. Hopefully, you have mastered the red flags of agreement illiteracy to the degree that you realize *it don't* and *he done* are incorrect. However, many agreement errors are very common with beginning (and even some advanced) writers.

You have learned that pronouns have four properties. Agreement affects three of these: person, number, and gender. In your study of verbs, you learned the five properties of verbs. Of these, person and number are involved in agreement. Your study of nouns included number (singular and plural); this property is of great importance in subject-verb agreement.

Remember from your study of Unit 1 that subjects and verbs are the two essential parts of a sentence and that subjects can be either nouns or pronouns. For a sentence to be clear, these essential elements must agree in number and person. For example, notice the difference between these sentences:

Mr. Rodriquez *sends* the notification.

Mr. and Mrs. Rodriquez *send* the notification.

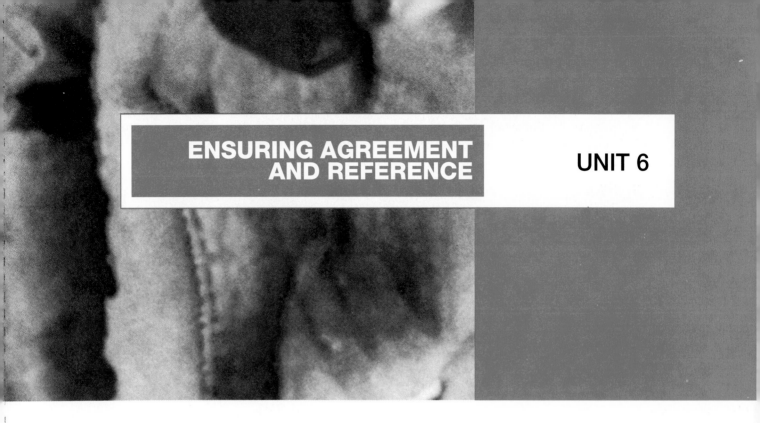

Often, you use verbs because they "sound right" in the situation. However, many times this informal approach will be inappropriate. Lesson 26 includes the principles of agreement of subjects and verbs. You will want to pay close attention to those principles that are unfamiliar to you. Nonagreement of subjects and verbs is one of the most-common red flags that separate poor writers from good ones.

After you are sure the subjects and verbs in the sentence are in agreement, you will want to turn your attention to the other parts of the sentence. Another important agreement principle is making pronouns agree with their antecedents. From your study of pronouns, you should remember that antecedents are the nouns to which the pronouns refer. Consider the antecedents of the following sentences:

Mrs. Rodriquez sends the notification from her office.

Mr. and Mrs. Rodriquez send the notification from their office.

You also learned that every pronoun needs an antecedent, even though the reference may not occur within the same sentence. Lesson 27 covers the rules governing agreement of pronouns and antecedents.

Without clear antecedents, pronouns may cause confusion. Even though the antecedent may be included, readers sometimes may have difficulty determining which noun is the antecedent. This concept is known as *reference*. Notice the pronoun and its antecedent in the following sentence:

Our copies of the reports did not contain the signatures of the authors, so you should return them.

Although you can easily find the pronoun *them*, you cannot easily find the antecedent. Is it *copies, reports, signatures,* or *authors*? The confusion created by the sentence could result in various plans of action by the reader. As a careful writer, you will want to take care to ensure the antecedent for each pronoun is clear. The principles of reference are also included in Lesson 27.

SUBJECT-VERB AGREEMENT
LESSON 26

Making subjects and verbs agree in a sentence is vital to effective writing. Yet many writers (and speakers) have much difficulty with this task. Agreement requires that the writer understand two basic components: recognizing the true subject and understanding verb conjugation. Your goal throughout this lesson is to master the process of finding the true subject and making the verb agree with it.

You know that subjects are either nouns or pronouns. In Lesson 2, you were introduced to subject recognition; and in Unit 5, you learned the details of nouns and pronouns. As you will see from this lesson, however, you must take care to find the *true* subject, as it is not always the most obvious noun or pronoun in the sentence.

During your study of verbs in Unit 2, you should have learned to distinguish singular from plural verbs. Remember that third-person singular verbs end in *s*. Be careful not to confuse these singular verbs with nouns, which commonly end in *s* in their plural form.

Pretest

In each example, underline the true subject and circle the correct verb.

1. The winners of the most-recent contest (is, are) eligible for a scholarship.

2. In the closet (is, are) Mylvia's summer and winter clothes.

3. Neither of the honor students (was, were) present for the exam.

4. Half the bicycles (contains, contain) missing parts.

5. A number of employees (is, are) unhappy with the new vacation policy.

6. Four years (seems, seem) like a long time to get a bachelor's degree.

7. The staff (is, are) getting new office furniture.

8. Everyone in the corporation (has, have) the proposals in writing.

9. The pen and the pencil (is, are) in the desk drawer.

10. Each boy and girl in the class (brings, bring) a textbook each day.

11. The professor or the lab assistant (was, were) available for help with our questions.

12. Neither the president nor the officers (believes, believe) we should implement the new ideas.

Key: (1) are—plural subject *winners*; (2) are—plural subject *clothes*; (3) was—singular subject *neither*; (4) contain—"portion subject" *half* refers to plural *bicycle*; (5) are—plural subject *a number*; (6) seems—singular unit *four years*; (7) is—singular unit *staff*; (8) has—singular subject *everyone*; (9) are—plural subjects *pen* and *pencil* joined by *and*; (10) brings—*boy* and *girl* are the subjects, but the addition of *each* makes the meaning singular; (11) was—*professor* and *lab assistant* are subjects joined by *or* requiring a singular verb; (12) believe—*president* and *officers* are subjects joined by *nor* requiring a plural verb to agree with *officers*, the subject closer to the verb.

Terminology

Collective noun—A noun that names a group or collection of persons or things *(class, jury, team, staff)*. Collective nouns may be either singular or plural depending on their function within the sentence.

Indefinite pronoun—A pronoun that classifies a group of persons or things rather than a specific person or thing *(each, anyone, nobody, many)*.

Inverted sentence—A sentence that does not begin with the subject. Inverted sentences may have the verb split by the subject (as in a question) or have the true subject following the verb.

Rules

1. **Make the verb agree with the subject in number and in person. Singular subjects take singular verbs; plural subjects take plural verbs. Verbs of pronoun subjects must also agree in person.**

   An old *habit is* difficult to change. (singular subject and verb)

   Old *habits are* difficult to change. (plural subject and verb)

   He agrees with the solution to the current problem. (third-person singular pronoun, singular verb)

   They agree with the solution to the current problem. (third-person plural pronoun, plural verb)

   The challenge in subject-verb agreement is identifying the real subject of the clause and determining whether that subject is singular or plural.

   Learning Hint 1.   Mentally omit any prepositional phrases or other modifiers that come between the subject and the verb.

NO   The *subject* of the letters *are* our new billing procedures.
       The *reply*, along with the enclosures, *were* in yesterday's mail.

YES   The *subject* of the letters *is* our new billing procedure.
       The *reply*, along with the enclosures, *was* in yesterday's mail.

Learning Hint 2.   When sentences are not written in normal order (subject/verb/completer), mentally reword the sentence to help you determine the real subject; then make the verb agree with the true subject.

On the shelf in the bookroom (is, are) the new novels.

NORMAL ORDER: The new *novels are* on the shelf in the bookroom.

Easily seen from the hall (was, were) the visitors in the boardroom.

NORMAL ORDER: The *visitors* in the boardroom *were* easily seen from the hall.

Sentences that begin with the word *there* will always have the true subject following the verb. Because *there* is not the true subject of the clause, does not usually add meaning to the sentence, and detracts from conciseness, careful writers avoid its use. Try to acquire the habit of revising your sentences to omit the expletives.

NO   There are three reasons to avoid expletives in writing.

YES   Good writers avoid expletives for three reasons.

Use T26-1 here

2. **Use singular verbs with most indefinite pronouns** (*any, another, anyone, anything, each, either, everybody, neither, nobody, someone, somebody*). **Use plural verbs with indefinite pronouns that express plural ideas** (*few, many, most, several, some*).

   Everybody is trying to increase productivity in the company.

   Each of the boys *has* a new suit for the event.

   Neither of the answers to our question *was* a correct one.

   Many are called, but *few are* chosen.

   The indefinite pronouns *everyone* and *anyone* are written as two words (*every one* and *any one*) when followed by an *of* prepositional phrase or when the writer wants to stress individuality.

   Everyone is coming to the party later.

   Every one of the employees is coming to the party later.

Use T26-2 here

3. **Make the verb agree with the prepositional phrase following part or portion words** (*all, some, most, half, two-thirds, part*).

   SINGULAR   *Most* of the *flour is* gone.
                Three-fourths of the *camping equipment has* been rented.
                Some of the *knowledge is* outdated.

   PLURAL   *Most* of the *cookies are* gone.
                Three-fourths of the new *videos have* been rented.
                Some of the *ideas are* outdated.

Remember from your study of Unit 4 that *of* is normally omitted when using *all*. However, the same agreement principle still applies.

All the material *is* available.

All the patterns *are* available.

The pronoun *none* may take a singular verb even with a plural noun antecedent if the emphasis is on the idea of *not one*.

None of the *information* is missing from the report. (The antecedent *information* is singular.)

None of the *data* are missing from the report. (The antecedent *data* is plural.)

None of the *facts* is missing from the report. (Although the antecedent *facts* is plural, the emphasis is that *not one of the facts is missing*.)

Learning Hint 3.   *A number* is a plural subject and takes a plural verb; *the number* is a singular subject and takes a singular verb.

SINGULAR   *The number* of candidates for our program *is* decreasing.

PLURAL   *A number* of candidates *are* applying to our program.

Learning Hint 4.   Numbers take a singular verb to indicate a unit of measurement and a plural verb to emphasize individual parts.

SINGULAR   *Twelve hours is* the minimum time required.
                      Five dollars was all I had in my pocket.

PLURAL   *Twelve hours have* elapsed since I began writing.
                      Five dollars were added to the poker bet.

4. **Use a singular verb with collective nouns that are acting as a unit; use a plural verb with collective nouns that are acting individually.**

SINGULAR   The *class is* studying English usage on the job.
                      The *jury has* been deliberating for hours.

PLURAL   The *class are* divided in their opinions.
                      The *jury are* disagreeing on the verdict.

Because the sentence may sound awkward when a plural verb is matched with a collective noun, some writers prefer to change the sentence to avoid the situation.

The *students in the class are* divided in their opinions.

The *members of the jury are* disagreeing on the verdict.

Examples of typical collectives are *association, audience, board, class, committee, company, council, couple, crowd, department, family, firm, group, jury, majority, management, minority, number, pair, press, public, staff, team,* and *tribe.*

5. **Use a plural verb to agree with two separate subjects joined by *and*.**

> *Reading* and *writing* are important communication skills.
>
> *Eating* popcorn and *watching* movies are their favorite hobbies.

Learning Hint 5.   Some nouns joined by *and* are not separate subjects. If the two subjects cannot be separated, use a singular verb. If only the first of the two subjects contains an article (*the, a, an*), assume you have a singular subject.

SINGULAR   *The editor and reporter* on the staff *needs* a computer. (one person with two assignments)
Bacon and eggs is my favorite breakfast. (one meal)

PLURAL   *The editor and the reporter* on the staff *need* a computer. (two people)
The bacon and the eggs are in the refrigerator. (two separate items)

Learning Hint 6.   The words *each* and *every* denote a singular idea, even though two items may be joined by *and*.

NO   *Every* man and woman *are* entitled to a fair deal.
Each car and truck on the lot *are* for sale.

YES   *Every* man and woman *is* entitled to a fair deal.
Each car and truck on the lot *is* for sale.

Although the sentence may sound plural, the writer is conveying a singular idea about ''every single'' item.

6. **Use a singular verb with two singular subjects joined by *or* or *nor*; use a plural verb when both subjects are plural. When one of the subjects is plural and one is singular, make the verb agree with the subject closer to the verb.**

NO   Either the software or the hardware are not working.
The department heads or the vice presidents is responsible for the agreement.
Neither the dean nor the professors was available for a conference.

YES   Either the software or the hardware is not working.
The department heads or the vice presidents are responsible for the agreement.
Neither the dean nor the professors were available for a conference.

The last sentence is also grammatically correct as

Neither the professors nor the dean was available for a conference.

However, the sentence sounds awkward with a singular verb when the writer may mean several professors. Therefore, many writers prefer to always place the plural subject last; then, the plural verb is correct. We suggest you follow this procedure, and the exercises in this lesson will reflect this recommendation.

Posttest

In each example, underline the true subject and circle the correct verb.

1. The tree, along with its leaves and fruit, (is, are) plagued with insects.

2. Downstairs in the storage areas (is, are) the book you need.

3. Either of the proposals (is, are) acceptable to the committee.

4. Three-fourths of the questionnaires (has, have) been returned.

5. The number of available summer activities (has, have) decreased this year.

6. Two years (seems, seem) like a long time for us to be apart.

7. The crowd (is, are) getting unmanageable.

8. Some of the criteria (has, have) been reviewed by the committee.

9. The cake and ice cream (was, were) served at the party.

10. Every actor and agent (believes, believe) a raise is essential.

11. A cat or a bird (is, are) good company for a senior citizen.

12. Neither the football team nor the coaches (believes, believe) we can possibly lose the title.

Key: (1) is—singular subject *tree*; (2) is—singular subject *book*; (3) is—singular subject *either*; (4) have—"portion subject" *three-fourths* refers to plural *questionnaires*; (5) has—singular subject *the number*; (6) seems—singular unit *two years*; (7) is—singular unit *crowd*; (8) have—plural subject *some* because it refers to the plural term *criteria*; (9) was—subjects *cake* and *ice cream* joined by *and* are used as a singular unit; (10) believes—*actor* and *agent* are subjects, but the addition of

LEVEL A

Name _____

Exercise
26–1

On the lines below, write **T** if the statement is true and **F** if the statement is false.

__T__ 1. To make verbs agree with the subject, you must first be able to recognize the *true* subject.

__F__ 2. Like plural subjects, plural verbs often end in *s*.

__F__ 3. Because collective nouns imply a group, they always take plural verbs.

__T__ 4. Normally, you will mentally omit prepositional phrases when making the verb agree with the subject.

__F__ 5. The true subject is simple to find because it always precedes the verb in the sentence.

__T__ 6. *There* is an example of an expletive that should be avoided in writing because expletives are wordy and do not add meaning to the sentence.

__F__ 7. Indefinite pronouns used as subjects always require singular verbs.

__T__ 8. Some indefinite pronouns are written as two words when followed by a prepositional phrase beginning with *of*.

__T__ 9. The pronoun *none* may take either a singular or plural verb depending on the intent.

__T__ 10. Portion words, such as *some* or *most*, may take singular or plural verbs depending on the prepositional phrase that describes the portion or part.

__F__ 11. *A number* is a singular term that requires a singular verb.

__F__ 12. When used as subjects, numbers always indicate a unit of measurement and, therefore, take singular verbs.

__T__ 13. Two subjects joined by *and* take a plural verb if the subjects can be separated.

__T__ 14. When *every* is used with two subjects, a singular verb is required because a single idea is intended.

__F__ 15. Two singular subjects joined by *or* require a plural verb.

__T__ 16. When a singular and a plural subject are joined by *nor*, the plural subject should be placed last.

__F__ 17. Sentences written in inverted order are always questions rather than statements.

__F__ 18. *No one, either, several*, and *anybody* are examples of indefinite pronouns that require singular verbs.

__T__ 19. *There* may never be the subject of a sentence.

__T__ 20. Some sentences that have two subjects joined by *and* are still correct with a singular verb.

Exercise 26–2 Some verbs have been omitted from the following sentences. Write **S** if the omitted verb should be singular and **P** if it verb should be plural.

_S_ 1. Everybody in the corporation but Mr. Kaminski _____ received a copy of the report.

_S_ 2. The fax machine, as well as the new computers, _____ intimidating to some of the employees.

_P_ 3. Meeting with the management team _____ the chairman of the board and the president.

_S_ 4. The set of glasses _____ broken when we opened the package.

_P_ 5. The arrest and the conviction _____ recorded on the court records.

_S_ 6. Our understanding of the policies and procedures _____ important to the success of the program.

_P_ 7. Neither the producer nor the stars _____ informed of the cancellation of the show.

_S_ 8. Much time and effort _____ expended to make the new program a success.

_S_ 9. A committee of three managers and two supervisors _____ approved to study the problem.

_S_ 10. None of the people on the committee _____ able to meet with us yesterday. [Intent is _not one_ of the people]

_P_ 11. Either the secretaries or the accountants _____ planning to rewrite the payroll policy.

_S_ 12. Every man, woman, and child _____ excited about Christmas.

_S_ 13. Either of the solutions _____ acceptable to the committee.

_S_ 14. Four hours _____ not enough time to master the subject matter for the test.

_P_ 15. Two-thirds of the women involved in the makeup demonstration _____ convinced to change to our products.

_P_ 16. Beside the car _____ the flat tires that must be repaired.

_P_ 17. Few salespeople _____ the ability to sell these ineffective products.

_P_ 18. Three days _____ required as a ''cooling-off'' period for home sales.

_S_ 19. A total of three days _____ required as a ''cooling-off'' period for home sales.

_S_ 20. The emphasis on both speed and accuracy in keyboarding _____ stressed in the textbook.

_S_ 21. The secretary and treasurer of the organization _____ completed the reports.

_S_ 22. Any one of the people on the committee _____ eligible to be selected as the chair.

_P_ 23. The dining room and the living room furniture _____ delivered last week.

_S_ 24. Each of the new contestants _____ been informed of the guidelines for the competition.

_P_ 25. Not only the professor but also the students _____ willing to change the date of the exam.

LEVEL B

Name _____

Exercise   Write the letter of the sentence or sentences with correct usage of subject-verb agree-
26–3   ment. In some cases, more than one sentence may be correct.

_c_   1. *a.* Neither fundamental business skills nor computer technology are required in the humanities curriculum.
      b. Only one of the members were able to complete the requirements on time.
      c. Yoshie, along with the other department personnel, was ready to leave by noon.

_a,c_   2. *a.* The desk next to the filing cabinets needs to be straightened.
      b. The reason for the changes in policies are a reduction in paperwork.
      c. The analyses presented by the department head make a lot of sense.

_a_   3. *a.* On the wall in Judy's office are four marks left from the bookcase that was removed.
      b. Where's the brochures we had printed to distribute to the new customers?
      c. Each of the problems were studied in depth before solutions were furnished.

_a,b_   4. *a.* None of the assistants was available to help me with the experiment.
      b. The dealers who are involved in the upcoming sale are eager to receive our promotional material.
      c. Neither an ardent salesperson nor severe objections changes my opinion of the product.

_a_   5. *a.* Some of your income-tax returns, along with this year's refund, are being questioned.
      b. Most of the office furniture have been delivered to our new building.
      c. Conducting the evaluation of the program is the advisory committee and the board chair.

_a,b,c_   6. *a.* One-third of the administrative assistants are poor in spelling.
      b. The number of jurors chosen has decreased over last month.
      c. Between Broadway and Main Streets is located the largest business-equipment company.

_a,c_   7. *a.* Mr. Smigelski's use of good manners proves he is a caring person.
      b. Each computer, printer, and calculator need to be serviced this week.
      c. The data from your printout have been copied for the board meeting.

_b,c_   8. *a.* When is the video recorders scheduled to be returned from the repair shop?
      b. Nearly 80 percent of the surveys were returned with important information missing.
      c. Do you understand what the bases are for his final decision?

_a,c_   9. *a.* A few members of our football team were reluctant to play the stronger opponents.
      b. Two fundamental rules of office etiquette is to avoid gossip and to offer assistance.
      c. The board were unable to agree on the direction we should pursue.

_a,b,c_   10. *a.* Among the stack of papers on Karl's desk were the missing contracts.
      b. Either Mr. Rory or his brothers are expected to continue running the chain of men's stores.
      c. A number of the materials for the conference were delivered to your office.

_a, b, c_ 11. *a.* The china and the silverware were packed carefully in preparation for our move.
       b. The china, along with the silverware, was packed carefully in preparation for our move.
       c. Neither the china nor the silverware was packed carefully in preparation for our move.

_a, c_ 12. *a.* Be sure that parentheses are used when additional information is needed.
       b. The first parenthesis were omitted from your initial paragraph.
       c. The curricula were divided into three important study sessions.

_a, c_ 13. *a.* The headquarters office has been moved from Tampa to Tallahassee.
       b. The scissors are too dull to cut the paper and needs to be sharpened.
       c. The children were eager to see how many fish are in the aquarium.

_c_ 14. *a.* Anyone of the applicants is qualified for our new position.
       b. Any one of the applicants are qualified for our new position.
       c. None of the applicants is qualified for our new position.

_a, b_ 15. *a.* A number of people have criticized Aiano's promotion because he has limited experience.
       b. The number of people who have criticized Aiano's promotion has diminished since he has proven himself.
       c. Every one of the people who criticized Aiano's promotion have apologized.

_a, b, c_ 16. *a.* With the girls as they entered the auditorium was the city mayor.
       b. All the cookies Mrs. Pendleton baked have been eaten by the children.
       c. The carton of business-communication texts has finally arrived.

_b, c_ 17. *a.* Most of the lots chosen for the housing development has been sold.
       b. The criteria used to evaluate the program are outlined in the introduction of the report.
       c. One of the topics to be discussed at the meeting is the new housing development.

_a, b, c_ 18. *a.* The china cupboard and the curio cabinet were delivered yesterday.
       b. The china cupboard and curio cabinet was delivered yesterday.
       c. The china cupboard or the curio cabinet was delivered yesterday.

_b, c_ 19. *a.* The data was delivered to the president for her recommendation.
       b. The secretary to both committees was eager to review his notes from the meeting.
       c. The right parenthesis was missing from the document's title page.

_c_ 20. *a.* The crises was resolved before the committee adjourned for lunch.
       b. The director for the Distinguished Service Award and the Outstanding Employee Awards were not able to attend the meeting.
       c. The addendum was omitted from the report our committee received.

_a, c_ 21. *a.* The tomato and tuna salad was our most popular menu item.
       b. Neither the mother nor the children was willing to wait for the next show.
       c. The class were busy working on their individual assignments.

_b_ 22. *a.* One hundred dollars were the cost of the table we purchased last week.
       b. Neither of the proposed guidelines was acceptable to the board.
       c. The set of eight coasters were given to the retiring committee member.

LEVEL C

Name _____

Exercise
26–4

Underline the true subject or subjects in the following sentences. Then choose the verb to agree with the subject. Write **A** if the first verb is correct and **B** if the second verb is correct.

_A_ 1. The <u>couple</u>, along with the wedding guests, (is, are) leaving for the reception.

_A_ 2. In the freezer that is next to the storage shelves (is, are) the <u>meat</u> for the barbecue.

_A_ 3. <u>Either</u> of the committee members (is, are) a satisfactory replacement for Mr. Hzan.

_A_ 4. Only <u>part</u> of the playground equipment in the park (has, have) been repaired.

_B_ 5. The <u>number</u> of times you repeat the task (determine, determines) your eventual proficiency.

_A_ 6. <u>Ten dollars</u> (has, have) been added to the wholesale price of the equipment.

_A_ 7. The <u>class</u> (has, have) pooled the resources from several sources for the project.

_A_ 8. <u>Anyone</u> who is interested in the results of our campaign (wants, want) a copy of the details.

_B_ 9. The <u>monitor</u> and the <u>keyboard</u> (is, are) upgraded from the previous computer system.

_A_ 10. Every financial <u>planner</u> and <u>broker</u> in the state (has, have) been invited to our convention.

_A_ 11. A <u>pen</u> or a <u>pencil</u> (was, were) included in each registration folder.

_B_ 12. Either the <u>advisor</u> or the student body <u>officers</u> (is, are) in charge of the homecoming activities.

_A_ 13. <u>One</u> of the most-important points in financial analysis (is, are) determining the original cost.

_A_ 14. <u>Anybody</u> who will try to increase the profit from our consulting services (is, are) worthy of a promotion.

Exercise
26–5

Compo-
sition

Compose sentences meeting the following stipulations.

1. A number used as a unit of measurement.

_____

_____

2. A number emphasizing individual parts.

_____

_____

3. A collective noun acting as a unit.

_____

_____

4. A collective noun acting individually.

_____

_____

5. An indefinite pronoun expressing a singular idea.

_____

_____

6. An indefinite pronoun expressing a plural idea.

_____

_____

7. Two subjects joined by *or* that require a singular verb.

_____

_____

8. Two subjects joined by *or* that require a plural verb.

_____

_____

9. Two subjects joined by *and* that require a singular verb.

_____

_____

10. Two subjects joined by *and* that require a plural verb.

_____

_____

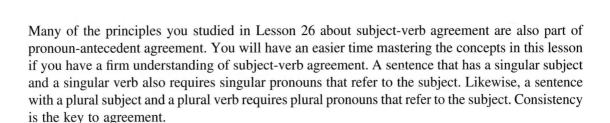

PRONOUN-ANTECEDENT AGREEMENT AND REFERENCE

LESSON 27

Many of the principles you studied in Lesson 26 about subject-verb agreement are also part of pronoun-antecedent agreement. You will have an easier time mastering the concepts in this lesson if you have a firm understanding of subject-verb agreement. A sentence that has a singular subject and a singular verb also requires singular pronouns that refer to the subject. Likewise, a sentence with a plural subject and a plural verb requires plural pronouns that refer to the subject. Consistency is the key to agreement.

Just as finding the true subject is essential for successful subject-verb agreement, identifying the true antecedent is the fundamental point in pronoun-antecedent agreement. Placing the antecedent in a preceding sentence is grammatically correct. However, as a careful writer, you want to be sure the pronoun's antecedent is clear to your reader. Vague or missing pronoun referents can cause much confusion in writing, and the reader may infer an illogical or incorrect conclusion.

As you learned in Unit 5, pronouns have four genders: masculine, feminine, neuter, and common. Plural pronouns are in the common gender; they refer to both males and females and cause few problems for writers. Singular pronouns, however, require that you determine whether the antecedent is a male, a female, or an animal or inanimate object requiring a neuter form.

Pretest

For each sentence, write **C** or **I** to indicate correct use of pronoun-antecedent agreement.

1. Please remove our stock of cleaning supplies from their cabinet.

2. A few members of the team agreed to sign their contracts.

3. Each clerk received a commission based on their sales.

4. For an employee to be successful in the business world, you must expend total effort.

5. You must examine these type of error in proofreading your writing.

6. Everyone who is attending the concert has been asked to bring a visitor with them.

7. Senator Inouye is one of the congressmen who has been in office for several terms.

8. The chair told Lorraine that she will change offices next month.

9. If you cannot find the text in my bookcase, ask Ms. Elliott about it.

10. When the students were interviewed, it was a helpful event.

11. Silila expanded his knowledge through continued education, which resulted in a promotion.

12. It is either Steve or Ron who has the latest information on the subject.

Key: (1) I—singular antecedent *stock* requires *its*; (2) C; (3) I—singular antecedent *each clerk* requires *his or her*; (4) I—*you* should be *he or she* to avoid a shift from third person to second person; (5) I—singular *type of error* requires *this* or *that*, or plural *types of errors* require *these*; (6) I—to be consistently singular, antecedent *everyone* requires pronoun *her or him*; (7) I—*have* because the referent is *several congressmen*; (8) I—vague reference of *she* should be reworded; (9) I—unclear reference of *it* should be changed to *ask Ms. Elliott about the book*; (10) I—implied reference of *it* should be reworded, *The students' interviews were helpful events*; (11) I—unclear reference of *which* should be reworded to *continued education; this learning resulted in a promotion*; (12) I—expletive *it* should be changed to *Either Steve or Ron has the latest information on the subject*.

Terminology

Antecedent—The noun to which a pronoun refers. The antecedent is sometimes called a referent, especially when the noun is in another sentence.

Common-gender nouns—Nouns that may refer to either masculine or feminine people (*customer, manager, executive, secretary*).

Gender—Classification of words into masculine, feminine, neuter, and common-gender categories.

Neuter—Neither masculine nor feminine in gender, such as the pronoun *it*.

Rules

Use T27-1 here

1. **Make pronouns agree with their antecedents in number, in person, and in gender.**

   The *politician* has agreed to present *his* platform at our forum. (singular antecedent and singular masculine pronoun, indicating the politician is a male)

   The *politician* has agreed to present *her* platform at our forum. (singular antecedent and singular feminine pronoun, indicating the politician is a female)

   The *politicians* have agreed to present *their* platforms at our forum. (plural antecedent and plural pronoun, indicating the politicians may include both males and females)

*Use
T27-2
here*

Learning Hint 1. Avoid the pitfall of using male pronouns with common-gender nouns. Although this practice was common and previously accepted in business writing, the trend has changed. When using a common-gender noun, you must acknowledge the fact that the reference may be to a female as well as to a male.

NO   Every *secretary* in the company has assignments that *she* must complete.
   Any competent corporate *president* is concerned with *his* employees.

YES   Every *secretary* in the company has assignments that *she or he* must complete.
   Any competent corporate *president* is concerned with *his/her* employees.

Of course, if you know the gender of the noun, you are correct to use only *he* or *she* (or *she* or *he*).

The personnel secretary has assignments that *he* must complete. (The writer knows the secretary is a male.)

Our corporate president is concerned with *her* employees. (The writer knows the president is a female.)

Because using *he/she* in a sentence may sound awkward, many writers (and speakers) ignore the rule of consistency and use a plural pronoun with a singular antecedent. This approach is not grammatically correct.

NO   Any customer who wants to receive your catalog must leave *their* name and address with us.

YES   Any customer who wants to receive our catalog must leave *his or her* name and address with us. (Use both a masculine and a feminine pronoun.)

Repeated use of *she or he* (or *he/she*) notations may be wordy and awkward in writing. Therefore, you may prefer to use an alternative approach.

Any customer who wants to receive our catalog must leave *a* name and address with us. (Omit the necessity for a pronoun.)

Any customer who wants to receive our catalog must leave *the person's* name and address with us. (Repeat a noun rather than substitute a pronoun.)

All customers who want to receive our catalog must leave *their* names and addresses with us. (Change sentence to plural, and use a common-gender pronoun.)

All the preceding examples are correct. As a writer, you have the option of choosing the example that best fits your situation. However, you must observe the original principle to be consistent in using singular or plural pronouns and antecedents.

Learning Hint 2. Do not use the second-person pronoun *you* in third-person situations. A common error of beginning writers is using *you* to avoid the problem of pronoun gender.

NO   Any customer who wants to receive our catalog must leave *your* name and address with us.

You is correct in second-person situations only—that is, if you are speaking *to* the person.

YES   If *you* want to receive our catalog, please leave *your* name and address with us.

2. **Follow the subject-verb agreement rules by using singular pronouns with singular subjects and verbs and plural pronouns with plural subjects and verbs. Do not shift from singular to plural.**

   NO   Each student must bring *their* book to class.
           Neither the dean nor the assistant dean has completed *their* part of the progress report.
           A person needs to know *they have* a place to go for answers.

   YES   Each student must bring *his/her* book to class.
           Neither the dean nor the assistant dean has completed *her or his* part of the progress report.
           A person needs to know *he or she has* a place to go for answers.

3. **Make demonstrative pronouns agree in number with the nouns to which they refer. *This* and *that* are singular; *these* and *those* are plural.**

   SINGULAR   Please give us your feedback on *this form.*
                Please give us your feedback on *that form.*

   PLURAL   Please give us your feedback on *these forms.*
                Please give us your feedback on *those forms.*

   Grammatically, *this* and *that* are interchangeable. The only distinction is location—where the writer (or speaker) is in relation to the thing spoken about. The same is true with *these* and *those.*

   Learning Hint 3.   The pronouns *it, this, that,* and *which* are often used to introduce clauses that have unclear references to their antecedents. Be sure the referent is clear to the reader.

   NO   We have produced several commercials to describe our products, *which* will begin next week. (What—the commercials or the products?)

   YES   We have produced several commercials, *which* will begin next week, to describe our products.
           We have produced several commercials to describe our products; the commercials will begin next week.

   Sometimes, repeating the noun instead of using a pronoun makes the meaning clear and avoids the unclear reference.

4. **Make the verbs and pronouns in a relative-pronoun clause agree with the noun antecedent.**

   Have you seen the computer *printout* that *includes* our data on *it*?

   Did Helen and Mary tutor the *student* who *was* failing *his* classes?

   When the sentence contains (1) the phrase *one of the, one of these,* or *one of those* and (2) a relative clause, the antecedent of the relative pronoun is the plural word in the prepositional phrase. Therefore, the relative clause requires a plural verb. When the sentence contains (1) the phrase *the only one of* and (2) a relative clause, the antecedent of the relative pronoun is the singular *one*; and the relative clause requires a singular verb.

SINGULAR Chen is *the only one of* the teachers who *is* willing to help with the project. (Only one is willing.)
The only one of the math problems that *is* correct is the first one. (Only one is correct.)

PLURAL Chen is *one of the teachers* who *are* willing to help with the project. (More than one are willing.)
One of the math problems that *are* correct is the first one. (Several are correct; the first problem is one of those.)

5. **To avoid ambiguity or confusion, make the pronoun reference clear. Vague or implied antecedents make writing unclear to the reader.**

NO The manager told Mr. Trout that he was increasing *his* workload. (Whose—the manager's or Mr. Trout's workload?)
The customers did not sign the checks, so we are sending *them* back. (Which—the checks or the customers?)
Although the professor lectured for over an hour, *it* was an interesting experience. (The antecedent of *it*—lecture—is implied but not stated.)

YES Mr. Trout was given an increased workload by the manager.
We are returning the unsigned checks to the customers.
Although the professor talked for over an hour, the lecture was an interesting experience.

Many beginning writers have problems with pronoun reference. You will want to ensure that your pronouns not only agree with the antecedent but also refer clearly to that antecedent.

Learning Hint 4. An expletive commonly used in writing is *it*. When used without a pronoun antecedent, *it* becomes an expletive.

NO *It* is important to write good reports. (Expletive construction—no pronoun antecedent)

YES Writing good reports is important.
Writing good reports is important; *it* is a vital task. (A correct use of *it*, referring to the concept of *writing reports*.)

As mentioned in Lesson 26, careful writers avoid expletive constructions in their writing.

Posttest

For each sentence, write **C** or **I** to indicate correct use of pronoun-antecedent agreement.

1. Allyson's family will be taking their vacation next month.

2. Every employee in the office needs their own phone.

3. Each governor distributed his proposal at the conference.

4. Everyone should write your name on the paper before starting the test.

5. Be sure you check for this kind of error in your other writing samples.

6. When someone loses a possession, they should check the Lost and Found Department.

7. Josef is the only one of the immigrants who know American history.

8. When the professors met with the students, they seemed anxious to end the discussion.

9. After you have finished using my computer to write your report, please return it.

10. Although the magician performed for several minutes, it was not successful.

11. The letter is on my desk that arrived yesterday.

12. It is important to cover the key items on the agenda.

Key: (1) I—singular antecedent *family* requires *its*; (2) I—singular antecedent *every employee* needs *his or her*; (3) I—common-gender antecedent *governor* requires *her or his* unless the writer knows that all governors are male; (4) I—*you* should be *his or her* to avoid a shift from third person to second person; (5) C; (6) I—to be consistently singular, the antecedent *someone* requires *she or he*; (7) I—*knows* since the referent is *the only one*; (8) I—vague reference of *they* should be reworded, *The students seemed anxious to end their discussion with the professors*; (9) I—unclear reference of *it* should be changed, *Please return my computer when you have finished using it for your report*; (10) I—implied reference of *it* should be reworded to *the show was not successful*; (11) I—unclear reference of *that* should be reworded, *The letter that arrived yesterday is on my desk*; (12) I—expletive *it* should be reworded: *The key items on the agenda must be covered.*

LEVEL A

Name _____

Exercise 27–1

On the lines below, write **T** if the statement is true and **F** if the statement is false.

_T_ 1. A sentence with a singular subject and verb must also have singular pronouns that refer to the subject.

_T_ 2. A pronoun's antecedent may also be called the *referent* if the noun appears in another sentence.

_F_ 3. Pronouns have only three genders: masculine, feminine, and neuter.

_F_ 4. Common-gender nouns are used to refer to both males and females, so neuter pronouns are used for agreement.

_T_ 5. Making pronouns agree with their antecedents in number refers to the use of plurality.

_F_ 6. The use of masculine pronouns with such words as *executive, employee,* and *supervisor* is always acceptable in business writing.

_T_ 7. To avoid wordiness in using *her or his* repeatedly, a writer may prefer to rewrite the sentence in plural form.

_F_ 8. To avoid gender problems with pronouns, a writer may switch from third person to second-person *you* within the sentence.

_T_ 9. *These* and *those* may be used interchangeably, as they are grammatically equal.

_T_ 10. Omitting the pronoun and repeating the noun are acceptable in business writing if you are trying to avoid unclear pronoun reference.

_F_ 11. The phrase *one of* always indicates a singular idea that requires a singular pronoun.

_T_ 12. The phrase *the only one of* indicates a singular idea that requires a singular pronoun.

_F_ 13. Using implied antecedents is acceptable in business writing.

_T_ 14. Using *it* in a sentence without a pronoun referent is an example of an expletive construction.

_F_ 15. *The billboard stands over 8 feet high; it is easily seen from the street* is an example of an expletive construction.

_F_ 16. A company name is an example of a common-gender noun, and a neuter pronoun is required.

_F_ 17. Because words such as *secretary* and *nurse* most often refer to women, using feminine pronouns in a general sense with these terms is acceptable business writing.

_T_ 18. To avoid the problem of male-gender pronouns, a writer may elect to use second-person pronouns.

Exercise 27–2 Some pronouns and verbs have been omitted from the following sentences. Write **S** if the pronoun or verb should be singular and **P** if the pronoun or verb should be plural.

S 1. A chairman must rely on the information _____ receives from subordinates.

S 2. Everyone who wants to receive additional dividends on _____ investment should read our new pamphlet.

P 3. Many pilots and flight attendants in our company have invested _____ money in our stock.

S 4. My business partner and friend received a bonus for _____ ideas.

S 5. I am not sure whether Craig or Merlene has made _____ reservations for the conference.

S 6. Our Honolulu office is the only one that _____ financially stable.

S 7. In the opening speech, the president of the two corporations indicated that _____ found listening to customers was a most-important key for success.

S 8. The investigators have found _____ kind of evidence in every room.

P 9. Dr. Rothwell is one of those professors who _____ interested in _____ students.

P 10.

P 11. _____ types of situations seem to be occurring most often in recent years.

P 12. This room contains the typewriters that _____ already been sold.

P 13. Specialists, Inc. is one of those businesses that _____ offering a discount to build up _____ business.

P 14.

S 15. Either Mahana or her mother will give _____ speech at the assembly.

S 16. Our government requires each citizen to be responsible for _____ family first because neither the state nor national leaders _____ able to care for everyone.

P 17.

S 18. Although the crisis may be over, _____ effects will still be felt throughout the company.

P 19. Jeanette's analysis proved to be one of those problems that _____ not easily understood on _____ own merits.

P 20.

P 21. All the employees in the company had an opportunity to assess _____ standing in our corporation.

S 22. Marshall is the only employee who knew _____ importance to the company.

P 23. How many of the salespeople _____ able to meet the quota that _____ set for _____ ?

S 24.

P 25.

LEVEL B

Name _____

Exercise **Some pronouns have been omitted from the following sentences. Write the letter that**
27–3 **matches the gender the missing pronoun should have.**

M Masculine	**N** Neuter
F Feminine	**C** Common (includes M and F and plural)

_N_ 1. Hahn's, Inc. is developing a brochure highlighting _____ new products and services.

_C_ 2. Employees wanting to discuss _____ salary must make an appointment with the personnel director.

_C_ 3. Has either Michael or Anna distributed copies of _____ recommendations?

_M_ 4. Has either Daniel or his son finished _____ application yet?

_F_ 5. Angela is the only secretary who showed _____ ingenuity with the project.

_C_ 6. Neither Huhn nor his assistants could find _____ copy of the proposal.

_N_ 7. The committee has been in _____ meeting session for over two hours.

_N_ 8. Neither the cat nor the dog looks _____ age, as reported by the owner.

_F_ 9. If Ms. Jarret or Ms. Hardy places an order today, _____ will receive a discount.

_C_ 10. Nicolette is different from the other employees who remained calm when _____ faced disaster.

_N_ 11. You will be pleased to learn that the board of directors agreed on _____ decision to expand operations.

_C_ 12. Neither Ms. Clark nor her assistant remained in _____ office during the break.

_C_ 13. Peggy is one of those employees who felt comfortable with _____ positions in the company.

_F_ 14. Maria indicated that none of the materials had yet been delivered to _____ office.

_C_ 15. An efficient secretary will transcribe _____ notes as soon as possible after a meeting.

_C_ 16. Both Teresa and Michael are eager for _____ summer separation to end.

_N_ 17. The parrot has lost most of _____ tail feathers in the last few days.

_N_ 18. My car's left rear tire is flat, and _____ must be repaired as soon as possible.

_C_ 19. Either Sarah or Norm will bring _____ recommendations to the committee meeting next month.

_C_ 20. A president who agrees to answer _____ own phone will make a good impression on a client.

Exercise 27–4 Write the letter of the sentence or sentences with correct usage of subject-verb agreement. In some cases, more than one sentence may be correct.

_c_   1.   *a.*   Mimi is interested in improving her writing, which she acquired in a class at the community college.
         b.   If your computer is giving you inadequate information, let us do it for you.
         c.   Neither Mrs. Anderson nor the other managers are willing to help their customers satisfactorily.

_a, b_   2.   *a.*   Each of the applicants was cautioned to complete his/her application carefully.
         b.   One of the student's mothers volunteered to contribute two hours of her time each week.
         c.   Larry met my brother, and I learned how impressed he was with the operation.

_c_   3.   *a.*   Gerald's automobile is parked in the driveway, and it needs attention.
         b.   Jeanne asked if it were possible to see the results of the survey.
         c.   Did both branch stores show increases in their income statements?

_c_   4.   *a.*   Has the alumnus followed through on their commitment to build a new stadium?
         b.   The sales letter was sitting on my desk, and it was a mess.
         c.   The policy of our company regarding promotions is well known by all its employees.

_c_   5.   *a.*   For our employees who have additional education and don't know it, you are entitled to a raise in your salary.
         b.   After cleaning the room, I opened the window, which was a great improvement.
         c.   Both Rose and Donna are taking their books home with them.

_c_   6.   *a.*   After an adult changes occupations, you must relearn the company politics.
         b.   I do not want to make the trip because it is difficult to return the same day.
         c.   Someone must have left his or her keys in the cafeteria.

_a, b_   7.   *a.*   One of the officers added a postscript to the memo he received.
         b.   Several of the staff wanted their vacations the end of August.
         c.   William drove the van for several hours through a traffic jam; this was exhausting.

_a, c_   8.   *a.*   Neither of the applicants had her or his qualifications questioned.
         b.   If a person wants to master business principles, you should study marketing, management, and finance.
         c.   Either of the administrative assistants will help you when he or she is finished.

_c_   9.   *a.*   Mr. Sefallus admired the theater and its marquee, which showed all the newest releases.
         b.   Please ask everyone on the staff to make their reservations early.
         c.   All members of the jury cast their votes in favor of the defendant.

_a_   10.   *a.*   Either Elaine or Roxanne will be called on to read her poem in class.
         b.   Neither Duane nor his brother could find his wool suit in the closet.
         c.   Never before has the game ended in a tie; it is a first.

LEVEL C

Name _____

Exercise 27–5   Edit the following sentences to avoid awkward or unclear pronoun references.

1. When the inventory at the warehouse is low, we have to order supplies from our competitor;
   ordering this way
   ~~this~~ can cause us problems.

2. Cliff and Andrea have been working on the income statement and balance sheet for many
   this task
   hours; ~~it~~ has been difficult.

3. The increased cost of fuel for our trucks ˄*,which concerns us all,* will be discussed in our upcoming board meeting ~~,~~.

   ~~which concerns us all~~.

4. We will now give discounts to keep our best customers happy because ~~it~~ means *good public relations* more sales

   for us.

5. Dr. Pierce's goal is to improve the efficiency of the process for arranging schedules ~~; which is~~ *the current*
   system is
   ~~currently~~ impractical.

6. I have not finished analyzing your report; ~~it~~ *the task* has been ~~a~~ difficult ~~task~~.

7. Although the professor repeated the procedure to be followed, ~~it~~ *the process* was not easy to understand.

8. You will be introduced at the meeting directly after the president's status report ~~;~~ *your introduction* ˄ ~~which~~ is

   scheduled for 8:25.

9. Rico has recently advanced to a new position with additional responsibilities; this ˄*advancement* will require

   increased training on his part.

10. Jared completed his report quickly under the assumption that top management would approve

    his recommendations ~~; which~~ *his assumption* was in error.

Exercise **Compose sentences that fulfill the following directives.**
27–6

Compo-
sition

1. Use the pronoun *it* in an example that is not an expletive construction.

_____

_____

2. Use the phrase *the only one of* in a correct example.

_____

_____

3. Use the phrase *one of* in a correct example.

_____

_____

4. Use pronouns to correctly refer to the common-gender noun *executive.*

_____

_____

5. Use a relative pronoun clause in which the reference to the antecedent is clear.

_____

_____

6. Use *each* as part of the complete subject, and include correct agreement of verbs and pronouns.

_____

_____

7. Use *neither* with a compound subject, and include correct agreement of verbs and pronouns.

_____

_____

Exercise 27–7

Edit the following sentences to reflect the principles you learned in Units 4, 5, and 6 involving connectives, nouns and pronouns, and agreement and reference.

Cumulative Editing

1. Please ask one of the managers if ~~they~~ *she or he* can tell us ~~what is involved in~~ *about* the problem and ~~the chances of solving the situation.~~ *about possible solutions.*

2. *The idea of* ~~Can you imagine~~ Kathie and ~~I~~ *me* on a deserted island running a business, ~~which is fiction,~~ *fictitious* and also unrealistic?

3. One of the most-common factors ~~which is~~ *that are* part of the decision-making process an executive employs is defining the problem.

4. A person's knowledge of business communication, along with other important curriculum areas, ~~are~~ *is an* important factors in determining future success and ~~to improve your~~ *in improving his or her* career.

5. Teaching economics involves ~~the opportunity for~~ a lot of creativity; ~~which increases~~ *this task* students' enthusiasm, *for retention of* and ~~retaining~~ the principles.

6. A student must ~~both~~ understand internal and external credit to comprehend the effect finance has on ~~your~~ *her or his* business enterprise.

7. Do students believe that professors ~~must be~~ either research experts in ~~his or her~~ *their* field or ~~experienced in~~ *must have experience* working in the profession?

8. Commitment is the only important part of the procedures that ~~have~~ *has* not yet been considered in determining an instructor's competency and mastery of the subject area.

9. If ~~they are~~ *she or he is* interested in the new service, a customer should call our special number, which is listed in our brochure ~~and~~ that illustrates examples of the service.

10. Society would be better off if we worried less about our differences, which are trivial and ~~of relative unimportance,~~ *relatively unimportant* and concentrated instead on our similarities; this *approach* suggests developing sensitivity.

11. Humans in a society tend to be gregarious~~,~~ *;* and ~~we~~ *to* form groups ~~both~~ according to ~~our~~ *both* interests

    and strengths~~,~~ *;* ~~which~~ *these groups* vary with each person's effort.

12. The subject of time management, ~~that~~ *which* is part of the upcoming conference, is one of the topics

    that ~~is~~ *are* most interesting to me because ~~it is so important~~ *of the importance of managing time* in the business world.

13. Jerry is the only one of the new worker~~'s~~ *s* whose benefits *either have* ~~has~~ been ~~either~~ paid already or will

    be paid in a separate check by the end of the month.

14. Each client ~~that~~ *whom* we talked with in the past month and who ~~want~~ *wants* to test our new fax services

    has arrived for the initial planning-committee~~'s~~ *e* meeting with the board and ~~we.~~ *us.*

15. As you are aware, neither the administrative assistants ~~or~~ *nor* the word-processing operators in

    our headquarters office ~~has~~ *have* proven ~~there~~ *their* competency with the new software program.

16. I believe ~~your~~ *you're* right about ~~him~~ *his* agreeing to help with the project~~,~~ *;* therefore~~,~~ I will not only invite

    ~~he~~ but~~,~~ *him also* his partner to join us for a dinner meeting.

17. All the ~~criterion~~ *criteria* used by ~~she~~ *her* and her staff in the management decision were appropriate in

    analyzing, ~~making the choice,~~ *choosing* and ~~implementation of~~ *implementing* the decision.

18. The signer was either I or my assistant~~,~~ *;* however~~,~~ nobody in the company who has seen the

    contracts ~~believe~~ *believes* we should continue with the contracts as ~~it is~~ *they are* written.

19. Mr. Griffiths, ~~which~~ *who* is witty, creative, and ~~has a great deal of intelligence,~~ *intelligent,* is one of the

    employees ~~that is~~ *who are* very adept at ~~his job~~ *their jobs;* and we agree with ~~him~~ *his* relating our position to top

    management.

20. On the computer table in my office are the printouts that will reveal the analyses and that will

    substantiate the decisions made by us and our advisory committee.

LESSONS IN THIS UNIT

28. ADJECTIVES AND ADVERBS

29. COMPOUND, COORDINATE, AND CONSECUTIVE MODIFIERS

30. MISPLACED AND DANGLING MODIFIERS

You likely have given little or no thought to just how important modifiers are in your writing. That's because we are accustomed to seeing modifiers—and hearing them—in our language every day. Modifiers—words that describe—are used in the communication process by almost everyone.

Nearly all sentences contain modifiers. These words are essential in giving our writing the descriptive power it needs to be clear and accurate. Even the simple sentence that follows contains five modifiers. Can you identify them?

The student received a high grade on her first paper.

Two of the modifiers in the preceding sentence are the articles *The* and *a*; the other three modifiers are *high* (modifying *grade*), *her*, and *first* (both modifying *paper*). Just for fun, remove the modifiers from the sentence and see how it sounds.

We can write sentences without modifiers, of course; and most of us do on occasion. Consider the following sentences that contain no modifiers:

Money talks.	Virtue triumphs.
Jesus wept.	Truth endures.
Honesty pays.	Death and taxes await.

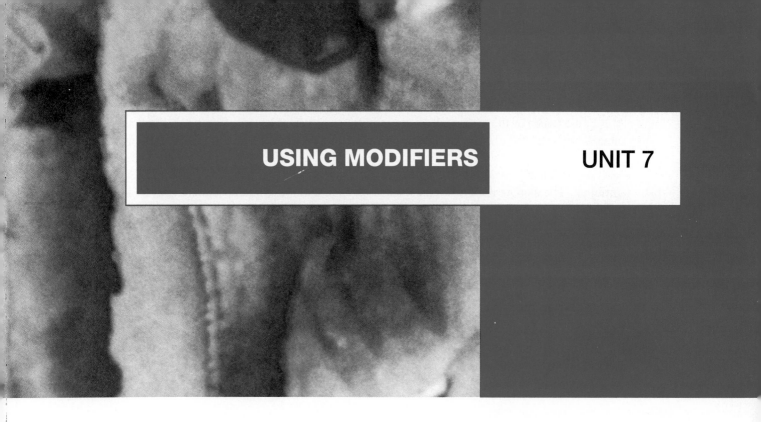

These sentences contain only subjects, verbs, and one conjunction. They—and other sentences like them—can be used to good effect by the skilled writer. A steady diet of such sentences, however, soon becomes tiresome; and the writer's ability to describe and explain is severely limited. Thus, you will see very few sentences—either those you write or those written by someone else—that do not contain modifiers.

Modifiers are describing words—adjectives and adverbs—that give our writing color, texture, and interest. Modifiers help us describe the subject of a sentence, the action that takes place, and the relationships between things and ideas. Without modifiers, we would be seriously handicapped in conveying facts and expressing ideas.

Modifiers, then, are used to describe, limit, or make more exact the meaning of other words. When they are used properly, modifiers help make our writing both interesting and precise.

As useful as modifiers are, however, they can quickly get in the way of effective communication if they are not used properly. The following item appeared in the Lost and Found section of a local newspaper:

> Reward for nearly new tricycle lost in the vicinity of City Park by small girl with furry seat, shiny fenders, and twin tail lights. Call 464-0577.

All the modifiers in the preceding ad are useful—or would be if they were used properly. However, because some of the modifiers are positioned improperly with respect to the words they describe, the language is garbled. Thus, location as well as word choice is important in making modifiers do what is expected of them.

Modifiers go immediately to work wherever they are placed. They stick to the words they are near, even if such words are not the ones the writer intended to modify. The newspaper ad about the lost tricycle vividly illustrates this problem. Therefore, we must construct our sentences so that the modifiers are positioned as closely as possible to the words they are meant to describe.

In the hands of the informed writer, modifiers are versatile tools. We must guard against their abuse, however; for a writer can get into trouble quickly if modifiers are misused. Using too many modifiers is a major weakness for some writers. Putting modifiers in the wrong place is another writing deficiency. And choosing illogical or inadequately descriptive modifiers is still another problem. The alert writer knows these hazards exist and makes a conscious effort to avoid them.

As you will see in this unit, modifiers are typically classified into two categories—*adjectives*, including phrases and clauses that act as adjectives, and *adverbs*, including phrases and clauses that act as adverbs. You will learn how to identify adjectives and adverbs, how to distinguish them from each other, and how to use them to make your writing properly descriptive and exact. And, as you will see, the writer's judgment is crucial in determining what modifiers to use and where to place them in a sentence to achieve the desired result.

The guidelines that follow are intended to help you use modifiers correctly—a skill that will further strengthen your effectiveness as a writer. Study the guidelines carefully—they are important to your writing success.

ADJECTIVES AND ADVERBS

Adjectives are modifiers that describe nouns or pronouns. *Adverbs* are modifiers that describe verbs, adjectives, or other adverbs.

Adjectives answer such questions about the words they modify as *what kind? which one? how much? how many?* and *whose?*

> *New* cars are fun to drive. (*New* tells what kind.)
>
> *That* car is expensive. (*That* tells which one.)
>
> She has *little* available time. (*Little* tells how much.)
>
> *Two* cars are parked in the driveway. (*Two* tells how many.)
>
> I rode in *Nora's* car. (*Nora's* indicates whose.)

Adjectives usually are placed in front of words they describe. Sometimes, however, adjectives are placed after the words they describe for clarity or emphasis.

> *Weekly* reports will be required beginning October 1. (The adjective *weekly* is placed in front of *reports*, the noun it modifies.)
>
> Reports—*punctual* and *detailed*—are required weekly. (For emphasis, the adjectives *punctual* and *detailed* are placed after *reports*, the noun they modify.)

Adverbs answer such questions about the words they modify as *where? how? how much? when?* and *why?*

> Their sales representative will meet us *here*. (*Here* tells where.)
>
> The panel moderator spoke *softly*. (*Softly* tells how.)
>
> The game will be played *on September 2*. (*On September 2* tells when.)

Please interview Charlie *to get the facts*. (*To get the facts* tells why.)

Adverbs typically are placed after the words they modify. At times, however, adverbs appear before the words they modify. The choice of position is often a matter of judgment for the writer. Clear and comfortable language usually guides the writer in making the right choice.

Speaking *softly*, the nurse quieted the restless patient. (The adverb *softly* is placed after *speaking*, the present-participle form of the verb it modifies.)

Quickly reading the memo, the secretary found the information she needed. (The adverb *quickly* is placed in front of *reading*, the present-participle form of the verb it modifies.)

Some words may serve either as adjectives or as adverbs depending on their use. Following are a few examples of such double-duty words.

above	close	fast	much	soft
better	deep	hard	quick	very
clear	early	late	slow	well

Writers who use adjectives and adverbs skillfully strengthen significantly their communication skills. Use the guidelines in this lesson to improve your ability to use these important describing words in your writing.

Pretest

Write **C** or **I** to indicate whether modifiers are used correctly or incorrectly in the following sentences.

1. The foreman is the older member of the jury.

2. Of the three applicants for the position, Mrs. Doyle is least qualified.

3. Jane is a better speaker than any member of her club.

4. The division manager is believed to be the most dependable of the two executives.

5. The chairman of the board requested a honest reply from Mr. Li.

6. When your report is totally complete, please let me read it.

7. Norma Hobson is a stronger candidate in this year's election.

8. Mr. Wegemeir teaches more enthusiastic than any other teacher, as his students will tell you.

9. The supervisor reported an huge increase in the number of orders received for a deluxe automatic ice maker costing less than $100.

10. The program chair and featured speaker for the sales conference in Charleston are Rosalee Terris and Dominic Valisi, respectively.

11. As a self-employed interior decorator, Juana Perez manages her business affairs with an impressive degree of hard-earned, self confidence.

12. The Model No. 881 electric-powered lawn mower is featured in our buy-of-the-week ad on page C-12 of *The Morning Register*.

Key: (l) l—the superlative form *oldest* should be used in place of *older*; (2)C; (3) l—as a member of her group, Jane cannot be a better speaker than herself; change to *any other member*; (4) l—use the comparative form *more* in place of *most*; (5) l—use the article *an* in place of *a*; (6) l—the use of *totally* with the absolute adjective *complete* is illogical; (7) l—an incomplete comparison (stronger than what?); (8) l—add the *-ally* ending to *enthusiastic* to form the appropriate adverb; (9) l—use the articles *a* and *an* correctly: *a huge* and *an ice maker*; (10) l—if necessary, repeat an article that refers to two or more nouns to avoid confusion: *the program chair* and *the featured speaker*; (11) l—the comma after hard-earned should be deleted; self-confidence should be hyphenated; (12) C.

Terminology

Adjective—A word that describes a noun or pronoun.

Absolute adjective—A modifier that suggests extremes (*round, finished, dead*).

Adverb—A word that describes a verb, an adjective, or another adverb.

Articles—The three adjectives *the, a,* and *an*.

Comparative degree—A comparison of two persons or things.

Double comparison—The incorrect use of two comparative forms instead of one. (*The earlier you get up, the more sooner you will get to school.*)

Incomplete comparison—A confusing or unclear statement resulting from failure to name both terms of a comparison. For instance, *Our sales are higher this month in the Central Region*. Higher than what? Higher than some other month? Higher than some other region?

Irregular form—Comparisons in which the comparative words (modifiers) undergo changes that are not typical of most comparatives (*well, better, best; many, more, most*).

Modifier—A single word, a phrase, or a clause used to describe or define some element of a sentence.

Positive degree—Reference to a characteristic or quality of one person or thing.

Superlative degree—A comparison of three or more persons or things.

Rules

1. **Use the correct form or degree of a modifier to make clear and logical comparisons.**

    Adjectives and adverbs are often used to compare things. These modifiers change form to show a greater or lesser degree of a particular characteristic or quality. The three degrees of comparison are *positive (simple), comparative,* and *superlative*.

    The **positive** degree of an adjective or adverb merely describes or refers to a given characteristic. The **comparative** degree compares two persons or things (but not more than two); the **superlative** degree compares three or more persons or things.

    The **comparative** form compares two persons or things with each other by amount or degree. The comparative form results from the addition of *-er* to the positive form (*taller,* *nicer, sooner*) or from the addition of the words *more* or *less* before the positive form (*more intelligent, more beautiful; less capable, less efficient*).

The **superlative** form indicates the greatest or the least amount or degree of something. The superlative form results from the addition of *-est* to the positive form (*tallest player, longest report, clearest picture*) or from the addition of the words *most* or *least* before the positive form (*most helpful, most overrated; least understood, least effective*).

Adjectives.   Use the *-er* and *-est* endings to form the comparative and superlative forms of most one-syllable and many two-syllable adjectives. Use *more* (or *less*) and *most* (or *least*) with some two-syllable adjectives and with adjectives of three or more syllables. Note the following examples:

(handwritten in margin: Use T28-1 here)

Positive	Comparative	Superlative
small	smaller	smallest
young	younger	youngest
wealthy	wealthier	wealthiest
funny	funnier	funniest
tactful	more (or less) tactful	most (or least) tactful
creative	more (or less) creative	most (or least) creative
dependable	more (or less) dependable	most (or least) dependable
interesting	more (or less) interesting	most (or least) interesting

NO   Della is the *youngest* of the two secretaries.

YES   Della is the *younger* of the two secretaries.

NO   Sir Lancelot appears to be the nobler of the three knights described in the story.

YES   Of the three knights described in the story, Sir Lancelot appears to be the noblest.

NO   Dwayne is the *wealthier* son in a family of five boys.

YES   Dwayne is the *wealthiest* son in a family of five boys.

NO   LaNeeta is *dependabler* than her sister, Trudee.

YES   LaNeeta is *more dependable* than her sister, Trudee.

Adverbs   A few one-syllable adverbs form the comparative or superlative with the *-er* or *-est* endings. However, most adverbs—including all those that end in *-ly*—form the comparative and superlative with *more* (or *less*) and *most* (or *least*).

(handwritten in margin: Use T28-2 here)

Positive	Comparative	Superlative
fast	faster	fastest
loud	louder	loudest
hard	harder	hardest
carefully	more (or less) carefully	most (or least) carefully
skillfully	more (or less) skillfully	most (or least) skillfully
helpfully	more (or less) helpfully	most (or least) helpfully

NO   Mr. Sloane is the harder-working member of the City Council.

YES   Mr. Sloane is the hardest-working member of the City Council.

NO   Ron Ridder works the least skillfully of the two carpenters assigned to the project.

YES   Ron Ridder works less skillfully than the other carpenter assigned to the project.

As you may have noticed, the first three words in the preceding adverbs chart (*fast, loud, hard*), as well as their comparative and superlative forms, can serve as adjectives as well as adverbs.

Josh works *hard*. (*Hard* functions as an adverb.)

Josh welcomes *hard* work. (*Hard* functions as an adjective.)

Learning Hint 1.   Some modifiers are compared by means of ''irregular'' changes in the words themselves. Following are a few examples of these irregular comparisons:

Positive	Comparative	Superlative
well	better	best
bad	worse	worst
little	less, lesser	least
many, much	more	most
far	farther, further	farthest, furthest

Learning Hint 2.   Be careful to avoid confusion when comparing someone or something in a group with other members of the same group. Use the words *other* or *else* when making such comparisons.

NO   Dr. Huang is a better surgeon than any physician at the hospital. (Since Dr. Huang is one of the physicians at the hospital, this sentence illogically says that he is better than himself.)

YES   Dr. Huang is a better surgeon than any *other* physician at the hospital.

NO   Dixie received a bigger raise than anyone in her department. (As one of the employees in her department, Dixie can't receive a bigger raise than herself.)

YES   Dixie received a bigger raise than anyone *else* in her department.

Learning Hint 3.   Avoid double comparisons. Remember that a modifier's comparative is formed by using either *-er/-est* or *more (less)/most (least)*. Don't use both at the same time.

NO   The *most busiest* expressway in the city is Route 89.

YES   The *busiest* expressway in the city is Route 89.

NO   The sooner the project is completed, the *less busier* we will be.

YES   The sooner the project is completed, the *less busy* we will be.

Learning Hint 4.   Watch out for incomplete comparisons—a common language weakness for some writers. When two or more things are compared, your language must include everything necessary to make the comparison clear and complete.

NO   Jason Povik is a better analyst this year. (Better than what or whom?)

YES   Jason Povik is a better analyst this year *than he was last year.*

Jason Povik is a better analyst this year *than I expected him to be.*

Jason Povik is a better analyst this year *than Arthur Reynolds.*

Jason Povik is *the best analyst on our staff* this year. (The superlative form is required here since Jason is being compared to more than one other analyst.)

NO   Maggie's memo summarizes the facts better than Willa. (Is this comparison with Willa or with Willa's memo?)

YES   Maggie's memo summarizes the facts better *than Willa's.* (or *better than Willa's memo.*)

Maggie's memo summarizes the facts better *than Willa summarized them* in today's meeting.

NO   You relate better to that kind of customer than I. (Do you relate to the customer better *than I do*, or do you relate better to the customer *than you relate to me*?)

YES   You relate better to that kind of customer *than I do.*

You relate better to that kind of customer *than to me.*

Learning Hint 5.   Some adjectives such as *correct, perfect, priceless, complete, hopeless, dead, endless, straight,* and *unique* are called *absolute adjectives.* They suggest extremes and are poor choices for making comparisons. Expressions such as *more correct* and *less perfect* make little sense. Similarly, something is either unique or it isn't; it cannot be more unique or less unique.

NO   Even the *most-perfect* paper is unlikely to satisfy the professor.

YES   Even a *perfect* paper is unlikely to satisfy the professor.

NO   You are *completely correct* in your assumption.

YES   You are *correct* in your assumption.

NO   The proposed concept involves a *totally unique* method of inventory control.

YES   The proposed concept involves a *unique* method of inventory control.

NO   The analysis is *less complete* than it should be.

YES   The analysis is *incomplete.*

2.   **Avoid dropping the -ly ending from frequently used adverbs.**

The sentences *Drive careful* and *Mary sure sang well* illustrate a common grammar error—the omission of the *-ly* ending from adverbs that require it.

Drive carefully and *Mary surely sang well* are the correct usages for these sentences. The words *carefully* and *surely* both modify verbs and are, therefore, adverbs. In both cases, the *-ly* ending is needed. Without the *-ly* ending, these words become adjectives—and adjectives do not modify verbs.

Do not use the adjective form of the modifier to describe verbs—an error that may be tolerated in casual conversation but one that definitely should be avoided in our writing.

Many adverbs are formed by adding the *-ly* ending to an adjective, as shown in the following illustrations:

Adjective	Adverb
nice	nicely
real	really
bad	badly
sure	surely
slow	slowly
cautious	cautiously
careful	carefully

Adjective	Adverb
beautiful	beautifully
helpful	helpfully
predictable	predictably
respectful	respectfully
resourceful	resourcefully

Not all adverbs end in *-ly*, of course, and not all words that end in *-ly* are adverbs. The ability to determine whether a modifier is an adjective or an adverb is essential if you are to know how to use the *-ly* ending correctly.

NO   The protesters behaved *bad.*

YES   The protesters behaved *badly.*

NO   Maurice paints *beautiful.*

YES   Maurice paints *beautifully.*

NO   Speak *cautious* when you give unsolicited advice.

YES   Speak *cautiously* when you give unsolicited advice.

NO   You still have time to get to the meeting if you don't walk too *slow.*

YES   You still have time to get to the meeting if you don't walk too *slowly.*

Learning Hint 6.   If a linking verb (the various forms of the verb *to be;* the verbs *seem, appear, become, remain,* and *stay;* and the sense verbs *feel, look, smell, sound,* and *taste*) is followed by a modifier that suggests action, use an adverb as the modifier. If the modifier does not suggest action, use an adjective.

Use T28-3 here

The message *appeared promptly* on the screen. (The modifier *promptly* that follows the linking verb *appeared* suggests action; the modifier, therefore, takes the adverb form.)

Monique *looked anxiously* out the window. (The modifier *anxiously* that follows the linking verb *looked* suggests action; the modifier, therefore, takes the adverb form.)

The witness *looks confused* by the question. (The modifier *confused* that follows the linking verb *looks* does **not** suggest action; the modifier, therefore, takes the adjective form.)

Carter *felt uneasy* in the darkness. (The modifier *uneasy* that follows the linking verb *felt* does **not** suggest action; the modifier, therefore, takes the adjective form.)

3. **Use correctly the definite article *the* and the indefinite articles *a* and *an* to properly reflect their functions as adjectives.**

Use of the definite article *the* seldom causes problems. On the other hand, when to use the indefinite articles *a* and *an* is not always clear.

Use the article *a* when the next word begins with a consonant sound.

a door
a building
a hallway
a proposal
a promotion
a Utah native (*Utah* begins with the sound of the consonant *y*)
a historical document (*historical* begins with the sound of the consonant *h*)

Use the article *an* when the next word begins with a vowel sound.

an envelope
an organization
an apple
an income-tax statement
an umbrella
an honest man (*honest* begins with the sound of the vowel *o*)

Remember, the sound of a word, not its spelling, determines whether *a* or *an* is the correct choice.

an X-ray (the initial sound of *X-ray* is the vowel *e*)
an M.B.A. degree (the initial sound of *M.B.A.* is the vowel *e*)
a ukelele (the initial sound of *ukelele* is the consonant *y*)
a union contract (the initial sound of *union* is the consonant *y*)
a hypothesis (the initial sound of *hypothesis* is the consonant *h*)
an honorarium (the initial sound of *honorarium* is the vowel *o*)

Learning Hint 7. If an article refers to two or more nouns, repeat the article if necessary to avoid confusion.

The meeting will be attended by *the* secretary and treasurer. (one person, two positions)

The meeting will be attended by *the* secretary and *the* treasurer. (two people, two positions)

The recipe book and dieting guide can be obtained from Delaware Publishing, Inc. (one publication—a combination recipe book and dieting guide)

The recipe book and the dieting guide can be obtained from Delaware Publishing, Inc. (two publications)

For her birthday, Tomiko received *a* radio and phonograph. (one instrument—a radio-phonograph combination)

For her birthday, Tomiko received *a* radio and *a* phonograph. (two instruments—one radio and one phonograph)

Do you have *a* driver and car to take you to the airport? (One article may refer to two or more nouns if confusion does not result.)

4. **Avoid excessive use of modifiers in your writing.**

Although modifiers are useful tools for a writer, they sometimes get in the way of effective communication. This problem often occurs when a writer uses more modifiers than needed to express an idea. Don't let modifiers get away from you! Use them judiciously and with restraint to produce clear writing that is both concise and suitably descriptive.

NO   Marietta's polished recital and musical renditions thrilled and excited the enthusiastic and appreciative audience of music lovers.

YES   Marietta's polished recital thrilled the appreciative audience.

NO   According to the detailed and up-to-date file maintained by the principal's very competent secretary, the student's school attendance record for this entire school year is considered to be anything but satisfactory.

YES   The student's file shows his attendance this year is unsatisfactory.

As a writer, you must determine what modifiers are needed to express your thoughts. Your writing can be condensed—and improved—if you eliminate modifiers that serve no useful purpose.

Learning Hint 8.   Avoid vague and overworked modifiers in your writing. Such modifiers as *good, nice, fine, great, super, really,* and *surely* have been used so often they no longer enjoy precise meanings. You will do well to select adjectives and adverbs that clearly and accurately describe the words they modify.

NO   I saw a *good* movie recently.

YES   I saw a *suspenseful* and *well-acted* movie recently.

NO   Antonio wrote a *fine* report.

YES   Antonio wrote a *brief* but *well-documented* report.

NO   Mrs. Crackin is *really* pleased with your *super* performance, Todd.

YES   Mrs. Crackin is pleased with your *outstanding* performance, Todd.

Mrs. Crackin is *particularly* pleased with your *outstanding* performance, Todd.

Posttest

Write **C** or **I** to indicate whether the use of modifiers is correct or incorrect in the following sentences.

1. Dr. Case suggested the creation of an hospital fund for the elderly.

2. Roger is the oldest of Mrs. Henderson's two grandsons.

3. The May report is the more accurate of the four reports received thus far.

4. As an auditor, Mrs. Palaski is more thorough than anyone in her group.

5. At age 28, Donna Goldberg is the youngest member of the board of directors.

6. The completely correct computations were achieved on the first attempt.

7. Mr. Dougherty is more busier now than he has ever been.

8. Jodie is more familiar with Celia's work than you.

9. Marcie received a grill and waffle maker for Christmas that are sure to be used often by her family.

10. The head of Accounting, Reese Murwin, is paid more money per month than anyone in the firm's Division of Financial Operations.

11. The Winter King snow thrower priced at $595 is self propelled and comes equipped with steel blades and a 5 horsepower self lubricating motor.

12. The beautifully arranged display room at Warmley Brothers, Inc. features rich, comfortable furniture and an unusual assortment of modernistic floor lamps.

Key: (1) I—replace *an* with the correct article *a*; (2) I—the comparative form *older* should be used in place of *oldest*; (3) I—the superlative form *most* should be used in place of *more*; (4) I—an illogical statement; Mrs. Palaski cannot be more thorough than herself; change to *than anyone else*; (5) C; (6) I—the use of the modifier *completely* with the absolute adjective *correct* is illogical; (7) I—use the comparative form *busier* instead of the double comparative *more busier*; (8) I—this statement is an incomplete comparison; (9) I—use the article *a* both with *grill* and with *waffle maker* to indicate two items rather than one combination item; (10) I—as an employee in Financial Operations, Reese cannot be paid more money than himself; (11) I—self-propelled, 5-horsepower, and self-lubricating should be hyphenated; (12)—C.

LEVEL A

Name _____

Exercise
28–1

On the lines below, write **T** if the statement is true; write **F** if the statement is false.

_T_ 1. A modifier may be a single word, a phrase, or a clause.

_F_ 2. An adjective may describe another adjective.

_T_ 3. The word *greatest* is the superlative form of the word *great*.

_F_ 4. The positive degree compares two (but not more than two) persons or things.

_T_ 5. The words *more* and *less* are used to indicate the comparative degree.

_T_ 6. Both adverbs and adjectives may be expressed in the positive, comparative, and superlative degrees.

_F_ 7. The words *farther* and *further* are the irregular comparative and superlative forms of the word *far*.

_F_ 8. The three comparative forms of the word *bad* are *bad, badder,* and *baddest.*

_F_ 9. The sentence *Elvin is younger than anyone on his team* is an example of a double comparison.

_F_ 10. Absolute adjectives suggest extremes and are, therefore, good choices for making comparisons.

_T_ 11. The words *correct, priceless,* and *alive* are good examples of absolute adjectives.

_T_ 12. The sentence *Lorna answered all test questions as complete as possible* is incorrectly formed because of the omission of the *-ly* ending.

_T_ 13. The adjective form of the adverb *really* is *real.*

_F_ 14. All adverbs end in *-ly.*

_F_ 15. The article *a* is used when the next word begins with the sound of a vowel.

_F_ 16. *An* is the correct choice of article for use with the word *union.*

_T_ 17. The sound of a word, not its spelling, determines whether *a* or *an* should be used.

_T_ 18. The terms *history, historical,* and *historical figure* all should be preceded by the article *a* rather than *an* because the initial sound of each term is that of a consonant.

_T_ 19. If an article refers to two nouns in the same sentence, the article is sometimes—but not always—repeated with the second noun.

_T_ 20. The sentence *Ms. Conak works faster than anyone in the office* is weakened by a confused comparison.

_T_ 21. The definite article *the* and the indefinite articles *a* and *an* are all modifiers.

_F_ 22. The article *an* is used correctly in the sentence *The event is described by some authors as an historical accident.*

Exercise 28–2 Write **C** if the bold modifier is used correctly; write **I** if it is used incorrectly.

_I_ 1. Cassia met this morning with **the** secretary and treasurer, Nelda Garcia and Juan Mendez.

_I_ 2. The **smartest** of the two students is Melissa Falacci with a 3.9 grade-point average.

_C_ 3. Dan is **less** tactful than I in making recommendations for improved service to our customers.

_I_ 4. Of all your friends, I want to be considered one of the **better** ones.

_I_ 5. Your attendance, Reese, is **better** than the rest of the class.

_C_ 6. In her group, Marianna has gone **farthest** toward completing the work assigned.

_I_ 7. Professor Prudkin stated that we will be even **more busier** near the end of the semester.

_I_ 8. Your critique of the proposal is **more** detailed than Seth.

_C_ 9. The more people who help, the **less** tired we will be when we finish.

_C_ 10. **An** original Hawaiian ukelele may be purchased at the music store for about $150.

_C_ 11. The **smallest** travel bag in the group belongs to me.

_I_ 12. Plan B is clearly **more unique** than Plan A.

Exercise 28–3 Write **C** if the use of modifiers is correct. Write **I** if the use of modifiers is incorrect.

_C_ 1. Our Milwaukee field manager—the youngest of the three nominees—is scheduled to meet with you tomorrow morning at nine o'clock.

_I_ 2. Both customers filed complaints with the store, but Mrs. Doogins will be the most difficult to please.

_C_ 3. The smallest annoyance is enough to cause Mr. Prithering to fly into a rage.

_C_ 4. Notify the agency that none of the five applicants referred to us is satisfactory, although Miss Derwinsky comes closer to meeting our needs than any of the others.

_C_ 5. The faster car in the race is No. 37, even though the other car in the event is reported to be equipped with a new turbo-thrust engine.

_I_ 6. Bob Webley, in Car No. 16, has won more prize money this year than any driver entered in today's events.

_I_ 7. Which engineer do you suppose feels worst about the flaw in the mechanical design—Ray DeBakey or Bruno Greene?

_I_ 8. Actually, the design error is less worrisome to us than are several other problems related to the project.

_I_ 9. All the officials agreed that Bob Webber is a much-better driver this season.

_C_ 10. The driver's assessment of the problem suggests he has a better grasp of the facts than does the president of the drivers' association.

LEVEL B

Name _____

Exercise 28–4   Write the letter identifying the statement that reflects the preferred usage of modifiers.

_a_ 1. *a.* One characteristic of a good organization is the ability to serve the needs of its members.
  b. The cost of an union membership is expected to rise 20 percent this year.
  c. An extra-large envelope and a air-mail label will be needed for this mailing.

_c_ 2. *a.* Mrs. Crystal Partridge, the owner and the managing director of The Prowess Agency, will be the featured speaker at the symposium.
  b. The doctor prescribed a high-protein diet and a intensive exercise program for the final phase of the patient's rehabilitation.
  c. The word processor is considered an indispensable tool in the modern business office.

_a_ 3. *a.* Brady's small dog, Popeye, is even smaller than the family cat and is, in fact, the smallest dog in the neighborhood.
  b. Even though Popeye is smaller than might be expected, he is definitely the most noisiest dog on the street.
  c. Brady claims that Popeye's bark is the most-funnier bark of any dog the family has ever owned.

_b_ 4. *a.* Is Lonnie the stronger member of the wrestling team, as he claims?
  b. Is Maggie a better hitter than any other member of the volleyball team?
  c. Is Coach Pruitt the most-hardest-working member of the coaching staff?

_c_ 5. *a.* We expect the team to be better prepared on Saturday.
  b. The pitcher, Ryan Pearson, is probably more talented than any member of the team.
  c. The best-conditioned athlete on the team is undoubtedly Harrison Despain, the catcher.

_c_ 6. *a.* The Fairborne Company's proposal is less detailed than the Claxton Company.
  b. Furthermore, the Fairborne Company's ideas are more unique than any we have heard thus far.
  c. I believe the Fairborne concept is more promising than any the planning committee has considered.

_b_ 7. *a.* All players must pay an uniform fee of $40 by Monday.
  b. An athletic participation fee of $25 is also required for each sport.
  c. In some cases, a exception is made if a student participates in three or more sports.

_a_ 8. *a.* I really believe you should proceed slowly in making your decision.
  b. A refusal letter that is worded careful has been drafted by the architect.
  c. I feel badly that only one of the excellent proposals we received can be funded.

_c_ 9. *a.* I'm sorry to say that Mr. Taggart's line of reasoning seems to me to be completely hopeless.
  b. Kelly is the older of the triplets by less than three minutes.
  c. Miss McKelling is a more-experienced advisor than either Miss Ling or Miss Garza.

_b_   10. *a.*   The quality of personal integrity is thought by many to be the most priceless of all human attributes.

             b.   An eagle and a unicorn appear on the logo of the World Tours travel agency.

             c.   Jose definitely handles angry customers' complaints more skillful than Carlos.

_c_   11. *a.*   Mr. Skorney reported that the audience's response to his presentation was the deadest he had ever seen.

             b.   Austin said he has never worked with a more-happier person than Kylie Fleming.

             c.   Anatole Daviden's critique of *None but the Valiant* was the funniest of the three reviews he presented to the Middleburg Book Club.

_a_   12. *a.*   Is the girl with the red hair the younger of the two swimmers?

             b.   No, she is the older of the two swimmers as well as the older of the four girls in her family.

             c.   As the oldest girl, Hannah has a special responsibility for Dorothy—the younger of Hannah's three sisters.

_a_   13. *a.*   Alexandra earned the best grades in her writing class this term.

             b.   In her class of 25 students, she was judged to be better in both keyboard composition and creative writing.

             c.   Alexandra found the research paper to be the most-hard assignment given in the course.

_a_   14. *a.*   Thanks to your careful planning, the fund-raising drive was—predictably—a huge success.

             b.   Can I count on you, as team captain, to exhibit more leadership than anyone on the team?

             c.   The direction lines you have drawn on the map need to be more straight.

_c_   15. *a.*   The announcement indicated the reception is to be held at a Elk Ridge Drive address.

             b.   Colder temperatures have been forecast for the Uinta Mountains.

             c.   Although Andreas is not an officer in the organization, he is, nevertheless, a union member who lives in an Oregon city.

_c_   16. *a.*   Of the two Italian restaurants in Wittberg, Luigi's is the best.

             b.   The better menu item at Luigi's is Veal Marsalla.

             c.   The service at Luigi's Restaurant is better now than it has ever been.

_a_   17. *a.*   The teacher looked sad when the announcement was read.

             b.   The players spoke excited about their narrow victory.

             c.   Leaking chemicals smelled badly to everyone near the scene of the accident.

_c_   18. *a.*   All agreed that the cherry pie tasted deliciously.

             b.   We hope everyone will feel happily about this new opportunity.

             c.   What makes you sound so concerned?

_b_   19. *a.*   Do you feel that Marissa is the best of the two applicants?

             b.   The manager feels happy about your promotion.

             c.   I have been told you feel badly about my transfer.

_b_   20. *a.*   Saturday is the better day of the week for the reunion.

             b.   What is your best cost estimate for this project?

             c.   After comparing Don's plan with Dave, I believe Don's plan is best.

LEVEL C

Name _____

Exercise 28–5

Editing

Determine whether the bold words are used correctly in the following sentences according to the guidelines given in this lesson. If they are not, edit them to make the necessary corrections. Two of the sentences are correct in their present form.

1. Today is the **happiest** day of my life!

2. I consider Mrs. Locker's comment to be the ~~**more**~~ *most* profound statement made thus far in the seminar.

3. Moon Lake is **larger** than Trial Lake, but both of them are **smaller** than Crater Reservoir.

4. The architect recommended that **an** additional entrance **nearer ~~a~~** *an* elevator be provided in the remodeled building for the physically handicapped visitors.

5. Of the two drafts the student submitted for review in Technical Writing 100-A, the second draft is definitely ~~the **best**~~ *better*.

6. The book you asked about is checked out **more often than any** *other* **book** in our school library.

7. The office manager believes ~~**farther**~~ *further* work will be needed before we take our projections to the finance officer.

8. Can the St. Louis office process the financial data **more efficiently than** ~~**New Orleans**~~ *the New Orleans office can*?

9. The new model is the ~~**most-perfect**~~ *best* product available in the commercial manufacturing industry.

10. Wadkins Construction Company has given us ~~**a**~~ *an* estimate based on **an** unusual assumption related to expected company growth.

11. **The printer and** *the* **word processor** shown on page 206 of the catalog appear to be ideal for our office.

Exercise 28–6

Editing

Edit the following sentences where necessary according to the guidelines presented in this lesson on the use of modifiers. Two of the sentences are correct in their present form.

1. Royce is easily the ~~more~~ *most*-interesting person on the jury.

2. However, his views are ~~least~~ *less* likely to sway the other jurors than those of the jury foreman, Mr. Tyler Waltripp.

3. As an attorney, Ms. Kymert appeared ~~most~~ *more* skilled in handling the jury's emotions than her opponent, Mr. Kattelle.

4. Students in Art 111 are expected to provide paints, paint brushes, canvas, and ~~a~~ *an* easel for their own use during the course.

5. After looking at both locations, the planning director determined that the Skyline Drive site offers the ~~most~~ *more*-promising possibilities for a new restaurant.

6. The June sales performance of the Southwest District is the ~~stronger~~ *strongest* of the performances by the firm's eight districts in the U.S.

7. The television promotion campaign launched in the fall seems to have produced an endless stream of new customers for our products.

8. Mr. Telford, at age 71 the ~~older~~ *oldest* member of the board of directors, still conducts each meeting with his customary wit and good humor.

9. To no one's surprise, a traffic survey recently determined that the ~~most~~ noisiest street in the city is Central Boulevard.

10. We have learned that an unsold piece of property on the West Side may offer the least-expensive location for the proposed warehouse.

11. Just between you and me, Jon's performance on the Spokane project is noticeably better *than his performance on the Boise project.*

Exercise 28–7

Cumulative Editing

Edit the following sentences according to (1) the guidelines given in Unit 5 for using nouns and pronouns and (2) the guidelines presented in this lesson for using modifiers. Two of the sentences in their present form use nouns, pronouns, and modifiers correctly.

1. The ~~more~~ *most* qualified of the three candidates for Vice President of Consumer Affairs is ~~her~~ *she.*

2. Because these are Lilah's belongings, they will be forwarded to her in Baltimore immediately.

3. The best-liked directors of the research center in its 30-year history are Gerald Tobler and ~~him~~ *he.*

4. ~~Us~~ *We* students agree that the requirements of this class are ~~more~~ heavier by far than we expected.

5. According to Dennis, Cassie is as well prepared for graduate school as ~~him~~ *he is.*

6. In the future, all new employees will be required to have ~~a~~ *an* interview with ~~myself~~ *me* before they begin work.

7. The department chair challenged ~~we~~ *us* instructors to be better teachers than anyone *else* in our school.

8. Except for ~~he~~ *him*, the entire squad played better in last night's game *than in the previous game.*

9. Without warning, the boss ordered Vanessa and ~~she~~ *her* to cancel all meetings and interviews scheduled for Thursday afternoon.

10. You yourself know that the most-motivated workers in our present group of 12 trainees likely will be offered permanent positions with the firm.

11. None of the proposals submitted by ~~we~~ *us* three designers was given even so much as ~~a~~ *an* honorable mention in the final judging.

12. We are not surprised that more people are parking in Lot No. 36 *than in Lot No. 35* this semester, as predicted by ~~myself and~~ the campus traffic office *and me.*

13. ~~Who~~ *Whom* do the humidifier and the air purifier belong to?

Exercise 28–8

Edit the following sentences according to (1) the guidelines given in Unit 5 for using nouns and pronouns and (2) the guidelines presented in this lesson for using modifiers. If you can, find the two sentences that are correct in their present form.

Cumulative Editing

1. Archie Cox, ~~that~~ *who* is always the ~~less~~ *least*-prepared member of the group, has submitted his resignation.

2. The company policy that is under review forbids workers to accumulate more than three weeks of unused sick leave.

3. Miss Tompkin's recommendation, which came as no surprise, is better than any of the *other* recommendations she has submitted thus far.

4. Only the person in charge, ~~which~~ *who* everyone knows is Mrs. Wennert, can make that decision— one that could be the ~~more~~ *most*-important step of her career.

5. Ruth Wharton, the secretary whom you met yesterday, apologized for speaking ~~bad~~ *badly* about her supervisor.

6. The bicycle ~~which~~ *that* we found in the street has ~~a~~ *an* identification tag on the handlebars.

7. The man who called about the bicycle and ~~that~~ *who* offered ~~an~~ *a* reward for its return has a ~~most~~ unique voice.

8. The book that you borrowed yesterday and its author, ~~which~~ *whom* you met this morning, will leave you with two of your ~~more~~ *most*-pleasant memories.

9. You may not understand Ivan's English as well as Brandon's, but Ivan is the person who has helped us most and to whom we should express our sincere thanks.

10. Trina drove her old car to work because her new car, ~~that~~ *which* has ~~a~~ *an* engine problem, is in the repair shop on Cumberland Avenue.

As describing words, modifiers can act individually or together to define or limit other words. Modifiers that act alone are called *individual* or *independent modifiers*. Two or more modifiers that act together are called *compound modifiers*.

Note the following sentences:

The *young* worker asked an *unusual* question.

The *old cathedral* spire is a campus landmark.

The *intelligent, resourceful* secretary deserves a raise.

The *newly hired* executive submitted a *well-stated* proposal.

In the first sentence, the words *young* and *unusual* act as independent modifiers.

In the second sentence, the words *old* and *cathedral* are consecutive, independent modifiers. Because these consecutive modifiers are not equal in rank, they are not separated by a comma.

In the third sentence, the words *intelligent* and *resourceful* are equal in rank and are, therefore, separated by a comma. They are said to be *coordinate modifiers*.

In the fourth sentence, the words *newly* and *hired* act together as one compound modifier; the words *well* and *stated* act together as another compound modifier.

As shown above, commas are used to separate coordinate modifiers, but not consecutive modifiers. Hyphens are frequently used with compound modifiers. And in some cases, compound modifiers occur in a series that requires the use of both hyphens and commas.

The proper order and form of consecutive modifiers, coordinate modifiers, and compound modifiers will be discussed in this lesson. As you become familiar with the guidelines provided, your confidence in your ability to use modifiers effectively in your writing will increase.

443

Pretest

Write **C** or **I** to indicate whether modifiers are used correctly or incorrectly in the following sentences.

1. Barney Olds is considered to be a blue-ribbon soccer player.

2. Mr. Tolliver, our high school principal, received his master's degree from Florida State University.

3. The sales meeting was especially well-planned by the headquarters staff.

4. Our visit to the University-of-Washington campus went exactly as planned.

5. A stop at the little doughnut shop on Ninth Avenue is always a treat.

6. The accident occurred at a crowded, dangerous intersection in the downtown area.

7. Miss Tiners must be considered a thoroughly prepared applicant for the position in Minneapolis.

8. The professor told his students to avoid long rambling sentences in their writing.

9. The least expensive items in the Danton family's yard sale were no more than 25 cents each.

10. Row after row of bright shiny new cars may be seen on the attractive, display lot on Million Dollar Drive.

Key: (1) C; (2) I—the compound modifier *high school* should be hyphenated; (3) I—the modifiers *well planned* are not followed by a noun and, therefore, should not be hyphenated; (4) I—the proper adjective *University of Washington* should not be hyphenated; (5) C; (6) C; (7) C; (8) I—the modifiers *long* and *rambling* should be separated by a comma to avoid confusion; (9) I—*least expensive* should be hyphenated; (10) I—commas are needed after the coordinate adjectives *bright* and *shiny*, but no comma is needed after the consecutive adjective *attractive*.

Terminology

Compound modifier—Two or more words acting together as a single adjective. Some compounds consist of adverb-adjective combinations (*well-behaved* youngster, *best-looking* daughter); other compounds consist of adjective-adjective combinations (*old-fashioned* clothes, *left-hand* column).

Consecutive modifiers—Two or more modifiers in an uninterrupted series of modifiers that are unequal in rank and that are, therefore, not separated by commas (*delicious apple* pie, *comfortable rocking* chair).

Coordinate modifiers—Two or more modifiers that describe the same word; that are equal in rank; and that are, therefore, separated by commas (*tall, dark* stranger; *attractive, modern* office).

Independent modifier—A single-word modifier (*long* report; *dependable* worker).

Proper adjective—A capitalized term that names a particular person, place, or thing and that functions as a modifier rather than as a noun (*Thanksgiving Day* dinner; *Acme Tool Corporation* employees).

Rules

Use
T29-1
here

1. **Place a hyphen between the words of a compound modifier that precedes a noun.**

Two or more words acting together as a single modifier are called a **compound modifier**. Join such modifiers with a hyphen when they precede a noun.

> a *first-place* trophy
> her *get-well* card
> the *well-qualified* instructor
> an *up-to-date* resume
> Ben's *never-say-die* attitude

NO   Dave Boley is our *best known* representative in the East.

YES   Dave Boley is our *best-known* representative in the East.

NO   The burro is known as a *sure footed* animal.

YES   The burro is known as a *sure-footed* animal.

NO   Jeff's get up and go approach to his work nearly always leads to blue ribbon results.

YES   Jeff's get-up-and-go approach to his work nearly always leads to blue-ribbon results.

Learning Hint 1.   Knowing whether to hyphenate modifiers that precede a noun often depends on the writer's ability to identify the noun in question. Consider the following sentences:

> When do you expect to deposit your *social security check*?

> Dwight will receive his *high school diploma* in May.

In the first sentence, is the term *social security check* a noun; or is *check* the noun with *social* and *security* acting as modifiers?

In the second sentence, is the term *high school diploma* a noun; or is *diploma* the noun with *high* and *school* acting as modifiers?

Answers to these questions will vary—even among the "experts." A thoughtful look at these statements, however, will help you make the correct choice.

In the first sentence, the word *social* modifies *security*, not *check*. The words *social* and *security* thus join logically together to form a compound modifier that describes *check*. As a compound modifier, *social-security* should be hyphenated.

Similarly, in the second sentence, the word *high* modifies *school*, not *diploma*. The words *high* and *school* join logically together to form a compound modifier that describes *diploma*. As a compound modifier, *high-school* should be hyphenated.

Some writers regard terms like *social security check* and *high school diploma* as multiple-word nouns. In this text, for purposes of consistency and simplicity, we have taken the position that in most such cases the last word in the series is the noun. The words preceding the noun are considered modifiers. For that reason, the proper form of these two sentences is as follows:

When do you expect to deposit your *social-security check*?

Dwight will receive his *high-school diploma* in May.

Most compound modifiers reflect two or more adjectives that modify a noun (*student-authored paper, middle-class American, career-driven person*). As such, these compound modifiers are often called **compound adjectives**.

However, some compound modifiers are adverb-adjective combinations (*most-qualified candidate, least-expensive purchase, much-improved growth*). Style manuals are not consistent in dictating whether the hyphen should appear in such adverb-adjective compound modifiers.

For consistency purposes in this text, we hyphenate adverb-adjective modifiers unless the adverb ends in *-ly*. (See Rule 3 for a further discussion of *-ly* adverbs.)

NO best informed person
    above mentioned facts
    most prized possessions
    carefully-prepared presentation
    slightly-built man
    nicely-phrased compliment

YES best-informed person
     above-mentioned facts
     most-prized possessions
     carefully prepared presentation
     slightly built man
     nicely phrased compliment

Note the difference in meaning when the hyphen is used or not used in such sentences as the following:

We need more-qualified employees than we presently employ.
We need more qualified employees than we presently employ.

The large-appliance industry is growing rapidly.
The large appliance industry is growing rapidly.

Learning Hint 2.   As stated in Learning Hint 1, your expertise in hyphenating compound modifiers depends on your ability to identify the noun in a multiple-word expression.

Nouns may consist of one word only or of two or more words without hyphens. For example, the following multiple-word terms are nouns without hyphens:

gross national product
conflict of interest
condensed balance sheet
cost of goods sold

In a similar respect, nouns that follow compound modifiers can be one word or more than one word. For example:

fair-trade *price*   Indefinite-life *intangible fixed asset*
carry-forward *working papers*   full-paid *capital stock*

How do you determine what noun is in relation to the modifiers in such expressions? One technique that works well in most instances is called the *cadence test.*

To use the cadence test, simply put a dramatic pause between the various options in a multiple-word expression. When your ear tells you the pause is a natural one, more than likely you will then know what the noun is and, therefore, what the compound modifer is.

For example, apply the cadence test as you read the following options out loud. Give a lengthy pause where indicated, and then decide whether the expression following the pause is a normal one. In each instance, you're trying to determine whether the italic item following the pause is the noun.

full   *faith and credit debit*
full faith   *and credit debit*
full faith and   *credit debit*
full faith and credit   *debit*

Obviously, the cadence test tells you Item 4 is the logical choice. Therefore, you know that *debit* is the noun and that hyphens must appear in the compound modifier as follows: *full-faith-and-credit-debit.*

If you are having difficulty determining the noun in relation to the compound modifier in a multiple-word expression, try the cadence test.

Learning Hint 3.   Hyphens are usually omitted in compound modifiers that follow a noun.

The car has *well-worn* tires.
The car has tires that are *well worn.*

The Cougars have a *strong-armed* quarterback.
The Cougars have a quarterback who is *strong armed.*

Send this memo to every *part-time* student.
Send this memo to every student who attends school *part time.*

Learning Hint 4.   With few exceptions (such as *selfish* and *selfless*), *self* words are written as hyphenated compounds whether they precede or follow a noun.

self-sufficient employee
an employee who is *self-sufficient*

self-protected software
software that is *self-protected*

self-lubricating machine
a machine that is *self-lubricating*

Learning Hint 5.   Compound modifiers that are multiple-word **proper adjectives** are not hyphenated.

NO   The new automobile will be built and assembled at the *Chrysler-Corporation* plant in Midland.

YES   The new automobile will be built and assembled at the *Chrysler Corporation* plant in Midland.

NO   The *Auburn-University* stadium will undergo renovation later this year.

YES   The *Auburn University* stadium will undergo renovation later this year.

NO   A *White-House* ceremony is scheduled for 11 a.m. on July 4.

YES   A *White House* ceremony is scheduled for 11 a.m. on July 4.

Learning Hint 6.   Some adjectives that occur in a series of two or more terms before a noun do not form logical compound modifiers. These modifiers are either **coordinate** or **consecutive**, depending on whether they are equal in rank. They function as separate modifiers rather than as compounds. In such cases, the use of a hyphen is illogical.

Do not hyphenate two or more adjectives that precede a noun if they do not act jointly to form a single compound modifier.

NO   my *new-straw* hat (*new* and *straw* do not join together logically to modify *hat*)

YES   my *new straw* hat (*new* and *straw* are consecutive modifiers)

NO   Robin's *restored-antique* car

YES   Robin's *restored antique* car

NO   a *popular-rock* song

YES   a *popular rock* song

The incorrect examples in this group of illustrations demonstrate the illogical pairing of adjectives that function properly as *consecutive* modifiers.

Use T29-2 here

2. **Use a comma to separate coordinate adjectives that precede a noun.**

Notice how the commas inserted in the following expressions improve the flow and clarity of the language.

a long, winding road

the cool, cloudy weather

our old, outdated equipment

your intelligent, energetic secretary

the difficult, frustrating examination

Remember that coordinate adjectives are separated by commas; consecutive adjectives are not. The italicized adjectives in the following sentences are **coordinate** adjectives.

NO   The meeting will begin with a *brief entertaining* greeting from the mayor.

YES   The meeting will begin with a *brief, entertaining* greeting from the mayor.

NO   A *bright energetic trustworthy* manager is needed for the Cedar City office.

YES   A *bright, energetic, trustworthy* manager is needed for the Cedar City office.

NO   The work crew transformed a *small dreary* entrance into a *comfortable convenient good-looking* reception area.

YES   The work crew transformed a *small, dreary* entry into a *comfortable, convenient, good-looking* reception area.

Learning Hint 7.   If you are uncertain whether to use a comma between nonhyphenated modifiers that precede a noun, try this simple, two-step test. Mentally switch the modifiers' positions with each other and see if the sentence makes sense. Then insert the word *and* between the modifiers and, again, see if the sentence reads logically. If the sentence "feels" comfortable and its meaning remains essentially unchanged **with both parts of the test**, use a comma between the modifiers. Otherwise, leave the comma out.

NO   Mr. and Mrs. Peck recently moved into a *fine, brick home*. (*A brick fine home* doesn't sound right; neither does *a fine and brick home*. Therefore, omit the comma.)

YES   Mr. and Mrs. Peck recently moved into a *fine brick home*.

NO   We awakened to a *dark dreary day*. (*A dreary dark day* sounds logical; so does *a dark and dreary day*. Therefore, a comma should be inserted after *dark*.)

YES   We awakened to a *dark, dreary day*.

NO   I plan to hire a *pleasant efficient receptionist*. (*An efficient pleasant receptionist* sounds right; so does *a pleasant and efficient receptionist*. Therefore, a comma should be inserted after *pleasant*.)

YES   I plan to hire a *pleasant, efficient receptionist*.

I plan to hire a *pleasant and efficient receptionist*. (The conjunction *and* is interchangeable with the comma in this sentence.)

You must occasionally use your own judgment in deciding whether modifiers that precede a noun should be separated by a comma. Even authorities on language usage don't always agree on this point. If you observe the guidelines presented in this lesson, however, you will usually make the right choice.

Use T29-1 again here

3. **Do not hyphenate a compound modifier if one of the words in the compound is an adverb ending in *-ly*.**

The hyphen is not needed to indicate that an adverb ending in *-ly* and some other word act jointly as a compound modifier. Since the hyphen serves no useful purpose in such constructions, it is omitted—whether the modifiers occur before or after the words modified.

NO   a *beautifully-played* concerto
Wendell's *carefully-written* manuscript
her *kindly-worded* letter
the *hastily-called* press conference

YES   a *beautifully played* concerto
Wendell's *carefully written* manuscript
her *kindly worded* letter
the *hastily called* press conference

a concerto that was *beautifully played*
Wendell's manuscript that is *carefully written*
her letter that is *kindly worded*
the press conference that was *hastily called*

Posttest

Write **C** or **I** to indicate whether modifiers are used correctly or incorrectly in the following sentences.

1. The Calgary Stampede celebration offers outstanding entertainment to all who attend.

2. The angry-frustrated customer demanded a full refund of his airfare.

3. The chief suspect claimed he carried a gun strictly for self defense.

4. That modern-looking structure is both attractive and well-built.

5. The clean-shaven recruit was complimented on his appearance.

6. All recently-approved guidelines go into effect tomorrow morning.

7. The lower-parking level is now completely filled.

8. Our northern territory offers many promising, exciting opportunities for a hard-working salesman.

9. Merle Jones recommends the Barton-Street location as the most promising site for another Sunshine convenience store in this city.

10. A complete physical-examination has been ordered by Dr. Jurelski for the ailing elderly patient in Room 701 in the transitory care unit.

Key: (1) C; (2) I—the coordinate modifiers *angry* and *frustrated* should be separated by a comma; (3) I—*self defense* should be hyphenated; (4) I—the compound modifier *well-built* should not be hyphenated because it does not precede a noun; (5) C; (6) I—the adverb *recently* ends in *-ly* and, therefore, should not be hyphenated; (7) I—the words *lower-parking* should not be hyphenated because they do not act together logically as a single modifier; (8) C; (9) I—the multiple-word proper adjective *Barton-Street* should not be hyphenated, whereas the compound modifier *most promising* should be hyphenated; (10) I—omit the hyphen in *physical examination*, and separate the coordinate adjectives *ailing* and *elderly* with a comma.

LEVEL A

Name _____

Exercise
29–1

On the lines below, write **T** if the statement is true; write **F** if the statement is false.

_T_ 1. Two words that act jointly to modify or describe another word are called a compound modifier.

_T_ 2. Compound adjectives are hyphenated if they are followed by a noun.

_F_ 3. Consecutive modifiers are sometimes—but not always—separated by commas.

_F_ 4. In the sentence *George is late,* the word *George* is a proper adjective.

_F_ 5. In the expression *long hot summer,* the words *long* and *hot* should be hyphenated.

_T_ 6. If two adjectives can have their positions reversed and the conjunction *and* placed between them without changing the meaning of the sentence, the adjectives should be separated by a comma.

_T_ 7. Hyphens are usually omitted in a compound modifier that follows a noun.

_F_ 8. In general, *self* words are hyphenated if they precede a noun; they are not hyphenated if they follow a noun.

_F_ 9. Multiple-word, proper adjectives should be hyphenated.

_T_ 10. Coordinate adjectives that precede a noun always should be separated by a comma.

_F_ 11. Adverb-adjective combinations that precede nouns should be hyphenated if the adverb ends in *-ly.*

_F_ 12. The hyphen is used correctly in the expression *Miss Trager's criticism is well-meant.*

_T_ 13. Modifiers that occur in a series may require the use of both hyphens and commas to satisfy established usage standards.

_F_ 14. All modifiers meet acceptable standards of good form in the sentence *A suitably-pre-pared student is nearly-always successful.*

_F_ 15. Two or more words that act jointly to modify another word are always hyphenated.

Exercise
29–2

Write **C** if the italicized modifiers are used correctly; write **I** if they are used incorrectly.

_C_ 1. Jilean's diamond ring is definitely in the *high-price* category.

_I_ 2. This year's *Christmas-Day* parade will include more than 100 entries.

_I_ 3. The *slightly-built* man demonstrated remarkable physical strength.

_I_ 4. A *new synthetic, rubber* plant will soon be constructed on the outskirts of town.

_C_ 5. The city is in need of an *attractive, spacious, well-constructed* civic arena.

_I_ 6. The model constructed by the architect appears to be made entirely of a *newly-developed* fiberglass compound.

_I_   7. A *top, notch* player of Wendy's caliber comes along only *once-in-a-while*.

_C_   8. A *much-improved*, medical-insurance package is a *badly needed* addition to the firm's *employee-benefits* program.

_I_   9. The *State-of-California* legislature is expected to pass *major, insurance* legislation this spring.

_C_ 10. Mrs. Dagglin introduced her literature class to a *beautifully written* sonnet.

_I_ 11. As predicted on *last-night's* weathercast, today has brought an abundance of *windy blustery* weather.

_C_ 12. Mr. Adams' dog, Pretty Lady, has a *three-strand* identification choker around her neck.

_C_ 13. The Model 300-ZT is a *quick-starting* machine preferred by business firms that do a lot of *word-processing* work.

_I_ 14. This year's basketball tournament will follow a *round robin* format in determining a tournament champion.

_I_ 15. Sonora is confident that a *properly-placed* advertisement in the Ponca City News will produce a buyer for her *ten-speed* bicycle.

Exercise 29–3   Write **C** if the use of modifiers is correct; write **I** if the use of modifiers is incorrect.

_C_   1. The most-current data available indicate a new shopping plaza is badly needed in this area.

_C_   2. Your energetic, intelligent secretary is a terrific asset in your office.

_C_   3. As a result of his test scores, Freddy is recognized as a sure-fire prospect for admission to the Air Force Academy.

_I_   4. In May, the United-States-Army Band will make an appearance in the Salt Palace.

_I_   5. We have heard over-and-over again that the site of the new high school is not going to be changed.

_C_   6. Professor Fuad's most-promising students are Gretchen, DaLynn, and Samantha.

_I_   7. Remember, Ms. Sabatini, all out of town calls are to be charged to the customer-relations account.

_I_   8. One largely-overlooked possibility is Leila Tonne's suggestion that we transfer our operations to Miami.

_C_   9. The Texas Railroad Company bid is very much in line with our expectations.

_I_ 10. The expert work of Harry Pawner—a last-minute substitute—saved us from losing the biggest most-profitable account we have.

_I_ 11. Please report to my office on Monday morning to review the quarterly, financial reports from our seven regional offices.

_C_ 12. A five-step program of plant improvement has been given the green light by the CEO and the board of directors.

LEVEL B

Name _____

Exercise 29–4 Write the letter identifying the statement that reflects the preferred usage of modifiers.

c 1. *a.* Please furnish the foyer with comfortable attractive furniture.
   b. A tactfully-presented alternative seems likely to be well received.
   c. A good bet is that our new manager will prove to be a truly capable executive.

a 2. *a.* A three-minute egg is the beginning of a nutritious breakfast.
   b. Only once this month has a poorly-prepared estimate been submitted for review.
   c. Few believe the contract was not carefully-reviewed and double-checked before it was signed.

b 3. *a.* Randy has been working at the old, flour mill since September 1.
   b. Is that his bright-red sports car parked in the employees' parking lot?
   c. Without a doubt, that car is a powerful exciting road machine.

a 4. *a.* The creative-writing class offered by Waterford College is one of the best around.
   b. I'd like a strawberry ice cream cone, please.
   c. The brick-building on the corner of State and Main is the tourist information center you asked about.

c 5. *a.* The well staged production of *The Old Man and the Sea* now playing at the Bijou Theater is absolutely first-rate.
   b. None of the performers has been in a big time production previously, I was told.
   c. The theater's technical equipment—up to date in all respects—contributes much to the production's success.

c 6. *a.* A little success does a lot to build one's self confidence.
   b. Yes, without a doubt, Mr. Goodin is a selfmade man.
   c. To get along in your work and at the same time retain your self-respect, just do the right thing every time you make a choice.

c 7. *a.* The Dixon-Manufacturing plant in Charleston employs upwards of 2,000 people.
   b. Few events are as colorful as the Parade-of-Roses in Pasadena, California.
   c. The grueling Indianapolis 500 racing spectacle is one of the major sporting events in the U.S. each year.

a 8. *a.* When the project can be suitably funded, we will get the green light to proceed.
   b. A fully-accredited college is the goal of the Marion County School Board.
   c. A heated discussion of bonding options for school construction needs led to a proposal that was quickly accepted.

b 9. *a.* We now subscribe to *The Trumpet,* Porter City's popular, daily newspaper.
   b. Rush, Inc. is well known for its speedy, reliable, overnight delivery service.
   c. The prospect of converting the dilapidated, train depot into a recreation center for the elderly is widely supported.

c 10. *a.* This year, the Rocky-Mountain Rodeo will be held in West Valley City, June 16–22.
   b. Car No. 6 is the highly favored entry in this year's Skyline-Ridge race.
   c. The cross-country runners followed steep, mountain trails to reach the finish line.

_c_ 11. *a.* A fair, minded approach should be taken in the matter if we want to avoid injured feelings.

        b. In about one hour, the new products manager will meet with us in his private office.

        c. As a matter of fact, the judges gave the first-place rating to your performance on the parallel bars.

_b_ 12. *a.* According to the defense attorney, a calmly-stated review of the evidence is likely to have the desired impact on the jury.

        b. The timid, frightened witness was admonished by the judge to answer the attorney's questions truthfully.

        c. As the jury returned to the courtroom, the confident self-assured defendant rose to her feet to hear the verdict.

_c_ 13. *a.* Parry won the championship with the help of his favorite-tennis racket.

        b. Parry won the championship with the help of his favorite, tennis racket.

        c. Parry won the championship with the help of his favorite tennis racket.

_a_ 14. *a.* Lucy's long-awaited appointment to the Central Planning Commission is hardly unexpected.

        b. Delta's unusually-candid article was not only accepted for publication but also given priority placement in the September issue.

        c. The firm's budget projections for the coming year—extremely conservative though they may be—are mostly-accurate estimates, according to the finance department.

_b_ 15. *a.* A short-term appointment is definitely preferable to an assignment for a much, longer period.

        b. A steadily increasing flow of traffic over the Causeway Bridge resulted in tougher safety guidelines from the State Traffic Council.

        c. On-site inspections by the Safety-Standards-Board inspectors can be expected with ever-increasing frequency in the coming year.

_a_ 16. *a.* A neatly written note of appreciation was received today from the office of the managing director.

        b. Crisp clean linens are provided each day by the housekeeping staff at the Regis-Towers Hotel.

        c. Miss Tann submitted a brief interesting summary of the contract negotiations conducted in Bangor, Maine, last week.

_b_ 17. *a.* The main objection to the document is that it is not a fully-documented publication, according to the research analyst.

        b. Mr. Fronze's self-serving decision to let the original judgment stand is considered selfish by everyone affected.

        c. The City Council determined that the high rise condominiums on Lake-Front Drive violate the zoning code that applies to that part of town.

LEVEL C

Name _____

Exercise
29–5

Editing

Determine whether the bold modifiers are used correctly in the following sentences according to the guidelines given in this lesson. If they are not, edit the modifiers to make the necessary corrections. One of the sentences is correct in its present form.

1. In his **state-of-the-union** address, the President noted with pride the country's economic growth during the past four years.

2. The **soft-spoken** stranger commanded immediate respect with his **unparalleled grasp** of the facts.

3. As the **crowded subway** train pulled into the station, the four transit officers took their positions on the loading platform.

4. As a final gesture of her **solid unwavering** support, Martha spoke eloquently to the Appeals Committee on Delora's behalf.

5. As events turned out, the **once-in-a-lifetime** opportunity proved to be a **surprising, memorable** experience for the team of **professional mountain** climbers.

6. The admonition, ''Run to daylight, Mister,'' was the coach's challenge as his team's **first-string** halfback entered the game.

7. Marsha was a **hardly noticed** addition to the office staff when she was hired, but that changed quickly when her work proved to be **first rate.**

8. All those who finished the course in advanced writing reported an increased sense of **self-confidence** and of **selfworth.** *self-worth*

9. Mrs. Daw is the **first-grade** teacher at **Union Elementary** School this year.

10. Your car's tires—both **front and rear**—are **badly worn** and should be replaced immediately.

Exercise 29–6 Edit the following sentences where necessary according to the guidelines presented in this lesson on the use of modifiers. One of the sentences is correct in its present form.

Editing

1. As a graduate student seeking a master's degree, Bob found that his worn-out dictionary had become a valued, trusted friend.

2. The notion that all graduate classes observe an open-admission policy is a widely-held misconception on some college campuses.

3. Professor Tarbett's letter of recommendation is a very-fine statement of Dwayne's truly-impressive credentials.

4. The newest business entry in Crossroads Mall is the Santa-Claus Shop on the third-floor plaza.

5. I can give you a quick 30-second rundown of our day-to-day progress, if you like.

6. On Monday next, Mr. W. T. Breem will be named an elementary-school principal in the Gantwood School District.

7. As a modern-school administrator, Mr. Breem has a no-nonsense view of daily-homework assignments for young students.

8. The self-study conducted by the Brigham Young University School of Management will be completed by August 1.

9. The health-insurance program offered by Globe, Inc. is inexpensive and worry-free.

10. Up-to-the-minute weather reports are provided each evening on Channel 14 in a fresh, entertaining format that appeals to most viewers.

11. The small-grocery store on the corner of Main and Stradling Avenues has been sold.

12. Following his lecture at Monarch College in Pellham, Professor Plethrowe will hold a question-and-answer session for all interested graduate students.

Exercise 29–7

Cumula-tive Editing

Edit the following sentences according to (1) the guidelines given in Unit 5 for using nouns and pronouns and (2) the guidelines presented in this lesson for using modifiers. Two of the sentences in their present form use nouns, pronouns, and modifiers correctly.

1. The recently͜delivered shipment contained seven boxes of books and two cardboard cartons of school supplies.

2. Have you invited the Hernandezes to participate in the neighborhood clean-up drive?

3. All grade-one ~~secretarys~~ *secretaries* in the department will receive a 6 percent raise on January 1.

4. Both of Cecelia's ~~sister-in-laws~~ *sisters-in-law* have applied for entry˄level positions with a rapidly͜growing firm in Billings.

5. The Kecker Construction Company specializes in all˄tile patios at very reasonable prices.

6. All three remote-control TV's in the house are in badly͜neglected condition.

7. Over 3,000 ~~alumnuses~~ *alumni* attended the tense͜exciting football game played in Brisco Stadium.

8. Of the different media available for advertising, we believe that widely circulated newspapers will serve our purposes best.

9. The State Wildlife Service reported a below˄average harvest of 1,800 deers during the carefully controlled October hunt in Southern Utah.

10. Four of the one-year-old ~~calfs~~ *calves* entered in the Nebraska͜State͜Fair livestock competition came from the Rawson Ranch.

11. Do you know whether ~~Don~~ *Don's* and Daryl's contracts have been signed and returned as requested by the school˄district superintendent?

12. A fully͜formed weeping˄willow tree adds a great deal to the appearance of the cemetery's south entrance.

Exercise 29–8

Edit the following sentences according to (1) the guidelines given in Unit 5 for using nouns and pronouns and (2) the guidelines presented in this lesson for using modifiers. If you can, find the two sentences that are correct in their present form.

Cumulative Editing

1. Phyllis's bell-chime telephone is defective. Please ask for a pretested, desk-top replacement.

2. The buses' parking zone is the blacktop area next to the ~~girl's~~ *girls'* gym.

3. Please call me when Charles's and Monica's student-officer jackets arrive from the manufacturer.

4. As a new member of the club, you are entitled to a night's stay without charge at the highly regarded Palace Hotel in Philadelphia.

5. Have you asked ~~you're~~ *your* attorney whether the case is going to be as successfully prosecuted as most well-informed people believe?

6. Don Jones' note indicated that the automatic door opener will prove to be a convenient, inexpensive addition to ~~they're~~ *their* garage.

7. An up-to-date roster of officers will be distributed by the chairman-elect's assistant at the next meeting of the Personnel Advisory Board.

8. Mr. Moorman learned that ~~Sid~~ *Sid's* and Phil's spring-term grades will be delayed because of unpaid library fines.

9. May I speak to Mrs. Wadsworth's and your secretaries about the urgently needed blue-and-white carpet they ordered for their offices?

10. Rex's time card and Ross' current-period paycheck are inside the black, locked briefcase by the door.

Misplaced and dangling modifiers are common writing errors. They cause our writing to be ambiguous, strange, or—sometimes—just plain silly.

The order in which words occur in a sentence is critical to clear communication. The placement of words, phrases, and clauses suggests the relationship of these expressions to other elements in the same sentence. Even well-chosen describing words may confuse the reader if they are improperly placed in the sentence or if they have nothing logical to refer to.

The reader depends on the location of a modifier in a sentence to know which word or words are being described. If the geography of a sentence places a modifier in the wrong position, the reader can be easily confused.

Some publications on language usage draw no distinction between misplaced modifiers and dangling modifiers. Although related, these problems usually are different writing errors—as this lesson points out.

Both misplaced modifiers and dangling modifiers are serious obstacles to effective writing. The skillful writer is able to avoid these troublesome barriers to clear communication and to recognize and eliminate them when they occur.

Pretest

Write **C** or **I** to indicate whether modifiers are used correctly or incorrectly in the following sentences.

1. The sealed envelope is in my car containing $2,000 in traveler's checks.

2. To get your proposed changes approved, the vice president of public affairs is the person you should talk to.

3. May I have a cold glass of milk?

4. The manager's new office—comfortable and well lighted—is on the northwest corner of the ninth floor.

5. Placing the finished report on the boss' desk, a smile of satisfaction appeared on the secretary's face.

6. The salesperson promised after the order was placed that delivery would take place within three days.

7. To become law, the governor must sign the bill before midnight on March 31.

8. I almost think the truckers' strike is over.

9. After speaking to reporters at the airport, a police escort rushed Ambassador Donatelli to the Italian Embassy on Fourteenth Street.

10. Because she changed her travel plans, Mrs. Brickert wants the cost of her airline tickets refunded in full.

Key: (1) I—place the modifying phrase *containing $2,000 in traveler's checks* immediately after *envelope*; (2) I—the introductory phrase is a dangling modifier; (3) I—the modifier *cold* should be placed in front of *milk;* (4) C; (5) I—the introductory phrase is a dangling modifier; (6) I—this sentence contains a *squinting* modifier—was the salesman's promise made before or after the order was placed?; (7) I—the introductory phrase is a dangling modifier; (8) I—place the modifier *almost* in front of *over*; (9) I—the introductory phrase is a dangling modifier; (10) C.

Terminology

Dangling modifier—a phrase stating an action or condition that does not logically and grammatically attach to the subject of the main clause of the sentence.

Limited adverbs—a small group of modifiers (*actually, almost, also, just, merely, nearly, only,* and *quite*) that are particularly troublesome if not placed immediately before the words they are intended to modify.

Misplaced modifier—a word, phrase, or clause (usually a phrase) that is not positioned properly with respect to the word or words it is meant to describe.

Squinting construction—usually a phrase (a modifier) that is improperly placed in a sentence with the result that it appears to apply to two terms rather than one. (Example: *The teacher consented **after the assignment was completed** to change the student's grade.* Does the modifying phrase *after the assignment was completed* refer to *consented* or to *to change?*)

Rules

1. **Place modifiers as closely as possible to the words they modify.**

   Write this rule indelibly in your mind. The rule applies to all modifiers—single words, phrases, and clauses.

   The sensible placement of modifying words in a sentence contributes directly to language clarity. Good language geography is a must for the skillful writer. Indifference to the proper placement of modifying words often results in murky and ambiguous writing.

   NO   The book is in the library that relates to animals and zoos.

   YES   The book that relates to animals and zoos is in the library.

   NO   The candidate was interviewed by the personnel manager who applied for the job first.

   YES   The candidate who applied for the job first was interviewed by the personnel manager.
   The personnel manager interviewed the candidate who applied for the job first.

   Learning Hint 1.   Place a single-word adjective immediately before the word it modifies.

   NO   A young group of children will be waiting for you at the gate.

   YES   A group of young children will be waiting for you at the gate.

   NO   I hope this hot cup of tea makes you feel better.

   YES   I hope this cup of hot tea makes you feel better.

   NO   The university plans to demolish the old women's dormitory.

   YES   The university plans to demolish the old dormitory for women.

   Learning Hint 2.   A few adverbs (*actually, almost, also, just, merely, nearly, only,* and *quite*)—referred to as *limited adverbs*—are particularly troublesome. They should appear in front of a word only if they are intended to modify that word. Note how the meaning of the language changes depending on where the adverb is placed in the following sentences:

   Only Rose can write the research proposal. (No one but Rose can write it.)

   Rose can *only* write the research proposal. (Rose can write the proposal, but that's all she can do.)

   Rose can write *only* the research proposal. (The only document Rose can write is the research proposal.)

   Rose can write the *only* research proposal. (Only one proposal will be written, and Rose can write it.)

   Make a special point of placing these particular adverbs as closely as possible to the words they describe.

   NO   Mr. Trotter *almost* believes Susan is eligible for promotion. (Mr. Trotter doesn't quite believe it.)

   YES   Mr. Trotter believes Susan is *almost* eligible for promotion. (Susan isn't quite eligible.)

(handwritten margin note:) Use T30-1 here

NO   Clive Yorgasen *actually* addressed a group of people who are millionaires. (Clive definitely gave a speech.)

YES   Clive Yorgasen addressed a group of people who are *actually* millionaires. (The people Clive addressed are definitely rich.)

Learning Hint 3.   Multiple-word modifiers are usually placed before the nouns they modify. For clarity or emphasis, however, these modifiers are **sometimes** placed after the words they modify. Compound modifiers that follow a noun are written without hyphens, even if the modifiers are placed after the noun for purposes of emphasis.

The personable, confident applicant answered all questions without hesitation. (The modifiers *personable* and *confident* appear in the customary position before the noun *applicant.*)

The applicant—personable and confident—answered all questions without hesitation. (For emphasis, the modifiers are placed after the noun they describe.)

The good-natured, happy-go-lucky student is pleased by his limited academic success. (The modifiers *good-natured, happy-go-lucky,* and *limited* are properly placed before the nouns they describe.)

The student, good natured and happy go lucky, is pleased by his academic success—limited as it is. (Emphasis is given to the modifiers by placing them after the nouns they describe. Because the modifiers *good natured* and *happy go lucky* follow the nouns they modify, the modifiers are not hyphenated.)

Learning Hint 4.   Modifying phrases—like single-word adjectives—should be logically positioned in sentences to avoid absurdities or unintended humor.

Use T30-2 here

Strange things happen to our writing when we are careless about the placement of modifying phrases. Note the following sentence:

The keynote speaker is a pretty, smiling woman with blue eyes weighing less than 100 pounds.

The sentence is confusing because the modifying phrase *weighing less than 100 pounds* is incorrectly positioned in the sentence. The phrase seems to refer illogically to *eyes* rather than to *speaker*. Following are preferred constructions for this sentence:

The keynote speaker—weighing less than 100 pounds—is a pretty, smiling woman with blue eyes.

The keynote speaker, who weighs less than 100 pounds, is a pretty, smiling woman with blue eyes.

Weighing less than 100 pounds, the keynote speaker is a pretty, smiling woman with blue eyes.

Misplaced modifying phrases can be found at the beginning, at the end, or in the middle of the afflicted sentences. Avoid placing these modifiers where they distort or muddle the language.

NO   Standing on the patio, the swimming pool appears cool and inviting to Linda. (The swimming pool is standing on the patio.)

YES   To Linda standing on the patio, the swimming pool appears cool and inviting.

The swimming pool appears cool and inviting to Linda standing on the patio.

NO   Professor Moyle looks forward to returning to the college where he began his professional career after 20 years as a university administrator. (The professor worked for 20 years before he began his career.)

YES   After 20 years as a university administrator, Professor Moyle looks forward to returning to the college where he began his professional career.

Professor Moyle—after 20 years as a university administrator—looks forward to returning to the college where he began his professional career.

NO   The automobile registration papers were found by the worried driver hidden in the trunk. (The driver was hiding in the trunk.)

YES   The worried driver found the automobile registration papers hidden in the trunk.

The automobile registration papers—hidden in the trunk—were found by the worried driver.

Learning Hint 5.   Avoid placing modifiers where they seem to apply to two different words. These *squinting* constructions require the reader to guess which word the writer means to describe. The following sentence contains an example of a *squinting* modifier:

NO   The teacher told the student *at the end of class* the assignment would be required.

Is the assignment due when class ends? Or was the student told at the end of class that the assignment would be required later? The modifying phrase *at the end of class* should be logically placed in the sentence to convey clearly the writer's intended meaning.

YES   At the end of class, the teacher told the student that the assignment would be required.

During class, the teacher told the student the assignment would be required at the end of class (or when the class ended).

NO   The foreman said after the project was completed new safety procedures will be observed.

YES   After the project was completed, the foreman said new safety procedures will be observed in the future.

The foreman said that following the completion of the project, new safety procedures will be observed.

Learning Hint 6.   Avoid placing long, complex modifying phrases at the end of a sentence. Such phrases weaken the impact of otherwise good writing. Place these modifiers—if they are needed—before the main clause of a sentence.

NO   No further reservations can be accepted because our facilities are inadequate to accommodate the large number of people who want to attend the workshop.

YES   Because our facilities are inadequate to accommodate the large number of people who want to attend the workshop, no further reservations can be accepted.

NO   Attend class regularly to get help with the writing assignments to be completed this semester.

YES   To get help with the writing assignments to be completed this semester, attend class regularly.

2. Avoid dangling modifiers resulting from illogical or ungrammatical sentence structure.

Use T30-3 here

Dangling modifiers are phrases that cannot logically and grammatically attach to the subject of the main clause in the sentence.

Dangling modifiers cause language to be awkward, confusing, and implausible. They are often good examples of a writer's saying one thing but meaning another. Frequently (but not always), modifiers that dangle occur at the beginning of a sentence; and they are usually phrases.

Dangling modifiers can be eliminated in one of two ways: (1) by adding words that clarify the language or (2) by changing the structure of the sentence to cause the modifiers to refer clearly to the right word.

NO   Although only 15 years old, the state approved Harriet's application for a learner's permit. (The introductory modifying phrase *Although only 15 years old* does not logically attach to the noun *state*, the subject of the main clause that follows.)

YES   Although Harriet is only 15 years old, her application for a learner's permit was approved by the state. (The addition of *Harriet* to the introductory modifying phrase clarifies the language and makes the sentence a logical statement.)

Although only 15 years old, Harriet was issued a learner's permit by the state. (The introductory modifying phrase attaches logically to *Harriet*, the subject of the main clause that follows.)

NO   Firing a completed pass into the end zone, the winning touchdown was scored with just ten seconds left in the game. (The modifying phrase *Firing a completed pass into the end zone* does not logically attach to the noun *touchdown*, the subject of the main clause that follows.)

YES   Firing a completed pass into the end zone, the quarterback scored the winning touchdown with just ten seconds left in the game. (The introductory modifying phrase attaches logically to the noun *quarterback*, the subject of the main clause.)

With just ten seconds left in the game, the quarterback scored the winning touchdown by firing a completed pass into the end zone.

Learning Hint 7.   One easy way to recognize a dangling modifier is to find the subject of the independent clause following the modifying phrase. Then, put the subject in front of the modifying phrase and read the remainder of the sentence. If the rearranged sentence is not logical, you have a dangling modifier.

The following sentence seems suspect and may contain a dangling modifier:

With hooves pounding and tail flying, the youthful jockey rode Gallant Warrior to a thrilling victory.

To determine whether the introductory modifying phrase is a dangling modifier, place the subject of the main clause—*the youthful jockey*—in front of the modifying phrase. The sentence now reads as follows:

The youthful jockey, with hooves pounding and tail flying, rode Gallant Warrior to a thrilling victory.

Sure enough—the introductory modifying phrase in the original sentence is a dangling modifier. *With hooves pounding and tail flying* illogically attaches to the jockey instead of the horse. By revising the sentence, we eliminate the dangling modifier and get the following sensible sentence:

With hooves pounding and tail flying, Gallant Warrior was ridden by the youthful jockey to a thrilling victory.

Try this easy—and usually dependable—test on modifying phrases you suspect may be dangling modifiers.

Learning Hint 8.   As you may already have noticed, one way to eliminate a dangling modifier is to change the subject of the main clause of the sentence to give the modifying phrase something to which it can logically attach.

NO   To meet Mr. Gale's three o'clock flight, my interview with Sam will have to be postponed. (The interview can't meet the flight.)

YES   To meet Mr. Gale's three o'clock flight, I will have to postpone my interview with Sam. (The introductory modifying phrase now attaches logically to *I*, the subject of the main clause.)

NO   As the senior engineer in the division, your ideas will be considered carefully. (Ideas are not engineers.)

        As the senior engineer in the division, careful consideration will be given to your ideas. (Careful consideration is not an engineer.)

YES   As the senior engineer in the division, you will have your ideas considered carefully. (The introductory modifying phrase now attaches logically to *you*, the subject of the main clause.)

Learning Hint 9.   Another way to remove a dangling modifier at the beginning of a sentence is to change the modifier that dangles to an introductory clause with a subject of its own. Be careful to avoid the shift in voice that often occurs when this approach is used.

NO   In summarizing her presentation, only the most important points were emphasized. (The most important points can't summarize.)

YES   When Carole summarized her presentation, she emphasized only the most important points.

NO   As the supervising physician, the patient wants your opinion on whether surgery is necessary. (The patient is not the supervising physician.)

YES   Because you are the supervising physician, you have been asked by the patient whether surgery is necessary.

NO   To reduce expenses, travel requests will be screened carefully in the future. (Travel requests do not reduce expenses.)

        Since the firm must reduce expenses, travel requests will be screened carefully in the future. (Although the sentence no longer contains a dangling modifier, it now contains a shift from active to passive voice.)

YES   Since the firm must reduce expenses, we will carefully screen travel requests in the future. (Both the dangling modifying phrase and the shift in voice have been eliminated.)

Posttest

Write **C** or **I** to indicate whether modifiers are used correctly or incorrectly in the following sentences.

1. The announcement of Mr. Trumble's election was in last night's newspaper to the school board.

2. A close group of friends has offered financial support to the candidate.

3. Because everyone else is unavailable, Terri Carr will just be able to represent our firm at the Chamber of Commerce luncheon.

4. My car is parked just beyond the stop sign with a flat tire.

5. After the data have been collected, organized, and carefully analyzed on the computer by the Stat-Rite statistical procedure, the results must be reported promptly.

6. As the youngest member of the group, CoraLee presented her proposal last.

7. Arriving at her office early, the agenda was completed by Miss Jackalone just moments before the meeting began.

8. If the boss is right, we will see a 60 percent increase in profits in the coming year.

9. As a specialist in office automation, we are fortunate to have Professor Lorimar's expertise to guide us.

10. The invoice containing the error is in the top drawer of the gray file cabinet in the outer office.

Key: (1) I—place the modifying phrase *to the school board* after *election;* (2) I—place the modifier *close* before the noun *friends;* (3) I—place the modifier *just* before the noun *Terri;* (4) I—place the modifying phrase *with a flat tire* after *car;* (5) C; (6) C; (7) I—the introductory phrase is a dangling modifier; (8) C; (9) I—the introductory phrase is a dangling modifier; (10) C.

LEVEL A

Name _____

Exercise 30–1   Write **T** if the statement is true. Write **F** if the statement is false.

_F___ 1. Misplaced modifiers and dangling modifiers are the same things.

_T___ 2. Dangling modifiers are usually phrases.

_F___ 3. Misplaced modifiers are usually single words.

_T___ 4. A *squinting* construction allows a modifier to appear to refer logically to two words or ideas.

_T___ 5. The modifiers *almost, just,* and *only* are all limited adverbs.

_T___ 6. All modifiers should be placed as closely as possible to the words they modify.

_F___ 7. Single-word adjectives usually are placed after the words they modify.

_T___ 8. Multiple-word modifiers usually come before the words they modify, but they may come after such words for purposes of clarity or emphasis.

_____ 9. If long, complex, modifying phrases must be used, they should be placed at the end of the sentence.

_T___ 10. Dangling modifiers have nothing logical to refer to.

_T___ 11. One way to eliminate a dangling modifier is to change the subject of the main clause in the sentence.

_F___ 12. The sentence *When Mr. Tabbon arrived, the visitor rose to greet him* contains a misplaced modifier.

_F___ 13. The sentence *The manager agreed to approve Fred's promotion* contains a dangling modifier.

_T___ 14. A misplaced modifier may occur at the beginning, at the end, or in the middle of a sentence.

_T___ 15. In the sentence *Please give me a hot bowl of soup,* the word *hot* is a misplaced modifier.

Exercise 30–2   Write **C** if the bold modifiers are used correctly; write **I** if they are used incorrectly.

_I___ 1. My schedule is very busy this week; therefore, I can **only** meet with you on Thursday at 3 p.m.

_C___ 2. Of all our field representatives, **only** Marvin Ho reached $1 million in sales last year.

_I___ 3. **In making the announcement,** the employees were disappointed to learn from the CEO that the customary salary increase based on merit will not be given this year.

_I___ 4. **Running to catch the train,** the tickets fell unnoticed from the passenger's coat pocket.

_I___ 5. As the Leland County Fair opened to the public, an **excited** bus full of schoolchildren arrived at the entrance.

_I_ 6. The kindly bus driver **quickly** opened the door **grinning from ear to ear**.

_I_ 7. **Wanting to be the first person off the bus,** Tommy's shoe got stuck in the doorway.

_C_ 8. **In submitting her application,** Phyllis is hoping **just** to be among the finalists for the four-year scholarship to Rutgers University.

_I_ 9. The manual we ordered has arrived from the publisher **concerning software development and copyrighting.**

_I_ 10. **Unless completed by Friday,** we cannot consider your proposal **for improved parking facilities.**

_C_ 11. **As Miss Warmley's note pointed out,** Megan Drewe is the unexpected winner in this year's competition.

_I_ 12. Miss Drewe agreed to a radio interview **following the awards ceremony**.

_I_ 13. On our trip to Kansas, we drove for miles and miles through **tall fields of corn**.

_I_ 14. The program director said **at the end of the meeting** refreshments will be served.

_I_ 15. **When lodging the complaint,** the company's decision to require employees to work additional overtime was blamed.

Exercise 30–3 Write **C** if the use of modifiers is correct; write **I** if the use of modifiers is incorrect.

_I_ 1. The picture is hanging on the wall that won first place in the art exhibit.

_C_ 2. Only Rosalie can write the research proposal.

_I_ 3. The old stack of business correspondence should be taken to the shredder.

_I_ 4. The fresh box of strawberries you ordered will be delivered within an hour.

_C_ 5. The newly elected mayor—smiling and waving—arrived at City Center Plaza to acknowledge his victory.

_I_ 6. Chatting with reporters following the election, a decrease in taxes is to be the mayor's first order of business.

_I_ 7. The student submitted her assignment in a folder provided on letter-quality paper.

_I_ 8. After consulting with her attorney, the defendant changed her plea from not guilty to guilty at the last possible moment.

_I_ 9. Cut excessive duplicating costs immediately by screening very carefully the various copy center projects that are submitted from the marketing, advertising, and finance departments as well as from the main executive offices.

_C_ 10. In response to the award received for outstanding performance, Miss Drewe wrote the screening committee a note of appreciation.

LEVEL B

Name _____

Exercise
30–4
Write the letter identifying the statement that reflects the preferred usage of modifiers.

a 1. *a.* The announcement concerning the factory recall of trucks with defective axles is in tonight's newspaper.
  b. The letter is on your desk regarding the shipping errors that occurred on December 12.
  c. The customer wants to talk to you on the telephone who wrote the letter of complaint.

c 2. *a.* The magician performed today for an old group of people at the Community Seniors' Center.
  b. A straight-A group of high-school students will be honored at Friday's awards assembly.
  c. The management-training program for a team of new employees gets underway next week.

b 3. *a.* I can only talk to you on Friday because I will be out of town during the rest of the week.
  b. Dagmar called to say she had just heard of your resignation.
  c. The manager will see you when you arrive, and I can talk with you also while you are here.

b 4. *a.* The audit report—revised—was submitted to the client yesterday morning.
  b. The personnel-committee decision—unexpected and irrevocable—was reluctantly accepted by the employees.
  c. According to the investigating officer, the accident—near fatal—could have been easily prevented.

a 5. *a.* The busy, successful executive interviewed the young woman with an M.B.A. degree from Stanford University.
  b. Please take the luggage to my car at the curb with the Kansas license plates.
  c. Will you speak to our service club about managing money on Wednesday, October 10?

a 6. *a.* Leaving the bus, the distracted passenger was nearly struck by an oncoming car.
  b. After making the telephone call, the decision was quickly made in favor of Miss Gooding's request.
  c. While preparing to graduate, a part-time job will enable you to pay your tuition and other school expenses.

c 7. *a.* The boss told her secretary at the end of the day the mail must go out promptly.
  b. In her note of explanation, the receptionist said after the package was delivered the customer raised no objection.
  c. As I indicated to you yesterday, we should prepare a letter of agreement following our meeting with the client.

_a_   8.   *a.*   To reduce the rapidly rising costs from the inefficient and expensive air-conditioning equipment in the Red River plant, keep windows and doors closed.

          b.   Give us your individual application promptly if you wish to be considered for one of the recently approved $1,000 employee-performance awards to be given this coming summer by the firm's present board of directors.

          c.   Treat all existing customers very courteously at all times to foster the best possible customer relations, to promote a decidedly positive public image, and to quickly attract promising new customers.

_b_   9.   *a.*   Speaking to the graduating class of police cadets, the rising crime rate was emphasized by the Commissioner of Public Safety.

          b.   Running to catch the elevator, the delivery boy stumbled and fell to the floor.

          c.   To meet the deadline you have given us, an additional $3,000 will be required for equipment and supplies.

_C_   10.   *a.*   The manager's wallet was finally found by his secretary in the waste basket.

          b.   Have you seen the umbrella I keep in my private office with the gold handle?

          c.   With a smile and a handshake, the owner welcomed each customer to the grand opening of her new restaurant.

_C_   11.   *a.*   To apply for the position now open in Sales, a letter of application and a resume must be sent to the Director of Personnel.

          b.   In reaching a decision, all relevant facts were considered by the review committee.

          c.   We have been told that, after investigating the accident, the police department is ready to file a complaint.

_a_   12.   *a.*   The view of the superintendent is that only Carmine deLuca is eligible for early retirement with full benefits.

          b.   As a guest professor this semester, we understand that Dr. Timothy Earle will teach a class in advanced electronics.

          c.   Please review this graduate thesis on the hazards of toxic waste by Heather O'Toole.

_C_   13.   *a.*   Upon being sued by an unhappy patient, an appointment was made with a competent attorney by the hospital administrator.

          b.   After earning a 4.0 GPA, Carleton College admitted Rhonda as a freshman before she was 16.

          c.   A gray sedan with four doors and a white top struck the motorcycle parked in front of the red brick house on Sunrise Avenue.

_a_   14.   *a.*   You will need a pair of warm boots if you hike in the cold and rugged Wasatch Mountains.

          b.   While you were at work, your neighbor left this tasty bottle of peach marmalade.

          c.   We drove home in the bright red convertible sitting in the driveway with chrome bumpers and recessed headlights.

_b_   15.   *a.*   The Dorchester Exhibit is featuring an abstract collection of fine paintings by promising, young artists.

          b.   At the end of her performance, the soloist was given a bouquet of flowers by the leader of the orchestra.

          c.   While speaking to the congregation, the microphone slipped from the minister's hand.

LEVEL C

Name _____

Exercise 30–5

Edit the following sentences where necessary according to the guidelines presented in this lesson on the use of modifiers. One sentence is correct in its present form.

Editing

1. Mr. Dunnigan's raincoat is hanging on the foyer coat rack with his gloves in its pockets.

2. To get your money refunded, ~~a telephone~~ *you must* call ~~should be made to~~ the Customer Complaint Department.

3. For just $7, you can buy a freshly picked box of King Richard apples ~~from~~ *at* the fruit stand on the highway.

4. Your salary increase goes into effect immediately, substantial and well-deserved.

5. As class president, *you must attend* all student council meetings ~~must be attended~~—even those that conflict with your work.

6. The coach instructed the team to leave the playing floor immediately after the game and to go directly to the dressing room.

7. To qualify for the Dean's List, *you must give* your studies ~~must be given~~ top priority while you are in school.

Exercise 30–6

Edit the following sentences where necessary according to the guidelines presented in this lesson on the use of modifiers. One sentence is correct in its present form.

Editing

1. A stack of old yearbooks was given to the school library this week by a former principal.

2. I believe *only* David Yancey, our club president, can ~~only~~ draft a document of such importance as that.

3. A picture of the car was in the *Tallahassee Tribune* that crossed the finish line first.

4. The old headquarters building—too small and poorly located—will be sold *for cash* to the highest bidder. ~~for cash.~~

5. To be successful in the real-estate business, ~~property~~ *you must sell* ~~must be sold~~ quickly and customers ~~must~~ *treat* ~~be treated~~ with courtesy and respect.

6. The audience was delighted when the program director said during the seminar that partial refunds will be mailed to all participants.

7. *Even the* ~~The~~ slowest runner can ~~even~~ complete the course in less than one hour.

Exercise 30–7

Cumulative Editing

Edit the following sentences according to (1) the guidelines given in Unit 6 for ensuring proper agreement and reference and (2) the guidelines presented in this lesson for using modifiers. Two sentences are correct in their present form.

1. The reporters and the editor ~~is~~ *are* willing to run the story—factually stated and objectively written—in tomorrow's edition.

2. The intent of the six mathematics teachers ~~are~~ *is* to assign grades to all students based on merit.

3. In the briefcase on the floor ~~are~~ *is* the revised group of contracts you requested for the meeting.

4. Neither of the customers ~~seem~~ *seems* to understand that to qualify for a discount, ~~we must receive~~ their payments *must reach us* within ten days after ~~their~~ orders are shipped.

5. As stated in *The Employees' Handbook*, everybody should be aware ~~they will have~~ rapid opportunities for advancement *are available* in this firm.

6. Within a week, two-thirds of the money was spent on the 30 cartons of supplies needed for the trip.

7. In analyzing the information collected, *I have concluded that* none of the data is ~~considered to be~~ reliable.

8. The professor said *, after the meeting,* all the research completed by the graduate students ~~are~~ *is* going to be examined by a team of scholars.

9. In recognition of his professional accomplishments, Dr. Whitney, the consultant and writer, is to be awarded an honorary doctorate by the University of Alabama.

10. Although completed last week, neither the secretaries nor the office manager ~~have read~~ your report on employee turnover *has been read by*

Exercise 30–8

Cumulative Editing

Edit the following sentences according to (1) the guidelines given in Unit 6 for ensuring proper agreement and reference and (2) the guidelines provided in this lesson for using modifiers. If you can, find the two sentences that are correct in their present form.

1. As you know, every customer who wants his *or her* name placed on our mailing list must ~~return~~ *sign* a postcard ~~with a signature addressed~~ *and return it* to our shipping department.

2. To pay ~~their~~ tuition by mail, any student may use a personal check or a money order.

3. Every employee—male or female, young or old—is required to update ~~their~~ *his or her* personnel files each year during the month of January.

4. We have learned that employees who plan to use the firm's lodge *on Far-Away Mountain* must make ~~your~~ reservations ~~on Far-Away Mountain~~ with the scheduling office on the fourth floor.

5. Four new hardware products *if they are* will be placed in numerous department stores in various cities in the coming months ~~if they are~~ approved by the marketing division.

6. Mr. Dudley is the only one of the counselors who is nearly certain that next term's class schedule is final.

7. A complete vote of confidence was given to the directors *by the workers* who made the final decision.

8. The evidence suggests that the company's medical insurance is almost exactly what the consultant recommended in her report.

9. Because of the strike, ~~it seems likely that~~ the ~~policy proposed~~ *proposal made* by the Employees' Council ~~giving~~ *to give* all workers three weeks of vacation *probably* cannot be implemented this year.

10. The sharp increase in product demand was called a ~~fresh~~ *fresh* breath of̷ air by the president and

the vice president in ~~his~~ *their* remarks.

Exercise 30–9 Write sentences that will correctly complete the following composition and editing exercises.

Cumula-
tive
Compo-
sition and
Editing

1. Use the words *beautifully written* as a compound modifier preceding a noun.

   _____

   _____

2. Use a compound modifier that precedes a noun and a compound modifier that follows a noun.

   _____

   _____

3. Rewrite this sentence to eliminate the two expletives it contains.

   It seems to us there is a need for further discussion.

   _____

   _____

4. Use a hyphenated compound modifier that properly uses the word *jury* with a plural verb.

   _____

   _____

5. Use the words *everyone* and *every one* in a single sentence.

   _____

   _____

LESSONS IN THIS UNIT

31. WORDY EXPRESSIONS
32. CONFUSABLE WORDS
33. NONSEXIST WRITING

The major components of a written presentation can be broken down into three areas:

1. **Content**—described by the statement "what is said."

2. **Organization**—described by the statement "where and when it is said."

3. **Style**—described by the statement "how it is said."

Most of the content of this business English book deals with the third component—style. By now, you know the business world has rather precise guidelines to follow when we write a sentence and decide, in the process, "how to say something."

Style can be broken down further into two components:

1. **Mechanics**—the principles and rules of grammar with which most of this textbook is concerned.

2. **Language usage**—the preferred choice of words to express thoughts.

You've already studied many things in this textbook that touch on language usage. For example, Lesson 4 on confusing words is a language-usage lesson. And many of the grammar rules, such as those in Lesson 13 on mood, have language-usage overtones.

We could devote hundreds of pages in this textbook to the language-usage dimensions of style. However, space will not permit our doing so. Therefore, we are giving you a brief exposure to language usage in this unit by including only three lessons.

If you were to examine the contents of these three lessons as applied to your own language usage, you would probably find you presently violate many of the preferences for language usage. That is, you probably use expressions that sound correct to you and that seem to communicate just fine in your speaking and writing. Indeed, what is correct or incorrect in language usage is sometimes a matter of personal choice or of personal opinion.

Through Unit 8, we'll share with you numerous language-usage preferences. We recommend you do your best to learn to recognize weak (though not necessarily *incorrect*) language usage in your writing and in the writing of others. Try to internalize the preferred language usage so the preferred expressions become part of your ''toolbox of writing skills.'' You probably will not remember all of the preferred expressions in Unit 8, but you'll undoubtedly change many of the expressions you presently use.

In doing so, you'll find you have certain ''pet peeves'' in your own language usage; and you'll probably find yourself being critical of others who violate these pet peeves. For instance, a notorious wordy expression is *whether or not*. Usually, we can merely say *whether* and convey the same meaning as *whether or not*. Once a writer has internalized the preference for *whether*, he or she tends to be somewhat critical of other writers who continue to use *whether or not*. We're not saying that's good or bad; we're merely suggesting you individually will master some of the language-usage items more readily than others. Obviously, you should attempt to internalize as many of them as you can during the time you spend with Lessons 31 through 33.

Business executives often state that conciseness is one of the most-important writing principles. Obviously, *conciseness* is the opposite of *wordiness*. As a writer, you will achieve conciseness when you say what you have to say in the fewest possible words.

In analyzing weak writing, we often notice that such writing uses wordy expressions. Perhaps unsure writers feel that the more they say, the more they know or the more the reader will think they know. Or perhaps such writers feel that the more obscure their writing is, the more profound their thoughts are.

Wordiness in writing is a flaw of style—how we say what we say. Perhaps wordiness is the biggest obstacle to clear writing. To overcome that obstacle, we should learn to identify wordy expressions used by other writers and by ourselves. When we can identify wordy expressions, we can improve both others' and our own writing through the editing process.

Pretest

Underline all wordy expressions in each sentence.

1. On more than one occasion, we have donated a sizable percentage of our profits to charity.

2. Sally, our 15-year-old cocker spaniel, is no longer with us; we had her put to sleep about a month ago.

3. Mr. Fields' behavior at the meeting goes to show that he is sick and tired of assuming a secondary leadership role.

4. In the eventuality that the Hudson contract materializes, please call me immediately.

5. The first and foremost reason for selecting Boston is that I can pick and choose my own accounts.

6. I was totally overwhelmed by your firm commitment to the Logan project.

7. The inclusion of children in the annual social event means the acceptance of new roles by the organizers.

8. The new guidelines do not make a distinction between a congenital anomaly and a chronic illness.

9. In the event that you want to change the plans over the duration of the project, please call Ms. Baxter.

10. As a matter of fact, I do take exception to the new policy.

Key: (1) circumlocutions—*on more than one occasion, a sizable percentage of*; (2) euphemisms—*no longer with us, put to sleep*; (3) cliches—*goes to show, sick and tired*; (4) polysyllabic words—*eventuality, materializes*; (5) couplets—*first and foremost, pick and choose*; (6) extraneous adverbs and adjectives—*totally overwhelmed, firm commitment*; (7) noun phrases—*the inclusion of, the acceptance of*; (8) verb phrase—*make a distinction*; (9) prepositional phrases—*in the event that, over the duration of*; (10) idioms—*as a matter of fact, take exception*.

Terminology

Circumlocution—A roundabout expression that evades preciseness. (For example: *in the near future* rather than *soon*.)

Cliche—A trite or overused expression. (For example: *consensus of opinion* rather than *consensus*.)

Couplet—Two similar words that are joined by *and* that have one meaning. (For example: *first and foremost* rather than *first* or *foremost*.)

Euphemism—An inoffensive phrase that substitutes for a phrase that might be considered offensive. (For example: *correctional facility* rather than *prison*.)

Idiom—An expression that is peculiar to itself grammatically or that cannot be understood from the individual meanings of its elements. (For example: *in a nutshell* rather than *briefly*.)

Polysyllabic word—A word that has more than three syllables. (For example: *materialize* rather than *happen*.)

Discussion

As we edit material to eliminate wordy expressions, we tend to do one of three things with them, as follows:

*Use
T31-1
here*

1. Reduce the number of words in a phrase.

2. Substitute a single word for a phrase or a short word for a long word.

3. Delete the extraneous word or phrase.

Knowing which to do is largely a function of recognizing the most frequently used wordy expressions and of becoming familiar with their "feel." The key to effective editing is to question the value of every word or phrase in a sentence. Ask yourself whether the word or phrase is needed, whether it contributes to or interferes with the meaning, or whether it adds something to the meaning that another word does not.

As you question each word or phrase, look carefully for wordiness in prepositional, verb, and noun phrases. Look also for extraneous adjectives and adverbs. And be wary of euphemisms, circumlocutions, cliches, idioms, polysyllabic words, and couplets. At times, you may have difficulty classifying a wordy expression—for example, whether it is a wordy prepositional phrase or a cliche. The important thing is that you recognize the wordy expression and substitute a more concise one.

Books could be consumed with examples of wordy expressions, so we have tried to be judicious in selecting the expressions to include in this lesson. The ones that follow are widely used and are reflective of those that might appear in a comprehensive listing. Our suggested alternatives are not comprehensive in every case, but they do reflect potential revisions. Study the lists carefully to become familiar with each wordy expression and its suggested revisions. The expressions are presented in alphabetical order. We cannot say that all the expressions should be avoided in every instance. However, those that follow are indicative of the wordy expressions we should try to avoid.

Prepositional Phrases.   Look carefully at all prepositional phrases—but especially those that are longer than two words. A wordy prepositional phrase can usually be reduced to a single word or be deleted altogether. For example:

Instead of	Use
about the fact that	because, that
along the same line	likewise, similarly
for the purpose of	to
for the most part	chiefly, mainly, mostly
for the present	for now
for the time being	for now
go along with	agree with, favor, support
in accordance with	according to, by, to
in actuality	actually, indeed, truly
in addition to	besides, beyond
in all probability	likely, probably
in any way, shape, or form	at all, in any way
in a position to	able to, ready to
in attendance	present
in brief summary	briefly, in short
in conjunction with	combined, together
in connection with	along with, with
in consequence of the fact	because
in light of the fact that	because, considering
in like fashion	likewise, similarly
in large part	largely, mainly, mostly
in order for	for
in order that	for, so, so that, that
in order to	to

Instead of	Use
in regard to	about, regarding
in relation to	about, regarding
in respect to	about, regarding
in spite of the fact that	although, even though, though
in such a way	so, so that
in such a fashion that	so, so that
in terms of	by, for, in, of, regarding
in that regard	about, that [or delete phrase]
in the absence of	having no, lacking, without
in the amount of	for, of
in the direction of	on, to, with
in the event that	if, should
in the final analysis	in the end, ultimately
in the first place	first
in the meantime	meantime, meanwhile
in the near future	soon, shortly
in the unlikely event that	if
in the vicinity of	close by, near, nearby
in view of the fact that	because, when
over the duration of	during
under certain circumstances	at times, on occasion
under no circumstances	in no way, never
up to a maximum of	up to
up to and including	through
up to the current time	so far, to date, until now
with reference to	about
with regard to	about, concerning, regarding

Verb Phrases. Many expressions we loosely call ''verb phrases'' are wordy. In wordy verb phrases, two or more words usually perform the work of one word. For example:

Instead of	Use
add together	add
add up	add, sum, total
analyze in detail	analyze, detail
attach together	attach
come to a conclusion	conclude, finish, stop
come to grips with	accept, face, understand
communicate in writing	write
considering the fact that	because
cooperate together	cooperate
divide up	divide
enter into an agreement	agree, contract
extend an invitation to	invite
expresses regret	regrets
figure out	decide, determine
form an opinion	conclude, resolve
gather together	gather
get across	convey, explain
get divorced	divorce
get in touch with	call, phone, visit

Instead of	Use
get married	marry
give us encouragement	encourage us
given the fact that	because, considering
has an influence upon	acts on, affects, influences
has a tendency to	tends to, will
has got	has
has reference to	concerns, deals with
has the ability to	can, is able to
has the appearance of	appears
have a considerable impact	considerably impact
have in my possession	have, possess
help out	help
hold a meeting	meet
incorporate into	add, include
is an acquaintance of	knows
is an illustration of	illustrates
is appreciative of	appreciates, approves of
is at variance with	differs from
is of the opinion	believes
is concerned with	concerns, deals with
is contingent on	depends on
is deficient in	lacks, wants
is dependent on	depends on
is evidence of	proves, shows
is familiar with	knows
is lacking in	lacks
is knowledgeable in	knows, understands
is reaching the conclusion	is concluding
is under the assumption that	assumes, believes, thinks
join together	join
make a distinction	distinguish
merge together	merge
mix together	mix
owing to the fact that	because
pick up the phone and call	call, phone
place pressure on	pressure
predict ahead of time	predict
provided that	if
put an end to	cease, complete, finish, end
put heavy emphasis on	heavily emphasize
put in alphabetical order	alphabetize
put in an appearance	appear, arrive, show up
put two and two together	conclude, deduce, infer
raise questions about	challenge, dispute, question
reach a conclusion	conclude, decide, resolve
reach an agreement	agree, decide, settle
refer back	refer
return back	return
render assistance to	help
seesaw back and forth	seesaw
share together	share

Instead of	Use
take into consideration	consider
to give expression to	to express
to take the time to thank	to thank
to take this opportunity	[delete this phrase]
to tell you the truth	actually, frankly, truthfully
unite together	unite
voiced disapproval	disapproved
wait around	wait
want to have	want
will come to an end	will end

Noun Phrases.   Wordy noun phrases often begin with an article followed by a noun and the word *of*. In other instances, several words are used when one or two words are sufficient. For example:

Instead of	Use
course of action	action, direction, strategy
place of employment	business, firm, office
plan of action	action, plan, strategy
point of view	belief, position, view
the acceptance of	accepting
the conversion of	converting
the development of	developing
the inclusion of	including
the installation of	installing
the maintenance of	maintaining
the marketing of	marketing
the opposite sex	female, male, man, woman
the processing of	processing
time of day	time

Extraneous Adjectives and Adverbs.   For forceful writing, writers sometimes couple adjectives and adverbs to nouns or verbs. The result is wordy expressions such as the following:

Instead of	Use
absolutely essential	essential
actively involved	involved
actually submit	submit
basic fundamentals	fundamentals
blatantly evident	blatant, evident
brief summary	summary
cautiously optimistic	optimistic
current status	status
duplicate copy	copy, duplicate
exact duplicate	duplicate
exact same copy	same copy
exactly identical	identical
firm commitment	commitment
first introduced	introduced
general consensus	consensus

Instead of	Use
general public	public
general rule	rule
general vicinity	vicinity
honest truth	truth
huge throng	throng
important essentials	essentials
intellectual ability	ability, capacity, intellect
most important	foremost, main, principal
mutually beneficial	beneficial
mutual friendship	friendship
necessary prerequisite	prerequisite
necessary requirement	requirement
original inventor	inventor
overwhelming preponderance	almost all, the percent
past history	history
popular consensus	consensus
preliminary draft	draft
previous experience	experience
qualified expert	expert
quickly expedite	expedite
real attempt	attempt
record high	record
totally overcome	overcome
whole idea	idea

Euphemisms.   We create a euphemism when we substitute an inoffensive phrase for one considered offensive. Many euphemisms deal with sex or death—topics we often consider too delicate for straightforwardness. Others deal with expressions of politeness or deception. We need not avoid all euphemisms; but we should avoid wordy euphemisms when a short expression will not offend. For example:

Instead of	Consider using
advanced in years	old
comfort facilities	rest room
correctional facility	prison
economic adjustments	price hikes
human resources	employees, people, workers
loss-prevention specialist	guard
negative feelings	dislike, hate
no longer with us	dead
passed away	died
put to sleep	destroy
revenue enhancers	taxes
succumb to injuries	die

Circumlocutions.   If we *circumvent* something, we get around it. Similarly, a circumlocution is a roundabout word or phrase. Sometimes we want to use a circumlocution if we want to evade an issue, if we do not want to commit ourselves to a cause, or if we do not want to be held accountable for supporting or for not supporting a cause. Circumlocutions usually mean something far different from what a reader might imagine. For example:

Instead of	**Use**
a limited number	[use the precise number]
an overwhelming majority of	most
a significant proportion of	some, a majority
a sizable percentage of	many
for an indefinite time period	for a while, indefinitely
in a few minutes	briefly, quickly, soon
in excess of	above, greater than, more than
in many circumstances	frequently, normally, usually
in most regards	mostly, often, usually
in much the same fashion	much as, much like
in my estimation (opinion)	I assert, I feel, to me
in the foreseeable future	before long, soon, next month
in the immediate future	at once, presently, soon
in the near future	soon
in the neighborhood of	about, close to, near
make a statement saying	say
on a number of occasions	frequently, often
on more than one occasion	[use the precise number]
over the long term	ultimately
to a certain extent	in part
to a large degree	largely

Cliches. A cliche is a trite or overused expression. When cliches are initially coined, they may be effective. However, they often become overused; and they lose power when we rely on them because we are too lazy to express thoughts without being wordy. For example:

Instead of	**Use**
all done	done, complete, finished
all of a sudden	suddenly
after all is said and done	finally, ultimately
as a consequence of the fact	because, in that
as a matter of course	commonly, normally, usually
as luck would have it	by chance, luckily, unluckily
as the need arises	as needed
as time goes on	in time, later, sometime
at some point along the way	at some point, at some time
at the present time	at present, presently
because of the fact that	because, in that
by one means or another	by some means, in some way
by reason of the fact that	because
by way of example	for example, to illustrate
consensus of opinion	consensus
despite the fact that	although, even though
due to the fact that	because
during the course of	during, throughout
fear and trembling	dread
first of all	first
for all intents and purposes	essentially, virtually
free of charge	free
from beginning to end	completely, totally
goes to show	proves
in a timely fashion	promptly

Instead of	**Use**
in all probability	most likely
inasmuch as	because, as
irregardless of	despite
irrespective of the fact that	although, even though
it goes without saying that	clearly, obviously
it is imperative that	must
kinder and gentler	humane
know for a fact	know
more often than not	commonly, customarily, usually
on the other hand	but, conversely, however
out of the question	impossible, unthinkable
par for the course	typical
regardless of the fact that	although, even though, yet
sick and tired	annoyed
the truth of the matter is	actually, in reality
when all is said and done	all in all, overall
whether or not	if, whether
window of opportunity	opportunity, chance

Idioms.   An idiom is an expression that is unique to a language and that has little or no meaning on the surface—especially to a person who is not familiar with the idiom. The literal meaning of an idiom is often different from its actual meaning. Some idioms play distinctive roles by stating cleverly what other words cannot, but many idioms are wordy expressions that should be avoided. For example:

Instead of	**Use**
a feather in your cap	an honor, a compliment
as a matter of fact	in fact
before long	soon
beyond a shadow of a doubt	certainly, undoubtedly
bite a person's head off	speak angrily
brand new	new
burn the candle at both ends	work hard
burn the midnight oil	work overtime
bury one's head in the sand	avoid reality
by the skin of your teeth	barely
day in and day out	every day
dead as a doornail	dead
down in the mouth	depressed
fly in the face of	disobey, defy
high and dry	alone, helpless
high and low	everywhere
high and mighty	arrogant
in a nutshell	briefly
in due time	in time, someday, sometime
kick the bucket	die
let the cat out of the bag	divulge the truth
on the part of	by
all your eggs in one basket	risk everything
once in a blue moon	seldom
put on an act	pretend
put your foot down	be firm

Instead of	Use
put your foot in it	blunder
rub a person the wrong way	annoy, offend, irritate
run of the mill	average, common, typical
see eye to eye	agree
take exception	object
take offense to	resent
the long and the short	the gist, the essence
turn over a new leaf	change
up in the air	unanswered, unsure

Polysyllabic Words.   Nothing is wrong with big words. However, we can often communicate better by using small words rather than polysyllabic words. The dictionary defines a polysyllabic word as one with four or more syllables. Some three-syllable words might be classified as big words, but the words that follow are truly polysyllabic. For example:

Instead of	Use
accommodations	rooms
alleviate	lessen, reduce
ameliorate	heal, help, improve
appellation	name, title
approximately	about, roughly
effectuate	bring about, carry out
eventuality	event
facilitate	help
incarcerate	jail
incremental	minute, slight, small
indebtedness	debt
indication	clue, hint, sign
individuals	people
inflammable	flammable
innumerable	countless, endless, infinite
instantaneously	at once, instantly
institution	hospital, jail, prison, school
interestingly	[delete this word]
limitation	limit
literally	[delete this word]
locality	area, region, site
materialize	happen
methodology	method
motivation	motive
multitudinous	endless, many, numerous
multiplicity	many
necessitate	require
necessity	need
notwithstanding	despite
parameter	limit
potentiality	potential
practically	almost, nearly
prioritize	arrange, list, order, rank
probability	chance, likelihood, prospect
profitability	profits
proliferate	spread

Instead of	Use
proximity	closeness, nearness
remunerate	pay
substantiate	confirm, prove, verify
unnecessarily	needlessly
unsubstantiated	unfounded
utilization (utilize)	use
whensoever	whenever
wheresoever	wherever

Couplets.   One dictionary definition of a *couplet* is "two similar things." Under the umbrella of wordy expressions, therefore, a couplet is two words that are connected by *and* and that have one meaning. We sometimes feel we can reinforce a meaning if we use two words for emphasis. The truth is that the second word is usually redundant and adds no additional meaning. For example:

Instead of	Use
above and beyond	above, beyond
aid and abet	aid, abet
and so on and so forth	and so on, and so forth
any and all	any, all
anything and everything	all, anything, everything
bits and pieces	bits, pieces
bound and determined	determined, resolved
calm, cool, and collected	calm, cool, collected
cease and desist	cease, desist
compare and contrast	compare, contrast
complete and utter	complete, utter
each and every	each, every, all
facts and information	facts, information
fair and equitable	fair, equitable, just
few and far between	few, infrequent, scarce
first and foremost	first, foremost
good and sufficient	adequate, good, sufficient
hale and hearty	hale, healthy, hearty, well
hard and fast	firm, fixed, steadfast
here and now	now, presently, the present
honestly and truly	honestly, truly, truthfully
hope and expect	hope, expect, trust
hue and cry	clamor, hubbub
if and only if	if, only if
if and when	if, when
neat and tidy	neat, tidy
new and innovative	new, innovative
null and void	null, void
one and only	one, only
one and the same	identical, one, the same
peace and quiet	peace, quiet
pick and choose	pick, choose
plain and simple	plain, simple
rant and rave	rant, rave
rules and regulations	rules, regulations
separate and distinct	separate, distinct

Instead of	**Use**
then and then only	only then, then
until and unless	until, unless
various and sundry	various, sundry

Being able to identify a wordy expression by name is useful. However, more important goals are to recognize that an expression is wordy and to edit the expression properly.

Posttest

Underline all wordy expressions in each sentence.

1. Our move to a new locality necessitates a change in insurance agents.

2. The rules and regulations will be null and void if we change the bylaws.

3. As a matter of fact, the long and the short of his message is that sexual harassment will not be tolerated.

4. It is imperative that you fly in the face of Mr. Holmes by seeking redress for your grievances.

5. Mr. Leavitt, one of the loss-prevention specialists, succumbed to injuries received during the robbery.

6. Ms. Wentworth is of the opinion that the specifications are at variance with those you stipulated.

7. We are moving in the direction of liberalism in such a way that you will feel comfortable being an officer.

8. Byron is dependent on his mother for financial support.

9. The installation of a new water heater and the conversion of the furnace from oil to gas will be completed by April 1.

10. From previous experience, I think that reconciliation will be mutually beneficial to Richard and Jodi.

Key: (1) polysyllabic words—*locality, necessitates*; (2) couplets—*rules and regulations, null and void*; (3) idioms—*as a matter of fact, the long and the short*; (4) cliches—*it is imperative that, fly in the face of*; (5) euphemisms—*loss-prevention specialists, succumbed to injuries*; (6) circumlocutions—*is of the opinion that, are at variance with*; (7) prepositional phrases—*in the direction of, in such a way that*; (8) verb phrase—*is dependent on*; (9) noun phrases—*the installation of, the conversion of*; (10) extraneous adjectives and adverbs—*previous* experience, *mutually* beneficial.

LEVEL A

Name _____

Exercise 31–1   On the lines below, write **T** if the statement is true and **F** if the statement is false.

_T_   1. The key to effective editing of wordy expressions is to question the value of every word or phrase in a sentence.

_T_   2. A wordy prepositional phrase can usually be reduced to one word or be deleted altogether.

_T_   3. In wordy verb phrases, two or more words usually perform the work of one word.

_F_   4. A euphemism is a trite or overused expression.

_F_   5. A circumlocution occurs when we substitute an inoffensive phrase for one considered offensive.

_F_   6. A cliche is an expression that is unique to a language and that has little or no meaning on the surface.

_F_   7. By definition, a polysyllabic word is a word with three or more syllables.

_F_   8. For the best business writing, all polysyllabic words should be avoided.

_F_   9. A couplet occurs each time we connect two words with *and*.

_F_   10. *In any way, shape, or form* is an example of a couplet.

_T_   11. The following sentence contains a wordy noun phrase: *I will supervise the installation of the new milling machine.*

_F_   12. A couplet occurs when we couple adjectives and adverbs to nouns or verbs.

_T_   13. The following sentence contains an example of an extraneous adjective: *Please send me a preliminary draft of your report on the Ricks College project.*

_T_   14. The following sentence contains an example of a circumlocution: *A sizable percentage of the workers participated in the sick-out.*

_F_   15. Good advice to business writers is the following: Avoid all euphemisms.

_F_   16. The following sentence contains a euphemism: *The consensus of opinion is that the sick-out will get the appropriate attention from management.*

_T_   17. The following sentence contains an example of a cliche: *On the other hand, we might be wise to ignore the sick-out for at least a week.*

_F_   18. The literal meaning of an idiom always has a close resemblance to the idiom's actual meaning.

_F_   19. The following sentence contains an example of a cliche: *The primary effect of the sick-out was that questions about employment of part-time workers were left up in the air.*

_F_   20. The following sentence, by definition, contains three polysyllabic words: *When you terminate, please help facilitate the paperwork by giving Mr. Jex an indication of your future plans.*

_T_ 21. A wordy expression is used in the following sentence: *The boys were ordered to stay after school each and every time they were tardy.*

_T_ 22. The following sentence contains two idioms: *In a nutshell, you will have run-of-the-mill accommodations when you stay with Uncle George.*

_T_ 23. The following sentence contains examples of cliches: *Irregardless of your wishes, Ms. North plans to offer you full-time employment at some point along the way.*

Exercise 31–2 Mark the sentence **Y** if it contains one or more wordy expressions or **N** if it contains no wordy expressions.

_Y_ 1. I wrote the article in order to explain the controversy about ethics.

_N_ 2. I have concluded that accountants must behave ethically.

_Y_ 3. Will you extend an invitation to Alyssa to attend your reception?

_Y_ 4. We must hold a meeting to talk about rendering assistance to the homeless.

_N_ 5. Accepting responsibility to be honest is one of my beliefs.

_Y_ 6. I need a duplicate copy of your report about the conversion of our boilers.

_Y_ 7. The general consensus is that we must unite together to get Jemma elected.

_N_ 8. Troy seems to have the intellect and experience to qualify him for the job.

_Y_ 9. My grandmother is advanced in years; she almost succumbed to the injuries she suffered when she fell down the strairs.

_Y_ 10. As luck would have it, an overwhelming majority of the employees are willing to work overtime next Saturday and Sunday.

_N_ 11. The consensus is that taking the stray dogs to the animal shelter is the humane thing to do.

_Y_ 12. I know beyond a shadow of a doubt that I will be able to attend in place of Corey.

_Y_ 13. Please confirm whether or not you will attend the seminar.

_Y_ 14. Notwithstanding my broken leg, I will attend the writing seminar.

_Y_ 15. Each and every student is expected to follow all rules and regulations.

_N_ 16. For now, I refuse to affiliate with the National Business Teachers Association in any way.

_Y_ 17. Elisabeth scored the highest grade on the exam in spite of the fact that she was absent for two weeks.

_Y_ 18. What time of day will April want to have the meeting on computer security?

_Y_ 19. Please cease and desist your efforts to develop a new and innovative space heater.

_N_ 20. Honestly, we are determined to give employees the best health-care plan we can.

LEVEL B

Name _____

Exercise   Write the letter that matches the wordy expression in each sentence.
31–3

A   prepositional phrase   G   circumlocution
B   verb phrase   H   cliche
C   noun phrase   I   idiom
D   extraneous adjective   J   polysyllabic word
E   extraneous adverb   K   couplet
F   euphemism

_K_   1. We hope to get fair and equitable pay for our work.

_I_   2. Mr. Weiss reviewed the long and the short of the situation.

_G_   3. Your raise will be in the neighborhood of $1,000.

_J_   4. I hope the new copy machine materializes soon.

_H_   5. First of all, we want you to move to Genoa.

_F_   6. My uncle is too advanced in years to accept employment with you.

_C_   7. Mr. Tessel will be responsible for the installation of the new boiler.

_E_   8. The relationship will be mutually beneficial for Ms. Rieske and Ms. Birkedahl.

_B_   9. I personally have in my possession two of the necklaces.

_A_   10. Will you please work next Saturday in order to help us complete the project.

_H_   11. We must work on Saturday regardless of the fact that Penn State plays football that day.

_J_   12. Buying a new computer will help ameliorate the wounds of the July 4 robbery.

_I_   13. Janie has a brand new car that was given to her by her grandfather.

_A_   14. Yes, we stayed overnight at the Hotel Delta in accordance with your wishes.

_B_   15. We plan to place pressure on Dr. Geurts to sell the old computers and buy new ones.

_G_   16. You are right—the senator has been accused of sexual harassment on more than one occasion.

_I_   17. Mr. Stocks is not quite so high and mighty since he lost his job at Future Software, Inc.

_J_   18. When we connected the television set to the cable system, we instantaneously got clear reception.

_K_   19. To my complete and utter surprise, Victoria did very well as host of the talk show.

_D_   20. I'm not sure whether Bell was the original inventor of the telephone.

_E_   21. Garth became actively involved in the finance club soon after he joined.

Exercise Write the letter that identifies the best sentence.
31–4

_c_   1.   *a.*   Honestly and truly, we must replace the ceiling fan in the conference room.
           b.   For the time being, we have no plans to replace the ceiling fan.
           c.   Actually, I doubt we will replace the ceiling fan this summer.

_a_   2.   *a.*   To my complete surprise, Mr. Nawahine has decided not to return to Hawaii.
           b.   Please get in touch with me when you return from your vacation.
           c.   You will pay about $5,000 in interest over the duration of the loan.

_c_   3.   *a.*   We will restrict smoking in order to protect the rights of nonsmokers.
           b.   I feel a necessity to place restrictions on smoking in offices.
           c.   The consensus of the executive board is that we must restrict smoking.

_b_   4.   *a.*   Sergio has been down in the mouth because his son is ill.
           b.   Whether Sergio decides to sign up for payroll savings is his decision.
           c.   Sergio has decided to turn over a new leaf by getting to work on time.

_a_   5.   *a.*   Clearly, the company must decide whether Martin Luther King Day is a paid holiday.
           b.   McRay is under the assumption that next Friday is a state holiday.
           c.   We need to hold a meeting to talk about paid-vacation holidays.

_b_   6.   *a.*   In the first place, Chad failed to sign his income-tax return.
           b.   Please ship the parts we ordered on P.O. 346-462.
           c.   Please get in touch with us if you have further questions.

_c_   7.   *a.*   Write the letter in such a way that you will not get a negative reaction.
           b.   Are you willing to enter into an agreement to sublease your apartment?
           c.   Mr. Murdock died in his sleep at 10:30 p.m. on March 12.

_a_   8.   *a.*   Frequently, we cannot use the company car because it won't start.
           b.   I cannot meet with you on May 30 because of the fact that I am getting married that day.
           c.   Joseph Murphy was sentenced to five years in the correctional facility.

_b_   9.   *a.*   LaDawn let the cat out of the bag when she told me she was getting married.
           b.   Seldom do we have a chance to leave work early for a game of golf.
           c.   In a nutshell, we have been cleared of any sexual-harassment charges.

_c_   10.   *a.*   The inflammable liquid was spilled on the carpet in innumerable places.
           b.   In approximately a month, we hope to have computer terminals at every desk.
           c.   For now, we have no plans to change our health-insurance benefits.

LEVEL C

Name _____

Exercise 31–5   Edit the following sentences by eliminating all wordy expressions. Each sentence contains two similar wordy expressions.

1. ~~In the final analysis~~, we accepted your proposal ~~in accordance with~~ your father's wishes.
   Ultimately   *according to*

2. Please ~~enter into an agreement~~ to ~~extend an invitation to~~ all the junior executives.
   agree   *invite*

3. My ~~point of~~ view is that we must continue ~~the marketing of~~ the book until we cover all our expenses.
   to market

4. I was ~~totally~~ overcome by the ~~whole~~ idea of your traveling to Egypt next summer.

5. She feels that her cousin is too ~~advanced in years~~ to spend another night in the town's ~~correctional facility~~.
   old   *jail*

6. ~~Over the long term~~, you might default on your car payments ~~on more than one occasion~~.
   Ultimately   *two or more times*

7. At some point, ~~along the way~~ we must know whether ~~or not~~ Winston plans to attend the conference.

8. ~~As a matter of fact~~, Wilma did not ~~take offense to~~ the professor's remarks.
   In fact   *resent*

9. ~~Practically~~ all the employees expected to be ~~remunerated~~ for their after-hours work on the company picnic.
   Nearly   *paid*

10. The new ~~and innovative~~ toys we have developed this year are surely ~~few and far between~~.
    scarce

Exercise 31–6   Edit the sentences by eliminating the two wordy expressions in each sentence.

1. In ~~approximately~~ a week, we hope to contact all the former employees, ~~despite the fact that~~ 25 of them have moved.
   about   *although*

2. ~~In the unlikely event that~~ the students get homesick, we are ~~bound and~~ determined to help them cope.
   If

3. Mark plans to ~~prioritize~~ *order (or arrange)* his time so he can ~~get married~~ *marry* during the holidays.

4. Every student in the class has the ~~intellectual~~ ability to satisfy the ~~necessary~~ requirements for college admission.

5. To Wes' complete ~~and utter~~ surprise, Paula memorized the Sermon on the Mount ~~from beginning to end~~.

6. ~~In order that~~ *So* the parts will be ready, we have ~~reached a conclusion~~ *concluded* that about 50 hours of overtime will be required.

7. ~~Under no circumstances~~ *In no way* can we hold the rally ~~in the vicinity of~~ *near* Pioneer Park.

8. ~~In all probability~~ *Most likely*, I will be able to finish the course ~~in the immediate future~~ *soon*.

9. The team will divide ~~up~~ the assignments among themselves if ~~and when~~ Mr. Bona approves the project.

10. I know ~~for a fact~~ that a foreign language is a ~~necessary~~ prerequisite for admission to Costa Mesa University.

Exercise 31–7 Edit the sentences by eliminating the three wordy expressions in each sentence.

1. ~~In the absence of~~ *Without* enough evidence, I have ~~come to the conclusion~~ *concluded* that our best ~~course of action~~ *strategy* is to compromise.

2. ~~In my opinion,~~ *I feel* Ms. Crenshaw is ~~a qualified~~ *an* expert on ~~economic adjustments~~ *price hikes* in the housing industry.

3. ~~As a matter of fact,~~ *In fact* the average cafeteria lunch will cost ~~in the neighborhood of~~ about $7 because ~~of the fact that~~ the minimum wage is increasing.

4. ~~Under no circumstances~~ *In no way* will ~~each and~~ every office get the results ~~instantaneously~~ *instantly* without a local area network.

5. We ~~honestly and~~ truly ~~hope and~~ expect to get the rules ~~and regulations~~ approved at the next executive committee meeting.

6. I see no reason to ~~hold a~~ *meet,* ~~meeting irregardless of the fact that~~ *even though* Mr. Western ~~succumbed to his injuries.~~ *died.*

7. ~~In due time,~~ *Some day* you will ~~reach the conclusion~~ *conclude* that ~~the development of~~ *developing* a new lighting system is crucial.

8. ~~Notwithstanding~~ *Despite* my biases ~~in connection with~~ *about* the North Ogden project, we will not ~~enter into an agreement~~ *contract* with General Pipeline Company to build the pipeline.

9. When we ~~first~~ introduced the idea of separate ~~and distinct comfort facilities~~ *rest rooms* for white- and blue-collar workers, we were accused of discrimination.

10. We will ~~take into consideration~~ *consider* the ~~probability~~ *prospect* that he will accept the job ~~in order~~ to live close to his parents.

Exercise 31–8 Edit the sentences by eliminating all wordy expressions in each sentence.

1. ~~In that regard,~~ you can remove the file name from the directory ~~in such a fashion that~~ *so* the file appears, ~~for all intents and purposes,~~ to be deleted.

2. The ~~long and the short~~ *intent (or nature)* of the decision is that I expect ~~in the foreseeable future~~ *sometime soon* to ~~effectuate~~ *bring about* a change ~~with regard to~~ *in* fringe benefits.

3. ~~It goes without saying that~~ *Clearly,* if you want to ~~alleviate~~ *reduce* overtime hours, you must ~~place~~ pressure on the workers to speed up production ~~by one means or another.~~ *in some way*

4. ~~The truth of the matter is that~~ *Actually,* each ~~and every~~ person ~~in attendance at~~ *attending* the seminar is ~~an acquaintance of mine.~~ *knows me.*

5. We ~~substantiated~~ *confirmed* the teaching ~~methodology~~ *method* through ~~the use of~~ *using* random procedures.

6. ~~Owing to the fact that~~ *Because* Mary and Martha seesaw ~~back and forth~~ on formatting decisions, the ~~general~~ rule I propose is that we ~~alleviate~~ *reduce* friction by following Irwin's style manual.

7. ~~In light of the fact that~~ *Because* we ~~put heavy emphasis on~~ *emphasize* performance, ~~it goes without saying that~~ *clearly* we should ~~prioritize~~ *rank* our performance criteria.

8. ~~By one means or another~~, *In some way,* we plan to ~~enter into an agreement~~ *contract* with South-Side Storage to ~~make full utilization of a limited number~~ *use six or seven* of our storage units.

9. ~~Irregardless of the fact that~~ *Even though* we supposedly set a record ~~high~~ for monthly sales during May, I know ~~for a fact~~ that our sales volume in December was above ~~and beyond~~ our sales in May.

10. Honestly ~~and truly~~, Joe, we ~~unnecessarily~~ *needlessly* left you ~~high and dry~~ *helpless* in Sacramento and took away your ~~window of opportunity~~ *chance* to sell the Comstock account in San Francisco.

11. Ashley ~~has a tendency~~ *tends* to brag when he talks about his ~~one and~~ only son.

12. ~~In accordance with your instructions~~, *As you instructed,* we will send you a replacement certificate that is ~~exactly~~ identical to the original.

13. Mr. Husberg is ~~bound and~~ determined he will be calm, ~~cool, and collected~~ throughout the budget hearings.

14. ~~The overwhelming preponderance of~~ *Almost all the* evidence shows that the ~~original~~ inventor of television is indeed Mr. Farnsworth.

15. ~~In the foreseeable future~~, *Soon* we hope ~~and expect~~ to provide stock incentives ~~in such a way that~~ *so* all employees will participate.

16. Mr. Hymas' illness ~~necessitates our hiring~~ *requires us to hire* another receptionist for ~~an indefinite period of time~~ *a few weeks*.

17. We will ~~make a real~~ attempt to computerize our billing system ~~in order~~ to ~~totally~~ overcome the billing delays we have experienced recently.

In Lesson 4, you learned to choose correctly between *confusing words*—words that usually occur in pairs and that have similar sounds, similar spellings, or similar meanings. We were quite selective in determining the limited list of words to include in Lesson 4.

In a unit on language usage, we naturally might expect to learn about additional words that are confusing. To distinguish Lesson 4, ''Confusing Words,'' from Lesson 32, we have opted to call Lesson 32 ''Confusable Words.''

The confusable words in Lesson 32 occur in pairs. The words might have similar sounds, similar spellings, or similar meanings. Some of the words occur more frequently than others in the business vocabulary, but all are useful words that should be used correctly. Study the pairs of confusable words carefully, and then use them correctly in your writing.

Pretest

Underline the ten confusable words that are used incorrectly. Above or beneath each incorrectly used confusable word, write the correct word.

1. Mr. Bryson, an amiable person, proved himself to be an authoritative person throughout the balance of his term in office.

2. Many of the colonists emigrated to New England regardless of the continual hardships they knew they faced upon landing.

3. Ms. Patrick agreed to make several discrete prophesies about the death-row prisoners who had opted to be hung.

4. The data shows that Governor Bangerter is not adverse to running a second time, and I know he is under no illusion about his chances of winning.

5. While Ida's invention is an ingenuous one, we are not eager to bankroll its manufacture.

Key: (1) authoritative—authoritarian; balance—remainder; (2) emigrated—immigrated; continual—continuous; (3) prophesies—prophecies; hung—hanged; (4) data shows—data show; adverse—averse; (5) while—although; ingenuous—ingenious.

Terminology

Countable—Capable of being counted. For example, you cannot count wheat; but you can count sacks of wheat. When you apply the ''countable principle'' to *amount/number* and to *fewer/less*, you will choose *number* and *fewer* if you are referring to countable items.

Mass noun—A noun that names a concept or a substance that cannot logically be counted—for example, *honesty*, *oil*, *gravel*, or *water*. In English, a singular mass noun is preceded by modifiers such as *some* or *much* rather than *a* or *an*. The confusable words *amount* and *less*, rather than *number* and *fewer*, are used with mass nouns.

Discussion

As you study the pairs of confusable words, give special attention to the usage comments and to the hints that will help you choose correctly between any two words. The pairs of words are alphabetized and therefore are not presented in any order of priority or of frequency of usage.

A/An.   Usage guidelines governing the choice between *a* and *an* are very simple:

1. Use *a* before all words beginning with a consonant sound, including words beginning with *h* when the *h* is pronounced in such words as *home* and *honey*. Use *a* also before words that begin with the sound of *y*, such as *united* and *use*.

2. Use *an* before all words beginning with a vowel sound, including words that begin with an *h* that is not pronounced, such as *honest* and *hour*. Do not use *an* before words that begin with *h* in which the *h* is pronounced, such as *hotel* or *historical*. For example, *an historical novel* is not in keeping with normal English pronunciation, even though you might see such usage in some written documents.

Adapt/Adopt.   *Adapt* is a verb; its noun form is *adaptation*. *Adapt* means to conform, to change, or to modify to suit different conditions. *Adopt* is also a verb; its noun form is *adoption*. *Adopt* means to accept as a person's own something that belongs to someone else (such as a child). *Adopt* also means to select and to pursue a plan or to assume or to take on something.

Adverse/Averse.   *Adverse* means unfavorable, antagonistic, or hostile, such as *adverse criticism*. However, a person cannot be adverse. *Averse* reflects a feeling of great distaste, aversion, or opposition on the subject's part—for example, *He was averse to running for governor*.

Allusion/Illusion.   An *allusion* is an indirect but pointed or meaningful reference—something that is alluded to, as in *Please don't make allusion to my father's gray hair.* An *illusion* is an erroneous perception of reality, a fancied vision, the appearance of something that is imaginary, or a false impression, as in *The dry lake bed had the illusion of real water.*

Although/While.   *Although* means in spite of the fact that, or even though. *While* is generally used to mean during the time that or at the same time. *While* indicates a duration of time; *although* shows contrast or comparison.

Alumnus/Alumna.   *Alumnus* and *alumna* are used, often incorrectly, to refer to graduates of a school or a college. An *alumnus* is a male graduate; the plural is *alumni*. An *alumna* is a female graduate; the plural is *alumnae*. When both males and females are graduates, *alumni* is used.

Amiable/Amicable.   Both *amiable* and *amicable* have similar meanings associated with friendliness. However, *amiable* is used to characterize people and other living things; and *amicable* is used to refer to relationships, documents, and things. For example, *Bryce is an amiable leader; he and Victor reached an amicable agreement.*

Amoral/Immoral.   *Amoral* is used to describe a person who lacks or has no morals. Such a person does not have the slightest idea of what others consider to be moral behavior. An amoral person is neither moral nor immoral; such a person does not care about right and wrong. *Immoral* is used to describe a person who is not moral—a person who has bad morals. Therefore, an immoral person is one who is familiar with moral behavior but chooses to act otherwise.

Amount/Number.   *Amount* refers to quantity, bulk, or mass; *number* refers to countable units.

Anxious/Eager.   Colloquially, *anxious* and *eager* have interchangeable meanings. However, in formal writing, the distinctions should be observed. *Anxious* means filled with anxiety as in *We anxiously waited for news about the accident.* *Eager* means earnestly longing or intensely desirous of something—but not anxious, as in *We eagerly opened Grandmother's letter.*

Appraise/Apprise.   To *appraise* something is to estimate its value, quality, amount, size, or other features. To *apprise* someone of something is to give notice to or to inform. For example, *The jeweler appraised the ring at $4,000; I apprised my father of the ring's increase in value.*

Authoritarian/Authoritative.   *Authoritarian* and *authoritative* are both derived from *authority*. *Authoritarian* means exercising authority or favoring absolute obedience to authority. *Authoritative* means approved or validated by authority; official. Therefore, a person or a government might be authoritarian or domineering; and a reference manual might be considered authoritative.

Balance/Remainder.   Except in accounting circles, *balance* should not be used as a substitute for *remainder*. *Balance* has the meaning of equilibrium; *remainder* means residue—that which is left over. *Balance* is used in connection with financial matters, such as that which is left at a bank after withdrawals have been made. *Remainder* is used to refer to that which is left when something other than money is taken away.

Compare/Contrast.   In general, *compare* is used to emphasize the similarities between or among things; and *contrast* is used to emphasize the differences. However, when *compare* is used, the differences may also be inherent in the comparison.

Compare usually takes *to* when we denote the act of stating or representing that two things are similar, as in *He compared her to an angel. Compare* usually takes *with* when we denote the act of examining the ways in which two things are similar, as in *The expert compared Hoffman's handwriting with the handwriting in the forgery. With* is also used when compared means worthy of comparison, as in *The artist's rendition cannot be compared with Rembrandt's original.*

Contrast is usually followed by *with, between,* or *to*: *My boss stresses the contrasts between his office today and his office of 30 years ago. The mannerisms of George contrast nicely with those of Teddy Roosevelt. In contrast to your earlier poems, your latest ones are brilliant.*

Connote/Denote. *Connote* is used when we want to suggest or to imply something in addition to literal meaning, as in *To many people, the word* cowboy *connotes blue jeans and country-western music. Connote* is also used to show a condition or a consequence, as in *A blush usually connotes embarrassment.*

Denote is used to indicate, to mark, to signify, or to refer to specifically, as in *Cold weather denotes the coming of the flu season.*

When applied to words, *denote* indicates the thing a word names and *connote* indicates our association with the word, as in *The word* spinster *denotes an unmarried woman and often connotes a life of loneliness.*

Continuous/Continual. *Continuous* means without interruption or cessation, and *continual* means repeated regularly and frequently—at close intervals. Typical phrases with these words in them are as follows:

> *continuous* hiccuping
>
> a *continuous* vigil
>
> the *continuous* improvement in technology
>
> *continual* complaining
>
> the *continual* banging of the shutters
>
> *continual* work stoppages

Data/Datum. Formally, *data* is the plural of *datum,* as indicated in Lesson 24. However, *data* has been misused so much, especially by computer specialists, than it is often used with a singular verb and a singular pronoun of reference. In casual speech or writing, *data* might be acceptable as a singular noun. In formal writing, we recommend that *data* be used in a plural sense only, as in *These data are inconclusive.*

Deprecate/Depreciate. *Deprecate* means to express disapproval of, to belittle, or to mildly disparage, as in *Ben treated Wilma in a very deprecating way. Depreciate* means to lessen the value of something or to diminish in value, as in *Your car will depreciate about 25 percent in the first year.* Although *depreciate* is often used in place of *deprecate,* we recommend that *deprecate* be used to distinguish among the meanings given above.

Different From/Different Than. In the United States, *different from* is considered correct and *different than* is considered incorrect. That distinction is not as evident in Great Britain.

Discreet/Discrete.   *Discreet* means prudent or tactful and is often used to describe situations in which information is to be kept quiet, private, or secret, as in *Ms. Venice won't say anything about the incident because she is so discreet. Discrete* means separate or distinct, as in *I have three discrete reasons for preferring football to baseball.* In mathematics, a *discrete variable* is a variable that assumes only whole-number values.

Disinterested/Uninterested.   *Disinterested* means free of bias or prejudice; impartial. Judges should be disinterested because they should not make decisions that are influenced by personal motives. *Uninterested* means without interest; indifferent. A person who is uninterested in the outcome of an event does not care which way the outcome goes. A person can be both disinterested and uninterested. For example, an umpire should be disinterested (no bias or prejudice toward either team) and may also be uninterested (perhaps bored with the process or the game).

Egoist/Egotist.   An *egoist* is a person devoted to his or her own interests and advancement. On the other hand, an *egotist* is a person who is conceited and boastful. The similarities of the two words are obvious, and you can see that an egoist may be an egotist and vice versa. Derivatives of the words are *egoism* and *egotism.* Perhaps the best way to distinguish between the two words is through the *t* in *egotist/egotism.* A person who is clearly an ego*t*ist or who clearly practices ego*t*ism *t*alks about himself or herself.

Emigrate/Immigrate.   A person who departs from a country permanently or for a long period of time *emigrates from* the country. A person who emigrates for political reasons is called an *emigre*; if the person merely leaves, he or she is an *emigrant.* To *immigrate* is to enter and settle in a country or region to which a person is not native. Such people are known as *immigrants.* If the place of departure is mentioned, the preposition is *from,* as in *Because many people emigrated from England, the population declined.* However, if the move refers to destination and emphasizes movement there, the correct word is *immigrate* and is followed by *to,* as in *Because many Scots have immigrated to the United States, its population is increasing.*

Extrovert/Introvert.   *Extroverts* are affable and outgoing and are interested in others as opposed to themselves. *Introverts* are thoughtful and quiet and tend to keep their thoughts to themselves. In general, the extrovert externalizes everything; and the introvert internalizes everything.

Fewer/Less.   *Less* is often incorrectly used for *fewer,* but the reverse seldom occurs. However, *less* is used before a mass noun, which is the name of something that is not countable, such as *less music, less rice,* and *less sugar. Fewer* is correct when used with a countable noun, such as *fewer sheets of music, fewer grains of rice,* and *fewer ounces of sugar.* In addition, *fewer* is correctly used only before a plural noun. *Less than* is used before a noun that involves a measure of time, amount, or distance, as in *less than two months, less than ten years old,* or *less than $50.*

Good/Well.   *Good* is properly used as an adjective with state-of-being verbs such as *be, seem,* or *appear.* For example: *The future looks good. The meal tastes good. Well* rather than *good* should be used as an adverb with other verbs, as in *His motorcycle runs well.* Notice the correct use of *good* and *well* in the same sentence: *Tom's suit fits well and looks good.*

Good is used to refer to proper behavior and morality—as opposed to *sinful* or *evil. Well* is used to mean in satisfactory health or spirits. *Good* is always an adjective. *Well* can be either an adjective (*Nancy is finally well*) or an adverb (*Nancy did very well on the test.*).

Hanged/Hung. People are *hanged*; pictures and similar items are *hung*:

Past Tense: The sheriff *hanged* Tom Dooley at dawn.
Martha *hung* the stockings with care.

Past Participle: Tom Dooley was *hanged* at dawn.
The stockings were *hung* by Martha.

Ingenious/Ingenuous. *Ingenious* means showing great skill in creating or devising; resourceful; characterized by originality. *Ingenuous* means without sophistication or worldliness; naive; innocent. Although the two words came from the same source originally, as you can see, their meanings have little resemblance today.

Material/Materiel. *Material* is used to refer to any substances of which something is made, such as sand, water, cement, cloth, or steel. *Materiel* is used to refer to all the parts and equipment required in an undertaking or by an organization. *Materiel* is used especially in military circles to refer to military equipment and supplies, such as guns and ammunition.

Practical/Practicable. *Practical* is used to refer to something that is sensible and worthwhile. *Practicable* is used to describe something that is workable or that can be put into practice. Usually, if something is not practical, the likelihood that it ever will be is remote. However, if something is not practicable, that might be because someone has not yet invented a way to make it so. For example, getting to work by helicopter for the average citizen might be practicable, but doing so routinely would not be practical.

Prophecy/Prophesy. A *prophecy* is a prediction or is the inspired utterance of a prophet. The word *prophecy*, therefore, is a noun. On the other hand, *prophesy* is a verb that means to reveal by divine inspiration; to predict; to speak as a prophet. The final syllable of *prophecy* rhymes with *see*; and the final syllable of *prophesy* rhymes with *sigh*.

Use T32-1 here

Posttest

Underline the ten confusable words that are used incorrectly. Above or beneath each incorrectly used confusable word, write the correct word.

1. Mack appraised us of his feelings by stating that hiking the 95 miles to Williams Lake to fish might be a practical solution; but doing so is not practicable.

2. Adopting the resolution to store the war material at Tooele Ordnance Depot posed ramifications that are different than those for storing it at Dugway Proving Grounds.

3. Nick reported that his car finally runs good after its continuous trips to the repair shop.

4. Although Coach Bradley is uninterested in choosing the five most successful alumnus of the college, she might be biased in favor of her basketball players.

5. Please don't deprecate Bryan for believing that the groundhog's shadow signifies six more weeks of winter and that the event is an historically proven fact.

Key: (1) appraised—apprised; practical—practicable; practicable—practical; (2) material—materiel; different than—different from; (3) good—well; continuous—continual; (4) uninterested—disinterested (logically, if she is either of these, she is probably disinterested, but she might be uninterested); alumnus—alumnae or alumni; (5) an—a.

LEVEL A

Name _____

Exercise
32–1

On the lines below, write **T** if the statement is true and **F** if the statement is false.

_F_ 1. In general, *compare* is used to emphasize the differences between or among things.

_T_ 2. *Number* is used when you are referring to countable units.

_F_ 3. *Continuous* means repeated regularly and frequently—at close intervals.

_F_ 4. *Balance* is used to refer to that which is left when something other than money is taken away.

_T_ 5. *Data* is the plural of *datum* and has been misused so much that it is often used with a singular verb and a singular pronoun of reference.

_F_ 6. *Deprecate* means to lessen the value of something or to diminish in value.

_F_ 7. *Denote* is used to show a condition or a consequence, as in *Shifty eyes often denote guilt.*

_T_ 8. A prophet can make a *prophecy*; a prophet can also *prophesy.*

_F_ 9. *Ingenuous* means showing great skill in creating or devising; resourceful; characterized by originality.

_F_ 10. An *egoist* is a person who is devoted to his or her own interests and who constantly talks about himself or herself.

_F_ 11. In general, an *introvert* externalizes everything; and an *extrovert* internalizes everything.

_T_ 12. An *emigrant* is a person who departs from a country permanently or for a long period of time.

_F_ 13. *Discrete* means prudent or tactful, as in *I was discrete about the special considerations given me.*

_T_ 14. A person can be both *disinterested* and *uninterested.*

_T_ 15. People are *hanged*; pictures are *hung.*

_F_ 16. If you *apprise* something, you estimate its value, quality, amount, or other features.

_F_ 17. An *amoral* person is a person who is familiar with moral behavior but chooses to act otherwise.

_T_ 18. Both *adapt* and *adopt* are verbs; *adapt* means to conform, to change, or to modify to suit different conditions.

_F_ 19. *Anxious* means earnestly longing or intensely desirous of something.

_T_ 20. The article *a* is used before all words beginning with a consonant sound, including words beginning with *h* when the *h* is pronounced.

_F_ 21. An *alumna* is a male graduate; the plural is *alumni.*

_F_ 22. *Amicable* is used to characterize people, as in *Marylu is certainly an amicable person.*

F 23. *Adverse* reflects a feeling of great distaste, as in *Tucker was adverse to accepting the nomination.*

I 24. *While* indicates a duration of time; *although* shows contrast or comparison.

F 25. In *I feel good after my bout with the flu,* the word *good* is correctly used as an adverb modifying *feel.*

Exercise 32–2 Mark **C** if all confusable words are used correctly; otherwise, Mark **I.**

I 1. The theme of the junior prom is an adoption of Irving Berlin's "Deep Purple."

I 2. We experienced some severe averse winds when we sailed to Catalina Island.

C 3. Your allusion to our deer-hunting experiences brought back fond memories.

I 4. Dr. Bert Taylor is perhaps the most amicable professor I know.

C 5. Members of the gang who murdered the children are simply amoral individuals.

I 6. Wilmer is the person who appraised me of Mr. Yanno's heart condition.

C 7. Your dictionary is not as authoritative as the one I'm currently using.

I 8. When I went to Peru, I withdrew the remainder of the funds in my savings account.

I 9. Your writing proficiency today cannot be contrasted with your writing of a year ago.

I 10. The term *balmy* connotes a person who reflects eccentric behavior.

C 11. Gerta's continual nagging almost drove her husband to take up drinking.

I 12. The data we have accumulated supports our decision to buy a new company car.

I 13. We plan to deprecate the duplex over a ten-year period.

I 14. The second edition of the textbook is very different than the first edition.

I 15. Herbert's statistical formula contains three discreet variables.

C 16. Margie and her husband have a minor conflict because she is so uninterested in football.

I 17. When your grandparents immigrated from Ireland, did they settle in Chicago?

I 18. The new shopping mall resulted in less downtown stores for shopping.

C 19. George indeed looked well following the open-heart surgery.

I 20. As you requested, we hanged the picture of George Washington on the north wall.

C 21. Merrill's remarkable spare-tire cover is indeed an ingenious invention.

I 22. Following World War II, war-surplus stores sold millions of dollars worth of war material left over from the war.

I 23. Winston is a very practicable person because of his attitude toward luxury cars.

C 24. What happened to Douglas' prophecy about the fourth-quarter stock market?

LEVEL B

Name _____

Exercise 32–3 Write the letter that identifies the sentence with the correctly used confusable word(s).

_b_ 1. *a.* While you have the skills, you do not have the required bachelor's degree.
   b. I am not averse to your suggestions about office protocol.
   c. We must be very discrete about Que's decision to leave the company.

_a_ 2. *a.* You are probably an introvert if you are thoughtful and quiet and keep to yourself.
   b. You are probably an egoist, not an egotist, if you are boastful about yourself.
   c. A person who is immoral probably does not have the slightest idea of what others consider to be moral behavior.

_c_ 3. *a.* The museum appraised the painting at $5,000; I appraised Mr. Winters of the appraisal's discrepancy.
   b. Marshall contrasted Mr. Welling to an nineteenth-century robber baron.
   c. When we finish, bring the remainder of the empty boxes into my office.

_c_ 4. *a.* The emigrants to Minnesota settled in the St. Anthony area.
   b. I am eager to know whether my sister died in the accident.
   c. When I was a boy, the passing of Thanksgiving denoted the imminence of Christmas.

_b_ 5. *a.* Our home on Freedom Boulevard deprecated when the new mall was announced.
   b. Dr. Yeltsin's book represents an authoritative work on the Cold War.
   c. Ms. Hollings is an alumnus of the Waterford School class of 1952.

_b_ 6. *a.* Mikhail's continuous references to the rules of order caused us to resent his presence at the meeting.
   b. Your datum identifying the number of murders in the state is not correct.
   c. We are an united group in our resolve to solve the crimes.

_a_ 7. *a.* Kelly's allusion to the crime statistics was a brilliant statistical move.
   b. The President's prophesies about the economy proved to be correct after all.
   c. The council passed the resolutions with no allusions about the outcomes.

_c_ 8. *a.* How many outlaws were hung during the Wyatt Earp series?
   b. Mario's successful first week in New York City proved how ingenuous he was.
   c. Diverting more water from the Colorado River to satisfy the thirst of Southern California is a practicable, but not a practical, solution.

_a_ 9. *a.* Much of the materiel left over from the Gulf War was given to Saudi Arabia.
   b. Luke's new clothes seem to fit him very good, and he is well pleased with his tailor.
   c. We will adopt the procedures so they conform to our thinking about the zoning ordinances.

_c_ 10. *a.* The procedures we follow today are certainly different than those we followed a year ago.
   b. The amount of dollars we expended for Christmas exceeded our budget considerably.
   c. Amy showed how amiable she is when she invited the international students to dinner.

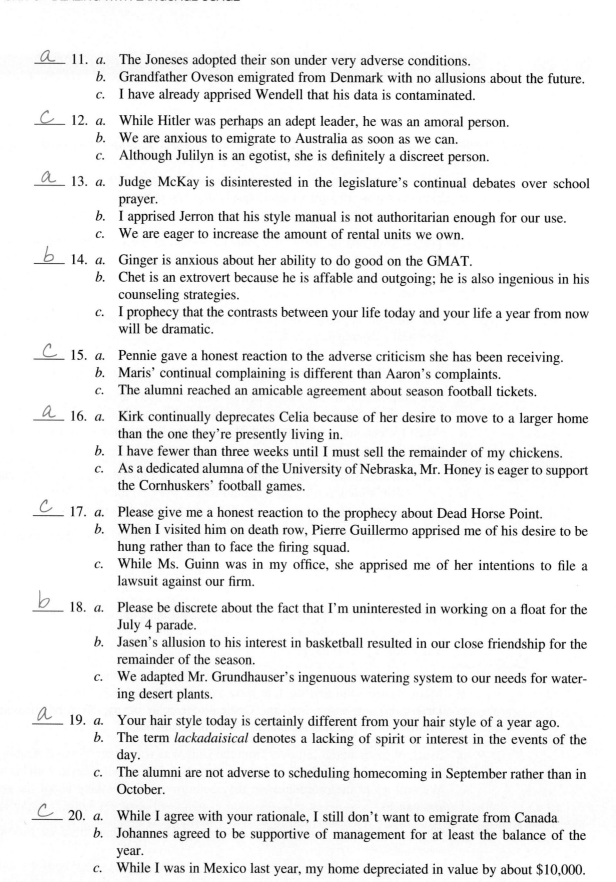

_a_ 11. _a._ The Joneses adopted their son under very adverse conditions.
        _b._ Grandfather Oveson emigrated from Denmark with no allusions about the future.
        _c._ I have already apprised Wendell that his data is contaminated.

_c_ 12. _a._ While Hitler was perhaps an adept leader, he was an amoral person.
        _b._ We are anxious to emigrate to Australia as soon as we can.
        _c._ Although Julilyn is an egotist, she is definitely a discreet person.

_a_ 13. _a._ Judge McKay is disinterested in the legislature's continual debates over school prayer.
        _b._ I apprised Jerron that his style manual is not authoritarian enough for our use.
        _c._ We are eager to increase the amount of rental units we own.

_b_ 14. _a._ Ginger is anxious about her ability to do good on the GMAT.
        _b._ Chet is an extrovert because he is affable and outgoing; he is also ingenious in his counseling strategies.
        _c._ I prophecy that the contrasts between your life today and your life a year from now will be dramatic.

_c_ 15. _a._ Pennie gave a honest reaction to the adverse criticism she has been receiving.
        _b._ Maris' continual complaining is different than Aaron's complaints.
        _c._ The alumni reached an amicable agreement about season football tickets.

_a_ 16. _a._ Kirk continually deprecates Celia because of her desire to move to a larger home than the one they're presently living in.
        _b._ I have fewer than three weeks until I must sell the remainder of my chickens.
        _c._ As a dedicated alumna of the University of Nebraska, Mr. Honey is eager to support the Cornhuskers' football games.

_c_ 17. _a._ Please give me a honest reaction to the prophecy about Dead Horse Point.
        _b._ When I visited him on death row, Pierre Guillermo apprised me of his desire to be hung rather than to face the firing squad.
        _c._ While Ms. Guinn was in my office, she apprised me of her intentions to file a lawsuit against our firm.

_b_ 18. _a._ Please be discrete about the fact that I'm uninterested in working on a float for the July 4 parade.
        _b._ Jasen's allusion to his interest in basketball resulted in our close friendship for the remainder of the season.
        _c._ We adapted Mr. Grundhauser's ingenuous watering system to our needs for watering desert plants.

_a_ 19. _a._ Your hair style today is certainly different from your hair style of a year ago.
        _b._ The term _lackadaisical_ denotes a lacking of spirit or interest in the events of the day.
        _c._ The alumni are not adverse to scheduling homecoming in September rather than in October.

_c_ 20. _a._ While I agree with your rationale, I still don't want to emigrate from Canada.
        _b._ Johannes agreed to be supportive of management for at least the balance of the year.
        _c._ While I was in Mexico last year, my home depreciated in value by about $10,000.

LEVEL C

Name _____

Exercise
32–4

Edit the following sentences by using the correct confusable words. Two of the sentences are correct.

1. *Smith's Bible Dictionary* is an ~~authoritarian~~ *authoritative* source for biblical events and traditions.

2. While the band played, the audience anxiously awaited word about Senator Hodges.

3. Thomas Edison's work resulted in one of the most ~~ingenuous~~ *ingenious* inventions ever—the electric light.

4. Regardless of your predictions, the Holzapfel prophecy came to pass on January 1 of last year.

5. Members of the group reached an ~~amiable~~ *amicable* understanding of the role each member must assume.

6. All of the 1935 ~~alumnus~~ *alumni* of Delta High School met at a class reunion on July 5.

7. The ~~averse~~ *adverse* criticism caused me to lose faith in our study group.

8. I made far ~~less~~ *fewer* mistakes on the exam when I took it a second time.

9. Thousands of converts ~~immigrated~~ *emigrated* from England during the 1850s.

10. Be sure you identify the ~~discreet~~ *discrete* variables in each of the homework problems.

Exercise
32–5

Edit the following sentences by using the correct confusable words. Two of the sentences are correct.

1. Oscar thinks you are ~~a~~ *an* honest person—in spite of your being such an extrovert.

2. Judge Carley was ~~disinterested~~ *uninterested* in the game until Coach Newton put the judge's son in for the ~~balance~~ *remainder* of the game.

3. Benjamin proved himself to be ~~a amoral~~ *an immoral* person—he violated two of the commandments even though he believed in them.

4. ~~While~~ *Although* I thought I would have an ~~averse~~ *adverse* reaction to the penicillin, I had no choice but to take it because I was so sick.

5. Before we adapted the play, we apprised Ms. Snelling of our intention to make the changes.

6. We ~~contrasted~~ *Compared* our governor to President Kennedy because both had no illusions about their leadership roles.

7. To me, the name of the group, The Lonely Hearts Club, connotes a group of introverts whose lives have been affected by divorce.

8. Percy talks so much about himself that he clearly is an ~~egoist~~ *egotist* who is ~~anxious~~ *eager* to brag whenever he gets a chance to do so.

9. Do you know the ~~amount~~ *number* of murderers who were ~~hung~~ *hanged* in the Utah Territory in the 1860s?

10. Suzanne is an introvert and an ingenuous person who does ~~good~~ *well* in her schoolwork.

Exercise 32–6 Edit the following sentences by using the correct confusable words. Two of the sentences are correct.

1. The continual ringing of the bell denoted an end to the strike.

2. Marsh is a ~~practicable~~ *practical* man who refuses to deprecate his wife under any circumstances.

3. I want to author ~~an~~ *a* historical novel about the outlaws who were hanged during the Gold Rush days.

4. The ~~materiels~~ *materials* you will need for the job are two-by-four studs, shelving, 8-penny nails, and whisper-white paint.

5. Monica looks ~~well~~ *good* in her new dress; her appearance these days is certainly different from her appearance of a month ago.

6. We studied the prophecies of Ezekiel, but we had no illusions about our ability to interpret them correctly.

7. The agreement between Wilson and Michael is an ~~amiable~~ *amicable* one—they adopted the maxim, "We agree not to disagree."

8. When you get the jewelry ~~apprised,~~ *appraised,* don't bother telling Bradford about the results unless the total appraisal is ~~fewer~~ *less* than the retail value of your car.

9. For the ~~balance~~ *remainder* of the semester, the seminary students studied the ~~amoral~~ *immoral* behavior of selected seventeenth-century church leaders. ** Could be amoral if such leaders did not care about right or wrong.*

10. The data you have collected ~~is~~ *are* going to be ~~contrasted~~ *compared* with the data Ms. Bryant collected.

Exercise 32–7 Edit the following sentences by using the correct confusable words. Two of the sentences are correct.

1. ~~While~~ *Although* your research results are different ~~than~~ *from* the results of my study, I don't think we will face any ~~averse~~ *adverse* criticism.

2. When the alumnae ~~contrasted~~ *compared* the present team's strengths and weaknesses with last year's, the girls became ~~eager~~ *anxious* to begin competition because they were sure their team was going to lose.

3. In ~~an~~ *a* historical sense, the name *George Washington* ~~connotes a~~ *denotes an* honest individual who's averse to telling lies of any kind.

4. You should have no ~~allusions~~ *illusions* about why Dr. Grover is ~~authoritative~~ *authoritarian* in his role as coordinator of the Wasatch Academy ~~Alumnus~~ *Alumni* Association.

5. Your ideas about a new keyboard are ~~ingenuous~~ *ingenious* and practicable, but we have ~~less~~ *fewer* dollars to invest in market research this year than we did last year.

6. Mr. Farmer, who ~~depreciates~~ *deprecates* his children continually, is an ~~adapted~~ *adopted* child who may have suffered abuse as a child.

7. The Andersons emigrated from Denmark seven years ago and have done well in no fewer than five business ventures.

8. Although Ms. Gough made the prophecy this week, she still does not know the men were hanged last week.

Exercise 32–8 Compose a sentence in which you correctly use all three of the following confusable words.

1. authoritarian, averse, deprecate

_____

_____

2. although, egoist, well

_____

_____

3. anxious, less, ingenious

_____

_____

4. prophesy, different from, disinterested

_____

_____

5. extrovert, discreet, alumna

_____

_____

The following letter was received in response to a survey whose cover letter contained the salutation *Dear Sir*. Imagine your feelings if you were the recipient of this letter.

> Thank you for your letter. We have responded to your survey.
>
> I would be remiss, however, if I did not point out my disappointment at the use of the masculine salutation in your introductory letter. I am not, nor is our other owner, a ''Dear Sir.'' Nor are we the only women in this year's ''INC 500.'' When God distributed the intelligence mentioned on your letterhead, it was not to men only! I am sorry, and so should you be, that the person who programmed your word processor believed otherwise and that no one seemed to notice.
>
> Such an error is not merely careless, inaccurate or even rude; it is discriminatory, insulting, and anti-women!

The letter is a classic reaction to an unintentional but sexist incident in business correspondence. You will be wise to write so you do not offend your readers, whether male or female, through the use of sexist writing.

In the 1970s, an abrupt change in writers' approaches to gender impacted the English language in America. In many instances, new words or new uses for old words took root. Such words as *chairperson, firefighter*, and *Ms.* were used to avoid sex stereotyping.

The trend toward nonsexist writing came about because of the inherent nature of the English language. Structurally, English is one of the least sex-conscious languages. Unlike French, German, Spanish, and others, English essentially lacks grammatical gender. Many languages other than English commonly divide nouns among masculine, feminine, and neuter classes and require precise gender agreement of adjectives, pronouns, and verbs.

When you understand that language is a living thing shaped by the needs of society, you'll know that business writers today must avoid sexist writing to be accepted positively by society.

Your task in Lesson 33 is to acquaint yourself with techniques to follow so you can recognize sexist writing by other writers and also avoid sexism in your own writing. Sexist writing in English comes from the stereotyping of males and females through the generic use of the masculine, singular pronouns; through the generic use of *man*; through the use of masculine-marker words; and through sex-role stereotyping in words and phrases.

You'll have to decide how far to go in avoiding sexism in your writing. For example, such words as *brotherhood, craftsman, freshman, horsemanship, manpower, sportsmanship,* and *weatherman* reflect masculinity. Does that mean you should avoid using some of these words or all of these words? Facetiously, you'll have to decide whether *manhole cover* should be *personhole cover, peoplehole cover, sewer lid,* or whatever. The guidelines that follow are safe guidelines that give good advice about nonsexist writing, but you'll have to make decisions about how far to go in achieving an appropriate balance between masculinity and femininity in your writing.

Pretest

Mark the item **S** (sexist) if it reflects potentially offensive sexist terms; mark it **NS** (nonsexist) if it reflects no potentially sexist writing.

1. If a student wants an appointment, he can see me after class.

2. The policemen arrived at the scene within 15 minutes of his phone call.

3. Dr. Devern Davenport did her word-frequency study with financial support from Delta Pi Sigma. [Writer does not know Devern Davenport personally.]

4. We use only manmade materials in the soles and heels of our shoes.

5. The girls in Mrs. Alice Libbey's office gave her a roasting during her farewell party.

6. By the 15th of each month, each engineer will report the progress of her/his current projects.

Key: (1) S—change *student, wants,* and *he* to plural; or use *he or she* or *she or he*; (2) S—change *policemen* to *police officers*; (3) S—change *her* to *the*; or verify the person is a woman; (4) S—change *manmade* to *synthetic*; (5) S—change *girls* to *ladies* or *women*, and use *Mrs.* only if that is the preference of Alice; (6) NS.

Terminology

Courtesy title—A polite title used before a person's last name—for example, *Miss, Ms., Mr., Mrs.*

Gender—Classification of words into masculine, feminine, common, and neuter categories.

Generic—Descriptive of an entire group or class; general. In this lesson, a *generic* word is one that is neither masculine nor feminine, such as the pronouns *them* and *they.*

Neuter—Neither masculine nor feminine in gender, such as the pronoun *it.*

Sex stereotyping—The process of associating a person, group, event, issue, or word with masculinity or femininity.

Sexism—Discrimination based on sex, most frequently applied to women; attitudes or circumstances that promote stereotyping of social roles based on gender.

Sexist writing—Writing that potentially reflects sexism. Sexist writing is associated with singular masculine pronouns, the generic *man*, masculine markers, and sex-role stereotyping.

Discussion

Although the suggestions that follow for nonsexist writing are stated in the imperative mood, they are not rules. Choose the suggestion that fits the situation as you deal with the singular, masculine pronouns; the generic *man*; masculine markers; and sex-role stereotyping.

Use T33-1 here

1. **Avoid sexism in writing by choosing an appropriate alternative to the singular, masculine pronouns *he*, *him*, and *his*.**

   Prior to the 1970s, usage books advocated using singular, masculine pronouns as generic words to refer to both males and females. The trend has now come full circle to the point where writers must choose one of many alternatives to singular, masculine pronouns.

   Some writers feel that society has gone too far in attempting to deal with the masculine pronoun. For example, at least one new version of the Holy Bible expunges all references to God as ''He'' and thereby eliminates the ''male bias'' that supposedly is found in the Hebrew and Greek Scriptures and in subsequent English translations.

   Some attempts have been made to replace the singular, masculine pronouns with new, nonsexist words. For example, one unsuccessful proposal was to use *E* as a singular pronoun that is neuter—neither masculine nor feminine. Presently, the chances of replacing the singular, masculine pronouns with nonsexist, singular pronouns seem very remote.

   In your writing, you must decide how to deal with singular, masculine pronouns. Following are various alternatives from which you may choose.

   Eliminate the singular, masculine pronouns.

   NO   The student must read *his* text, study *his* notes, and get help from *his* teacher.

   YES   The student must read *the* text, study notes, and get help from *the* teacher.

   Use a plural pronoun.

   NO   When *a worker* uses a company car, *he* must keep accurate expense records if *he* expects to be reimbursed.

   YES   When *workers* use a company car, *they* must keep accurate expense records if *they* expect to be reimbursed.

   Use genderless words.

   NO   *He* will not receive the benefits to which *he* is entitled unless *he* plans for the future.

   YES   *You* will not receive the benefits to which *you* are entitled unless *you* plan for the future.

Use job titles or functions.

NO   *He* cannot cope with 60 students in a classroom.

YES   *The teacher* cannot cope with 60 students in a classroom.

Use T33-2 here

Change the pronoun to an article.

NO   When an employee uses *his* personal vehicle . . . .

YES   When an employee uses *a* personal vehicle . . . .

Use the passive voice.

NO   *He should spend* considerable energy convincing employees they should give up smoking.

YES   Considerable energy *should be spent* convincing employees they should give up smoking.

Use the person's name.

NO   When *the district manager* conducts exit interviews, *he* follows the guidelines in our policy manual.

YES   When *Nathanial Bankhead*, the district manager, conducts exit interviews, *he* follows the guidelines in our policy manual.

Repeat the noun.

NO   If the driver is intoxicated, *he* will undoubtedly be cited.

YES   If the driver is intoxicated, *the driver* will be cited.

Include the feminine pronoun.

NO   If the driver is intoxicated, *he* will undoubtedly be cited.

YES   If the driver is intoxicated, *he or she* [or *he/she, she or he*, or *she/he*] will be cited.

When including the feminine pronoun, be judicious in favoring neither the masculine nor the feminine. For example, for every *he or she* [or *he/she*] you use, include a *she or he* [or *she/he*] for equal treatment of the masculine and the feminine.

Use T33-3 here

2. **Avoid sexism in writing by choosing an appropriate alternative to the generic use of the word *man*.**

NO   man, men, mankind

YES   human(s), person(s), individual(s), people, humanity, human being(s), human race, men and women, women and men

NO   The observant *man* will be aware of neighbors' needs.

YES   The observant *person* will be aware of neighbors' needs.

3. **Avoid sexism in writing by choosing substitutions for *man* suffixes and prefixes.**

NO   businessman, businessmen

YES   businessperson, business executive(s), manager(s), business leader(s), industrialist(s)

NO   chairman

YES   chair, chairperson, presiding officer, group leader

NO   manmade

YES   handmade, machinemade, manufactured, hand-built

NO   manpower

YES   human resources, workforce

NO   salesman, salesmen

YES   salesperson(s), salespeople, sales agent(s), sales representative(s), sales force

NO   spokesman, spokesmen

YES   spokesperson(s), representative(s), advocate(s), proponent(s)

4. **Avoid sexism in writing by choosing appropriate substitutions for occupational titles containing the suffix *man*.**

NO   deliveryman, foreman, draftsman, repairman, salesman, serviceman, yardman, etc.

YES   delivery clerk, deliverer, supervisor, drafter, repairer, salesperson, sales representative, sales agent, yard worker, etc.

When the U.S. Government finally dealt seriously with appropriate substitutions for occupational titles containing *man*, the entire *Dictionary of Occupational Titles* had to be rewritten. This publication is an excellent source for occupational titles that are not sexist.

5. **Avoid sexism in writing by eliminating sex-role stereotyping in words and phrases. Eliminate the following:**

Language that is demeaning or patronizing.

NO   acted like a woman, woman driver, the weaker sex, weak sister, the fairer sex, man-sized job, old-maidish, the little woman, the better half, etc.

Adjectives that unnecessarily identify gender.

NO   female doctor, male nurse, male secretary, female driver, etc.

YES   doctor, nurse, secretary, driver

Nouns that unnecessarily identify gender.

NO   coed, housewife, poetess, usherette, etc.

YES   student, homemaker, poet, usher

Male or female language that sex-stereotypes jobs or roles.

NO   secretary . . . she; nurse . . . she; receptionist . . . she; executive . . . he; attorney . . . he; truck driver . . . he; etc.

Adult feminine references that might be demeaning.

NO   the girls, the females, the opposite sex, the fairer sex, etc.

YES   the women, the ladies

Feminine courtesy titles that might offend.

Unless you know that a woman is married and prefers to be called *Mrs.* or that she is single and prefers to be called *Miss,* you should always use *Ms.* as a courtesy title.

An alternate suggestion is to avoid the courtesy title, particularly if you cannot tell from the name whether the person is a man or a woman. You cannot rely on the typical feminine or masculine spelling of a name (such as *Marian/Marion*) as a clue to whether the person is a man or a woman.

Courtesy titles are particularly troublesome in business-letter salutations. For example, if the addressee's name is Marian Jones, the writer might face a dilemma. If *Dear Ms. Jones* is used, the addressee might be a male. If *Dear Marian* is used, the addressee might be offended by the first-name familiarity. The writer might use *Dear Marian Jones* as the salutation, but that also might be offensive to the addressee.

One logical solution to potentially offensive salutations is the Simplified letter style discussed in Unit 10. This style eliminates the salutation. A second solution is to make a discreet telephone call to the organization to verify whether the addressee is male or female.

Posttest

Mark the item **S** (sexist) if it reflects potentially offensive sexist terms; mark it **NS** (nonsexist) if it reflects no potentially sexist writing.

1. The honorable man recognizes his duties before he demands his rights. [statement from a fraternity initiation ceremony]

2. The founding fathers of our nation were inspired when they prepared the Bill of Rights.

3. An accurate typist will make no more than two errors per minute when she takes a timed writing.

4. Jane is a highly successful lady advertising executive who will be a CEO in the future.

5. When the secretary does the office payroll, he or she shall verify all overtime with department supervisors.

6. Ms. Parent's son, Jimmy, took it like a man when he was cut from the basketball squad.

Key: (1) S—change *honorable man* to *honorable people* and change the singular, masculine pronouns to *they*—even if *fraternity* suggests masculinity; (2) S—change *founding fathers* to *founders*—even if the founders all were men; (3) S—change *she* to *he or she* or *she or he*, or make everything plural; (4) S—delete *lady*; (5) NS—you may prefer *she or he* to *he or she*; (6) S—change *took it like a man* to *acted maturely*.

LEVEL A

Name _____

Exercise 33–1   On the lines below, write **T** if the statement is true and **F** if the statement is false.

_T_ 1. The salutation *Dear Chair* may reflect appropriate nonsexist writing.

_T_ 2. Business writers today must avoid sexist writing if they desire to be accepted positively by society.

_F_ 3. The lesson stipulates ten categories of potentially sexist writing.

_F_ 4. *Caveman, fellowman*, and *kinsman* cannot be considered sexist terms.

_F_ 5. The words *person* and *human* are sexist terms because they contain the words *son* and *man*.

_F_ 6. At no time in the history of American English has *he, him*, and *his* been acceptable as a generic, nonsexist, singular pronoun.

_T_ 7. A writer typically has several revision choices to eliminate singular, masculine pronouns.

_F_ 8. *He or she* should always be used in preference to *he/she*.

_F_ 9. *He or she* should most often be used in preference to *she or he*.

_T_ 10. Sometimes, a good alternative to avoid sexism is to use an alternative to the generic use of the word *man*.

_F_ 11. *Man* as a prefix is usually sexist, but *man* as a suffix is seldom sexist.

_F_ 12. Occupational titles that contain the suffix *man* are nonsexist if the occupations are clearly staffed by males only.

_F_ 13. *Male nurse* and *female driver* are terms that reflect sex-role steryotyping.

_T_ 14. Even if a woman is married, the appropriate courtesy title in nearly every instance is *Ms.*

_F_ 15. A writer can usually assume safely that the following names are clearly the names of women: *Shirley, Kay*, and *Kelly*.

_F_ 16. You can avoid sexist writing altogether if you use the Simplified letter style.

_T_ 17. The following statement is an example of sex-role stereotyping: *A business man is aggressive; a business woman is pushy.*

_F_ 18. A logical alternative term is not available for the male and female job titles of *steward* and *stewardess*.

_F_ 19. If you were trying to eliminate sexism in the Bible, you would consider the following statement an appropriate, nonsexist statement in its own right: *Thou shalt not covet thy neighbor's wife.*

_F_ 20. German, French, and Spanish have built-in sexism-in-writing problems that are similar to those of English.

__T__ 21. English is a male-oriented language as spoken traditionally.

__F__ 22. If you know a woman is single, you can safely assume she prefers to be called *Miss* as a courtesy title.

__T__ 23. Logically, for every *he or she* you use in a written presentation, you should use a *she or he*.

__F__ 24. English is a particularly troublesome language because it has no genderless pronouns.

__T__ 25. One way of avoiding sexism associated with singular, masculine pronouns is to replace the pronoun with an article.

Exercise 33–2 Mark **C** if the sentence contains no offensive language; mark **I** if sexist language is used in the sentence.

__I__ 1. When the serviceman comes, tell him to check the feed mechanism carefully.

__I__ 2. When Brandon saved Mavis from drowning, he performed a manly act of courage.

__C__ 3. The women in the office plan to petition us for an extra day of Christmas vacation.

__I__ 4. As soon as I return to my office, I'll have my girl check the addresses for accuracy.

__I__ 5. Pamela Drexler certainly performs her job as a CPA as well as any man.

__I__ 6. Ms. Greer is a highly successful lady advertising executive.

__I__ 7. When a salesman uses a company car, they must get clearance from me ahead of time.

__C__ 8. LesliAnn Greathouse is the first female executive in our organization.

__C__ 9. If an employee is injured, she/he must fill out an injury report within 24 hours.

__I__ 10. How many coeds plan to attend the initiation ceremonies?

__I__ 11. If your secretary uses our style manual, she will find answers to all her grammar questions.

__I__ 12. Two of the doctors at the Larsen Clinic are female doctors.

__I__ 13. Ms. Greene has been foreman of the sheet-rocking crew for about five years.

__I__ 14. If a coed's computer is old, she can trade it in for at least $500 toward a new machine.

__C__ 15. In today's society, the diligent manager will be aware of a worker's needs.

__C__ 16. Any farmer may sell her or his livestock at the June 15 Ralston Cooperative Livestock Show.

__I__ 17. The spouse who survives such an accident may request the insurance company to buy him a new car.

__C__ 18. When we hire a bus driver, he or she must complete four weeks of training before a permanent route is assigned to him or her.

__I__ 19. I was sure the driver of the vehicle was a woman driver.

LEVEL B

Name _____

Exercise 33–3 Write the letter identifying the sentence that best avoids sexist language.

_c_ 1. *a.* Each participant will receive the new guidelines in her packet.
    b. The chairman of any committee must submit his expense report by October 15.
    c. When an employee travels by bus, she or he will receive bus fare but not a mileage allowance.

_c_ 2. *a.* The sculptress completed the statue in time to display it at the art show.
    b. Any congressman who expects to represent his district should hold town meetings.
    c. You may be surprised to know that half of our flagpersons are women.

_a_ 3. *a.* Ms. Chalmers gave permission for women workers to wear slacks in the office.
    b. Karl complained because his new responsibilities seemed like woman's work to him.
    c. Each youngster was counseled to complete his or her work as well as a full-grown man would do so.

_b_ 4. *a.* When a swing-shift nurse cannot work her schedule, she will be expected to find a replacement from among coworkers.
    b. If he or she wants to be a lawyer, then she or he must plan for an additional three years of schooling.
    c. Senator Fogbound reported in his speech that housewives are complaining about high prices.

_b_ 5. *a.* A worker who participates will receive her/his recognition when they attend the year-end banquet.
    b. If you think you need additional insurance, you should attend the orientation meeting.
    c. When a coed is initiated into a sorority, she makes a host of new friends.

_c_ 6. *a.* Will the gentleman who parked his car illegally please move it immediately!
    b. Henry has his heart set on working as a car salesman when he finishes high school.
    c. You and your spouse are invited to attend Ms. Inouye's class for modern homemakers.

_a_ 7. *a.* Each teacher should consult his or her chair for instructions about travel clearance.
    b. Marjorie thinks she has an excellent chance of becoming a mailman within a year.
    c. If a chief executive officer wants to change the hiring policies, he is at liberty to do so.

_b_ 8. *a.* Mr. Burdick had a man-to-man talk with his twin sons before he sent them away to college.
    b. When Ms. Tedesco's boys grow to adulthood, she hopes they have an appreciation for classical music.
    c. The executive committee worked out a satisfactory gentlemen's agreement with the disgruntled workers.

_c_ 9. *a.* As we look back upon man's achievements, the airplane stands out as a singular event.

    b. Boyd Takasaki plans to get his journeyman plumbing experience in Flagstaff, Arizona.

    c. The men and women who served in the Gulf War were praised for being courageous soldiers.

_a_ 10. *a.* If the price is right, the farmer will sell on the open market; if the price is too low, he or she will wait until spring to sell.

    b. The senior employee may not receive all the benefits to which he is entitled.

    c. Each sales manager will be given the freedom to schedule a meeting with his salespeople.

_c_ 11. *a.* Matthew Gonsalves is definitely an example of a man on the way up.

    b. In your phone survey, did you pointedly ask to talk with the lady of the house?

    c. Mr. Gough will be responsible for inviting employees and their spouses or guests to the annual company picnic.

_a_ 12. *a.* What does the average person on the street think about the new bus routes?

    b. In layman's terms, how do you tell employees about potential civil-rights violations?

    c. Hereafter, each employee will complete his own time sheet and hand it personally to his supervisor.

_a_ 13. *a.* Our survey will sample the attitudes of all sales managers in the Albuquerque store.

    b. Noah Goss and Ms. Gooch will both receive promotions at the start of the fourth quarter.

    c. The ladies and the men will share round-table discussion responsibilities at the convention.

_b_ 14. *a.* Six of the coeds made excellent suggestions about the cafeteria service in Old Main.

    b. How many women students from Wasatch State University will register for the tour of the national parks?

    c. My article contains the story of a woman who, as a manager, somehow keeps up with shopping and cooking as well as her duties as department head.

_c_ 15. *a.* Did you make a gentlemen's agreement to share the costs of the banquet?

    b. Glenn's invention also represents one small step for man and one giant step for mankind.

    c. The Physical Facilities Department hired several women and men to work as part-time laborers responsible for keeping the campus beautiful.

_b_ 16. *a.* If the auditor makes a mistake, he undoubtedly will be reprimanded.

    b. As subjects for the study, Shay selected six male and six female salespersons.

    c. No matter what you say, I maintain that handling 100-pound sacks of potatoes is not a job for the weaker sex.

_a_ 17. *a.* Mr. Gillespie and Mrs. Gladden gave excellent reports of their research on sex-role stereotyping.

    b. Do we have enough manpower lined up to help the Gillsons move next Saturday?

    c. All females will hereafter be permitted to wear slacks to work during the winter months.

LEVEL C

Name _____

Exercise 33–4 Edit the following material to avoid sexist writing reflected in singular, masculine pronouns.

Honorable people
~~The honorable man~~ conscientiously seek*s* to recognize, to uphold, and to encourage that which is ethical and that which is just. With humility, *they* ~~he~~ acknowledge*s* human failings that tend to induce the sacrifice of lofty ideas for base gains. *They are* ~~He is~~ aware of the difficulty of distinguishing right from wrong when confronted by a variety of alternative goals and a multitude of pressures to achieve those goals. But *their* ~~his~~ honor is coupled with resolute courage. *They* ~~He~~ may falter, and *they* ~~he~~ may fall. Yet *they* ~~he~~ rise*s* with renewed determination to do what is right. *Their* ~~His~~ reputation is *their* ~~his~~ most priceless possession.

Honorable people
~~The honorable man~~ recognize*s* *their* ~~his~~ duties before *they* ~~he~~ demand*s* *their* ~~his~~ rights. *Such people* ~~He~~ respect*s* law and promote*s* order not because of a negative fear of sanctions but because of an affirmative conviction that a good society requires the stability that order provides.

Exercise 33–5 Edit the following sentences by eliminating all potentially sexist language. Two of the sentences contain no sexist language.

1. According to the present guidelines, no employee is obligated to retire when he *or she* reaches the age of 65.

2. All ~~stewardesses~~ *flight attendants* must have ~~her~~ *their* uniforms cleaned regularly.

3. In addition to a ticket for the one who wins the drawing, we will send travel tickets for ~~his~~ *his or her spouse* ~~better half~~ and for two other members of ~~his~~ *the* family.

4. All veterinarians who complete ~~his~~ *their* schooling ~~is~~ *are* assured of work somewhere in the West.

5. The personnel manager advised each employee of his or her opportunities for advancement.

6. Yesterday, one of the ~~female~~ office workers challenged our records about how many sick days ~~they~~ *she* had accumulated.

7. All of the ~~girls~~ *workers/women* in our office have been lobbying to have ~~her~~ *their* working hours reduced.

8. Unless care is exercised, a ~~policeman~~ *police officer* may not get all the retirement benefits to which ~~they~~ *she or he is* ~~are~~ entitled.

9. Someone on the girls' junior-varsity team misplaced her basketball shoes.

10. Because of the noisy crowd, nobody could hear ~~their~~ *her or his* name called by the committee ~~chairman~~ *Chairperson.*

Exercise 33–6   Edit the following sentences by eliminating all potentially sexist language. Two of the sentences contain no sexist language.

1. The executive vice president called a meeting of all the ~~men and girls~~ *employees* in the Accounting Department.

2. ~~A female~~ *An* attorney is expected to exercise the caution that a reasonable ~~man~~ *person* should possess before accepting a case that *he or* she has doubts about.

3. Raymond Parsons, the vice president, took his time explaining to the salespeople why they should feature merchandise in special displays.

4. If a ~~fellow traveler~~ *travel companion* decides to rent a car~~, in his name,~~ he *or she* will not get reimbursed for ~~his~~ *the* rental car's expenses.

5. The individual ~~female~~ *worker* in the word-processing center should determine which software functions she *or he* has not mastered and then ask for help from me.

6. Our ~~spokesman~~ *spokesperson*, Carla Cintra, has agreed to talk about liability insurance to the newly hired *stuntperson* ~~stuntmen.~~

7. Each worker and supervisor was notified when her/his yearly dental checkup was due.

8. Seventy miles an hour, under the circumstances, is faster than a cautious ~~policeman~~ *police officer* should drive ~~their~~ *his or her* patrol car.

9. Under federal regulations, each ~~salesman~~ *salesperson* has the right to examine his *or her* personnel file.

10. Any applicant for the position of bat ~~boy~~ *handler* must submit a medical report signed by ~~his~~ *a* family doctor.

Exercise 33–7 Edit the following sentences by eliminating all potentially sexist language. Two of the sentences contain no sexist language.

1. At very few hospitals in the state ~~is a nurse~~ *are nurses* required to provide ~~her~~ *their* own ~~uniform~~ *uniforms.*

2. Mr. Gunderson hired a ~~female~~ nurse to help with ~~woman's~~ work around the house while ~~his~~ *Ms. Gunderson* ~~better half~~ recovered from back surgery.

3. Mr. Breinholt told his disappointed son to ~~take it like a man~~ *be courageous* because doing so ~~separates the men from the boys.~~ *helps a person become a mature individual.*

4. If ~~the consumer~~ *Consumers* think~~s he~~ *they* will get a lower price by waiting, ~~he~~ *they* will find ~~he is~~ *they are* mistaken.

5. By filing an amendment to her/his motion, a participant might strengthen his/her status in the eyes of the chair.

6. The sales manager must provide ~~his~~ sales representatives with updated software as soon as ~~he can~~ *possible.*

7. According to the professor, the economic factors that must be present are ~~men~~ *human resources*, money, and machines.

8. According to Professor Malthus, ~~man~~ *the human race* will become extinct if ~~he~~ *humans* fail~~s~~ to control the population growth.

9. One of the members of the boys' choir lost his music just before the program began.

10. The ~~spokesman~~ *spokesperson* for the group, Rico Mendez, gave his permission for us to use the gymnasium.

**Exercise
33–8** Edit the following sentences by eliminating all potentially offensive language.

1. How can we use ~~layman's~~ *simple* terms so employees will understand the new procedures?

2. ~~Juanita~~ *Ms.* Gillett and Mr. Glain have been approved to attend the Grand Forks seminar.

3. The men and the ~~ladies~~ *women* will not have separate seating arrangements.

4 Several ~~coeds~~ *students* have complained about the cafeteria service in Benson Hall.

5. Did your ~~gentlemen's~~ agreement take into account the wishes of Ms. Densley?

6. If you hire ~~a female~~ *an* architect, be sure to tell her *or him* about the needed auditorium capacity.

7. ~~The weaker sex~~ *Some participants* may not be able to handle the rigors of the 50-mile hike.

8. The ~~females~~ *women* in the Englewood office voted in favor of four-day work weeks.

9. Do members of the sugar lobby plan to lobby all ~~congressmen~~ *members of Congress* or just a select sample?

10. For separate analysis, we will look at the responses from respondents who are ~~just housewives.~~ *homemakers*

11. During my stay in the hospital, I was surprised at the ratio of ~~female~~ *male and female* doctors and ~~male~~ nurses.

12. Any secretary who agrees to work overtime will receive double-overtime pay in ~~their~~ *his or her* April paycheck*s*.

13. Since she was a small child, Tamara has had her heart set on becoming a ~~fireman.~~ *firefighter*

14. If ~~a salesperson~~ *salespersons* sign*s* up now for payroll savings, ~~he or she~~ *they* will be pleasantly surprised at the accumulated savings they will experience in ten years.

15. Do you really think ~~females~~ *women* should be permitted to go into military combat? *(The content of the sentence itself may be offensive.)*

LESSONS IN THIS UNIT

34. WRITING SENTENCES AND PARAGRAPHS
35. ACCESSING BUSINESS DOCUMENTS
36. USING PREWRITE, WRITE, AND REWRITE STRATEGIES

In Unit 8, we considered the importance of words and of choosing the right words for business messages. In Unit 9, we will examine the process of grouping words in sentences and paragraphs to achieve specific goals in business writing. We will also review the techniques and the advantages of **access** in business documents as a way of simplifying the reader's task and encouraging reader understanding. And we will discuss a writing strategy known as **Prewrite, Write, Rewrite** that may be used to improve your writing effectiveness.

Sentences and Paragraphs.   Words are seldom used alone in business writing. Occasionally, we see individual words such as *hello, goodbye, congratulations, welcome,* and *thanks*. But even these words, when used individually, are generally preceded or followed by other words grouped in sentences that give meaning to the individual words.

   Most writing consists of words strung together in sentences and of sentences grouped in paragraphs. Therefore, a writer must be able to construct effective sentences and paragraphs. Helpful guidelines for accomplishing this task are emphasized in this unit.

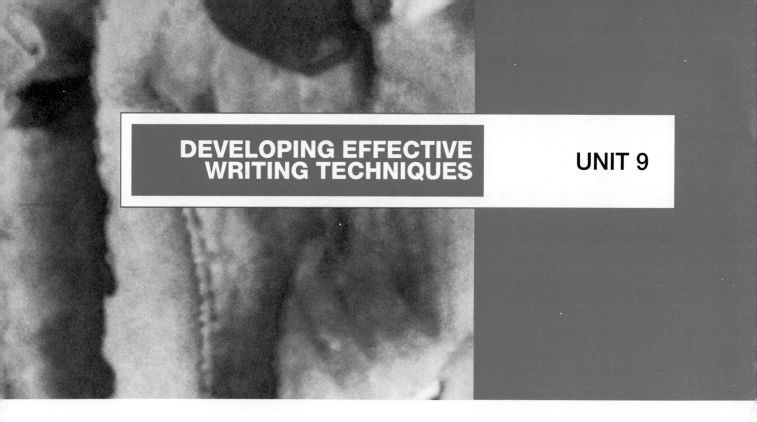

DEVELOPING EFFECTIVE WRITING TECHNIQUES

UNIT 9

Accessing Business Documents.   Business documents with good **access** are business documents with proper **emphasis**. When business documents are properly accessed—or emphasized—they offer the reader easy entry and ready comprehension. In fact, the copy you are reading at this moment is characterized by a number of access techniques.

The skillful writer knows that an important message poorly presented is unlikely to accomplish its purpose. Access keeps the reader in mind. It makes the reader's task easy by providing a quick preview of the contents of a message. And access enhances the writer's chances of making clear and effective contact with the reader.

By itself, access cannot guarantee effective writing; but effective writing without good access is a rarity. In this unit, you will become acquainted with a variety of proven access techniques that can significantly improve the communicative power of your writing.

Prewrite, Write, and Rewrite.   How often have you heard a writer say "I know what I want to say, but I don't know how to say it" or "I just can't seem to get started"? You may have even said something like that yourself. Getting started on a writing project, working through it without delays, and bringing it to a successful conclusion are often difficult and frustrating tasks. Writing is creative work and often very hard work at that.

Most writers have, at times, come face to face with writer's block—the inability to find the words needed to move the writing process forward. One method of combatting writer's block is the **prewrite-write-rewrite** process—a writing strategy used successfully by many writers. It offers guidelines for planning and carrying out a writing task successfully. It draws on a writer's knowledge, motivation, and self-discipline to produce effective writing. And it suggests strategies for minimizing wasted time and writer frustration.

The **prewrite-write-rewrite** process isn't the only way to write, of course. But it offers one useful alternative that many writers have used successfully. You will definitely want to consider the possibilities it offers you.

Put to work the concepts and writing strategies you will study in this unit. They will further strengthen your writing skills as you make them effective weapons in your writing arsenal.

WRITING SENTENCES AND PARAGRAPHS

LESSON 34

As we have seen in earlier lessons, the writer's ability to choose words correctly is critical to clear and effective communication. However, business messages are not conveyed by individual words. Instead, the words chosen by the writer must be formed into sentences; and sentences in turn must be formed into paragraphs. Even well-chosen words become ineffective if the sentences and paragraphs in which the words appear are poorly constructed.

Words travel most often in groups—in sentences and paragraphs. Just as a passenger in an automobile will not get far in a car that sputters and stalls, words can't achieve their objective in sentences and paragraphs that stumble because of faulty construction.

Business messages communicate through well-chosen words, clear sentences, and unified paragraphs. The successful writer uses these tools skillfully to produce effective business messages.

Pretest

Write **T** or **F** to indicate whether the following statements are true or false.

1. A sentence expresses a complete thought and contains both a subject and a verb.

2. The following is an example of a sentence: *As you interview Miss Muranka to make sure her qualifications are satisfactory and discuss with her the question of salary.*

3. The statement *The ad was placed in the Help Wanted section of the newspaper* illustrates the use of active voice.

4. The statement *Mr. Potemka wrote letters to the mayor and the members of the City Council* illustrates parallel grammatical form.

5. The recommended average sentence length in most business messages is approximately ten words.

531

6. Paragraph unity is promoted by the use of topic sentences.

7. The expressions *consequently* and *on the other hand* are examples of transitional language used to promote coherence within paragraphs.

8. For purposes of consistency, most paragraphs in a business document should be approximately the same length.

Key: (l) T; (2) F—a sentence fragment; (3) F—passive voice; (4) F—. . . *to the mayor and to the members* . . . ; (5) F—17–18 words; (6) T; (7) T; (8) F.

Sentences

You have learned previously that a sentence expresses a complete thought and must contain at least a subject and a verb. Most sentences contain other components as well.

We use sentences to group words, phrases, and clauses in chunks of writing to inform, to persuade, to create interest, and to promote goodwill. Sentences permit us to blend individual words into the language of business and are the basis of clear, informative, and interesting writing.

The ability to construct strong, clear sentences is indispensable to the successful writer. Observe the guidelines presented in this lesson to help you write effective sentences.

Rules

1. **Write sentences that express complete thoughts; avoid sentence fragments.**

   One common writing weakness is the construction of a sentence fragment—a group of words that is punctuated as a sentence but that does not express a complete thought. Be on guard against these confusing—and annoying—red flags of illiteracy.

   NO: When you prepare well and then work hard to ensure a successful outcome to your efforts.

   YES: Prepare well and then work hard to ensure a successful outcome to your efforts.

   If you prepare well and then work hard to ensure a successful outcome to your efforts, you are likely to succeed.

2. **In most cases, prefer active voice to passive voice.**

   In general, active voice expression is more concise, more interesting, and more easily understood than passive-voice expression. Although passive-voice language is desirable in certain circumstances (as noted in Lesson 14), most business writers should emphasize active voice in their writing.

   NO: The meeting was attended by the entire faculty.

   YES: The entire faculty attended the meeting.

   NO: As you were told when you were hired, every opportunity for advancement will be given to you by Camtex, Inc.

   YES: As we told you when you began working for us, Camtex, Inc. will give you every opportunity for advancement.

Use
T34-1
here

3. Write sentences that reflect parallel grammatical form.

Parallel writing is writing that is characterized by consistency in the expression of words and ideas. When logically parallel words or ideas are placed in grammatically parallel constructions, clear communication is encouraged.

NO: She stopped at the market and the cleaners.

YES: She stopped at the market and at the cleaners.

NO: Lorna has an appreciation and a background in the fine arts.

YES: Lorna has an appreciation for and a background in the fine arts.

NO: The student is bright, energetic, and works hard.

YES: The student is bright, energetic, and hard working.

4. Write sentences with words that are accurate, appropriate, and easily understood.

Clear communication depends in large part on a writer's ability to choose words correctly. Using ''almost'' the right word may result in ''almost'' a correct understanding. Which of the words in parentheses do you consider the better choice in the following sentence?

Ben is (eager, anxious) to receive a grade report for last semester.

Actually, either word may be a good choice, depending on Ben's frame of mind. If he is looking forward to getting his grades (because he expects them to be good), *eager* is the right choice. If he is worried about getting his grades (because they may be bad), *anxious* is the better choice. (The common substitution of *anxious* for *eager* is a good example of improper word selection. Lessons 4 and 32 contain many examples of words that are often incorrectly substituted for each other.)

NO: *While* no rules were broken, the student's behavior was severely criticized.

YES: *Although* no rules were broken, the student's behavior was severely criticized.

NO: Did the boss *infer* that she disagreed with your conclusion?

YES: Did the boss *imply* that she disagreed with your conclusion?

Be especially vigilant toward words that are likely to be unfamiliar to or overly difficult for your audience. Big words, technical words, or infrequently used words often fall into this category.

NO: Most employees considered the supervisor to be *persnickety*.

YES: Most employees considered the supervisor to be *fussy*.

NO: The doctor gave special attention to the patient's *physiognomy*.

YES: The doctor gave special attention to the patient's *facial features*.

NO: The buyer was advised to *peruse* the agreement carefully.

YES: The buyer was advised to *examine* the agreement carefully.

Big words and technical terms may be used appropriately, of course, if they are suitable for the intended audience. Such words often communicate ideas more precisely and with less wordiness than do other words that might be used. One engineer writing to another, for instance, can be reasonably certain the reader will understand the jargon of the engineering profession. In such instances, some words may be big or technical or both. The writer has the responsibility of making certain the words used convey the intended message accurately and understandably to the reader.

5. **Write concisely to avoid wordy and confusing sentences.**

Wordy expressions are thought by many writing authorities to be clear communication's worst enemy. Using an excess of words to express an idea is a common writing weakness. And when wordy writing is sprinkled with big words, technical terms, and unfamiliar words, good communication suffers. Note the following examples:

NO: In order to facilitate a satisfactory final outcome to the Newton Springs project, the construction phase of this undertaking should be initiated at the earliest opportunity by those assigned to this important task.

YES: To make sure the Newton Springs project succeeds, the contractors should begin construction immediately.

Both sentences say the same thing, but the first sentence is ponderous and wordy. It is bloated by three times as many words as the second sentence. It tests both the patience and the endurance of the reader.

The second sentence, on the other hand, is crisp and clear. It says what needs to be said and stops. It is a good example of concise writing—the kind of writing that is prized in business messages.

Lesson 31 identifies many frequently used, wordy expressions that should be avoided in favor of more concise writing.

6. **To promote reader interest, vary the length of your sentences.**

Short sentences (under 10 words), medium-length sentences (10–25 words), and long sentences (over 25 words) are all used effectively by the skillful writer. Although short sentences and medium-length sentences are generally preferred to long sentences in business writing, long sentences are sometimes useful, too. All the following sentences, although they vary in length, are examples of clear writing.

Please sit down. (3 words)

Will you read this report today? (6 words)

Pay close attention to the conclusions and recommendations on the final pages. (12 words)

Outline in detail the procedures we should follow to attract investors with enough money to pay for the planning and development stages of the project. (25 words)

Evaluate the report's assumptions, stated on page 8, that (1) consumer demand for our products will grow at an annual rate of 10 percent during the next decade and (2) we can maintain our present market position only if we successfully introduce at least one new product each year. (49 words. Note that each number is counted as a word.)

Note that the short sentences are easier to read and to understand than the long sentences. Long sentences require the reader to work harder than do short sentences to grasp the writer's meaning. Readers often get lost in long sentences. In fact, the last of the example sentences just seen resorts to numbers in parentheses to break the sentence into smaller, more understandable parts. In general, you should avoid sentences that are as long as the last example. Use long sentences sparingly and only if they contribute to clear communication.

Some studies have suggested that the average sentence length of effective business writing should be 17–18 words. Obviously, most sentences are either shorter or longer than the average. A steady string of short sentences is likely to result in choppy, monotonous copy. Messages containing many long sentences are likely to be difficult for the reader to understand. Therefore, most of the sentences we write for business purposes should be short or medium-length sentences. Use long sentences infrequently—especially those that contain more than 30 words.

7. **To promote goodwill, write sentences that reflect appropriate tone.**

What is your reaction to the following statements?

Please send your check in the enclosed envelope.

Send your check to us in the enclosed envelope.

Send your check to us in the enclosed envelope immediately!

We expect you to send your check to us in the enclosed envelope without further delay!

Although the objective of the four messages is essentially the same, the tone of the language—and therefore the message itself—changes from sentence to sentence.

Well-written sentences not only convey information but also make the desired impression on the reader. The tone of a sentence is determined by the writer's words as well as by the sentence's structure and punctuation.

The tone of most business writing is meant to be friendly, helpful, and businesslike. Occasionally, however, we may prefer the tone to be firm, insistent, or even demanding. The circumstances related to the message together with our past experience with the reader help us decide what tone our writing should reflect.

Paragraphs

Paragraphs are short pieces of writing that consist of one or more sentences and that are developed around a central thought or main idea. Paragraphs usually begin with a topic sentence that identifies the paragraph's main idea, although the topic sentence may be positioned in the middle of or at the end of a paragraph if the writer prefers.

In business writing, short paragraphs are generally preferred to long ones. Short paragraphs are usually easier to read than long ones, and the visual impact on a reader of a short paragraph is more favorable than that of a long paragraph.

Rules

8. **Use topic sentences to promote paragraph unity.**

A well-written paragraph is characterized by unity—that is, it concerns itself with only one topic or idea. Note the following example of a paragraph that lacks unity.

> An analysis of the third-quarter data has been completed. We are pleased that gross sales are much higher than they were for the third quarter last year. We have planned a new advertising campaign for several of our products. Fewer employees left the firm, and supervisors report improved worker morale. We expect to expand our sales efforts in the East in the near future. We are continuing the hiring and training program that we introduced earlier this year for sales representatives.

Because the paragraph lacks a topic sentence to provide a suitable focus, the reader wanders through a series of sentences that seem unrelated and without direction.

Now look at a unified paragraph that is anchored by a well-stated topic sentence and properly sequenced sentences.

> The firm's new hiring and training program for sales representatives is working well. One result, for instance, is that the performance of the sales staff improved noticeably during the past quarter. Furthermore, lost work time due to employee absences decreased by 30 percent. In addition, gross sales more than doubled over the same period last year. And finally, supervisors report higher worker morale and a sharp decline in employee turnover.

The paragraph begins with a strong topic sentence followed by other sentences related directly to the topic sentence and, therefore, to each other. The result is a clear sense of paragraph unity. The support sentences combine under the umbrella of the topic sentence and use transitional language to give the paragraph a focused and integrated feeling.

Note also that the paragraph can be easily rearranged to position the topic sentence in the middle of or at the end of the paragraph if the writer believes such an arrangement will serve a useful purpose.

If a paragraph consists of a single sentence, that sentence is, by definition, the topic sentence, as illustrated by the following one-sentence paragraph.

> The announcement made by the vice president means that those employees who have worked for Pembroke Papers for 20 years will be eligible for early retirement with full benefits.

Often, a single-sentence paragraph conveys all that needs to be said about the main idea or topic. When that is the case, a one-sentence paragraph is entirely appropriate.

Most paragraphs, of course, are longer than one sentence. Remember that a well-written, multiple-sentence paragraph contains a readily identifiable topic sentence with good support sentences that properly develop the paragraph's main idea.

9. **Use logical sentence order and transitional language to achieve coherence within paragraphs.**

Coherence is the quality of "tightness" and "good flow" that occurs in a paragraph when sentences follow each other in logical order and fit together comfortably. By contrast, note the illogical sequence and the poor fit of the sentences in the following paragraph.

Ms. Lundeen encouraged the class to begin the group project assignment immediately. A few groups have already begun. Most have not. The projects will take longer to complete than expected, according to Ms. Lundeen. The group project is the most demanding assignment in the course. Penalties will be assessed against project reports that are submitted late. Students will learn how to work effectively as members of a team. They will also learn a great deal from this group experience.

Now, let's reorder the sentences, revise the language slightly, and use transitional language where appropriate to improve the flow and fit—the coherence—of the paragraph.

Ms. Lundeen said the group project is the most demanding assignment in the course. Consequently, students will learn a great deal from this activity, including how to work effectively as members of a team. Because the projects will take longer than expected, Ms. Lundeen urged students to begin work immediately. Although a few groups have already begun their projects, most have not. Remember, the students have been told that penalties will be assessed against project reports that are submitted late.

The coherence achieved in this paragraph through well-ordered and comfortably fitting sentences simplifies the reader's task and contributes to easy comprehension.

Did you notice the use of such transitional terms as *consequently*, *although*, and *remember*? These terms and others like them are the "glue" that connects sentences and other language segments together comfortably and logically. Become well acquainted with these useful expressions, and use them to strengthen your writing skills.

Following are some—but not all—of the transitional terms that good writers use to give cohesion to their written communication.

accordingly	however	nevertheless
also	in addition	otherwise
as a result	in fact	so
besides	in the same manner	similarly
conversely	in other words	that is
consequently	likewise	then
for example	on the contrary	thus
for instance	on the other hand	yet
furthermore	moreover	
hence	namely	

10. Vary paragraph length, but avoid overly long paragraphs.

A business document containing several paragraphs is likely to be more readable and have a better appearance if the paragraphs vary in length. Just as effective sentences vary in length, so do well-written paragraphs.

Of course, paragraphs may be as short as one line. Note the following one-line closing paragraphs from typical business letters.

Thank you for your interest in our products.

Use T34-2 and T34-3 here

We hope the information provided will be helpful.

If we can be of further help, please let us know.

Most paragraphs in business messages, of course, are longer than one line. We often need several lines of copy to properly develop the content that accompanies a paragraph's topic sentence. Discussion and explanation require space, sometimes quite a lot of it. Six-, eight-, and ten-line paragraphs are common in good business writing. Some writers believe that an **average** paragraph length of five to seven lines is about right for most business documents.

On the other hand, paragraphs that get too long can be troublesome. They look like "hard work" to the reader. The human eye tends to be repelled by long blocks of solid print. Good writers guard against overly long paragraphs because such paragraphs discourage the reader and increase the difficulty of comprehension.

In determining appropriate paragraph length, the writer should take into account the nature of the message as well as the length of the document. Documents that use technical language or other difficult words probably should use more short paragraphs than documents that use less-difficult words. Similarly, short documents like most business letters and memos that are no longer than one page should emphasize short paragraphs.

What, then, is an "overly long paragraph?" As a rule of thumb, a paragraph that exceeds ten lines of copy should be considered a candidate for division into two or more shorter paragraphs. Occasionally, you may want to leave a long paragraph intact, but you should do so only because the paragraph cannot logically be divided into two or more shorter ones.

Posttest

Write **T** or **F** to indicate whether the following statements are true or false.

1. Most sentences contain components in addition to a subject and a verb.

2. The following sentence illustrates the use of active voice: *The report contains a summary as well as conclusions and recommendations.*

3. The statement *Sit down* is an example of a sentence fragment.

4. The following is an example of a **short** sentence: *All boys and girls under ten years of age may attend.*

5. The characteristic of coherence is effectively illustrated in the following sentence: *Jay will arrive at 10 a.m.; Reba, however, cannot come before noon.*

6. The sentence *Floyd is anxious to go* means Floyd is looking forward with pleasure to going.

7. One-sentence paragraphs do not contribute to effective business writing.

8. Some writers recommend an average paragraph length of five to seven lines of copy.

Key: (l) T; (2) T; (3) F—a complete sentence; (4) F—a medium-length sentence; (5) T; (6) F—*anxious* indicates *anxiety* or *worry*; (7) F; (8) T.

LEVEL A

Name _____

Exercise 34–1 On the lines below, write **T** if the statement is true; write **F** if the statement is false.

_T_ 1. A properly constructed sentence must express a complete thought.

_T_ 2. Active-voice language is generally preferred to passive voice in business writing.

_T_ 3. Parallel language is language that is logically and grammatically consistent.

_T_ 4. Technical language is likely to be helpful in a message from one scientist to another.

_F_ 5. Technical language is usually wordier and less precise than other words that might be used in its place.

_F_ 6. Both an unfamiliar word like *queue* and a big word like *immediately* should be avoided in ordinary business writing.

_T_ 7. A 20-word sentence is considered a medium-length sentence; a 30-word sentence is considered a long sentence.

_F_ 8. Writers should avoid one-sentence paragraphs.

_F_ 9. Writers should definitely avoid one-line paragraphs.

_T_ 10. The suggested **average** length of paragraphs in a business message is five to seven lines of copy.

_T_ 11. A paragraph with more than ten lines of copy should be considered for division into two or more shorter paragraphs.

_F_ 12. The recommended **average** sentence length in a typical business message is 25 words.

Exercise 34–2 Write **C** if the sentence expresses a **complete thought**; write **I** if it does not express a complete thought.

_I_ 1. To complete the audit by the deadline and then prepare a report that is both accurate and readable for Dansey Tools, Inc. of St. Louis.

_C_ 2. Although the deadline was met by the auditors, our client was dissatisfied with the procedures used to gather and analyze the financial data.

_I_ 3. At 3 p.m. on Wednesday, March 20, the Board of Trustees, responding to the stockholders' demand that a complete review be conducted of officers' salaries.

_I_ 4. In a last-minute attempt to resolve the conflict blocking the merger of two companies that will definitely benefit from a joint operation.

_C_ 5. As explained in the brief filed with the county attorney, the defendant possesses no assets other than those identified at the August 4 hearing.

Exercise 34–3 Write **C** if the bold words represent effective use of **transitional language**; write **I** if they do not.

_I_ 1. I cannot attend the conference. **In addition**, I plan to obtain a copy of the printed conference proceedings.

_C_ 2. Your shipment left Portland on December 9; **hence**, it should reach you no later than December 12.

_I_ 3. We can definitely meet the shipping deadline you specified. **On the other hand**, you should receive the complete order well in advance of your spring sale.

_C_ 4. Please contact me immediately. **However**, if you cannot reach me, leave a message with my assistant, Roy Faux. **Moreover**, plan to come to the home office for a personal interview before the end of the month.

_I_ 5. Both managers, **namely** Mrs. Dollag and Mr. Golde, were invited. **Likewise**, Randy Truex, in the White Plains office, was not contacted.

Exercise 34–4 Write **A** if the sentence uses active voice; write **P** if the sentence uses passive voice.

_P_ 1. Your suggestions will be considered by Mr. Willett at the Honolulu meeting.

_P_ 2. An analysis of stock market trends was provided by our chief economist in New York.

_A_ 3. Near the end of the month, Julie Tuck will transfer to the research division to work on the quality-control project.

_A_ 4. Send your estimates as soon as possible to the architectural firm of Bookings and Prine.

_P_ 5. When was the request for better data received?

Exercise 34–5 Write **C** if the sentence is a suitable **topic sentence** for a paragraph; write **I** if it is not.

_C_ 1. Shipping problems will delay the arrival of your order by one week.

_C_ 2. My interview with Ms. Hart was more successful than expected.

_I_ 3. The postmark on your letter is October 3.

_I_ 4. In only one class, trigonometry, was a grade lower than a B received.

_C_ 5. The student-parking situation at Crossland College has become intolerable.

LEVEL B

Name _____

Exercise 34–6   In each of the four sections in this exercise, write the letter that identifies the preferred application of the language-usage principle or writing technique indicated in the section heading.

Parallel Language

_a_   1.   *a.*   The qualifications needed in a new supervisor include knowledge, leadership, and sound judgment.

      b.   She is enrolled in chemistry and physics this semester.

      c.   Mr. Royster plans to meet with the president, vice president, and the CEO this afternoon.

_a_   2.   *a.*   James possesses a good understanding of and broad experience in mail-order sales.

      b.   Our attorney, Ruthe Glazier, has impressed us with her honesty and her mind is lightning-quick.

      c.   Flight No. 866 is scheduled to stop in Chicago, Denver, and also in San Diego.

_b_   3.   *a.*   Sonja's answer was not only correct but it was complete, too.

      b.   Neither you nor I was selected for the award.

      c.   Both Eddie as well as Lora are eligible to participate.

_c_   4.   *a.*   As the manager, you are expected to (1) set the example, (2) motivate the employees, (3) creative ideas, and (4) strong leadership skills.

      b.   Neither the driver of the car or the bus saw the approaching train.

      c.   The legislature will focus on recruiting new employees and on training presently employed workers.

Sentence Structure

_b_   5.   *a.*   Do not begin the project unless the firm that made the proposal and guaranteed that adequate funding will be available for your needs.

      b.   Place the file here.

      c.   Not more than one-third of the employees contributing to the United Way fund-raising drive this year.

_c_   6.   *a.*   No nominations for team captain have yet been received the level of interest is surprisingly low.

      b.   Attracting highly qualified employees, has been more difficult than we expected.

      c.   When you complete the proposal, take it immediately to the project director, Eve St. Clair, who wants to read it before circulating it to the staff.

_b_   7.   *a.*   Promoting a new product by means of radio and TV ads that are cost effective from management's point of view.

      b.   What will be your response if you are asked to transfer to another region that offers fewer opportunities than this one?

      c.   As I explained yesterday to Miss Rabinski, the service representative from Gayson, Inc. who has been instructed to help us get our copying equipment working properly.

a   8. *a.* As I told Mike Rogers when he called this morning, the copying equipment has been serviced by the field representative from Gayson, Inc. and now works satisfactorily.

  b. Traveling to Houston for the leadership conference on March 10 and returning via Indianapolis on March 12 if necessary travel arrangements can be confirmed.

  c. Call me when you arrive then I will introduce you to our Reno staff all of whom are eager to meet you.

Topic   *c*   9. *a.* Fred Moranga will be the keynote speaker.
Sentences   *b.* Current sales practices will be reviewed.
  c. The Houston sales conference promises to be a very successful event.

a   10. *a.* Preparations are now complete for the restaurant's grand opening.
  b. Furniture has been installed and menus have been printed.
  c. We placed ads in local newspapers.

b   11. *a.* The article's main points have been appropriately highlighted.
  b. In general, the abstract does a good job of summarizing the author's message.
  c. As requested, the abstract is limited to one page.

c   12. *a.* The car needed new tires and new paint.
  b. Furthermore, we believe employee morale is improving.
  c. I am pleased to have this opportunity to review your performance as production specialist during the past six months.

Transi-   *b*   13. *a.* Tess will meet your plane. However, she will also help you get through Customs, and she will drive you to your hotel.
tional
Language   *b.* Try to submit all travel documents requested. Moreover, notify the office immediately of any changes in your itinerary.

  c. Please visit the London agency in July prior to returning to the U.S. from Amsterdam. Conversely, have you contacted our London representative?

b   14. *a.* My speaking schedule is more crowded than ever this summer; consequently, I will be able to address your group on July 21.

  b. Overhead costs for the first quarter are not as high as expected. On the contrary, they are 5 percent lower than a year ago.

  c. Our plans call for a personnel review every year. In other words, we believe our employees will applaud this policy.

c   15. *a.* We intend to close the Fort Meyers outlet soon. Likewise, new stores are planned for Baltimore and Trenton.

  b. Thank you for your interest in our computer products. In the same manner, we are pleased to have this opportunity to serve you.

  c. The results of the new ad campaign are favorable. For example, gross sales in the Midwest during May alone are up nearly 20 percent.

c   16. *a.* We expect business to improve this year; namely, an aggressive product-development program will be an important part of our strategy.

  b. Increased funding has helped us expand our operations. Besides, we may soon reach a point where we cannot provide adequate customer support.

  c. The strength of our work force has never been better. However, we intend to continue our efforts to recruit increasingly creative and well-trained workers.

LEVEL C

Name _____

Exercise 34–7   Make the following statements more concise by editing the wordy expressions in bold print.

Editing

1. *Frequently, Occasionally*
   ~~On a number of occasions thus far,~~ products have been returned to the factory because of poor workmanship.

2. *soon, sometime soon*
   We know that ~~at some point in the near future,~~ changes must be made in our inventory-control procedures.

3. A research survey shows the **consensus ~~of opinion~~** among our employees is that working conditions in the assembly plant must be improved.

4. *because*
   Sales are down in all regions **due to the fact that** consumer interest in our products has declined.

5. *Thank*
   ~~I want to take this opportunity to~~ thank you for your patience with our efforts to eliminate delays in shipping your orders.

Exercise 34–8   Improve the coherence of the following statements by editing the transitional expressions in bold print.

Editing

1. *therefore, consequently*
   We welcome your inquiry; **however,** we are forwarding the samples you requested.

2. *Accordingly, Consequently*
   Your business is very much appreciated. **Similarly,** we will continue to give your orders our highest priority.

3. *However, Conversely*
   Price reductions on most models are expected in March. **For instance,** current prices are at an all-time high.

4. *For instance, For example*
   Wages paid throughout the industry rose only slightly last year. **Moreover,** average increases
   Moreover, Furthermore
   in worker pay amounted to less than 2 percent. **As a result,** the outlook is equally gloomy this year.

5. Congratulations! All June production goals were reached. ~~On the contrary,~~ *Furthermore* we expect to do even better in July. ~~Nevertheless,~~ *In addition* our performance for the current year may be our best ever.

Exercise 34–9

Editing

Edit the following sentences, revising as necessary to improve the tone reflected in the language. Don't permit your revisions to change the intended meaning of the original statements.

1. *Please* Send your check in the enclosed envelope.

2. The shipment ~~you claim is overdue~~ *overdue* should have reached you by now.

3. ~~The answer to your surprising~~ *We are glad to answer your* question about our firm's pricing policies ~~is simple.~~

4. ~~Surely you must know that we give~~ Customer discounts ~~only~~ *are gladly given* when bills are paid in full within ten days of the statement date.

5. ~~We assure you that~~ Your order of copper gizmos was shipped promptly. ~~Any~~ *The* delay you have experienced ~~in receiving your order should be blamed on the shipping company, not on us.~~ *apparently occurred after the shipping company took the order from our warehouse.*

Exercise 34–10

Composition

In each of the following items, write a short paragraph that uses the sentence provided as your topic sentence. Include three or four additional sentences in each paragraph.

1. The results of our survey on consumer attitudes toward Sparkle mouthwash are encouraging.

_____

_____

_____

_____

_____

2. Sentences that are overly long are obstacles to clear communication.

_____

_____

_____

_____

_____

3. As you know, all preparations for moving to the firm's new administrative offices on Ocean Drive must be completed by September 20.

_____

_____

_____

_____

_____

Exercise 34–11

In each of the following items, write a brief paragraph (four to five sentences) on a business topic of your choice. Underline the topic sentence in each paragraph, and use the transitional expressions indicated to promote coherence in your language.

Compo-
sition

1. (however, as a result, for instance)

_____

_____

_____

_____

_____

2. (thus, similarly, in addition)

_____

_____

_____

_____

_____

3. (consequently, on the other hand, in fact)

_____

_____

_____

_____

_____

Exercise
34–12
Each of the following paragraphs contains sentences that are approximately the same length. As a result, the writing is dull and monotonous. Rewrite each paragraph by varying the lengths of the sentences and using appropriate transitional language to make the sentences interesting and readable. Use at least three transitional terms in each paragraph, and underline each term. Substitute words if you wish, but avoid changing the intended meaning of the existing language.

1. **Henry Tawne's report will be on your desk tomorrow morning. Review the report carefully prior to Tuesday's meeting. Pay special attention to the conclusions and recommendations. Note the projected costs summarized on page 20. Be prepared to answer questions about Henry's projections.**

_____

_____

_____

_____

2. **The Model No. 335 electric fan you wrote about on January 12 has a 180-degree oscillation arc with automatic reverse and features a convenient three-speed, finger-tip control. The fan is sold in most high-quality home-appliance stores nationwide and is priced just under $60 with vinyl cover and double-insulated cord.**

_____

_____

_____

_____

Business writing should be easy to read and easy to understand. Unlike some other kinds of writing, business writing is meant to require minimum effort by the reader to understand clearly the writer's intended message.

Some business messages, of course, are unavoidably more difficult than others. Language difficulty is controlled to some degree by the subject matter discussed. Nevertheless, the business writer is expected to write with the reader in mind—and that means to simplify the reader's task. One of the important tools a writer uses to achieve this goal is **access.**

Access is a strategy used to emphasize important ideas in business writing and to simplify its comprehension. Good access, then, is good emphasis. The purpose of access is to make messages easy to read and to comprehend. The writer thus aids the reader by providing easy entry, or access, to the message.

One major difference between business writing and so-called literary writing is the attention given by the writer to document access. In literary prose, the reader is expected to extract meaning from the narrative with little help from the writer. Such writing rarely has strong access. In business writing, on the other hand, the writer uses access extensively to help the reader ''get the message.''

A message that has good access is one that is open, that is easily entered by the reader, and that uses emphasis to communicate clearly. Through a variety of access signals, the writer leads the reader to an easy recognition of the major elements of the document and to a fast and accurate grasp of the main points of the message.

Pretest

Write **T** or **F** to indicate whether the following statements are true or false.

1. In effective business writing, to access something is to emphasize it.

2. Printed copy that is double spaced has better access than printed copy that is single spaced.

3. Good business writing should require a minimum of effort by the reader to understand the message.

4. Captions, bullets, and pictures are all effective access techniques.

5. As an access technique, enumerations may use any of the following: *1, 2, 3, 4; A, B, C, D; first, second, third, fourth; I, II, III, IV.*

6. One effective way to encourage good document access is to limit the amount of white space around the printed copy.

7. Captions and headings should be avoided in documents that are no longer than two or three pages.

8. Of the two following statements, the first reflects better access than the second:

    To clean your car properly, wash it with soap, wipe it dry, spray it with water, and wet it down.

    To clean your car properly, wet it down, wash it with soap, spray it with water, and wipe it down.

Key: (1) T; (2) T; (3) T; (4) T; (5) T; (6) F; (7) F; (8) F—the second example illustrates a more logical sequence than the first.

Access Guidelines

Access signals fall into three categories of emphasis—verbal, visual, and psychological.

Verbal Emphasis.   As the term implies, verbal emphasis uses language—words—to tell the reader what is most important in a message. Two kinds of verbal emphasis are especially useful.

1. **Word Signals.** Words—alone or in groups—may be used to give obvious emphasis to message elements the writer wants the reader to notice and remember. Some examples of these important word signals are the following:

    "*Remember*, the final step in the procedure is . . ."

    "One *especially important* fact to note is . . ."

    "Pay *particular* attention to the following instructions. . . ."

    "*Above all*, give first priority to . . ."

2. **Repetition.** Deliberate, purposeful repetition can be used to achieve appropriate emphasis. We often repeat things to give them special impact (*No, no, no!*). A name, an address, a telephone number, or the cost of something is more likely to be remembered if it is mentioned several times than if it is mentioned only once.

Note the repetition in the following paragraph of a sales message:

A *Perfection* blender is a modern-day mechanical marvel. With a *Perfection* at your fingertips, you can make dozens of delicious drinks and dishes instantly. Your *Perfection* blender may be the most versatile and often-used appliance in your house. Many a satisfied owner has said that a *Perfection* blender is almost, well, perfection!

We should avoid excessive repetition, of course. Repetition carried to an extreme annoys the reader and serves no useful purpose. Unintended repetition—redundancy— makes our writing wordy by repeating something that usually need not be repeated. When used properly, however, repetition is an effective emphasis technique in business writing.

Visual Emphasis.   Visual emphasis is achieved through the use of numbers, letters, symbols, pictures, color, lines, and other signals that catch the reader's eye. Words may be used for visual emphasis, too; but they are used differently from the way they are used in standard prose.

Be sure to use visual emphasis signals **logically**. If such signals are improperly positioned or attached to words that do not need emphasis, the signals may cause awkward language and confuse the reader.

*Use
T35-2
here*

1. **Enumeration.** Numbering is used to break up long language segments into small, easily digested parts.

   Complete the first phase of your assignment by (1) writing the proposal, (2) constructing a document outline, (3) attaching a bibliography, and (4) preparing an estimate of costs.

   Other enumeration choices include the following:

   A, B, C, D, etc.

   I, II, III, IV, etc.

   first, second, third, fourth, etc.

   Use enumeration when you are dealing with several items in a series, particularly if the items consist of more than two or three words.

2. **Listing.** Place items in columns; and introduce the items with numbers, letters, bullets, or some other mark of emphasis.

   - Write the proposal.

   - Construct a document outline.

   - Attach a bibliography.

   - Prepare an estimate of costs.

   A combination of enumeration and listing is particularly effective.

   1. Contact your insurance agent.

   2. Complete an accident report.

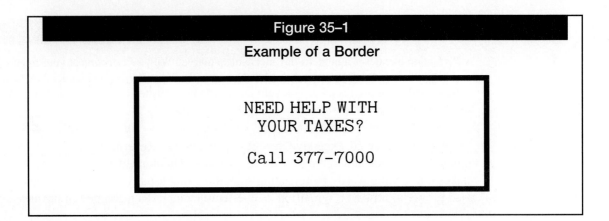

Figure 35–1

Example of a Border

NEED HELP WITH
YOUR TAXES?

Call 377-7000

   3. Take your car to the Customer Claims Office for a damage assessment.

   4. Have the car repaired.

   5. Submit all bills to Customer Claims for payment.

3. Bold print. Words and letters in **bold print** attract immediate attention, don't you agree?

4. Underlined words. Note how the underlined word—a very important element in the following sentence—catches the eye.

   Mr. Pursing will arrive at your office tomorrow at 3 p.m., not at 4 p.m. as you were previously told.

5. Borders. Use borders (Figure 35–1) to set off and emphasize important information in your messages. Have you noticed that some items in the classified ads section of the newspaper have borders around them? The borders cost extra, but they are effective attention getters.

6. Capitalization. Words in SOLID CAPITAL LETTERS get definite emphasis.

   If all words in a long sentence or a paragraph are in caps, of course, little emphasis occurs. In fact, some studies indicate that messages consisting entirely of capital letters are more difficult to read than messages consisting primarily of lower-case letters. Use caps selectively to give appropriate emphasis to your writing. Bolding or underlining the caps provides added emphasis.

7. Print variation. The printers used today to prepare business documents offer many choices in print styles and sizes. A few of the possibilities are shown in Figure 35–2.

8. Graphics. Pictures stay in our memories longer than words. Along with charts, diagrams, and other visuals, pictures are powerful emphasis techniques (Figure 35–3).

9. Shading, color, and highlighting. The use of shading, color, and other highlighting techniques is an appealing and an effective emphasis strategy. Many home and office printers give the writer one or more eye-catching options, one of which is shown in Figure 35–4.

Figure 35–2

Samples of Print Styles

CG Times 12 pt.   Universe 12 pt.   Courier 12 cpi

Line Printer 16.67 cpi   *CG Times 24 pt.*   **Universe 20 pt.**

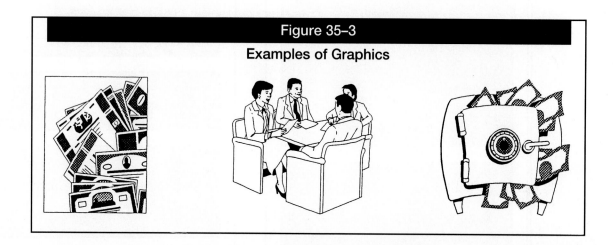

Figure 35–3

Examples of Graphics

Figure 35–4

Example of Highlighting

Emphasis usually determines what the reader sees first and remembers longest in a message.

A creative writer who uses emphasis techniques skillfully has a definite advantage over the writer who doesn't.

Don't fail to include these effective writing weapons in your communications arsenal.

---

10. **White space.** Business mesages with plenty of white space are received more favorably than messages with little white space. All the following locations in a business document invite the use of white space as an emphasis strategy:

- between letters
- between lines
- between paragraphs
- between sections
- in margins—top, bottom, and side

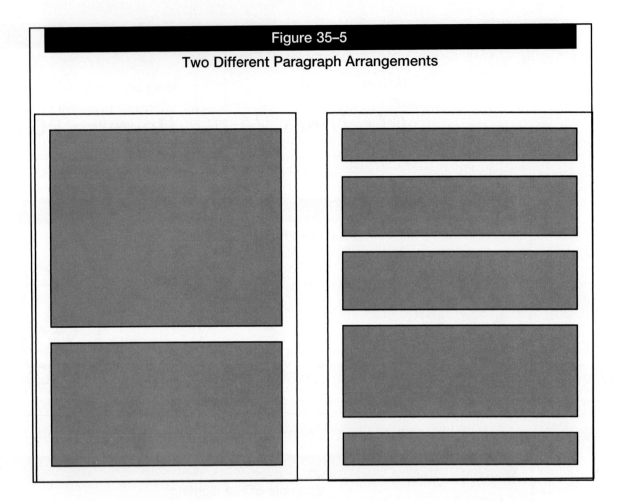

Figure 35–5

Two Different Paragraph Arrangements

White space can be used effectively to break up large blocks of single-spaced copy. Short paragraphs with plenty of white space around them look better to the reader than big chunks of solid copy. Long, uninterrupted paragraphs suggest hard work is ahead for the reader; short paragraphs suggest the task will be easier. How do you react to the paragraph arrangements shown in Figure 35–5?

Use T35-3 here

Psychological Emphasis.   Psychological emphasis occurs when the mind reacts favorably to the arrangement of copy, the use of white space, and other strategies designed to make a strong impression on the reader. Space, order, imagination, and reader interaction are four techniques the writer can use to achieve psychological emphasis.

1. **Space.** In general, the more space given to something in our writing, the more that ''something'' is emphasized. As the space allocated to a topic or an idea increases, so does the emphasis given to the message.

   However, we should exercise good judgment in our writing to avoid overkill. Wordy discussions tire the reader and obscure important points. Short, direct sentences often give more emphasis than long ones. Even so, the amount of space consumed by the discussion of a particular point or idea is one indication of emphasis given to the information presented.

2. **Order.** The human mind responds best to information when the information is logically ordered. That is why business messages should have a beginning, a middle, and an end that are easily recognized.

Usually, we have several ideas, facts, or pieces of information to present to the reader. Good access is encouraged when the indidvidual parts of the message are arranged in an order that is both comfortable and logical to the reader's mind.

3. **Imagination.** Fresh and creative approaches in business writing—when used in good taste—are effective emphasis techniques. How do you react to the following variations of the opening sentence in a typical business message?

☞   Thank you for the invitation to a workshop on business writing.

☞   I was glad to hear of the workshop you plan to hold on business writing.

☞   The workshop to be held on business writing sounds interesting.

☞   A workshop for business writers—a *good* idea!

The first three examples are adequate but strictly routine. The language of the fourth example is fresh and shows imagination. Such writing is more interesting than ordinary prose. It is different but still in good taste. It thus achieves a degree of emphasis not present in the first three examples.

With good taste as a guideline, use your imagination to make your writing as fresh and as original as possible.

4. **Reader interaction.** Strong emphasis occurs when the reader is active rather than passive in the communication process. Use techniques like the following to involve your reader:

• Ask questions. (*Have you thought about this?*)

• Issue challenges. (*Ask yourself these questions.*)

• Use thought-provoking language. (*Somewhere a child will be born with a birth defect while you are reading this letter!*)

Now that we have discussed and illustrated several access techniques, let's integrate some of them in a typical business document.

Note that in Figures 35–6 and 35–7, the messages are essentially the same; but their appearances are very different. Figure 35–6 is unappealing to the eye. It suggests hard work for the reader. Few clues are given about the content of the message until the document is read in its entirety.

Figure 35–7 is much more appealing than Figure 35–6. Its use of white space and emphasis makes it look less formidable and more ''digestible'' than Figure 35–6. Numerous signals tell the reader at a glance something about the memo's message. Even without reading the entire document, the reader gets a good indication of what the message contains.

When you give your written messages strong access, you simplify your reader's task and increase the likelihood of clear and effective communication. Make a conscious effort to use these helpful access tools in your writing.

Posttest

Write **T** or **F** to indicate whether the following statements are true or false.

1. In business writing, good access is good emphasis.

2. One similarity between business writing and traditional literary writing is the attention given by the writer to document access.

3. Access signals fall into three categories: verbal, visual, and psychological.

4. Word signals are examples of psychological emphasis.

5. The following statement contains an example of a word signal: *The meeting is scheduled to begin at 10 a.m. Monday morning.*

6. Enumerations, bold print, capitalization, and imaginative writing all are examples of visual emphasis.

7. Asking a question can be an effective way to promote reader interaction.

8. The following statement effectively illustrates verbal emphasis: *The three most-important priorities in building or buying a home are location, location, and location.*

Key: (1) T; (2) F; (3) T; (4) F—verbal emphasis; (5) F; (6) F—*imaginative writing* is psychological emphasis; (7) T; (8) T.

Figure 35–6

A Business Document with Weak Access

TO: Tom Miles, Personnel Director

FROM: Leah Ross, Vice President

DATE: June 1, 19xx

SUBJECT: EMPLOYEE COMMUNICATION

You will recall the recent survey we conducted to determine why so many of our workers leave our firm to take jobs elsewhere. The analysis of the data gathered on employee terminations has been completed. Our investigation resulted in two findings that are particularly noteworthy. Most workers who leave our firm to work elsewhere do not leave because they believe they are poorly paid. Their primary complaint is that they did not have satisfactory working relationships with their supervisors while working for us. The need for better communication throughout our work force is clear. Accordingly, the following steps will be taken to meet this important need. All supervisors will interview their subordinates once each quarter rather than once each year, as in the past. Also, seminars in management-communication skills will be provided for all supervisors and department heads to help them develop more effective communications techniques. We believe these efforts will open channels of communication among our employees and eliminate most of the frustration revealed by former workers in our recent survey. We have also designated an employee-relations officer to personally deal with worker complaints of a particularly serious nature. Finally, a company newsletter will be published monthly to provide an opportunity for employees to express their views publicly and to improve the flow of information throughout the firm. Appointments to the newsletter staff will be announced shortly.

These changes will go into effect on July 1 and will be officially announced to all employees the previous week in the first edition of the newsletter. We believe these initiatives will be effective in our efforts to improve communications among employees, upgrade worker morale, and reduce the firm's costly and disruptive employee turnover problems. We will need your support as well as that of other first-level officers if the desired results are to be obtained in this undertaking. Feel free to make suggestions or recommendations that you believe may be helpful. We are hopeful that these changes will be well received by employees at all levels.

Figure 35–7

A Business Document with Strong Access

TO: Tom Miles, Personnel Director

FROM: Leah Ross, Vice President

DATE: June 15, 19xx

SUBJECT: EMPLOYEE COMMUNICATION

We have completed the analysis of the data gathered recently on employee terminations. The results are interesting.

Research Methods

Over 200 former employees who terminated within the past five years were surveyed by telephone to determine why they left us to work for someone else.

Survey Findings

Two particularly significant findings resulted from our survey.

- Poor worker/supervisor communication is a serious problem.

- Inadequate pay is *not* a major cause of employee turnover.

Action to be Taken

The Executive Committee has agreed that **five steps** must be taken immediately to reduce employee frustration and the worker terminations it causes. Accordingly, the following actions will be implemented on **July 1**.

1. Supervisor/worker **interviews** will be held quarterly.

2. **Training** in management-communication skills will be offered to all supervisors and department heads.

3. An **Employee Relations Officer** will be designated to personally handle all serious worker complaints.

4. A **newsletter** will be published monthly to give employees a public voice in company affairs.

5. An **incentives program** will reward workers who identify effective ways to improve communications at all levels.

These initiatives will be effective, we believe, in strengthening employee morale and reducing costly and disruptive employee-turnover problems in our firm. We request your strong support.

LEVEL A

Name _____

Exercise 35–1   On the lines below, write **T** if the statement is true; write **F** if the statement is false.

_T_   1. In business writing, *access* and *emphasis* have the same meaning.

_T_   2. Business writing is meant to be easy to read and to understand.

_T_   3. A business document with strong access provides easy entry for the reader.

_T_   4. The three categories of emphasis in business writing are verbal, visual, and psychological.

_F_   5. Good business writing and good literary-style writing are likely to provide equally strong access for the reader.

_F_   6. Verbal emphasis uses numbers and letters to achieve good access, whereas visual emphasis uses symbols, pictures, and color.

_F_   7. *Repetition* and *redundancy* mean the same thing and should be avoided in business writing.

_F_   8. The use of the words *first, second, third,* etc. to refer to a series of items in a sentence is an example of listing.

_T_   9. Bold print, double spacing, and underlined words are all recommended techniques for achieving emphasis in written messages.

_F_   10. Borders may be used with pictures and other visuals, but they should not be used with words.

_T_   11. Several short paragraphs are generally preferable to one or two long paragraphs.

_T_   12. White space can be used to advantage between paragraphs as well as in the margins of a document.

Exercise 35–2   Write **C** if the sentence uses an access technique *effectively*. Write **I** if it does not.

_C_   1. The newly appointed committee chairperson, Monique LaDieux, takes office tomorrow morning.

_C_   2. Your interview with Mr. Reedy should allow you to (1) assess his academic background, (2) review his work experience, and (3) evaluate his leadership skills.

_C_   3. Don't forget—the meeting will begin at 1 p.m. sharp.

_I_   4. Applications for the position of systems analyst will be accepted until the end of the month.

_I_   5. No **matter** what conclusions are drawn in Kellie's memo, Mr. Dreyfuss **will make** the final decision.

_I_ 6. WE ARE PLEASED TO HEAR THAT YOU AND NEIL WATSON WILL BOTH VISIT THE SEATTLE AND PORTLAND OFFICES TO MEET WITH PROJECT MANAGERS DURING YOUR FORTHCOMING TRIP TO THE WEST COAST.

_C_ 7. Our experiences with this customer have reinforced two important principles:

- Investigate an applicant's credit worthiness thoroughly.

- Set realistic credit limitations for all customers.

_C_ 8. If you want to earn an A in this course, you must attend class regularly, complete all assignments, and do superior work.

_I_ 9. The Oklahoma City site is preferred over the other locations because (A) consumer demand for our products is strong, (B) the labor supply is plentiful, and (3) local taxes and construction costs are favorable.

_C_ 10. Shouldn't your family be able to enjoy all the advantages that a home computer has to offer?

Exercise 35–3 Write **VR** if the sentence illustrates verbal emphasis; write **VS** if the sentence illustrates visual emphasis; write **PS** if the sentence illustrates psychological emphasis.

_VS_ 1. Rotate your car's tires every 5,000 miles to assure their long life and best performance.

_VR_ 2. To conduct a successful interview, do three things—listen closely, listen closely, and listen closely.

_VS_ 3. Judy's essay, "How to Get an A From a Teacher Who Rarely Gives One," received a B+.

_PS_ 4. When I saw your suggestion, I knew immediately you were on the right track!

_VS_ 5. The key to success in our firm is simple:

→ Work Hard
→ Work Even Harder

_VS_ 6. In the future, annual raises will be based exclusively on merit.

_PS_ 7. Can you name the capitals of at least 40 states in no more than three minutes?

_VR_ 8. Get the budget estimates ready before the meeting begins, no matter what.

_VS_ 9.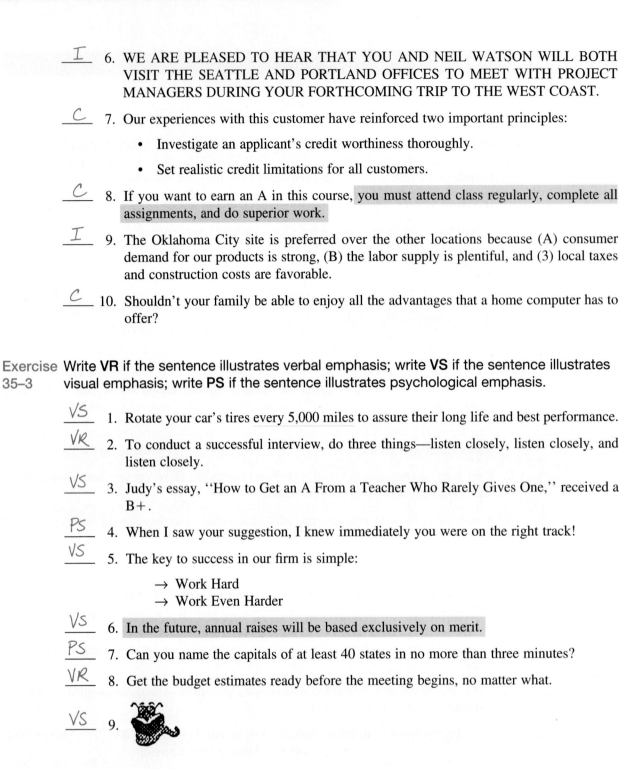

LEVEL B

Name _____

Exercise
35–4

In the following items, one of the three statements uses an access technique effectively. The other two statements do not. Write the letter of the statement that uses access effectively.

_b_ 1. *a.* The planning meeting has been postponed one week.
  b. The registration deadline is June 15—one week from today.
  c. Another attempt will be made this afternoon to reach an agreement with Mr. Cornwall's attorney.

_c_ 2. *a.* Anyone who misses the final exam will **receive** a failing grade in the course.
  b. Anyone **who** misses the final exam will receive a failing grade in the course.
  c. Anyone who misses the final exam will receive a **failing grade** in the **course**.

_b_ 3. *a.* To win the contract, we must (A) submit the lowest bid, (B) post a $1 million bond, and third, agree to pay a penalty if we fail to meet the completion deadline.
  b. If you were in my place, how would you answer this complaint?
  c. To complete the project on time, (1) increase the labor force and work two 8-hour shifts every day through the month of October.

_a_ 4. *a.* Today, Mr. DeLong seems to want only to grumble, grumble, grumble.
  b. The lesson to be learned from this experience is clear:
  • Prepare well, and prepare early
  c. Thank you for inviting me to address the graduating class at Rooster Cogburn Tech.

_c_ 5. *a.* I may not remember to return your call.
  b. I am certain I will remember to return your call.
  c. Remember, please, to return my call.

_a_ 6. *a.* Will you be able to afford proper medical care in your old age?
  b. Discontinue the use of your credit card until the balance on your account is less than $2,000.
  c. Once you make a purchase, you will have two months to send your payment in full.

_b_ 7. *a.* As you know, Ms. Pennert, we have written you several times about the unpaid balance of $130 that still shows on your account.
  b. PLEASE, Ms. Pennert, won't you send your check for the unpaid balance of $130 on your account?
  c. If you have questions about the unpaid balance of $130 still owed on the dishwasher YOU PURCHASED on February 17, please let us hear from you.

_c_ 8. *a.* When you receive the kit, first verify that its contents are complete, secondly read the instructions carefully, then assemble the parts, and finally mail the warranty card immediately.
  b. As we hoped, contract negotiations resumed this week in Detroit.
  c. Question-and-answer sessions for new employees will be held on Monday, September 12, and Friday, September 30, in the first-floor conference room.

Exercise   In the following items, write the letter that identifies the statement using the emphasis
35–5   technique (verbal, visual, or psychological) indicated in the section caption.

Verbal   *c*   1. *a.*   In approximately three weeks, the Cincinnati agency will be closed; and most of
                            the work force will be transferred to Columbus.
                  b.   One result of the revised accounting procedures is a monthly statement that reflects
                            accurately the firm's financial strengths and weaknesses.
                  c.   Read very carefully the conclusions on pages 20–21.

            b   2. *a.*   • Arrange to meet the director personally.
                  b.   The cost of the cruise is just $495 per person—that's right, only $495 for seven
                            days and nights on the Caribbean Star.
                  c.   Why do you suppose most dieters fail to reach and maintain their weight-loss goals?

Visual   *a*   3. *a.*   AN ANALYSIS OF COMPUTER SOFTWARE PIRACY
                  b.   Don't forget to mail your tax returns by April 15.
                  c.   Yes, Marie, I won the scholarship—just as you predicted.

            a   4. *a.*   Nothing short of total surrender will satisfy the commander.
                  b.   When did you last have a blood-cholesterol check?
                  c.   First you must consult with the mayor, and then you must appoint your campaign
                            committee.

            c   5. *a.*   Are you personally convinced the governor will veto the crime-control bill even
                            though the legislature voted for it overwhelmingly?
                  b.   My analysis of your ad campaign will be on your desk by nine o'clock Monday
                            morning.
                  c.   The Peterson plan is superior to other proposals in (1) design, (2) location, (3)
                            market analysis, and (4) profit potential.

Psycho-   *a*   6. *a.*   How certain are you that you will be able to afford to send your children to college?
logical   *b.*   Arbor College no longer admits students with high-school **grade-point averages
                            below 3.3**.
                  c.   A record snowfall in the northern states this winter means two things:
                            • Plenty of water next summer
                            • A profitable season for the northern states' ski industry

            c   7. *a.*   First, make hotel reservations; second, mail your deposit; third, arrange transpor-
                            tation.
                  b.   The fabric of choice this season may surprise you. It's cashmere! That's right, it's
                            not wool, it's not cotton, and it's not polyester—it's cashmere.
                  c.   Our records show you have used your AAA membership card four times this year,
                            but do you know your membership expires this month?

            c   8. *a.*   The first time you see one you'll love it; the first time you drive one you'll love it,
                            and the first time you own one you'll love it.
                  b.   Cash discounts are given with every purchase.
                  c.   Dear Mr. Wynne: You wouldn't be getting this letter if we didn't have very good
                            news for you.

LEVEL C

Name _____

Exercise 35–6 Reposition the underlines and caps in the following sentences to achieve stronger emphasis.

Editing

1. Return the <u>enclosed</u> card no later than <u>December 31</u>.

2. A <u>third</u> advantage of this investment program is its guaranteed liquidity.

3. Interest rates are expected to <u>decline</u> in the coming months.

4. Ask for new ~~Scrubber~~ *SCRUBBER* cleaner at your favorite ~~GROCERY~~ *grocery* store.

5. ~~Only~~ *ONLY* True Blue Casualty offers these unique ~~ADVANTAGES~~ *advantages*.

Exercise 35–7 Use each of the verbal access techniques provided below (word signal or repetition) to write a sentence with strong emphasis.

Composition

1. don't forget

   _____

   _____

2. please remember

   _____

   _____

3. $75, $75

   _____

   _____

4. first priority

   _____

   _____

5. save, save, save

_____

_____

Exercise 35–8 In each of the following items, write one sentence that effectively uses the access technique indicated at the beginning of the item.

Composition

1. Underlining

_____

_____

2. Caps

_____

_____

3. Enumeration—three items

_____

_____

4. The verbal signal **remember**

_____

_____

5. Repetition of the term **Dancer shirts**

_____

_____

6. The verbal signal **the most important**

_____

_____

7. A three-item list that introduces the items with bullets

_____

_____

_____

_____

8. An enumeration that uses the words **first, second,** and **third**

_____

_____

9. The verbal signal **please note** and one or more words in caps

_____

_____

10. A question that achieves effective reader interaction

_____

_____

Exercise 35–9 Write an effective sentence as directed to achieve the particular kind of access or emphasis indicated.

Composition

1. Use a verbal signal to achieve strong emphasis.

_____

_____

_____

2. Use a psychological signal to achieve strong emphasis.

_____

_____

_____

3. Use visual signals to achieve strong emphasis (two sentences).

(*a*) _____

_____

_____

(*b*) _____

_____

_____

Exercise 35–10 Use access devices as directed in the following composition exercises to achieve effective emphasis in your writing.

Compo-
sition

1. Write a sentence that uses the words *pen, wallet, notebook,* and *handkerchief* in an **enumeration** (not a listing).

_____

_____

_____

2. Write a statement that uses the following terms in a **listing** and that introduces each term with an appropriate mark of emphasis: *effective leader, competent planner, strong organizer, skillful communicator, creative problem solver.*

_____

_____

_____

_____

_____

USING PREWRITE, WRITE, AND REWRITE STRATEGIES

So, you need to write a paper—a school assignment, a business document, an application letter for a job, or a personal message. Your task is clear; getting it done is another matter.

Getting started on a writing project is often difficult and frustrating. For many writers, getting started is the hardest part of the task. And one of the chief obstacles to getting started is **writer's block**.

Writer's block is a mental wall—a barrier that stops writers before they get started and disrupts them along the way. Few writers have not met writer's block firsthand on more than one occasion.

Perhaps the best way to avoid—or at least to minimize—writer's block is to use proper planning and writing techniques. These techniques are referred to here as the **prewrite-write-rewrite** process.

Pretest

Write **T** or **F** to indicate whether the following statements are true or false.

1. Writer's block is rarely a problem for most writers.

2. In the prewrite stage of the writing process, the writer actually should write nothing with pen, pencil, or word processor.

3. The write stage is the drafting stage.

4. Most of the editing is done during the rewrite stage.

5. Grammar and punctuation errors should be corrected during the write stage.

6. Effective writers do not impose time limits on themselves when they write.

7. Anticipating the reader's response should occur during the prewrite stage.

8. If you get stuck during the write stage because you can't think of the right word, leave a blank space and go on.

Key: (1) F; (2) F; (3) T; (4) T; (5) F—during rewrite; (6) F; (7) T; (8) T.

Prewrite

Use T36-1 here

Prewriting is the process of planning—of getting **ready** to write. It prepares the writer properly for the writing task ahead. Effective preparation increases the prospects for success in most things we do—and that includes writing.

The experienced writer knows better than to jump right in and begin writing without making appropriate preparations. We know what happens when we speak before we think. We are often embarrassed or wrong or both.

Writing is much the same. If we write before we have prepared to write, we will likely confuse, mislead, or irritate the reader. Prewriting reduces the probability of weakness and error in our writing and helps us achieve our writing objective.

Prewriting—properly preparing to write—requires the writer to do four things:

1. Identify the writer's goal.

2. Anticipate the reader's response.

3. Choose the content of the message.

4. Determine the general order of presentation.

When the writer meets these four requirements in the prewrite stage of the writing process, the prospect of success is greatly increased.

Identify Your Goal.   What do you want to accomplish with your message? Do you intend to inform, to persuade, to present bad news, or to do something else? You must be clear about your objectives. Ask yourself ''Where am I going with this message? What do I want the outcome to be?''

Anticipate Reader Reaction.   Knowing how your reader will react to your message makes the writing process easier. Visualize your reader as clearly as possible. Put yourself in the reader's place, if you can. Anticipating the reader's response to your message will help you write effectively to achieve your goal.

Choose Message Content.   Select thoughtfully the main facts and ideas to be presented in your message. Construct either a mental or a written outline to identify and assemble these important pieces of information. Don't give much thought at this point to the sequence in which these items will be covered in your message. Concentrate primarily on pinning down the substance of your message—the points you plan to emphasize in your writing.

Determine Order of Presentation. Taking into account the expected reaction of the reader, decide whether to write inductively or deductively. The direct (deductive) approach is used to convey good news or to present routine information that is unlikely to have an emotional impact on the reader. The indirect (inductive) approach is used to convey bad news or to present information that may not be readily accepted or believed. The skillful writer uses order of presentation as a helpful tool in achieving the desired outcome of the message.

Write

Now, you are ready to write. The prewriting phase is behind you, preparations are complete, and your writing pad (or the computer screen) is waiting. The **writing** phase can begin.

Writer's block sometimes occurs at this point. But because you have completed the prewriting stage properly, you are unlikely to be blocked. Instead, move quickly and confidently into the writing stage. Record your thoughts and ideas in rough form. Write in a rapid, free-flowing manner. Don't worry about whether your thoughts are organized or clearly expressed. For now, ignore such matters as grammar, spelling, punctuation, and precise word choice. Write quickly, forcing yourself to get your thoughts in print without hesitation or delay. Your first priorities are substance and speed. Give little thought to form or language usage; you'll get to these matters later.

This rapid-writing process is known by various names: free writing, raw writing, rough writing, quick-and-dirty writing, etc. In this text, we call it **fast writing**. The intent is to let go, take off the brakes, slip into high gear, and go for broke!

Fast writing is the **drafting** stage. It is the process used to quickly transfer your thoughts to paper or screen. Most writers lose time *between* sentences, not *within* them. Therefore, force yourself to begin a new sentence *immediately* after completing the previous one. Concentrate on *what* you want to say; give little attention to how you say it or to the order in which you get your thoughts in print.

Don't get blocked because you can't think of the right word or expression. If necessary, leave a blank space to be filled in later; and keep going. Use a circle or an underline to identify a trouble spot you will come back to later.

Don't worry about captions and headings as you fast write. If they occur to you as you write and you can insert them in your copy quickly, that's fine. But don't fuss over precise wording or location. You can take care of that later.

Write the various parts of the document in any order you choose. If writing the conclusions or recommendations first makes starting easier, do it—even though these elements typically appear near the end of a document. Begin writing whichever part of the message seems easiest. In fast writing, nothing is sacred about the order in which the various parts of the document are written. In fact, the notion that "anything goes" applies nicely to the fast-write phase of message development.

As you fast write, keep going. Don't stop. Keep plugging away until you have said what needs to be said. This first draft will be rough. That's all right—it's expected to be. What matters is that the "meat" of your message is in printed form—rough and awkward though it may be. Most of the important stuff is on your paper or screen. The good news is that now the hardest part of your task is behind you.

Rewrite

Use T36-2 here

With the fast-write phase behind you, the most difficult part of the writing task is over. Words and sentences have given form and meaning to your thoughts and ideas. Your message—rough as it is in its present form—is in place and ready for the third and final stage of the writing process—**rewriting**.

Rewriting is the revising—or polishing—stage in your writing. Rewriting tightens the content and improves the flow of ideas and facts to give unity and coherence to your writing. It smooths out the language to produce a message that is clear and logical to the reader. And it cleans up the grammar and the mechanics to eliminate distractions and stumbling blocks that get in the reader's way. In short, it puts the finishing touches on your writing and gets you to the goal that you identified at the beginning of the writing process.

The rewrite phase focuses on four important factors: content, organization, language and readability, and grammar and mechanics.

During rewriting, each of these message elements undergoes close scrutiny to make certain it contributes effectively to the success of the message.

Content.   During the rewriting stage, the writer examines carefully the content—or substance—of the written message. Did you leave out anything of importance? Should you omit anything in your rough draft? Have you covered the topic adequately without being redundant? This is the time to fill in any holes in your message and to eliminate anything that now seems to be unimportant or unrelated. Double check facts, names, dates, and figures.

Be thorough. Unlike prewriting when speed is a priority, rewriting is the time to slow down, to take your time, to be sure of your ground.

Organization.   Rewriting for effective organization of content leads to unity and coherence in your writing. Unity occurs when each paragraph has a topic sentence and when other sentences in the paragraph relate to and support the topic sentence. Paragraphs should follow each other in logical order, and transitional language should be used to connect sentences to sentences and paragraphs to paragraphs.

Use the rewrite stage to move your sentences and paragraphs around to achieve the desired effect. Be ready to change the sequence of the sentences in a paragraph, to move sentences from one paragraph to another, and to alter the order of the paragraphs. And look for opportunities to use transitional language to strengthen paragraph unity and to give your message the coherence that results in easy and comfortable reading.

Except in short documents, include appropriate captions and headings in your writing to give your document good access. Start with the headings you may have inserted during the fast-write stage; change the wording and reposition the headings as necessary. Then provide additional headings if needed.

Language and Readability.   Rewriting to improve language usage and readability directly affects the ease with which the reader understands your message. Because you probably gave little thought to the words selected in the fast-writing stage, take time now to be sure your language does what you want it to do. Observe the following guidelines to strengthen your language and to improve its readability:

- Change words as needed to improve the precision and clarity of your writing.

- Use easy, familiar words rather than hard, unfamiliar ones.

- Check the tone of your message. Do you sound friendly, helpful, and interested in your reader?

- Avoid words or expressions that irritate or offend.

- Use active voice and plenty of action verbs to make your writing lively and interesting.

- Shorten or divide most of those long sentences.

- Use specific rather than vague or overly general language.

- Avoid overworked and fuzzy words like *very* and *really*.

- Minimize or eliminate the use of the lazy expletives *there* and *it*.

- Avoid technical terms unless you are sure your audience will understand them.

- Avoid overloading your sentences with too many modifiers.

As a writer, you are in the business of using words. The rewriting stage of the writing process provides you with your best opportunity to use words with power and skill. Make the most of this opportunity if you want your message to succeed.

Grammar and Mechanics.   Remember that we said not to worry about grammar, spelling, punctuation, appearance, etc. during prewriting, because we would get to these matters later? Well, *this* is the later we were talking about. The writer who expects a message to get a good reception **must** be concerned about grammar violations and the mechanics bugs that creep into practically *every* fast-write effort.

Proofread your work carefully. Correct the errors you find in grammar and mechanics. Then proofread again and again—until you proofread the entire message without finding *any* errors. Don't trust this responsibility entirely to a secretary or an assistant. The message is yours; you are responsible for it. Your signature likely will be on it, and your image and reputation are on the line.

Use the dictionary. If you are writing on a computer screen, use a spell checker (and a grammar checker, if you wish). Let someone you trust proofread your message, too. Two heads usually *are* better than one in the proofreading process.

Go after these grammar and mechanics gremlins with a vengeance. Demand clean, error-free copy that is unmarred by annoying distractions. A grammar violation, a misspelled word, a typo, or a similar error is a sure-fire eye catcher. It distracts the careful reader—interrupting, inhibiting, and often annoying your audience.

The successful writer knows that time spent in rewriting the grammar and mechanics of the fast-write draft to remove any troublesome errors is time well spent. The effectiveness of otherwise well-presented messages is often seriously damaged by the impact of unwelcome grammar and mechanics weaknesses.

Summary

You have just had a good look at the complete writing process divided into three stages—prewrite, write, and rewrite. The process is designed to make you efficient and effective. The process works well for many writers and for most messages longer than just a few lines.

The more you use the prewrite-write-rewrite process, the more proficient you will become. With experience, you will find ways to refine the process to fit your own needs and abilities. Many possibilities exist.

For instance, some writers set time limits to force themselves to move quickly through the three stages. A writer who has three to four hours to prepare a short report may allocate 30–45 minutes to the prewrite stage, 60–90 minutes to the write stage, and 60–90 minutes to the rewrite stage. Using the clock as a pacer and adhering to pre-set time limits push the writer to be productive.

Whatever personal variations you devise, use the prewrite-write-rewrite strategy to strengthen your writing. It offers both novice and experienced writers proven opportunities to refine their planning, drafting, and revising skills. The result can be both improved writing and a more productive use of the writer's valuable time.

Posttest

Write **T** or **F** to indicate whether the following statements are true or false.

1. **Fast writing** occurs during the drafting stage.

2. The writing stage of the prewrite-write-rewrite process should produce a reasonably polished product.

3. The content, organization, language, and mechanics are carefully reviewed and refined during the rewrite stage.

4. One good proofreading effort should be sufficient during the rewrite stage.

5. Of the three stages in the prewrite-write-rewrite process, the writer should spend less time in prewrite than in either of the other two stages.

6. During the write stage, the writer should concentrate on what to say, not on how to say it.

7. During the prewrite stage, the writer should do all of the following: identify the writer's goal, anticipate the reader's response, choose message content, and determine order of presentation.

8. Most writers lose more time **within** sentences than **between** sentences.

Key: (1) T; (2) F; (3) T; (4) F; (5) T; (6) T; (7) T; (8) F.

LEVEL A

Name _____

Exercise
36–1

On the lines below, write **T** if the statement is true; write **F** if the statment is false.

_T_   1. The preparation that precedes the composition of a message is called *prewrite*.

_F_   2. Drafting takes place during prewrite.

_F_   3. The first step in prewrite is to choose the content of the message.

_T_   4. Determining the order of presentation includes deciding whether a message should be written inductively or deductively.

_F_   5. Prewrite has little or no relationship to writer's block.

_F_   6. Anticipating the reader's reaction is the first step in prewrite.

_T_   7. Writers lose more time between sentences than they do within sentences.

_T_   8. *Fast write* and *quick-and-dirty writing* refer to the same thing.

_F_   9. Fast write precedes drafting.

_T_   10. Both fast write and drafting occur during the write stage of the writing process.

_T_   11. A writer who gets hung up trying to think of the right word or expression should leave a blank space in the copy and move on without delay.

_T_   12. A writer who writes the last part of a document before writing the first part may be doing a smart thing.

_F_   13. Captions should be omitted entirely during the drafting stage.

_F_   14. Effective fast write emphasizes content and language usage but not grammar or mechanics.

_T_   15. The fast-write process is esentially the same whether the writer is using a computer screen or a pencil and paper.

_T_   16. The writing process consists of three distinct stages.

_F_   17. Rewrite is the most difficult stage of the writing process.

_T_   18. Polishing is the chief emphasis in rewrite.

_F_   19. One thorough proofreading of a document is generally sufficient to identify and correct all writing errors.

_T_   20. A topic sentence is an important factor in paragraph unity.

_T_   21. Coherence in business messages is encouraged through the use of transitional language.

_T_   22. Double-checking facts, names, dates, and figures should take place during rewrite.

_F_   23. Most readers understand that the person who signs a document is not necessarily responsible for errors in the document's grammar and mechanics.

_F_ 24. Although some writers impose time limits on themselves during the writing process, such a practice is discouraged because it often creates writer tension.

_F_ 25. The four message elements that are scrutinized during rewrite are content, language usage, message unity, and mechanics.

Exercise 36–2 Write **Yes** if the statement applies to the *prewrite* stage of the writing process. Write **No** if it doesn't.

Yes 1. Identify the writer's goal.

_No_ 2. Record facts and ideas in rough form.

_No_ 3. Insert captions and headings as they occur to you.

_No_ 4. Use action verbs to make your writing interesting.

Yes 5. Decide whether to use inductive or deductive organization.

Yes 6. Develop either a mental outline or a written outline of your message.

Yes 7. Choose the content for your message.

Exercise 36–3 Write **Yes** if the statement applies to the *write* stage of the writing process. Write **No** if it doesn't.

Yes 1. Ignore such things as grammar, spelling, and punctuation.

_No_ 2. Determine, if you can, your reader's probable reaction to your message.

Yes 3. Use fast write to draft your message.

_No_ 4. Examine closely the organization of your message.

_No_ 5. Shorten or divide most long sentences.

Yes 6. Concentrate on *what* you say; give little thought to *how* you say it.

_No_ 7. Pause for thought between sentences.

Exercise 36–4 Write **Yes** if the statement applies to the **rewrite** stage of the writing process. Write **No** if it doesn't.

_No_ 1. Start a new sentence *immediately* after completing the previous sentence.

_No_ 2. Decide which part of your message to write first.

Yes 3. Check the tone of your message.

Yes 4. Eliminate sexist terminology.

Yes 5. Use a dictionary or a spell checker or both.

Yes 6. Set a time limit to pace yourself.

Yes 7. Examine message content carefully.

LEVEL B

Name _____

Exercise 36–5 In the following items, write the letter of the statement that reflects the correct application of the writing stage indicated in the section heading.

Prewrite   _a_   1. *a.* Decide whether to begin the message by presenting the main idea first.
          b. Consider eliminating words like *salesman, spokesman,* and *chairman.*
          c. Prepare a rough draft of the message.

          _c_   2. *a.* Fast write your thoughts and ideas.
          b. Use a spell checker.
          c. Develop an outline.

          _a_   3. *a.* Attempt to predict the reader's response.
          b. Record your thoughts quickly without interruption.
          c. Polish the grammar.

          _a_   4. *a.* Set a time limit.
          b. Check to see whether your language sounds friendly and helpful.
          c. Revise the content.

          _b_   5. *a.* Slow down; do a thorough job.
          b. Determine the main points of your message.
          c. Leave a blank space if you can't think of the right word.

Write   _c_   6. *a.* Proofread carefully.
          b. Eliminate spelling errors and typos.
          c. Move quickly from one sentence to the next.

          _a_   7. *a.* Don't worry about precise wording.
          b. Substitute words to improve clarity.
          c. Use a grammar checker, if you wish.

          _a_   8. *a.* Complete the hardest part of your writing task.
          b. Prepare well to avoid writer's block.
          c. Use active voice.

          _b_   9. *a.* Visualize your reader.
          b. Use fast write to prepare your first draft.
          c. Ask yourself what you want your message to accomplish.

          _c_   10. *a.* Look for excessive modifiers.
          b. Get rid of fuzzy words like *very* and *really.*
          c. Be more concerned with *what* you say than *how* you say it.

Rewrite   _b_   11. *a.* Make substance and speed your first priority.
          b. Revise and reposition captions.
          c. Determine whether a business letter will be a routine, persuasive, or bad-news message.

_c_ 12. *a.* Write rapidly; keep going; don't stop!
   b. Use a circle or an underline to identify a trouble spot to come back to later.
   c. Move sentences and paragraphs around to improve unity and flow.

_b_ 13. *a.* Write *The caller was identified by Mr. Tewker* instead of *Mr. Tewker identified the caller.*
   b. Write *I am delighted you can attend* instead of *I am really happy you can attend.*
   c. Write *If a student wants to succeed, he must study hard* instead of *Students who want to succeed must study hard.*

_c_ 14. *a.* Begin writing in the middle of a message if that's the easiest place to get started.
   b. Never use technical terms.
   c. Write *We will meet at 10 a.m.* instead of *There will be a meeting at l0 a.m.*

_a_ 15. *a.* Use transitional language to improve coherence.
   b. Get the meat of your message in print.
   c. Avoid losing time between sentences.

Exercise 36–6 Write the letter of the statement that reflects a correct application of the language-usage guidelines given in the *rewrite* discussion in this lesson.

_c_ 1. *a.* We expect Lena's report to be long.
   b. We expect Lena's report to be between 40 and 60 pages.
   c. We expect Lena's report to be approximately 50 pages.

_c_ 2. *a.* The language in her report is ponderous.
   b. The language in her report is stolid.
   c. The language in her report is dull.

_c_ 3. *a.* This is in reference to the questions raised in your recent letter.
   b. I have been assigned to reply to your letter of February 10.
   c. I am pleased to answer the questions in your February 10 letter.

_b_ 4. *a.* Every successful manager knows that leadership skills are essential in his work.
   b. An employee will be promoted only if he or she is fully qualified.
   c. Anyone who selects nursing as a profession knows her services will be in demand.

_a_ 5. *a.* At eight o'clock this morning, J. T. Reuker, financial vice president, announced the reopening of the Tallahassee office.
   b. A press conference was held by Mr. Reuker later in the day.
   c. When I introduced Mr. Reuker at the press conference, he was given a standing ovation by the audience.

_c_ 6. *a.* We really appreciate your willingness to assist us.
   b. We are very happy you can assist us.
   c. We are delighted you can assist us.

_a_ 7. *a.* The interview will be held in Roy's office at 10:30; we will meet you there.
   b. When we arrived, it surprised us to find the office empty.
   c. There is, no doubt, a logical explanation for the confusion.

LEVEL C

Name _____

Exercise
36–7

The words printed in bold are typical of the usage violations encountered in the rewrite stage of the writing process. Edit the statements to correct the violations shown.

Editing

1. ~~**There**~~ ~~will be~~ *F*urther information *will be* provided following the audit.

2. **Please answer Mr. Tashki's recent memo and tell him we have approved his request thus making it possible for him to begin construction on the Grand Forks project by August 1, barring any ~~unforseen interuptions~~ or delays.** *unforeseen interruptions*   *Long sentence; various possibilities.*

3. Every voter in the general election should ~~inform~~ **~~himself~~** *be informed* on the issues before **~~he votes.~~** *voting*

4. I believe **~~it is unlikely~~ ~~there~~** ~~will be~~ further concessions by either side, *are unlikely*

5. The **~~metamorphasis~~** *development* of the document led to the removal of a decidedly **~~obstreperous~~** *cranky* tone. (Do you have a dictionary handy?)

6. Your flight time from Philadelphia to Honolulu is expected to take **~~the better part of a day.~~** *7½ hours.*

7. We are **~~really~~ pleased** ~~and excited~~ to learn that the shipment will arrive in Boise on time; we are ~~**very appreciative** of~~ your efforts. *appreciate*

8. In one week, ~~a special preferred-customer sale~~ **~~will be held by~~** the J. & J. Department Store in downtown Bloomington, *will hold a special preferred-customer sale.*

9. **You will** ~~have a plane~~ **change** in Pittsburgh. Your pilot will let you know whether **he** expects *planes* / ~~any~~ delay in your departure for Los Angeles. *to*   *a*

10. *We are glad to do whatever we can to solve the problem.*
We **doubt** ~~the problem is as big as you~~ **claim** ~~it is,~~ **but we are willing** to do **~~what we can to~~** ~~try to~~ **satisfy you.**

Exercise
36–8

Editing

Following are two examples of the same short paragraph as it might appear in the **write** and **rewrite** stages of the writing process. Note the rough form of the first example typical of the fast-write approach. Then compare the first version of the paragraph with the polished rewrite version of the same paragraph.

A Draft Paragraph (from the Write stage)

We need to get bussy on next years cost estamates right awray. Tell all teh middle mangers to get their estimats of next years expenses in pronto because if there late agin this year the boss is going to hve another fit and make sure thay are based on good data this time. We have to pro-jexct next years operatng buget on these estmatees so wewill be in truble if they contane errors and other prblems like sum of them had last year.

The Revision (from the Rewrite stage)

Ask all mid-level managers to submit by December 1 their cost estimates for the coming year. To make sure the reports are not late, emphasize December 1 as a *firm* due date. Mr. Tweed will be satisfied with nothing less!

Estimates must be as accurate as possible. Remind managers that data used to make projections must be documented in every case. Next year's projections will be only as reliable as the data managers use in their estimates.

––––––––––––

Now, **you** try it. Here is another short paragraph drafted during the write stage of the writing process. **Rewrite** it. In your revision, keep the content consistent with that of the draft version. Use transitional language and rearrange sentences, if necessary, to improve the paragraph's organization. Strengthen the language and polish the grammar and mechanics as needed.

The copy is double spaced for your convenience in revising it. Make whatever changes are needed to produce a ready-to-use, **final version**. Write your revision on a separate piece of paper.

A Draft Paragraph (from the Write stage)

Merchendise items in our stock will no longr be manualy counted and recordedd so errors in

inventry control will be grately reduced in the futur. New inventory managment proceedures

will go into affect on Sept. 1, and after that updatged and accurate inventory information can be

instantly available upon demaand. A modern and computerized record kekeping system have

been designned and tried out for our firm.

LESSONS IN THIS UNIT

37. CORRESPONDENCE FORMATS
38. GOOD-NEWS MESSAGES
39. BAD-NEWS MESSAGES
40. PERSUASIVE MESSAGES

When you have mastered the principles in Units 1 through 9, you are ready to put them into practice. Business correspondence encompasses many of these principles. Through the lessons in this unit, we will discuss correspondence both inside and outside the company.

Although most business people are involved in business correspondence to some degree, many of them do not understand the principles that will make their compositions convincingly meet the needs of their readers as well as the needs of their own companies. As a competent writer, you will want to ensure that your document is as effective as possible.

One of your first tasks in written business correspondence is to determine the purpose of your message. As you will learn in this unit, that purpose must be evident to your reader. However, you will also discover you can influence the receiver of the message by the location of the purpose statement within the message. The placement of the purpose statement depends on the kind of news being presented.

Business writers are also concerned with the reaction of the reader. One of the main goals in business correspondence is to give the messages a *you* approach. You can accomplish this goal by putting yourself in the reader's place to determine how he or she will react to your message. Lesson 38 will discuss the *you attitude* in detail. Related to this principle is the concept of goodwill.

Regardless of the type of information you are giving to your reader, you still want to maintain goodwill with the person—whether inside or outside your business. Sometimes special care must be taken to ensure the reader will not be offended or angered by the message.

Several other important principles will be discussed in the lessons of this unit. Although this unit is not all-inclusive, we have attempted to present those principles we believe are most important in an overview of business correspondence.

One of those principles is tone. You can influence your reader not only by what you say but also by the way you say it. Many times you state information in a slightly different way and cause the reader to have a different reaction. The old adage of the glass being *half full* instead of *half empty* can be used effectively to influence your reader's reaction to your message. Another psychological concept is that of emphasis. Along with *what* you say and *how* you say it, you can also influence your readers by *where* you say it. The ability to emphasize or deemphasize your information is important if you are to meet your goals of maintaining goodwill while accomplishing the purpose of your message.

Besides the message itself, the presentation of the information is important. Lesson 37 presents conventional formats for your business correspondence. Messages used within the business are written in memo form, whereas messages sent outside the company are written in letter format. Because you want to ensure that the first impression your reader gets from your message is as effective as the message itself, you will want to master these commonly used and accepted correspondence formats.

Readers' reactions to business messages may be classified in one (or more) of the following four ways: pleased, displeased, interested, and uninterested.

One of the factors in the decision of which type of message to write is your determination of the reaction the reader will have to your message. Lesson 38 presents the **direct format** that is used when your reader will react to your message with pleasure or interest. Good- and neutral-news messages traditionally use this direct format.

Lesson 39 introduces the **indirect format** that is used when the reader will be displeased with the information presented.

Closely related to bad-news messages, **persuasive messages** also use a type of indirect format. This plan, used when readers will be uninterested in the message, is explained in Lesson 40.

You can write most kinds of business correspondence using one of these three plans. A thorough understanding of the basics of these concepts will give you an edge over many people who write business documents every day but have no understanding of the effect their messages may have on their readers.

The effectiveness of your communication, of course, is determined by the content and language used in your message. In addition, your message's impression is also affected by its appearance. Just as the way you present yourself may affect the way people treat you, the appearance of your letter will determine how your reader reacts to your message.

You have learned the principles of correct grammar, punctuation, and language usage. The *format* is the presentation of communication principles in business correspondence settings. Because the first impression of your message may be formed by the package, you will want to be sure your format is correct and does not detract from the purpose of your presentation.

Pretest

Write **T** in the left margin if the statement is true and **F** if the statement is false.

1. Both memos and letters must include the receivers' inside addresses.

2. The two-letter state abbreviations may be written with or without periods.

3. The salutation of the letter should include the person's title and complete name.

4. An enclosure notation indicates something else is to be included with the letter.

5. A modified-block letter may or may not include indented paragraphs.

6. The purpose of a memo is to present information informally to customers.

7. Mixed punctuation may include a comma or a colon after the salutation.

Key: (1) F—a memo does not include the inside address; (2) F—the state abbreviations should be written without periods; (3) F—either the receiver's title and last name or the receiver's first name should be included in the salutation; (4) T; (5) T; (6) F—a memo is used within the business; (7) F—the salutation contains a colon; the closing uses a comma.

Letter Parts

Although every letter does not contain all the following parts, you will want to have a clear understanding of all components so you can use them when the occasion arises. Using the correct terminology of parts will also help you communicate about correspondence with others.

Letterhead/Return Address.   Most businesses use printed letterhead stationery for their correspondence outside the company. This letterhead includes not only the company name but also the address and other vital information. This printed letterhead assures business writers that the receivers will have the address readily available for return correspondence.

If the correspondence is personal and if a letterhead is not available, the writer replaces the printed stationery with his or her return address. When this method is used, the return address is the first item on the page. Note that the return address should not include the writer's name (which appears at the bottom of the message) and that it is located directly above the date with no space between (see Figure 37–1). This position is the same regardless of the format used for the letter.

Date.   The date appears directly after the return address of a personal letter or as the first item of a message written on letterhead paper. The beginning line for the date depends on the length of the message and the size of the letterhead printing. The message should be reasonably centered vertically on the page.

Inside Address.   The address of the person being written to is called the *inside address*. It is usually keyed four lines after the date, although this practice may vary with the length of the document. The address may be from three to six lines in length and is always placed at the left margin. If possible, use a courtesy title (*Mrs., Mr., Dr., Professor*, etc.) with the name. When you are not sure of a woman's title, *Ms.* is always appropriate and has become the standard courtesy title for females.

The use of two-letter post-office abbreviations is encouraged in both return and inside addresses. The zip code must accompany the two-letter abbreviation, and no periods or extra space is used. Otherwise, spell the state name in full. A complete list of state abbreviations is found in Lesson 7.

Attention Line (optional).   When addressing a letter to an organization, you may use an attention line to direct the letter to a specific individual or position within the organization. Your other option, of course, is to include the name as part of the address. When using an attention line, however, you must be sure to make the salutation agree with the inside address, as the total organization is actually the receiver of the letter. The colon after the word *Attention* is optional.

Salutation.   The salutation is the greeting to the receiver of the letter. The preferred greeting, of course, is the individual's name. If you know the person well enough, you may use a first name in the salutation. Otherwise, a courtesy title and the last name are preferred. If your inside address is to an organization, the salutation must agree. Because women are also part of the organization, using *Ladies and Gentlemen* is preferred to the more traditional *Gentlemen. Dear Sir or Madam* may also be used as a salutation and is preferred over *To Whom It May Concern.*

Subject Line (optional).   The purpose of a subject line is to give the reader a brief idea of the objective of the letter. The subject line may be written in all capitals or in upper- and lower-case letters. A colon may or may not be included after the word *Subject*. Including a subject line is not required in most letters. Simplified letters are an exception; they are discussed later in the lesson.

Body.   The message is presented according to the type of letter. These letter plans will be discussed in following lessons. The message should be single-spaced with double spaces between paragraphs.

Complimentary Close.   Just as the salutation is the greeting, the complimentary close is the ending. As the writer, you have many options for the closing; however, *thank you* is not among the commonly accepted choices. If your closing has more than one word (e.g., *Sincerely yours*), only the first word is capitalized.

Signature Block.   The writer's name and title are keyed several lines (usually four) below the complimentary close. This space allows room for the writer's signature. If both the writer's name and title are short, they may be keyed on the same line, separated by a comma. Otherwise, the title appears directly under the name.

Reference Initials.   If someone other than the writer keys the letter, his or her reference initials usually appear on the left side of the document below the signature block. If the writer also keys the letter, however, reference initials are not required.

Enclosure Notation.   When other items are being sent with the letter, an enclosure or attachment notation is used. This comment reminds the person mailing the letter to enclose or attach the additional information. The notation may be written as *Enclosure* or may include the specific items to be included (*Enclosure: Reply envelope*). If the items are stapled or clipped to the letter or memo, this notation is called *Attachment*.

Copy Notation.   A copy notation indicates that copies of the letter are being sent to other people. The comment may be noted as *cc* (courtesy copy), *pc* (photocopy), or *c* (copy). Including a colon between the notation and the name is optional.

Document Formats

Although you may find some variation in format among businesses, four commonly accepted document styles are illustrated in this lesson. Study the characteristics of these styles until you are comfortable using each format. The specific formatting information is included in the body of each illustration. Reading the example as well as looking at the document will give you the details of each style.

Use T37-1 here

Block Format.   Figure 37–1 illustrates a block format. Notice that all letter parts begin at the left margin. Because you do not have to remember what parts to indent, this style is the easiest and is very popular.

Use T37-2 here

Modified-Block Format.   Figure 37–2 shows a modified-block letter. Notice that the date and the signature sections both begin at the center. Although the paragraphs are indented in this illustration, modified block may also have blocked paragraphs.

Use
T37-3
here

Simplified Format. The simplified format is noted for the omission of the salutation and complimentary close. This style is illustrated in Figure 37–3. A simplified letter can be very useful when you do not want to include a salutation to a company or do not know to whom to address the letter. Because the salutation is omitted, the subject line is *not* optional in this style. Notice that the word *subject* is omitted and that the subject line information is all in capitals. Also, the writer's name and title in the signature block are capitalized.

Use
T37-4
here

Memo. Memos are becoming the most commonly used document in the business world. The main difference between using a memo and a letter is the purpose of the message. Whereas letters are sent to customers and others outside the company, memos are used within the business, even though the office may be in a different city.

Notice in Figure 37–4 that a memo is more informal than a letter. The inside address and signature blocks are omitted, and a simple arrangement is used at the top of the document. Although many variations of the form are used, this example is a common style. Because the document is sent within the business, a signature is not required. If you want to personalize the document, you may initial or sign it by the keyed name at the top of the form.

Punctuation Styles

Two types of punctuation are used in business letters—open and mixed. These terms refer to the presence or absence of punctuation marks after the salutation and the complimentary close of the letter.

Open-punctuation letters have no punctuation marks after either the salutation or the complimentary close. Figure 37–1 illustrates a letter with open punctuation.

Mixed punctuation letters include punctuation in both places—a colon after the salutation and a comma after the complimentary close. Figure 37–2 illustrates mixed punctuation.

Figure 37–1

Personal Business Letter, Block Style with Open Punctuation

800 South Pioneer Road
Riverton, WY 82501
August 24, 19xx

Professional Development, Inc.
Attention Word Processing Department
321 Hardy Avenue
Las Vegas, NV 98765

Ladies and Gentlemen

Subject: Block Letter Style

The block letter is a format with all elements aligned with the left margin. Without a letterhead (as in this illustration), begin the top line no higher than 2 inches, and key the return address (without name) just above the date. If a printed letterhead is used, place the date several lines below the letterhead, depending on the length of the message. Quadruple-space to the inside address. Double-space between the inside address and the salutation. Key the subject line, if used, a double space below the salutation; and double-space again to the first line of the message. Key the optional attention line as part of the inside address. However, the salutation still must refer to the entire company.

Single-space the paragraphs, and use double spacing to separate them from each other. Indent displayed enumerations and long quotations from each side.

Double-space after the last line of the message to the complimentary close. Quadruple-space to the signature; (this space allows for the signature). Block the signature and title (if needed) under the complimentary close. If the letter is a personal business letter (as illustrated here), no reference initials are required because the writer probably also keyed the letter.

Sincerely yours

Tania L. Adamson

Figure 37–2

Modified Block Business Letter with Mixed Punctuation

 IRWIN

Richard D. Irwin, Inc.
1818 Ridge Road
Homewood, IL 60430
312 798-6000

March 7, 19xx

Dr. Linda M. Ross
Eastern Washington, Inc.
275 Court Street
Spokane, WA 99218

Dear Dr. Ross:

SUBJECT: MODIFIED-BLOCK LETTER

The modified-block letter includes features similar to those of the block letter with the exception of the positioning of the date and the signature block. The paragraphs may be indented (as shown here) or blocked as they are in a block letter.

The subject line as it is positioned here is set flush left. If an attention line had been used, it would also have been positioned flush with the left margin.

The complimentary close—aligned with the date—appears a double space below the last message line. Three blank lines (a quadruple space) have been allowed for the written signature. The signature block is then aligned with the complimentary close.

Other notations, such as reference initials, enclosure notations, and a list of copy recipients, are placed a double-space below the signature block, flush with the left margin.

Very truly yours,

Kathleen Day
Executive Vice President

tds

Enclosures

c   Mr. William Ryan
    Mr. Andrew Sweeney

Figure 37–3

Simplified Business Letter

Richard D. Irwin, Inc.
1818 Ridge Road
Homewood, IL 60430
312 798-6000

October 20, 19xx

HCI Corporation
112 East 100 North
Denver, CO 84216

SIMPLIFIED LETTER

This letter is an example of the simplified letter. It is a clean format that saves time, boosts productivity, and streamlines the look of the document.

If you do not know the name of the person to whom you are writing and do not want to use ''Ladies and Gentlemen,'' the simplified format is a good alternative. Because no salutation is used, the gender question is solved on letters to correspondents who have signed previous letters with their initials and a surname only.

A capitalized subject line is a triple space below the last line of the inside address. Although a subject line is optional with other styles, one must be used with a simplified format. The subject line is positioned flush with the left margin, and the word *Subject* is omitted.

The message begins a triple space below the subject line. All paragraphs are set flush left. Enumerated lists and tabular data, if included, are set flush left with double spacing separating one item from another. Items are single-spaced internally.

The simplified format has no complimentary close. Quadruple space to the signature block and key the writer's name and title in capital letters flush with the left margin. Depending on the length of the name and title, key them on the same line or on two consecutive lines. The writer then signs the letter in the space allowed.

The reference initials are keyed a double space below the signature block. If a copy or enclosure notation is required, key the material a double space beneath the reference initials.

JANE M. DOE, SENIOR EDITOR

rdb

Figure 37–4

Memo Format

IRWIN

Inter-office Correspondence

TO: All Employees
FROM: Dennis Phillips
DATE: May 1, 19xx
SUBJECT: FORMAT FOR INTERBUSINESS MESSAGES

When sending messages to another person within the office, either this branch or our others located around the country, use this standard memo format. The message may be addressed to an individual, a department, or the entire organization. Although you do not sign the memo, you may want to put your initials by your name.

Be sure to include the subject of the memo. This notation not only gives the reader an overview of the memo but also helps in filing.

The body of the memo is usually single-spaced with double spacing between paragraphs; however, some short memos may be double-spaced. Enumerated items are set flush left with double spacing separating one item from another.

The typist's reference initials are placed at the bottom of the memo.

Times Mirror
Books

csb

Posttest

Write **T** in the left margin if the statement is true and **F** if the statement is false.

1. Because most letters require a reply, you must always key your return address at the top of the letter.

2. Both an attention line and a subject line are optional on a block letter.

3. The writer's title is always written one line below the typed name.

4. A copy notation may be shown as either *cc* or *c*.

5. The date and signature sections should be centered on a modified block letter.

6. The simplified letter format is useful when the name of the recipient is unknown.

7. Open punctuation means no punctuation should be included in the inside address.

Key: (1) F—the return address is included when the letter is not written on letterhead stationery; (2) T; (3) F—the title may also be written on the same line with a comma if the name and title are short; (4) T; (5) F—they begin at the center point; (6) T; (7) F—open punctuation includes no punctuation after the salutation and complimentary close.

LEVELS A, B, and C

Name _____

Exercise 37–1
On the lines below, write **T** if the statement is true, **F** if the statement is false.

_F_ 1. All letters should include a return address as the first keyed item so the receiver has a ready address for reply.

_F_ 2. The writer's name should be included as part of the return address.

_F_ 3. The date always appears flush with the left margin of the letter.

_F_ 4. The courtesy title and complete name are preferred in the salutation of a business letter.

_F_ 5. If the letter is addressed to a company and if an attention line is used, the salutation should be addressed to the individual mentioned in the attention line.

_F_ 6. *To Whom It May Concern is* a preferred salutation when the receiver's name is not known.

_T_ 7. The two-letter postal abbreviations should only be used with zip codes.

_F_ 8. Only simplified letters include a subject line.

_F_ 9. The writer's name and title should always be placed on two successive lines.

_F_ 10. *Thank you* is a preferred complimentary close if you want to establish goodwill.

_F_ 11. A block letter may include indented paragraphs.

_F_ 12. Mixed punctuation includes commas after the salutation and the complimentary close.

_F_ 13. Memos are used within an organization and are more formal than letters.

_T_ 14. The writer's name and title should be written in all capitals in a simplified letter.

_T_ 15. A simplified letter format is helpful when you do not know the name of the person to whom you are writing.

_F_ 16. *Wy* is the correct way to write the two-letter postal abbreviation for *Wyoming*.

_F_ 17. If the message is correct in grammar, punctuation, and word usage, the format used really is not important.

_F_ 18. The specific letter style used depends on the type of message being sent.

_F_ 19. The subject line is always written in all capitals.

_F_ 20. The two-letter state abbreviation may either omit or include periods.

_T_ 21. The letter format is important in the overall impression the reader will have of the message.

_T_ 22. The enclosure notation may be written as ''Attachment'' if the additional items are stapled to the document.

Exercise 37–2

Edit the following message. Look for capitalization, punctuation, spelling, grammar, and number-usage problems.

Editing

You are ~~amoung~~ among a ~~prefered~~ preferred group of Anderson charge customers who ~~is~~ are being invited to save 20 to 30% percent on our collection of fine appliances. For ~~2~~ two days, you will have ~~a opportunity~~ an opportunity to ~~chose~~ choose from appliances, that ~~has~~ have been collected from all our stores, just for this exciting ~~sell~~ sale. This event will not be ~~advertized~~ advertised to the ~~general~~ public.

Now is your chance to save money on washers, ~~and~~ dryers, freezers, and all large and small kitchen appliances. Mark June ~~15th~~ 15 and ~~16th~~ 16 on your ~~calender~~ calendar and join us in the Appliance Department at Anderson's in the ~~c~~Crossroads ~~m~~Mall. Bring the ~~inclosed~~ enclosed authorization letter with you. We look forward to seeing ~~their~~ you there.

Exercise 37–3

On a separate sheet, rearrange the following letter parts to form a correct block letter with mixed punctuation. Use the paragraphs from Exercise 37–2 for the body of the letter.

Sincerely yours

Dear Mr. and Mrs. Greenwood

Enclosure

March 20, 19xx

Wayne A. Grover
Sales Manager

Subject   APPLIANCE SALE

mbj

Mr. and Mrs. Jerry Greenwood
1808 Hollow Circle Road
Milwaukee, WI 53704

Exercise 37–4

Using the necessary information from Exercise 37–3, rearrange the message into a memo format.

See the Instructor's Manual for sample solutions to these exercises.

Most people prefer writing about good news. Think about your own experiences. Wouldn't you rather tell someone *yes* than have to say *no* and provide an explanation? Approach good-news messages the same way you do personal conversations. Rather than using a formal, stilted style, write as if you were discussing the situation with the reader in person. You will discover that the process is simple and that the results are effective.

Good-news messages are written using the direct plan. This plan is appropriate whenever the receiver will be pleased by or interested in the news. Letters that request, acknowledge, order, inform, or respond affirmatively are written using the direct approach. As you study this lesson, you will see how this approach is used to present good news effectively.

Pretest

Write **T** in the left margin if the statement is true, **F** if the statement is false.

1. Emphasizing *you* in a letter will encourage your reader to react positively to your message.

2. Good-news messages should be written in a direct way.

3. The first part of a sentence deserves special attention because it is the most emphatic.

4. Using more *you* references than *I* or *we* references will ensure goodwill.

5. The more specific a goodwill ending is, the more effective it will be.

Key: (1) T; (2) T; (3) T; (4) F—not necessarily; *you* references can be used in a negative way; (5) T.

You Attitude

Use
T38-1
here

One of the most important principles in business correspondence is putting yourself in the reader's position. This ability is known as using the *you attitude*.

If I want to convince you to buy the encyclopedias I am selling, I will not be very successful by selling to you from *my* point of view. Will you buy a set so I can win a free trip to Europe? I imagine not. I must convince you that the encyclopedias will be valuable to your education, your children's future, and your scholastic achievement. Otherwise, you will put your money into something else. You are more concerned about *you* than about *I* or *we*. Therefore, to be effective in communicating with you, I must play on the logic of the *you attitude*.

One way to ensure the *you attitude* is to replace *I* or *we* references with *you* and *your* ideas. Notice the pronoun references in the preceding paragraph. The first few sentences are loaded with *I* pronouns, and the emphasis of the ideas is on the writer. The next few sentences use *you* pronouns, putting the emphasis on the reader.

Another key to *you attitude* is the use of emphasis. Because the most emphatic part of a sentence is the beginning, we can often rearrange the idea to stress the reader's viewpoint. Notice the difference in emphasis in the following examples:

> *We* are excited about *our* new computer software.
> *We* want to tell you that your order will arrive next week.

> *You* will find the new computer software will save *you* time.
> *Your* order will arrive next week.

Because the beginning of a message has the greatest emphasis, a good business writer will generally avoid opening a letter with *I* or *we* beginnings. The editing process of any business correspondence should include looking for *we*-oriented ideas and replacing them with *you*-oriented ideas.

This *you*-oriented approach is well known in marketing. It is also essential in effective business correspondence, not only in good-news messages but also with the other kinds you will study in the next lessons. When you begin planning a message, think how the receiver will react to your message. What does he or she most want to know from your message? What comments will make the reader feel most positive about you and your business? Answers to these questions will help determine how to begin your letter and what the best approach to your message will be.

Goodwill

Another major principle in business correspondence is the concept of *goodwill*. Although goodwill is significant, it is difficult to define. Related to the *you attitude*, goodwill illustrates the repeat business and public relations maintained between business and patrons. Goodwill is often listed as an asset on a balance sheet and results from satisfying the customers' needs. Because business messages ''sell'' the organization to the reader, goodwill is important in writing just as it is in face-to-face communication with customers. Compare the following messages:

You must come to our office to sign the forms. We cannot submit your application until you do.

Please stop by our office at your convenience to sign the forms. We will then be able to submit your application quickly.

Putting yourself in the reader's position will help the message to reflect goodwill. Using positive language and *you*-oriented messages will establish goodwill in your communications and result in effective messages. Although goodwill is not often the major reason for writing your message, it is considered a secondary purpose in most business correspondence.

Organization Plan

A good-news letter should be written in a direct approach; that is, the message should begin with the main point. When you are telling someone *yes*, that is what he or she most wants to hear. Suppose you have written a letter to Dr. Saunders, asking her to speak to your professional association. Her answer begins:

> Your letter has just arrived. Thank you for asking me to speak at your upcoming meeting. Your professional association has provided much service in the community over the years and is well respected by all who know of it.

As the reader of the message, your reaction is likely to be, "When will she get to the point?" How much more effective is the message that begins:

> Yes, I will be pleased to speak at the March meeting of your professional association.

You will be more likely to react positively to her information if the main point is given at the beginning of the message. Effective good-news messages should be complete yet concise in transmitting the good news. Neither the writer nor the reader wants to get bogged down in unnecessary information.

Use the following direct (sometimes called *deductive*) organization plan to write good-news messages:

Use T 38-2 here

1. Main idea

2. Details

3. Goodwill ending

Establishing the objective of the message is an important first step in writing an effective good-news message. Determining the purpose not only will tell you whether the message is good news and should in fact be written using a direct approach but also will help you start the message. The initial statement is often the most difficult to write. Once you have the purpose written, the rest of the message will follow easily. Add the necessary details, and close the message with a positive statement to promote goodwill between the writer and the reader.

Using the three-step direct approach will also help you organize your information into paragraphs. Often, you can make each item a separate paragraph. Sometimes, however, your purpose statement and the details are short and closely related. In that case, put both items together in one paragraph; and make the goodwill the second paragraph. Other times, you will have many details that will require more than one paragraph. A direct-news message does not have a set number of paragraphs; however, you will want to have a minimum of two paragraphs in your message.

When ending your message with goodwill, be careful to make the statement specific to your letter. If a goodwill statement is generic enough to be used in almost any letter, chances are the statement is ineffective and will not promote much goodwill. Because you want your statement to be credible to the receiver, you will want to take care to make the goodwill statement original.

This direct plan is also used for routine and good-news memos. Although your message is not being sent outside the organization and although a different format is used, a direct approach and use of goodwill are still important. Maintaining a good relationship with people within the organization is as important as goodwill with outside businesses and customers. Using this three-step approach to direct-news messages will help your good news to be received positively and effectively by your reader.

Use T38-3 and T38-4 here

Figures 38–1 and 38–2 illustrate two ways of presenting the same message. Read the first letter (Figure 38–1) and analyze its effectiveness. Then read the second letter (Figure 38–2) and compare your impressions of the two letters.

As you can see, the second letter is more effective than the first. Through the use of access techniques, the writer has made the message easy to follow. Whereas the first message has little or no goodwill and is very *I* oriented, the second message avoids overusing *I* and ends on a goodwill note.

| Posttest |

Write **T** in the left margin if the statement is true, **F** if the statement is false.

1. Using the *you* attitude is important in letters but not necessary in memos.

2. Using a direct approach means beginning with the details and building up to the main point.

3. Rearranging the information in a sentence to stress the reader's viewpoint will help achieve *you* attitude.

4. Goodwill is usually the major purpose for most good-news messages.

5. A direct-news organization plan is used for both good-news and routine messages.

Key: (1) F—both letters and memos should include *you* attitude; (2) F—the direct approach begins with the main point; (3) T; (4) F—but goodwill is usually a secondary purpose; (5) T.

Figure 38–1

229 North 320 West
Providence, UT 84322
August 30, 19xx

Seagull Office Supply
800 West 1200 South
Salt Lake City, UT 84111

To Whom It May Concern:

I recently received your fall catalog, and I desire to order some items for my copier. If possible, will you send them by UPS. I need 5 bottles of toner (No. 86254), 3 boxes of transparencies (No. 86287), 4 cases of white paper (No. 76298), and 4 reams of blue cover stock (No. 78098).

I hope you will send these items as soon as possible.

Thank you,

Rae Fairmont

Figure 38–2

229 North 320 West
Providence, UT 84322
August 30, 19xx

Seagull Office Supply
800 West 1200 South
Salt Lake City, UT 84111

Ladies and Gentlemen:

Please send me the following items from your fall catalog:

5 bottles	No. 86254	Toner
3 boxes	No. 86287	Transparencies
4 cases	No. 76298	Paper—white
4 reams	No. 78098	Cover stock—blue

Please send the items by UPS and bill my account (528 2654). I look forward to your usual prompt service.

Sincerely,

Rae Fairmont

LEVELS A, B, and C

Name _____

Exercise
38–1

Write **T** if the statement is true, **F** if the statement is false.

_T_ 1. Effective good-news messages are written in a direct manner.

_F_ 2. Business correspondence should be written formally rather than in a conversational style.

_F_ 3. The direct plan is used when the reader will be pleased or uninterested in the information.

_T_ 4. Using the *you attitude* means looking at the information from the reader's point of view.

_T_ 5. Because the beginning of a message is the most emphatic, the use of *you* rather than *we* is encouraged.

_T_ 6. *Goodwill* means keeping customers happy with your business.

_F_ 7. Using goodwill is important in good-news messages but really is not essential in direct-plan memos.

_T_ 8. Determining the purpose is the first step to writing effective direct-news messages.

_F_ 9. Direct-plan messages should always have three paragraphs, one to correspond with each item in the plan.

_F_ 10. Using *I* often in a letter will achieve a conversational style in your writing.

_F_ 11. The *you attitude* will be assured if you have more *you* references than *I* references.

_F_ 12. Because you are conveying positive information, you need not worry about tone; it will be positive.

Exercise
38–2

Change the following sentences to reflect the principles of the *you attitude*.

1. I appreciate your taking the time to interview me last Wednesday.

_____

_____

2. I would like to order six copies of your book on time management.

_____

_____

3. I am pleased to tell you that I will be able to speak to your women's group next month on the topic of professionalism.

_____

_____

4. I enjoyed listening to your recent presentation and want to order a written transcript.

_____

_____

5. We have an opening for a marketing representative that we believe is for you.

_____

_____

6. I want to reserve a hotel room for two for December 5 to 7.

_____

_____

7. I will be arriving at 4 p.m. on August 7 to speak at your convention. Will you pick me up?

_____

_____

8. Because I received only a partial shipment of the merchandise that I ordered from you last month, I am requesting your help in locating the balance.

_____

_____

9. In reply to your letter of February 24, I wish to advise you that the book you requested will be off the press next week.

_____

_____

10. I am writing this letter to inform you your automobile insurance policy expires on June 1.

_____

_____

Exercise 38–3   The following cases require good-news messages. Using the direct-news plan learned in this lesson, write the document for each situation. Supply addresses and other necessary details not provided. Determine whether letterhead should be used for the messages. If so, create the letterhead as part of your document.

1. As an assignment in one of your classes, you need to write a paper on the outlook of your future career. As part of this paper, you must interview a person currently working in the occupation who can give you insight about the expectations for the future, advancement opportunities, etc. Write to your selected person asking for an interview and explaining your purpose and the time required of the interviewee.

2. As the personnel director of Smyrna Temporary Services, you are responsible for placing administrative assistants in temporary assignments. The Smyrna Medical Center has requested a replacement executive assistant for three weeks beginning the first of next month. You need to let the center know you are sending Anne Richards. She has excellent shorthand, computer, and human-relations skills. You will request an evaluation from the center at the end of the assignment.

3. Part of your responsibility as an adjuster for the San Juan Mutual Insurance Company is to settle claims. Your client, Kirk Sharp, has sustained injuries in an automobile accident in which he was not at fault. Dr. Jim Pinnock has been treating him. Write to Dr. Pinnock requesting medical information on Mr. Sharp's condition, expected recovery time, and estimated expenses. Enclose the release form signed by Mr. Sharp.

4. You are in charge of the upcoming company picnic. Because you have a limited budget, you need to shop for the best prices. Write a letter to Foodmart asking for prices on your needed items. You anticipate 400 people will attend the event. If their business proves dependable, you will recommend they be used for all future company celebrations.

5. You recently ordered a full-length, etched-glass mirror. Cache Trucking Company delivered the mirror yesterday. When you unpacked it, you found a large crack in the upper left side of the mirror. You want the mirror for the entry hall of your new home, and you need a replacement before the open house in two weeks. Request that the trucking company replace the mirror.

6. One of your frequent assignments as manager of the Rexton Hotel is acknowledging reservations. Most times your assistant sends a form letter. However, President and Mrs. Lexington of American International Corporation have made reservations for the Christmas holiday. You feel you must acknowledge this reservation personally. The only problem is they want to stay for nine days, and you have a suite available for the first seven days only. Send an appropriate acknowledgment letter.

7. You have just graduated with your degree and have begun the job hunt. An opening with Novell Corporation is available—just the position you are seeking. You need letters of recommendation to accompany your application. Write to one of your former professors, asking him or her to write a letter for you. Be sure to include the address of the company. The recommendation letter will be more credible if your professor sends it directly than if you send it.

8. You recently invited Ms. Marian Cartwright, vice president of operations with your company, to speak to your Rotary Club about the future direction and opportunities in the technological industry. She did an excellent job, and you have been complimented by many members of your organization on her fine speech. Write her a thank-you message; because she is part of your company, send the message as a memo.

See the Instructor's Manual for sample solutions to the letters in this exercise.

BAD-NEWS MESSAGES | LESSON 39

As you learned in Lesson 38, good-news and routine messages are written in a direct way. That plan works well when you are saying *yes*.

> Yes, your group is welcome to tour our department.

Imagine the effect the message would have if you were giving bad news.

> No, your group may not tour our department.

As the writer, you do not have much chance to build goodwill after beginning with the bad news. In fact, the reader is not likely even to finish reading the message. Obviously, your message will not be effective; and your secondary purpose of goodwill will not be achieved. Therefore, you will want to use an **indirect** (or **inductive**) approach any time the reader will be displeased with the news. This lesson will teach the indirect technique of putting the purpose later in the message, which will make the bad news more effective than it is in a direct approach.

Pretest

Write **T** in the left margin if the statement is true, **F** if the statement is false.

1. Because bad-news messages say *no*, goodwill is not an important consideration.

2. Stating the bad news without using the word *no* is more effective than using the word *no*.

3. Words such as *misfortune* and *problem* increase the negative image of a message.

4. The bad news can be deemphasized by putting it in a short sentence.

5. Including an alternative after presenting the bad news is not encouraged because the impact of the message may be lessened.

6. The letter should end on a positive note because that is the part the reader will most likely remember.

7. Referring to the bad news at the end of the message is desirable because the reader will remember your purpose.

Key: (1) F—even though the news is negative, you still want to retain the reader's goodwill; (2) T; (3) T; (4) F—short sentences emphasize; (5) F—the alternative will deemphasize the effect of the bad news and increase the goodwill; (6) T; (7) F—referring to the bad news will emphasize its effect and deter from the goodwill.

Positive Tone

Use T39-1 here

One of the important concepts that should be reflected in the writing of bad-news messages is maintaining a positive tone. Using a positive tone is easy with good news. However, the task is not so simple when you are sending news that will not please the receiver. Remember, you want to maintain the reader's goodwill even though you are saying *no* at the present time. Notice the difference in tone of the following messages:

> Your carpet order has been delayed and will not be delivered until next Friday.

> Your carpet order will be delivered next Friday.

Although the message is essentially the same, how differently will the reader react to the news? People subconsciously respond differently to positive terms than to negative terms. Such words as *no* and *not* as well as words beginning with *un-* and *in-* (meaning *no*) or ending with *-n't* imply negative meanings. Other words with negative connotations include *unfortunately, problem, claim,* and *complaint.* Careful writers work to avoid using these negative-sounding words in presenting the information.

By stating what can be done rather than what cannot be done, you can often control the reader's reaction to your message. When editing messages, be sure to look for potentially negative words and determine whether you can state the same information in positive terms.

Emphasis and Deemphasis

Use T39-2 here

In the last lesson, we learned that good news should be stated first in the most emphatic position. Using the same logic, you will want to address the bad news in a way that will give it less emphasis. Many deemphasis techniques are available, but none can be used in every situation. You will want to become familiar with several deemphasis techniques so you can find one to fit your specific situation.

Location.   As we have discussed, putting something at the beginning provides emphasis. Thus, the first word in the sentence, the first part of the paragraph, and the first sentence in the message receive emphasis. The second most emphatic location is the end—the last word, the last part of the paragraph, and the last sentence in the message. Therefore, you will want to avoid putting bad news in any of these locations.

Sentence Length.   Short sentences are more emphatic than long ones. Consequently, you will want to put good news in a short sentence but make sure the bad news is included in a longer one. As you will recall from the beginning of your study of business English, simple sentences are usually short, whereas compound and complex sentences are longer. These longer sentences are more effective for bad news than are simple sentences. When you analyze a compound sentence, however, you realize that both parts are equal in importance because they are both independent clauses. A complex sentence, however, includes both a dependent and an independent clause. Because the independent clause is more emphatic than the dependent one, you will want to put the bad news in the dependent clause. Notice the difference in the following complex sentences containing bad news:

> Although Ron is congenial with coworkers, he has difficulty with time management.
>
> Although he has difficulty with time management, Ron is congenial with coworkers.

Notice the difference in emphasis of the bad news. Using the name with the positive information and the pronoun with the negative news is another way of achieving emphasis and deemphasis because the noun is more emphatic than the pronoun.

Implied Bad News.   Many times you can imply the bad news without stating it directly. Suppose Mr. Lindsay has asked you for information about prescription-drug reactions. Although you want to be helpful, he is asking for a multitude of information. If you had a clear idea of which reactions he was concerned about, you could help him. Notice the difference in the way your reply can indicate you are not complying with his request:

> Because the list of prescription-drug reactions is almost limitless, we cannot send you the information you need.
>
> The list of prescription-drug reactions is almost limitless. If you will use the enclosed list to mark the drugs that concern you, we will be happy to provide the information you requested.

Although neither example gives Mr. Lindsay the information he requested, he will likely feel positive about the implied statement in the second sentence. Consequently, you will meet your primary purpose of denying his request while achieving your secondary objective of maintaining goodwill.

You will also want to be careful not to offend the reader with the bad news. Rewording the information may be necessary to be sure you have addressed diplomacy as well as the purpose of the letter.

> If you had read the tag, you would know the dress is not washable.
> The tag indicates the dress should be dry cleaned only.

Passive Voice.   You will recall from your study of verbs that using passive voice is a method of deemphasizing the doer of the sentence. To avoid laying blame on the reader, you can use passive voice to present the bad news. How differently will the reader react to these two statements?

> You gave Jader incorrect information about the event.
> Jader was given incorrect information about the event.

As you have learned, passive sentences are less common in writing than active sentences; but presenting bad news is one specific instance in which passive voice is effective.

Subjunctive Mood.   You will recall from your study of verbs that subjunctive mood is used to express doubt or a condition contrary to fact. Therefore, subjunctive mood becomes another effective method of presenting bad news. Phrases such as *I wish I could* or *I would like to* are effective in suggesting that you will not be able to comply with the request while indicating your willingness to do so. Compare the following statements:

> Because I will be out of town, I will not be able to speak to your group.

> If I were going to be in town, I would be pleased to speak to your group.

By using subjunctive mood, you can often eliminate the negative words in the refusal.

Third Person.   The use of second-person pronouns (*you, your*) emphasizes your information. This situation is desirable when presenting good news—the idea of *you* attitude. However, when presenting bad news, you can deemphasize the information by using third-person pronouns *(he, she)*. Notice the difference in emphasis in the following sentences:

> When *your* payment is late, our financial situation is affected.

> When *a customer's* payment is late, our financial situation is affected.

Instead of laying the blame on the reader, this approach generalizes the situation to another party.

Organization Plan

When presenting bad news to the reader, we will be more effective using an indirect approach than using a direct one. Because more tact is required, these messages are usually longer than those presenting good news.

*Use
T39-3
here*

Use the following indirect organization plan to write bad-news messages:

1. Neutral Statement

2. Reasons

3. Refusal

4. Alternative, if possible

5. Goodwill ending

Of course, the purpose of our message is to present the bad news, but using this approach deemphasizes the bad news by putting it in the middle of the letter. The two most emphatic parts of the message—the beginning and the end—will have no mention of the bad news.

The beginning neutral statement should introduce the subject without giving away the purpose. The statement should be one that neither implies *yes* nor indicates *no*.

Next, put the reader on your side by explaining why. Initial reaction to a *no* answer is usually *why?* If you can explain the reasons objectively and clearly to your readers, they will better understand why you are saying *no*, even though they may not agree with your decision.

Once you have established the background, then present the bad news using the deemphasis techniques presented earlier in this lesson. You will have been successful if you can state the refusal without using any negative-sounding words. Be sure to present the bad news as quickly as possible; don't dwell on it.

The impact of the bad news will be lessened if you can present an alternate idea. For example, although you cannot speak to the group this month, you will be available next month. The use of an alternative leaves a "better taste in the reader's mouth" about you and your organization. Although an alternative may not always be possible, most times you can find one with some thought.

Because the receiver will likely remember the last thing he or she reads, you will want to end on a goodwill note. Again, tact becomes very important. If you have just denied a customer's claim or refused a request, an ending such as *If I can be of further assistance, please let me know* will not be effective. The reader is likely to believe you have not been of any help yet, and this ending may cause more harm than goodwill. Keep several points in mind when creating your goodwill endings:

1. Don't refer to bad news. You don't want to emphasize it.

2. Don't apologize. If you were at fault, you would not be saying *no*.

3. Don't ask for follow-up correspondence. You really do not want to go through the trauma with the receiver again!

Use T39-4 and T39-5 here

When you have finished the goodwill statement, read it in context with the rest of the letter to be sure the ending sounds sincere.

Suppose you have submitted a proposal for funding to obtain computers for teaching business communication. You have spent considerable time organizing and writing the proposal. You just received one of the following answers to your request. Analyze the effect created by each letter.

Dear Grant Applicant:

It is with regret that we must inform you that your proposal was not selected.

The staff spent many hours weighing the merits of the 325 projects. The review process included a reading by four different individuals. After long hours of discussion, the top proposals were selected.

We certainly wish we had more favorable news for you. Please do not interpret our inability to support your project as an indication that it should not be implemented. It is our hope that you will find a way to resolve the problems that you have described so carefully in your proposal.

Only those of you with limited budgets who must choose how to allocate those resources can understand how sincere is our regret that we cannot support all the proposals we received.

Thank you for taking the time and effort to prepare your proposal. We are truly sorry that we were unable to reward your efforts with a grant.

Sincerely,

Dear Dr. Neal:

Thank you for the proposal you recently submitted. Your project has a great deal of merit in teaching business communication.

As you can imagine, many excellent ideas were presented in the 325 proposals received. The staff had a difficult choice and spent many hours carefully reviewing each project. We wish we could grant all submissions. However, funding is limited.

The next proposal submissions will begin in six months. We hope you will request a copy of the new guidelines and resubmit your project at that time. Best wishes as you educate students on the important topic of business communication.

Sincerely,

Posttest

Write **T** in the left margin if the statement is true, **F** if the statement is false.

1. An indirect approach to bad news will make your reader more likely to read your entire message than will a direct approach.

2. Stating the bad news using the word *no* is more emphatic than not using the word *no*.

3. The bad news can often be implied instead of stated directly.

4. Both subjunctive mood and passive voice will emphasize the bad news.

5. Putting the reasons before the refusal can help avoid a negative reaction by the reader.

6. Including an apology after the bad news is encouraged to help the reader appreciate your situation.

7. *If you have further questions, please don't hesitate to call* is an effective ending for a bad-news message.

Key: (1) T; (2) T—however, emphatic is what you want to avoid; (3) T; (4) F—both will deemphasize the bad news; (5) T; (6) F—apologies will usually hinder your message; (7) F—besides being trite and negative, you don't want to continue the correspondence.

LEVELS A, B, and C

Name _____

Exercise 39–1 On the lines below, write **T** if the statement is true, **F** if the statement is false.

_T_ 1. A careful writer will try to state the bad news without using any negative words.

_F_ 2. An indirect plan puts the bad news last rather than first as in a direct plan.

_T_ 3. You can deemphasize the bad news by stating it in the middle of the paragraph.

_F_ 4. Short sentences usually have less emphasis than long sentences.

_F_ 5. You want to be sure you state the purpose; simply implying the bad news is not an effective method.

_F_ 6. Passive voice is effective in presenting bad news because the doer, rather than the action, is stressed.

_T_ 7. You can use subjunctive mood to present the bad news without using negative words.

_F_ 8. Third-person pronouns emphasize information; second-person pronouns deemphasize it.

_T_ 9. Presenting an alternative plan will help ease the impact of the bad news.

_F_ 10. Ending the bad-news message with an apology will help ensure reader goodwill.

Exercise 39–2 Change the following sentences to reflect the principles of positive tone.

1. If you had paid within 10 days, you could have taken the discount legally.

_____

_____

2. We cannot send your order because you failed to sign the check.

_____

_____

3. You won't be considered for the position without at least three references.

_____

_____

4. We cannot possibly send a repairman for two weeks.

_____

_____

5. We are sorry, but the product you requested is no longer available in blue.

_____

_____

6. Because we are a wholesale outlet, we do not sell our products directly to consumers.

_____

_____

7. We cannot send your order because you did not specify sizes and colors.

_____

_____

8. Unfortunately, I will be unable to donate to your charity because I have already spent our allotment for the year.

_____

_____

9. Brent may be a good leader, but he is not a good follower.

_____

_____

10. We are turning down your request for an extended vacation.

_____

_____

11. I cannot offer you the position because you do not have the qualifications we are looking for.

_____

_____

Exercise
39-3

The following cases require bad-news messages. Using the indirect-news plan learned in this lesson, write the document for each situation. Supply addresses and other necessary details not provided. Determine whether letterheads should be used for the messages. If so, create simple letterheads as part of your letters.

1. You own a business that sells appliances by mail. You have recently received a letter from Mrs. Wanda Wade, who is not happy with the VCR she purchased. She has returned the VCR and wants either a refund or a new machine because this one is defective. Your repair department has determined that Mrs. Wade is at fault because she pushed the tape in upside down and has ruined both the tape and the machine. You can repair the machine, but she certainly must pay the bill. She should have read the instruction booklet she received with the machine to know how to operate the equipment.

2. You have been asked to speak to the Phi Beta Lambda (PBL) Chapter at Valley Community College. Although you would usually be pleased to accommodate the organization, you cannot because of a conference of your own to be held out of town at the same time. Write to Mr. Brooks Fletcher, the president, suggesting another idea.

3. You recently hired an accountant from Savers Employment Agency. You trusted its testing scores and recommendation; however, Ms. Johnson was not satisfactory. Although you have had positive experiences with Savers previously, in this instance you feel you have been betrayed. Apparently, the agency knew certain details about Ms. Johnson that they failed to pass on to you. You feel they should make the situation right with your company. Write to the personnel director.

4. As personnel director of Word Exact Corporation, you receive a large number of applications for employment each week. Because you cannot interview all these prospective employees, you have a committee who screens the applications and determines which candidates will be interviewed. To avoid spending an excessive amount of time responding to these rejected applicants, you need to develop a form letter. The letter should be flexible enough to allow you to enter specific details about different applicants or positions.

5. You have recently received an order from Ms. Mika Kurashi for office supplies. Although you can send her most of the items, her request for business cards must be delayed for two weeks because your printing equipment is being repaired. The other problem with her order is that she has used an old catalog, and the prices have increased for all items. Before you send the rest of the order and print the cards, you need to write her to find out if she still wants them at the new price. Supply any necessary details.

6. For the last few months, the long-distance phone calls placed from your company have increased considerably. In reviewing the bills, you believe that many of the calls are personal. Write a memo to your employees regarding this problem. They need to realize they must pay for these calls!

7. As chair of the Educational Endowment Institute of the National Business Bureau, you are in charge of granting funding to colleges and universities. This year you were able to grant funds to 14 schools for their projects. However, you must inform the other 745 applicants that their projects will not be funded. They can, however, reapply next year. Write the form letter to be used.

8. Your assignment in the accounting department of Braxton Industrials is accounts receivable. You recently received a check from Steve Durfey for his purchases last month. You appreciate the check, but one problem exists. The terms of the credit agreement are 2/10, n/30. Mr. Durfey agreed to these terms when he was first granted credit with your company. Until now, he has been good about paying his bill on time to receive the discount. This month, however, he took the discount but did not pay the bill until the 21st day of the credit cycle. Your company policy is very strict about not granting discounts after the 10-day period has passed. This policy was part of the agreement Mr. Durfey signed. Write requesting the additional payment. Supply necessary details.

See the Instructor's Manual for sample solutions to the above letters.

PERSUASIVE MESSAGES

Often, as a business writer, you want to convince your reader to act in a certain way or comply with a specific request. When you are not sure whether the reader will readily agree with your purpose, you will want to be diplomatic in making your request.

In Lesson 39, you were introduced to the indirect plan of business correspondence for presenting bad news. Many of the same principles also apply to persuasive messages. Imagine beginning a persuasive message in a direct format starting with the purpose as you do with good or neutral news.

Look at the following examples of potential beginnings for persuasive messages:

Please send your contribution to the homeless shelter.

I am looking forward to a refund for the shoes I am returning that I have only worn twice.

Send for a jar of our tar remover by enclosing your check today.

You can quickly see that your message will not be effective. Neither your goal to achieve *you attitude* nor your endeavor to promote goodwill for you and your company will be served.

In this lesson, you will learn persuasive communication techniques to use when you want to convince your reader to take some action.

Pretest

Write **T** in the left margin if the statement is true, **F** if the statement is false.

1. The reader's attitude can be influenced by the way the message is worded.

2. Appealing to the reader may be an effective persuasive technique.

3. All claim letters should be written in a persuasive format.

4. Getting the reader's attention is the first step to convincing him/her of your purpose.

5. When presenting a sales message, you will be more successful if your message presents the price first to set the stage for the selling points of the product.

6. Persuasive messages are best written in a direct format to let the reader see your point of view.

Key: (1) T; (2) T; (3) F—routine claim letters are written in a direct (good-news) format; (4) T; (5) F—the reader will better accept the price after he/she has been convinced of the importance of the product; (6) F—an indirect format will be better than a direct format in convincing the reader.

Persuasive Technique

Using an indirect approach allows you to influence the reader's attitude in the desired direction. Instead of beginning with the request, you attempt to win the reader over to your point of view before the actual purpose of the letter is revealed. Consider the expected reactions when the reader's point of view is taken into account.

If the reader understood the nature of the charity and its accomplishments, he or she would probably be more willing to contribute to the cause.

If you first explained why you believe you should receive a refund for the shoes even though you have worn them, the business may be more willing to comply with your request.

If you want a potential buyer to purchase your product or service, you must first tell the customer why he or she wants it.

To be effective with persuasion, you must begin with a logical foundation. Once you have put the reader "on your side," you are more likely to have him or her comply with your request.

Successful use of persuasion involves appealing to the reader. The appeals may be physical, emotional, spiritual, or intellectual. Determining which appeal or combination of appeals to employ lies in putting yourself in the reader's position (the *you attitude*). What would make you want to comply with the request? Use your own experience as a basis for determining how to appeal to the reader. Sometimes you must be a creative writer to determine the reader benefit in some persuasive requests.

Organization Plan

Many different types of messages use this persuasive plan. They can be classified in the following three divisions:

1. Persuasive claims, which differ from the routine claims that will be granted willingly.

2. Special requests, which may or may not have much benefit to the receiver.

3. Sales messages, including job applications, in which the writer is trying to market a product, service, or himself/herself.

Although the persuasive plan may be used in a variety of situations, the general plan is similar. Using an indirect plan will better meet your purpose in persuasive messages than a direct plan will. Although the persuasive plan has some similarities with the bad-news plan, you will see some differences because your purpose is to convince rather than to present negative news.

Use the following indirect organization plan to write persuasive messages:

1. Capture attention

2. Present persuasion

3. Request action

Use T40-1 here

Before you can convince the reader to comply with your request, you must first get the reader's attention. The attention-getter will differ with the kind of persuasive message but is an important beginning to a persuasive message. Remember, even though the attention-getter is not the purpose of the communication, it is in an emphatic position and may determine whether the receiver continues reading the message. Consider the effect of the following attention-getting statements for the previous examples:

> A cozy bed . . . a hot meal . . . someone to listen. Imagine life without these necessities!
>
> Alexander's has a reputation for exceptional customer service and quality merchandise.
>
> Where were you when the hot tar hit the fan? If you were within 50 feet, Strip-Off Tar Remover is for you; if not, Strip-Off Tar Remover is for your car!

Once you have gained the reader's attention, your next step is to present the persuasion. Again, the specific information and presentation order will vary with different persuasive messages. Keep in mind the goal of achieving *you attitude* while presenting the purpose of your message.

> If your purpose is a favorable request, present the situation and make the appropriate appeal to the reader.
>
> If your purpose is a persuasive claim, show the reader how compliance will be in his or her best interest.
>
> If your purpose is a sales message, present the selling points of the product or service in terms of benefits to the reader.

The message is not complete, however, until you have requested action. One common problem of many persuasive messages is the lack of the action ending. Your persuasion may be splendid, but the action ending is as important to completing the persuasion as the attention-getter is to beginning the persuasion. The action statement may be considered the true purpose of your message. Everything else in the message is leading up to your request for action. Consider the following endings:

> Your contribution to the homeless shelter can make the simple necessities possible for many under-privileged members of our community. Please use the enclosed envelope to send your tax-deductible donation today.

Because Alexander's has always stood for excellence, I am looking forward to receiving a prompt refund for the enclosed shoes.

Use the enclosed order blank to send for your free sample of Strip-Off Tar Remover before the next hot summer day arrives. Both you and your car will be delighted you did.

Use
T40-2
and
T40-3
here

When you use persuasive techniques such as these, you will be able to write effective persuasive messages.

Posttest

Write **T** in the left margin if the statement is true, **F** if the statement is false.

1. Persuasive messages are most effective when they begin with the request.

2. Appeals to the reader may take an emotional or intellectual approach.

3. Because job-application letters are unique, they should not be written in a persuasive plan.

4. Persuasive communications are more similar to good-news messages than to bad-news messages.

5. Showing the reader how she or he will benefit from complying with your request will help make your persuasive message effective.

6. The actual purpose of a persuasive communication is best presented at the end of the message.

Key: (1) F—the messages are more effective if they begin with an attention getter; (2) T; (3) F—application letters are often most effective as a persuasive message; (4) F—persuasive messages, like bad-news messages, are written in an indirect format; (5) T; (6) T.

LEVELS A, B, and C

Name _____

Exercise 40–1 On the lines below, write **T** if the statement is true, **F** if the statement is false.

F 1. A persuasive plan is used when you believe the receiver will readily accede to your request.

F 2. A persuasive plan is more similar to the good-news plan than to the bad-news plan.

F 3. Appealing to the reader means changing the request to agree with the reader's belief.

T 4. Using your reaction to a request is a good way to determine what reader appeal to use.

T 5. Successful persuasion may include a physical, emotional, intellectual, or spiritual appeal.

T 6. Finding a reader benefit may be difficult in some persuasive requests.

T 7. A letter applying for a job may be considered a type of persuasive message.

F 8. An attention-getting statement should reveal the purpose of the message to the reader.

F 9. Goodwill is not a necessary part of a persuasive message.

T 10. The real purpose of the persuasive message is usually found at the end of the letter in the action statement.

Exercise 40–2 Create attention-getting openings for the following persuasive situations.

1. A memo to your supervisor requesting additional vacation days.

_____

_____

2. A letter to a customer requesting payment for a past-due account.

_____

_____

3. A request for a refund on a cassette that was damaged in shipment.

_____

_____

4. A request by a student group to tour a high-security plant.

_____

_____

5. A letter to a magazine publisher asking for permission to copy and distribute a recent article to use in an upcoming professional presentation you are giving.

_____

_____

6. A memo to convince your supervisor to try a new idea you have been developing.

_____

_____

7. A request to the city mayor to address your community meeting.

_____

_____

8. A letter to sell a new innovation. (You create the product.)

_____

_____

9. A letter to a popular software company requesting free use of its product for a professional seminar.

_____

_____

10. A request to fill out a questionnaire for a research study.

_____

_____

11. A request to your insurance company to reevaluate your recent surgery claim.

_____

_____

12. A memo to the company president requesting a reevaluation of your performance review.

_____

_____

**Exercise
40–3**
The following cases require persuasive messages. Using the plan learned in this lesson, write the document for each situation. Supply addresses and other necessary details not provided. Create simple letterheads as part of your letters.

1. Write a memo to your supervisor, George Daniels, requesting funds to attend the upcoming National Communication Conference in Honolulu. The conference is scheduled over the Christmas holiday weekend. The estimated cost for the conference is $950. Although the location may be indicative of a vacation, you believe the conference will be beneficial in your position as the communication director for the company. Persuade him to pay your expenses.

2. You recently attended a conference in Nashville. Your connecting flight from Houston to Nashville was canceled, and you were delayed and then rerouted on a different flight. When you arrived in Nashville, you found your luggage had not been rerouted with you. Consequently, you were without the luggage for 24 hours until it arrived. You believe you should be compensated for expenses incurred during that time. Write a persuasive letter to National Airlines explaining your situation and requesting compensation. Supply appropriate details.

3. As a long-time citizen of Newton, you are concerned about the changes taking place. People in the adjoining city, Springfield, are trying to rezone portions of your smaller, rural town to their advantage. You are chair of a grass-roots committee formed to combat these developers. You need to send a letter to the citizens of Newton to persuade them to attend the City Council meeting and to express their opinions.

4. Although you consider yourself a good credit risk and have always paid your bills on time, you now find yourself in a difficult situation. Since you were injured in an automobile accident four months ago, you have not been able to work. Your sick leave has expired, and so has your paycheck. Because your doctor indicates you will not be able to work for at least six more months, you will not be able to keep up with your bills. Your job will be waiting for you when you can return, and you know you eventually will be able to resume payments. Write a letter to People's Savings and Loan requesting an extension on the $25,000 still owing on your condominium loan.

5. You have developed a new product that is not currently on the market. Create a sales letter to be sent to all your customers persuading them to try the product. Use your creativity to explain the product and its benefits to the customers.

6. As manager of the sales department of Valley View Production, you send a unique Christmas gift to your customers each year as a goodwill gesture. This year you bought Old World Chocolates for your 987 active accounts. Old World agreed to send the candy directly to your customers two weeks before Christmas along with a card from your company. By now, the end of January, you have received thank-you notes from only a small percentage of those you usually hear from. Doing some informal checking, you believe only about one-third of the gifts were actually delivered. Write to Old World requesting adjustment of the problem. Your credibility is at stake, and you are determined that Old World must make compensation.

7. You work as an administrative assistant to the vice president in your company. You have been assigned to raise funds for the United Way campaign from your organization. Laurelton is making a push to get 100 percent participation from all employees in each company in the community. Write a persuasive memo to your employees convincing them to get involved even if they can afford only a small donation.

8. As a member of the Founders' Day committee, you are in charge of the concession booths. Write a form letter to be sent to all restaurants in Danbury inviting them to establish a booth as part of ''A Taste of Danbury.'' Because you are expecting several thousand people, the participants should earn a good profit.

See the Instructor's Manual for sample solutions to the above letters.

A

A/an, usage, 500
Abbreviations, 4
   general directives, 89–90
   plurals of, 367–68
   rules for, 91–95
   terminology, 91
Abridged dictionaries, 105, 106
Absolute adjective, 427
Abstract nouns, 32
Academics, capitalization rules, 76
Accent marks, 108
Access
   in business documents, 530
   guidelines, 548–53
   strong, 556
   weak, 555
Acronyms, 91
Action verbs, 121
Active verbs, 123
Active voice
   definition, 202
   illogical shifts in voice, 205
   preference for, 201
   rules for, 203
Adapt/adopt, usage, 500
Addresses, comma use, 282
Adjectives, 5
   comparative forms, 106, 427
   definition, 425, 427
   extraneous, 484–85
   function, 8–9
   predicate, 124
   proper, 444
   superlatives, 107
   verbals as, 122
Adverbial clauses, 248
Adverbs, 6; *see also* Relative adverbs
   comparative forms, 106, 427, 428–
      30
   conjunctive, 10
   definition, 425–26, 427
   endings, 430–31
   extraneous, 484–85
   function, 9
   limited, 460
   superlatives, 107
   verbals as, 122
Adverse/averse, usage, 500
Agreement
   of pronouns, 407–11
   subject-verb, 392–93
Allusion/illusion, usage, 501

Although/while, usage, 501
Alumnus/alumna, usage, 501
Amiable/amicable, usage, 501
Among/between use, 321–22
Amoral/immoral, usage, 501
Amount/number, usage, 501
Antecedent, 6
   definition, 339, 408
   for pronouns, 7–8
   rules for, 408–9
Antonyms, 106
   in dictionaries, 109
Anxious/eager, usage, 501
Appendage, 261–62
   definition, 263
Appositives, 261
   comma use, 266
   definition, 263, 339
Appraise/apprise, usage, 501
Archaic words, 106
Articles, 6
   definition, 427
   function as adjectives, 9
   rules for, 431–32
Artistic works, capitalization rules, 79
As-if statements, 191
Associations, abbreviations for, 93–94
Astronomical bodies, capitalization
    rules, 76
Attention line, 582
Authoritarian/authoritative, usage, 501
Auxiliary verbs; *see* Helping verbs

B

Back matter of dictionaries, 107
Bad-news messages, 601–6
Balance/remainder, usage, 501
Beside/besides use, 322
Between/among use, 321–22
Block format, 583
Body of letter, 583
Bold print, 550
Borders, 550
Brackets, 285–86
Broadcasting stations, abbreviations,
   93–94
Business correspondence
   accessing, 530, 547–53
   bad-news messages, 601–6
   examples, 585–88
   formats, 581–88

Business correspondence—*Cont.*
   good-news messages, 591–94
   persuasive messages, 611–14
   tone, 579
Business organizations
   abbreviations for, 93–94
   capitalization rules, 76–77

C

Calendar events, comma use, 281
Calendar items
   capitalization rules, 77
   comma use, 281
Capitalization, 75, 550
   of abbreviations, 91
   learning hints, 80
   rules for, 4, 76–80
   of words in titles, 284
Case
   objective, 125, 130–32, 336
   possessive, 378
   of pronouns, 8
   subjective, 336
Cipher, 62
Circumlocution
   definition, 480
   examples, 485–86
Clauses, 19, 221
   colon use, 282
   definition, 222
   restrictive and nonrestrictive, 354
Clichés
   definition, 480
   examples, 486–87
Collective nouns
   definition, 396
   and verb agreement, 398
Colloquial words, 106
Colon, use of, 282
Comma
   in addresses, 282
   with appositives, 266
   with calendar events, 281
   with conjunctive adverb, 304
   with coordinate adjectives, 447–48
   with coordinating conjunction, 303
   with dependent clauses, 248–50
   in direct address, 281
   with Inc. or Ltd., 282
   with introductory phrases, 250–51
   with introductory words, 251
   with Jr. and Sr., 282

Comma—*Cont.*
with parenthetical statements, 266
with place names, 282
and quotation marks, 283
rules for, 223–24
with series, 263–65
to set off interrupters, 265–66
with subordinating conjunctions,
305
terminology for, 222–23
with transitional elements, 265–66
Commands, period use, 281; *see also*
Imperative sentences
Comma splice, 19, 23
correcting, 223
definition, 222
Common-gender nouns, 408
Common noun, 6, 7
Comparative forms, 427
rules for, 427–30
Comparative words, 106
Compare/contrast, usage, 501–2
Comparison, types of, 427
Compass directions
abbreviations for, 92
capitalization rules, 77
Complements, 18–19
definition, 19
Complete predicate, 126
Complex sentences, 19, 22, 248
Complimentary close, 584
Compound adjectives, 446
Compound-complex sentences, 19, 22,
248
Compound modifiers, 443–49
definition, 444
omitting hyphens, 448–49
rules for, 445–47
Compound nouns
definition, 366, 378
rules for, 380
Compound sentences, 19, 22, 222
Compound subjects, 17–18
Compound verbs, 18
function, 129–30
lack of comma, 224
Conciseness, 479
Conclusion, 188
Concrete nouns, 32
Confusing/confusable words, 3, 47
examples, 48–51
terminology, 500
usage guidelines, 500–504
Conjugation, 122
definition, 123
function, 124
Conjunctions, 6; *see also* Coordinating
conjunctions *and* Subordinating
conjunctions
function, 10

Conjunctive adverbs, 10
comma and semicolon use, 236–37
definition, 234, 302
rules for, 304
Conjunctive joiners, 222, 301; *see also*
Connectives
Connectives/connectors
conjunctions, 10
prepositions, 9
rules for, 303–7
simple prepositions, 319
terminology for, 302–3
Connote/denote, usage, 502
Consecutive modifiers, 443–49
definition, 444
Consonants, 32
Content
prewriting stage, 566
rewrite stage, 568
Continuous/continual, usage, 502
Contractions, 91
Coordinate adjectives, rules for, 447–
48
Coordinate modifiers, 444
Coordinating conjunctions, 10, 222
comma use, 223
definition, 302
rules for, 303–4
semicolon use, 237–38
verb agreement and 399
Coordination function, 298
Copy notation, 583
Correlative conjunctions, 10
definition, 302
rules for, 306–7
Correspondence formats, 581–88
direct and indirect, 579–80
document format types, 583–84
examples, 585–88
parts of a letter, 582–83
punctuation styles, 585
Countable, 500
Couplet
definition, 480
examples, 489–90
Courtesy titles
definition, 514
feminine, 518

D

Dangling modifiers, 459–65
definition, 460
rules for, 463–65
Dashes
for emphasis, 266
with parenthetical statements, 266
types, 267

Data/datum, usage, 502
Date line, 582
Decimal fractions, 64
Declarative sentences, 19, 23
Definite numbers, 62
Definitions, in dictionaries, 108
Demonstrative pronouns, 336
agreement of, 410
Dependent clauses, 20–22
comma use, 248–50
definition, 235
with subordinating conjunctions,
304–5
Deprecate/depreciate, usage, 502
Derivative words, 32
capitalization rules, 77
Dialect, 106
Dictionaries
components, 107–9
terminology for, 106–7
use, 4
uses and types, 105–6
Different from/different than, usage,
502
Direct address, comma use, 281
Direct format, 579–80
Direct object, 18
definition, 20
Direct object completers, 21
Discreet/discrete, usage, 503
Disinterested/uninterested, usage, 503
Distances, 65
Districts, abbreviations for, 92–93
Double comparison, 427
Double quotation marks, 283
Drafting stage, 567

E

Effective writing
accessing business documents, 547–
53
psychological emphasis, 552–53
verbal emphasis, 548–49
visual emphasis, 549–52
Egoist/egotist, usage, 503
Electronic spellers, downfalls, 31
Ellipsis
definition, 280
use of, 285
Em and en dashes, 267
Emigrate/immigrate, usage, 503
Emphasis/de-emphasis, in bad-news
messages, 602–4
Enclosure notation, 583
End-of-sentence prepositions, 320–21
Enumeration, 549
Essential, 248

Et cetera, 264
Etymology, 106, 108
Euphemisms
    definition, 480
    wordiness, 485
Exclamatory sentences, 20, 23
Extrovert/introvert, usage, 503

F

Family titles, capitalization rules, 78
Fast writing, 567
Feminine courtesy titles, 518
Fewer/less, usage, 503
Finite verbs, 124
    definition, 171
    function, 174
Foreign expressions, abbreviations, 95
Foreign nouns
    definition, 366
    plurals of, 368
Fractions, 64
Fragments, 20, 532
    definition, 174
    nature of, 22
    with verbals, 173
Front matter, of dictionaries, 107
Future-perfect-progressive tense, 162
Future-perfect tense, 145
    rules for, 161
Future progressive tense, 162
Future tense, 145
    usage, 147–48

G

Gender
    definition, 408, 514
    in pronouns, 335
Genderless words, 515
Generic, 514
Gerund, 122
    definition, 174, 378
    rules for, 381
    usage, 173
Goal identification, 566
Good-news messages
    examples, 595–96
    guidelines, 591–94
Good/well, usage, 503
Goodwill, 592–93
Government agencies
    abbreviations, 93–94
    capitalization rules, 78
Grammar, rewrite stage, 569
Graphics, 550

H

Hanged/hung, usage, 504
Hard space, 280–81
Headings, capitalization rules, 79
Helping verbs, 6, 8, 125
    usage, 127
He/she, usage, 409
Historical present, 145
    usage, 146
Homonyms, 107
Hyphenated words, capitalization rules,
    78
Hyphens
    omission with compound modifiers,
        448–49
    use with compound modifiers, 445–
        47

I

Idiomatic prepositions, 322–23
Idioms, 107
    definition, 319, 480
    in dictionaries, 109
    examples, 487–88
If/then statements, 189, 190
Illogical shifts
    in mood, 191–92
    in tense, 148, 162
    in voice, 205
Imagination, 553
Imperative mood
    definition, 188
    rules for, 190
    usage, 187
Imperative sentences, 20, 23
Inc., with comma, 282
Incomplete comparison, 427
Indefinite number, 62
Indefinite pronouns, 336
    definition, 396
    verb agreement, 397
Independent clauses, 20, 22
    comma use, 223–24, 248–51
    joining process, 221
    punctuation issues, 221–22
    semicolon use, 233–38, 307
    terminology for, 222–23
Independent modifiers, 444
Indicative mood
    definition, 189
    rules for, 189
    usage, 187
Indirect commands, 191
Indirect format, 580
Indirect object, 18
    definition, 20

Indirect question, period use, 281
Infinitives, 122, 125
    definition, 174–75
    split, 176
    usage, 172–73, 175–77
Inflection, 107
    characteristics, 125
    in dictionaries, 108
Ingenious/ingenuous, usage, 504
In/into use, 322
Inside address, 582
Intensive pronouns, 336, 337–38
    definition, 339
    rules for, 342–43
Interjections, 6, 10
Interrogative pronouns, 336
Interrogative sentences, 20, 23
Interrupters, 261
    comma use, 265–66
Intransitive verbs, 107, 125
    definition, 202
    usage, 130–32
Introductory clauses, 247
    terminology for, 248
Introductory phrases, comma use, 250–
    51
Introductory words, comma use, 251
Inverted order, 20
Inverted-order sentence, 21, 396
Irregular forms of comparisons, 427
Irregular verbs, 125
    compound, 130
    frequently occurring, 128–29
Italics
    definition, 281
    use of, 284–85

J

Joint ownership
    definition, 378
    rules for, 380–81
Jr. and Sr., with comma, 282

L

Labor unions, abbreviations, 93–94
Languages, capitalization rules, 78–79
Language use, 476–78
    confusable words, 499–504
    nonsexist writing, 513–18
    rewrite stage, 568–69
    wordy expressions, 479–80
Letterhead/return address, 582
Letters, 582–83; *see also* Business
    correspondence

Like, use of, 322
Limited adverbs, 460
Linking verbs, 6, 8, 123
  definition, 202
  function, 125
  rules for, 205
  usage, 127
Listing, 549–50
Literary works, capitalization rules, 79
Logical sentence order, 536–37
Ltd., with comma

M

Main verbs, 125, 127
Mass nouns, 500
Material/materiel, usage, 504
Measurements, abbreviations, 94–95
Memo format, 584
  example, 588
Message content, 566
Metric units, abbreviations, 94–95
Misplaced modifiers, 459–65
Misspelled words, 36–37
Mixed numbers, 62
Mnemonic, 32
  spelling rules, 34, 35–36
Modified-block format, 583
Modifiers, 8, 9, 422–65; *see also*
    Adjectives *and* Adverbs
  compound and consecutive, 443–49
  excessive, 432–33
  misplaced and dangling, 459–65
  participles, 126
  placement of, 461–63
  rules for, 427–33, 461–65
  terminology, 427, 444, 460
  types of, 422–23
Money amounts, 64
Mood, 122
  definition, 189
  function, 125, 187
  imperative, 187
  indicative, 187
  rules for, 189–92
  subjunctive, 188
  terminology for, 188–89

N

Names, capitalization rules, 78
Nationalities, capitalization rules, 78–79
Neuter, definition, 408, 514
Nicknames, capitalization rules, 78

Nominative pronouns; *see* Subjective pronouns
Nonessential words
  comma use, 251
  definition, 248
Nonfinite verbs
  definition, 171, 175
  function, 125
  as verbals, 124
Nonrestrictive clauses
  definition, 354
  rules for, 354–55
Nonrestrictive modifier, 265
Nonrestrictive words, 263
  definition, 248
Nonsexist writing
  guidelines, 515–18
  terminology, 514–15
  trend toward, 513–14
Normal order, 20
Noun phrases, wordy, 484
Nouns
  abstract and concrete, 32
  appendage, 263
  in apposition, 263, 266
  capitalization rules, 76–80
  common, 7
  common and proper, 6
  common-gender, 408
  as direct object, 18
  function, 7
  gerunds as, 173
  plural forms, 365–69
  possessive, 377–81
  predicate, 124
  proper, 7
  subjects of sentences, 17–18
  terminology, 378
  verbals as, 122
Number(s), 4
  capitalization rules, 79
  in pronouns, 335
  rules for, 63–64
  terminology for, 62
  usage, 61–65
  verb inflection, 125

O

Objective pronouns, 336
  definition, 339
  rules for, 340–42
Objects
  of transitive verbs, 130–32
  of verbs, 125
Obsolete terms, 107
Order of information, 553

Ordinal numbers, 62
  in sentences, 65
Organization
  of bad-news messages, 604–6
  of good-news messages, 593–94
  of persuasive messages, 612–14
  in rewrite stage, 568

P

Paragraphs
  effective writing, 529
  function of, 535
  rules for, 536–38
Parallel grammatical form, 263, 301, 533
  by correlative conjunctions, 306–7
  definition, 302
  use of connectives for, 298–99
Parenthesis, 266
Parenthetical statements, comma use, 266
Participles, 122
  characteristics and types, 171–72
  definition, 175
  function, 126
  present, 157–58
  types, 159
  usage, 175
Parts of speech
  adjectives, 8–9, 425–33
  adverbs, 9, 425–33
  articles, 9
  conjunctions, 10
  connectives, 298–307
  in dictionaries, 108
  interjections, 10
  mood of verbs, 187–92
  nouns, 7
  perfect tense, 157–61
  plural nouns, 365–69
  possessive nouns and pronouns, 377–81
  prepositions, 9, 317–23
  progressive verb forms, 157–61
  pronouns, 7–8, 407–11
  relative pronouns, 353–57
  subjective and objective pronouns, 337–43
  subject-verb agreement, 395–99
  tenses of verbs, 143–48
  terminology, 5–7
  use of modifiers, 422–65
  verbals, 171–77
  verb basics, 120–32
  verbs, 8
  voice of verbs, 201–5

Passive verbs, 123
Passive voice
  avoidance of, 532
  in bad-news messages, 603
  definition, 202
  general avoidance of, 201
  and illogical shifts in voice, 205
  rules for, 203–4
Past participle
  definition, 159, 202
  function, 171
  usage, 159–60
Past-perfect-progressive tense, 162
Past-perfect tense, 145
  rules for, 160
Past-progressive tense, 162
Past tense, 145
  usage, 147
Percentages, 64
Perfect infinitive, 172–73, 175
  usage, 177
Perfect participle
  definition, 159, 175
  function, 172
  usage, 175
Perfect tense, 145
  definition, 159
  function, 157
  rules for, 159–60
  time framework, 157–58
Period
  and quotation marks, 283
  uses, 281
Person
  in pronouns, 335
  of verbs, 126
Personal business letter, 585
Personal names, with abbreviations, 91
Personal pronouns, 336
Personal titles, capitalization rules, 79
Persuasive messages, 580, 611–14
Persuasive techniques, 612
Phrasal preposition, 319
Phrases, 20
  definition, 234
  function, 21
Place names, comma use, 282
Plural nouns
  rules for, 366–69
  terminology, 366
Polite requests, 20, 23
  periods with, 281
Polysyllabic words, 480
  examples, 488–89
Positive degree
  of adjectives, 427
  definition, 427
Possessive case, 378

Possessive nouns
  rules for, 378–80
  use, 377
Possessive pronouns
  rules for, 380
  use, 377
Practical/practicable, usage, 504
Predicate, 18, 127
  definition, 20
  in sentences, 126
Predicate adjective, 124
Predicate noun, 124, 124
Prefix, 32
  spelling rules, 34–35
Prepositional phrases
  avoidance of, 320
  definition, 319
  versus possessive forms, 381
  and verb agreement, 397–98
  wordy, 481–82
Prepositions, 6
  function, 9
  rules for, 319–23
  selection of correct type, 317–18
  terminology for, 319
Presentation, order of, 567
Present infinitive, 172–73, 175
  usage, 175–76, 177
Present participle
  definition, 159, 175
  function, 171–72
  in progressive forms, 157–58, 162
  usage, 175
Present-perfect-progressive tense, 162
Present-perfect tense, 145
  rules for, 159–60
Present-progressive tense, 162
Present tense, 145–47
Prewrite stage, guidelines, 566–67
Prewrite-write-rewrite process, 530–31
Principal parts of verbs, 126
Print variation, 550
Products, capitalization rules, 79
Progressive forms/tenses, 145
  definition, 159
  rules for, 162
  usage, 157–58
Pronouns, 6; *see also* Relative
    pronouns
  antecedent agreement and reference,
    407–11
  case, 8
  categories of, 336
  as direct object, 18–19
  function, 7–8
  masculine, 515
  possessive, 377–81
  predicate, 124
  properties of, 335–36

Pronouns—*Cont.*
  relative, 353–57
  rules for, 339–43
  subjects of sentences, 17–18
  terminology, 339, 408
Pronunciation, symbols in dictionaries,
    108
Proper adjectives
  definition, 444
  unhyphenated, 447
Proper nouns, 6
  function, 7
Prophecy/prophesy, usage, 504
Provinces, abbreviations, 93–94
Psychological emphasis, 552–53
Publications, capitalization rules, 79
Public officials, capitalization rules, 78
Punctuation
  of abbreviations, 91
  colon, 282
  comma, 221–24, 248–51
  in correspondence formats, 584–86
  independent clauses, 221–22
  need for consistency, 218–19
  objectives of, 219
  period, 281
  quotation marks, 283–84
  restrictive clauses, 355
  semicolon, 233–38
  with series, interrupters, appositives,
    or appendages, 261–67
  terminology for, 280–81
Punctuation marks
  brackets, 285–86
  ellipsis, 285

Q–R

Quotation marks
  for direct quotations, 283
  with titles, 283–84
Races and ethnic groups, capitalization
    rules, 78–79
Readability, 568–69
Reader interaction, 553
Reader reaction, 566
Recommendation, 189
Reference, 393
  of pronouns, 407–11
  rules for, 411
Reference initials, 583
Reflexive pronouns, 336, 337–38
  definition, 339
  rules for, 342–43
Regional dialect, 106
Regular verbs, 126
Relative adverbs, 303, 306

Relative clauses, 353
Relative-pronoun clause, 411–12
Relative pronouns, 336
    cases, 353
    definition, 303
    rules for, 305–6, 354–57
    terminology, 354
Religions, capitalization rules, 78–79
Repetition, 548–49
Restrictive clauses
    definition, 354
    rules for, 354–55
Restrictive words, 248
Rewrite stage, guidelines, 568–69
Rule of ten, 62
Rules of spelling, 33–37
Run-on sentences, 20, 23
    definition, 223

S

Salutation, 582
Semicolon
    characteristics, 233–34
    with conjunctive adverbs, 304
    with coordinating conjunction, 303–4
    rules for, 235–38
    in series, 265
    terminology for, 234–35
    use without connectives, 307
Semiperiod, 235
Sentence interrupters, 235
Sentences
    categories of, 23
    complements, 18–19
    effective writing, 529
    ending with prepositions, 320–21
    inverted, 396
    parallelism in, 298–99, 301
    patterns, 20–21
    predicates, 18, 126
    problems with, 22–23
    required components, 123–24
    rules for, 532–35
    split construction, 319
    subjects, 17–18
    terminology for, 19–20
    types, 21–22
    use of, 532
    use of connectives, 298–300
Separate ownership, 378
Series, 261
    comma use, 263–65
    definition, 263

Sexism
    avoiding, 515–18
    definition, 515
Sexist writing, 515
Sex stereotyping, 514
Shading, color, and high-lighting, 550
Shift of tense, 145
    avoidance, 148
    rules for, 162
Shifts in mood, 191–92
Shifts in voice, 205
Signature block, 583
Simple predicate, 126
Simple preposition, 319
    as connective, 319
Simple sentences, 22
Simple tenses, 145
Simplified business letter, 587
Simplified format, 584
Single compound noun, 366
Slang, 107
Societies, abbreviations, 93–94
Soft space, 281
Space allocation, 552
Spacing, in abbreviations, 91
Spelling, 31
    in dictionaries, 107
    frequently misspelled words, 36–37
    problems, 3
    rules, 33–37
    terminology for, 32–33
Split construction
    definition, 319
    preposition use, 321
Split infinitives, 176
Squinting construction
    definition, 460
    example, 463
State-of-being verbs, 126, 202; *see also* To be
States, abbreviations, 93–94
Subject, 20
Subject/action verb/direct object sentence, 21
Subject/action verb/indirect object/ direct object sentence, 21
Subject complement, 18, 20, 124
    definition, 203
Subjective case, pronouns, 336
Subjective pronouns
    definition, 339
    rules for, 339–40
Subject line, 582–83
Subject/linking verb/subject complement sentence, 21
Subjects, 17–18
Subject-verb agreement, 122
    pronoun use, 410

Subject-verb agreement—*Cont.*
    rules for, 396–99
    terminology, 396
Subject/verb sentence, 20
Subjunctive mood
    in bad-news messages, 604
    definition, 189
    rules for, 190–91
    usage, 188
Subjunctive mood noun clause, 191
Subjunctive should, 189
Subordinating conjunctions, 10
    definition, 248
    rules for, 304–5
Subordination function, 298
Suffix, 32
    spelling rules, 33–34
Suggestions, period use, 281
Supercomma, 235
Superlatives, 107
    definition, 427
    rules for, 427–30
Syllabication, 33, 107
    in dictionaries, 108
Symbols, abbreviations, 95
Synonyms, 107
    in dictionaries, 109

T

Tenses
    definition, 121, 145
    frequently used, 144
    function, 126, 143–44
    of participles, 171–72
    perfect, 157–61
    in progressive forms, 157–61
    rules for, 146–48
    terminology for, 145
Territories, abbreviations, 93–94
That clauses, 265
That/which, usage, 305–6
Third-person pronouns, 604
Time of day/time zones, abbreviations, 94
Titles
    capitalization rules, 78, 79
    use of italics, 284–85
    use of solid capitals, 285
To be, 126
    function, 8
    as linking verb, 127
    in progressive tenses, 157
Tone
    in bad-news messages, 602
    in business correspondence, 579

Topic sentences, 536
Trade names, capitalization rules, 79
Transitional phrases, 235
    comma or semicolon use, 236–37, 265–66
    as conjunctive adverbs, 304
Transitional terms, common, 537
Transitive verbs, 107, 126
    definition, 203
    usage, 130–32

U

Unabridged dictionaries, 105, 107
Underlined words, 550
Usage labels, in dictionaries, 108–9
Usage notes, in dictionaries, 108

V

Verbal emphasis, 548–49
Verbals, 122
    definition, 175
    function, 171
    gerunds, 173
    infinitives, 172–73
    nonfinite verbs, 124
    participles, 171–72
    rules for, 175–77
    terminology for, 174–75
Verb phrase, 126
    and main verb, 127
    wordy, 482–84

Verbs
    agreement rules, 396–99
    classes of, 121
    compound, 129–30
    definition, 126
    function, 8
    intransitive or transitive, 107
    irregular, 128–30
    linking, 127
    linking and helping, 6
    main and helping, 127
    moods of, 122, 187–92
    objects of, 18–19
    perfect tenses and progressive forms, 157–61
    predicates of sentences, 18
    principal parts, 122, 128
    properties of, 120–21
    in relative-pronoun clauses, 410–11
    sentence requirement, 123–24
    subject-verb agreement, 395–99
    tenses of, 122, 143–48
    terminology, 123–26
    transitive and intransitive, 130–32
    voices of, 122, 201–5
Visual emphasis, 549–52
Vocabulary; *see* Confusing words *and* Wordy expressions
Voice
    definition, 122, 203
    function, 126
    rules for, 203–5
    terminology for, 202–3
    as verb property, 201
Vowels, 33

W–Y

Webster's Ninth New Collegiate Dictionary, 109, 110
When/where, use, 306
Which clauses, 265
Which/that, usage, 305–6, 355–57
While, usage, 306
White space, 551–52
Whole numbers, 62
    in sentences, 64
Who/whom, usage, 305–6, 355–57
Wordiness, 534
Word Perfect, 267
Word processing
    hard space, 280–81
    soft space, 281
    types of dashes, 267
Words
    confusing, 47
    connectives, 298–300
    sentence interrupters, 235
    terminology for, 106–7
Word signals, 548
Wordy expressions, 479–90
    eliminating, 480–90
    terminology, 480
Write stage, guidelines, 567
Writing techniques, scope of, 528–30
You attitude, 592

Frequently Misspelled Words

absence	accessible	accidentally	accommodate
acknowledgment	acquaintance	acquisition	adolescence
alignment	all right	a lot	analyze
apparent	argument	attendance	beginning
believe	beneficial	benefited*	bookkeeper
brief	brochure	calendar	canceled*
careful	catalog	category	cemetery
changeable	commitment	committee	comparative
competent	competitive	concede	conceivable
congratulate	consensus	consistent	convenience
criticism	curriculum	deductible	defendant
definite	dependent	describe	description
desirable	develop	disappear	disappoint
eligible	embarrass	employee*	enclosure*
entrepreneur	equipped	equivalent	exaggerate
excellent	existence	explanation	extension
familiar	feasible	fluorescent	foreign
forfeit	fulfill	gauge	grammar
grateful	grievous	harass	height
helpful	hindrance	hopeful	implement
incidentally	interference	irrelevant	judgment*
label	liable	liaison	library
license	likable*	maintenance	mileage
miscellaneous	misspell	mortgage	necessary
noticeable	obsolescent	occasionally	occurrence
omission	opportunity	pamphlet	parallel
perceive	permanent	permissible	persuade
possession	practical	preferred	prejudice
presence	privilege	procedure	prominent
pronunciation	pursue	questionnaire	receive
recommend	reference	referring	remuneration
restaurant	rhythm	satellite	separate
serviceable	similar	sincerely	sizable*
sophomore	summarize	superintendent	supersede
surprise	synonymous	temporary	thorough
transferred	traveler*	truly	usable
vacuum	visible	volume	withhold
writing	yield		

*Preferred business-world spelling.